Encyclopedia of Ancient Myths and Culture

ENCYCLOPEDIA OF ANCIENT MYTHS AND CULTURE

Eagle
Editions

A QUANTUM BOOK

Published by Eagle Editions Ltd
11 Heathfield
Royston
Hertfordshire SG8 5BW

This edition printed 2003

ISBN 1-86160-786-5

QUMTEOA

Manufactured in Singapore by
Pica Digital (Pte) Ltd
Printed in Singapore
by Star Standard Industries (Pte) Ltd

Contents

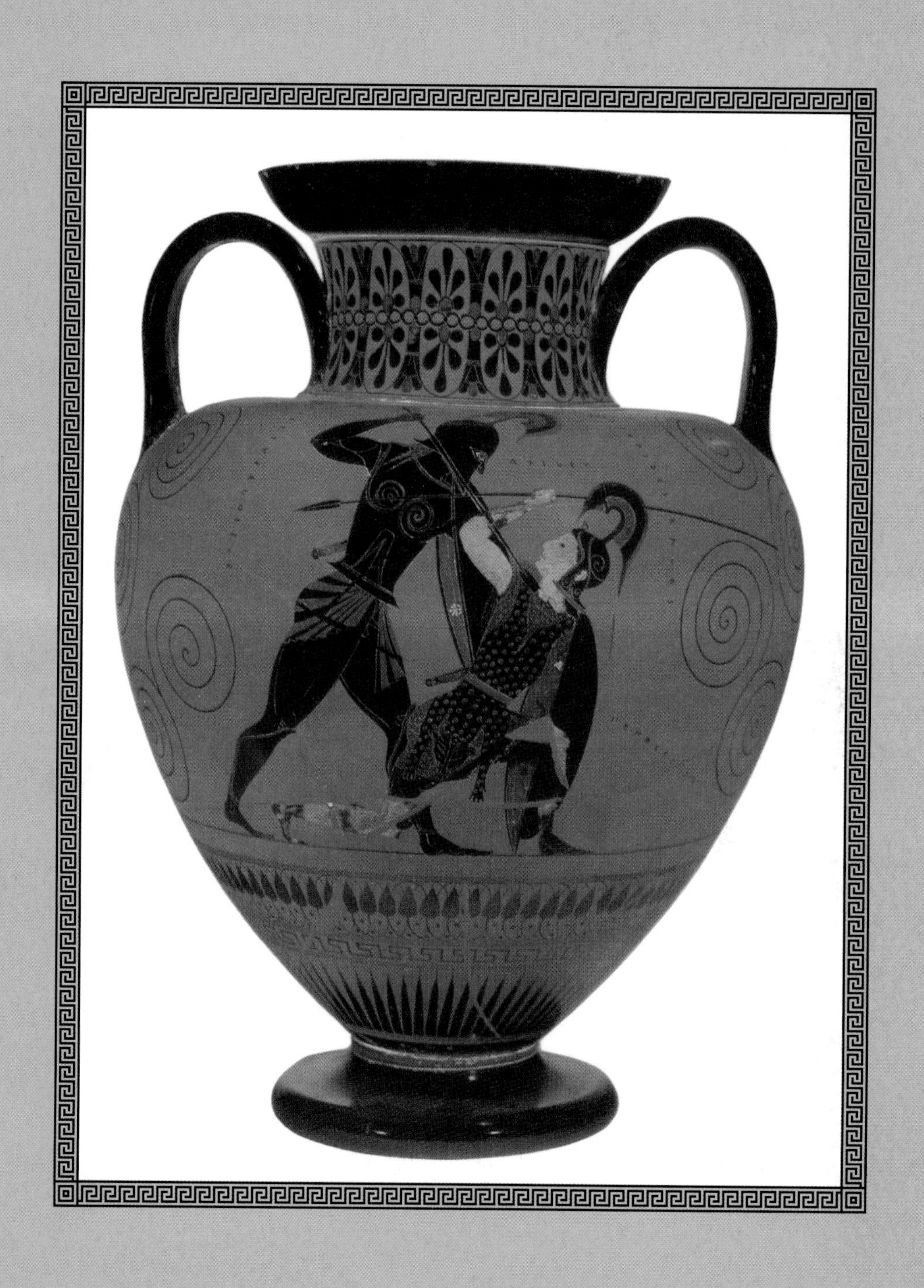

Greek Mythology

Introduction

Our word 'myth' derives from the ancient Greek word *muthos* which originally meant 'utterance' and came to mean 'a spoken or written story'. The Greek word *mythologia* meant 'talking about, or retelling stories'. Today, 'mythology' refers both to the body of myths of a society and to the study of those myths. There is, however, no precise definition of the word myth and scholars tend to divide myths into three main types: legends, folktales and 'pure' myths.

LEGENDS The importance of mythology to the ancient Greeks can be gauged by the subjects of their earliest surviving poems. In the 8th century BC, the poet Homer produced the first written version of the legends surrounding the Greek siege of Troy; these have survived as the epic poems the *Iliad* and the *Odyssey*. Legends deal with real events and people, but contain unreal elements normally associated with myth: meetings between mortals and gods, superhuman feats, magic and monsters. There are several possible reasons for this mixture of the real and the fantastic. The actual events of the Trojan War occurred some four centuries before Homer, at a time when the Greek world was run by kings who lived in luxurious palaces defended by high stone walls. Though these royal communities were relatively civilized, there was no written literature; therefore the history of events such as the Trojan War had to be passed down from generation to generation by poets relying on memory. This early poetry was designed to entertain and instruct the members of the royal courts, who identified with the heroes of the stories – after all, these heroes were their ancestors. Therefore, it is hardly surprising to find the poets glamourizing the Greek heroes as well as embroidering the facts with mythical stories of gods and monsters.

'PURE' MYTHS Hesiod, a contemporary of Homer, wrote the *Theogony* in which the Greek account of the creation of the world and its giants, gods and mortals was recorded for the first time. Again, there must have been many different versions of the story, passed down through the preceding centuries by the oral poets. Although Hesiod's poem is basically a catalogue of the divine family tree, the poet occasionally breaks the monotony by relating a self-contained 'pure' myth – that is, a myth relating directly to religion and ritual. For example, Hesiod's myth of Prometheus defined the early relationship between man and gods and 'explained' the nature of the animal sacrifices in Greek religious rituals. Likewise, Hesiod's myth of the 'Ages of Man' sought to explain why the Greek world of the 8th century BC was a violent and greedy place. There had once been a 'Golden Age' in which mortals and gods lived happily together on earth; Mother

BELOW *View of Mycenae: the Classical Greeks romanticized their prehistoric Mycenaean ancestors, believing that the huge stone walls had been built by the giant Cyclopes race: we still call this architectural style 'Cyclopean'. Traditionally the palace of King Agamemnon, who led the Greek army against Troy.*

Earth produced everything for man's consumption and manual labour was unnecessary. Unfortunately, the men became inquisitive and began to sail their ships to foreign lands from which they would return laden with riches; this newly acquired wealth had to be defended and the first city walls were built. Mother Earth was shut outside and men had to extract her natural gifts by force, using the same iron for their ploughs which they had used for their weapons. With the advent of greed and war the gods departed to the heavens in disgust. According to Hesiod, Greek culture had regressed from the Age of Gold, through the Silver and Bronze and Heroic Ages to his own Iron Age. However, there was an educational motive for this myth: Hesiod pleaded with his royal audience to refrain from greed and violence so that the Golden Age might return, a plea that was repeated by later poets.

ABOVE *View of the countryside at the monastery of Osios Loukas near Athens. The landscape, with its olive groves and wild limestone hills, has hardly changed since Classical times.*

FOLKTALES As the name suggests, folktales were mythical stories intended for the uneducated farming communities outside the palaces and cities. The heroes of folktales were often ordinary men and women as opposed to the royal princes and princesses of the poetic myths. Generally the social purpose of folktales was moral and cautionary rather than religious and ritualistic. Myths tended to come in the form of highly sophisticated poetry, whereas folktales were told as straightforward prose narratives or simple poems.

It is impossible to say whether all Greeks actually believed in their myths. By the Classical period (5th century BC) the Greek city-states had become complex social structures; wealthy citizens were educated in a wide range of subjects and although they read mythical and legendary poetry, they also studied philosophy which had developed rational explanations for most natural phenomena. Therefore myths might no longer have been seen as 'true stories' in sophisticated circles, but they continued to be referred to in every type of writing.

Our knowledge of Greek myths derives mainly from their literature, but it is rare to find a complete myth contained in a single piece of literature. As already referred to in the case of Homer and Hesiod, writing had developed relatively late in Greece, by which time the myths and legends were widely known from the oral tradition. Later writers could therefore depend on this knowledge in their audience, and concentrate on certain undeveloped aspects of the earlier stories. The consequent fragmentation of the surviving myths was accelerated by later poets who tended to alter them, giving different endings or explanations for a character's behaviour. These changes were not for variety only, but often reflected contemporary social attitudes. The female poet Sappho defended the behaviour of Helen of Troy as being divinely inspired, whilst male writers tended to blame the Trojan war on what they saw to be either feminine weakness or whorish behaviour. Likewise the writers of tragedies used the mythical framework of their plays to air the political and social problems of the day: thus legendary kings were often represented as contemporary tyrants threatening the new democracy of Classical Athens.

The Greek poet would use the myth as an entertaining story that would retain the audience's attention while allowing the poet to make contemporary implications. Theseus was seen in the 5th century BC as the hero of the new Athenian democracy and artists depicted him defeating uncivilized giants and Centaurs, symbols of the barbarian Persians who had invaded Greece earlier in the century.

Greek mythology bears many similarities to other ancient mythologies. This is particularly evident in the relationship of gods and heroes. In Norse mythology the god Odin can be compared to the Greek Zeus: Zeus ruled in Olympus, Odin in Valhalla;

ABOVE Charon on the River Styx; *Athenian white-ground* lekythos *(funerary oil container), late 5th century* BC. *Terracotta vases are a visually important source of our knowledge of the Greek myths and the subjects usually reflect their function: Charon is apt for a vase used in burial rituals.*

both used thunderbolts as weapons and both had angry wives, Hera and Frigg, ever-jealous of their affairs with mortal women; each had a favourite warrior daughter, Athene and Brunhild. The three Moerae (Fates) of Greek mythology sat and span mortal destinies; the Norns did the same in Norse mythology. The Norse heroes performed similar super-human exploits. Thus Siegfried slew the dragon Fafnir and fell in love with the divine Brunhild.

Since the 19th century this comparative mythology has become a serious academic discipline and many other links have been discovered between the myths of cultures as far apart as India and Celtic Britain. The Greek hero Heracles has been compared to both the Indian Sisupala and the Germanic Starkadr: for example, each hero was born with too much strength, had a divine helper and a divine enemy, and became immortal by a suicide brought about by a mortal assistant whom they rewarded with a supernatural gift: thus, in some traditions, Heracles gave his magic bow to Philoctetes who lit the hero's pyre. So striking are the similarities that scholars have used the comparison as evidence for a common 'Indo-European' cultural heritage.

ABOVE The introduction of Heracles to Olympus by Hermes and Athene; *Athenian black-figure* lekythos *(funerary oil container), 6th century* BC. *The deification of the mortal hero was an appropriate subject for this vase destined for an Athenian grave.*

In the 20th century we have created our own myths. Popular comic-strip heroes such as Superman and Wonderwoman often reflect the ancient Greek heroes. Wonderwoman was actually born from Greek myth as Diana, daughter of Hippolyte, Queen of the Amazons. Her creator, Charles Moulton, introduced her in 1941: 'At last, in a world torn by the hatreds and wars of men, appears a woman to whom the problems and feats of men are mere childsplay. With a hundred times the agility and strength of our best male athletes and strongest wrestlers, she appears as though from nowhere to avenge an injustice or right a wrong. As lovely as Aphrodite, as wise as Athena, with the speed of Mercury and the strength of Hercules, she is known only as *Wonderwoman!*'.

Modern heroes, like their ancient counterparts, exhibit extraordinary physical powers. The Greek Achilles was invulnerable except on his heel and Superman could only be destroyed by green Kryptonite: these weak points enable ordinary mortals to identify with the heroes. The heroes also tend to fall in love with someone they save: thus the Greek Perseus married Princess Andromeda after rescuing her from the sea-monster; Wonderwoman likewise fell in love with the airline pilot whom she had rescued after a crash.

The Greeks sometimes turned living men into heroes. Alexander the Great died in 323 BC; he was only 33 years old, but had built an empire from India to Egypt. In imitation of the mythical heroes such as Heracles, he argued that his father was Zeus and proceeded to 'prove' his divine parentage to the rest of the world by means of his heroic military campaigns. After his tragic early death his life-story was mythologized and the more youthful Greek and Roman military leaders regarded him as their hero, to the extent of even copying his famous hairstyle in their portraits. We have similar 20th-century 'living legends' whom we have likewise transformed into mythical figures by confusing their glamourized and hyped media images with reality.

In this book many of the myths have been grouped according to types of subject, such as heroic tales and tragic romances: this will enable the reader to appreciate the different kinds of story that interested the Greeks, but it will be noticed that many of the individual stories contain a mixture of legend, folktale and 'pure' myth. I have used the traditional Romanized spellings of names, but have retained the Greek forms of names like Heracles and Hermes (not the Roman Hercules or Mercury – see the Appendix for a list of comparative Greek and Roman name forms).

Finally, for the sake of narrative flow, I have selected my own favourite versions of the myths and only occasionally refer to alternate versions.

ABOVE *Silver coin showing Alexander the Great and Zeus, and a marble copy of the original portrait head by the sculptor Lysippos. On the coin, Alexander wears Heracles' lion-skin, raising him to superhuman levels. The reverse depicts Zeus with his eagle – Alexander, like Heracles, claimed Zeus to be his real father. Alexander controlled his image by allowing only one sculptor (Lysippos) and one painter (Apelles) to portray him. The dramatic deep-set eyes, rather anxious heavy forehead and windswept hair, parted off-centre, were immediately recognizable in antiquity; these features were repeated in images of later generals who wished to emulate Alexander's heroism.*

ONE

The Birth of the Gods

The earliest and also the fullest account of the creation and the birth of the giants and gods is to be found in Hesiod's poem, the 'Theogony' (literally, 'The Birth of the Gods'). Hesiod lived in the 8th century BC *at the time when the Greeks first introduced writing skills. We must assume that his account is the culmination of centuries of poems told from memory and handed from generation to generation in an oral tradition. As with other Greek myths, it cannot therefore be considered the only version of the story, but Hesiod's was the most influential source for later poets. There are remarkable parallels with the creation myths of the Hittites and Babylonians, whose literary versions were produced five centuries earlier. Recent archaeological and literary studies have suggested a much greater level of contact between Greece and the Orient than was previously thought for this early period, and Hesiod is now considered to have produced a mixture of oriental and Greek mythology. There was no single divine creator in Greek mythology; the Earth and the Sky 'emerged' from the void and together gave birth to worldly life forms.*

First there was Chaos, a chasm without shape or light. The ample-breasted Gaia (Mother Earth) emerged, where one day gods and men would dwell; deep beneath her swirled the mists of Tartarus, later the prison of rebellious giant Titans; and then appeared the most handsome god of all, Eros (Sexual Love), who numbs our limbs and defeats our reason – he has the same effect on the immortal gods. No birth of gods, giants, animals or men would have taken place without his power of attraction.

From the chasm came the two dark ones, Erebus (Dark Underworld) beneath Gaia and Nyx (Night) above her. Eros was present; Nyx and Erebus made love and Nyx gave birth to her brilliant and beautiful children; Aether (Upper Air) with his azure satin cloak stretched across the top of the sky; and his sister Hemera (Day) who steps out of Tartarus bringing us light and returns in the twilight, greeting her mother, Nyx, on the other side of the road.

THE BIRTH OF THE TITANS

Meanwhile lonely Gaia felt the touch of Eros and produced a lover of herself and for herself; his name was Uranus (Heaven) and he covered her with his black velvet cloak, decorated with glittering stars, amongst which the gods would later make a home. Gaia twisted and turned and formed Ourea (the mountains), the home of Oreads (mountain-nymphs); from her came also never-draining Pontus (sea).

Eros produced a longing in Gaia for her own son Uranus, who showered her with heavenly rain and produced the swirling depths of Oceanus, the river which encircles mother Gaia. Oceanus was the first of the Titans, children of Gaia and Uranus. Next came Thea and Phoebe and their famous sisters, Tethys of the sea, Themis and Rhea of the earth, and Mnemosyne (Memory) who helps us to recall our myths; their brothers were Coeus, Crius and Iapetus and dazzling Hyperion of the sun. But the youngest was wicked little Cronus, whose schemings would later dethrone lusty Uranus, the father he despised. Later still, the three Cyclopes were born. They had only one eye at the centre of their foreheads and were skilful and crafty smiths. Their names were Brontes (Thunder), Steropes (Lightning), and Arges (Whitebolt); it was they who later forged the mighty thunderbolt of Olympian Zeus. More children were born to Gaia and Uranus, each one more monstrous then the last: the three Hecatoncheires brothers – Cottus, Gyes and Obriareus – each with 100 hands and fifty heads. Their appearance was abhorrent to Uranus, who feared and loathed his own offspring. As they were born, he pushed them back into the cavernous recesses of Gaia's womb, and delighted in her painful groans.

Gaia in her despair made a huge scythe from grey adamant and, showing it to her imprisoned children, said, 'My dear ones, would you dare to put an end to your father's evil ways?'. Young Cronus replied, 'I am not afraid of my cruel father. It would be right to put an end to his unspeakable behaviour; after all, it is of his own doing.' Gaia explained her plot to Cronus, handed him the awesome sickle and took him to a shady place for the ambush.

At twilight lusty Uranus appeared, walking alongside Nyx, his aunt. In his usual violent manner he mounted Gaia, smothering her with his black bejewelled cloak. Immediately Cronus grabbed Uranus's genitals and, with one sweep of the sharp-toothed sickle, cut them off and threw them carelessly behind him. The drops of blood which bespattered Gaia produced the Erinyes (Furies), who in memory of their birth haunt those who murder their own kin. The genitals themselves landed on the beach. The waves caressed them in the presence of Eros and Himerus (Desire) and soon white foam appeared and a girl was born. She came ashore on Cythera, then appeared in Cyprus as a beautiful goddess, and, because she was born from the foam, was named Aphrodite (literally 'foam-born').

Uranus in his anger gave his children the unflattering name of Titans. We also call them Giants.

BELOW *Sandro Botticelli (1444–1510),* The Birth of Venus. *Using ancient literary descriptions Botticelli 'recreated' lost easel-paintings by famous Greek painters which would have pleased his classically educated patrons. In this painting Aphrodite appears in a well known Hellenistic pose which Botticelli adapted from an antique statue. The shell appeared in ancient versions of the birth.*

NYX AND HER CHILDREN

Meanwhile Nyx produced many children of her own. From her came many of the dark and gloomy forces which oppress us: she it was who gave us our Fate and our Death, our Sleep and Dreams, and Misery with whom no god will sleep. As a reason for the gods to despise us she produced Nemesis, the goddess of retribution, who inspires both the gods and mortals with feelings of resentment when our fellow men misbehave. Dreadful Nyx gave us the facts of life we curse: Old Age, Deceit and hard-hearted Eris (Strife), who in turn bore Battles and Slaughter, Pretence and Arguments between neighbours, and Oath who strikes when we swear a falsehood.

LEFT *Eustache Le Sueur (1616–55),* The Sea Gods and the God of Love. *Two sailors (left) are approached by Poseidon with his trident, Tritons blowing conch shells, and Nereids. The presence of Cupids would suggest the impending mermaid-like 'marriage' of the doomed sailors to the Nereids.*

NEREUS

Pontus (Sea) produced with his mother Gaia the resplendent gods of the sea: from them came Nereus, the Old Man of the Sea, so kind and trustworthy and blessed with many lovely children – fifty girls who play in the watery lap of their grandfather Pontus. Such wonderful names they have: Speo the swift, rosy-armed Hipponoe, Galatea the beautiful, Amphitrite of the pretty ankles and Halimede with her gleaming diadem, floating beside Euarne with her perfect figure, a joy to behold.

Gaia lay with her son Nereus and bore huge Thaumas who married Electra, a daughter of deep Oceanus. Thaumus and Electra had peculiar children: Iris, a messenger of the gods, fleet of foot she is, and when she sometimes stops to catch her breath, we see a rainbow, carrying all the colours of heaven down to earth; how she raises our spirits after the storms created by angry Zeus! Yet the sisters of Iris are the Harpies, they look so pretty with their lovely hair, racing along in the storm-gales faster than birds, but many have they snatched from the earth as they fly, friends whom we never meet again.

THE CHILDREN OF CETO AND PHORCYS

The brother of Thaumas was noble Phorcys, who, admiring the splendid cheeks of his sister Ceto, lay with her to produce the Old Women, the Graeae; grey haired, they have only a single tooth and one eye between them, which they share. Ceto also bore the Gorgons; they live near Oceanus in the farthest regions of the earth, past the Atlas mountains, neighbours of Nyx and the sweet-singing Hesperides sisters, who guard the golden apples of the tree given by Gaia to Hera when she married Zeus. The Gorgon sisters are Stheno, Euryale and Medusa. Unlike her sisters, Medusa was mortal and one day when she was sitting in a meadow, surrounded by the first flowers of spring, the god with the sable locks,

LEFT The Gorgon Medusa; *painted terracotta plaque, 6th century* BC. *Such 'apotropaic' plaques decorated the roofs of Greek temples and were intended to frighten away evil spirits. The kneeling pose was used by Archaic Greek artists to suggest a running figure.*

Poseidon, made love to her; but she never saw her children for the hero Perseus cut off her head as a gift for a king. From her neck sprang Chrysaor with his golden sword, father of the three-headed giant Geryon whom Heracles killed for his cattle, and Pegasus, the wonderful winged horse.

As if that were not enough troublesome children for Ceto and Phorcys, one day a real monster was born to them, Echidna by name; the gods gave her a cave deep beneath the earth, because neither they nor mortal men could bear her, for although she looked quite normal from the waist up, her lower half was serpent, all snake-like and slippery.

THE CHILDREN OF ECHIDNA

Typhon, the Titan offspring of Gaia and Tartarus, became Echidna's friend and a number of fearsome offspring were produced, some of them now famous: Orthus the two-headed dog who helped to guard Geryon's cattle, but was killed by an arrow of Heracles; and the much more formidable guard-dog of Hades, Cerberus; some say he has as many as fifty heads and a resounding bark like a bronze cauldron struck by a sword. There was also the terrible Hydra of Lerna, object of one of Heracles' labours; you cut off one head and she grew two more. A worthy sister for the Hydra was the fire-breathing Chimaera; now she had just three heads, but one was a lion, one a goat, and one a snake. The hero Bellerophon would one day kill her, helped by his winged steed Pegasus. Echidna did not mind whether she loved Titan or monster, and even had children by her own son, the dog Orthus; to this couple were born the famous riddling Sphinx, who brought death to so many Thebans before Oedipus solved the problem, and the Nemean Lion, whose pelt Heracles wore after slaying it for his first labour.

The last of Echidna's children was the serpent Ladon that guards the golden apples of the Hesperides.

THE CHILDREN OF TETHYS AND OCEANUS

Tethys, lovely daughter of Gaia and Uranus, lay with brother Oceanus and their children were the elegant-ankled Oceanids (sea-nymphs) and the river-gods of the earth – the Nile, the fair-flowing Danube, and those that run through Greece. The Oceanids were also joined by other beautiful nymphs, spirits of nature: the Naiads who swim in the rivers and springs; the Dryads who dwell in the trees; the Oreads of the mountains;

RIGHT Nereid riding the waves on a sea-bird; *late 5th century* BC. *She was one of several Nereids standing between the columns of a royal tomb at Xanthus in East Greece: in this funerary context the figures were probably symbolic of the journey to the after-life. The drapery is suitably wet and clinging.*

the Nereids of the sea. Lucky the man who glimpses them, for they bring good fortune to those who treat them with respect; but woe to that man who abuses them, who cuts a sacred tree or pollutes a spring.

THE CHILDREN OF THEA AND HYPERION

Thea and Hyperion, sister and brother of Tethys, also had children: the mighty Helius (the Sun) took after his father; by day he is woken by his rosy-fingered sister Eos (Dawn) and rides across the sky in a four-horse chariot, sinking into Oceanus at dusk to refresh his tired horses; at night he floats eastwards along Oceanus in a golden bowl. His shining sister Selene (the Moon) drives her chariot by night, a dimmer light so as not to wake us.

THE CHILDREN OF EOS AND ASTRAEUS

Astraeus was born to two other children of Gaia, Crius and Eurybia. Mist-born Eos and starry Astraeus gave birth to the bright Morning Star and many other shining ones in the garland of heaven; to them were born also the flint-hearted Winds: Zephyrus comes with his clearing breezes from the west; Boreas rushes down from the north; Notus comes up from the south and Argestes blows from the east.

THE CHILDREN OF STYX AND PALLAS

Pallas was a brother of Astraeus and together with the stream of Styx, an Oceanid, brought into the world Aspiration and winged Nike (Victory) with her trim ankles, and their outstanding brothers Power and Strength; all four never leave the side of thundering Zeus, they sit beside his throne and follow him wherever he goes. On that fateful day when Zeus summoned the immortal gods to Mount Olympus for a counsel of war against the Titans, he pledged, 'I shall give to any of you who fight alongside me all the privileges and honours which our cruel father Cronus denies you. This shall be our justice and revenge.' Oceanus sensibly sided with the Olympians and sent his ever-flowing daughter Styx to pledge the family's eternal loyalty. Zeus blessed her waters and made her a symbol of oaths taken by the gods and he took her children under his protection.

THE CHILDREN OF PHOEBE AND COEUS

The Titans Coeus and Phoebe were brother and sister of Cronus, and to these two were born Leto of the sable gown, loved by men and gods for her gentleness and as mother of the two Olympians, Apollo and Artemis. Her grand-daughter was Hecate, one of the few Titans not despised by Zeus, who made her the nurse of our young children; powerful Hecate moves between heaven, earth and sea, and brings success by standing beside all who worship her, be they fighters, farmers, athletes or fishermen.

THE CHILDREN OF RHEA AND CRONUS

At last some gods were born to Cronus and his sister Rhea: Hestia who protects the hearth of our houses; Demeter who dwells beneath the earth and sends up cereal crops through the soil; Hera of the golden sandals who blesses marriages and the birth of our children; merciless Hades, the unseen, unmentionable lord of the dead who dwells with his sister Demeter under the earth – we prefer to call on Plutus (the giver of wealth) to grant us the fruits of the Underworld; booming Poseidon, who rules the waves and brings earthquakes to the land – he is also lord of horses and keeps his own stables at the bottom of the sea; and the father of us all, gods and men, mighty Zeus who shakes the wide earth with his thunder.

But their father Cronus was worried about these children, as his own father Uranus had rightly been about Cronus, who had deposed him. Gaia and Uranus had warned Cronus that the same fate would befall him, that one day he too would be defeated by a child of his own. Whereas Uranus had pushed his babies back into Gaia's womb, Cronus, knowing how his mother had deceived Uranus, would not trust Rhea to keep them and he would therefore swallow them as they were born. But Rhea had a plan of her own; when she was expecting her sixth child, Zeus, she appealed to starry Uranus and Gaia to help her in avenging the wrongs of scheming Cronus. They told Rhea to come, when she felt that the baby was due, across the sea to the island of Crete. When Rhea felt the birth pangs, she travelled swiftly through the dark night until she found a hidden cave at Lyktos on Crete. There she left her baby in the care of Gaia and some nymphs, and back she rushed to

LEFT *Goya (1746–1828),* Cronus Devouring One of his Children. *The painter has emphasized the pre-civilized nature of the Titan, enjoying his cannibalistic meal against the dark backdrop of Chaos.*

Cronus, presenting him with a rock, bound in swaddling clothes, which he promptly swallowed.

Meanwhile Zeus grew into a strong young man, and the nymphs told him of his father's cruelty. Zeus married the Titan Metis (Thought) who slipped an emetic into Cronus' wine; a moment later up came the rock, which you can still see at Delphi, followed by the brothers and sisters of Zeus, first Poseidon, then Hades, Hera, Demeter and Hestia. Zeus also freed the Cyclopes; one day they would return his help by providing him with weapons of thunder and lightning against the Titans.

THE OLYMPIANS

The Children of Zeus

Zeus took the Oceanid Metis (Cunning Resourcefulness) as his first wife. Now Uranus and Gaia gave him the same advice that they had given Cronus, namely that he should beware his offspring. When one day he discovered that Metis was with child, he swallowed her, and prevented the birth of a son who would certainly have usurped his power; but the birth of a grey-eyed daughter Athene was allowed, and she had the wisdom of her father.

He then married slender Themis (Righteousness), Titan daughter of Uranus and Gaia, who gave birth to the three Horae sisters who watch over the affairs of mortals; they usher in the seasons of spring, summer and winter, and their names are Eirene (Peace), Eunomia (Order), and Dike (Justice). Three more daughters she had: Clotho, Lachesis and Atropos, the Fates who spin, measure out and cut the threads of our lives, apportioning both good and bad things.

Attracted to an Oceanid called Eurynome, who had her mother Tethys's lovely looks, he had by her the three Graces; they melt our flesh with loving glances from their incredibly beautiful eyes; they fill our hearts with delight. They are aptly named Aglaea (Splendour), Euphrosyne (Good Cheer) and Thalia (Festivity).

With Demeter Zeus had white-armed Persephone, whom Hades snatched from the land of the living with her father's blessing.

By Mnemosyne he had nine daughters, the Muses; each wears a golden diadem to set off her lovely hair, inherited from their mother. They attend us at our feasts when we sing our songs of love and war. Their home is on Mount Pieria, near Olympus, but they also join musical Apollo at Mount Parnassus above Delphi, and have been seen on Helicon in Boeotia, anywhere where poets find their inspiration.

ABOVE The three Graces: *Pompeian wall-painting, 1st century* AD. *One of several versions of the group appearing as decorations on the walls of private Roman houses. The painting probably copied a lost Hellenistic sculpture and depicts the figures in a formal dance-like arrangement with flowers in their hands and hair.*

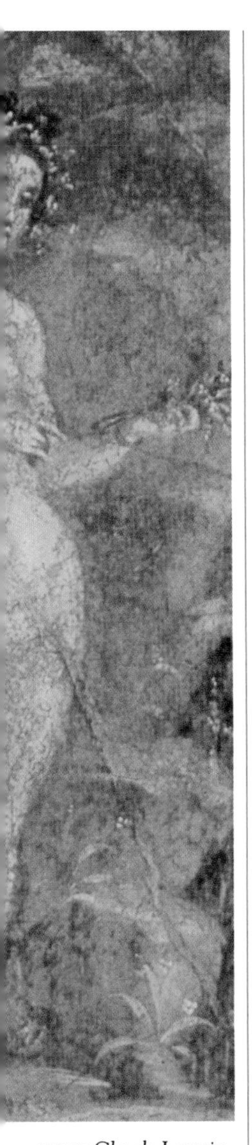

The king of gods and men finally married his sister Hera and she bore Ares the war god, Hebe goddess of youthful beauty who is cup-bearer to the Olympians and would one day marry the deified Heracles, and Eileithyia goddess of childbirth.

Without a woman's help was born Athene, who rouses our spirits to battle and leads our armies, loving the noise of the battlefield. Hera was furious and, as an act of revenge on her husband, produced Hephaestus the skilled craftsman of the Olympians.

Other Divine Births

The sea-goddess Amphitrite was loved by Poseidon the earth-shaker, but she refused his affections and fled to Atlas for protection. Poseidon in his despair sent his scouts our searching for her, and it was Delphinus who found her; as a reward, Poseidon placed him in the night sky as the constellation we call the Dolphin. Poseidon and Amphitrite had a powerful son Triton who lives with his parents in a house of gold at the bottom of the sea.

Aphrodite and Ares, the piercer of shields, had two formidable sons, Terror and Fear, who go into battle with their father the city destroyer, breaking the tightest of battle-lines. Their daughter Harmonia married Cadmus the Theban king, and their own children were to meet tragedy after tragedy; Agave would one day kill her son Pentheus in the worship of Dionysus; Autonoe was the mother of Actaeon, a victim of his own hunting-hounds; and Polydorus was

BELOW Zeus and Hera; *Greek sculpted metope, early 5th century* BC. *Hera is depicted drawing aside her wedding veil in her marriage to Zeus. The stylized patterning of the drapery folds is typical of Archaic art.*

RIGHT *Claude Lorrain (1600–82),* Apollo and the Muses on Mount Helicon. *The painter has depicted Greek Helicon in a misty northern landscape. The Classical temple probably adapted a Roman model.*

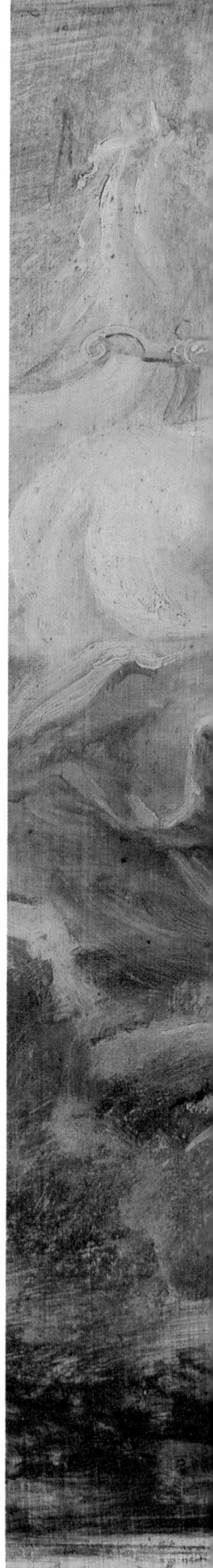

ABOVE *Peter Paul Rubens (1577–1640),* Jupiter and Semele. *Hera tricked the mortal Semele into making her lover appear in his true divine guise. Rubens depicts Zeus (Jupiter) with his thunderbolts destroying Semele.*

RIGHT *Peter Paul Rubens (1577–1640),* Aurora and Cephalus. *Eos (Aurora), the goddess of Dawn, invites the tired hunter into her chariot. His sleeping dogs are contrasted with the wide-awake horses.*

the ancestor of ill-fated Oedipus. They also had Semele who slept with Zeus and had a divine son, merry Dionysus of the golden locks, who one day would marry the auburn-haired Ariadne, daughter of King Minos of Crete; Zeus made her ageless and immortal for his son. The hero Heracles was born from another union between immortal and mortal, Zeus and Alcmene; after completing his labours, he was granted eternal life.

Maia the daughter of Atlas, climbed Olympus and had a glorious child by Zeus, Hermes the herald of the gods.

Zeus and Leto had two children, the loveliest of the gods in the heavens, Artemis and Apollo.

The Oceanid Perseis and Helius, tireless god of the Sun, had a daughter Circe the sorceress who would one day give brave sons to the hero Odysseus, and a son Aeetes, king of the land of the Golden Fleece. With another Oceanid, Idyia of the lovely cheeks, Aeetes had slender-ankled Medea.

Children of The Goddesses

The noble goddess of cereals Demeter lay with the hero Iasion in a fertile Cretan field that had been ploughed three times, an ancient ritual. Their son was the beneficient god Plutus (Agricultural Wealth) who walks the earth and gives riches and good fortune to anyone he meets.

Eos (Dawn) desired Cephalus, son of Hermes, and their son Phaethon, who was godlike in his beauty, attracted the attention of Aphrodite, lover of smiles; she carried him off to be a priest in her Syrian temple.

Aphrodite with the gleaming diadem made love to mortal Anchises of Troy and their son was heroic Aeneas (who would one day found the Roman people).

The daughters of Nereus, the Old Man of the Sea, had amorous adventures too. Thetis of the silvery feet was pursued by the mortal Peleus, changing shapes to avoid his grasp; their child was Achilles the lionheart.

BELOW *Jan Cossiers (1600–71),* Prometheus Carrying Fire. *The rebellious Titan is shown bringing the blazing light of Olympus to dark earth; the stolen fire is hidden in a hollow fennel stalk.*

Prometheus, Champion of Mankind

The story of Prometheus the Titan appears in the earliest Greek literature and figurative vase-painting. His enduring popularity throughout the Classical period is surely due to his defiance of divine authority in order to provide mankind with the essentials of civilized life. It is no surprise that the Early Romantic artists such as the composer Beethoven and the poet Shelley became fascinated by Prometheus as a symbol of the superhuman struggle for justice. Here is Hesiod's account.

Iapetus was yet another Titan brother of Cronus; he went to the bed of the fine-ankled Oceanid Clymene, who bore him the strong-armed Atlas, whose punishment from Zeus one day would be to hold up the heavens from the earth; and Prometheus, such an intelligent schemer, like his uncle Cronus; and Epimetheus, his fool of a brother.

Prometheus fashioned clay objects, presenting the finished works to Olympian Zeus for approval. One day he invented man in the shape of Phaenon, a boy of beautiful features. Knowing Zeus' unbridled attraction to both boys and girls, Prometheus kept Phaenon from him. Zeus saw the youth from the clouds and sent his eagle down to snatch him. The king of the gods refused to hand back Prometheus' most prized creation and placed him in the heavens as the planet Jupiter. Prometheus defiantly made more from the same mould – thus the race of men came into being.

The gods demanded sacrifices of oxen from the men, more than they could give. Prometheus persuaded Zeus to accept only a part of each ox, but Zeus demanded that he be allowed to choose the best cut. Crafty Prometheus butchered an ox, wrapping the inedible bones and innards in tasty looking fat; the other portion consisted of the best meat, but was wrapped in unappetizing ox-hide. Zeus made the wrong choice, and being god of oaths, was compelled to receive the same tripe at every future sacrifice.

Zeus refused men the civilizing gift of fire; Prometheus stole it for his protégés, concealing it in the hollow stalk of fennel. As punishment, Zeus had Prometheus nailed to a cliff and every evening sent his eagle to peck at his liver, which each night regenerated, thus prolonging his agony. Thirty-thousand years later, Herakles shot the eagle with an arrow and freed Prometheus from his torment.

In the meantime life on earth had become too comfortable. Therefore Zeus commanded the smith-god Hephaestus to match Prometheus' beautiful creation with something that would plague men for ever. Hephaestus decided to create something that men would find beautiful, but discover to be bad at the core, just like the deceitful sacrifices which men offer gods. He created woman and called her Pandora. Grey-eyed Athene made a shining white dress for her, drew a beautiful embroidered veil over her head, but most wonderful of all was the golden crown which she placed on Pandora's lovely head; on this Hephaestus had hammered and chased all the animals of the earth and fish of the sea, and so lifelike they were that you could almost see them move and hear their different voices.

Pandora was presented to Epimetheus (whose name means 'think later'). His brother Prometheus (whose name means 'think first'), had warned him never to accept gifts from the gods. But Pandora came with a rich dowry and a sealed jar with the words 'DO NOT OPEN' written on its neck. Epimetheus immediately opened it and all the troubles of the world flew out; only Hope was left at the bottom.

BELOW The creation of Pandora; *Athenian red-figure vase painting, early 5th century* BC. *(Left to right) Zeus, Hermes, Hephaestus, Pandora, with Eros floating above Pandora's head.*

THE BATTLE OF THE TITANS AND OLYMPIANS

Beneath Mount Olympus is the plain of Thessaly, on the other side of which stands another mountain called Othrys; on high Othrys the proud race of giants, the Titans led by Cronus, had built a great fortress, from which they fought the gods whose leader was Zeus. The war had been going on for ten years, neither side gaining the upper hand. One day Zeus freed the Hecatoncheires, the three giants with 100 hands each, most terrifying children of Gaia and Uranus. He fed his new allies nectar and ambrosia, food of the gods, and as they sat and ate together with the Olympians, Zeus stood and addressed the three brothers, Cottus, Gyes and Obriareus:

'Now listen to me, children of Gaia and Uranus, and let me tell you what I really think. We have been fighting your brother and sister Titans for many years; the victory will bring us total power. Will you now repay us for giving you freedom after so many years spent beneath the earth in darkness? Let us see you making good use of those 100 hands by wielding many swords and spears against the Titans.'

Cottus immediately stood up and replied from one of his fifty heads:

'You are our friend indeed, great Zeus. You do not have to remind us of the time we have spent in our gloomy prison, humiliated by cruel Cronus, unable to put our strength to good use. We can see that you have great intelligence and profound understanding, which you have used to save the immortals from grave danger, and now you have brought the three of us out of darkness into light and we are eternally in your debt. To show our gratitude we will make sure that you will gain a final victory over the Titans; there will be terrible bloodshed and great slaughter on that day.'

BELOW Athene fights Alcyoneus and Gaia; *relief sculpture from the altar of Zeus at Pergamon, early 2nd century BC. Athene wears the aegis (breastplate) with Medusa's head attached. Gaia emerges from the earth to help her son. Winged Nike (right) awards Athene the victory crown. The dramatic 'baroque' style with its contorted, emotional figures is typical of Hellenistic art.*

LEFT *Giovanni Battista Tiepolo (1693–1770)* Olympus. *Zeus sits in majesty on a cloud, while Hermes performs aerobatics above; Aphrodite sits with Eros (Cupid) aboard a chariot pulled by her sacred doves; Athene appears below. Tiepolo's skill at decorating palatial ceilings with divine skyscapes is exhibited here on canvas.*

The Olympian gods, sitting round the great table, applauded the speech and raising their cups of nectar, made a toast to their strange new allies. The thought of victory after so many years inspired a yearning for battle in their hearts and the Hecatoncheires led the charge across the plains of Thessaly to the Titan stronghold. They discarded the spears and swords given to them by the gods, finding them of little use against the strong walls built by the Titans. Instead they tore entire cliffs from the mountain and hurled these uncouth but effective missiles at the Titan defences. In their turn, the Titans retaliated, and never have the earth, sea and sky been so near to collapsing than on that day. Their battle-cries shook the very top of Mount Olympus and resounded down to the dark depths of Tartarus and way up again into the heavens; even the stars were shaking.

Zeus, seeing that his splendid palace, the work of Hephaestus, was in imminent danger of collapsing, grew angry and displayed his full powers for the first time. He was fearful to behold as he reached into the starry heavens for his thunderbolts. Out of the huge gates of Olympus he came, fury in his eyes, blinding sparks of lightning flashing around his majestic body as he strode across the plain. Nothing was safe from his destruction on that day; he left scorched footprints in the life-giving earth, and the forests crackled with fire as he passed. Soon the flames were everywhere, licking the flat earth and lashing out at the heavens; if you could have borne to look at it, you would have seen into the deepest parts of the chasm, so bright was the fiery glare, and intense the heat. There was a mighty crash as though Uranus had collapsed with all his weight on top of Gaia, and the winds came from all sides to magnify the might of Zeus. To tip the scales of the battle the Hecatoncheires took a rock in each hand, and soon the sky was darkened by 300 missiles, which hurtled down upon the Titans within their stronghold. They could no longer resist the terrible onslaught, and the gods chased them down the mountain and beneath the earth into dark Tartarus, which is as far below earth as heaven is above it – a bronze anvil, dropped from earth would take ten days to hit the bottom of Tartarus.

THE UNDERWORLD AND ITS INHABITANTS

Tartarus is like a huge jar enclosed in three layers of pitch darkness, with a stopper of bronze to keep the Titans from earth. Cottus, Gyes and valiant Obriareus stand guard over it; and inside they say there are violent gusts, the only sensation in the terrifying darkness; even the gods do not like to think about the place. Nearby stands the gloomy house of Nyx (Night) with its thick black curtains. By day Nyx lives there, but at night she leaves it and greets her daughter Hemera (Day) whom she passes on her way to the house, which they share but where they can never be found at home together. While Hemera carries light around the earth, Nyx sits at home, brooding over her children, beautiful young Hypnos (Sleep) and his ugly elder brother Thanatos (Death). Helius never sees either of them: Hypnos moves quietly over sea and land, gentle and mild towards mankind; but Thanatos struts about at random, with heart of iron and merciless soul of bronze, destroying anyone he comes upon.

In a magnificent palace with silver columns supporting a roof of long rocks, lives Styx, the goddess who makes even the immortals shudder; for when there is a dispute among the gods on Olympus, or one of them is accused of speaking a lie, Zeus sends rainbow-bodied Iris down into the depths of the underworld to bring the great oath of the gods back from the river Styx (which they swear by). The water

ABOVE *Joachim Patinir (c1480–1524)* Charon Crossing the River Styx. *Angel-like figures (left) escort the dead from the land of the living, with its fantastic crystal domes, to the banks of the River Styx. Charon ferries them to Hades (right), where Cerberus guards the gates; the fires and scenes of death together with the angels suggest a Christian vision of Hell. The painting is typical of the cool expansive landscapes of northern Renaissance artists.*

enters the Styx from a great height, cascading down a high cliff, at the bottom of which Iris collects the water in a golden jug. Any god who breaks an oath sworn over that holy water, can expect to lie in a coma breathless for a year without touching his food of nectar or ambrosia; and that is only the beginning of his ordeal, for after his illness he is exiled from the snowy peak of Olympus. After nine years he can once again join the immortals at their meals.

ZEUS FIGHTS TYPHON

After Zeus had pushed the Titans out of heaven and earth, there was a brief time of peace, while the smouldering lands and forests tried to recuperate after the battle. But Gaia decided to have yet another child, this time with dark Tartarus, inspired by golden Aphrodite; his name was Typhon, and he is one of the most terrifying creatures, with 100 heads like snakes with flickering black tongues and sinister eyes glimmering with fire beneath the brows; but most remarkable were the different voices that could be heard from each head. You could sometimes hear the bellowing of a mighty bull, and at other times the roar of a wild lion, or the howling of a pack of hunting-dogs; and sometimes he would seem to utter in crystal tones for the ears of the gods, or they would all hiss together echoing in the surrounding hills. This proud son of Tartarus and Gaia had a high ambition, no less than to rule the heavens and the earth.

Luckily Zeus became aware of his scheming, and out he strode to defend Olympus a second time. Once more the earth and sky resounded with his thunder and even the dark violet sea was set alight as Typhon the giant fought Zeus the god with his fiery breath. Beneath the earth Hades himself trembled with fear, and Cronus and the Titans down in Tartarus also heard the fearsome noise of fighting. Zeus stood on Olympus and reached into the heavens for his lightning and thunderbolts. Suddenly he leapt from the mountain down onto the monster's back, pummelling him with blow after blow. Typhon gradually weakened and as he hit the ground, his mother Gaia groaned under his huge weight. The land for miles around was scorched by the heat of his crippled body, in places it melted like tin when heated in crucibles by metalworkers, or when iron is smelted by the craft of Hephaestus. Before any more damage could be done, Zeus hurled the hefty body down into Tartarus, a fine companion for the Titans. Typhon brings violent winds and havoc to sailors at sea, and his typhoons are destructive to the work of men too; crops and flowers are uprooted by his gusts and the air is filled with dust.

LEFT Zeus hurling a thunderbolt; *hollow-cast bronze discovered in the sea off Cape* Artemisium, c460–450 BC. *One of the few surviving Classical bronze orginals. The weapon is lost and some identify him as Poseidon throwing a trident; however the short Greek thunderbolt appears to fit the hand better than a trident, which would also interrupt the view of the face. Nudity is a feature of Greek gods and heroes in action; originally the statue would have been more lifelike with glass/stone eyes, polished tawny flesh and (probably) red copper-coated lips and nipples.*

RIGHT Apollo; *hollow-cast bronze discovered in the ancient Athenian port of Piraeus, c530–520* BC. *He originally held a bow in his left hand and a sacred bowl in his right. His frontal and symmetrical 'Egyptian' pose is typical of Archaic art.*

BELOW Kleobis and Biton; *discovered at the Sanctuary of Apollo at Delphi, early 6th century* BC.

GREEK SCULPTURE

Stylistic periods of Greek Art:
c650–490 BC: ARCHAIC
c490–450 BC: EARLY CLASSICAL
c450–400 BC: HIGH CLASSICAL
c400–323 BC: LATE CLASSICAL
c323–30 BC: HELLENISTIC

In prehistoric times, Greek artists had created images of gods and goddesses from tree-trunks and beaten metal. In the 7th century BC they learnt from the Egyptians how to carve marble statues; this tradition continued throughout the Classical period. In the 6th century BC they also learnt the technique of casting large, hollow bronze statues. During the Archaic period there was little physical distinction between gods and men. The statues were used as offerings to the gods (male nudes for gods, draped females for goddesses) to stand around their temples; but were these representations of the god or the worshipper? They were also used as tomb monuments to commemorate the deceased. In the Archaic period, sculptors, painters and even potters and painters of vases begin to sign their work and to label figures with names, suggesting a degree of respect for their work by socially superior patrons, as well as a relatively high standard of literacy.

A pair of Archaic statues which can be identified are Kleobis and Biton; they were set up at Delphi in the early 6th century BC to commemorate the heroic deed of the two brothers. The Greek historian Herodotus tells us that their mother wished to attend the festival of Hera at Argos; as the temple was several miles away she asked her farmer husband for the use of his oxen to take her by cart, but he replied that they were needed in the fields. Therefore her two sons, Kleobis and Biton, offered to pull the cart. At the festival

ABOVE Poseidon, Apollo and Artemis; *from the Athenian Parthenon frieze, 447–432* BC. *This slab comes from the east end, where the gods were shown presiding over the procession which decorated the rest of the 525-foot/160-metre frieze. The designer, probably Phidias, exhibits qualities typical of High Classical sculptors: a mixture of naturalism and idealism in drapery and anatomy; an avoidance of monotony by varying the poses and gestures of the figures.*

their mother prayed at night to Hera to grant her sons the greatest of divine rewards; the next morning she woke to find them dead and their immortality was assured by the sending of these two marble statues to Delphi. The dedication is certain owing to the preserved inscription on the statue base.

By the 5th century BC these bronze and marble figures could represent both gods and men, and had reached a high degree of naturalism which always conformed to an ideal of beauty. The marble statues were always painted in increasingly lifelike colours. The bronzes were also more naturalistic than they now appear; they would be polished to a tawny, flesh-like surface with red copper lips and nipples, silver-coated teeth and realistic eyes of coloured stone. The gods are recognizable by their attributes: Apollo holds a bow, Athene wears armour, Zeus holds a thunderbolt, Poseidon a fish or trident.

RIGHT Apollo Belvedere; *Roman marble copy of 4th-century BC original by Leochares. In the early 5th century BC sculptors broke away from the stiff symmetrical poses of the Archaic period and created standing statues in naturalistic 'relaxed' poses with the weight shifted onto one leg. The contrast between drapery and anatomy is typical of Late Classical art. The tree-trunk support would not have been necessary in the bronze original.*

Mythical narratives generally require more than one figure and in the Classical period sculptors began to create statue groups in tableaux representing crucial moments in the stories. Religious buildings were often decorated with sculptures which also tended to represent myths. One of the most famous temples, the Parthenon at Athens, was decorated in the High Classical period with marble sculptures depicting several mythical subjects. The pediments contained 'in-the-round' sculptures representing the birth of Athene and her contest with Poseidon for the patronage of Athens; the 'metopes' (square slabs positioned above the external colonnade) were decorated in 'high relief' with scenes of Lapiths fighting Centaurs, Greeks fighting Amazons, gods fighting giants and Greeks fighting Trojans: all symbolic of the conquest of barbarians by civilized Greeks. The low-relief frieze ran around all external sides of the inner temple and represented the Panathenaic procession at the climax of which a new gown was placed on the old wooden status of Athene in the presence of the gods. Within the temple stood a huge chryselephantine (gold and ivory) statue of Athene designed by Pheidias.

These statue types continued into the later Classical and Hellenistic periods, but styles changed: more sensual, earthly figures were created in the 4th century BC while the Hellenistic period saw a wider range of subject, from babies to drunken old women, as well as a more dramatic and 'realistic' style. These changes reflected the tastes of the new royal patrons, who required visually exciting statues of new subjects in novel poses to decorate their palaces – for the first time perhaps artists were producing 'art for art's sake'.

RIGHT 'Varvakeion' Athene; *Roman marble copy of Phidias' lost 5th-century BC chryselephantine cult statue of Athene Parthenos (see opposite); discovered in Athens, 2nd century AD. Such Roman copies provide invaluable evidence for lost works and, combined with written descriptions, enable art historians to reconstruct the original statues.*

LEFT Athene Parthenos; *model reconstructed from ancient copies (see bottom left) and literary descriptions, 447–432* BC. *Phidias' cult statue (now lost) was designed as an impressive monument to the Greek victory over the Persians; it was built on a wooden frame with ivory for the flesh and gold for the drapery; it stood about 11 metres tall. The shield was decorated with reliefs depicting Greeks fighting Amazons and Gods fighting Giants, the sandals with Lapiths fighting Centaurs – all symbolic of the triumph of civilization – Nike (Victory) stood on Athene's right hand and on the base the birth of Pandora was depicted. The sculpture is typical of High Classical standing female figures with its weight shifted to one leg and the other bent at the knee. A pool of water was placed before the statue to reflect the gold and moisturize the ivory. Phidias was accused of embezzelling the gold and it had to be removed and weighed. It was also said that he portrayed himself as one of the Greeks on the shield which, if removed, would bring the whole statue crashing to the floor.*

TWO

The Olympian Gods

The Olympian gods traditionally number twelve: Zeus, Hera, Athene, Hephaestus, Ares, Aphrodite, Apollo, Artemis, Demeter, Hestia, Poseidon and Hermes. Dionysus often replaces Hestia in the ancient lists. Other residents on Mount Olympus include Heracles after his deification; his wife Hebe, daughter of Hera, cup-bearer to the gods and goddess of youth; Eros, boy god of sexual passion, companion to Aphrodite; Iris, a Titaness, messenger to Zeus then later to Hera, appearing to men as a rainbow; Ganymede, cup-bearer to Zeus. Hades remained in the Underworld.

After his victory over Typhon, Zeus apportioned the gods with their various realms and powers and they were forbidden to overreach themselves: thus Aphrodite, being a non-military love-goddess, was chided by Zeus for appearing on the Trojan battlefield, and only Hermes had access to Heaven, Earth and the Underworld. In literature, the divinities are given their own epithets or stock descriptions, for example: Zeus 'Gatherer of Clouds', 'ox-eyed' Hera, Athene 'of the flashing eyes'. In the visual arts, they are recognized by their age, dress and attributes, though these are not consistent in early Greek art.

RIGHT Zeus and Hera; *black-figure* lekythos *(funerary oil-vase) discovered in the* Athenian Agora *(market-place), mid* 6th century BC. *Hera ties a wreath round the head of Zeus who wields his thunderbolt. The gods are welcoming Heracles (other side of vase) into* Olympus, *the entrance to which is marked by a temple column.*

ZEUS

Son of Cronus and Rhea, he proved his superiority in single combat against Typhon and in the battle with the Titans and became king on Mount Olympus. After having a number of children with Titanesses, he married his sister Hera; although they had several important children, their marriage was far from happy, mainly owing to Zeus' tendency to lust after mortal women. A common pattern emerges in these relationships: Zeus is attracted to a woman and is compelled to visit her in disguise (his true appearance with thunder and lightning would destroy a human being); Hera discovers the affair and seeks revenge against her husband by punishing the woman or the offspring of the liaison.

Zeus (meaning 'to shine') was god of the sky in all its moods, from the clear bright light to the darkest storm. He administered justice and protected oaths sworn in his name. In art he appears as a long-haired (sometimes plaited up), mature and somewhat imposing figure; he is represented in heroic nudity as well as in full regalia; his attributes are his throne, sceptre, thunderbolt (not our modern zigzag design, but rather like an exploded fat cigar), diadem and eagle. His most important sanctuary was Olympia where all Greek states were entitled to compete in the games held in his honour every four years. A rich temple was built there in the 5th century BC which housed the gold and ivory statue of the god seated on his throne; it was made by Pheidias and became one of the Seven Wonders of the World.

HERA

A daughter of Cronus and Rhea, Hera was one of the gods to be swallowed by Cronus; when she was vomited back up by the Titan, she did not join the battle with her brothers and sisters against the giants, but was put into the care of Oceanus and Tethys. She became the permanent wife of Zeus after his relationships with other goddesses, and became the guardian of marriage and childbirth; her character in the myths reflects this role and she is constantly venting her anger at her husband's infidelities. Her children by Zeus were Ares, Hebe (guardian of youthful beauty and divine cup-bearer) and Eileithyia (goddess of childbirth); in angry response to the birth of Athene without a mother, Hera bore Hephaestus without a father.

In art Hera is depicted as a mature woman, sometimes with an elaborate crown and sceptre and holding a wedding veil aside from her head. Her most important cult centre was at Argos.

ATHENE

Virgin goddess of war as well as the arts and crafts and in later times of general wisdom, Athene had an extraordinary birth. Zeus had been warned by his grand-parents, Gaia and Uranus, that his first wife, Metis,

LEFT The birth of Athene; *red-figure* pelike *(possibly a container for perfumed oil) discovered in an Etruscan tomb at Vulci, early 5th century* BC. *A miniature Athene, fully armed, pops out of Zeus's head which has been split by Hephaestus' axe. The smith-god wears the craftsman's short tunic. Poseidon holds his trident; Zeus his sceptre.*

would have a son who would overthrow Zeus as he had his own father. Zeus therefore swallowed Metis, who was pregnant, and forgot all about her until one morning he awoke with a terrible headache and a rattling sound in his head. Hephaestus was called in to crack open Zeus' skull to see what the trouble way; the smith-god obliged and out jumped Athene in full armour – she became Zeus' favourite. Her titles 'Promachos' (the Champion) and 'Ergane' (Worker) reflected her dual role as a goddess of war and everyday work.

In art she appears as a tall, slim, noble woman with helmet, spear and shield and her special breastplate, the aegis, decorated with the head of the Gorgon Medusa, worn over a long tunic. Her main sanctuary was on the Acropolis at Athens where an ancient wooden image of her was worshipped in the Erechtheion, while Pheidias constructed a huge gold and ivory statue of the goddess for the magnificent Temple of Athene Parthenos ('Virgin'), called the Parthenon. The Panathenaic Games were held in her honour every year, while every four years there was a special festival during which a new tunic was placed on the old wooden statue.

RIGHT Mourning Athene; *votive relief from the Athenian Acropolis, c470* BC. *Athene probably contemplates a tombstone which lists the Athenians who died in the Persian wars. Traces of blue pigment were found on the background. The goddess wears her helmet and peplos dress, belted at the overfold; she carries her spear but has removed her aegis (breastplate).*

Long ago the Athenians had built up a prosperous city and desired a god to protect them. Both Poseidon and Athene wanted the honour and began to fight for it. The Athenians suggested a more peaceful way of settling the dispute: whichever of the two gods gave them the greatest gift would be awarded the city. Poseidon went first and thrust his trident into the Acropolis rock to bring forth a salt-water pool which threatened to flood the city; the Athenians protested that their rich farmland would be spoilt and asked Athene to produce a more useful gift. Athene struck the rock with her spear and immediately an olive tree sprouted; the Athenians realised that its fruit would provide them with oil for cooking, lighting and perfume and awarded the city to her protection. The marks of the trident and the sacred olive tree remained for centuries.

On one occasion Athene was bringing a huge rock to plant as a natural defensive barrier for Athens; Hephaestos saw her coming and attempted to make love to her as she flew towards the walls. She managed to fend him off and the rock fell to the ground to become the conical hill Lykabettos, while his seed fell onto the Acropolis and Erichthonius, the future King of Athens was born. Athene not only fought with the Athenians but accompanied many Greek heroes on their adventures.

RIGHT Poseidon; *red-figure wine-cup painted by Oltos, late 6th century* BC. *Vase-painters often painted figures in the actual bowl of wine-cups, which would generally become visible as the person drank. Poseidon, seen here with his trident and fish as attributes, would thus have appeared running through a sea of wine. The signature around the border is that of the potter:* Kachrylioni epoiesen *('Kachrylion made this').*

POSEIDON

Son of Rhea and Cronus, god of the sea, earthquakes and horses, Poseidon received dominion over the sea when he drew lots with his brothers Zeus and Hades. His adventures often resemble those of Zeus, involving the

seduction of mortal women in the guise of animals, including a ram, a dolphin and a bird; and like Zeus, he also fell in love with men, taking Pelops to Olympus as his lover and presenting him with winged horses to win a chariot-race to obtain his wife; Pelops gave his name to the Peloponnese. Poseidon was constantly fighting for dominion of places on the land including Athens, which he lost to his niece Athene, and Corinth, where Helius received the hill of Acrocorinth and Poseidon was given the Isthmus which forms the bridge to Attica. An important sanctuary was dedicated to him at the Isthmus. In art he is similar to Zeus, perhaps lacking his more domineering attitude, and identifiable by his trident; sometimes he holds a sea-creature.

ARTEMIS

Daughter of Leto and Zeus and sister of Apollo, Artemis, like Athene, was a virgin goddess; she was given the wild areas outside city walls as her realm where she both hunted and protected the wild animals; she was also goddess of childbirth. Her encounters with men generally involve the administering of cruel punishments for their attempts to rape or spy on her. In art she appears as a beautiful huntress, usually in short tunic and bearing quiver and bow; in later art she can appear with the crescent moon on her head – a sign of her lunar associations.

When King Agamemnon was about to lead the Greek fleet to Troy to recapture his brother's wife Helen, who had been abducted by Paris, he stupidly boasted that he was a better hunter than Artemis. She punished him by refusing winds for his sailing ships unless he sacrificed his young daughter Iphigeneia to the goddess. The girl was taken to the altar but Artemis took pity on her and replaced her with a deer, carrying her away to be her priestess in the land of the barbarian Taurians where she would sacrifice all visiting strangers to Artemis.

LEFT Artemis of Versailles; *Roman marble copy of 4th-century BC Greek original. The virgin goddess is here portrayed with short tunic and quiver while a sacred stag runs beside her. The sculpture reflects her dual role as both hunter and protector of wild animals.*

APOLLO

Son of the Titaness Leto by Zeus, and brother of Artemis, Apollo was born on the island of Delos which remained sacred to him. While still a boy, Apollo journeyed to Delphi where he killed a huge snake called Python and took control of the Pythian oracle. He appeared as a dolphin to Cretan

RIGHT Apollo 'Sauroctonos' (Lizard-Slayer); *Roman marble copy of 4th-century* BC *Greek original by Praxiteles. The god is poised to throw a dart at a lizard as it climbs the tree. The softness of the flesh is typical of Praxiteles' treatment of marble; also Praxitelean is the sinuous pose.*

BELOW RIGHT Apollo; *Roman wall-painting, 1st century* AD. *Apollo appears with his attributes of lyre (god of music) and quiver (the hunter).*

sailors and took them to Delphi, ordering them to guard his oracle and build a temple to Apollo Delphinius (of the Dolphin). Apollo and Artemis defended the honour of their mother when Niobe, Queen of Thebes, boasted that she had more beautiful children: they shot the Niobids with their arrows.

Apollo was god of prophecy and healing, and became associated with music and cultural activities; he was worshipped as a rational god, defending intellectual pursuits, the opposite of Dionysus. He had many affairs with both male and female mortal lovers. In art he appears as a beardless handsome youth with long hair, often plaited up; he holds a bow, lyre or his sacred laurel branch.

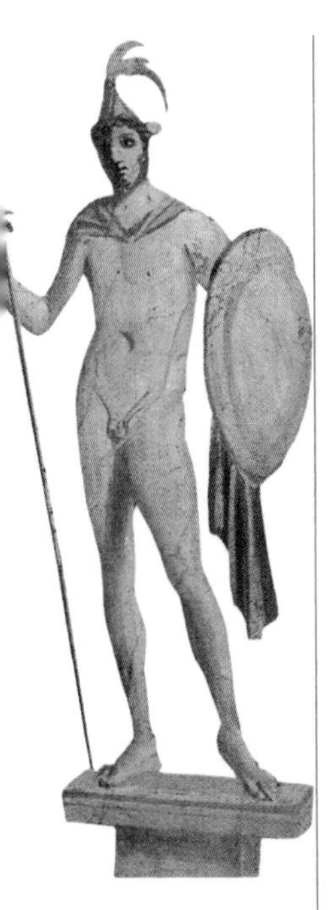

ABOVE Ares; *Roman wall-painting from the House of the Venus, Pompeii, 1st century* AD. *It was fashionable for Romans to decorate their gardens with marble copies of Greek sculptures. On the garden wall of a private house the painter has created the illusion that the real garden continues past the wall and contains a statue of Ares surrounded by plants and birds.*

LEFT *Titian (c1488–1576),* Venus with a Mirror. *Titian has painted Aphrodite (Venus) the goddess of love as a model of Renaissance Italian beauty. In Renaissance paintings, as in late Greek art, she was often shown admiring herself in a mirror, held here by Cupids.*

ARES

Only son of Zeus and Hera, Ares was the god of war. He appears in art as an ordinary Greek warrior, with helmet, shield, sword and spear. His association with warfare is far from glamorous: generally we see him generating as much trouble as he can on the battlefield to cause the maximum bloodshed on both sides. His fellow Olympians do not care for him, apart from Aphrodite, who was his lover. On one occasion Hephaestus left Olympus and stayed for a while on the island of Lemnos. His wife Aphrodite called Ares into her bed, but Hephaestus had hung a net of fine wire over his bed, which fell upon them; they became completely tangled and Hephaestus invited all the other Olympians to laugh at the expense of the god of war and goddess of love. The smith god let them go free and Aphrodite returned to Cyprus and Ares returned to Thrace, a centre for his worship.

APHRODITE

The most famous account of the birth of the goddess of erotic love is that she appeared out of the sea-foam surrounding the severed genitals of Uranus; her name means 'born from foam'. Homer makes her a daughter of Zeus and the Oceanid Dione. Likewise Eros, the god of sexual desire, is her son by Ares in many accounts, though Hesiod has him welcoming the goddess ashore at her birth. Many Greeks associated her with Eastern love goddesses such as Ishtar; these were also war goddesses and this might explain Aphrodite's links with Ares, god of war. Her husband on Olympus was the lame god Hephaestus.

In art she appears at first as an attractive young woman, wearing pretty clothes and often holding a flower and a dove. Her most famous statue was made by Praxiteles for her shrine on the island of Kos, but when it was unveiled the town council rejected it, shocked by its nudity. The people of Knidos bought it for their sanctuary to the goddess, placing her in a romantically positioned circular temple. The temple, which became one of the most important cult centres of the goddess, was recently discovered by the aptly named Professor Love; the statue has long since disappeared, but its base and a Greek inscription telling us the artist and subject were found. She stood with her back to the setting sun and the sea. There was a story that a man, lusting after the statue, made love to it one night; this story emphasizes her physical sexual presence in antiquity rather than the more romantic view that developed later.

The depiction of Aphrodite as a beautiful mature woman preparing to bathe influenced all later representations of the goddess. She regularly appears with Eros, who is symbolized in early art as a beautiful youth with long wings and hair, holding the bow and gold-tipped arrows with which he pierces the hearts of lovers. In later art he multiplies into many children (Erotes or Cupids) with short wings, precursors of Renaissance 'putti'.

Aphrodite had both mortal and immortal lovers. Hermes was rejected by her, so Zeus sent his eagle to snatch her sandal and take it to Hermes, who would not return it until she had submitted. Their son was the beautiful youth Hermaphroditus with whom the Naiad Salmacis fell in love whilst he was bathing in her spring. As they made love, she clung to him so fast that their bodies fused into one. In art Hermaphroditus appears as a woman with male genitals.

HEPHAESTUS

Hera probably produced this son without a father in retaliation to Zeus who had given birth to Athene without a mother. Hephaestus was rejected by Hera because of his lameness; she threw him out of Olympus into Oceanus where Thetis rescued him. When he grew up he punished his mother by making her a magical golden throne, but when she sat on it she found herself stuck fast. The gods tried to persuade Hephaestus to return to Olympus and forgive his mother; he refused until Dionysus gave him wine and led him back drunk on an ass to the great mirth of his fellow Olympians.

Hephaestus was associated with fire and the crafts of blacksmithing and metalwork and his workshop was thought to be beneath volcanoes such as Etna in Sicily. In art he often appears in a craftsman's short tunic, holding a double axe or a pair of blacksmith's tongs; his lameness is sometimes suggested by his leaning on a crutch. His temple in the Agora at Athens was close to potters' workshops and contained statues of both himself and Athene who was also associated with crafts.

BELOW Hephaestus and Thetis; *Roman wall-painting from Pompeii, 1st century AD. Thetis sits in the smith-god's workshop and waits for the completion of her son Achilles' new armour. The shield is held up for inspection and the goddess is reflected in its polished surface; the helmet is still being hammered. Thetis is portrayed as a noble matron while Hephaestus wears the craftsman's tunic and skullcap.*

HERMES

Offspring of Zeus and one of the Pleiades, Maia, Hermes was born in a cave on Mount Cyllene in Arcadia. He was a precocious child and, on the very day of his birth, he climbed out of his cradle and killed a tortoise outside his cave and, using the shell as a sound-box and sheep-gut for strings, invented the lyre. Later the same day, Hermes stole cattle belonging to Apollo and led them back to his cave, where he lay down in his cradle pretending innocence. Apollo eventually caught up with the thief (Hermes was later a god of thieves) and demanded the lyre in place of the cattle, in return for which he made Hermes god of herds and herdsmen. When he grew

RIGHT Hermes with the infant Dionysus; *Praxiteles, 4th century* BC. *This rare original Greek marble by a known artist was discovered in the Temple of Hera at Olympia. Hermes is depicted carrying baby Dionysus to the nymphs on Mount Nysa and teases him with a bunch of grapes (now lost). The contrast of drapery with anatomy and the sinuous pose and soft flesh are typical of Late Classical sculpture.*

up, Zeus made him the messenger of the gods; only Hermes was allowed free passage between Olympus, the Earth and the Underworld and he escorted dead Greeks to the ferryman Charon, who for a small coin would carry the dead across the river Styx to Hades.

Hermes, like Apollo, had many love affairs. There is argument as to the mother of his most famous son Pan, who became god of shepherds. In art, Pan appears as a lusty human figure, sometimes with goats' legs and horns and sometimes with goat's head and human body; he often plays the rustic pan-pipes. Hermes appears with his *kerykeion*, a magic wand entwined with snakes which gives him access to all places. He is often bearded and wears traveller's clothes, including a sun-hat, short tunic and cloak; his hat and boots are sometimes winged for flight.

BELOW *Peter Paul Rubens (1577–1640),* Artemis and her Nymphs Attacked by Pan with Satyrs. *Artemis (right) hurls an arrow at lusty Pan (left), who has come with satyrs to molest the virgin goddess while she is out hunting with her nymphs.*

DEMETER, PERSEPHONE AND HADES

Daughter of Cronus and Rhea, Demeter, goddess of corn and fertility, was seduced on earth by a prince called Iasion; their children were Plutus (Wealth) and Philomelus, who was made into the constellation Bootes ('the wagon'), which he invented. Zeus killed Iasion with a thunderbolt for presuming to love a goddess; Zeus then made love to Demeter himself and she bore a daughter named Persephone. Hades, brother of the Olympians and god of the Underworld, asked Zeus for Persephone as his wife. Zeus agreed, but, thinking that Demeter would not accept the match as she would lose her daughter forever to the Underworld, assisted Hades in Persephone's abduction. He asked Gaia to send up many lovely flowers near where Persephone dwelt; whilst she was picking them with her friends, Hades came up from the Underworld in a chariot and took the poor girl back with him. Demeter searched the world for many days and nights in the guise of a mortal. At every town she visited, she told men the secrets of the harvest; one of these towns, Eleusis, became a centre for her mystery cult. Demeter threatened famine to the earth unless her daughter was returned; but Persephone had eaten several pomegranate seeds which meant that she would have to stay in Hades for one-third of the year, during which period Demeter refused to allow the crops to grow. Festivals were held for the return of Persephone every spring. At Eleusis, Demeter lent her winged chariot, drawn by dragons, to the youth Triptolemus; he was to use it every year to scatter seed over the earth. In art, mother and daughter sometimes wear crowns and carry torches or ears of corn.

LEFT *Sir Edward Coley Burne-Jones (1833–98),* The Rape of Proserpine *(1883–4); pencil drawing, touched with orange and red chalk. Hades emerges from the Underworld through a chasm in a four-horse chariot. Winged figures bear Persephone (Proserpina) away from her friends who tear their hair in grief. A many-headed snake appears from the cleft.*

RIGHT Demeter, Triptolemos and Persephone, *relief from* Eleusis, Greece, c40–30 BC. *Demeter, holding a sceptre, hands ears of corn (originally added in metal) to the young Triptolemos; Persephone holds a torch.*

DIONYSOS

Also known as Bacchus, the god of wine and vegetation, his mortal mother was Semele of Thebes, whom Zeus had taken as a lover. Jealous Hera appeared to Semele in the guise of her old nurse and dared her to demand that Zeus appear in his real form. Semele was incinerated by his thunderbolt, but Zeus salvaged the unborn boy and sowed him into his thigh; a few months later Dionysus was born and given to Hermes to entrust to the care of nymphs on Mount Nysa. When he grew up these nymphs became his female devotees, the Maenads. Hera drove him mad and he fled to the east where the oriental earth goddess Cybele cured him. He then returned to Greece, establishing his cult in different places and proved to the world that his father was Zeus.

In Classical art he appears as a beautiful youth with long hair and a thyrsos, a wand bound with ivy and topped with a pine cone; round his head he wears an ivy wreath and often carries an upturned wine cup. In later art he becomes increasingly effeminate in appearance.

His female followers, the Maenads, are human in form, but carry thyrsoi and wear skins from the animals they have slaughtered during the rites; often they wear ivy or even snakes for headbands. His male followers, the Satyrs,

RIGHT Dionysus, *Roman wall-painting, 1st century* AD. *The god holds his thyrsus and wears his ivy crown. In late Greek and Roman art the god appears increasingly effeminate; here he has the large hips and small breasts of a Classical female nude.*

appear as men with horses' tails, pointed ears, and erect penises, signs of the irrational animal nature that is freed by the worship of Dionysus; we often see them drinking or in lusty pursuit of Maenads.

HESTIA

The eldest child of Cronus and Rhea, Hestia guarded hearth, fire, house, family and community. She remained a virgin goddess, though both Poseidon and Apollo had wished to marry her. She rarely appears in art and has few shrines, her home being at the hearth.

ABOVE AND LEFT Satyrs drinking; *Athenian red-figure* psykter *(wine-cooler) discovered in an Etruscan tomb at Cerveteri, painted by Douris in the early 5th century* BC. *The* psykter *was filled with ice and placed in wine to cool it. The potter balanced the vase so that it floated at the base-line of the figure-scene. The drinker could spin it round and the satyrs would appear to dance on the wine. The satyrs pour wine from rustic animal-skins as well as civilized pottery vases, representing the use of wine to bring out man's animal nature at the urban symposium (drinking-party).*

BELOW Introduction of Heracles to Olympus; *Athenian black-figure* oinochoe *(wine-jug) by the* Amasis Painter, *mid* 6th *century* BC. *In black-figure pottery, female flesh is often painted white to contrast with the darker, tanned male flesh; white flesh was a sign of rich women who did not often go outside of the house. The only other added colour was purple, seen here on Hermes' cloak and hat and on Athene's shield device (the owl was her sacred bird). Details of embroidered drapery and anatomy are incised through the black 'paint' before firing. The signature between Athene and Hermes reads* Amasis m'epoiesen *('Amasis made me').*

GREEK PAINTING

Ancient writers speak of renowned easel painters, but unfortunately none of their originals have survived. Mythical scenes formed a large part of their output; Roman interior decorators often painted copies of them, and surviving examples give us some idea of their original quality and style. By the Late Classical period painters had broken away from the Egyptian pictorial style with its flat images, and were using changing hues of colour and light and shadow effects to suggest solid figures within a three-dimensional space; this technique of 'chiaroscuro' had to be rediscovered by Italian Renaissance painters.

From the Archaic period onwards the vases used by Greeks for their symposia were painted with mythical scenes. There were two main styles: 'black-figure', in which the images were black silhouettes incised with details of dress and anatomy; and 'red-figure', in which the figures were reserved in the red of the oxidized clay and their details were painted in with a brush. The applied black 'pigment' was a refined version of the clay of the vase. The clay was shaken in water and left for a few days; fine metallic elements were held in suspension in the water and a paste was produced by evaporation; this iron-rich paste was used as the 'paint'. During firing the iron in the clay

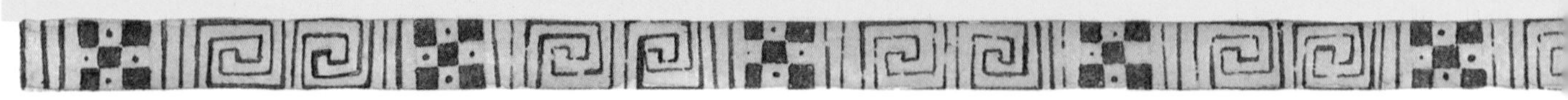

was oxidized to become red iron oxide; the potter then closed the air supply and the resulting carbon monoxide turned the iron oxide into black ferrous oxide. For the final stage oxygen was allowed back into the kiln and the ordinary clay of the vase turned back to red iron oxide whilst the iron rich 'paint' remained black.

Black-figure vases first appear in the Archaic period and continue into the Classical period; the silhouetted figures are effective against the red clay background, but are flat and unnaturalistic, with profile legs and heads and unrealistic frontal eyes and torsoes. Red-figure vases appear in the Late Archaic period (*c*530 BC); this technique allows for a more naturalistic representation with light figures spotlighted against the black background; drapery and anatomical lines are now painted with the more fluid brush and this allows the painters to produce apparently three-dimensional figures. Three-quarter views of figures and profile eyes appear for the first time in the history of art. The Archaic and Classical artists relied on simple gestures and the viewer's knowledge of the myth rather than the overt expressions of emotion which were features of Hellenistic art.

The most popular scenes were not surprisingly Dionysiac. Other myths went in and out of fashion; Heracles was popular at the time of the tyrants during the Archaic period, but representations of Theseus were popular during the Classical period of democracy. Theseus, who had saved the Athenian youths from the Minotaur, was regarded as a democratic hero; Heracles who had risen above his fellow men and become a god would have been associated with tyrannical aspirations. It would therefore appear that, as in literature, the myths were not purely decorative, but could reflect political and social changes.

LEFT Selene and Endymion; *Roman wall-painting from a Pompeian house, 1st century* AD. *In the 1st century* AD *it was fashionable for Romans to decorate the walls of their houses with frescoes giving the illusion of an art gallery. Copies of earlier Greek 'Old Masters' (collected by connoisseurs) would be painted in the centres of the walls as if the original easel-paintings were hanging there. In this painting 'windows' appear on either side of the painting to give the impression of a townscape outside: the perspective colonnades increase the illusion. The 'easel-painting' depicts Selene, head surrounded by the moon, approaching her sleeping lover Endymion. These paintings provide valuable information about the Greek easel-paintings, none of which have survived. In particular, they exhibit the 'chiaroscuro' (light and shade) technique, invented by Greek painters around 400* BC *to create realistic three-dimensional effects.*

BELOW Athene; *Athenian red-figure amphora, early 5th century* BC. *The red-figure technique allowed the painter to produce a more naturalistic image with anatomy and drapery lines painted with a brush. This also facilitated the painting of three-quarter views and foreshortened limbs, as with Athene's left foot.*

Italian Renaissance artists revived the Classical myths, but in most cases the only evidence they had for their representation in art was in literary descriptions of the lost ancient masterpieces. They would therefore 'reproduce' the paintings in their imagination and often dress the mythological figures in contemporary dress and locate them in Italian landscapes. The Florentine painter Botticelli made several paintings based on mythological subjects, including Aphrodite (Venus) subduing Ares (Mars) while her Erotes play with his armour. They lie in an Italian landscape and 'Venus' wears contemporary clothes. Renaissance artists and their patrons were highly sophisti-

cated in their interpretations of mythology and often read several meanings into the same image. Thus, *Venus and Mars* might also be seen as the marriage of Alexander the Great to the exotic princess Roxanne – the ancient writer Lucian describes the lost painting of this subject by Apelles and refers to 'Erotes' playing with the divine king's armour. Botticelli's Erotes are more like little horned devils, perhaps suggesting a more Christian idea of the temptation of man by woman. There is no evidence that Botticelli himself named his painting *Venus and Mars*, and therefore any of these interpretations might be correct.

BELOW *Sandro Botticelli (1445–1510)*, Venus and Mars.

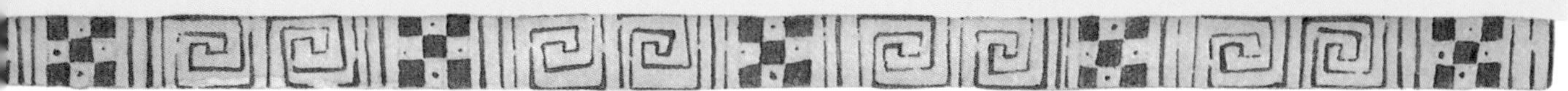

THREE

Tales of Greek Heroes

Apart from the legendary warriors of Homer's epic poems who fought at Troy, several heroes existed who were the central subjects of lengthy sagas. All exhibited super-human strengths, clearing the world of its troublesome monsters, and generally experienced a number of love affairs.

Heracles and Theseus were contrasted in both art and literature. As a boy, Heracles rejected his education and relied on sheer brute strength in his later encounters with men and monsters. He was deified at death and was later worshipped as a god by military men. Theseus was seen as an educated and civilized version of Heracles and became the hero of Athenian democracy in the 5th century BC. *He performed similar super-human tasks as Heracles, but introduced more 'gentlemanly' fighting skills. In art Theseus appears short-haired and clean-shaven, while Heracles, easily recognized by his lion skin and club, sports long, shaggy hair and a beard. Perseus (meaning 'slayer-destroyer'), like Heracles, appears to have represented the earlier, more violent stage of Greek mythology. In art Perseus is usually depicted in the winged sandals and magic hat used on his quest for the head of Medusa.*

HERACLES

As King and Queen of Tiryns and Mycenae Perseus and Andromeda had many children, but this tale concerns just two of their sons, Alcaeus and Electryon. Alcaeus had a son named Amphitryon, who married his cousin Alcmene, the daughter of Electryon. Amphitryon wanted to become king, but his uncle Electryon stood in his path so he murdered him; the attempted coup failed and Amphitryon and Alcmene were exiled. They travelled to Thebes where King Creon welcomed them. Alcmene would not sleep with Amphitryon until he had avenged her brothers who had been killed by pirates. He returned in triumph one night and they made love whilst he told her of his adventures. Imagine her surprise when the next day he walked in and told her the same stories all over again, as if for the first time. They called in Teiresias the prophet who told them that Zeus had visited Alcmene in the guise of her husband. Amphitryon was willing to forgive Alcmene, but problems arose when Alcmene became pregnant; the whole Theban court waited to see whether the child would be Amphitryon's or Zeus'.

LEFT Heracles in the garden of the Hesperides; *Roman wall-painting from the villa at Oplontis, 1st century* AD. *A sun-tanned Heracles carries his club and looks up at the golden apples; the special tree is marked with a ribbon.*

Meanwhile on Olympus, Zeus boasted that a son of his was about to be born on earth who would be a great ruler. Hera, understandably angry and jealous, sent Eileithyia, goddess of childbirth, to delay Alcmene's labour and speed up the birth of Eurystheus, grandson of Perseus, and great-grandson of Zeus, to ensure his inheritance of the throne of Tiryns in place of Alcmene's child. The next day Alcmene gave birth to twin sons, named Iphicles and Heracles, but no one was able to say whether either was the god's progeny. The problem was solved when Hera sent two snakes into the babies' cots as they slept. Iphicles screamed but, to the surprise of Amphitryon and Alcmene, little

LEFT The infant Heracles strangling the snakes; *Roman wall-painting from the House of the Vettii, Pompeii, 1st century* AD. *Heracles has laid aside his tiny baby's club to deal with the snakes. His mortal father Amphitryon raises his hand in wonder at the child's strength, whilst the eagle reminds us of his real father Zeus. This might be a copy of a well known lost original of the scene by the 4th-century* BC *Greek painter Zeuxis, the inventor of the 'chiaroscuro' technique which is fully apparent in this painting; note the shading and highlights on Amphitryon.*

Heracles took the snakes by the necks and strangled them; there was no doubt that this was a son of Zeus.

Heracles received the normal royal education: his step-father taught him to drive the chariot, and various experts were called in to teach him to fence, wrestle and use the bow and arrow; but Heracles showed little interest in these gentlemanly skills, finding that it was quicker and easier to dispatch his opponent with one blow of the fist or a swing of his club. This rather worried his mortal parents, and they thought that some training in the arts would make him behave a little more gracefully. Orpheus's brother Linus, himself a wonderful musician and teacher, was called in to give Heracles music lessons. Heracles proved to be a slow learner and one day Linus lost his temper and struck him; Heracles angrily brought his lyre down on Linus's head killing him instantly; the boy did not know his own strength, nor where it came from.

Amphitryon thought it would be sensible to send him away from the city for a while and Heracles spent many happy summers on the royal cattle farm. In his spare time he would practise with his bow and arrow on the slopes of Mount Cithaeron; he never missed, but found that there were certain creatures whose skins could not be pierced with arrows, so Heracles would wrestle with them. However, there was one that eluded him, a lion that had been eating the flocks of Thespius, their royal neighbour. To get him in a good mood and to see how strong this young man really was before asking him to kill the lion, Thespius invited Heracles to supper and plied him with gallons of wine. That night Thespius sent all fifty of his daughters to his guest's room; the next morning each swore that Heracles had made love to them, but Heracles could not remember anything. On his way back to Thebes he killed the lion with his own bare hands. Nearing Thebes, he encountered some ambassadors on their way from Orchomenus in Minya to collect their annual tribute from Thebes; Heracles in his anger, cut off their noses and ears, and hanging them round their necks, sent them back home with what he called their tribute.

War followed and Heracles led the Thebans to victory. Creon rewarded him with his daughter Megara.

Heracles had been away on business and several years later on his return to Thebes found that Creon had been murdered by a Euboean called Lycus, who was about to execute Heracles' wife and their children. Heracles killed Lycus, but as he was embracing Megara, Hera never forgetting her grudge, brought a fit of madness upon him, and he killed both his wife and his children. Coming to his senses he saw with horror what he had done and took his impure body away from Thebes and walked to Delphi to seek advice from the Pythian Oracle. She pronounced that to atone for his crime, he must travel to Tiryns and ask King Eurystheus to set him ten trials of his strength and courage. Heracles turned to go with face downcast; humiliated that this weakling of a king, Eurystheus, who sat on the throne which he himself would have held if Hera had not tricked his father Zeus, was to have such power over his fate; but the Pythia called after him that if he succeeded in the ten labours he would achieve immortality. Heracles rose to the challenge and was impatient to begin the first of his labours.

I *The Nemean Lion*

Heracles' euphoria faded, however, when he stood in Tiryns before the throne of his rival Eurystheus who smirked and demanded the pelt of the Nemean Lion, one of the monstrous sons of Orthus and Echidna, which had been ravaging the surrounding countryside. On his way to Nemea, Heracles stayed for the night in the hut of a peasant named Molorchus, who, when he heard what Heracles was attempting, offered a sacrifice to him. Heracles told his to delay the sacrifice for a month, after which if he had not returned, the sacrifice should be made to Heracles the Hero; but if he returned in triumph, the sacrifice must be made to Zeus the Saviour.

Molorchus pointed out the long path to the lion's cave and wished him luck. Fifteen days later Heracles could hear its distant roaring for several

RIGHT Heracles and the Nemean Lion; *black-figure* oinochoe *(wine-jug), late 6th century* BC. *Heracles has hung up his quiver and bow on a tree and wrestles with the lion.*

hours before he eventually found himself peering through the bushes at a cave with two entrances. Heracles strung his bow and, without making a sound, fitted an arrow; he then flung a rock against the nearest mouth of the cave. Immediately a lion, twice the size of the one he had strangled on mount Cithaeron, leapt out of the cave, roaring and spitting with rage at being disturbed. Heracles let his arrow fly and, true as ever, it found its mark between the eyes of the magnificent beast, but Heracles' heart sank as it bounced straight off again. 'What a wonderful warm and light coat of armour that pelt would make, if Zeus would help me to kill the lion!', thought Heracles. Zeus heard him from Olympus – they were all up there watching – and sent his warlike daughter, Athene of the flashing eyes, down to help. Unknown to Heracles, she gave him new courage and he stepped out into the open, rolling a stone in front of one of the entrances; he entered the other one and slew the lion, strangling it as easily as he had the snakes when he was a baby.

Meanwhile Molorchus was preparing to sacrifice to Heracles the dead hero, it being a month since Heracles had left him. Upon seeing the hero returning with the dead Nemean lion over his shoulder, Molorchus praised Zeus and burnt the sacrifice to the Gatherer of Clouds, reserving the meat for a night of feasting and drinking in celebration of Heracles' victory. The local peasants joined them in dancing well into the night; at last they could work in the fields without fear of the monster.

Eurystheus was annoyed when Heracles entered Tiryns in triumph; he was expecting never to see him again and what is more was terrified when he saw the lion which looked as if it might spring to life at any moment. Eurystheus jumped into a storage jar to hide; Heracles could not conceal his amusement and Eurystheus angrily vowed that Heracles would not be laughing when he heard what his next labour was to be. Hera rewarded the lion's vain attempts to defy Heracles by setting it as the stars in the heavens known as the constellation Leo.

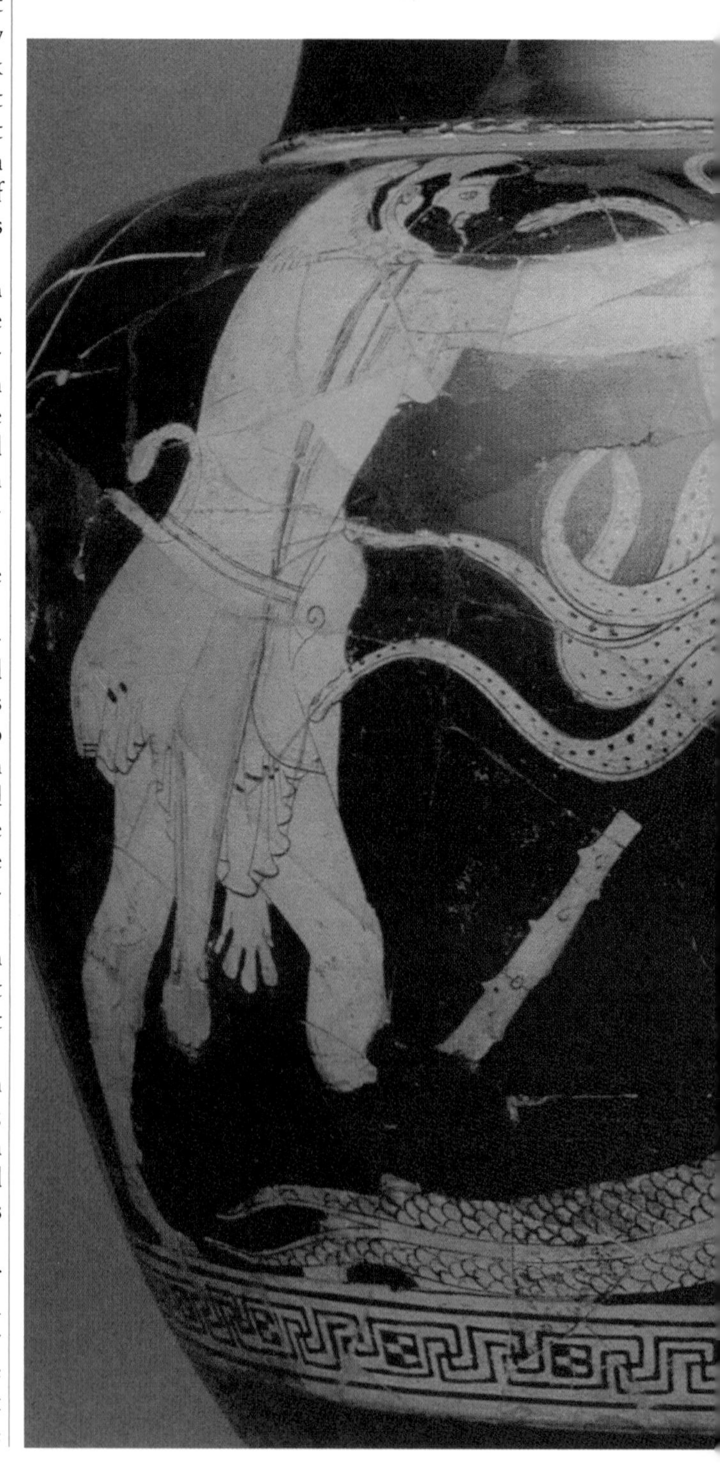

II *The Hydra*

The Hydra was the half-sister of the Nemean Lion, spitefully chosen by Eurystheus as the object of Heracles' second labour as he knew that the Hydra would be yearning to avenge her relative's death. The Hydra had the venomous nature of her father Typhon, who lay crushed by Zeus under Mount Etna, breathing his fires. Heracles left Tiryns, wearing the magnificent pelt of the Nemean lion, its scalp protecting his head like a hood, and as soon as he was clear of the gates, Eurystheus had them bolted and shouted after him from the ramparts that he was to leave any further trophies outside the city walls. Heracles laughed and went on his way in high spirits, accompanied by his nephew Iolaus, who had volunteered to be his charioteer.

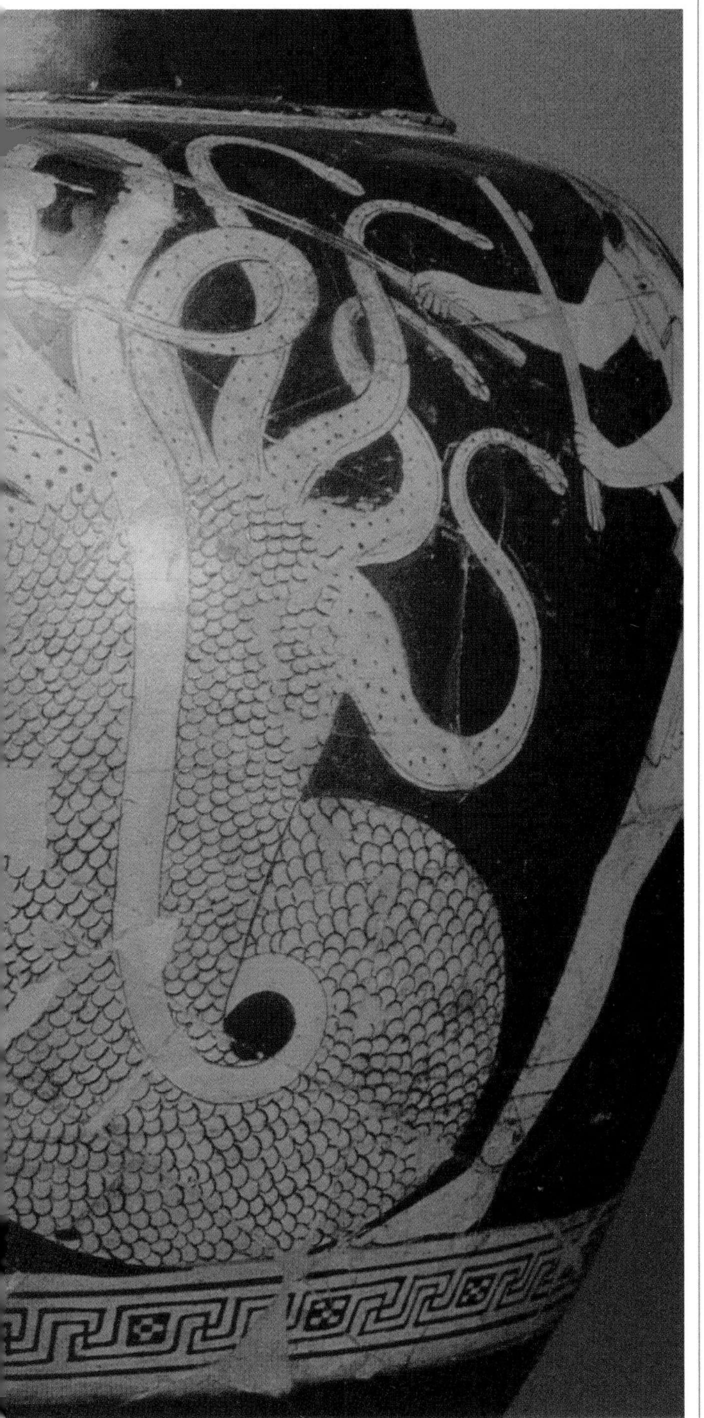

LEFT Heracles and the Hydra; *Athenian red-figure* stamnos *(wine-jar) by the Syleus Painter, early 5th century* BC. *Heracles (left) has laid aside his club to sever the snake-heads while his companion Iolaus cauterizes the open wounds with torches.*

The Hydra lived in a pool formed by the freshwater spring Amymone at Lerna. The spring had once been crystal clear and a source of drinking water for the people of Lerna. Now it was polluted and they had to draw their water from a well some distance away, and this meant passing by the Hydra's lair; many of them never returned, finding themselves in one of the jaws of the monster, who would lie in wait for them with its accomplice, Cancer the crab, who would run out and grab the feet of unsuspecting travellers. Heracles approached the pool without fear and fired burning arrows into the cave behind the pool where the Hydra was supposed to live. Out she came, and Heracles was surprised at seeing so many heads, for no one had seen the monster and lived to tell the tale. He did not have time to reflect and found himself hacking away at its heads with his sword; but for every head lost, it immediately grew two more, and he found himself cornered when the giant crab sallied out to bite his ankles. He called to his charioteer Iolaus for help, and the clever youth brought burning torches with which he cauterized the wounded necks as Heracles removed the heads. At last only its huge central head was left; Heracles cut it off with a final blow and buried it beneath a large stone which still lies beside the road outside Lerna. He dipped his arrows into the dead Hydra's poisonous blood and returned to Tiryns in triumph, but Eurystheus refused to acknowledge the labour as one of the ten as Iolaus had helped the hero.

III *The Cerynitian Hind*

For his third labour, Heracles was ordered to capture the golden-horned deer known as the fabulous Cerynitian Hind. The problem for Heracles was that he was to bring it back alive; moreover, the hind was sacred to the goddess Artemis. It had last been seen in the woods around Oenoe in Argolis, a short journey for Heracles. He tracked it down after a year and had little trouble dragging it away with nets. But on the way to Tiryns he encountered Artemis and Apollo who demanded that he return the deer. Heracles blamed Eurystheus, and they let him pass, so long as he did not harm the creature.

IV *The Erymanthian Boar*

Eurystheus now tried to exhaust Heracles, immediately sending him back down to Arcadia to capture alive a huge boar which was terrorizing the shepherds on Mount Erymanthus. On his way Heracles stayed for the night with Centaurs on Mount Pholoe; in the evening they held a banquet, and Pholus, the host, brought out wine for his guest, a drink never before tasted by the Centaurs; the moment they smelt it they became intoxicated and began to cause an uproar. Heracles fought with them and they fled to their mountain homes. The banquet was resumed with soft drinks and Heracles sang of his labours; when he reached the story of the Hydra, Pholus asked to see the poisonous arrows, but still a little drunk, he dropped one on his foot and was dead in an instant. Heracles would one day encounter the Centaurs again.

Heracles had no difficulties in trapping the boar, using the same nets with which the Cerynitian Hind had been ensnared. He was beginning to tire of the labours and when he reached Tiryns, entered the city against the orders of Eurystheus, and threatened to throw the monster into the storage jar in which Eurystheus had fled for refuge.

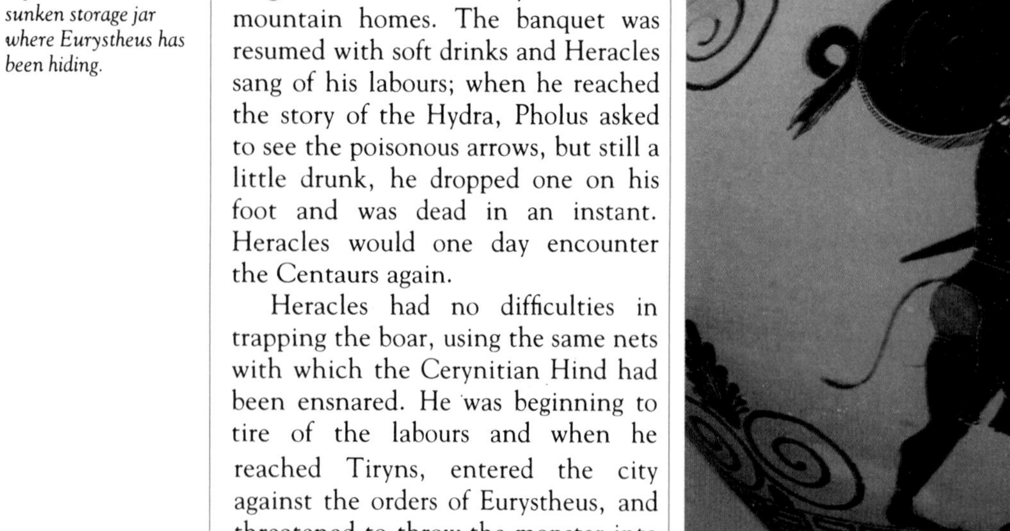

RIGHT Heracles hurls the Erymanthian Boar at Eurystheus; *Athenian black-figure amphora, mid 6th century* BC. *Heracles threatens to put the captured boar into the sunken storage jar where Eurystheus has been hiding.*

V *The Cleansing of the Augeian Stables*

After absconding with Jason and the Argonauts on their quest for the Golden Fleece, Heracles returned to Tiryns for his fifth labour set by Eurystheus, angry at Heracles' recent disappearance. In a single day Heracles was to muck out the stables of the cattle of Augeias, King of Elis in the Peloponnese. Augeias' wealth depended on large herds of cattle, but there were so many of them that their dung lay too thickly on the fields for them to be tilled. Heracles demanded a payment of one-tenth of the cattle, and then proceeded to break a hole in the wall of the enclosure at a weak point shown to him by Athene, who was now his patron deity. He dug channels from the rivers Alpheius and Peneius and the area was flushed clean. Augeias refused to hand over the cattle and Heracles returned enraged to Tiryns where, to add salt to his wound, Eurystheus again refused to count it as a labour since Heracles had demanded a payment.

RIGHT Heracles and Athene cleaning the Augeian Stables; *metope sculpture from the Temple of Zeus at Olympia, c460* BC. *Athene points to a weak spot in the river bank for Heracles to break and flood the land. This was the last of twelve sculpted metopes depicting the Labours; it was placed at the climax because the Labour was local to Olympia. Heracles' hair was left flat for paint and a metal helmet was attached to the holes in Athene's head. Athene's rather heavy drapery and relaxed standing pose are typical of Early Classical art.*

VI *The Stymphalian Birds*

Eurystheus sent Heracles back into Arcadia where a flock of birds, to escape local wolves, had settled on an island in the middle of Lake Stymphalus where they were now creating a nuisance to the local fishermen. The birds were hiding in the rushes when Heracles arrived armed with a pair of bronze castanets forged for him by Hephaestus. He climbed to the top of a mountain overlooking the lake and began to clash the castanets with all his might. Alarmed, the birds took flight in different directions; but Heracles had his catapult at the ready and many of them fell into the lake, others escaping never to return again.

VII *The Cretan Bull*

To date, all of Heracles labours had been in the Peloponnese on mainland Greece; there were no more monsters left for him to kill, no more fabulous creatures to bring home alive, and no more public nuisances to be cleaned up, so now Eurystheus asked his friends overseas if they had any similar problems. King Minos of Crete sent word that there was a wild bull roaming the fields outside of his palace at Knossos. In fact this was the bull that his wife Pasiphae had tricked into making love to her; she had been inspired with lust for the creature by Poseidon when Minos had refused to sacrifice this particularly handsome

LEFT Heracles and the Stymphalian Birds; *Athenian black-figure amphora, mid 6th century* BC. *Heracles uses a catapult to kill the birds, some of which can be seen falling from the sky while others continue to glide gracefully along on the lake. The painter has applied much purple and white to give colour to the exotic birds.*

bull to the god. Every morning she would go out into the fields and attempt to seduce it, but to no avail – it was more interested in the dewy grass. The great craftsman Daedalus was asked to find a solution, and a few days later he presented her with a hollow wooden cow on wheels, which the next morning was pushed into the bull's field with a rather uncomfortable Pasiphae inside. It had the desired effect and Pasiphae's next baby had the head of a bull and was therefore named the Minotaur (Minos-Bull). Minos and Pasiphae were so embarrassed that they instructed Daedalus to construct the Labyrinth, a vast network of vaults beneath the palace, as a home for their curious son. Perhaps Minos wished to do away with his son's real father, and Heracles was the man to do it. The bull was brought back alive to Eurystheus, and one evening broke its tether and wandered off to Marathon ravaging the countryside until the arrival of Theseus.

VIII *The Mares of Diomedes*

Eurystheus heard that in Thrace there existed four horses, mares owned by the wicked king Diomedes, which lived on human flesh; with any luck they would be hungry when Heracles arrived to capture them for his eighth labour. Heracles made the long journey to Thrace by ship with Abderus, the young lover he had taken after the tragic loss of Hylas. Together they overpowered the grooms, but the alarm was raised and as they rushed the horses down to the waiting ship, Diomedes and his guard came in pursuit; Abderus went ahead with the mares while Heracles turned to kill Diomedes and sent his men running for cover. But when Heracles arrived at the beach he found that the four mares had proved too wild for his young friend and were finishing their tasty meal. Heracles drove them into the ship's hold and returned to bury what remained of Abderus, founding the city of Abdera on the burial mound in his memory. The mares were taken to Tiryns, where Eurystheus freed them; on their way back to Thrace they were attacked by wolves on the slopes of Mount Olympus.

IX *The Belt of Hippolyte*

The next labour turned into a romantic adventure. Eurystheus' daughter Admete had as a child been told stories about the Amazons, a race of female warriors who lived beside the Black Sea on the River Thermodon. In her imagination she developed an admiration for their leader, Queen Hippolyte, who apparently wore a beautiful belt, studded with jewels. Admete suggested that Heracles should fetch it for her, and off he sailed with a crew of heroes. After a number of hostile encounters they arrived at last at Themiscyra, where the queen had her palace. Hippolyte was invited to a banquet on board during which she was struck by the charm of these handsome Greek heroes and wishing to ally herself to them, promised her belt to Heracles. Hera, annoyed at how smoothly Heracles was handling the task, disguised herself as an Amazon and informed the others that their queen was about to be kidnapped. The Amazons immediately attacked the ship and Heracles, thinking that Hippolyte had set him up, killed her and took the belt. Meanwhile, Prince Theseus, one of Heracles' companions, had fallen in love with Antiope, Hippolyte's sister, and he took her with him back to Athens.

X *The Cattle of Geryon*

Heracles delivered the belt to Eurystheus who gave it to his delighted daughter on her next birthday. There were three more labours left and Eurystheus was starting to panic, for he knew full well that if Heracles completed them he would claim his right to the throne at Tiryns. For the tenth labour therefore he decided that a really long journey to bring back the cattle of Geryon, a man with three heads, would exhaust

Heracles and that he would fall easy prey to one of the many monsters encountered on the way: there were plenty of them, for Heracles had never travelled westwards before. Geryon was King of Erytheia (Cadiz), and employed the herdsman Eurytion with his two-headed dog Orthus, son of Typhon, to guard his fine cattle. Heracles enjoyed the outward journey, killing all sorts of beasts on the way, and when he arrived at Oceanus on the edge of the world, he set up a pillar on either side of the straits which divide Africa and Europe as a monument to his great voyage. (They are still there, one now named the Rock of Gibraltar, the other the Jebel Musa in Morocco.) The Pillars of Heracles also served to keep the hideous sea-monsters of Oceanus out of the Mediterranean – they were too large to squeeze through.

Heracles leaned back against one

LEFT Heracles in the bowl of the Sun; *Athenian red-figure wine-cup, early 5th century* BC. *The scene was painted in the bowl of the wine-cup, thus Heracles would appear to be floating in the wine when the cup was full. The sea is denoted by the octopuses and fish.*

of the pillars, feeling tired and irritable and extremely thirsty. In his anger at the intense heat of the sun he rashly let loose an arrow in the direction of Helius, charioteer of the Sun. Luckily for him, Helius was in a good mood and admiring the daring of the hero, actually lent him his great golden drinking-cup for his journey to Erytheia, not to drink from, but to sail in. Heracles, club in hand to fend off the sharks, made good progress in the magic cup and soon arrived at Mount Abas where Geryon's cattle were grazing. Eurytion and Orthus ran at him, the hound's two heads barking and snarling; Heracles swung his club killing dog and herdsman with one stroke and quickly made off with the cattle. However Geryon had seen the sun bowl glittering in Oceanus and, troops at the ready, was soon pursuing Heracles. The cattle came to a halt at the River Anthemus, where Heracles turned and shot Geryon with three arrows, one for each head. Heracles decided that the strange boat was drawing too much attention and returned it with thanks to Helius, explaining that the cattle would spoil it.

Thus began his long journey eastwards back to Greece, and as Eurystheus had foreseen this proved to be dangerous, as so many coveted the cattle and lay in ambush for them. In Liguria (southern France) he was attacked and fell to his knees, badly wounded. Zeus came to his rescue by sprinkling rocks around Heracles to shield him; Heracles then hurled them at the retreating Ligurians. (The rocks still lie scattered to the west of Marseilles.)

Heracles then made his way down the west coast of Italy, where unbeknown to him the giant Cacus stole some of the cattle and hid them in his cave, which unfortunately for Cacus stood ahead beside the road (on the future site of Rome). As Heracles drove the noisy herd past the cave, the cattle hidden in the cave answered back revealing their hiding-place. Heracles was furious and killed the giant in a wrestling-bout, to the joy of the local people whose lives Cacus had made a misery. News of Heracles the Hero travelled ahead and everywhere in Italy he was met by joyful crowds, cheering and begging him to dispatch their own local nuisance down to Hades. In the lovely regions beneath the volcanic Mount Vesuvius, he founded a town called Herculaneum in his honour, which was destroyed by a violent volcanic eruption many, many centuries later.

Heracles eventually arrived at the tip of the Italian boot, where Hera caused the finest bull in the herd to break loose and swim the narrow straits to Sicily. Heracles asked the god Hephaestus, who had his forge beneath Mount Etna, to come and look after his cattle and swam off to find the bull. Heracles chased it across the island as far as its westernmost tip where the local king Eryx put it in with his own herds. The king wagered his lands against all of Geryon's cattle in a boxing match with the hero; though Eryx, famous for his boxing skills, put up an entertaining fight, Heracles son of Zeus was simply too powerful and soon Eryx lay dead. Mount Eryx remains as a memorial to the king.

XI *The Apples of the Hesperides*

When Hera married Zeus she had received many fine wedding presents from gods, giants and mortals alike, but her favourite gifts were some golden-apple trees created specially by Gaia, the earth mother. They grew somewhere in the west, but no one knew quite where. Heracles, for his eleventh labour was to bring back the valuable fruit to Eurystheus. Only Nereus, the Old Man of the Sea, knew where they grew and Heracles caught him napping on the sea-shore. Nereus turned himself into all sorts of slippery sea-creatures in an effort to escape, but Heracles' grip was too strong and soon the old man was telling where they could be found. It would not be easy for they were tended by the

Hesperides, Daughters of Evening, who lived near their father where Helius drives his chariot into Oceanus; and the tree on which the apples grew was entwined by a 100-headed snake called Ladon. Heracles had encountered monsters of this type before and did not foresee any difficulties. But, on the way, passing through the Caucasus mountains, he found the Titan, Prometheus, chained to a rock as eternal punishment for deceiving Zeus and stealing fire from the gods to give to men; Zeus' eagle was busy pecking his liver, which was renewed every day. Heracles decided to free the hero and shot the eagle. Prometheus in return advised Heracles to ask Atlas, the Titan whom Zeus had forced to carry the sky, to fetch the apples for him.

ABOVE Heracles fights Antaeus; *Athenian red-figure* calyx crater *(wine mixing-bowl) signed by the painter Euphronios, late 6th century* BC. *The painter has used diluted 'paint' to depict the unkempt hair of the giant, who is in a highly contorted position while the hero's body is firm and true. The giant's right fingers are already limp as he begins to lose the fight.*

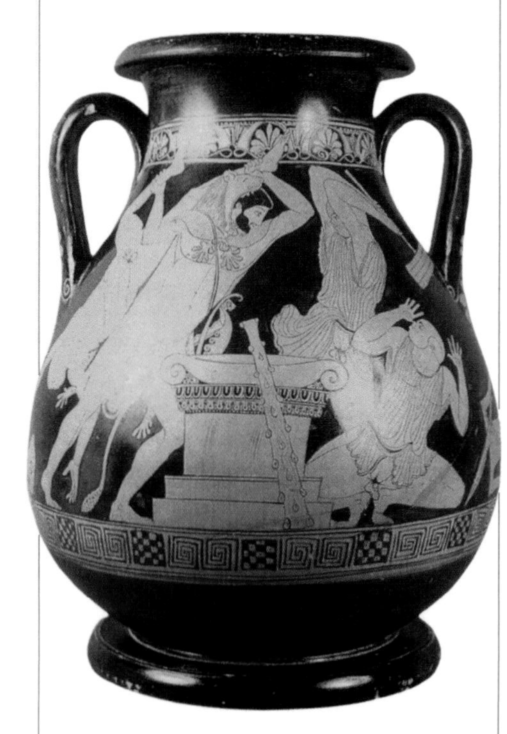

ABOVE Heracles and Busiris; *Athenian red-figure* pelike *(wine-jar) by the Pan Painter, early 5th century* BC. *The hero is shown flinging King Busiris onto the altar where he himself was about to be sacrificed. The Egyptians are depicted with Negroid features.*

Heracles passed through Arabia into Egypt, ruled at that time by the cruel king Busiris. At the start of his reign there had been terrible droughts which had led to famine. Busiris asked a seer from Greece for advice on what was to be done. The seer found that Zeus was angry with Busiris and was demanding the annual sacrifice of a foreigner in return for good harvests. Busiris was a practical man and the unfortunate seer became the first of a line of foreign visitors to Egypt to be sacrificial victims. Heracles would make a fine sacrifice and he was bound and adorned and dragged to the altar where his father Zeus recognized him. Heracles broke his bonds in fury and proceeded to kill Busiris, together with his son and the priests, laying them on the altar as that year's sacrifice to Zeus.

From Egypt he made his way along the North African coast and came to Libya, where an eccentric young king called Antaeus ruled. Antaeus would challenge heroic visitors to wrestling matches and had never been beaten; and he always fought to the death. Heracles could not resist the challenge but found Antaeus' abilities to be more than he bargained for; everytime he pinned him to the earth to deliver the final blow Antaeus would throw Heracles off with replenished strength. Then he remembered what he had been told about Antaeus' parentage; his mother was Gaia and he was strong only so long as he kept in contact with her. Heracles changed his tactics by holding Antaeus from mother earth as often as he could, draining his strength and eventually killing him with a bear hug.

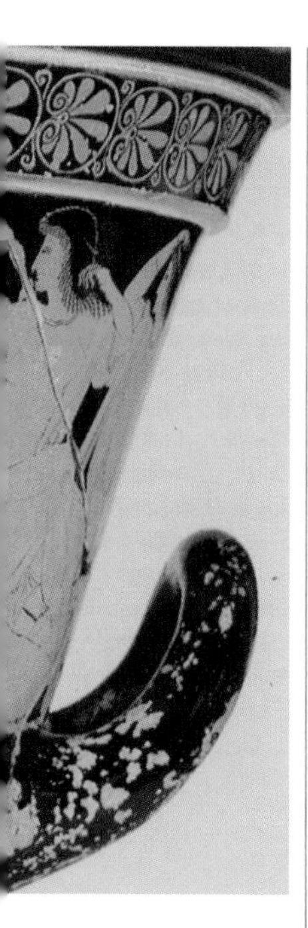

At last Heracles saw the faint blue line of the Atlas mountains on the western horizon, their white tops gleaming in the evening sun as he approached. Gradually the shape of two huge legs appeared and he greeted Atlas who was holding up the sky on his shoulders. Remembering the advice of Prometheus, Heracles offered to take the load if Atlas would go and fetch the golden apples from the grove of the Hesperides. Atlas was glad to get the weight off his back and obliged by pushing his way past the Daughters of Evening and strangling the hundred necks of Ladon. On his way back to the Atlas mountains, it dawned on him that he need never hold the sky again, and that Heracles could not come after him since he was unable to put down his load. He informed the hero that he felt like a walk and would take the apples to Tiryns himself. Heracles, for the first time in his life unable to use brute force to escape the predicament, had to rely on the few wits he had. He agreed to the proposal, and asked the Titan to hold the sky whilst he made himself more comfortable by placing a pillow on his shoulders. Atlas, who had no wits at all, laid down the apples and took the sky. Heracles took the apples and walked away laughing.

When he reached Tiryns, Eurystheus would not touch the apples, realizing that they were Hera's, so Heracles dedicated them at Athene's temple, since she had helped him to hold the sky. But she did not want them either and returned the sacred apples to the Hesperides.

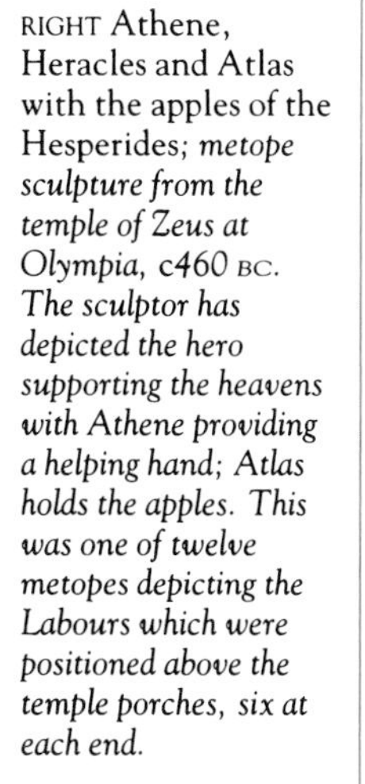

RIGHT Athene, Heracles and Atlas with the apples of the Hesperides; *metope sculpture from the temple of Zeus at Olympia, c460* BC. *The sculptor has depicted the hero supporting the heavens with Athene providing a helping hand; Atlas holds the apples. This was one of twelve metopes depicting the Labours which were positioned above the temple porches, six at each end.*

XII *Cerberus*

Eurystheus had to come up with something really lethal for the last labour. There were no more monsters or giants left on the earth; Heracles had annihilated them. 'Why not send him to the Underworld', thought Eurystheus, 'and let us see if he can bring Cerberus, the monstrous hound with three heads and a mane of snakes, up to the land of the living?' Cerberus undoubtedly held a grudge against Heracles for he had killed his brothers and sister: the Nemean Lion, the Hydra, and Orthus the dog.

To prepare himself for this twelfth and most difficult labour, Heracles was required to undergo ritual purification at Eleusis, where he was initiated into the secret Mysteries of Demeter and her daughter Persephone, goddess of the Underworld, to where Heracles now began his journey. Hermes was his guide into Hades' kingdom, and his patron deity Athene went with them as far as the gates near the birdless Lake Avernus. He tricked Cerberus by throwing him a cake soaked in opium, and while the dog snored Heracles pushed his way through the gates into the Underworld. As he became accustomed to the dark, he noticed the ghostly forms of the dead flitting away from him in fear; they appeared to be thirsty and Heracles killed one of the cattle of Hades and offered the blood to the shades as a drink. The cowherd protested and soon Heracles had cracked a couple of his ribs, only stopping when Persephone protested. In the mists he caught sight of two old friends, the heroes Theseus and Peirithous, who were seated in the two Chairs of Forgetfulness, Hades' punishment for attempting to carry off his wife Persephone. The chairs were of cold stone and anyone who sat in them turned to stone and became part of them, like enthroned statues of gods. He freed Theseus, but was afraid to untie Peirithous, the Lapith king, since the ground quaked as he approached him; Peirithous remains there to this day.

LEFT Heracles and Cerberus; *Athenian red-figure amphora by the Andokides Painter, late 6th century* BC. *The hero, holding a chain, approaches the dog with caution; Cerberus here has only two heads, each of which is surmounted by a cobra-like snake. Athene stands close by. The entrance to Hades is depicted as a temple porch.*

Hades, seeing the havoc that the heroes were causing, agreed to Heracles' request to take Cerberus to Tiryns, but stipulated that Heracles must try to tame him without weapons, and return him as soon as the people of Tiryns had seen him. Heracles reluctantly agreed; he felt naked without his favourite weapons, but Hades was a god and he dutifully laid down his club, quiver and bow. Again he had to use his brain, and it occurred to him that dogs always attacked people who appeared to be frightened of them; so Heracles walked up casually to Cerberus and, patting him on his three heads, put a chain round each one and took him for a walk to the world above. Cerberus was delighted with this attention and barked with joy all the way to Tiryns. Eurystheus could not believe the advanced warnings of the hound's approach and stood on the ramparts laughing and calling the people of Tiryns to rejoice with him that Heracles was dead; there was a sudden terrifying growl behind him (Heracles had already trained Cerberus to attack cowards) and Eurystheus was back in his jar in a flash of Zeus thunderbolt. Heracles was about to unchain his new pet, when Eurystheus reminded him that the labours were a sacred purification ceremony and that the gods would be angry if he let Cerberus loose. Heracles reluctantly agreed and took Cerberus back to the gates of Hades.

BELOW Heracles brings Cerberus to Eurystheus; *black-figure* hydria *(water jug), mid 6th century* BC. *The hero and king are both painted white, a colour normally reserved for women: perhaps it suggests their terror of the three-headed dog, whom the painter has depicted in black, white and purple with snakes on heads and paws.*

ABOVE Heracles and Omphale; *Roman wall-painting from a Pompeian house, 1st century* AD. *The gods (above) and Omphale (left) look on while Cupids remove the hero's club and quiver. The idea of Cupids draining the strength from heroes and gods was popular with Hellenistic and Roman poets and artists.*

Heracles and Omphale

The twelve labours were over and Heracles remembered the words of the Pythia, who had promised that he would now achieve immortality. But such a promise does not bring happiness on earth, and for the rest of his life Heracles received more than his fair share of human misery. He could never find himself a new wife, since the story of his insane slaughter of Megara and their children was too well known. King Eurytus, who had once taught Heracles archery, refused the hand of his daughter and Heracles took some of his cattle instead. When accused of the theft by Iphitus, son of Eurytus, Heracles threw him off the roof of his palace. The gods punished him with illness; once again he went to Delphi for advice, but the Pythia, considering that he had not grown wiser after the labours, refused to answer him. In his anger he stormed off, taking the sacred tripod of Apollo with him. A fierce fight broke out between him and Apollo for the tripod, Heracles' first encounter with an Olympian; he was doing well and Zeus stopped the fight with a well-aimed thunderbolt and then ordered the Pythia to advise him of his new punishment. He was to be sold into slavery for three years, the proceeds going to the orphans of Iphitus.

At the slave market he was bought at a high price by Omphale, the beautiful Queen of Lydia. He cleared her land of giants and monsters, and some say also served her as a lover. Later authors even suggest that at Omphale's suggestion he wore womens' clothes and took to spinning and playing the lyre. However he spent his time in Lydia, he was still under the orders of the queen and after three years had become healthy again.

Heracles and Deianeira

After years spent avenging himself on former enemies, Heracles went to live in the court of King Oeneus of Calydon. He fell in love with princess Deianeira, but had to

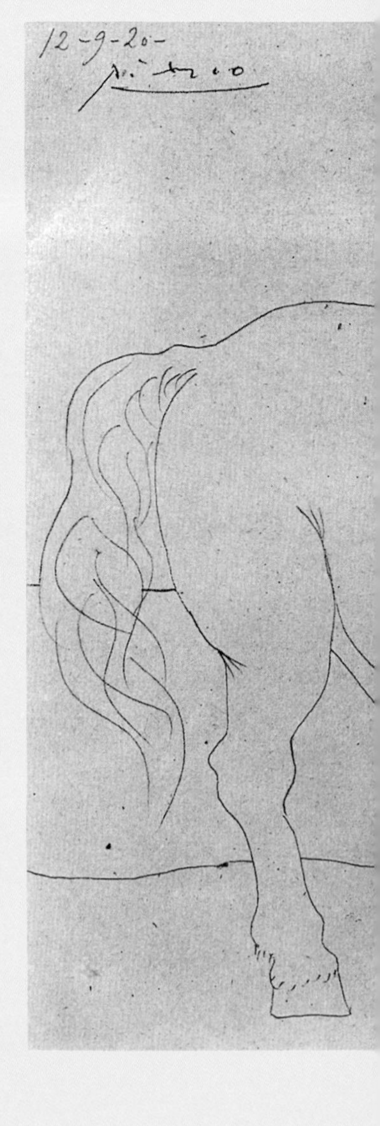

fight the local river-god Achelous for her hand; during the struggle Heracles broke off one of the god's horns which he later presented to the Hesperides, who filled it to the brim with fruit and named it the Cornucopia ('horn of plenty'). Heracles married Deianeira, but they were exiled from Calydon when Heracles, still not knowing his own strength, accidentally killed Oeneus's cup-bearer with a rap on the knuckles for spilling wine at a banquet. They made for Trachis and en route had to cross the wide river Evenus; Heracles was capable of swimming to avoid the high fees of the ferryman, the Centaur Nessus, so he put Deianeira on the ferry whilst he himself swam. In the middle of the river he heard the cries of his wife whom Nessus was trying to rape. Heracles reached the opposite shore and killed the Centaur with an arrow, dipped in the poison of the Hydra. As he lay dying, Nessus, pretending remorse, told Deianeira that she should smear his blood on Heracles' clothes as a magical love potion which would make him always attracted by her. Fearing that one day Heracles would leave her for another woman she bottled the potion for future use.

LEFT *Pablo Picasso (1881–1973),* Nessus and Dejanira *(1920). Picasso carried Classical subjects into the present century. He was particularly interested in figures symbolic of the animal nature of man and made many sketches of the Minotaur. Here he depicts another classic half-man/half-beast, the Centaur Nessus, attempting the rape of Deianeira. The pencil drawing exhibits Picasso's mastery of foreshortening by means of single lines in the manner of Athenian red-figure vase-painters.*

Heracles was welcomed by the people of Trachis and helped them in many battles. He had one last vendetta against King Eurytus of Oechalia, who had once refused him his daughter Iole, as the prize of an archery contest won by Heracles. Eurytus was defeated and on his way back to Trachis with his new concubine Iole, Heracles stopped at Cape Cenaeum on the island of Euboea to build an altar to Zeus. He had no clean clothes for the sacrifice and sent his herald to Trachis to ask Deianeira for a fresh tunic. Deianeira heard from the herald Lichas that Heracles was in love with Iole, and, remembering the Centaur's advice, smeared the tunic with the love potion. Heracles stood before the altar of Zeus in his new clothes. As he began the sacrifice his flesh began to burn; he ripped off the tunic, which took the flesh with it. In agony, he made his way back to Trachis where he found that Deianeira had committed suicide on learning that she had brought about the death of her husband.

The dying Heracles climbed Mount Oeta with his son Hyllus and ordered him to build a funeral pyre. The hero could not wait to die, but no one could bring themselves to light the pyre. At

last prince Philoctetes, who was passing by with his flocks, agreed to perform the sombre duty; Heracles rewarded him with his bow and arrows. A great crowd had gathered to witness the last moments of the great hero; they watched until the flames began to die away, and just as they were turning to depart a huge cloud rose above the pyre and there was a flash of lightning. The mists dispersed and no sign could be seen of the hero's body. Hyllus recalled the words of the Delphic oracle, related to his father many years earlier, that he would achieve immortality upon completion of the twelve labours.

Heracles was taken to Olympus by Athene and Hermes, where he was introduced to his divine father Zeus for the first time in his immortal life. He was reconciled with Hera, who gave him her daughter Hebe as a wife. Heracles continued to support his worldly allies against Eurystheus, who outlived Heracles on earth as king of Tiryns, and against the Trojans; Philoctetes was persuaded to join the Greeks on the Trojan plain where he killed Paris with the arrows of Heracles. Heracles remained hero of heroes for evermore.

LEFT The introduction of Heracles to Olympus; *Athenian black-figure wine-cup signed by the potter Phrynos, mid 6th century BC. This miniature scene was painted on the lip of the wine-cup. Athene, wearing her aegis (breastplate), introduces the hero to his father Zeus.* Phrynos epoiesen chairemen *('Phrynos made this and sends his greetings') is signed beneath the scene. It exhibits the fine use of both brush and incising tool by a group of painters known as the 'Little Masters'. On the opposite side of the cup the painter depicted the birth of Athene, emphasizing the brother/sister relationship of goddess and hero.*

Archaeology and Temples

Most Greek myths and legends had geographical locations in the real Greek world and covered the whole of the Mediterranean region. This does not necessarily mean that all Greeks had been to all places mentioned in the myths; the poets might have sometimes intentionally chosen unknown and therefore exotic settings for their stories which would have enhanced the magical and fantastic elements. (Shakespeare, for similar reasons, set many of his plays in real but exotic places where anything could happen.)

ABOVE *Mount Olympus, Greece; the snowy peak is nearly always obscured by clouds.*

Perhaps the most famous location is Mount Olympus, the mythical home of the Olympian gods. Its snowy peaks are rarely visible, often shrouded in clouds which added to the sense of awe felt by the Greeks towards this most sacred of places. Archaeologists have recently discovered a ruined temple on the summit (at 9,186 ft/2,800 m), almost certainly dedicated to Zeus, the king of the Olympian gods. It is unlikely that this inhospitably sited temple was often used for worship, but remains of animal sacrifices, dedicatory inscriptions, and coins have been found in the recent excavations. It was linked by a sacred way to the city of Dion, down in the valley; here there were many rich temples dedicated to various Olympians. A statue of Dionysus, not one of the original twelve Olympians, and a temple of the Egyptian goddess Isis have also been found; the temple of Isis was built during the later Hellenistic period when the Greek world had expanded to embrace alien cultures and their religions. Dion was also the original location of the Olympic Games, organized in honour of Zeus, before they were transferred in the 8th century BC to Olympia in the Peloponnese. One tradition also places the home of the nine Muses, daughters of Zeus and Mnemosyne (Memory), on nearby Mount Pieria.

Other locations included well-known natural features of the landscape: Mount Etna in Sicily (which was full of Greek colonies) was for some the workshop of Hephaestus; others located the divine smith on the island of Lemnos,

which had once been volcanic. Ancient writers of guidebooks, such as Pausanias in the 2nd century AD pointed out other peculiar natural features such as boulders and chasms and explained them with myths.

Archaeologists have discovered clues as to the possible origins of certain myths. Romantic 19th-century travellers thought that they had discovered the Labyrinth of the Minotaur at Knossos in Crete; what they actually saw was the many-corridored prehistoric Minoan palace, but even this might have suggested the Labyrinth to the ancient poetic imagination.

Excavations at Troy have uncovered many stages of the ancient city; there is one particularly imposing city (Troy VI) which suffered great devastation in the 13th century BC (dated by pottery); this date approximately accords with the traditional dating of the fall of Troy in the early 12th century BC. It is highly probably that there was a siege of Troy by a confederacy of Greek nations, and that legendary figures like Achilles, Paris and Helen did exist; it would have been quite natural for the epic poets to exaggerate their strength and beauty for the amusement of their audiences. Other 'mythical' features such as monsters and divine epiphanies can be 'explained' in the same manner.

BELOW *Troy and the Trojan plain; the site of Homer's Troy was already a place of pilgrimage in antiquity. Great generals such as Alexander the Great, Julius and Augustus Caesar visited it to pay their respects to the legendary heroes who had fought and died there. The Greek forces were encamped on the plain beside the sea. The site now bears the trenches and mounds of Schliemann's 19th-century excavations.*

BOTTOM *The Trojan walls; these are the remains of later walls and a tower, but they give some idea of the size of the Homeric city, described in the* Iliad *as 'spacious' and 'surrounded by rings of stone'.*

RIGHT *The Athenian Acropolis ('Top of the City') was the main sanctuary of Classical Athens. It rises steeply from the plain and overlooks the whole of the city. This is a view of the Propylaea (entrance gates) with the little Temple of Athene Nike to the right. On the extreme right appears the top of the Parthenon.*

BELOW *The Parthenon or Temple of Athene Parthenos ('The Virgin') was designed by the architect Ictinus and built between 447 and 432* BC. *Its partial survival is due to its conversion into a church and later a mosque. The many decorative sculptures have been destroyed or plundered over the years. Phidias's famous chryselephantine statue of Athene once stood inside.*

The Olympian gods were worshipped in walled sanctuaries. The most important building within the sanctuary was the temple, which was the home of the cult statue of the god; the temple was surrounded with a colonnade and was often decorated with sculptures referring to myths associated with the god (in much the same way as our churches have stained-glass windows illustrating bible stories). Before the temple, which faced the rising sun, was the altar where animal sacrifices were performed by priests or priestesses in front of worshippers who stood under colonnaded shelters called 'stoas'. Around the temple stood votive statues and other offerings dedicated by worshippers. Those who could not afford expensive bronze or marble statues would purchase terracotta images of the gods from booths outside the sanctuary; these were placed on the temple steps and later buried in sacred trenches which are today a rich source for our knowledge of Greek art and religion.

In the larger 'Panhellenic' sanctuaries such as that of Zeus at Olympia and Apollo at Delphi, city states would build their own treasuries along the sacred ways; these were often very fine buildings like miniature temples in which valuable offerings to the god were stored. Athletic competitions would be held every four years in honour of the gods; these sanctuaries therefore also contained stadia, gymnasia and statues of victorious athletes. A truce would be called throughout the Greek world whilst the games were being performed.

BELOW *The Sanctuary of Apollo at Delphi; the site was built on the side of a rocky mountain. In the foreground are the seats of the theatre with the Temple of Apollo behind.*

THESEUS

Aegeus, King of Athens, could not have children and sought the advice of the Delphic oracle. The Pythia's answer was that he should not loosen the spout of his wineskin until he arrived back at Athens. Aegeus did not understand the riddle and went to seek advice from his friend King Pittheus of Troezen before returning home. Pittheus grasped the Oracle's meaning immediately but pretended not to understand as he had hopes for his daughter Aethra; he plied Aegeus with wine and sent Aethra to sleep with him. The following morning the King of Athens left an ivory-handled sword and sandals beneath a huge rock in the palace yard, instructing the princess that if she bore a son who was able to lift the stone, she should send the boy to Athens with the sandals on his feet and the sword at his side. Little did he know that Poseidon came to Aethra on the same night.

The Labours of Theseus

Aethra did have a son and she named him Theseus. He grew into a strong and handsome young man, as might be expected, and believed his grandfather Pittheus who told him that his father was a god. Theseus loved to listen to the travelling poets with their stories of gods, giants and the heroes of Troy; but there was one hero who was still alive

LEFT The Labours of Theseus; *Athenian red-figure wine-cup, 5th century BC. In the centre Theseus kills the Minotaur and pulls the body outside the Labyrinth. Around the outside of the cup the hero punishes Sinis (tied to the tree), Sciron (note the turtle) and Procrustes (having his legs removed to fit the bed) and captures the Bull of Marathon.*

and yet was already the subject of epic tales. His name was Heracles, and Theseus wished that he could one day be the subject of such grand stories. Theseus differed from Heracles in one respect: he was quick-witted and cultured, turning the brutish sport of wrestling into an athletic event for the highly skilled. One day Theseus lifted the stone, which had always been an obstacle to his gymnastic training, and Pittheus told him the story of Aegeus' sword and sandals. Theseus decided to set out for Athens, but refused to take the short sea crossing across the Saronic Gulf, preferring to travel on foot across the Isthmus wnich joins the Peloponnese to Attica. His excuse was that he suffered from seasickness, but really he wanted a chance to encounter the monsters and giants who, it was rumoured, lived beside this well-trodden route.

All travellers from southern to northern Greece were compelled to cross the narrow Isthmus; therefore, not surprisingly, many robbers dwelt in the area and made a living as highwaymen. One of the most notorious and feared was the giant Sinis, known as Pityocamptes; this name meant 'Pine-Bender' and referred to the manner in which Sinis would slay his victims. He used two methods: in one he would help the traveller to bend the top of a pine to the ground, at the last moment letting go so that the unwary stranger was shot high into the air; the second method was more terrible, Sinis would attach the victim's legs one to each of two bent pines and then release the trees, tearing the stranger in two. Theseus dispatched Sinis by the second method.

On his journey to Athens, Theseus also discovereed wild beasts and monsters which had been left alone by Heracles. One of these was a huge sow called Phaea by her parents Typhon and Echidna, children of Titans; the beast was terrorizing the farms around Crommyon, but Theseus killed her with a single blow. Already Theseus was becoming renowned in Greece, and it was not long before rumours of this new hero had reached King Aegeus at Athens.

Beside the Isthmus are rocks and cliffs known as the Rocks of Sciron. Passing travellers would be welcomed by Sciron, offered a drink and told to put their feet up. After this refreshment he would ask them to wash his feet in return; but while they were drying his feet he would suddenly kick them unsuspecting over the precipice to fall into the jaws of a giant turtle waiting at the foot of the cliffs. Theseus accepted the hospitality, and returned the favour by washing Sciron's feet, considering this good behaviour for a royal prince. He was too skilled in the art of wrestling for the sudden kick to catch him off his guard and, taking hold of the robber's ankles, hurled him over his shoulders to become the turtle's last meal.

Theseus continued on his way to Athens and soon had reached Eleusis. Here he was welcomed by King Cercyon, who demanded a wrestling bout with the stranger. The king's style of fighting was barbaric and he had already killed a number of passing travellers by sheer brute force. In the palace at Troezen, Theseus had received a fine education in both fighting and the arts, and had developed rules and skills for the generally violent physical activities hoping to encourage sportsmanship among otherwise cultured peoples. Here at Eleusis was his chance to set an example; barbaric Cercyon smashed and grabbed, but Theseus used his skills and swift footwork to avoid and parry the blows, to the delight and applause of onlookers. Cercyon died of sheer exhaustion. Theseus set up a training school at Eleusis where athletes would be taught to box and wrestle in a civilized manner.

Theseus stayed the night just outside Eleusis at the inn of Damastes, whose nickname Procrustes ('Stretcher') was only understood when he showed his guests to their bedrooms. Wanting the tall ones to be comfortable, he made sure that their beds fitted exactly by sawing off any limbs which hung over the end of the bed. The short guests would have weights attached to their feet until they also fitted their beds exactly. Theseus put an end to the innkeeper's mad tricks by returning his gruesome hospitality.

On the following morning Theseus at last received his first glimpse of his destination; the palace and shrines on the Acropolis, the precipitous limestone hill which dominates the Athenian plain, were grander than any he had seen. As he was passing by the wayside Temple of Apollo Delphinius, some workmen on the roof of the temple jeered and whistled, thinking from his appearance that he was a young girl. Theseus was always well dressed as a civilized prince should be but he realised that his ankle-length gown was the fashion for Athenian women and that men wore a short tunic. However, he lost his temper and hurled two oxen from a passing cart up above the roof of the temple to the astonishment of the workmen.

King Aegeus had stopped at Corinth on his way back to Athens from Troezen; at the royal palace he had met the oriental princess Medea, who had been spurned by her husband Jason when he took a new wife at Corinth. Medea, famous for her witchcraft, had avenged herself on Jason by killing his new bride with a burning cloak, as well as murdering her two sons by him. She had flown to Athens in a dragon-drawn chariot, the gift of her grandfather Helius, and promised to bear Aegeus children if he would protect her at Athens. They had a son called Medus, whom Medea wished to see made king of Athens. Only she recognized Theseus as the boy whom Aegeus had once told her would one day come to Athens as the royal heir, but she kept this knowledge to herself. Aegeus held a splendid banquet for the new hero, whose exploits along the road from Troezen were already the subject of Athenian drinking songs; Theseus had become as renowned a hero as Heracles.

Medea, however, persuaded Aegeus that Theseus was actually an enemy who had come to overthrow the king; they sent him off to kill the bull of Marathon, which Heracles had brought from Crete years earlier as one of his labours. Medea and Aegeus knew that Theseus would be killed, and that being a hero he could not refuse the challenge. Theseus captured the bull on the plains of Marathon and triumphantly brought it back alive to prove his heroism to the people of Athens; he presented it to Aegeus for sacrifice. That evening at a celebratory banquet Medea slipped poison in the hero's cup; just as he was about to drink, Aegeus noticed the ivory-handled sword hanging at Theseus's side and knocked the poisoned cup from his hands. Theseus was welcomed as the new prince of Athens and the people rejoiced that such a brave and handsome hero would one day be king.

Theseus and the Minotaur

Later that year Theseus learnt of a disturbing event that took place every nine years at Athens. A generation earlier King Minos of Crete had attacked Athens and demanded tribute of seven boys and seven girls, who were to be sent to Crete as a nine-yearly feast for the Minotaur, his monstrous son born from the union of his queen, Pasiphae, and the bull of Marathon when it had lived on Crete; it had a bull's head and a man's body and represented to the Athenians all the uncontrolled lusts and animal qualities of uncivilized barbarians. Theseus asked Aegeus why his own name was not placed in the jar for the lottery which decided which unlucky children were to be sent to Crete; Aegeus laughed and answered that a prince did not count as a tribute. Theseus demanded that he should replace one of the chosen boys – he determined to slay the Minotaur.

The seven boys and seven girls of Athens sailed out from Piraeus, the port of Athens, in the black-sailed ship of Minos himself. Aegeus sadly told the captain to hoist a white sail on the return trip if Theseus was

RIGHT Theseus and Athene in the underwater palace of Amphitrite; *Athenian red-figure wine-cup, signed by Euphronios as potter and Onesimos as painter; early 5th century* BC. *The underwater scene with swimming dolphins and a Triton supporting Theseus' feet would have been enhanced by the sea of wine that covered it. The drapery is depicted swaying in the sea-currents.* Euphronios epoiesen *('Euphronios made this') is signed to the left of the young Theseus. On the cup exterior were painted further heroic exploits of Theseus.*

successful, so that preparations could be made for the triumphant homecoming. On the sea-journey to Crete Theseus, hearing the cries of one of the seven girls whom the lusty Minos was pestering, challenged him to a show of strength. Minos called on his father Zeus to hurl a thunderbolt into the sea as proof of his own divine parentage; a flash of lightning duly appeared, and Minos arrogantly threw his gold ring into the sea, challenging Theseus to prove that his father was Poseidon by retrieving it. Theseus dived without hesitation and had soon reached his father's palace; he was welcomed by Amphitrite, the lovely wife of Poseidon, who not only handed him Minos's ring, but also placed on his brow a beautiful wreath of roses and wrapped him in a purple cloak. Theseus was soon standing on deck miraculously dry. The Nereids rode the waves beside the ship and the Athenian children joined them in their songs of praise; Minos was greatly disturbed and left the girls alone for the rest of the journey.

On Crete, as was the custom on the night before feeding them to the Minotaur, Minos entertained his young guests at his palace at Knossos. At the banquet Princess Ariadne fell in love with Theseus and offered to help if he took her back to Athens with him. The Minotaur lived in a maze beneath the palace called the Labyrinth; Ariadne gave Theseus a plan of the Labyrinth which its architect, the famous craftsman Daedalus, had given her to spite King Minos. The next morning the young Athenians were thrown into the maze; Ariadne gave Theseus a ball of string and attached one end of it to the Labyrinth's exit. Theseus stepped into the darkness, unravelling the twine as he stepped over the skeletons of earlier victims. He heard the bellowings of the monster in the distance and made his way towards them; at last he found the Minotaur in a great hall at the centre of the maze about to strangle one of the children. Theseus used his wrestling skills, but finding that they were ineffective against the beast, killed it with a well-aimed blow of his fist. He gathered the Athenians together and, guided by the twine, was soon back in the open air. Ariadne had prepared the ship for sailing and soon they were safely on their way towards Athens. There was great rejoicing on board that night.

The ship stopped for water at the island of Dia (Naxos), where Theseus cruelly abandoned Ariadne on the beach. She watched his ship disappear over the horizon and, greatly distressed, prepared to hang herself; but as she placed the noose around her neck she heard distant music and singing. Coming towards her along the beach was a group of Maenads following a beautiful youth with ivy-strewn hair and a thyrsos in his hand. She knew immediately that this was the god Dionysus and their love lasted for many years. When she died Dionysus placed among the stars the crown which he had given her at their wedding, the constellation Corona Borealis.

LEFT Theseus fighting the Minotaur; *Athenian red-figure* stamnos *(wine mixing-jar) by the Kleophrades Painter, early 5th century* BC. *The hero's pony-tailed hair reflects the new 5th-century fashion for short or tied hair. Diluted 'paint' depicts blood on the Minotaur, who holds a stone as a weapon. Theseus' hat and scabbard hang on the wall.*

RIGHT Theseus and the Minotaur; *Roman wall-painting from a Pompeian house, 1st century* AD. *The Minotaur lies dead in the entrance to the Labyrinth. The hero is praised by both children and adults.*

RIGHT Dionysus and Ariadne; *red-figure wine-cup, 5th century* BC. *The drunken Dionysus, wearing an ivy wreath, holds a lyre and is supported by his mortal lover Ariadne. Eros, depicted in the 5th century* BC *as an adolescent youth with long hair and wings, plays a tambourine. The vine leaves and grapes which decorate the top of the bowl would be reflected in the wine.*

Perhaps Theseus' callous behaviour was repaid: as the ship approached Athens, the captain, caught up in the excitement of the rejoicing passengers, had forgotten to hoist the white sail. King Aegeus was standing on the edge of the Acropolis when he saw the mournful sign of the black sail; thinking his son dead, he jumped to his death.

Theseus, King of Athens

Theseus, after mourning his father, received a splendid coronation and set about improving the kingdom of Athens. He persuaded the outlying towns of Athens, the Demes, to support an Athenian commonwealth, and reduced his own royal powers; an early step towards democracy, which later took him as its hero.

Heracles honoured the new king by inviting him on an expedition, his ninth labour, to the Black Sea where the Amazons lived; his task was to bring back the belt of Queen Hippolyte as a gift for Eurystheus' daughter. Hippolyte and her relatives were invited to a banquet on board the Greek ship; Theseus fell in love with Antiope, sister to the queen, and took her back to Athens where they married and had a son called Hippolytus. Antiope was killed when an army of Amazons marched against Athens in an unsuccessful attempt to win her back.

Theseus thought it would be sensible to form a political alliance with Crete and arranged to marry Minos's daughter Phaedra – the abandonment of her sister Ariadne had apparently been forgotten. Demophon and Acamas were their two sons and became heirs to the Athenian throne; Hippolytus had already been sent to Troezen where he became heir to his great-grandfather Pittheus.

During an attempted political coup, Pallas, the half-brother of Aegeus, and his fifty sons were killed by Theseus; the oracle instructed Theseus to go into exile for one year as purification for the spilling of family blood. He decided to spend the year at Troezen. Theseus and his court were welcomed at Troezen by Hippolytus. When Phaedra saw him she shuddered as she recognized the beautiful young man she had once seen at an initiation ceremony to the goddess Demeter at Eleusis. Phaedra's love for this handsome stranger had been inspired by Aphrodite and Phaedra had built a shrine to the goddess on the corner of the Acropolis; on a clear day she could see Troezen, where she knew he lived, but until the day she arrived there with her husband she was unaware that this was the son of Theseus by another woman. Hippolytus himself had become a fine hunter and had vowed his chastity to the virgin goddess of the chase, Artemis.

BELOW *Peter Paul Rubens (1577–1640),* Battle of the Amazons. *Rubens represents a scene popular in Classical art: Greek males fighting the Amazon warriors. The Greeks used the subject to demonstrate the triumph of civilized patriarchal society over barbarian societies with feminine characteristics. The wives of Greek citizens lived in purdah.*

RIGHT *Pierre-Auguste Renoir (1841–1919),* Diana *(1867). Renoir has painted the virgin Artemis (Diana) as a contemporary beauty seated in a sunny French landscape. She wields a very unclassical longbow with which she has just killed a deer.*

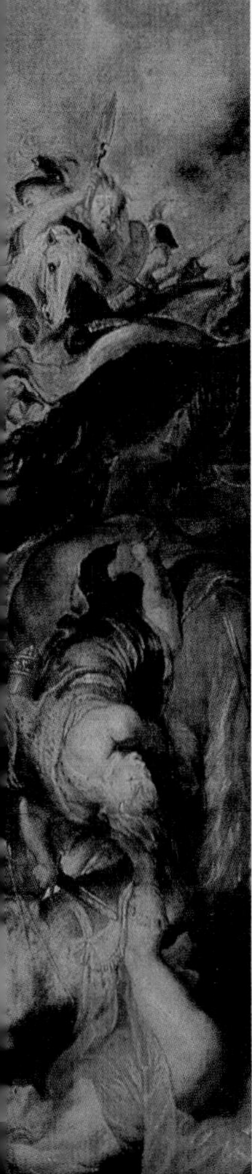

While Theseus was away at Delphi Phaedra found herself wasting away with unrequited love for her stepson. Her nurse secretly informed Hippolytus of Phaedra's feelings, but he was disgusted. Phaedra, driven to despair, committed suicide after writing a letter in which she spitefully informed Theseus that Hippolytus had raped her. Theseus returned and read the letter; refusing to believe his son's innocence, he called on his father Poseidon to destroy him. One day Hippolytus was riding his chariot along the beach when a huge bull rose from the sea and terrified the prince's horses; Hippolytus became entangled in the reins and was dragged over the rocks to his death. Theseus later learnt the truth from the priestess of Artemis; Aphrodite had arranged the tragedy because Hippolytus had refused to worship her, preferring chaste Artemis.

The Lapith King Peirithous invited Theseus to his marriage with Hippodameia. He also invited the Centaurs, who have the upper half of men but from the waist downwards are all horse. These semi-wild creatures had never drunk wine before and at the first taste their animal natures took control and they tried to rape the women. A fight ensued between Lapith and Centaur, and, with Theseus leading them, the Lapiths won.

LEFT Lapith fighting Centaur; *metope sculpture from the Parthenon, Athens, 447–432* BC. *The Parthenon's exterior Doric frieze was decorated with 92 sculpted metopes. Four subjects were represented, one for each side of the temple: Greeks fighting Trojans; Greeks fighting Amazons; gods fighting giants and Lapiths fighting Centaurs. The subjects symbolized the victory of the civilized Greeks over the Persians earlier in the century. Here the sculptor produces a circular tension between the man and half-beast, while the spread drapery makes an effective backdrop.*

After the deaths of Hippodameia and Phaedra, Peirithous and Theseus decided that they must find divine wives. Theseus forcibly abducted Helen, born from the egg of Zeus after he made love to Leda as a swan; but her heroic brothers, the Dioscuri, Castor and Polydeuces, won her back only to find her abducted again by Paris of Troy. Perithous decided to try to win Persephone from Hades; the two heroes were captured and imprisoned on the two chairs of Lethe (Forgetfulness), to make them forget their sacrilegious act. Heracles freed Theseus when he came on his last labour to capture the guard dog Cerberus.

Theseus, unlike Heracles, died an ignominious mortal death. He slipped over a cliff on the island of Scyros, where he had come to reclaim some lands which had once belonged to his grandfather; some say he was pushed. As he fell towards the rocks below, Theseus remembered the similar fates of the robber Sciron, of his beloved father Aegeus, and of his son Hippolytus.

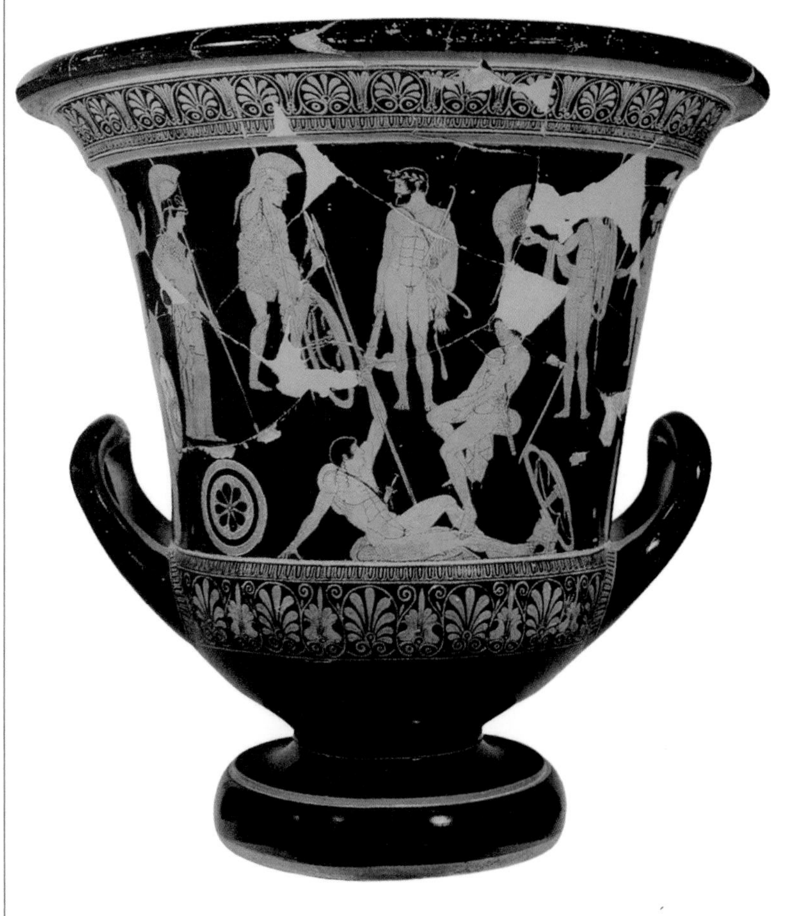

BELOW Theseus and Peirithous in the Underworld; *Athenian red-figure* calyx-crater *(wine-mixing jar) by the* Niobid Painter, *mid 5th century* BC. *The subject is disputed, but might well depict the two heroes seated in Hades with Heracles and Athene standing above them. The painter has attempted (for the first time in vase-painting) to convey an impression of depth by placing the figures on different levels; the rocky landscape is drawn in thin white lines.*

PERSEUS

Acrisius, the King of Argos, had been told by an oracle that he would one day be killed by a grandson. Therefore, he arranged for his daughter Danae to be locked in a cell of bronze until she was too old to have children; one day however he learnt that she had become miraculously pregnant. Zeus had plans for the future of Argos and had come to her one night through an air vent in the roof of the cell as a beautiful shower of gold dust. She bore a son and named him Perseus, but Acrisius had them thrown into the sea in a wooden chest. They were washed up on the island of Seriphos, where a friendly fisherman named Dictys gave them shelter. When Perseus reached manhood, Danae told him who his father was.

Perseus and Medusa

Dictys' lusty brother Polydectes was the King of Seriphos. He wanted to marry Danae but Perseus defended his unwilling mother. Angry at this rebuttal, Polydectes demanded horses from all the islanders as a gift to Hippodameia, daughter of King Oenomaus of Pisa, whom he now wished to marry. Perseus had no horses but said that he would provide anything else that the king might suggest, even the head of the Gorgon Medusa. Polydectes knew that no man had ever returned from visiting the Gorgons and confidently sent Perseus off to fulfil his rash promise.

Zeus sent Athene to give help and advice to his son. She directed him to a cave in Libya, where three hags called the Graeae dwelt; they would tell him where to find certain nymphs who were preparing special weapons to defeat the Gorgons. The Graeae, sisters of the Gorgons, refused to help Perseus. They possessed only one eye and one tooth between them and as one was passing the eye to the other

LEFT *Titian (c1487–1576),* Danae and the Shower of Gold, *(1554). The painting was commissioned as one of a number of erotic Classical subjects for Philip II of Spain. The painting depicts Danae not in the bronze prison of the Classical myth but in a luxurious bedroom complete with pet dog and a servant who tries to gather the gold in her apron. Titian described the painting as 'poesie' – a poetic fantasy of the myth.*

to look at the stranger, Perseus grabbed it and refused to return it unless they told him the whereabouts of the nymphs. He found them and they presented him with the weapons: a pouch in which to place Medusa's severed head; a pair of winged sandals to make a quick escape from her two immortal sisters, Stheno and Euryale, who had golden wings and hands of bronze; and a magical cap to make him invisible to perform the task. Hermes provided a sickle of sharpened adamant and helped him to polish his bronze shield until it shone like a mirror; this would be useful in enabling him to look at the reflected image of the Gorgons, who turned all who looked at them to stone.

Perseus recognized the approach to the Gorgons' lair by the petrified images of men and women who had caught sight of them; the sisters had placed them like marble statues on either side of the path. Invisible in his magic cap, Perseus approached Medusa, watching her reflection carefully in his shield. She was hideous, with snakes instead of hair and a huge red tongue hanging from her mouth between tusks. Perseus decapitated her with one swing of the sickle and, placing the head in the pouch, flew away swiftly in his winged sandals; Stheno and Euryale could not keep up with him and finally returned to mourn their dead sister.

On the way home Perseus stopped for the night in the land of the Hesperides. Atlas, who stood guard over their garden which contained the magic apples of Hera, had been told that one day a son of Zeus would come and steal them. He therefore tried to kill Perseus, who produced the Gorgon's head and turned the Titan into a high peak, Mount Atlas.

Perseus and Andromeda

As Perseus flew along the coast of Ethiopia he spied far below a naked girl chained to a rock by the sea. He flew nearer and heard her crying for help; two sad figures, her

parents King Cepheus and Queen Cassiopeia, were standing on the cliff and Perseus learnt from them what was happening: Cassiopeia had vainly boasted that her daughter was prettier than the Nereids; they had complained to Poseidon who had sent a sea-monster to terrorize Ethiopia. An oracle had told Cepheus that the monster would leave them alone only if he were to offer it his daughter Andromeda. Perseus promised to destroy the monster if the king and queen would allow him to marry Andromeda; at that moment the creature raised its long neck above the waves and dived, heading underwater for Andromeda's rock. Cepheus agreed and Perseus slew the monster with his sickle; it lay dead on the beach beneath the lovely Andromeda whom he unchained and delivered back to her parents. There was a celebratory banquet at the palace that night and Cepheus announced his daughter's marriage to the new hero, forgetting that he had already promised her to his brother Phineus. A fight started and Perseus, realizing that he was far outnumbered by Phineus and his troops, petrified them with the head of Medusa.

Perseus sailed to Seriphos with

RIGHT Perseus and the Gorgon Medusa; *Athenian black-figure* olpe *(wine-jug) by the* Amasis Painter, *mid* 5th century BC. *Medusa is depicted with fangs, sticking-out tongue and snake-locks. The hero averts his head as he decapitates Medusa so as not to be turned to stone by her gaze. Hermes stands watching.* Amasis m'epoiesen *('Amasis made me') is signed to the left of Theseus.*

LEFT Perseus and Medusa; *limestone metope sculpture from a Greek temple at Selinus, Sicily, mid 6th century* BC. *The winged horse Pegasus appears beside his mother Medusa, while Athene stands to the left. The profile bodies with frontal 'smiling' faces are typical of Archaic art.*

Andromeda and discovered on arrival that King Polydectes was still pursuing his mother Danae. Leaving Danae and Andromeda with Dictys, he went to the royal court and announced that he had returned with the gift for Hippodameia; out of its pouch came Medusa's head and all were turned to stone. He returned the magic cap, winged sandals and sickle to Hermes who took them back to the African nymphs; the head of Medusa was dedicated to Athene, who attached it to her aegis (breastplate) as a formidable weapon. Perseus decided to return to his birthplace at Argos and claim his inheritance from King Acrisius.

Though Perseus was prepared to forgive his past behaviour, Acrisius fled to King Teutamides, remembering the prophetic words of the oracle. Perseus left Danae and Andromeda at Argos and travelled to Larisa, where Teutamides was holding funeral games in honour of his father. Perseus could not see Acrisius among the crowds of spectators and decided to wait until the evening banquet; in the meantime he would compete in the games and introduced an event of his own called 'throwing the discus'. He took up the metal disk and hurled it into the open spaces of the stadium; but the wind suddenly diverted it and the discus landed in the crowd, killing Acrisius and thus fulfilling the prophecy.

Perseus returned to his mother and wife at Argos, but realized that the gods would consider it wrong for him to rule over the city of the man he had killed. He therefore exchanged Argos with nearby Tiryns where he ruled for many years, founding several other cities in the Argolid including Mycenae. Andromeda bore him several children and his grandson Eurystheus became the last of the Perseid dynasty at Argos. Perseus died a natural death.

LEFT *Sir Edward Coley Burne-Jones (1833–98),* The Doom Fulfilled. *Burne-Jones brings a Romantic medieval atmosphere to the myth of Perseus' rescue of Princess Andromeda. The hero's armour and winged greaves are distinctly exotic whilst the hair of Medusa's head spills from his shoulder-bag. Andromeda is free of her chains but awaits the outcome of the fight.*

The Greek Poets

RIGHT Rhapsode reciting; *Athenian red-figure amphora by the Kleophrades Painter, early 5th century* BC. *The painter has inscribed the start of an epic poem emerging from the poet's mouth: 'As once in Tiryns . . .'. Tiryns was a powerful Greek Mycenaean palace at the time of the Trojan war.*

In prehistoric Greece the myths were transmitted orally by professional poets called 'rhapsodes'. Their patrons were the Greek-speaking kings and aristocrats who governed relatively small areas of the Mediterranean. The rhapsodes would travel from court to court, often staying for several days to recite lengthy epic poems from memory: Mnemosyne (Memory) was the mother of the Muses who inspired poets. These epics were first recorded by poets such as Homer when writing was introduced in the 8th century BC. Their subjects concerned the origins of the gods and giants as well as legends of wars fought by their ancestors centuries ago. The most popular saga was the siege of Troy by the Greeks and their heroic adventures both before and after the siege. Relying on memory and wishing to hold the attention of their audiences, who would normally be wining and dining, the rhapsodes decorated their stories with superhuman activities and encounters with gods and monsters. Their language was suitably high-flown and the poems were sung in strict metre often to musical accompaniment.

Here is a description of the Greek hero Achilles from Homer's *Iliad*, translated by Alexander Pope in 1715:

The Hero rose;
Her aegis Pallas o'er his shoulders throws;
Around his brows a golden cloud she spread;
A stream of glory flamed above his head.
As when from some beleaguered town arise
The smokes high-curling to the shaded skies
(seen from some island, o'er the main afar,
When men distressed hang out the sign of war),
Soon as the Sun in ocean hides his rays,
Thick on the hills the flaming beacons ablaze;
With long-projected beams the seas are bright,
And heaven's high arch reflects the ruddy light;
So from Achilles' head the splendours rise,
Reflecting blaze on blaze against the skies.

There were also the lyric poets, who composed short poems for the symposia, intimate drinking parties held among a few close friends; they sung in short verses and accompanied themselves on the lyre – hence the name 'lyric'. Their subject matter was more personal than epic, dealing with apparently spontaneous outpourings of love, political satire and other themes relating to the lie of the *polis* (city-state). One of the earliest surviving lyric poets is

Sappho of Lesbos (c620–c550 BC), who recited her poems at symposia which seem to have been attended mainly by women.

In the following poem Sappho employs the myth of Helen to show the power of Aphrodite in influencing feelings of love. Sappho subverts the male values of war, preferring unadorned natural female beauty to the artificial glamour of armed warriors.

What is the most beautiful sight on this black earth?
Some will answer cavalry, or infantry, or warships;
But the woman I most love
Is lovelier than all these.

My answer is easily explained,
For Helen, more beautiful than all on earth,
Left doting parents, princely husband, child
To cross the sea for Troy: love at first sight.

After all, teenage brides have fragile hearts,
Which filled with passions newly poured
Are readily persuaded
By Aphrodite, Cypriot Queen.

I am no different when I think of Anaktoria
As she left me: at her sensual walk and glimmering
pearly face
I would prefer to gaze
than richly decorated Lydian chariots filled with
weapons.

(Translated by David Bellingham)

ABOVE Symposium and Gorgon's head; *Athenian black-figure wine-cup, mid 6th century* BC. *The drinkers hold similar wine-cups and one of them plays the aulos (double-pipe); a naked boy offers more wine. The Gorgon's head would appear as the drinker finished his wine.*

Choral odes were composed by lyric poets for more public occasions, such as weddings and religious festivals. These would include a colourful mixture of song and dance delivered by a chorus. They would employ myths to honour the patron, which might be a newly wed couple, a victor in the athletic games, or the *polis* itself. Bacchylides, writing in the 5th century BC, composed a choral hymn of praise to the hero Theseus, to be performed at a festival in honour of Apollo on his sacred island of Delos; it was sung by the poet's fellow islanders from Keos. King Minos of Crete, who is bringing Theseus and other young Athenian to offer as a sacrifice to the Minotaur, sends Theseus into the sea to fetch a golden ring to prove his heroism and divine favour. At the end of the poem Theseus emerges

from the sea triumphantly wearing a wreath given to him by the sea-goddess Amphitrite; the mythical narrative ends with songs of praise which return us to the present moment and the festival of Apollo:

He came to the surface beside the narrow ship's stern;
What a shock for the King of the armies of Knossos,
To see him standing there all dry.
All were amazed at the gleaming godly gifts he wore
And Nereids cried in delight from their glittering thrones
Riding the sea which echoed with their laughter.
The young Athenians praised him with songs of love.
Lord of Delos, your soul moved by our Kean voices,
Now send us your blessings from the heavens above.

(Trans. David Bellingham)

In the 5th century BC Athens was at the centre of Greek culture, attracting the best artists and writers with wealthy patronage. The most influential poetic form at this time was tragedy. Annual festivals to Dionysus culminated in dramatic competitions in the large open-air theatre of Dionysus on the slopes of the Acropolis. These plays took the form of trilogies performed in one day with a 'satyr play' in the evening to lighten the mood. Their subjects were drawn from mythology, but they usually dealt with matters of contemporary relevance: in the *Oresteia* trilogy by Aeschylus we are taken from the aftermath of the Trojan wars in the first two plays to contemporary Athens in the final play where we witness the first trial by jury under the new democracy. Other plays, such as Euripides' *Trojan Women* (415 BC), deal with Greek attitudes towards women; Andromache speaks:

The woman whom people really gossip about
Is the one who refuses to remain housebound.
I would love to have gone out, but dutifully
Stayed at home; and I did not answer back
Like some women do. My mind was sound enough
And taught me how to behave as nature intended.
What more did I need?
I would speak only when spoken to
And appear meek and mild before my husband.
I knew what was expected of me
And when to let him have his own way.

(Translated by David Bellingham)

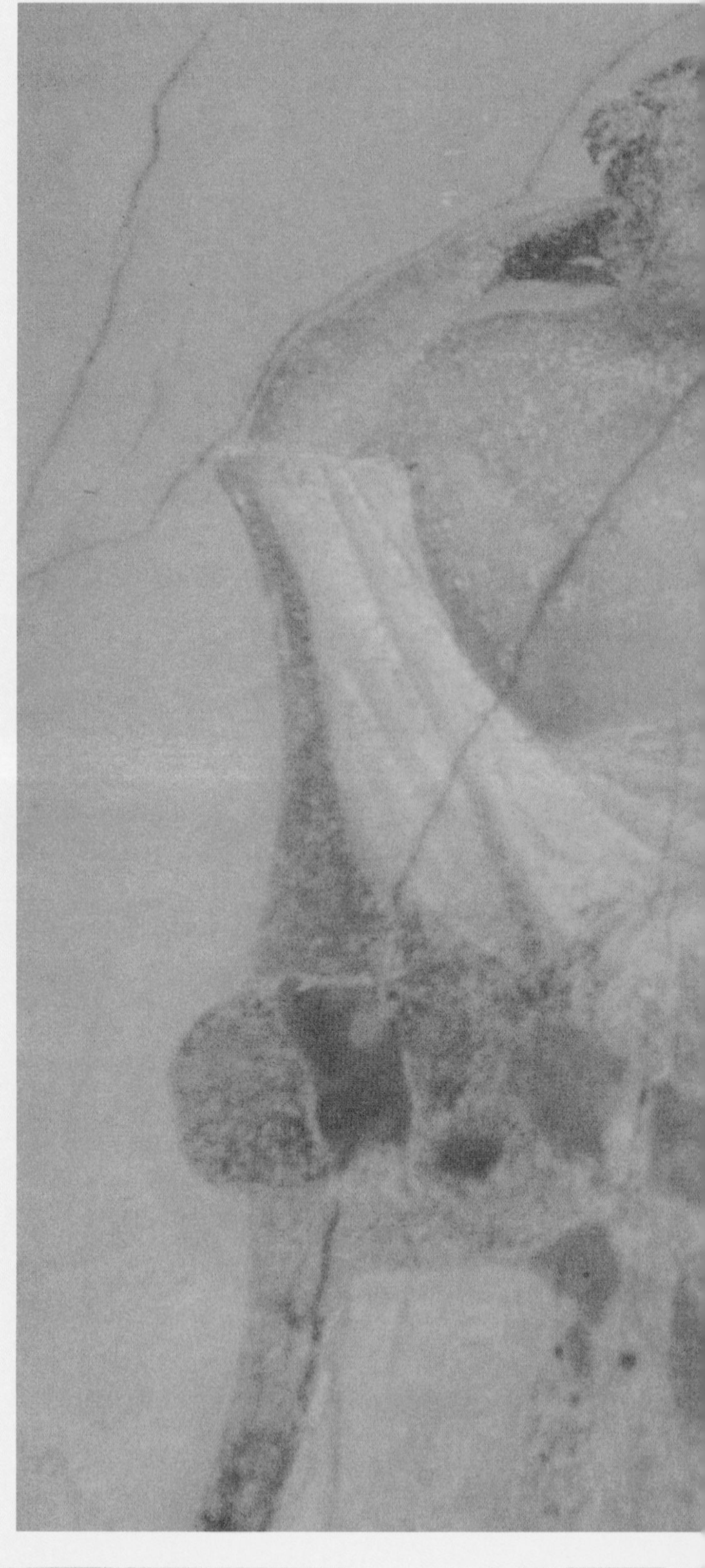

These early poetic uses of myth continued into the Hellenistic and Roman periods, but there are changes of emphasis. Greek poetry and art continued to be signs of high cultural attainment for Hellenistic kings and Roman emperors. Poets became increasingly learned in their use of myth and expected similar levels of understanding in their audiences. Callimachos, librarian at Alexandria in Egypt in the 3rd century BC, wrote for a royal patron and his court. An increasing tendency among poets in the Hellenistic period was to dwell on the minor details and previously unimportant episodes of the myths: the heroes and heroines became more human and Callimachos responded to a desire among the sophisticated urban elite for romantic images of country peasants. In the poem 'Hecale', Theseus is on his way to fight the bull of Marathon and seeks shelter from a storm in an old woman's cottage:

> Theseus threw off his soaking clothes
> And putting on a ragged tunic that she had laid out on the bed
> Made himself at home on her humble couch.
> She meanwhile had built a fire from wood stored long ago
> And brought him a cauldron of boiling water;
> 'Have you a bowl for me to soak my feet in?', asked Theseus.
> When he had finished she emptied the bowl and brought him
> Another cup of wine and water.
> She brought him black and green olives, which she had gathered wild
> In the Autumn, now swimming in brine;
> From a pipkin she served him loaves,
> And while Theseus ate the ploughman's lunch,
> Hecale told him the story of her life
> For she had once come from a wealthy family . . .

(Translated by David Bellingham)

LEFT The poet Menander; *Roman wall-painting from the House of the Menander, Pompeii, 1st century* AD. *Menander was a 4th-century* BC *writer of Greek comedy. He is shown here reading from a papyrus scroll, the normal medium for published poetry.*

FOUR

Tales of Gods, Heroes & Mortals

This chapter relates a number of short stories of various types, culled from many sources. They have been subdivided into 'Encounters with Monsters', 'Tales of Tragic Romance', 'Stories of Metamorphosis' and 'Stories of Divine Retribution'. As can be seen, the selected demarcations often overlap within a tale.

ENCOUNTERS WITH MONSTERS

Odysseus

Odysseus, King of the island of Ithaca, was one of the great Greek heroes who fought in the siege of Troy. On the return sea-journey he ran into storms caused by the gods, who were angry at the atrocities committed by the Greeks during the sack of Troy. Odysseus and his crew had many adventures before they reached their homes.

On one occasion Odysseus found himself near Sicily and went ashore with a few men to explore. They found a cave filled with food and wine and were about to take this booty back to the ship whey they heard giant footsteps approaching the cave. It was the Cyclopes Polyphemus, one of a race of giant shepherds who had just one eye in the centre of their heads. He entered the cave with his sheep and rolled a huge stone across the entrance. Odysseus expected the normal Greek hospitality, but the barbaric giant replied by eating two of the crew; this practice continued for several days, until cunning Odysseus thought up a plan. They offered Polyphemus some excellent wine which they had brought with them from Greece; he was soon intoxicated and the Greeks heated a pointed stake in the fire and thrust it into the single eye of the giant.

LEFT Polyphemus blinded by Odysseus and friends; *Athenian amphora found at Eleusis,* c650 BC. *The painting is a very early form of black-figure, with the painter experimenting with sketchy outlines for the figure of Odysseus. Polyphemus' intoxication is indicated by his wine-cup. The triangular torsos and profile legs and heads with frontal eyes are typical of Archaic art.*

Next morning the blind Cyclopes felt with his hands every sheep that went out of the cave and counted them in again in the evening, so as not to allow Odysseus and his men their escape. Odysseus thought up another clever plan. The following morning, Polyphemus counted the sheep out of the cave, feeling them carefully to check that they were not human, and rolled the stone across the entrance. Odysseus and his friends had tied themselves to the bellies of the sheep and thus escaped the blind giant's notice. They ran down to the ships and as soon as they were some distance from the shore, Odysseus foolishly began to shout insults at Polyphemus. The infuriated Cyclopes started to hurl boulders at random into the sea and the Greeks were lucky to escape; Polyphemus prayed to his father Poseidon to make trouble for the Greek sailors on their journey home.

After several other adventures the Greeks arrived at the island of Aiaia, off the west coast of Italy. Here lived Circe, lovely daughter of Helius and an Oceanid called Perseis, who was renowned for her knowledge of magical herbs and poisons. Odysseus, not wishing to stray too far from the ships after previous encounters with island monsters, sent scouts ahead to explore. They came to a house in the middle of the woods and were greeted by curiously well-behaved wolves and lions, who invited them to meet their mistress. Circe handed them drugged wine which turned them into pigs. One of the more cautious Greeks had stayed hidden in the bushes and he now returned to Odysseus and the others to tell them what marvels he had witnessed. Odysseus decided to investigate and on his way through the woods, Hermes, in the guise of a handsome youth, met him and offered him a spe-

RIGHT Odysseus and the Sirens; *Athenian red-figure* stamnos *(wine-mixing jar) by the Siren Painter; early 5th century* BC. *Odysseus is shown tied to the mast while his friends row past the Sirens with wax in their ears. The hero apparently enjoys the music, but the Sirens' spell is broken and they commit suicide by diving headlong into the sea.*

cial herb which would act as an antidote to Circe's drugs. Odysseus slipped it into the wine which Circe offered him; he then drew his sword and threatened to kill her unless she turned his friends back into human form. She obliged and after much feasting welcomed Odysseus into her bed. The Greek heroes stayed with Circe for a year; when they left, Circe advised Odysseus to visit the prophet Teiresias in Hades, for only a wise man could tell the Greeks how they might appease the gods and return home safely.

Circe had also warned Odysseus about other monsters who inhabited that part of the Mediterranean. These included the Sirens, women with the feet and wings of birds, who sang songs of such seductive beauty that many sailors had been lured to their rocky island, where they wasted away in yearning for the music. Odysseus wanted to hear the song and instructed the crew to row past the island with wax in their ears; he himself was lashed to the mast. The Sirens, fated to die if they were ever unsuccessful, crashed to their deaths in the sea below.

LEFT *J M W Turner (1775–1851),* Ulysses Deriding Polyphemus. *Polyphemus can just be seen in the misty light above the ship of* Odysseus *(Ulysses). Ghostly Nereids swim ahead of the ship, which is portrayed as a fantastic galleon. From the rigging flies a flag (hardly visible) depicting the Trojan horse outside the Trojan walls, referring to Odysseus' victory. Every feature of the painting veers between fantasy and reality: the arched rocks at times appear to be horses' heads rearing from the sea to pull the sun-chariot into the sky. A masterly Romantic treatment of the Classical myth.*

LEFT *Dosso Dossi (1474/9–1542),* Circe and her Lovers in a Landscape, *(c1525). Circe's woodland palace can be seen in the background. She holds a stone tablet inscribed with spells; a book lies at her feet with a magic pentagram on the open page. Dossi has transformed the Classical sorceress into a beautiful medieval witch.*

After many more adventures, Odysseus at last arrived at his home in Ithaca where his wife Penelope had been waiting for many years. While her husband was away she had been approached by princes from all over the Mediterranean who were intent upon marrying her. She refused to believe their false stories that Odysseus was dead, and told them that she would consider their offers only when she had finished weaving a funerary shroud for her father-in-law; every night she would unravel the day's work to delay its completion. Odysseus, disguised as a beggar, had arranged a contest for the suitors: they must string the bow of the absent Odysseus and fire an arrow through a row of twelve axe-heads; the prize would be Penelope. None of them were even able to string the bow and they all jeered at the beggar when he asked to have a go. Odysseus strung the bow with ease and his first arrow flew through each of the axe-heads; with the remaining arrows he killed the suitors.

ABOVE Penelope and Odysseus; *black-figure* skyphos *(wine-cup), late 6th century* BC. *A burlesque version of the myth: Penelope is shown beside her loom with the unfinished shroud; she mixes a drink for her returned husband in a cup of the same shape as the vase itself.*

Oedipus and the Sphinx

Oedipus' name means 'swollen foot': his father, King Laius of Thebes, had been told by an oracle that his son would one day kill him; therefore when his wife Jocasta gave birth to a boy, he was taken (as was the custom for unwanted children) into the mountains and exposed after having his feet pierced. A shepherd found the boy and took him to Corinth, where the childless king and queen adopted the boy, whom they called Oedipus because of his injured feet. One evening, when he had become a man, a drunken friend told

LEFT Oedipus and the Sphinx; *Athenian red-figure wine-cup by the* Oedipus Painter, *early 5th century* BC. *Oedipus is shown in travelling clothes and sun-hat; he is depicted with the 'thoughtful' gestures of crossed legs and hand to chin. The scene would have appeared as the drinker drained his cup.*

Oedipus that the king and queen were not his true parents. Oedipus could not rest until he had travelled to Delphi and asked the Pythia how he could find his real mother and father; the oracle replied that it would be better if he had not made the enquiry, for one day he would murder his father and make love to his mother. Oedipus in dismay decided never to return to Corinth in order to avoid the prophecy, for he still believed that the kind king and queen were his true parents; instead he made his way to Thebes. At a three-way junction in the road called the Cleft Way, a chariot approached Oedipus and the driver rudely shouted to Oedipus to get off the road. Oedipus' royal honour was wounded and he killed both charioteer and passenger.

When Oedipus arrived at Thebes he heard that a female monster, the Sphinx, had become a menace to the city. News of the death of King Laius on the roadside at the Cleft Way was brought to Creon, who was acting as regent in the absence of the king. Creon promised the hand of the king's widow, Jocasta, in marriage to any man who killed the Sphinx. Oedipus, with nothing to lose, decided to make the attempt. The Sphinx would fly onto the ramparts of the city and set a riddle to anyone she found there; if they were unable to answer it, she would eat them. Oedipus waited by the ramparts for the arrival of the monster, who asked him: 'What creature walks on four legs in the morning, on two at noon, and on three in the evening?' Clever Oedipus answered:

RIGHT *Girodet-Trioson (1767–1824),* The Sleep of Endymion. *The painter studied with David, whose cool severity can be seen here. However, there is an aspect of dreamy Romanticism already at work and Girodet-Trioson was admired by many early Romantics. Selene is present only as the light of the moon which Eros ushers into the woodland cave of the beautiful sleeping king.*

'The creature is man, for he crawls on all fours as a baby, walks on his two legs for most of his adult life, and resorts to a walking-stick in his retirement.' The Sphinx jumped to her death and Oedipus was welcomed as the new Theban hero and married Jocasta.

A new plague came to Thebes and Oedipus sent Creon to the Pythia to ask advice; she answered that the plague would not cease until Laius' murderer was exiled from the city. The prophet Teiresias was consulted, and unhappy Oedipus learnt the truth: he had killed his father on the Cleft Way and married his mother; the shepherd, who years ago had saved him from exposure, was called in as a witness to the truth of the prophet's words. Jocasta hanged herself and Oedipus, realizing his blindness to the truth, gouged out his own eyes. After his death he was buried outside of Athens by Theseus, who had learnt that the hero's tomb would protect the city.

TALES OF TRAGIC ROMANCE

Selene and Endymion

Endymion was a grandson of Zeus and founded the city of Elis, where he became king. Selene, who took the moon across the sky in her chariot, saw Endymion by the light of the moon one night and fell in love with him, for he was very handsome. Every night the two would meet in a cave and make love in the moonlight. Selene was so in love with Endymion that she could not bear to see his mortal beauty wane with age. Therefore one night, instead of visiting him in the cave, she touched his eyes with magic moondrops and put him to sleep for eternity. Every night she continues to gaze upon her lover from her chariot in the sky.

Cephalus and Procris

Cephalus, the Prince of Phocis, came to Athens to marry Procris, the daughter of King Erectheus. Cephalus would go out hunting very early and one morning was abducted by Eos the Dawn; he protested that he could not love the goddess, for he was betrothed to his mortal lover Procris. Eos threw him back down to earth, saying that he would regret his refusal of divine love. Cephalus suffered from a terrible jealousy of his lovely wife and would test her fidelity by trying to seduce her in the guise of a stranger. One day, however, Procris was told that her husband had been heard shouting the name of a woman named Aura while out hunting in the woods. Procris followed her husband next time he went hunting and hid in the bushes. Cephalus hurled his infallible javelin at what he thought was the rustling of a wild boar; as she lay dying in his arms he realized her grave mistake: he had indeed been calling on Aura, which means 'breeze', to cool his heated brow.

Achilles and Penthesileia

The mortal Peleus married the immortal Nereid Thetis. They were unaware that this marriage had been arranged by the gods who had been told that if Thetis were to have a son by a divine father, he would one day rule Olympus. All important gods and men were invited to the wedding feast; but Eris (Strife) was not invited, and she thought up an act of revenge which was to have dire and long-lasting consequences for mankind. She inscribed a golden apple with the words 'FOR THE MOST BEAUTIFUL' and cast it at the feet of the goddesses Hera, Athene and Aphrodite as they were coming home. They all claimed it, but Zeus suggested a beauty contest judged by the most beautiful man on earth, Paris, Prince of Troy. Each goddess tried to bribe the judge, and Aphrodite succeeded by offering him the most beautiful woman on earth as

LEFT *Claude Lorraine (1600–82),* Landscape with Cephalus and Procris Reunited by Diana. *Claude has typically chosen a Classical subject which requires a landscape. There is little sense of the impending doom of the myth in the idyllic and peaceful pastoral setting. The buildings are taken from the countryside around Rome which Claude loved.*

RIGHT Achilles kills Penthesilea; *Athenian black-figure amphora potted and painted by* Exekias, *mid 6th century* BC. Exekias epoiese (*'Exekias made this') is signed to the left of Achilles. Exekias has brilliantly evoked the tragedy by making the line of the spear run parallel to the eyes as the lovers meet for the first and last time.*

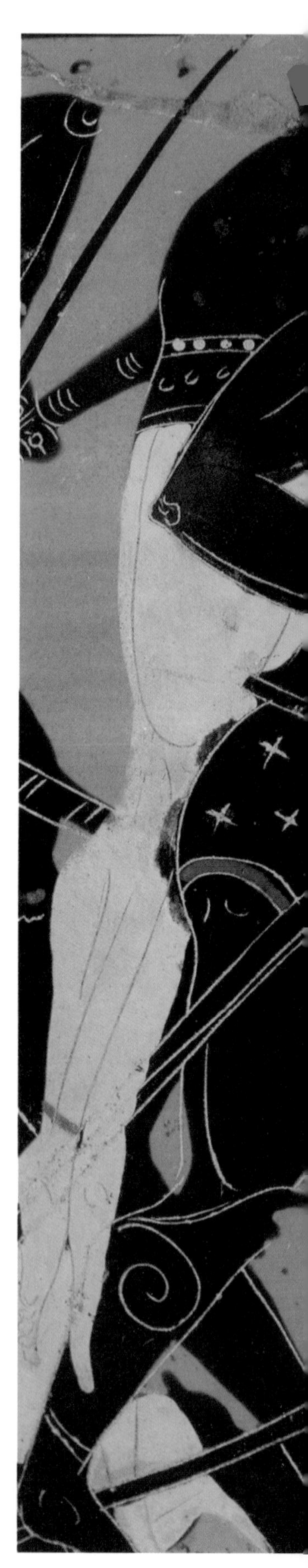

FAR RIGHT Achilles and Penthesilea; *Athenian black-figure vase, 6th century* BC. *Achilles carries the dead Amazon off the battlefield, her limbs limp and her eyes closed in death.*

his wife: this was Helen, the wife of Menelaus of Sparta. Paris visited Sparta and abducted Helen, taking her back to Troy. Menelaus and his brother Agamemnon, together with other Greek kings, besieged Troy for nine years.

Penthesileia was an Amazon queen who had accidentally killed one of her sisters. King Priam of Troy offered her purification if she would bring Amazon troops to help him fight the Greeks. One day she was out fighting on the Trojan plain when Achilles, son of Peleus and Thetis and King of the Myrmidons, singled her out in combat. They struggled for hours until at last Achilles drove his spear into her throat; at that moment his eyes met hers and he fell deeply in love with her, carrying her lifeless body from the battlefield in his grief.

The Greeks won the war and sacked Troy, but many of them died for Helen, including Achilles, who was shot by an arrow in the ankle, his one vulnerable point. One ancient tradition says that Thetis had dipped him as a child in the river Styx to make him immortal, but had forgotten to immerse the ankle by which she was holding him.

BELOW *Peter Paul Rubens (1577–1640),* The Judgement of Paris. *Paris, accompanied by Hermes, awards the golden apple to Aphrodite. To her right is Hera with her sacred peacock and to the left is Athene, armour laid aside; the Medusa head is here placed on her shield and not the aegis. In the sky appears the Fury, Alecto, symbolizing the tragedy to come.*

LEFT *Titian (c1487–1576),* Venus and Adonis, *(c1560). Titian evokes the impending tragedy by means of the stormy sky and cowering Cupid comforting the sacred dove. Adonis' boots are decorated with tragic masks. The figures are portrayed as contemporary Venetian lovers: Aphrodite (Venus) has a fashionable coiffeur whilst Adonis has his hunting dogs and wears one of Aphrodite's garters on his arm.*

Aphrodite and Adonis

The beautiful youth Adonis was born from the incestuous union of Myrrha with her own father Cinyras, King of Assyria. Aphrodite had caused this because the Assyrian queen had boasted that Myrrha was prettier than the goddess of love. Aphrodite fell in love with the young Adonis and handed him to Persephone to look after; but Persephone also desired Adonis and refused to return her charge. Zeus chose the Muse Calliope as an arbitrator and she judged that the two rival goddesses must share their lover. Some say that Aphrodite wreaked her revenge on Calliope for her decision by engineering the death of her son Orpheus. In any case, the story ends with the tragic, early death of Adonis during a wild boar hunt – perhaps the victim of Hephaestus or Ares, jealous husband and lover of Aphrodite. To commemorate her lover, the goddess created the red anemone flower from his blood.

Hylas and the Nymphs

On his voyage with the Argonauts to find the Golden Fleece, Heracles took with him a handsome boy as a travelling companion: his name was Hylas and he became Heracles' lover. During the journey, the heroes beached the magical ship *Argo* at Mysia in order to cut some new oars from the trees by the shore; Heracles sent Hylas off in search of fresh water. Hylas made his way slowly through the wild undergrowth, listening for the sound of running water. It was not long before he found himself lost, but he had discovered a clear pool and he leant over the still water to fill his jug. To his astonishment he found himself gazing into the eyes of several lovely Naiads, the nymphs who inhabited the lonely spring. In an instant, he felt himself being drawn down into the water to become the nymphs eternal lover. Heracles was heartbroken and roamed the woods for days crying for his lost friend.

BELOW *John Waterhouse (1849–1917),* Hylas and the Nymphs, *(1896). The Victorian painter sets the myth by a very English Romantic pool with flowering water-lilies and irises. Hylas carries his water-jar in his left hand but is soon seduced by the young nymphs. Waterhouse is one of the last in a long line of painters who used remote Classical themes as an excuse for blatant contemporary eroticism.*

Pyramus and Thisbe

In the city of Babylon there lived next door to one another two rival families. Pyramus had been a friend of his neighbour, Thisbe, since childhood, but as they grew older their respective parents forbade them to meet. Their bedrooms were next to each other and Pyramus managed to knock a small hole in the wall through which they could kiss and whisper. They fell in love and decided to marry against their parents' wishes. So, one night they arranged to meet by a tomb outside the city walls. Thisbe arrived first wearing a wedding veil; while she was waiting a lioness came to drink at a nearby pool – it was thirsty after a meal and its jaws were dripping with blood. Thisbe was alarmed and ran into a cave for shelter, dropping her veil in her haste. The lioness sprang after her but found only the veil which became stained by the bloody mane of the beast.

At last Pyramus arrived at their meeting place, only to discover the blood-stained veil and the paw-prints of the lioness. In his grief, Pyramus stabbed himself with his sword, staining the white fruit of the mulberry tree, which stood at the trysting-place, red. Thisbe, leaving her hiding place, found her lover dead and killed herself with Pyramus' sword.

Their parents were so stricken by the tragic deaths that they swore friendship and buried their children's ashes in a single urn. Two local rivers were named after the lovers and the mulberry tree continues to bear blood-red fruit to this day.

STORIES OF METAMORPHOSIS

Narcissus

Narcissus was the son of the nymph Leiriope and the river Cephissus. Leriope consulted Teiresias, the pro-

RIGHT Pyramus and Thisbe; *Roman wall-painting from a Pompeian House, 1st century* AD. *Thisbe kills herself on discovering her dead lover. The painting decorated an outdoor dining-couch and was coupled with a painting of Narcissus. Both stories were described in the 'Metamorphoses' of the contemporary poet Ovid, and it is likely that the paintings reflect the poem's popularity.*

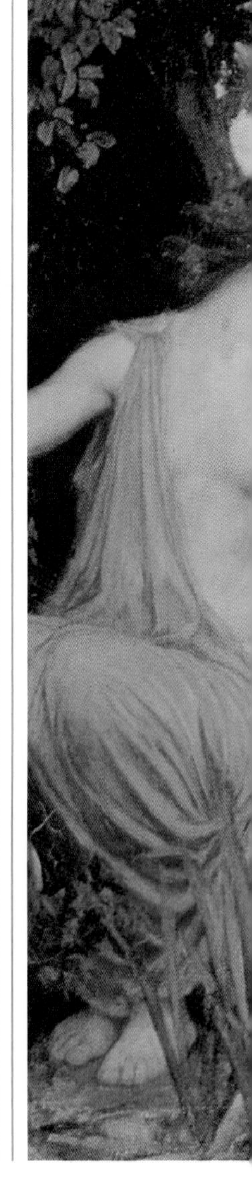

phet, and asked him if Narcissus would have a long life; Teiresias replied that he would so long as he did not know himself. Narcissus was admired by many girls and boys, but never returned their love. One, a nymph called Echo, fell hopelessly in love with Narcissus when she spied him hunting in the woods where she lived. Echo also suffered another affliction: her task had been to divert Hera's attentin with her constant chatter while her friends pursued their love affairs with Zeus, and, when found out, Hera punished her for her talkativeness by taking away her ability to utter anything but the last words of other people's sentences. Thus, unable to express her feelings for Narcissus, she had wasted away with unrequited love until she was merely a voice.

One boy prayed to Nemesis, the goddess of retribution, to punish Narcissus for his arrogance. One day, Narcissus was hunting on the slopes of Mount Helicon when he came to a clear pool; he stooped to quench his thirst and immediately fell in love with the beautiful boy reflected in the calm water. However much he talked to or tried to embrace him, the boy would not respond, but Narcissus would not leave his love and faded away like Echo, dying of starvation. The gold-centred, white-petalled flower that we call narcissus was all that remained when his friends discovered him by the pool.

BELOW *John Waterhouse (1849–1917),* Echo and Narcissus, *(c1903). A rather thin and wasted Echo gazes longingly at Narcissus who has laid aside his quiver to admire his own reflection in the pool, located in a very English-looking water meadow. By the boy's feet appear the flowers to which he will give his name.*

Baucis and Philemon

Baucis and Philemon were a poor, elderly peasant couple who lived in a hillside cottage in Bithynia. As Zeus and Hermes were wandering through this land, everywhere they went refused them hospitality. As the sun was setting they came to the old couple's home and were cordially welcomed. During the simple meal, Baucis and Philemon realized that their guests were not ordinary men since their wine-cups kept miraculously refilling. The next day the gods showed them the hostile village below: it was now a lake and their cottage was transformed into a beautiful marble temple. Granted a wish, Baucis and Philemon asked only to serve the gods in their new temple. When they died the loving couple were turned into an old oak and a linden tree to commemorate their goodness.

Apollo and Daphne

Daphne was a young Arcadian girl who used to hunt with her friends along the banks of the river Ladon. She worshipped the virgin goddess of hunting, Artemis, and had chosen to remain chaste herself. Eros assisted her chastity by firing a lead-tipped arrow into her heart; at the same time he shot Apollo with a gold-tipped arrow because the god had taunted him by telling him to leave archery to real men. Apollo fell in love with Daphne and pursued her through the woods; Daphne, realizing that she could not escape the god, prayed to Gaia for help. Gaia responded and transformed her into a laurel (Daphne means laurel). All that Apollo was left with was a branch torn from the lovely tree, which he placed as a wreath in his hair. The laurel tree remained sacred to Apollo.

RIGHT *Giovanni Battista Tiepolo (1696–1770),* Apollo Pursuing Daphne, *(c1775–1760). Tiepolo depicts Daphne stumbling into a river-god with Eros hiding from the angry Apollo. The sun is behind Apollo's head and he already wears the laurel which begins to sprout from Daphne's hands.*

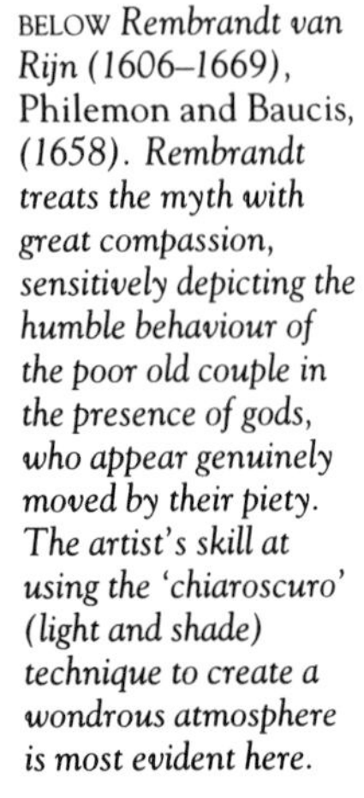

BELOW *Rembrandt van Rijn (1606–1669),* Philemon and Baucis, *(1658). Rembrandt treats the myth with great compassion, sensitively depicting the humble behaviour of the poor old couple in the presence of gods, who appear genuinely moved by their piety. The artist's skill at using the 'chiaroscuro' (light and shade) technique to create a wondrous atmosphere is most evident here.*

Zeus and Io

Io was a priestess of Hera at Argos. Zeus was attracted by her beauty and probably by the possibilities of annoying his wife Hera. He came and whispered to her in her dreams, inviting her to the meadows where her father, the local river-god Inachus, watched over his cattle. Io told her father of her strange dreams, and he sent enquiries to various oracles, all of which replied that Io must go into exile or the city would be destroyed by a huge thunderbolt. Io departed in low spirits but as she was passing through the river meadows Zeus approached; but Hera saw him from her temple and Zeus in his embarrassment turned Io into a beautiful white cow. Hera saw through the ruse and demanded the cow for herself, which she had tethered in an olive-grove at Mycenae and watched over by Argus Panoptes (All-Seeing), who had 100 eyes.

In retaliation, Zeus sent Hermes as god of thieves to steal the cow; Hermes, in the guise of a goatherd, played a lullaby on his pipes and soon all of Argus's eyes were closed. Hermes

RIGHT *Pieter Lastman (1583–1633),* Juno discovering Jupiter with Io, *(1618). Hera (Juno) appears with her peacocks (with the eyes of the dead Argus in their tails), outraged at her husband Zeus' (Jupiter) attempts to carry off Io, who he has transformed into a cow. The masked figure with the fox-pelt is a symbol of sly deceit.*

killed the guard, but Hera took Argus's eyes and placed them in the tail of her sacred bird, the peacock; she then sent a gadfly to sting the cow which broke away and escaped. After many months of wandering the cow arrived in Egypt and, beside the river Nile, Zeus made love to her in the guise of a bull. Io found herself a woman again and gave birth to a boy whom she named Epaphus ('touch of the god'); but jealous Hera sent the demon youths, the Curetes, to kidnap her son and take him to Syria. Zeus in his fury killed the Curetes even though they had once helped to protect him from his angry father when he was a boy in Crete. Io was guided to Epaphus and returned with him to Egypt where she married King Telegonus and instituted the worship of Demeter. Later Egyptians worshipped both Demeter and Io as Isis.

LEFT *Hendrick van Balen (died c1615),* Pan Pursuing Syrinx.

Pan and Syrinx

Syrinx was a woodland nymph who hunted in the forests of Arcadia with the goddess Artemis. The lecherous Pan, son of Hermes, who also lived in Arcadia, saw Syrinx one day as she ran past his cave pursuing a stag. He chased after her and Syrinx, who had vowed to the virgin Artemis that she would remain chaste, cried out to the nymphs of the River Ladon to help her. They quickly transformed her into a reed-bed, and when Pan reached the river all he found were the reeds swaying in the breeze. He cut them down, and trimmed them to different lengths to produce varied notes and bound them together in a row to make a set of pipes. He called these pipes 'syrinx' to commemorate his unfulfilled love.

STORIES OF DIVINE RETRIBUTION

Dionysus and Pentheus

The story forms the basis of The Bacchae, *a tragedy written by the playwright Euripides, when Classical Athens was at the height of its imperial power. It celebrates the introduction of a foreign religion into a highly conservative culture. The Dionysiac religion demanded irrationality in its devotees. This was highly disturbing to the normal rational thinking of Greek intellectuals, but worship of the god of wine was eventually welcomed as an essential part of human experience. A major annual festival was devoted to him at Athens, during which large terracotta phalli were carried in magnificent processions to his temple by the Acropolis. Nearby was the open-air theatre, in which tragedies (such as* The Bacchae*) were performed in his honour. Dionysus was also worshipped in the more intimate circumstances of the 'symposium', or drinking party, during which members of the Athenian elite would be joined by 'hetairai', courtesans who would sing poetry and entertain with sexual favours. During these orgiastic rites, the males would identify with the Satyrs, woodland followers of the god who were part goat or horse; the females would become Maenads or Bacchae; they wore fawn or panther skins and carried 'thyrsoi', wands wound with ivy and tipped with pine cones. Ivy or oak leaves were worn in their hair, and they danced wild, ecstatic dances in adoration of the god.*

Near the walled city of Thebes, on Mount Cithaeron, frenzied royal ladies roamed aimlessly. They included the sisters of Semele, mother of Dionysus, the beautiful youth who had not been

BELOW *Velazquez (1599–1660),* The Topers, *(c1629). Velazquez has typically mixed the Classical idealized figures of Dionysus and follower with realistically portrayed contemporary Spanish peasants.*

seen since his strange and miraculous birth. One of his aunts, Agave, was the mother of Pentheus the King of Thebes. The people of Thebes had refused to acknowledge the godhead in Dionysus, who had returned to his home after gathering devotees and establishing his cult throughout Asia. His devotees were the Maenads or Bacchae, Asian women who celebrated the god wherever he drove them, tempting the local women to abandon their husbands and homes and join them outside the city walls in orgiastic celebrations of wild nature. The rational Greek mind did not understand them and Pentheus suspected political rebellion. The Theban women had been driven mad by Dionysus for refusing to believe in him; on the mountain slopes they joined in with the song of the Bacchae:

From the high hills of Asia, exotic Mount Tmolus
We run and we run and we cannot stop running
Rejoicing in hard work and loving our leisure
Driven by Bacchus, his beauty and laughter.

Anyone present who's not of the god
Stay away from our ritual and keep your doors bolted
No listening, no peeping, O why don't you join us?
It's heavenly dancing the dance of the god.

Happy the man who seeks the wild country
Turning his back on the city of dreams;
His head crowned with ivy, not jewel-studded gold,
A branch for a sceptre, a heart for a stone.

His ecstacy drives us from out of the hills
Down into the city, the streets paved with stone,
Bringing the joys of the god born of god
Dancing the dreams of the spirit of wine.

Meanwhile, in the city of Thebes, Pentheus had heard news of these strange happenings; members of his family had already joined the cult, and both his mother Agave and his grandfather Cadmus attempted to persuade Pentheus to join them and welcome the new god Dionysus into their city. The seer Teiresias also joined the cult.

LEFT The death of Pentheus; *Roman wall-painting from the House of the Vettii, Pompeii, 1st century AD. This is possibly a copy of an earlier Greek original.*

Pentheus, fearing that this irrational worship might lead to anarchy in his city, had the young priest (Dionysus in disguise) arrested and interrogated him. He mocked his feminine softness and beautiful hair and threw him into prison. Dionysus miraculously broke the lock and appeared to Pentheus, who thus reaized his power. Dionysus tempted the young king to come and watch the Maenads performing their orgiastic dances; but he would have to go in secret, dressed as one of the women.

Dionysus then led Pentheus to the mountain, where he spied on the Maenads. One of them caught sight of the interloper and, together with her friends, chased him through the woods, thinking him a wild animal. They caught him and tore him to bits; Agave came back to Thebes with her victim's head as a trophy of her victory in the hunt. She showed the prize to Cadmus, who immediately realized her error.

Artemis and Actaeon

The story of Actaeon and his macabre fate remained a favourite with poets and artists throughout the Classical period. The nature of his punishment by Artemis remains the same, but his crime differs. Early writers say that he offended Zeus by wanting to marry the mortal Semele, who was pregnant with Zeus' child Dionysus, the god of wine. In the Classical period we see him boasting that he is a better hunter than Artemis. Hellenistic poets present him as a lusty and unashamed voyeur of the bathing goddess, deserving his punishment. The Roman poet Ovid, however, protests his innocence; he stumbled unawares upon the divinity and her retribution was therefore doubly cruel. The myth was particularly popular with wall-painters in Imperial Pompeii.

Actaeon hunted the stag. One morning he was woken by the full moon gazing in through the palace windows and the baying of his favourite pair of hounds. He swallowed cool water, threw on his cloak and, armed with spears, unlatched the kennel doors. Out they ran, Tracker and Blackfoot, their puppies Lightfoot and Tigress – their first hunt – and the old ones Storm and Blanche.

Outside the palace walls, the hounds veered from their usual direction. Turning tails on the rosy-fingered goddess of dawn, Eos, they headed for the pearly light of Artemis, goddess of the moon and the chase. Cool cypresses shadowed the path which soon led to tractless woodland and wilderness. Wild bramble gave place to apple. Actaeon stretched to taste the fruit, expecting bitterness; strange sweetness. Then great thirst and a search for water.

RIGHT *Titian (1478/90–1576),* The Death of Actaeon. *Beneath a stormy sky, Artemis (Diana) is shown loosing an arrow at stag-headed Actaeon, whose hounds have brought him down beside a woodland stream. Artemis is depicted with one breast bare in the manner of the Amazons.*

The hounds arrived first and were soon curled up asleep beside the stream. Actaeon had a desire to bathe and made his way towards the sound of falling water. Storm, wise and grizzled, raised and lowered an eyelid and returned to dreaming of stags. Actaeon approached the pool alone, but sounds of unearthly laughter stopped him in his tracks. Breath held – distant thunder – a splash – cautious peeping through the tangled branches. Actaeon's heart raced, he had spied the Dryads before, but always from the corner of his eye and never in the presence of the horned goddess. In an instant Actaeon was infatuated by Artemis the huntress, never before seen unclothed by mortal or indeed immortal eyes. The nymphs were merely stars in the presence of her glistening lunar beauty.

Artemis sensed the alien and threw water at his gaze. As his sight slowly returned, Actaeon felt panic. The pool, now still, mirrored his transformation. Even as he watched his forehead sprouted antlers, his feet and hands became furry hooves, and his neck extended. Blackfoot and Tracker woke to their master's musky scent and led the pack downstream. Actaeon, knowing his fate, attempted a scream and took to his heels. His hounds heard only the deep roar of the hunted stag and were hungry for the kill. Actaeon the hunter now knew, as he scrambled on all fours, what it felt like to be the hunted one.

He ran swiftly and came at last to a clearing in the forest. He stood, head held high, sniffing the damp night air. His hounds, as he himself had trained them, came at him from all sides, giving no quarter. Blackfoot and Tracker were the first. Actaeon tried to pat them as they jumped, but their enthusiasm was not the joy of greeting a master. They sank their teeth in deep, howling to their companions to join the feast. In the evening, beneath a crimson hunter's moon, the hounds sought in vain for their master. The horse-man Cheiron heard their sad howling and fashioned a statue of Actaeon to comfort them. This was set in the woodland shrine of Artemis, goddess of wildlife, as a reminder of her power.

Hermes alone among men and gods can pass unharmed between Heaven and Earth, or Earth and Hades. That same evening he escorted sad Actaeon through the gates which divide the living from the dead. Cerberus, triple-headed watchdog of the Underworld, had been trained by his master, Hades, to terrify only the proud. On this occasion he sensed the fear of dogs and Actaeon had safe passage.

ABOVE *Pieter Brueghel the Elder (c1525–69),* The Fall of Icarus. *The ploughman and shepherd continue their everyday work as Icarus falls into the sea in the lower right-hand corner of this expansive Northern European landscape; even the fisherman appears not to notice the crash beside him. The sun, which caused Icarus's death, is only just rising on the horizon.*

Daedalus and Icarus

Daedalus was a great craftsman and inventor who had been exiled from his home in Athens to Crete where King Minos employed him as his architect. When Theseus killed the Minotaur, Minos had Daedalus and his son Icarus imprisoned in the Labyrinth for their part in the plot. They escaped by making pairs of wings held together with bees-wax and were flying westwards when Icarus, who had been warned by his father to stay in the middle of the sky, flew upwards towards Helius. The sun-god, angry at the boy's attempts to approach the realms of the gods, melted the wax and Icarus crashed down into the sea which still bears his name, the Icarian Sea. His body was washed ashore on Icaria, where Heracles later buried him.

Laocoon

Laocoon, the Trojan priest of Poseidon, warned the Trojans not to accept gifts from the Greeks. One morning, they awoke to discover a huge wooden horse, which they thought must be a divine offering. Laocoon was suspicious and hurled his spear into the side of the horse; at that moment, two sea-serpents, at the command of Apollo whom Laocoon had once insulted, rose out of the sea and strangled the priest along with his two sons. Laocoon's fears were confirmed when the horse was dragged into the city: it contained Greek troops who emerged in the night and began the terrible sack of Troy.

Apollo and Marsyas

When Perseus killed the Gorgon Medusa, Athene was amazed at the strange sounds of lamentation made by her remaining sisters. She made a musical instrument which imitated their mournful notes: this was the 'aulos', a double flute played by blowing hard through a thin reed.

One day, as she played the aulos, Athene saw her face reflected in a pool and dismayed at the image of her contorted face, threw the pipes to the ground. Marsyas, a satyr, had been listening to her play from the bushes and tip-toed forward to claim the rejected aulos. He learnt to play it and challenged Apollo to a musical contest; the victor would win the right to use the other in whatever way he chose. The Muses were appointed as judges, but could not decide on a winner. Apollo then played his lyre upside down and challenged Marsyas to do the same. This was an impossible feat on the aulos and Apollo was declared the victor by default. Apollo claimed the prize, and he punished the satyr's audacity by tying him to a pine tree and flaying him alive.

RIGHT *El Greco (1541–1614),* Laocoon *(c1610). The violent subject, with its contorted, writhing figures provides a fitting subject for El Greco's anti-naturalistic style. However, though the figures are unnaturalistic, a real horse, representing the artificial wooden horse, approaches a medieval-looking Troy. On the left stand several figures, looking on helplessly like a Greek Tragic Chorus.*

BELOW *Domenichino (1582–1641),* The Flaying of Marsyas. *The artist, who worked in Rome, portrays the scene in a Roman countryside, with a medieval hill town in the background, and Italian shepherds mournfully observing the punishment.*

FIVE

The Constellations

Ancient Greek cartographers combined their researches in mapping the earth with the drawing of star charts. Unable to make any rational sense of the night sky, they equated the movements of the planets with various gods and imagined that the stars had been set into patterns by the gods to immortalize mythical characters. The early Greek astronomers, limited to the naked eye, saw only five planets which they associated with different gods according to their behaviour: Hermes (Mercury) moved swiftly; Ares (Mars) was blood-red and associated with war; Aphrodite (Venus) was bright and flirtatious; Zeus (Jupiter) moved majestically across the heavens; Cronus (Saturn) was dim, slow moving and distant – a nostalgic sign of the Golden Age.

The Milky Way, like many of the constellations (literally, 'star groups') was interpreted in several ways: the fiery gash burnt across the heavens by Phaethon when he drove his father Helius' chariot out of control or the stairway to heaven. The ancient astronomers also noted that the sun passed through twelve of their constellations, which became the signs of the Zodiac.

Andromeda, Cepheus and Cassiopeia

Cepheus and Cassiopeia, King and Queen of the Ethiopians, boasted that their daughter, Andromeda, was more beautiful than the Nereids, daughters of Nereus, the Old Man of the Sea. This act of hybris incurred the wrath of Poseidon who sent out one of his many sea-monsters to devastate the coastlands of Ethiopia. King Cepheus was advised by an oracle that there was only one way that he might placate the god's anger; he must sacrifice his daughter to the monster. Andromeda was bound with chains at the foot of a cliff, waiting for the tide to come in bringing the sea-monster; but the hero Perseus rescued her and took her home to Argolis in Greece where she bore him many children. Cepheus and Cassiopeia mourned the loss of their daughter and Poseidon, considering that they had been sufficiently punished, took pity on them by placing them in the heavens. Andromeda missed her parents and therefore, when she died, Athene also placed her among the stars, beside them. However, as an eternal warning against human pride, Poseidon has placed Cassiopeia on a chair, but upside down with her feet in the air.

Aquarius the Water-Bearer and Aquila the Eagle

People argue as to the mortal parentage of the young Trojan prince Ganymede, but whoever his father, he had the misfortune of being so beautiful as to attract the gods themselves. One day Zeus decided to have him brought to Olympus to be his own personal cup-bearer; hitherto Hebe had performed this task for all the gods. Zeus could never appear on earth as himself for his lightning-bolts would incinerate any mortal, but neither could he trust his fellow gods to abduct Ganymede on his behalf. So Zeus disguised himself as an eagle and flew down to Troy, where he swooped down on Ganymede and, grasping the boy in his talons, took him back across the sea to Olympus.

BELOW *Piero di Cosimo (1462–1521),* Perseus Rescuing Andromeda *(c1510). Piero has incorporated several episodes into the one painting: on the left the onlookers turn their heads aside in fear as the sea-monster approaches* Andromeda*. Perseus is shown both flying in from the right and standing on the monster's back swinging his sword. On the right, the king and queen receive their daughter and her new heroic husband to the sounds of music and rejoicing.*

ABOVE Zeus and Ganymede; *terracotta temple roof sculpture from Olympia, early 5th century* BC. *Traces of the paint which covered many clay and marble statues in the Classical world can be clearly seen on this lively group. Though bearing many Archaic features, the group has been dated to the Early Classical period.*

To console the parents for the loss, Zeus ordered the divine messenger Hermes to deliver to them a splendid gift: this was a grapevine of gold, the handiwork of Hephaestus. They continued to miss their fine son, so Zeus immortalized Ganymede's abduction by placing Ganymede and the eagle (Aquila) up amongst the stars for all to see at night.

Aries the Ram

Athamas was King of the Orchomenus in Boeotia. In spite of his great wealth he was one of the most unlucky men who ever lived. His children by his first wife Nephele were Phrixus and Helle; he took a second wife Ino, who also bore sons and she plotted to destroy Phrixus so that one of her own sons might succeed Athamas as king. Ino talked the Boeotian women who sow the grain seeds into parching it so that the next harvest was a disaster; Athamas sent messengers to seek advice from the oracle at Delphi; on the way back they were bribed by Ino into delivering a false report that Phrixus must be sacrificed in order to avert famine. Athamas reluctantly led his son to the altar of Zeus and raised the ritual knife to cut his throat; just at that moment a ram appeared and, with Phrixus and his sister Helle on its back, flew off towards the east.

On the journey they discovered that the creature could talk, and the beautiful ram whose fleece was of gleaming gold told them stories: he had been born to Poseidon and Theophane; Theophane had been turned into a ewe by Poseidon in order to fool her many suitors, so naturally Poseidon made love to her in the guise of a ram. As they flew over the straits where the Black Sea is joined to the Mediterranean, Helle lost her grip and fell into the sea; the straits are called the Hellespont in her honour. Eventually Phrixus landed at Colchis at the other end of the Black Sea, where the ram insisted that he sacrifice it and hang its golden fleece on an oak in a grove sacred to Ares the war god. Phrixus married a local princess and lived to a ripe old age, and he never forgot the ram who had saved his life; it was immortalized as the constellation Aries and the reason that its stars shine so dimly is that its shining fleece remained on earth, the object of the heroic quest of Jason and the Argonauts.

Auriga (The Charioteer)

The bright star Capella appears to stand behind two pairs of lesser stars. The Greeks realized that this represented the immortalized souls of a charioteer and his four horses, but could never agree on who it was: some said Erichthonius, legendary king of Athens; others Myrtilus, son of Hermes, who was bribed by Pelops to replace the lynch-pins of his master Oenomaus's chariot with wax so as to cause his death.

Cancer (The Crab)

Cancer lived in a swamp with the monstrous Hydra and when Heracles came along to kill her as one of his labours, the crab tried to help his friend by biting the hero's foot. Though this was unsuccessful, Hera rewarded the crab by transforming it into the constellation Cancer.

Capricorn

Aegipan (Goat-Pan) was the son of Zeus and a goat called Aex, whose skin Zeus took for his aegis when she died. In his battle with the monster Typhon, Zeus had lost his sinews which Typhon then hid. Aegipan and Hermes recovered their father's sinews, but Typhon chased them into Egypt where they disguised themselves by changing shapes; Aegipan turned his lower half into a fish to make his escape by sea. Zeus showed his gratitude by placing him in the heavens as the constellation Capricorn; he still has the top half of a goat and a fish's tail.

RIGHT The Punishment of Ixion; *Roman wall-painting from The House of the Vettii, Pompeii, 1st century AD. Probably a copy of a lost Late Classical Greek easel-painting. Hera (right) observes the punishment; Iris (or Hebe) stands behind and wears a 'nimbus', the divine aura which became the halo of Christian art; Nephele, the cloud-copy of Hera, sits below. Hermes, in the pose of a Classical sculpture, is about to wheel Ixion down to Hades (the dark bearded figure).*

The Centaur

The first centaur was Centaurus who was born from the union of the mortal Ixion and Nephele, a cloud that Zeus had substituted for his wife Hera when Ixion had dared to make love to her. Ixion was taken to Hades; he was lashed to a fiery wheel and rolled forever around the Underworld.

Centaurus, with his human head, arms and shoulders and body of a horse, represented the lustful side of man's nature, and the centaurs were often used in art to symbolize non-Greek, uncivilized barbarians. The centaur Cheiron was different; he was the son of Cronus and the Oceanid Philyra; in order to deceive his wife Rhea, Cronus turned into a stallion to make love to Philyra, but Rhea discovered them and Philyra fled to mountainous Pelasgia where she bore her strange child, who had a stallion's body from waist downwards. Zeus turned Philyra into a linden tree, but she need not have been ashamed of her son, for Cheiron, unlike Centaurus' descendants, became so wise and learned that many young Greeks were sent to be educated by him on Mount Pelion where he lived; these included Actaeon, Achilles and Jason. Cheiron was immortalized as the constellation named Centaur.

Canis Major and Canis Minor (The Great Dog and The Little Dog)

The larger of the two dogs was the hound of Orion the Hunter; the bright star Sirius (the dog star) was seen as a sign of coming droughts when it rose along with the smaller dog. The little dog was Maera, faithful hound of Icarius, the Athenian who was sent by Dionysus to introduce the gift of wine to the world; but the shepherds who received the first cups took it unwatered and clubbed Icarius to death for attempting to poison them, throwing his body into a well. Maera ran to fetch Icarius' daughter Erigone, who hanged herself from a tree above the well; poor Maera leapt into the well to join his master.

Cetus (The Whale)

This sea-monster was sent by Poseidon to devour Andromeda as a punishment for the boastings of her mother Cassiopeia; it was killed by the hero Perseus and appears alongside him and Andromeda.

ABOVE *Titian (1478/ 90–1576),* Bacchus and Ariadne. *Dionysus (Bacchus) leaps down from his leopard-drawn chariot. The god is followed by his Maenads and Satyrs who play music and hold the torn limbs of their animal prey. Ariadne's crown appears above her as the constellation Corona Borealis.*

Corona Borealis (The Northern Crown)

Ariadne received a glittering crown as a divine wedding gift, either from her earthly husband Theseus, presented by the Nereid Thetis, or from her divine lover Dionysus, presented by Aphrodite; it was Dionysus who set its jewels in the night sky to immortalize his love for Ariadne.

Corvus (The Crow or Raven)

Apollo made love to the princess Coronis. While pregnant with the god's son she lay with a young man called Ischys. She came with her father, King Phlegyas, to the festival at Epidaurus where in her shame she exposed the baby on Mount Myrtium. A goatherd discovered the boy, whose name was Asclepius, being suckled by his goats, but he fled when he saw lightning flashing around him. A white crow had seen Coronis with her mortal lover and it flew to tell Apollo; the god turned it from white to black and placed it in the night sky as a warning to those who would tell on others. Coronis was shot dead with the arrows of Artemis and Apollo, but her child Asclepius was taught medicine by the centaur Cheiron and became the god of healing; his main cult centre was at Epidaurus.

Crater (The Cup or Bowl)

An alternative story involving the crow of Apollo links the constellation to its neighbours, the Cup (which also has other stories) and the Serpent (usually seen as the Hydra). The crow had been sent to fetch a cup of water from a spring for Apollo. Beside the spring was a fig-tree covered with unripe fruit. The hungry crow delayed its return to Apollo in order to wait for the fruit to ripen. Apollo punished its delay by preventing it from drinking water during the season when figs are ripening. It was placed among the stars with the snake at its feet to stop it drinking the water in the bowl by its head.

Cygnus (The Swan)

King Tyndareus of Sparta married Leda; they had a number of famous children including Clytemnestra and Castor; but two of Leda's children, Helen and Polydeuces, had a divine father. Zeus was attracted to Leda and visited her as a swan; she laid an egg and Helen (of Troy) was hatched from it. Zeus reminded men of Helen's miraculous birth by placing the swan high up in the night sky.

Delphinus (The Dolphin)

The dolphin was such a revered creature in ancient Greece that its constellation has been attributed to various myths: the dolphin that swam the seas to find and persuade Amphitrite to marry Poseidon; or a symbol of the Etruscan pirates turned into dolphins by Dionysus when they jumped overboard in fear of the god.

Draco (The Serpent or Dragon)

There are many serpents, both of land and sea, in Greek mythology, and this constellation has been interpreted as a snake thrown at Athene during the battle with the giants; she caught it and threw it into the sky. It was also thought to be Ladon, the serpent who guarded the golden apples tended by the Hesperides for Hera.

Eridanus

Eridanus is a long meandering line of stars whose source is close to Orion the Hunter and which flows down to the horizon. Eridanus was a son of Tethys and Oceanus, and into his waters plunged Phaethon, struck by a thunderbolt hurled by Zeus to put an end to his destructive course across the sky in his father Helius's sun-chariot; on the way he managed to scorch a line across the sky (the Milky Way) and blacken the skin of those who live near the equator. Phaethon's sisters wept for him beside the river Eridanus and were turned into poplar trees which henceforth wept tears of amber. Ancient writers disagree as to which European river was Eridanus, but presumably it was one famous for its deposits of amber.

LEFT *Tintoretto (c1518–94),* The Origin of the Milky Way. *This version of the myth relates that Hera was tricked into nursing Heracles; upon discovering her mistake she had him snatched away, causing her milk to sprinkle across the heavens. The peacocks are her sacred bird; Zeus' eagle carries his thunderbolts.*

Gemini (The Twins)

Several pairs of men were thought to be represented by Gemini, but most agree that they are the Dioscuri, Castor and Polydeuces (or Pollux). They were the sons of King Tyndareus of Sparta and Leda and had two famous sisters: Clytemnestra (later wife of King Agamemnon) and Helen (of Troy). Their title 'Dioscuri' means 'sons of Zeus', though Castor and Clytemnestra were mortal children of Tyndareus whilst Helen and Polydeuces were fathered by Zeus. The two brothers performed many heroic exploits, their early adventures occurring on the voyage of the Argonauts, where Castor proved himself as a skilled tamer of horses and Polydeuces as a formidable boxer. Later they saved their sister Helen after her abduction to Athens by Theseus, who desired a daughter of Zeus for his wife. There seems to have been a general dearth of marriageable princesses in mythical times and the Dioscuri also went in search of wives, eventually settling on the two beautiful daughters of their uncle Leucippus, Phoebe and Hilaeira; they had to be taken by force as they were already betrothed to their cousins Lynceus and Idas. A fight ensued between the four cousins and when Castor was killed, Polydeuces prayed to his father Zeus that he might share his immortality with his beloved brother: thus they spent alternate days up on Mount Olympus and down in Hades. They were also placed as stars in the sky, forming the twin constellation Gemini, with its two bright stars, Castor and Pollux. They also guarded those in storms at sea, often appearing as balls of fire (later called St Elmo's fire) in the sky: one such ball was a bad omen, representing their sister Helen of Troy, but two balls together was a good sign, representing the twin heroes.

BELOW *Peter Paul Rubens (1577–1640),* Rape of the Daughters of Leucippus. *The Dioscuri, Castor and Polydeuces, appear with their two horses; Eros is present and invites the viewer to witness the abduction of the two 'Rubenesque' women.*

Leo (The Lion)

Placed in the sky by Hera to commemorate the Nemean Lion which fought Heracles without success.

Lepus (The Hare)

Hermes honoured the hare as a constellation for being a swift runner like himself. It appears beneath Orion the Hunter, who is more likely to be chasing Taurus the Bull as a more fitting adversary. The hare was considered an endearing creature and was often given as a love-gift; the people of the island of Leros imported some, but they bred rapidly and began to eat the crops threatening famine; the islanders marched in a line across the island driving the hares into the sea. Some say that the constellation was placed by Artemis as protector of animals.

Libra (The Scales)

Possibly the scales held by Dike, goddess of justice, if she is represented by nearby Virgo.

Lyra (The Lyre)

Orpheus was the son of the leader of the Muses, Calliope, and Apollo, and he inherited his father's skill with the lyre. In fact, Orpheus played his lyre so beautifully that the whole of nature was enchanted: even trees and rocks would gather around him while he played. He married a Dryad called Eurydice. One day, Aristaeus, another son of Apollo, was chasing Eurydice through the Thracian meadows, when the nymph trod on a snake which bit and poisoned her. Orpheus' sorrow was so great that he determined to rescue her from Hades. Cerberus and Charon allowed him to pass, lulled by his music, and Hades and Persephone were so moved by his lament that they allowed him to depart with Eurydice on the condition that he resisted the temptation to turn around and look at her until they reached Earth. As they approached the light of day, Eurydice refused to go further unless her husband looked at her; Orpheus could not refuse, and turning, saw her fade back into the mists of Hades. Orpheus was not allowed a second chance, and spent the rest of his earthly life in mourning for his doubly lost love.

One story says that Orpheus offended Dionysus because of his adherence to his father, the musical god Apollo, seen by the Greeks as a rational and intellectual deity in comparison to the irrationality and instinct embodied in Dionysus. Dionysus' Maenads tore him to bits, but the Muses gathered up his limbs and buried them in Pieria. They could not find his head or lyre, however, which floated down the river and across the Aegean Sea to the island of Lesbos, where the Lesbians were rewarded with the gift of song for giving his last remains a proper burial. The Muses carried his lyre into the night sky to become the constellation Lyra.

BELOW *Giovanni Bellini (c1430–1516),* Orpheus. *Representations of Orpheus, the bringer of music to mankind, always portray him with a contemporary stringed instrument: Bellini replaces the Greek lyre with an Italian viol while animals, nymphs and satyrs gather round – even a tree (right) has bent over to listen.*

Ophiuchus (The Serpent-Holder)

Many heroes fought serpents and this constellation therefore has many attributions, but most say that it represents Asclepius, son of Apollo and god of healing; he is often represented holding a snake, associated with his healing powers.

Orion (The Hunter)

In the night sky, the huge constellation of Orion is surrounded by animals; his hunting dog Canis Major runs ahead of him, the hare Lepus scampers away as does Taurus the Bull; some say that he is in endless lusty pursuit of Pleione's seven daughters, whom Zeus immortalized as the star-cluster Pleiades; it is a sign of good eyesight to be able to count all seven stars. Orion was the son of Euryale, daughter of Minos of Crete, and Poseidon. His father gave him the ability to walk over the sea and his adventures took him from island to island.

RIGHT The Gorgon Medusa; *sculpted pediment from the temple of Artemis at Corfu, early 6th century* BC. *Gorgons were often used on religious buildings to frighten away evil spirits. The kneeling pose was used by Archaic artists to denote running. Her children appear on each side in front of the leopards: Pegasus is damaged but his back legs are visible (left); Chrysaor appears (right). Fighting groups, probably from the Trojan legends, fill the corners. The frontal images and fractured composition are typical of early Archaic art.*

On Chios, Orion was invited by King Oenopion to hunt and destroy all the wild animals of the island; in return, Oenopion promised his daughter Merope in marriage to the giant. Orion cleared the island in a day and at the celebratory banquet demanded his prize; Oenopion denied all knowledge of the offer and plied his heroic guest with wine. That night the drunken Orion raped Merope and Oenopion had him blinded in revenge, dumping his body on the beach. Orion walked the waves across to Lemnos where Hephaestus worked a forge; Orion caught hold of Celadion, one of the divine blacksmith's apprentices, and made him stand on his shoulders to guide his way. The giant was lead eastwards and the light of Helius cured his blindness; he returned to Chios to kill Oenopion, but angry Hephaestus had hidden the king underground. Celadion was returned to Lemnos and Orion settled on Crete, where he hunted with Artemis.

Artemis' brother Apollo became jealous of the giant. One day when Orion was wading off the coast with only his head above the waves, Apollo pointed out what appeared to be a piece of driftwood to Artemis and gave her first shot at it as target practice. The arrow found its mark and the goddess set Orion among the stars. Some say, however, that he threatened to hunt down all the animals in the world; Gaia sent a scorpion to kill him and Zeus placed him in the night sky alongside the scorpion (Scorpio) at the request of Artemis.

Pegasus (The Winged Horse)

Pegasus was born from the neck of the Gorgon Medusa when Perseus cut her head off. His father was Poseidon, god of horses. Pegasus was tamed by the hero Bellerophon who killed many foes with the help of his magical steed, but when he tried to reach the heights of Olympus, Zeus sent a gadfly to sting the horse which reared up to dislodge his rider; Bellerophon fell to his death whilst Pegasus continued on to Olympus to become the bearer of Zeus' thunderbolts. Zeus honoured Pegasus with a constellation, depicting him on his way to heaven.

Perseus

The hero took his place among the stars standing above Cetus the sea-monster whom he slew to win the hand of Andromeda, who stands beside him.

Pisces (The Fish)

After the battle of the gods and Titans, Gaia gave birth to the monster Typhon as a last attempt to conquer the gods. Although Zeus eventually defeated him, the other gods turned and ran. Typhon encountered Eros and Aphrodite on the banks of the river Euphrates; they turned themselves into fish, leaping into the river to escape. These two gods thus appear as a pair of fish in the sky.

Pleiades (The Seven Daughters of Pleione and Atlas)

Merope alone took a mortal husband, and her star is therefore the dimmest of the seven. Her sisters had famous children by Zeus, Poseidon, Hermes and Ares; Zeus turned them into stars to escape the lustful approaches of the hunter Orion, but he too became a constellation and still pursues them across the night sky.

Scorpio (The Scorpion)

Although it appears on the other side of the sky from Orion, the constellation represents the huge scorpion sent as a punishment by Gaia to kill the giant hunter for his threat to destroy all the world's animals.

Taurus (The Bull)

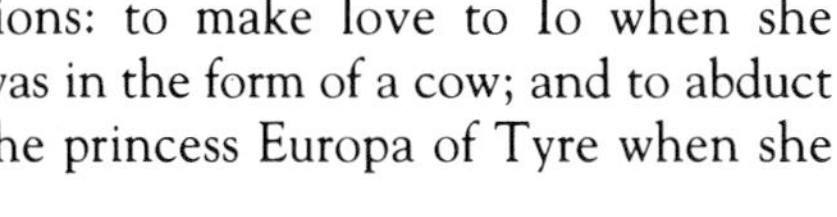

Zeus used the form of a handsome white bull on two amorous occasions: to make love to Io when she was in the form of a cow; and to abduct the princess Europa of Tyre when she was playing with her friends on the beach. Europa showed no interest in him until he lay down to chew a crocus; thinking him unusually sweet and gentle for a bull, she sat on his back but the laughter of her companions soon turned to screams as the bull swam out to sea with his new lover. They arrived at Crete and Europa had several children by the god including Minos; the bull and its horns remained important elements in Cretan art, myth and ritual. The bull was placed in the sky above Orion whom some say pursues it rather than the less noble hare.

Ursa Major and Ursa Minor (The Great and Little Bears)

The Great Bear was actually called Arctos (Bear) by the Greeks, Ursa Major being its Roman name. Zeus made love to Callisto, the Arcadian nymph and friend of Artemis, who was turned into a bear by Hera in her jealous anger. Callisto's son by Zeus was Arcas, who grew up in the woods where he one day shot his own mother, thinking her to be a wild boar. Zeus immortalized mother and son as constellations: Arcas became Arctophylax (The Bear-Keeper or Herdsman) who appears to watch over Ursa Major. Hera's anger increased at this celebration of Zeus' infidelity; she asked Tethys, her former nurse, and Oceanus never to allow the Great Bear to enter their waters, as the other constellations do when they set. Ursa Major was therefore doomed to wander together with Ursa Minor eternally around Polaris (the north star) and remains ever visible in the night sky.

Virgo (The Virgin)

Ancient writers disagree as to who is represented by this constellation; candidates include Dike (Justice) who might then be holding the scales of the neighbouring constellation Libra. Curiously the goddess Demeter is another suggestion, even though she had several children.

LEFT The Rape of Europa; *Roman wall-painting from a Pompeian house, 1st century* AD. *The pyramidal composition suggests that this copies a lost Late Classical Greek easel-painting. The princess is posed gracefully and no one seems aware of the bull's real identity except the bull himself, who looks out knowingly at the viewer.*

Appendix

SOURCES

The following ancient authors dealt with mythological subjects and can be readily obtained in translation in paperback editions:

GREEK AUTHORS

The tragedies of Aeschylus, Euripides and Sophocles
Herodotus, *The Persian Wars*
The poems of Hesiod, Homer, Pindar, Sappho, Theocritus
Pausanias, *Description of Greece*
Plutarch, *Parallel Lives*
The philosophical dialogues of Plato

ROMAN AUTHORS

The poems of Catallus, Horace, Lucretius, Propertius, Vergil and Ovid (especially his 'Metamorphoses' and 'Heroides')
Apuleius, *The Golden Ass*

FURTHER READING

The following modern studies of Greek Mythology are also of interest:

Bremmer, J (ed)
Interpretations of Greek Mythology
(London, 1987)

Dodds, E R
The Greeks and the Irrational
(Berkeley, 1968)

Henle, Jane
Greek Myths: A Vase Painter's Notebook
(Bloomington, 1973)

Kerenyi, C
The Gods of the Greeks
(London, 1974)

Kerenyi, C
The Heroes of the Greeks
(London, 1974)

Kirk, G S
The Nature of Greek Myths
(Baltimore, 1974)

Lefkowitz, M
Women in Greek Myth
(London, 1986)

Schefold, K
Myth and Legend in Early Greek Art
(New York, 1966)

Seznec, J
The Survival of the Pagan Gods; The Mythological Tradition and its Place in Renaissance Humanism and Art
(Guildford, 1961)

A NOTE ON GREEK AND ROMAN SPELLING

The Romanized spellings of Greek names have been used throughout, since they are the ones that generally occur in modern (post-Renaissance) literature and art. Moreover, many painters and writers have tended to adopt the Roman equivalent names of Greek gods and heroes. Below is a list of the more familiar Greek mythical figures together with their Roman spellings, Greek spelling where it differs and Roman equivalent names where they arise. Note that the Greek '-os' endings often become '-us' in their Romanized Latin forms and that, properly speaking, the 'c' in the Greek names (but not 'ch') should become a 'k' (for example, Achilleus, Narkissos, Kirke); likewise the Greek '-ai-' becomes Roman '-ae-'. Names that do not change have been omitted (for example, Echo, Prometheus, Theseus, Perseus).

ROMAN SPELLING	GREEK SPELLING	ROMAN EQUIVALENT
Achilles	Achilleus	—
Actaeon	Aktaion	—
Ajax	Aias	—
APHRODITE	—	VENUS
APOLLO	APOLLON	—
ARES	—	MARS
ARTEMIS	—	DIANA
Asclepius	Asklepios	Aesculapius
ATHENE (Athena)	—	MINERVA
Cephalus	Kephalos	—
Cerberus	Kerberos	—
Coeus	Koios	—
Crius	Krios	—
Cronus	Kronos	Saturn
Daedalus	Daidalos	—
DEMETER	—	CERES
DIONYSUS	DIONYSOS	BACCHUS
Eos	—	Aurora
Erebus	Erebos	—
Erinyes	—	Furies
Eros	—	Cupid (or Amor)
Gaea (or Ge)	Gaia (or Ge)	Tellus (or Terra)
Graeae	Graiai	—
HADES	HAIDES	PLUTO (or Dis)
Hebe	—	Juventas (or Juventus)
Helius	Helios	Sol
Hemera	—	Dies
HEPHAESTUS	HEPHAISTOS	VULCAN
HERA (or Here)	—	JUNO
Heracles	Herakles	Hercules
HERMES	—	MERCURY
HESTIA	—	VESTA
Iapetus	Iapetos	—
Icarus	Ikaros	—
Jocasta	Iokaste	—
Moerae	Moirai	Fates
Narcissus	Narkissos	—
Nike	—	Victory
Nyx	—	Nox
Oceanus	Okeanos	—
Oedipus	Oidipous	—
Olympus	Olympos	—
Persephone	—	Proserpina
Plutus	Ploutos	—
POSEIDON	—	NEPTUNE
Pyramus	Pyramos	—
Rhea	—	Ops
Seirenes	—	Sirens
Selene	—	Luna
Tartarus	Tartaros	—
Tyche	—	Fortune
Uranus	Ouranos	Caelus
ZEUS	—	JUPITER

Oriental Mythology

Introduction

This book attempts to introduce to the interested reader a taste of the myths and stories of more than one third of the population of the world. The peoples of India, China and Japan are spread over an area of approximately five million square miles, land which covers some of the highest mountain ranges on the globe, barren desert, and tropical forest. The banks of the three great arteries of India and China – the River Ganges, and the Yellow and Yangtse Rivers – are among the most densely populated places to be found on this earth. But also contained within these boundaries are vast tracts of land so inhospitable that they barely accommodate human life – the towering peaks of the Himalayas. As diverse as the geography of the region are the cultural and political experiences of the people: nomadic herdsmen and settled farming com-

ABOVE *The cave complex at Dunhuang in north-western China was begun in* AD *366, the first to be established in the country; illustrated is the cave of 1,000 Buddhas.*

LEFT *Hindu temple cut from the rock on the sea shore at Mahabalipuram in Madras, India.*

munities, fisher folk who need never set foot on dry land, workers in some of the most modern and innovative industries in the world. Patterns of living that have not changed for centuries exist if not alongside, then not very far from, the most advanced technologies.

The civilizations of the region include some of the most ancient and sophisticated ever to have existed. For more than 3,000 years, the peoples of the East have been trying to give a meaning and purpose to their existence on this earth. This urge to provide an explanation, to account for the otherwise random workings of nature and history, has been felt in all human societies since they came into being. Indeed, it is this need to explain and give significance to life that makes us human. The answers we have pro-

RIGHT *A sandstone bracket in the form of a* yakshi, *or tree-goddess, from a Jain stupa in Mathura, Uttar Pradesh.*

FAR RIGHT *The Heian shrine was founded in 1895 to celebrate Kyoto's 1,100 years as the capital of Japan.*

BELOW *The horse-shoe shaped ravine at Ajanta, central India, showing the entrances to the 29 Buddhist viharas (monasteries) and chaityas (temples) cut into the rock between the 2nd and 7th centuries AD; inside are some of the earliest surviving examples of Indian painting. Many of the frescoes illustrate the Jataka tales of the Buddha's previous incarnations.*

duced to questions about how the world came to be and our place in it are what we know as myth.

Myths also serve a function of justifying the social order and accounting for the existence of traditional rites and customs. The tales themselves, naturally as rich and diverse as the cultures of which they are a part, have changed as a result of differing social conditions over the centuries. As cultures merge or clash on meeting, so the myths develop and alter. Mythology is an organic tradition, living off and feeding back into the lives of the people whose existence it enhances.

Given the contrasting and various histories of peoples it is surprising to find that themes occur again and again all over the world. For example, the world-flood, or deluge, which is most familiar to western readers through the story of Noah and the Ark, is to be found in the mythologies of Ireland, Greece, Egypt, Persia, India, Indo-China, Korea, Siberia, Indonesia, the Philippines, Melanesia, Polynesia, Australia, North American Indians, South American Indians, Latin America, and even Africa. One of the main functions of myth is to present a cosmology – that is, to explain how the world came to be. In this book you will find resonances of the Chinese story of Pangu in the tales of Prajapati and Brahma, which originate in India. A symbol of fertility, the egg has been closely connected with creation and birth by many peoples: South Korean myth tells of an egg that contained a baby

ABOVE *Painting of Potala Palace in Lhasa, Tibet; despite the efforts of the Chinese authorities to dissuade the Tibetans – through propaganda and violent repression – from their belief in Buddhism, it remains a potent force.*

who grew up to be leader of the world. But even a concept with such enduring appeal as the egg can be altered and superseded. The ancient account of creation in which the Mediterranean goddess, Eurynome, laid the world-egg from which all nature sprang was replaced by that of Prometheus, who kneaded statuettes of human beings from mud – and the similarities with the Chinese tale of Nugua, which is told here, are striking. The incestuous marriage of Nugua and her brother Fuxi has its counterpart in the Japanese myth of the union of Izanami and Izanagi, almost certainly an example of the borrowing of Chinese ideas that had such important influence on the development of Japanese culture.

The importance that agricultural people attach to the cycle of the seasons and climatic conditions is clearly shown in their mythologies. In China, myths about controlling floods reflect the perennial concern of a farming people whose fortunes depended on channelling the flow of rivers to irrigate their paddy fields; in Japan, an

ABOVE *Gilded stone carving of the Buddha at Dazu, in central eastern China; 1,500 miles to the east lies Japan, 1,000 miles south is Thailand and a journey 800 miles west, skirting the foothills of the Himalayas, will bring you to Burma and India. Across these vast lands and thousands of miles further, radiates the spirit of the Buddha.*

BELOW *Modern Hindu temple at Matale, near Kandy, Sri Lanka, built in 1973. The tower above the main entrance depicts Hindu gods and heroes from the epic poems, the Mahabharata and Ramayana.*

LEFT *Rahu, one of the nine planets, about to swallow the sun and the moon, thereby causing an eclipse; from Konarak, Orissa, in north-eastern India (13th century).*

RIGHT *The Gion festival, at which prayers are offered for the happiness of the people, is one of the biggest in Japan, dating from the 10th century.*

appreciation of the natural world resulting from close observation is incorporated into the Shinto religion. A settled society relying on farming wants its world to follow an ordered and knowable pattern, and a high value is placed on social stability and cohesive family structure; sacrifices and rituals reinforce the sense of community and the greater good. The caste system, which was introduced to Indian caste system, first referred to in the Rig Veda of the Aryan invaders (*c* 1000 BC), is a system of ensuring her place and function in life. The influence of the caste system in defining individual destinies can still be seen at work today.

The belief in reincarnation, which was already widespread in India by the time of the Buddha, was refined and developed under the influence of Buddhism, which originated in northern India in the 6th century BC. The transmission of Buddhism across the whole continent of Asia – through

BELOW *Buddhist cave painting at Dunhuang depicting a group of mourners at a funeral. The paintings are strongly influenced by Central Asian and Indian artistic traditions.*

ABOVE *Contemporary Indian image of Durga, one of the incarnations of Parvati, Shiva's consort.*

India and Pakistan to neighbouring Nepal and Tibet, to Sri Lanka and southeast Asia, along the Silk Road to China and from there to Korea and Japan – shows us how a religion, and the myths that are associated with it, develops and grows under differing cultural conditions. The practice of Buddhism, and the art forms it gave rise to, link these countries more than any other factor. The great cave paintings at Dunhuang in the Gansu province of China, show strong Central Asian and Indian influences. As the Chinese civilization is much older than that of Japan, it is not surprising that much borrowing of ideas and techniques occurred. The propagation of Buddhism played an important role in the development of printing in the East, an art form which was to achieve its highest expression in Japan.

As in all cultures at all times, the mythologies of Asia have been the inspiration for artistic endeavour. Every area of the arts owes a debt to its mythological heritage: painting, sculpture, architecture, poetry, music – the list is endless. The symbols and stories that have been passed on from generation to generation are a rich and inexhaustible source of wisdom and pleasure. In much of the East, myth is not considered to be a 'dead' subject; it has a vital and necessary part to play in the business of living.

Economists predict that this part of the world will see the most dynamic growth as we enter the last years of the 20th century. It remains to be seen whether the traditions that today exist alongside modern industry and skyscraper cities will survive into the next century. The fact that myths and stories have been an essential part of human life since society came into existence implies that they will.

BELOW *12th–14th century Tibetan figure of Lokapala, Defender of the North, a Lamaistic Buddhist deity. He has nine heads and eighteen arms, and holds a conch, a skull, a toad, pearl, head and vajras. A body is draped over his shoulders, and the flayed skin of a head, hands and feet is draped around his waist. The same image of flayed skin is sometimes seen in Tibetan temple hangings. This one figure includes an amazing richness of symbolic, religious and mythical association.*

Chinese Mythology

The Chinese people have never demanded a clear separation of the worlds of myth and reality – indeed, they are so closely bound up that it is hard to say where one begins and the other ends. Historical figures are made into gods and myths are recounted as history. Even in revolutionary China, the same processes could be seen at work: Chairman Mao, in the heyday of the Cultural Revolution (1968–78), was often seen as the all-powerful god responsible for all good things that happen. When an airline hostess can offer the explanation that 'there is no need to wear a safety belt, because Mao, the Great Helmsman, is in charge', the feeling is that superhuman characters with fantastic powers, like those that inhabited the ancient texts, are alive and well in the 20th century.

An apsara, *a heavenly being, in the form of a musician flying on a cloud; this grey limestone carving dates from the early 6th century and comes from the Buddhist cave temples at Longmen, Henan province.*

Confusing though the tendency to intertwine fact and fantasy may be for the westerner, it indicates the power and importance of 'mythology' in the Chinese tradition. Chinese people chart their history in an unbroken line back through the dynasties to the world of Nugua and Fuxi, moving seamlessly from a historical to a mythical time-scale. The earliest archaeological evidence supports the existence of the Shang people in the 12th century BC in the basin of the Yellow River, 'the cradle of Chinese civilization', at about the same time as the beginning of Greek culture. As in Greece, by the 4th century BC, China had a society that was highly developed, and many of the distinguishing features of Chinese life then, have been passed down in recognizable form to the 20th century. The achievement of such a striking degree of stability in their social system is one of the Chinese people's most remarkable accomplishments.

The most important means that China used to secure the survival of its social system was its ability to modify and absorb foreign influences. Those who tried to conquer found themselves in confrontation with a society more complex and sophisticated than their own, and even when successful in their military endeavour, usually ended by adopting Chinese practices and political structures. This was the case when the nomadic Manchu tribes conquered China from the north and established the Qing dynasty in the 17th century. But the most significant influence on Chinese development to come from outside its boundaries (that is, until the 20th century and the introduction of

BELOW *Ceremonial axe-head in bronze dating from the Shang dynasty; bronze casting in Shang China was highly developed, in terms of both technique and decoration.*

19th-century Tibetan cloth painting depicting the gruesome fate awaiting sinners after death.

Marxism-Leninism) was not brought by invaders; Buddhism was introduced to China by traders travelling the Silk Road from India and Central Asia during the 1st century BC.

Two religions, or, more accurately, schools of thought, were already well established in China by this time – Confucianism and Taoism. Confucianism is named after its founder Kongfuzi, or Master Kong, who lived between 551–479 BC, during a period known as 'The Warring States'. After a lifetime spent trying in vain to persuade various nobles and rulers of small states to adopt his ideas on ethics and morals, Confucius died without ever seeing his theories put into practice. His thoughts were collected by his disciples and published posthumously, although it was not until the Han dynasty that Confucianism became the dominant ideology of the Chinese state.

Confucius argued for a highly structured, hierarchical organization of society in which the family was the mainstay of social cohesion. He believed that a state of harmony could be achieved if everyone was aware of their responsibilities and carried out the duties appropriate to their position. Preaching the virtues of filial piety and the veneration of those who had achieved old age ensured that the extended family remained closely knitted. Although he was non-committal about the existence of supernatural beings, sacrifices were a vital part of Confucius' vision. By carrying out such ceremonies, each was confirmed of his place in the wider scheme of things and reminded of his obligations and duties. For the individual, this took the form of ensuring that one's ancestors were happy and well catered for, both in their dotage and in the afterworld; at state level, the emperor made annual sacrifices to Heaven and Earth. Confucius' concern was a pragmatic one – to ensure the smooth running of a stable, well-ordered state. His philosophy cannot really be said to constitute a 'religion' as it lacks many of the features by which we identify religions, such as a priesthood.

The school of thought known as Taoism came into being about the same time as Confucianism. One of the earliest Taoist texts is a collection of observations, the *Tao Te Ching*, written by the Taoist sage Laozi, around the 6th century BC. At its most philosophical, Taoism argues that there is a natural order in the world that determines the behaviour of all things in existence. Early Taoist thinkers hoped that by studying the world of nature they would discover essential laws. This attention to the spirit of things – particularly naturally occurring phenomena like water or wind – led Taoists into a systematic investigation that became the begin-

ABOVE *17th-century Ming bronze of Laozi, the founder of Taoism. He is shown riding on the water buffalo which carried him away from China to the west.*

RIGHT Summer, *one of a set of paintings by Gong Xian (1652–82), depicting the seasonal changes in the landscape.*

ning of science in China. Later on, Taoism operated on a more popular level; the belief that inanimate objects had their own 'spirit' or 'god' gave rise to a system of worship designed to propitiate these powers which was far removed from the early Taoist principles. Taoist priests also practised the art of *fengshui* (wind and water), a method of determining the positioning of buildings so that they did not offend the spirit of the site. Taoism has had great influence on the development of landscape painting in China. Its preoccupations are reflected in the subject matter of the genre – the scholar gazing out from the shelter of a rustic retreat at pine-clad mountains shrouded in mist has been depicted over and over again.

One of the most important contributions that the introduction of Buddhism made to Chinese life was the concept of transmigration of souls. This belief in cyclical life, the view that souls return to the world in a

RIGHT *The Temple of Heaven in Peking, where the emperor conducted the annual sacrifice to Heaven and the prayers for a good harvest.*

form determined by their behaviour during their previous incarnation, offered some comfort to those who perhaps felt that their present existence left something to be desired. The mythology of Hell owes most to Buddhism: on arriving in the Underworld, the soul comes before Yen Wang, who examines the register recording all good and evil actions. Those who have done good deeds – for example, filial sons or believers – are able to proceed directly to join the Buddha himself, to go to Mount Kunlun, the home of the immortals, or to be reborn immediately as a human being. Sinners are required to come before one of nine judges who mete out the punishment appropriate to the offences committed. The taking of life was regarded as the most heinous of Buddhist sins, and it brought about a new respect for living things: vegetarianism became popular as a result of Buddhist influence.

The adage 'Confucian in office, Taoist in retirement and Buddhist as death draws near' sums up the pragmatic Chinese approach to religion. If we aim to rationalize and explain, to codify and authenticate these tales, then we will be exasperated and confounded by the tangled knot that is Chinese mythology. If, on the other hand, we can accept them as meaningful and vivid accounts of a way of experiencing the world, of drawing inspiration and comfort, then we enter a realm that will entrance and delight us.

RIGHT *The composition of the character* shou, *longevity, is designed to resemble the Taoist diagram of 'inner circulation'; Qing dynasty rubbing.*

RIGHT *The massive Leshan Buddha near Chngdu, Sichuan province, is carved out of a cliff overlooking a river.*

同治癸亥正月元日
八十五叟葉志詵

THE GIANT PANGU

At the beginning of time there was only dark Chaos in the universe. Into this darkness – which took the form of an egg – Pangu, the first living creature, was born. Pangu slept, nurtured safely inside the egg. After many years, when he had grown into a giant, Pangu awoke and stretched, thereby shattering the egg. The lighter, purer parts of the egg rose up to become the sky; the heavier, impure parts sank down to become the earth. This was the beginning of the forces of *yin* and *yang*.

The female element, *yin*, is associated with cold and darkness, the moon and the earth; the male element, *yang*, with light and warmth, the sun and the heavens. (These ancient Chinese concepts of *yin* and *yang* have become familiar to westerners through the popularization of the *I Ching*, or Book of Changes.)

Pangu feared that heaven and earth might merge together again so he placed himself between them, his head supporting the sky and his feet pressing down on the earth. For the next 18,000 years Pangu grew at a rate of 10 feet a day, increasing the distance between the two by the same amount. Eventually both heaven and earth seemed securely fixed at a gap of 30,000 miles, and Pangu fell into an exhausted sleep from which he never awoke. On his death, the different parts of his body were transformed into the natural elements: his breath became the wind and clouds; his voice turned into thunder and lightning; his left eye became the sun and his right the moon; his four limbs and trunk turned into the cardinal directions and the mountains; his blood formed the rivers and his veins the roads and paths; his flesh became trees and soil; the hair on his head became

the stars in heaven, and the skin and hairs on his body turned into grass and flowers; metals and stones were formed from his teeth and bones, and dew from his sweat. And the various parasites on his body became the different peoples of the human race. Thus was the universe created by the giant Pangu.

There are a number of versions of this myth – although broadly similar they differ in detail about the eventual outcome of the parts of Pangu's body.

LEFT *Taoist sages examining a painting of the yin/yang symbol; detail of porcelain dish, Kangxi period, Qing dynasty.*

BELOW *Here the yin/yang symbol is surrounded by eight trigrams used in divination. Fuxi, brother of Nugua, is usually credited with their discovery.*

Pangu is also sometimes credited with the power to control the weather, the outlook changing according to his temper. Another account of the origin of the human race is given in the following story:

NUGUA PEOPLES THE WORLD

There was once a goddess who was half human and half snake (some say half dragon). She had the ability to change shape and could do so many times a day. One day, as she wandered through this newly-created world, she felt that although there were many wondrous and beautiful things, it was a lonely place. Nugua yearned for the company of beings like herself, with whom she could talk and laugh. She came to a river and sat down on the bank, gazing at her reflection in the

BELOW *Interior of the Hall of Prayer in the Temple of Heaven, Peking.*

ABOVE *Mythical beasts on the eaves of buildings in the Forbidden City, Peking; it was believed that these ferocious animals would frighten away harmful ghosts and spirits.*

water. As she mused, she trailed her hand in the water and scooped up some mud from the riverbed. She kneaded the clay into a little figure, only instead of giving it the tail of a snake, like herself, she fashioned legs so it could stand upright. When this little creature was placed on the ground, it at once came to life, prancing around her and laughing with joy. Nugua was very pleased with her handiwork and determined to populate the whole world with these delightful little people. She worked all that day until nightfall, and started again at dawn the next day. But Nugua soon realized that the task she had set herself was immense, and that she would be exhausted before she had made enough people to fill the world. However, by using her supernatural powers, Nugua found she could achieve her wish. She took a length of vine, dipped it in the mud and then whirled it round in the air. The drops of mud that flew off the vine were transformed into little people when they touched the ground. Some say that those who had been formed by Nugua herself became the rich and fortunate people of the earth, and those formed from the drops of mud became the ordinary humble folk. Nugua realized that in order to save the human race from becoming extinct when her original people died, they would need a means of reproducing. So she divided the humans into male and female so they could produce future generations without her assistance.

Another story recounts that long ago there were only two people in the world, Nugua and her brother Fuxi. They wanted to marry and produce children, but were afraid to consummate an incestuous marriage without authority from heaven. One day they

LEFT *Earthenware figure placed in a tomb as a guardian, Tang dynasty.*

climbed the sacred Mount Kunlun in the west, and each built a bonfire. The smoke from the two fires mingled together and they took this as a sign that they should indeed become husband and wife. Out of modesty, Nugua made herself a fan of straw and with this she covered her face when they were joined together; it is still the custom today for a bride to hold a fan.

These tales contain a number of features that are common to the creation myths of many cultures. The idea of an egg as the beginning of the world occurs in Indian mythology, and the concept of a single progenitor of the human race can be found in cultures as diverse as those of Greece and Polynesia. Even within China, themes and motifs occur in numerous guises. A folktale recorded in Hebei province gives Pangu as the maker of the mud figures that became the first humans. And in another story, the union of Tianlong and Diya, attendants of Wenchang, the God of Literature, gives rise to the first humans. The universality of these motifs seems to indicate the similarity of concerns of people the world over, and the degree to which there is a shared human experience.

BELOW *Vase decorated with the animals that represent the 12 months of the year (5th–6th century* AD*).*

The structure of the classical Chinese world is indicated in several sources, and from these it is possible to see that there were a number of cosmographies (theories of the universe). Of the *suan ye* school, very little is known, save that its followers believed the sun and stars moved freely about the heavens. One school held that the universe was in the form of an egg, in which the sky was painted inside the upper part of the shell and the earth floated on the ocean that lay in the lower part of the eggshell. A still older tradition, the *zhou bei* school, held that the sky was an inverted bowl rotating around the axis of the Pole Star; the earth was a square underneath the sky, bordered on each side by one of the four seas. The sky was conceived as a solid dome, supported by four or eight pillars or mountains. The fact that the Pole Star does not occupy a central position in the firmament is ingeniously accounted for in the following myth.

GONGGONG'S DEFEAT

One day the gods Gonggong and Zhurong decided to do battle in order to find out which was the most powerful. After many days of fierce fighting, in the course of which they tumbled right out of the heavens, Gonggong was defeated. He was so ashamed that he resolved to kill himself by running against Mount Buzhou, one of the mountains holding up the sky. The mountain came off much the worse from this encounter, as a great part of it came crashing down. A jagged hole was torn in the sky, and great crevasses appeared in the earth. From these massive chasms fire and water spewed forth, causing a great flood that covered the surface of the earth. Those who escaped drowning saw their crops and homes consumed by the flames. Nugua, who had given these people life, could not bear to see them suffer so, and quickly acted to restore order. She chose some coloured pebbles from the river bed and melted them down into a viscous substance

RIGHT *Xiwangmu, Queen Mother of the West, rides on a deer holding a peach and a fungus, both symbols of long life (17th-century soapstone carving).*

ABOVE *Qing court robes were embroidered with dragons, symbols of imperial authority.*

with which she was able to repair the damage caused to the firmament. In order to be sure that the sky did not collapse again, Nugua slaughtered a giant tortoise and cut off its legs. These she placed at the four points of the compass as extra supports for the heavens. Nugua thus restored order to the world and enabled human beings to carry on their affairs in peace. However, Gonggong's collision with the mountain had caused the heavens to tilt in the direction of the north-west, leaving a void in the south-east. This is the reason all the great rivers of China flow toward the east, emptying their waters in that huge ocean.

It is clear that one of the great concerns of Chinese mythology is the maintenance of order and stability. The belief that natural calamities on earth were caused by disharmony in heaven is reiterated many times in the tales of ancient China, although there is only space here for a few of them.

CHANG E'S BETRAYAL

A giant mulberry tree called Fusang grew in the sea beyond the eastern ocean, and in this tree dwelt ten suns. These suns, who were the children of Dijun, God of the East, and Xihe, Goddess of the Sun, took it in turns to go out into the sky. Each morning one of the suns would be ferried across the sky in a chariot driven by his mother, thus bringing warmth and light to the world. One day the ten suns rebelled against the routine and all went into the heavens at once, frolicking across the skies. They enjoyed themselves greatly while they brought disaster down below. The earth dried up, causing all the crops to wither, and even the rocks began to melt. Food became scarce and there was hardly anything to drink. In addition, monsters and wild beasts emerged from the forests in search of prey. Dijun and Xihe took pity on suffering humanity and pleaded with their sons to behave, but without success. In exasperation, Dijun summoned the great archer, Yi, and handed him a quiver of white arrows and a red bow.

LEFT *Bronze mirror decorated with Taoist deities; (3rd century* AD*).*

'I depend on you to restore order on earth,' he said. 'Bring my sons under control and slay the wild beasts that are threatening the people.' Yi accepted the challenge and set off, accompanied by his wife, Chang E. It was clear to Yi that he would get nowhere with threats or persuasion so he fitted an arrow to his bow and shot it into the sky. A ball of fire exploded, and the air was filled with golden flames. A moment later, there was a thud as something fell to the ground. People rushed forward and discovered that one of their tormentors had been transformed into a three-legged raven. Yi loosed one arrow after another, each reaching straight to the heart of its target. And each time the soul of the sun fell to the ground in the form of a three-legged raven. The air promptly became cooler and, but for the quick thinking of the sage king Yao, all might have been extinguished. Realizing that one sun must remain to provide the earth with light and warmth, Yao counted the number of arrows in Yi's quiver and made sure that Yi would run out before he could shoot down the last sun.

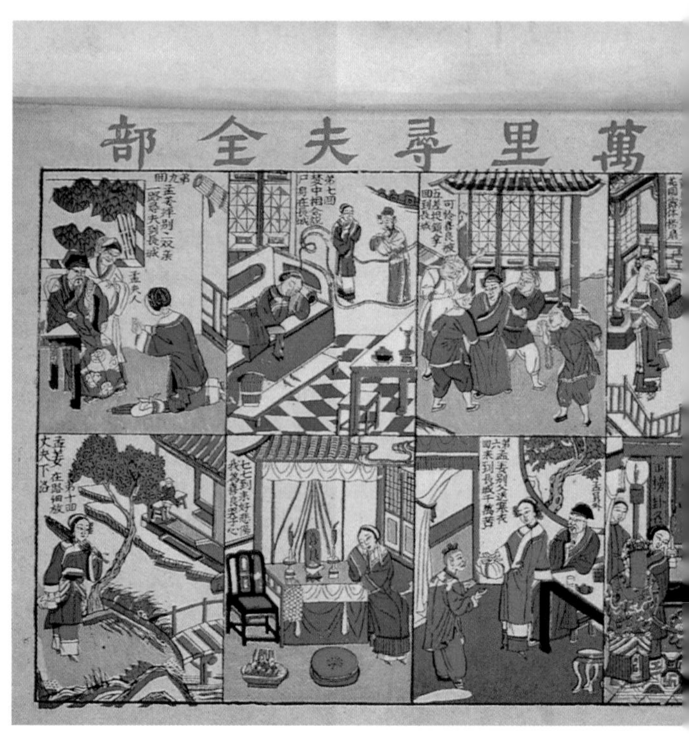

ABOVE *Early 20th-century New Year woodblock print telling the story of Meng Qiang nu, whose husband was enlisted to build the Great Wall during the Qin dynasty (221–206 BC). When he failed to return she set off to find him. On hearing that he was among the many who had perished in the course of the construction of the Wall, she began to weep and her tears caused the Wall to collapse. The beginning of the sorry tale is told here, starting on the right-hand side, moving top to bottom.*

BELOW *Earthenware figure of a guardian from a Tang dynasty tomb; (early 8th century AD).*

With this task accomplished, Yi now turned his attention to the monsters that still threatened the earth. With great skill and bravery, Yi despatched one fearsome beast after another until at last there was peace.

Yi was looked upon as a great hero and everyone was extremely grateful to him for saving them from a terrible fate. With the sounds of praise still ringing in his ears, Yi returned to heaven with his wife Chang E to report on his successful mission. But instead of welcoming him with open arms, Yi found that the god Dijun had shunned him.

'Although I cannot deny that you have only done my bidding, I find that I cannot bear to look upon you, you who have killed my sons. You and

Chang E must leave heaven and return to earth, to those you served so well.'

Chang E was furious at the injustice of this decision, and felt it was particularly unfair that she should be punished for her husband's actions. Reluctantly they packed up their things and moved down to earth.

Yi was able to fill his days with hunting, but Chang E could find no solace in their new home and mulled over their sorry state endlessly. 'Now we have been sent to live in the world of men, and one day, like them, we will die and have to descend to the Underworld. Our only hope is to go to the Queen Mother of the West, who lives on Mount Kunlun, and obtain the elixir of immortality from her.' Yi set off at once and, after many travails, he at last entered the presence of the Queen Mother. The Queen Mother was moved by Yi's sad story and agreed to help him and Chang E.

LEFT *Cakes in the shape of the full harvest moon are eaten during the mid-autumn festival.*

ABOVE *Embroidered pillow end showing the hare in the moon under a cassia tree, pounding the elixir of immortality.*

'This box contains enough elixir to give eternal life to two people, although you will still have to remain in the world of men. To obtain complete immortality you would need to take twice as much. Guard the box well, for all I have is contained therein.'

Yi returned home with the precious box and entrusted it to the care of his wife, planning to wait until a suitably auspicious day to take the drug. But Chang E mused, 'Why should I not take the whole amount, and be restored to my former status of goddess. After all, I have been punished quite without justification.' Immediately after she had taken the elixir, Chang E could feel her feet rise from the ground. Up and up she began to float, out of the window and through the night air.

'On second thoughts,' she said to herself, 'perhaps it would not be such a good idea to return straight to heaven: the gods might criticise me for not sharing the elixir with my husband.'

Chang E resolved to go first to the moon, which was shining overhead in

ABOVE *Embroidered pillow end showing Chang E on her flight to the moon.*

the clear, starlit sky. When she arrived on the moon Chang E found it to be a desolate place, empty except for a hare under a cassia tree. But when she tried to move on, Chang E found that her powers had deserted her and she was doomed to keep her lonely vigil to the end of time.

Yi was shocked and saddened when he found that his wife had betrayed him. He took on a pupil, Peng Meng, perhaps hoping that his skills at least would not die with him. Peng Meng studied hard and eventually reached the point where only Yi was better than him at archery. Peng Meng grew increasingly jealous of his master's superiority, and one day, in an opportune moment, killed him.

A very popular and well-known myth concerning stars in the sky is that of the ox herd and the weaving girl, who respectively represent the stars Altair and Vega, on either side of the Milky Way. This story holds particular significance for parted lovers; indeed, a husband and wife who have been assigned to work in different parts of the country are referred to in such terms.

LEFT *Folk papercut depicting the oxherd carrying his two children in baskets suspended from a pole, on his way to visit his wife in Heaven.*

RIGHT *18th-century soapstone figure of Shoulao, the star god of longevity, who is characterized by his bald head and staff. He holds a peach containing a crane, both symbols of long life.*

THE PARTED LOVERS

A poor young peasant lad just managed to make a living from his barren soil with the help of his most valued possession, his ox. He was honest, worked hard and was liked and respected by all, but the young man felt his life was empty without a wife and family. One day his ox revealed to his owner that he was in fact the Ox Star, sent to earth as a punishment for wrongdoing. 'As you have treated me kindly, I will reward you by helping you to find a wife.'

The Ox Star told the young man to go the next day and hide himself in the undergrowth surrounding a nearby pool, which he said was used by the Heavenly Maidens to bathe in. Following his instructions, the ox herd hid by the pool of clear water, and sure enough, before long a group of beautiful young girls arrived at the water's edge. They left their bright clothes on the bank and stepped into the water. While the girls were occupied with their toilette, the ox herd hid the pile of clothes that was nearest him. As the girls emerged from the water, the young man came out from his hiding place, causing the girls to panic, and grabbing their clothes, they flew off into the sky. One could not find her garments and was trapped on the ground, terrified. But when the young man spoke to her kindly, she realized he meant her no harm and agreed to be his wife. After their marriage, she divulged that she was in fact the granddaughter of heaven and the goddess of weaving. Thanks to the wife's skills, their fortunes pros-

pered and the young couple were very happy together, a happiness increased still further when they had two children, a boy and a girl.

But the gods were not pleased at the thought of the weaving maid remaining on earth and sent down messengers to snatch her back to her rightful abode. The ox herd and his children watched helplessly as the weaving maid was carried, weeping, back to heaven. The old ox came once more to the aid of his master: 'I shall die soon, and when I do, you must take my skin and wrap yourself in it, then you will be able to pursue your wife.' The ox herd did as he was told, and then, placing his children in two baskets suspended from a carrying pole across his shoulders, he set off.

The ox herd soon caught sight of

BELOW *Pagoda of the Six Harmonies, West Lake, Hangzhou; popular belief holds that building a pagoda will bring good luck to a place.*

his wife, but, before he could reach her, he was spotted by her grandfather, or some say, her grandmother, Xiwangmu, the Queen Mother of the West. A line drawn in the sky became a raging torrent, running between them. The little girl urged her father to use the ladle he had placed in the basket with her as ballast to empty the water from the river. The sight of the devoted family at their hopeless task touched the hearts of the gods, and it was decided that the family could be united once a year. On the seventh day of the seventh month, all the magpies fly up from earth and form a bridge across the river, enabling the ox herd to cross over and visit his wife. Some say that when rain falls on this day, it is the tears of the weaving maid as she weeps tears of joy.

The festival that is held on this date is the annual feast of young girls, in which they entreat the weaving goddess to give them skills in spinning, weaving and embroidery. It is said that the ladies of the Tang Emperor Xuan Zong would shut a spider into a box on this night, and take the web found the following day to be an indication of the skill of the one who imprisoned it.

ABOVE *The transplanting of rice seedlings is carried out today in the same back-breaking fashion as it has been for centuries; the overwhelming importance of a good harvest informs many of the myths of China.*

RIGHT *17th-century Ming dynasty ivory figure of the Taoist immortal, Chang Kuo Lao.*

Throughout the history of China, countless numbers of people have lived alongside the great rivers, the Yangtse and the Yellow River, knowing that the waters that provided them with the means of irrigating their fields could also one day deprive them of their life and livelihood. Although the deluge motif occurs in numerous myths the world over, it assumes a particular significance in Chinese mythology. The following tales illustrate the importance of controlling flood waters, and the degree of respect accorded to those who had such powers.

THE GREAT FLOOD

During the reign of the sage king Yao, Tiandi, the supreme god in heaven, sent a terrible flood down to earth to punish mankind for its wickedness. The waters covered the fields and villages, and people were forced to seek refuge in the mountains. They had to compete with wild animals for food and shelter and their suffering was very great. Of all the gods in heaven, only one took pity on the plight of those on earth, and his name was Gun. Gun felt that the punishment meted out was too severe and pleaded with Tiandi to end the deluge. But his entreaties were in vain.

One day, when he was racking his brains trying to think of a way to control the flood water, Gun came across an owl and a tortoise. When Gun told them of his concern, the owl and the tortoise replied, 'Tiandi has a magical substance, which looks just like an ordinary lump of earth. If you could get hold of a piece of this substance and throw it into the water, it would swell up into great barriers that would hold back the flood.'

Gun's determination to save the people was so great that he managed to overcome all obstacles and obtain a

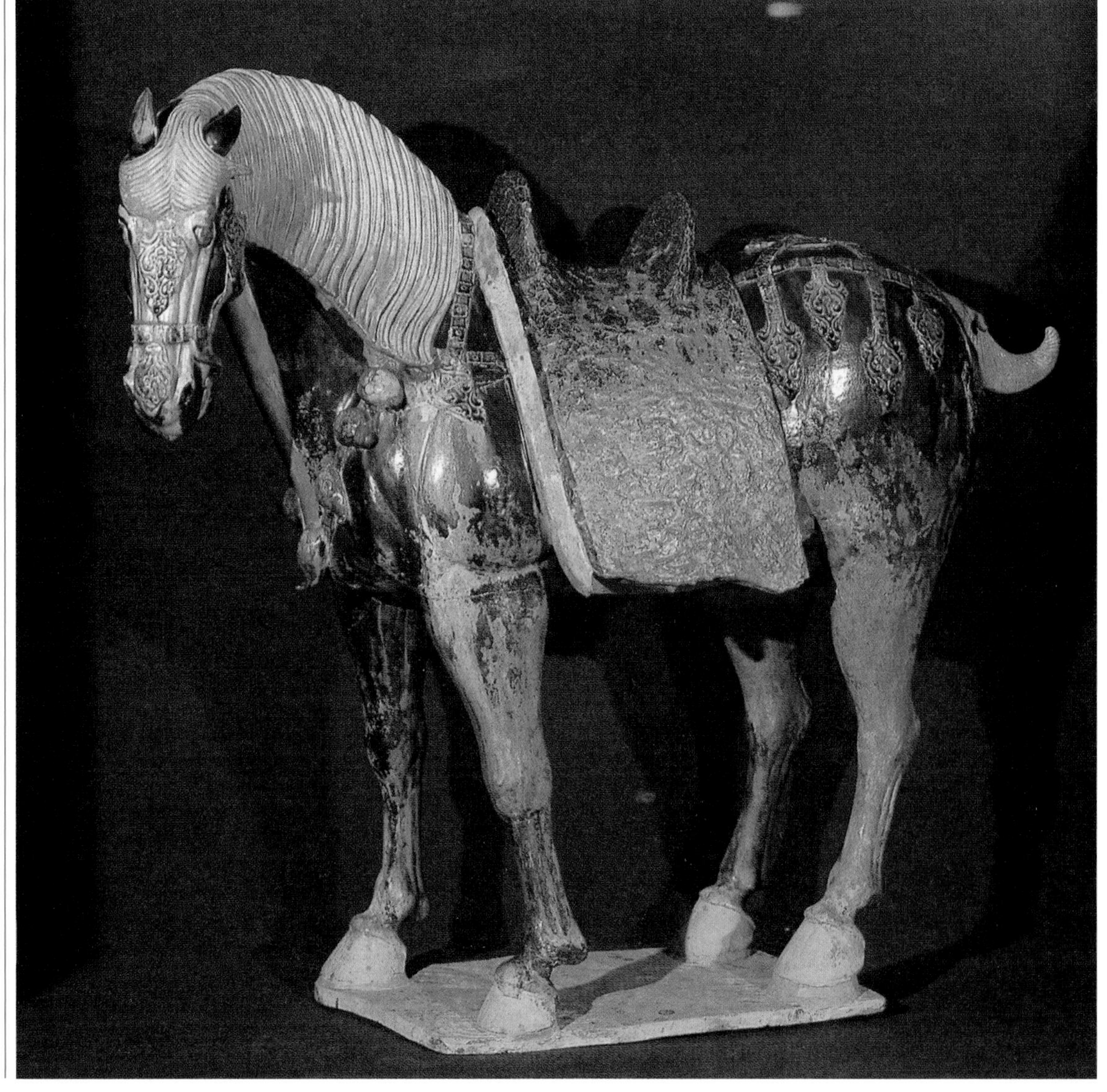

RIGHT *Glazed earthenware tomb figure of a horse from the Tang dynasty (7th–10th century AD).*

small piece of the magic soil. He immediately set off for earth and dropped a tiny lump into the water. At once, the soil started to heave and shift below the surface, and before long the tips of ridges and mountains could be seen. The flood waters were soon contained by these formations, and then dried up completely. The people were overcome with gratitude for Gun's actions, and danced and sang his praises. But Tiandi was furious when he discovered what Gun had done and sent the fire god Zhurong down to earth to seek revenge. Zhurong killed Gun and took what remained of the magic soil back to heaven, and floods again covered the world.

Although Gun had been killed, his spirit refused to die because he had not accomplished his task. New life began to grow inside his body, which would not decompose. After three years had passed, during which the mourning people had kept watch over the body of their saviour, Tiandi sent down a god with a sword to destroy Gun's remains. When the blade slashed at Gun's body, a terrible dragon was released. This dragon was none other than the Great Yu, Gun's son, who took on his father's unfinished mission and eventually brought the flood under control. Gun himself then turned into a yellow dragon and went to live at the bottom of the sea.

Dragons are the most important of all the mythical beasts to be found in the Chinese tradition. In contrast to western notions, Chinese dragons were believed to be generally well-disposed towards humankind, although subject to rather short tempers! Dragons represent the male *yang* element. From the Han dynasty on, the dragon was used as a symbol of the Son of Heaven, the emperor. The phoenix correspondingly represented the female *yin*, and the empress – together the dragon

RIGHT *Phoenixes dancing amid peonies and rocks; 16th–17th-century silk tapestry.*

RIGHT *18th-century porcelain figure of a phoenix, symbol of the empress.*

and the phoenix are used to indicate a state of marital harmony.

There is a particular affinity between dragons and water in all its natural forms: seas, rivers, lakes, rain. Four dragon-kings were believed to rule over the four seas that surround the earth, and dragon-kings could also be found in lakes and rivers inhabiting crystal palaces filled with precious treasure. Dragons were held to exercise control over rainfall, and are often depicted playing with a ball or pearl (symbol of thunder) among the rainclouds.

At the beginning of the Chinese year according to the lunar calendar, some time in February, a dragon dance is performed. A line of dancers each hold a stick supporting a section of the dragon's body, from head to tail. A lead dancer holds a lantern in the shape of a red ball. By moving up and down and back and forth, the dancers give the impression that the dragon is writhing around in pursuit of the ball. This dance, which may have originated in an ancient ritual to do with the preparation of the soil before the spring sowing, is performed by Chinese communities throughout the world. The dragon-boat festival of South China is held on the fifth day of the fifth month of the lunar calender (around the middle of June). Teams of men in long, narrow boats with dragon-shaped prows compete in a rowing race. The loss of a rower overboard was held to be a sacrifice to the dragon-god, and since many Chinese could not swim, this was a not unusual occurrence.

It was widely believed that the landscape was criss-crossed with 'dragon-lines', veins of the earth. Before building a house or choosing a burial site, people would consult a geomancer to ascertain whether the proposed development was likely to obstruct the natural forces flowing through the dragon lines, thus arousing the dragon's anger and causing

RIGHT *Chinese communities the world over perform the dragon dance at New Year in the Chinese calendar.*

ABOVE *Tang dynasty bronze mirror showing Chang E under the cassia tree with the hare that inhabits the moon.*

calamity. So strong are these beliefs that geomancers are regularly employed even in somewhere as relentlessly 20th century as Hong Kong. Although officially regarded as pedlars of feudal superstitious nonsense in China today, geomancers continue to advise, particularly in the countryside.

Chinese people believed that there was a great deal of communication between heaven and earth. In fact, heaven was generally conceived as reflecting the organization of society below: the emperor, who stood at the head of a vast bureaucracy, had his counterpart above, Shangdi. As on earth, Shangdi was served by numerous functionaries and officials. The supreme ruler, who was also known simply as Tian, or 'sky', appears in his Taoist guise as the Jade Emperor. An important functionary in the heavenly pantheon was the Jade Emperor's deputy, who headed an office concerned with all matters of life and death on earth. The officials in this ministry fixed the times of birth and death, determining the span of life of both human and animal life. This accorded with the Buddhist idea of reincarnation, in which one's soul can be reborn many times in higher or lower forms of human or animal life depending on one's conduct. This important deity was very popular with women anxious to give birth to a son.

Many of the gods lived on earth, and returned to heaven once a year to report on happenings in the affairs of men. Popular superstition held that many ordinary household objects had their own guardian spirit, and that they required offerings and sacrifices. Although such practices were generally looked down upon by the educated, the mistresses of most households took the precaution of not causing offence, just in case they should receive a bad report! One of the most important of these deities was the

LEFT *The dead were buried with all they might need in the afterlife, including attendants (Tang dynasty).*

kitchen, or hearth god. A statue or image of this god would be kept in a niche above the stove and during the course of the year, he would keep watch over the comings and goings in the house. At New Year, to ensure that he was in a good temper before his journey back to heaven, he would be offered a good meal and his lips were smeared with honey so that he could only utter sweet words. Then, to the accompaniment of fire-crackers, the soot-blackened image would be burnt to send it on its way. Like many other Chinese gods, the hearth god was thought to have originally been a human being. One story tells that he was a poor mason, in such straits that he was no longer able to support his wife. Forced to give her in marriage to another, he took to wandering the countryside, begging. By chance, he came one day to the house where his former wife lived. Overcome with shame, he tried to escape by climbing into the hearth, little realizing that it was alight. After his painful death, he was made into a god.

ABOVE *Qing dynasty print of a door god with the gods of wealth and acolytes.*

RIGHT *Qing dynasty New Year print of the Kitchen God.*

RIGHT *Guandi, the God of War, also epitomized justice. Parties involved in a legal dispute would present their case at temples dedicated to him.*

Many of the popular Chinese gods were historical characters with outstanding qualities who were deified after death. One of these was Guandi, the God of War, in whose name numerous temples and shrines were dedicated. Guan Zhong, as he was known in his lifetime, was one of a band of three brigands who lived at the end of the Late Han dynasty, a

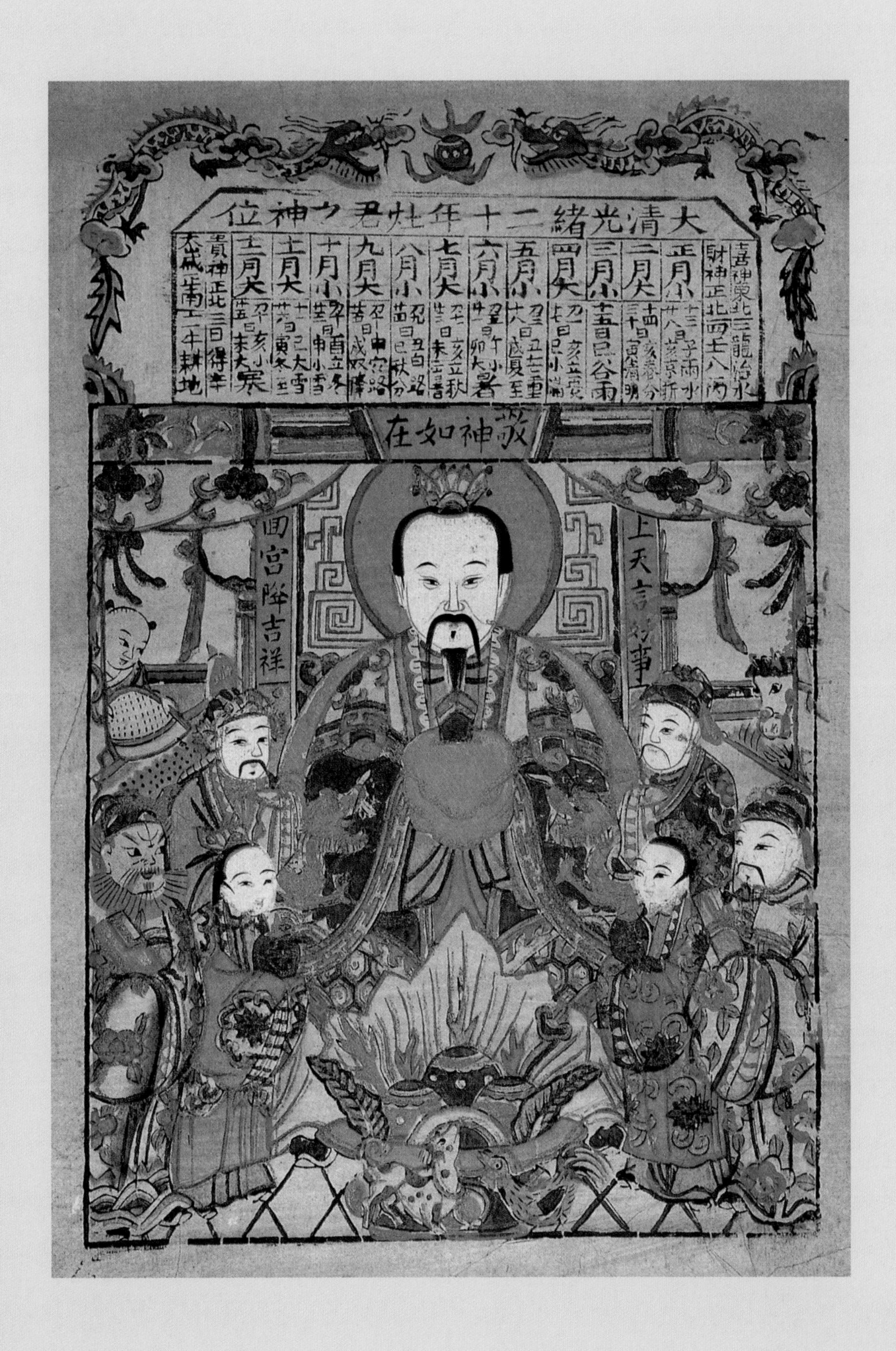

大清光緒二十年灶君之神位
正月小
二月大
三月小
四月大
五月小
六月小
七月大
八月小
九月大
十月小
十一月大
十二月大
敬神如在
上天言好事
回宮降吉祥

ABOVE *Gilt bronze statue of Bodhisattva sitting on a lotus leaf, a Buddhist deity who stayed in the world in order to save others; (Liao dynasty, 907–1125* AD*).*

period of great turmoil. The story of his life is recounted in *The Romance of the Three Kingdoms,* which was written at the beginning of the Ming dynasty although it purports to be a contemporary account of events, and it has been the inspiration for many plays and novels since. Guan Zhong first achieved renown for his military prowess, but came to be loved for great courage and loyalty. Guandi is instantly recognizable, as he is always portrayed with a red face.

The deity held most dear by the Chinese everywhere is Guan Yin, the goddess of mercy, who was originally the male Buddhist Boddhisatva, Avalokitsvara. This saint, whose name translated into Chinese means 'one who hears the cries of the world', is also the patron saint of Tibetan Buddhism. Guan Yin is often portrayed as a madonna with a child in her arms, and is worshipped by those hoping for a child. Fishermen consider her to keep particular watch over those in peril at sea, and she is sometimes identified with Mazu, whose cult has spread out from the coastal regions of south China. There are images of Guan Yin not only in temples and shrines, but also in homes and public places; her figure has been executed in all manner of media – she is the most revered of all gods in the popular pantheon. The following story indicates the degree of affection she inspires.

THE GIFT OF RICE

In the time when people lived by hunting and gathering, life was very hard and uncertain. When Guan Yin saw how people suffered and often died from starvation, she was moved to help them. She squeezed her breasts so that milk flowed and with this she filled the ears of the rice plant. In order to adequately provide for the people, she produced such quantities that her milk became mixed with blood towards the end. This is why there are two kinds of rice – white and red.

An alternative myth gives a dog the credit for introducing rice. After the great floods had been brought under control by Yu, son of Gun, people were forced to live by hunting as all the old plants had been washed away. One day a dog ran out of a waterlogged field and was found to be carrying long ears of rice that had got caught up in his tail. When the seeds were planted in the sodden fields they grew and ripened. In gratitude, the first meal after the rice harvest is shared with the dog.

Of all the animals that occur in Chinese myths, both real and fantastic, Monkey is in a class of his own. His story is related in *Xi you ji*, or *Journey to the West*, written by Wu Cheng'en in the 16th century. This novel purports to be a true account of the travels of the Buddhist monk Xuan Zang, who journeyed to India in the 7th century in search of Buddhist sutras. He returned to China after an absence of 16 years and spent the rest of his life translating the 520 cases of texts he had brought back with him. In the book, Tripitaka (as Xuan Zang is named after the Buddhist scriptures he seeks) is accompanied by Monkey and Pigsy, two creatures who have no historical basis whatsoever. Although Monkey has many wonderful and supernatural powers, and a sense of mischief and a temper to match, Pigsy is a completely down-to-earth character, who epitomizes the coarser human desires.

LEFT *18th century woodblock edition of* Journey to the West *by Wu Cheng'en. Monkey is at the top, the monk Tripitaka to the right and Pigsy centre left.*

BELOW *Life-size carved wooden figure of a Buddhist* lohan, *an enlightened holy man, (14th century).*

MONKEY'S IMMORTALITY

Monkey was born from a stone egg that had rested on the side of the Aolai Mountain in the Eastern sea ever since Pangu had created the world. Although in appearance there was nothing to distinguish this monkey from others, he was in fact possessed of magical powers. The tribe of monkeys with whom he lived recognized his special qualities and adopted him as their king. After he had been king for about 300 years, Monkey began to concern himself with the eventual fate that he and his tribe faced. He decided to seek the way of immortality that he had heard of through the tales of the Buddha and other deities. So Monkey left the mountain and travelled to the world of men. Here he found a master who agreed to take him on as a disciple. According to custom, Monkey was given a new name – Sun, the enlightened one, since *sun* is the Chinese word for monkey. After 20 years not only had Monkey learnt the secret of eternal life, but he had also acquired other valuable skills, such as the ability to change himself into any form, and fly through the air.

When Monkey returned to Aolai mountain, he found that a demon monster had taken over the monkeys' home. After defeating the monster in battle, Monkey decided he needed to get hold of a good magic weapon. He called on the Dragon King of the Eastern Sea, and against the dragon's will, carried off an iron pillar that had been used by the Great Yu, controller of the floods. The size of this pillar could be changed by its owner in an instant, so it could be made as small as a needle to be carried about and then turned at once into an eight-foot-long fighting staff.

One day, as he was feasting and drinking in the company of his fellow monkeys, Monkey was approached by two messengers from the Underworld. When they refused to take heed of his protest that he had become an immortal, Monkey became extremely angry. Laying about him with his magic cudgel, he knocked down his would-be guards, and charged off into the Underworld in a fury. The officials and judges at the courts of Hell were soon beaten into submission by the

BELOW *16th-century stoneware figure of a judge of Hell.*

ABOVE *Qing dynasty porcelain vase decorated in* famille rose *enamels. Peaches are credited with the power to ward off evil spirits, as well as being a symbol of immortality.*

furious Monkey. He demanded to see the Register of the Dead, and on finding his own entry 'Soul no. 1735, Sun the enlightened one: 342 years and a peaceful death', flew into a further rage. Monkey snatched up a brush and crossed out the lines referring to himself and his tribe. Throwing the book on to the floor, Monkey stormed out and returned to his mountain fastness.

However, news of Monkey's exploits was beginning to reach the ears of the great Jade Emperor. Both the Dragon King of the Eastern Sea and Yama, Lord of the Underworld, made complaints about Monkey's arrogant behaviour. It was decided that it would be a good idea to bring Monkey up to heaven where he could be kept under supervision. Monkey was offered the post of 'Keeper of the Heavenly Horses', and, thinking this was an important post in the heavenly bureaucracy, he duly accepted. After a short period in the job, Monkey started to make enquiries about his grade and salary and flew into a terrible rage when he discovered that his was an honorary post that carried no salary and was too lowly to figure in the heavenly hierarchy. The only way to persuade the proud Monkey to stay in heaven was to offer him the grand title 'Great Sage, equal of Heaven' (which sounded important but was in fact meaningless). After a time during which Monkey did nothing but amuse himself feasting and drinking with his friends, he was given the job of guardian of the Garden of Immortal Peaches in a desperate attempt to keep him out of trouble.

This garden belonged to Xiwangmu, Queen Mother of the West, and, every 6,000 years, when the fruit ripened, she would hold a great feast to which the immortals were invited in order to partake of the peaches and renew their immortality. It so happened that the peaches were nearly ripe and, of course, Monkey could not resist plucking one to see what it tasted like. It was so delicious that he ate one after another, until eventually he fell asleep in the branches of one of the trees. He was woken by a maid who had been sent to pick the peaches in preparation for the Queen Mother's banquet. Monkey was apoplectic when he learnt that he was not to be invited to the celebrations, and determined to seek revenge for being slighted. He had already eaten most of the ripe peaches in the garden and now proceeded to down great quantities of the fragrant wine that had been prepared for the feast. And when he came across gourds containing the elixir of immortality which Laozi was intending to bring to the occasion, well, he drank that too.

After a while, when he had sobered up a little, Monkey began to realize

LEFT *Ming ivory figurine of an attendant to Xiwangmu, Queen Mother of the West, holding three peaches of immortality.*

ABOVE *The Diamond Sutra scroll is the world's earliest example of a printed book; the frontispiece, which shows Buddha surrounded by his disciples, is dated 868* AD *and was found at Dunhuang, Gansu province.*

the enormity of the offence he had just committed. Feeling some remorse, he returned to the mountain and hid in his old home. The gods were livid when it was discovered what Monkey had done, and determined to punish him. After many great struggles, Monkey was brought before the Jade Emperor, bound hand and foot. Monkey could not be sentenced to death because he had consumed so many immortality-conferring substances, so it was decided that he should be burnt in Laozi's crucible. But 49 days of white-hot heat merely gave Monkey red rims to his eyes, and he leapt from the crucible ready to continue to do battle.

In desperation, the Jade Emperor called on Buddha himself for help. Buddha was amused by the antics of the insolent Monkey and, placing him in the palm of his giant hand, issued him with a challenge. 'If you can leap out of my hand, you can rule over heaven. If not, you must return to earth and work to achieve immortality.'

Monkey took a great leap into the air and hurled himself into the distance. When he landed on the ground at last, he found himself at the foot of a great mountain. Monkey plucked out one of his hairs and used it as a brush to write his name on the rocks. Then he urinated on the ground, like animals do to mark out their territory, before returning to Buddha. When Monkey claimed his right to be ruler of heaven, since he had been to the

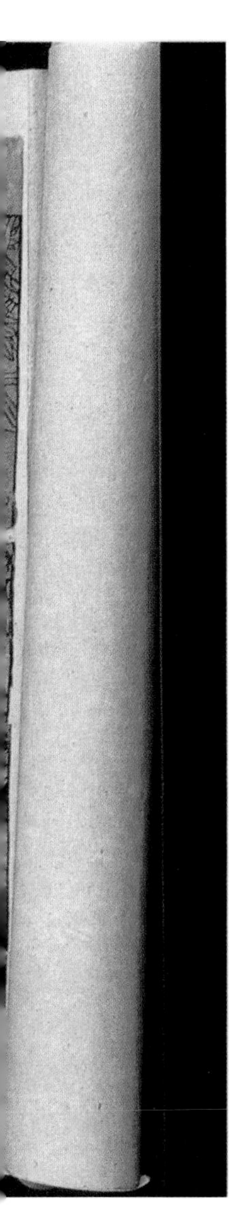

ends of the earth and back, Buddha burst out laughing,

'You never even left my hand! See, here is your name written on one of my fingers.' Monkey saw that there was no way he would ever be able to outwit Buddha, and tried to escape. But Buddha quickly created a mountain and imprisoned Monkey inside it, saying, 'There you will stay until you have paid for your sins'.

Five hundred years later, after Guanyin's intercession on his behalf, Monkey is released from his prison on the condition that he accompany the monk Tripitaka on his great journey to the West, and protect him from harm. The two travellers pick up a third companion, Pigsy, as they continue their dangerous and eventful journey, and after surviving 14 years and 80 perils, the little band finally come in sight of the Buddha's abode, the Mountain of the Soul. When they have received the scriptures from the Buddha himself, the three set off on their journey home. Thanks to Guanyin, this time they are able to travel in comfort, riding on a cloud borne by one of the Golden Guardians. This is brought abruptly to an end when Buddha decides they should face one more test, bringing the total trials they have undergone to the magic number of 81, nine times nine.

The three companions suddenly find themselves tumbling down to earth. On picking themselves up they recognize the spot as being the bank of a river they had crossed on their

RIGHT *Papercut image of Monkey about to eat a peach; his fur is covered with flowers, coins and swastikas, the latter a symbol of good luck in both India and China.*

outward journey on the back of a white turtle. The turtle appears to ferry them across again but, in mid-stream, enquires whether Tripitaka has indeed found out from the Buddha the life span of a turtle, a task that he undertook on their previous meeting. In the excitement of coming before the Buddha, Tripitaka had in fact completely forgotten about the turtle's query. On learning this, the turtle is so cross that he promptly tips them all into the water. Fortunately, they manage to swim to shore with their precious cargo, where they are received with great joy by the local people. On reaching the capital, Chang'an, they are brought before the emperor in a majestic ceremony. The three receive their final accolade in heaven, when Buddha announces that Tripitaka was once his disciple, who was sent to earth in punishment for his sins. Now Tripitaka is to be permitted to take up his place at the Buddha's side again, Monkey is made God of Victorious Battle, and Pigsy is created Chief Heavenly Altar Cleaner.

ABOVE *This page from a contemporary comic book telling the Monkey story indicates the enduring popularity of the tale.*

BELOW *Actors in Peking opera apply their own make-up. The patterns and colours all have a particular significance.*

The story of Monkey has been portrayed in every medium – book, play, opera, film – and continues to be greatly enjoyed by Chinese audiences. Monkey's mischievous antics and skill at martial arts delight people today as they have done for centuries.

Although China has such a long written history, there are difficulties for the student of mythology. As in the case of the *Journey to the West,* many texts are not as old as they purport to be, with material selectively incorporated by their authors in order to give credence to their own accounts. Often, the same basic myth exists in a number of variations, there is no one single authorized version. The *Shanhaijing,* the Mountain and Seas Classic, edited in the 1st century BC, and the *Huainanzi,* the writings of Marter Huai Nan, compiled in the 2nd century BC, are both rich sources of classical myths. During the Tang dynasty, one of the most artistically creative periods of Chinese history, there was much interest in magic and the supernatural, and themes from early myth and folklore were woven into stories written at this time.

The different contributions made to Chinese mythology by Confucianism, Taoism and Buddhism have already been indicated; it is worth remembering that the area of China covers a great variety of cultural and linguistic traditions. Han Chinese, who constitute 94 per cent of the one billion population of the People's Republic today, are only one of the 50 or so ethnolinguistic groupings identified within China's boundaries.

This diverse heritage has given rise to a body of stories that is a rich and vital part of Chinese life. It is impossible to make sense of Chinese literature without a knowledge of its myths, for they are constantly referred to. Today these tales are still the subject of numerous retellings – in book and comic form, or as plays, opera or even film. In festivals and holidays, in painting and sculpture, as figures of speech, the myths of ancient China live on in the lives of ordinary Chinese people everywhere.

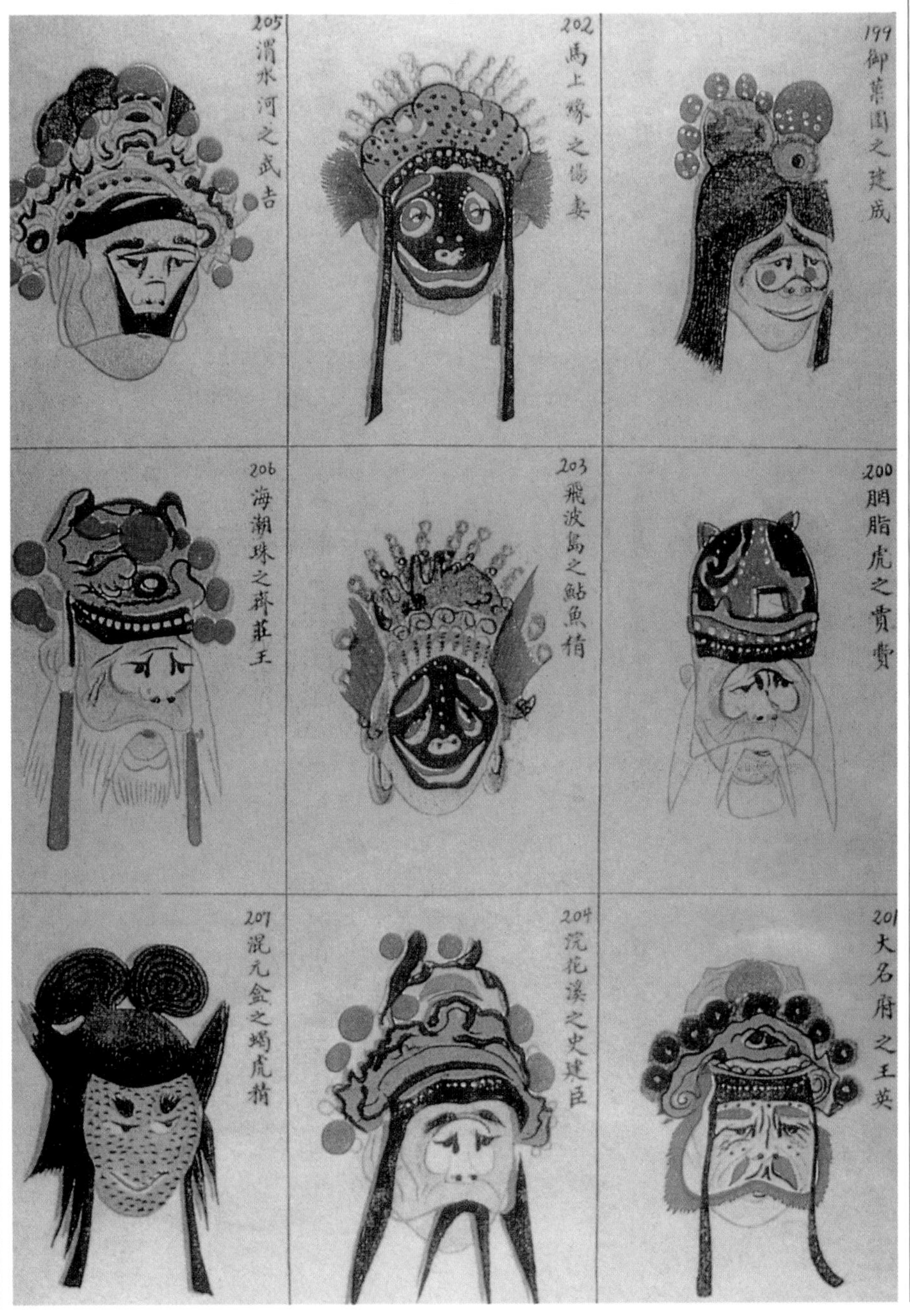

RIGHT *Designs for face make-up used in Chinese theatre; each design is for a specific character or type of character.*

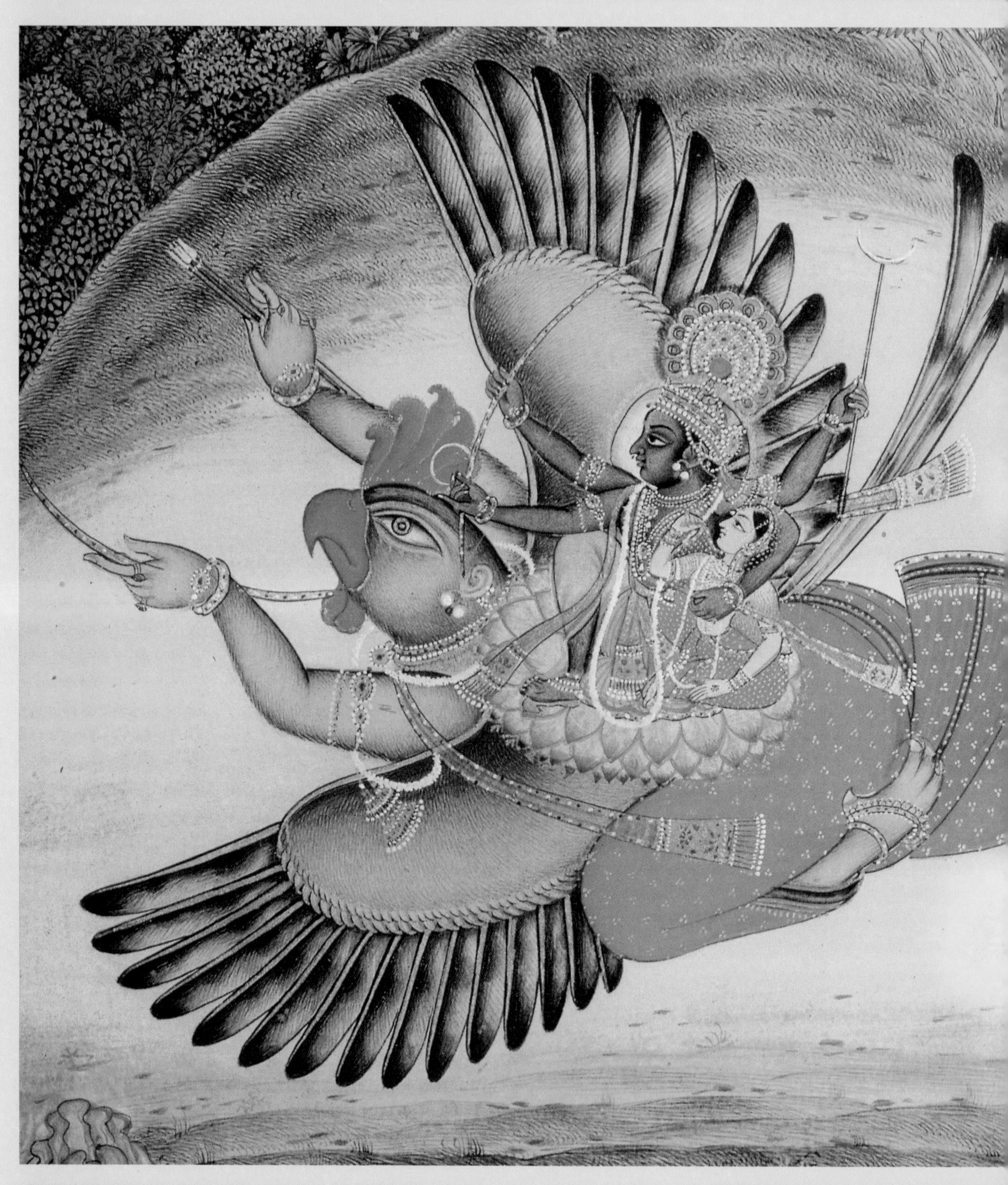

Indian Mythology

All over India millions of tiny oil lamps are lit as dusk falls. They shine out, row upon row of them, from rooftops and windowsills. It is autumn, the night of the great festival of Diwali. Children settle down around their mothers or grandmothers to hear the story of Lakshmi, the fickle goddess of wealth and good fortune. Hearing this tale, and countless others, at their mother's knee is their entertainment. They are absorbed in a rich fantasy world of gods and demons, princes and princesses, friendly animals and exciting adventures. Their psyches have free range over ideas of good and evil, exploring ways of living life and of facing death. They find these stories in books, films, theatre, dance, sculpture and painting, and in comics, but nothing compares with the power of an ancient tale directly told, handed down by word of mouth from generation to generation for thousands of years.

Vishnu, the most popular of the Hindu deities, and his consort, Lakshmi, ride on the bird-god Garuda; (18th-century Bundi painting from Rajasthan).

There is always a moral to the story: how to be the perfect wife or husband, how to be reborn as a better person, how to behave toward others, how to keep the gods happy with sacrifice and celebration. Much of Indian mythology holds a religious context, which speaks in particular to those holy men and women, priests, hermits and wandering ascetics who are searching for the key to the ultimate nature of reality, and for the way to escape the endless cycle of rebirth.

For the historian, the language and images of the ancient mythological texts present the ancient history of the land. The migrations of the Aryan peoples into India can be followed by tracing the burial and cremation practices of the region, as described in the ancient Vedic hymns. The cultural influences of the indigenous Dravidian peoples can be seen in the increased importance of the goddesses in subsequent sacred texts. The struggles of rival dynasties are vividly described in the great battles of the epic poems, the *Ramayana* and the *Mahabharata.* Indeed, Indian mythology is like a mirror that shows their hearts' desire to all who look into it.

Most of the stories in this introduction are Hindu tales, but other religions have not been overlooked. The story of the life of the Buddha, for example, is included. Although he is an historical figure, his life itself has been turned into an elaborate myth involving gods and demons, even though the Buddhist doctrine is atheistic. The Buddha is even sometimes described as an incarnation of Vishnu.

In the Indian Hindu tradition, the lives of famous holy men, saints, and the founders of other great religions are elaborated in similar ways. For instance, Mahavira, the founder of Jainism, was born after his mother had a visionary dream. The astrologers forecast his coming and the gods closely observed his young life full of heroic feats.

Traditional biographers also elaborated the life of the founder of Sikhism, Guru Nanak, who lived from 1469 to 1539. Although he believed in only one God, his birth was said to be witnessed by millions of gods who foretold his future as a great man. This greatness is exhibited in various feats of magic. For example, when his disciple Mardana was hungry, Guru Nanak turned poison berries into edible fruits. The story of his enlightenment is that he disappeared while bathing in the river and was presumed dead: After three days he returned and explained that he had been with God. His first words on his return were said to be 'There is neither Hindu or Muslim, so whose path shall I fol-

BELOW *The Jain saint Parsvanartha; (11th-century sculpture from Orissa). The austerity of Jain doctrine is expressed in the simple, continuous form.*

low? I will follow God's path. God is neither Hindu nor Muslim, and the path I follow is God's'. But even in the *Adi Granth,* or Original Collection of the hymns of the Gurus, the one God is sometimes described with reference to the Hindu deities: 'He, the One, is Himself Brahma, Vishnu and Shiva'.

Similarly, the animal stories of the Buddhist Jataka tales use all kinds of folk tales that have been used to illustrate Buddhist values. Some of these tales have been floating around the world for centuries and turn up in different forms in Homer, Boccaccio and Chaucer. They can be claimed by anyone! (Some students of Indian

LEFT *A Jain saint in the arms of his mother; (11th-century stone icon from western India).*

mythology believe that Hinduism claimed the epic poems of the *Ramayana* and the *Mahabharata* in the same way by inserting sacred texts, such as the *Bhaghavad Gita,* at appropriate points in the story.)

'Each myth celebrates the belief that the universe is boundlessly various, that everything occurs simultaneously, that all possibilities may exist without excluding each other' (Wendy O'Flaherty, *The Origins of Evil in Indian Mythology*). This is also a good way to describe the Indian subcontinent itself. It is geographically diverse, with the great Himalayan mountains in the north, rice- and wheat-growing plains, desert and tropical jungle, high, tea-growing plateaux and low-lying coastal areas with palm trees where the land is criss-crossed with waterways. The climate is extreme, the hot season brought to an abrupt end by the heavy monsoon rains. Although 8 out of 10 Indians are Hindus, India is the home of many followers of other great world religions, including Islam and Christianity.

IN THE BEGINNING

Some of the creation myths are very abstract, struggling with the concepts of existence and non-existence as in this extract from the hymn of creation from the *Rig Veda.*

'Neither not-being nor being was there at that time; there was no air-filled space nor was there the sky which is beyond it. What enveloped all? And where? Under whose protection? What was the unfathomable deep water? . . . Upon it rose up, in the beginning, desire, which was the mind's first seed. Having sought in their hearts, the wise ones discovered, through deliberation, the bond of being and nonbeing . . . Whereupon this creation has issued, whether he has made it or whether he has not – he who is the superintendent of this world in the highest heaven – he alone knows, or, perhaps, even he does not know.'

ABOVE *Three-headed icon of Brahma, the creator; early 11th-century Chola sculpture from south India.*

There are other stories where the gods actively create the world. The story of Prajapati, who rose from the primordial waters weeping as he was lonely and did not know why he had been born, for example. The tears that fell into the water became the earth, the tears that he wiped away became the sky and the air. Then he created people and spirits, night and day, the seasons and finally death.

In a creation myth using the concept of the egg – also found in Chinese and many many other mythologies – Brahma is the creator. The golden egg grew from a seed floating on the cosmic ocean for a year, and shone with the lustre of the sun. Brahma emerged from the egg and split himself into two people, one male and one female, the incestuous union of these two being the creative force. Brahma is also called Narayana (he who came from the waters) who is described as lying on a banyan leaf, floating on primeval waters sucking his toe – a symbol of eternity.

One fascinating creation myth

RIGHT *The Cosmic Egg according to Hindu theory; 18th-century painting (gouache on paper) from Rajasthan. At the bottom is Vishnu, reclining on the cosmic serpent. From his navel protrudes the lotus upon which sits Brahma. At the top is Vaikuntha, or paradise, where Krishna dwells.*

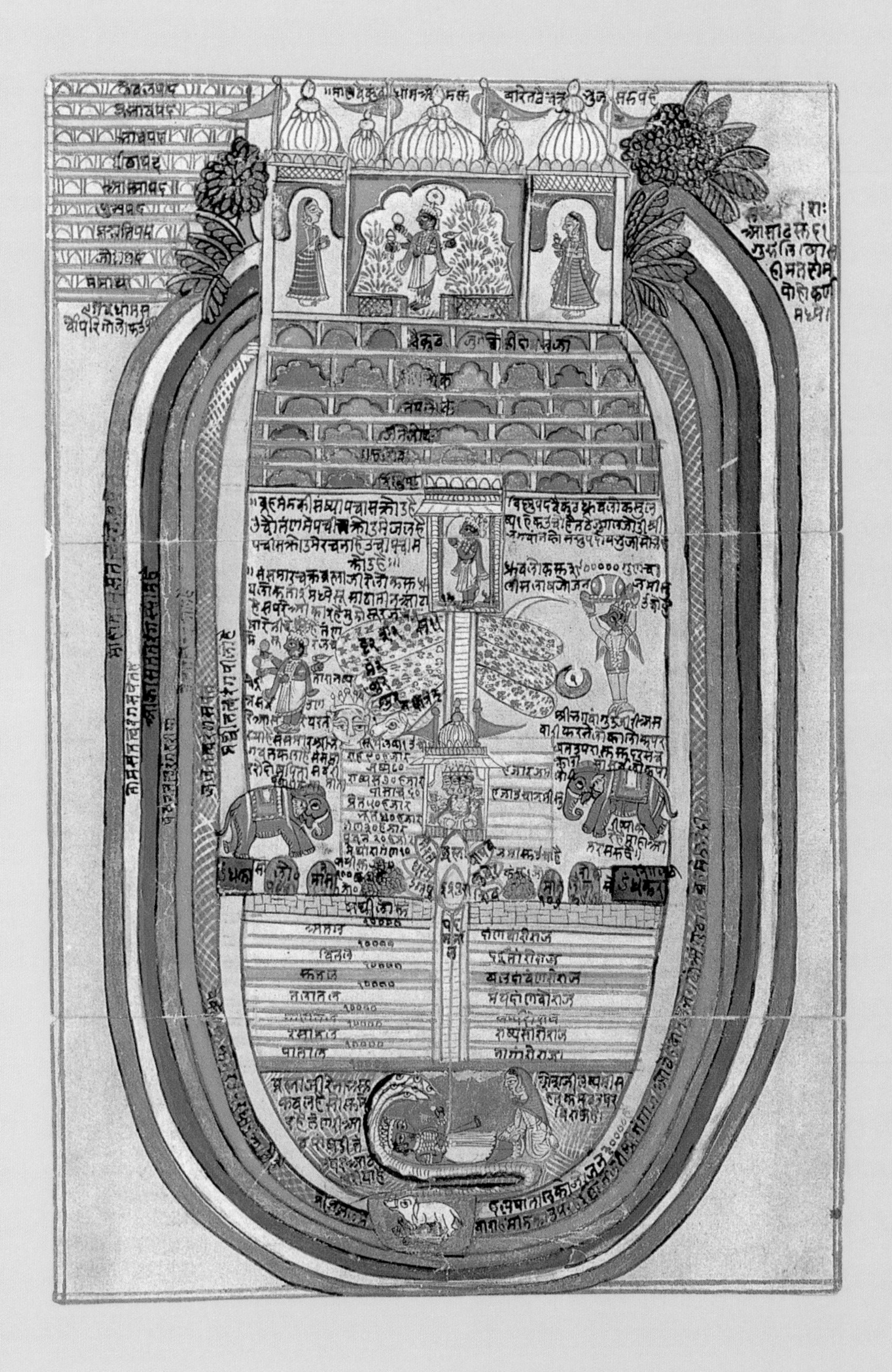

involves the sacrifice of Purusha, the cosmic person. The description of the sacrifice evokes the ritualistic atmosphere of the worship and the way in which the body of the victim is divided up is said to be the origin of the caste system. This is a translation of some of the verses of the Hymn to the Cosmic Person. It is part of the *Rig Veda,* the earliest book of the songs of the ancient seers which was composed by the Vedic Aryans who came into India from central Asia. They overran the already established Indus Valley civilization. The Vedic period spans approximately 2500 to 600 BC.

Indra was the most prominent god in the *Rig Veda.* He is identified with thunder and wields the *vajra* or thunderbolt, and his most significant deed is the slaying of the demon Vritra who holds captive the sun and the rain. This deed can be seen to represent either the conquest of India by Aryan warriors led by their champion, Indra; or as the cosmological allegory of the conquest of chaos and the release of the life forces of water, heat and light.

ABOVE *Impression of a Steatite seal from Mohenjo-Daro showing a humped Brahmani bull (Indus valley civilization c. 2500–2000* BC*). Seals like this one are the earliest art objects in India. Less than 2ins (4cms) high, the fine craftsmanship betrays a keen observation of animal form. Frequent portrayal of bulls on such seals suggest that they were religious symbols.*

RIGHT *Agni, the Vedic god of Fire; 11th-century bronze from Orissa.*

Agni is second only to Indra in the Vedic pantheon. He is the personification and deification of fire. His three forms are terrestial as fire, atmospheric as lightning, and celestial as the sun. He is a messenger between mortals and the gods and therefore particularly important as the sacrificial fire.

A thousand headed is the cosmic
person.
With a thousand eyes and feet,
Enveloping the earth on all sides,
And going ten fingers beyond.

When they divided the cosmic person,
Into how many parts did they divide
him?
What did they call his mouth? What
his arms?
What did they call his legs? What his
feet?
His mouth was the priestly class,

RIGHT *Putusa, the thousand-headed cosmic person, standing on Vishnu; 17th-century Nepali painting (gouache on cloth).*

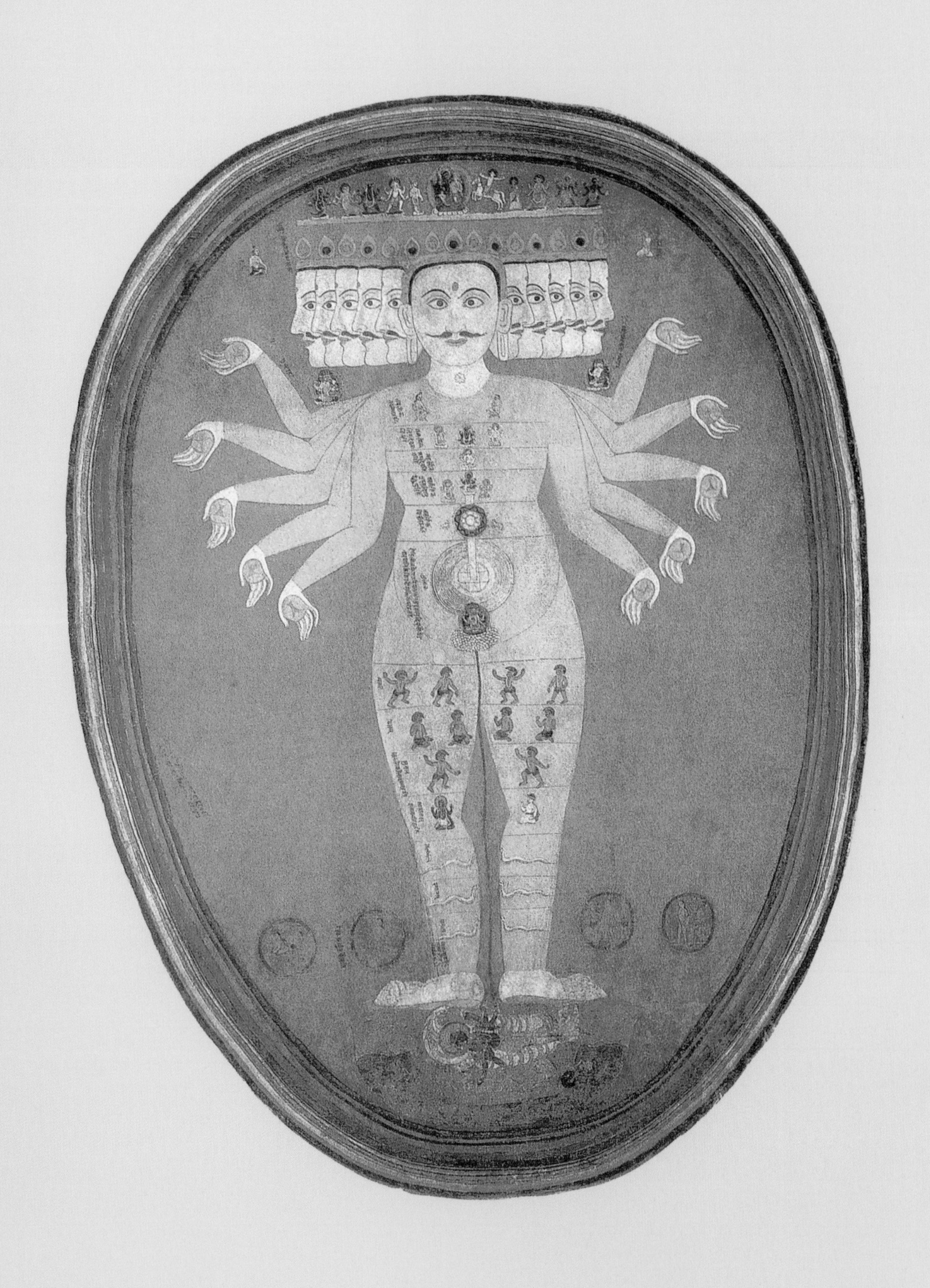

LEFT *The world in the form of a cosmic man; the middle world is at his navel. Below it are the levels of hell and above it the levels of the heavens; 17th century Jain painting.*

His arms the warrior-princes.
His legs were the producers,
His feet the servant class.

From his mind was born the moon,
From his eye was born the sun.
Indra and Agni came from his mouth,
And the wind was born of his breath

From his navel came the atmosphere,
The sky came from his head.
From his feet came earth, from his
ears the four regions.
Thus they formed the worlds.

(John M. Koller, *The Indian Way*)

MEASURING THE COSMOS

The legend which provides the key to Hindu cosmology and introduces us to the cyclical theory of time and to the theory of the transmigration of souls is the myth of the four Ages of Man.

The four Ages, or Yugas, are named after four throws of the dice. The Krita Yuga was the perfect age when there were no gods or demons, people were saintly and there was no disease. The Treta Yuga was when sacrifices began and virtue lessened a quarter. The Dwapara Yuga was a decadent age when virtue lessened one half and there came desire, disease and calamities. And the Kali Yuga is the degenerate age when only one quarter of virtue remains and people are wicked. The latter is, of course, the age that we live in.

The ancient mathematicians worked out that these four ages spread over 4,320,000 years, and that 1,000 of these periods equals one day of Brahma. At the end of each 'day' (*kalpa*), Brahma sleeps for a night of equal length, and before he falls asleep the universe is destroyed by fire and flood and becomes as it was in the beginning. He creates anew when he wakes the next morning. A year of Brahma is 360 *kalpas* and he endures for 100 years – and that is half of his existence. After another 100 years of chaos and disorder, a new Brahma will arise to create a new universe, and so the cycle will begin again.

This eternal cycle of creation and destruction is the backdrop to the eternal cycle of birth and death that those who believe in reincarnation

THE SPREAD OF BUDDHISM

The painting below is from a 19th-century Burmese book of illustrations of Buddhist heavens and hells. Buddhism has evolved according to national cultures to a bewildering extent: the Zen Buddhism of Japan, the Lamaistic Buddhism of Tibet, and Burmese and Sri Lankan Buddhism all have different emphases, Buddhist sects having quickly sprung up after the fifth century BC, basing their philosophies upon specific scriptures. Thus Zen Buddhism is based upon meditation in order to achieve 'sudden enlightenment', while Tibetan Buddhism, which arrived in the country and flourished in the 7th century AD, emphasizes the practices of the Tantra. Buddhism is divided into two main schools: the Theravada, or Hinayana, which predominates in Sri Lanka, Burma and Southeast Asia, and the Mahayana, found in China, Korea and Japan. A chief distinction is the Mahayana veneration of the Bodhisattva, a person who refuses to enter nirvana and escape the cycle of death and rebirth – even though he has earned the right – until all others have been similarly enlightened and saved.

LEFT *Painting of a scene from the epic poem the Ramayana.*

must endure. The atheistic Jains reject the doctrines of a divine creator. For them natural laws provide a more satisfactory explanation. They believe that the world is not created but is without beginning or end, existing under the compulsion of its own nature. Belief in a creator is considered an evil doctrine and makes no sense because '. . . If he were transcendant he would not create, for he would be free; nor if involved in transmigration, for then he would not be almighty.' (*Sources of Indian Tradition* ed. T. de Bary)

Although the great ascetic philosophy of Jainism rejected much of Hindu thought, the two beliefs shared one vision of the cosmos. The emphasis Jains laid on wisdom and teaching preserved and created many important learned texts on mathematics and other objects and also formed a body of popular literature in many different Indian languages. They have produced many beautiful maps of the cosmos, full of measurements and fine details.

Brahma, Shiva and Vishnu are the three most important of the Hindu gods. Brahma, the creator, is not worshipped as a personal god today and there is only one temple dedicated to him in the whole of India. His wife is Sarasvati, the goddess of learning and the patroness of arts, sciences and speech. Her earthly embodiment is the river Sarasvati, and as the river she presides over religious festivals

BELOW *Ephemeral clay figures of Sarasvati, the goddess of learning, wisdom, eloquence, music and the arts. She carries a Vina (a stringed instrument) and is mounted on a swan. During worship the clay figurines are carried in procession through the streets and then immersed in the Ganges or a nearby river or tank. Sarasvati is a popular deity in Bengal.*

LEFT *Stone icon of Harihari, or Shiva and Vishnu combined, (c. 1000* AD*).*

and gives fertility and wisdom to the earth. She may be portrayed holding the stringed instrument, the *vina*, a lotus bud, a book, a rosary, a drum or a stick of sugar cane.

Shiva is a very ancient god. He is still extremely popular today and is often worshipped in the form of a *lingam*, a stone phallus. He represents the underlying unity of existence in which all opposites are reconciled. He is creator and destroyer. As Lord of the Dance he dances out the awesome rhythms of creation and destruction, but as well as being a bringer of death, he conquers death and disease and is invoked to cure sickness. He is the great ascetic who has conquered desire, smeared with ashes and haunting the cremation grounds. But at the

RIGHT *Shiva the cosmic dancer; he dances the endless rhythms of creation and destruction. The significance of Shiva's dance becomes clearer if one remembers that a dance is at once a free expression of the will and an action directed by exterior laws – if you like, by the rhythm of the music of time. Thus Shiva is a god, but he is defined by larger ineffable patterns.*

same time he is erotic, the great lover and passionate husband.

To the philosopher these opposing qualities are a paradox, but to the worshipper they represent the richness of existence and the totality of the divine being. The ultimate reconciliation of the conflicts embodied by Shiva is brought about when half his body becomes female and half of him remains male. There are many stories about Shiva and his exploits. In this one he safeguards immortality:

LEFT *The Divine Couple, Shiva and Parvati, with their children at the burning-ground; behind them is Shiva's mount, the bull Nandi. Shiva's son, the elephant-headed Ganesh, helps him to make a necklace of skulls. Parvati holds the six-headed son Karttikeya; (18th-century).*

BELOW LEFT *Hindu temple sculpture of Shiva and Parvati as one, half male, half female figure.*

SHIVA'S BLUE THROAT

Following the advice of Vishnu, the gods and the demons were churning the celestial ocean of milk to obtain from it the nectar of immortality. For a churning rope they used the divine serpent Vasuki, and the great mountain Mandara was the churning rod. They churned furiously for 100 years. Among the first gifts of the celestial ocean were the beautiful goddess Lakshmi, who rose from a lotus flower floating on the rippling waves, and the divine cow Surabhi whose son Nandi, the snow-white bull, later became Shiva's companion and mount. The next gift was a crescent moon which Shiva snatched from the waves and placed on his forehead. Suddenly a terrible poisonous venom began gushing from the serpent's 1,000 mouths, threatening all existence. Moved by the request of the great Vishnu, Shiva swallowed the poison as if it were the nectar of immortality, thereby saving existence from extermination. The serpent's poison was harmless to the great Shiva but the venom stained his throat dark blue.

In painting Shiva is frequently portrayed with a blue throat and has acquired the epithet Nilakantha, or Blue Throat. A popular image of Shiva is that of Lord of the Dance, and he is frequently surrounded by a ring of sacred fire. This icon represents his five divine functions: creation, preservation, destruction, revelation (of the concealment of ignorance), and release (from rebirth).

But Shiva is most often worshipped as the *lingam*. The *lingam* is usually a cylinder of dark, shiny stone with a curved top set in a circular receptacle, or *yoni*, the symbol of female sexuality. Sometimes there are carvings of the five heads of Shiva on the *lingam*. It represents not only sexuality and the male creative force, but also chastity, as the seed is contained and controlled by yogic meditations. Mythology thrives on such paradoxes and there are many stories of the conflicts and

BELOW *Shiva Nataraja, Lord of the Dance (10th-century Chola bronze from Madras state, southern India); one of the most famous of all Hindu icons, still reproduced to this day. The legend associated with this image involves the subjugation of ten thousand heretical holymen. They sent a tiger against him but Shiva flayed it and took its skin as a cape. A poisonous snake attacked him and he just hung it round his neck as a garland. Next a black dwarf attacked him with a club, but Shiva put one foot on him and danced until the dwarf and the holymen acknowledged him as the supreme master. The drum he holds in his upper right hand beats out the rhythm of creation. The single flame in his upper left hand is the flame of destruction. His lower right hand is held in a gesture of benediction to his devotees. This is reaffirmed by his lower left hand which is drooping in imitation of an elephant's trunk and pointing towards his upraised left foot, a symbolic gesture promising release from* Samsara, *or rebirth, to his followers. His right foot crushes the demon of ignorance symbolized by the dwarf. The ring of sacred fire represents both the cosmos itself and also the final release from Samsara, by its association with the cremation ground.*

ABOVE *Stone Shiva icon in the form of a Lingam symbolizing divine power. The face carved on it represents the indwelling deity. A lingam occupies a sacred spot in all temples dedicated to Shiva (7th–8th century, Kashmir).*

struggles of Shiva as the erotic ascetic and of the problems of his unconventional married life. This tale tells of the rivalry between Shiva and Daksha, the father of his wife Sati. It is with reference to this story that the name Sati is given to the horrendous practice of throwing a widow on her husband's funeral pyre, imbuing what is an act of social and economic expediency with a ritual significance.

THE DEATH OF SATI

Daksha was holding a grand sacrifice to which all the gods were invited except Shiva. Sati was furious and decided to go since it was her own father's house. Shiva was pleased at

Ithyphallic figure of Shiva in his creative aspect; it is the double nature of Hindu gods that sometimes puzzles western observers (it is this confounding of opposites, this apparent lack of moral or metaphysical polarities, that destroys Mrs Moore in E. M. Forster's novel A Passage to India.

ABOVE *Shiva walking with the bull Nandi, followed by his consort Parvati; (c. 1730–40 painting from Mandi, north-west India).*

RIGHT *Stone icon of Shiva and Parvati.*

her loyalty and fervour but he warned her to be strong. 'Daksha will insult me and if you are unable to tolerate his insults, I fear you may come to harm,' he said. Sati arrived at the sacrifice and told her father, 'My lord is deep in meditation, I come alone.' Daksha laughed, seeing his chance to heap insults on his great rival. 'It is a disgrace for a god to wear filthy rags, to adorn himself with snakes and dance like a madman. I could never understand how a daughter of mine could wish for a creature like that for a husband.'

Sati, trembling with rage, denounced her father before the assembled gods. Since Shiva had instructed her not to take revenge she immolated herself on the sacrificial

RIGHT
The extremely popular elephant-headed god Ganesh, also known as 'The Remover of Obstacles'. His nature is gentle and affectionate and his image is found installed over the main entrance of many Indian homes to ward off evil. Symbolically, his round fat body contains the whole universe, his bended trunk can remove obstacles and his four arms represent the categories that the world can be divided into (that is the four castes). The sculpture is from Uttar Pradesh, c. 750 AD.

fire. Shiva's rage and torment at the loss of his beloved wife created a fearful demon who destroyed everyone who had been at the ceremony. Only when Vishnu interceded did Shiva relent and bring them all back to life. Daksha finally acknowledged that Shiva was a greater god than he, and as a sign of his foolishness he wore the head of a goat. Shiva fell into a profound meditation, waiting for the time when his beloved would be reincarnated as Parvati and be his wife again.

One of the children of Shiva and Parvati is Ganesh, the elephant-headed god. He is the general of Shiva's army, the patron of learning, the giver of good fortune and a popular deity today. At the beginning of books he is invoked by poets, his image is placed on the ground when a new house is built and he is honoured before a journey is begun or any business undertaken. This is the story of how he came to have an elephant's head:

THE ELEPHANT-HEADED GOD

Shiva had been away for years and Parvati was bored and lonely. She decided to make herself a baby to play with and fashioned a small roly-poly boy out of clay. One day when Parvati was bathing in a pool she asked her

RIGHT *The goddess Durga killing the buffalo demon Mahisha. In her eight arms she carries weapons lent to her by the gods; (13th-century stone sculpture from Orissa).*

son Ganesh to make sure no one disturbed her. Shiva arrived home at that moment and started to look for Parvati. The boy, not realizing who it was, stopped him from going near the pool. Furious at being opposed, Shiva immediately cut off the boy's head with his sword. Parvati's grief knew no bounds, she screamed and threw herself sobbing on the ground. To placate her, Shiva sent 1,000 goblins, demons and imps to look for the head of a male child. They searched all night but finding each baby animal asleep facing his mother they did not have the heart to cut off his head. Finally they found a baby elephant who was sleeping with his head turned away from his mother so his trunk didn't get entangled with his mother's and prevent them snuggling close together. Immediately Shiva's goblins removed his head and brought it to him. As he fitted the elephant's head onto his child's body he breathed life into it and waited for Parvati's reaction. To his surprise, she was delighted.

Shiva's bride is a perfect wife in the forms of Sati and Parvati, but like Shiva, she also has her horrible forms. As Durga she is the beautiful and ferocious warrior goddess, and as the hideous personification of death and destruction she is Kali, the black earth mother. As Kali, she is usually depicted naked save for a girdle of giant's heads suspended from her waist. She has long, flowing hair and a long necklace of giant's skulls around her neck. Like Shiva, she has a flaming third eye on her forehead. She is usually depicted with four arms: in one she holds a weapon, and in another the dripping head of a giant; two empty hands are raised to bless her worshippers. She is covered by a tiger skin and her long tongue protrudes, thirsty for blood. To her devotees, Kali is a divine and loving mother who reveals to them the reality of mortality. She not only destroys demons but also death itself. She appeals especially to those who find the mother–child relationship and symbol more satisfying as a revelation of the divine reality:

KALI'S DANCE OF DEATH

A wicked monster was ravaging the world. He seemed invincible because every drop of blood that he spilled came to life and became 1,000 more demons ready to battle. The gods summoned Kali and asked her to destroy the monster. Leaping into battle, the terrible goddess slayed 1,000 demons with her whirling sword. As she killed them she drank their blood,

RIGHT *Kali, the mother goddess in her horrible form; (9th-century stone icon from Orissa). She is holding a sword and wearing a garland of skulls.*

licking up the drops before they could touch the ground and produce more demons. Finally only the original monster was left and she consumed him in one gulp. Beginning her victory dance she became more and more frenzied and out of control, threatening all creation. Fearing that the universe would be destroyed, the gods came to her husband Shiva and begged him to intercede and stop her wild dance of destruction. But she paid no heed even to him, until in desperation he threw himself down before her. She began to dance on his body. Eventually, realizing what she was doing, she came out of her trance and stopped dancing. Thus the universe was saved from the ravages of the mad dance of Kali.

Vishnu is the most widely worshipped of the Hindu gods. He is all-

ABOVE *Vishnu in his 10th and future incarnation as the white horse Kalkin; (c. 1780 miniature from Bilaspur, Madhya Pradesh).*

LEFT *Vishnu worshipped in five manifestations; an illustration from the Hindu text* Vishnu Samabranahama. *(17th-century painting).*

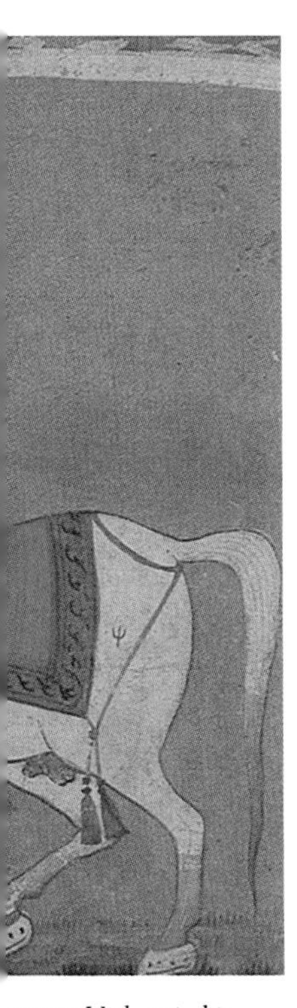

pervading, the preserver of the world, and his function is to ensure the triumph of good against evil. To this end he comes to earth on many occasions in different incarnations. The most famous are his lives as the epic heroes Krishna and Rama, but there are also the fish, the tortoise, the boar, the man-lion, the dwarf, Parashurama, Buddha and Kalkin.

These incarnations show how Hinduism has taken over and absorbed popular folk deities and the tales associated with them. Vishnu is often depicted with four arms. He holds in his hands the characteristic symbols of the wheel (the powers of creation and destruction), the conch shell (associated with the origin of existence through its spiral form, its sound, and its connection with water), and the club (authority or the power of knowledge), and his fourth hand has an upraised palm expressing reassurance.

Vishnu's consort in all his incarnations is Lakshmi, the popular goddess of wealth and good fortune. She is also known as the fickle one as she is a wanderer who never stays long with anyone. During the festival of Diwali in the late autumn, thousands of tiny lanterns are lit all over India, houses are cleaned and decorated until they too are sparkling, and fireworks are let off. All this is to please Lakshmi who is wandering from house to house looking for somewhere to spend the night and blessing with prosperity all those houses that are well lit.

In his incarnation as a fish, Matsya, Vishnu saved Manu from a great flood so that his descendants could people the world:

RIGHT *Vishnu in his Lion incarnation.*

FAR RIGHT *Vishnu in his Boar incarnation, lifting the earth-goddess Bhumi from the primeval ocean; (12th-century Chaunan-style stone icon from Punjab).*

VISHNU THE PRESERVER

While bathing in the river one day, Manu found a tiny fish. The fish begged him to rescue him from the other big fish who wanted to eat him. Manu scooped up the little fish and took him home in an earthenware pot. but Matsya, the fish, soon grew too big for the pot and Manu dug a pond for him to live in. When Matsya had grown too big for the pond he asked Manu to take him to the ocean and release him. As Manu tossed Matsya into the ocean, the fish turned and spoke to him. He warned Manu that in a year's time there would be a great flood, and told him to build a ship to save himself as the whole world would be submerged. Manu did as Matsya had told him and when the flood came he took refuge in his ship, praising Matsya for saving him. As the storms grew fierce and dangerous, Matsya appeared again. Now an enormous fish with golden scales and a horn, he attached the ship's cable to his horn and towed it along. Pulling the ship behind him, Matsya swam for many years until they reached mount Hemavat, the top of which was still above the water. Manu moored the ship to the mountain to await the end of the flood. Before he left, Matsya announced that he was really Vishnu the Preserver and had saved Manu from the flood in order that he might create new plants, animals and people for the world.

BELOW *Vishnu in his fish incarnation, Matsya.*

Krishna is the most beloved of all the Hindu gods. For his worshippers he embodies divine beauty, joy, and love. The playfulness of the divine child and the charming and tender love of the divine youth draw the devotees into the loving embrace of the supreme God. This is the story of the life of Krishna:

THE YOUNG KRISHNA

The gods wanted someone to destroy the evil king Kans of Mathura, so Vishnu resolved to be born as the eighth son of the king's sister Devaki. King Kans was warned of this scheme and he imprisoned Devaki and her husband Vasudev and killed each of their sons as they were born. But when Krishna was born Vishnu appeared to the couple and told them to exchange their baby son for the newborn daughter of a cowherd couple, Yasodha and Nanda, who lived in the village of Gokul across the river Yamuna. Vasudev found the doors of the prison miraculously open and set

ABOVE *Radha and Krishna in the Grove; (18th-century Pahari painting from the hill state of Kangra in Punjab). All nature rejoices in the couple's bliss and their embrace is echoed by the vine which encircles the tree in the foreground.*

off for Gokul with the child. He had to cross the river Yamuna in a terrible storm and feared for their safety. The baby Krishna touched the water with his foot and the waves parted, letting them through. Vasudev left the baby with Yasodha, who brought him up as her own son, and returned to jail with the baby girl who was no threat to King Kans. However, the king found out that Krishna had been saved and sent a demon nurse called Patoona to destroy him. The demon managed to deceive Yasodha and Nanda, but when she gave her breast to the baby Krishna he sucked and sucked until he had sucked all of Patoona's life away. As a child Krishna was playful and mischievous. Innocent and obedient in his mother's presence, he missed no opportunity for mischief when her back was turned. He untied the village calves and pulled their tails, mocked and laughed at his elders and teased

RIGHT *The young Krishna striking the cow with his cowherd's flask; his half-brother Balaram stands behind. The scene takes place beneath a Bo-tree; (10th-century stone relief carving).*

BELOW *Krishna subdues the snake demon by dancing on its head; (19th-century fragment of a temple painting from Madras).*

little babies until they cried, urinated in neighbours' houses and stole butter and sweets. But Yasodha and Nanda, who have no control over him, just laughed at his antics. When Krishna was about 12 he slew Kaliya, the five-headed serpent king who had been killing chickens, goats and cattle. He also destroyed the demon Trinavarta who was sent by King Kans disguised as a whirlwind. As a youth, Krishna enchanted and intoxicated the cowherd women with his flute playing. He teased them and made love to them. His favourite was the beautiful Radha, who took many risks to meet her dark lover:

How can I describe his relentless
flute,
which pulls virtuous women from
their homes
and drags them by their hair to
Krishna
as thirst and hunger pull the doe to
the snare?

Chaste ladies forget their lords,
wise men forget their wisdom,
and clinging vines shake loose from
their trees,
hearing that music.

(David R. Kinsley, *The Sword and the Flute*).

BELOW *Gopis (cowherds) begging Krishna to return their clothes. He has stolen them while the Gopis are bathing to tease them; (18th-century Kangra painting).*

Eventually, stories of Krishna's exploits reached King Kans and he resolved to try and kill him again.

THE WRESTLING CONTEST

The king announced a wrestling match and challenged the local young men to try and beat the court champions. His plan was to lure Krishna and his brother Balaram into the city and, pretending that it was an accident, release a wild elephant in their path. He felt sure that they would not survive such an encounter. Krishna and Balaram seized the chance to show off their prowess at wrestling and came to the city on the day of the festivities. When their turn came, they entered the ring to be faced by a wild elephant charging towards them

BELOW *A highly stylized 18th-century portrait of Radha from Kishangarh in Rajasthan. The painter Nihal Chand is thought to have derived this style from the poetry of his patron, Raja Savant Singh, describing his own beloved whose nose was 'curved and sharp like the thrusting saru cypress plant'.*

RIGHT *Rama with his bow; (16th-century bronze from Madras).*

trumpeting in fury. Without hesitating, Krishna leapt upon the elephant, and putting his mighty arms around its neck he squeezed until the creature fell beneath him dead. The crowd cheered and King Kans, more furious and frightened than ever, sent his fearsome champions into the ring. But they were no match for the brothers. Krishna soon broke the neck of the first, and Balaram squeezed the second in a great bear hug until his heart burst. Then Krishna leapt upon King Kans and flung him against the wall, killing him in front of the assembled crowds. He then freed his parents and his grandfather, who was the rightful king.

Many more exploits and marriages of Krishna are recounted in the epic poem, the *Mahabharata.* It is into his mouth that tradition puts the *Bhagavad Gita,* one of the most sacred books of modern Hinduism.

Rama is the hero of the other great epic, the *Ramayana,* and another incarnation of Vishnu, sent to earth to kill the demon Ravana. His wife, Sita, is considered to be the perfect wife and her behaviour is held up to young girls to emulate. Sita was abducted by

BELOW *A 20th-century depiction of Hanuman, the monkey god, causing mischief among people; note the flames he carries (top right). In the story related (right), Hanuman is protected by Agni, the god of fire.*

the demon Ravana and carried off to his Kingdom of Lanka and the distraught Rama went in search of her. In the forest he enlisted the help of the monkey god Hanuman. In this extract Hanuman uses his magic powers to reach Lanka and discovers Sita:

HANUMAN THE MONKEY GOD

Hanuman learned from Sampati, the brother of the king of the vultures, that Sita had been carried off to the distant island of Lanka, a hundred leagues over the southern ocean. Being the son of Vayu, the wind god, Hanuman resolved to use his powers to leap over the sea. He filled his lungs with sea wind and, with a mighty roar, rushed to the top of a mountain. Assuming a gigantic form, he leapt into the air and sped across the sea like an arrow. But his path through the air was impeded by demons. Surasa opened her enormous jaws to catch him, but he quickly shrunk to the size of a man's thumb and leapt in and out of her gaping mouth before she could close it. Next his shadow was grabbed by the she-dragon Sinhika who wanted to devour him. But he wounded and killed her and carried on to the island. Arriving at night he turned himself into a cat and crept stealthily around the sumptuous palace looking for Sita. Creeping up the jewelled stairways of gold and silver he came across the women's chamber. The perfumed forms asleep seemed like a wreath of lotus blooms awaiting the kiss of the morning sun. Outside, in a grove of Asoka trees, Hanuman saw the long-lost Sita. Guarded by fierce and ugly demons with the heads of dogs and pigs, she was without fear. Although Ravana came daily, threatening her with torture and death if she would not marry him, she rejected him. She would die before she was unfaithful to Rama.

LEFT *Hanuman, the monkey god, from a Vaishnavite shrine; (11th-century Tamilwork bronze from Sri Lanka).*

LEFT *The conception of the Buddha, Queen Maya's dream of the white elephant. Gandhara style sculpture c. 2nd century* AD.

Hanuman secretly approached the beautiful, sorrowing Sita and showed her Rama's ring that he was carrying. He offered to carry her away, but her modesty prevented her from touching the body of any man except her husband. Instead she gave him a jewel from her hair and begged him to tell Rama that she had only two months to live if he did not rescue her. Before he left, Hanuman decided to destroy as much of Ravana's kingdom as he could. Turning himself back into a giant monkey he started to uproot trees and devastate the countryside, but he was taken prisoner by Ravana's son, the mighty Indrajit, who shot him with a magic serpent arrow. As a gesture of defiance, Ravana set Hanuman's tail on fire and sent him back to Rama as an envoy. But Sita prayed that he would not burn and Agni, the god of fire, spared him. As he escaped from the kingdom of Lanka, Hanuman managed to accomplish great destruction by setting fire to many mansions with his flaming tail. When he returned, Rama was overjoyed that his beloved Sita had been found and immediately made preparations to go to her rescue.

SPIRIT OF THE BUDDHA

Buddhism originated in India but spread to the countries of south-east Asia where it has become a major religious and cultural force. Buddhist thought shares with Hinduism its cosmological vision of time, including the transmigration of souls. Gautama Buddha was born in northern India in the 6th century BC. But the story of his life has become a legend which illustrates the main precepts of Buddhist thought.

The spirit of the Buddha appeared to Queen Maya of Kapilavastu in a dream: an elephant floating on a rain-cloud, a symbol of fertility, circled around her three times and then entered her womb. Astrologers forecast that Queen Maya and King Suddhodana would have a son who would leave the palace to become a holy man. When the baby was born, a lotus sprang from the place where he first touched the ground. Fearing that Prince Siddhartha would leave as had been prophesied, the King surrounded him with luxury. At 16 he was married to the princess Yasodhara, and 12 years later their only child Rahula was born. At about this time Siddhartha's curiosity about the outside world was aroused and he ventured outside the palace grounds. Outside, he encountered for the first time old age, sick-

LEFT *Seated Buddha in Dharmachakra attitude; (c. 1st century AD Gandhara style sculpture from Yusufzai).*

RIGHT *Gautama Buddha 'The presentation of bowls'; (relief from Buner c. 2nd–3rd century AD Gandhara). A Buddhist monk's begging bowl is a concrete manifestation of his vow of poverty.*

ness and death and was awakened to suffering. He also met a wandering ascetic and resolved to leave his home and become a recluse. After six years of extreme asceticism he realized that he was no nearer enlightenment than he had been while living in luxury, and he resolved to follow a middle way to enlightenment, free from desire. While meditating, Siddhartha was tested by the demon Mara, first with fear and then with pleasure, but he was untouched. Eventually, he achieved insight into all his former existences. He became aware of how the terrible suffering that wastes human life is caused and how it can be eliminated, recognizing the four noble truths that became the basis of his teaching: that suffering exists; that it depends on certain conditions; that these conditions can be removed; and that the way to remove these conditions is to practise the eight-fold path – right views, right resolve, right speech, right conduct, right livelihood, right effort, right mindfulness, and right concentration. Forty-nine days later he set in motion the 'wheel of teaching' by preaching his first sermon in the deer park at Sarnath. His deep sense of compassion induced him to preach for the next 45 years.

The Jataka tales are a collection of 550 stories of the former lives of the Buddha. Some of these tales are peculiarly Buddhistic, but others are evidently part of the contemporary folk lore and have been incorporated into Buddhist mythology. They give us a vivid picture of the social life and customs of ancient India. Some of these tales are quite misogynistic; women are often viewed as the source of all treachery, as in this story about a demon – or *asura* – who used to come and listen to the preaching of the Boddhisattva. The story is a moral tale which warns against hankering after worldly pleasures, although an alternative interpretation might be that it is about the wiliness of women:

BELOW *The 'Sanci torso'; red sandstone torso of a Bodhisattva from Sanci (Gupta period, 5th–9th century).*

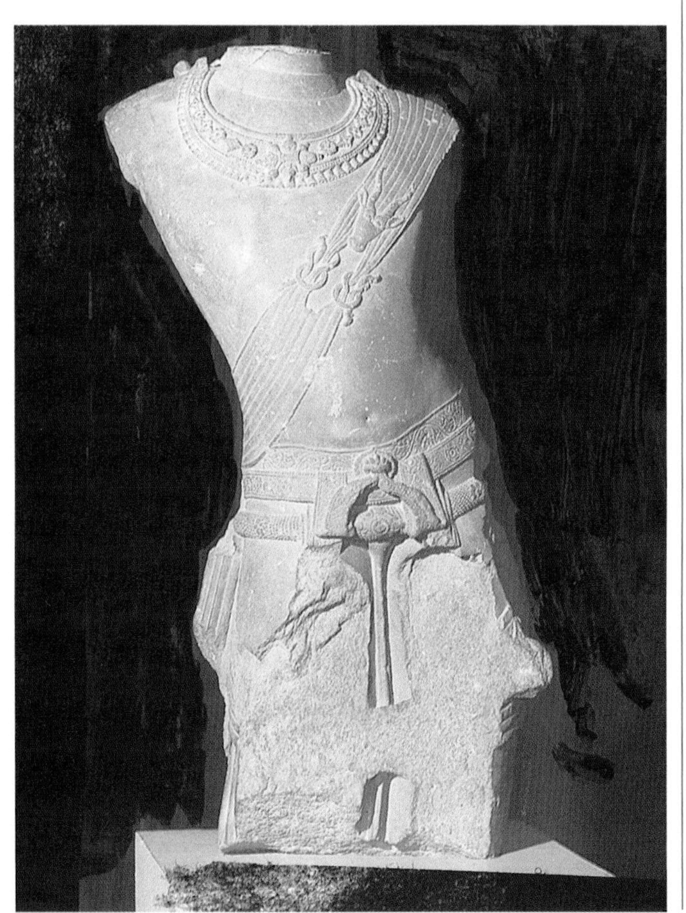

'WELCOME ALL THREE OF YOU'

The *asura* lived in the forest next to the highway. When he was not catching and devouring unwary travellers, the *asura* would go and listen to the teaching of the Boddhisattva. One day, he devoured the bodyguard of an exceedingly beautiful noblewoman of the area. She was so beautiful that he carried her off to his cave and took her for his wife. He brought her good things to eat, clarified butter, husked rice, fish, flesh and fresh fruit. He dressed her in rich robes and ornaments. And to keep her safe he put her in a box which he swallowed, thus guarding her in his belly.

One day, the *asura* went to the river to bathe. He threw up the box and let her out to enjoy herself in the open air while he bathed a little way off. While the *asura* was away she saw

BELOW *Stone relief representation of the great stupa at Amaravati (now destroyed) from its own casing; (Andhra Pradesh c. 150–200 AD). Buddhist stupas developed form burial mounds containing relics of the Buddha to vast representations of the cosmos and centres of Buddhist worship during the period of the Mauryan dynasty (c. 322–185 BC), when Buddhism was the imperial religion. The stupa was exported with Buddhism and in China evolved into the tiered tower pagoda.*

a magician flying through the air and beckoned him to her. When the magician came to her she put him into the box, covering him with her own body and wrapping her garments around him. The Asura returned and swallowed the box again, not thinking there was anyone but the woman inside it.

He decided to go and listen to the teaching of the Boddhisattva again, and as he approached, the holy man greeted him saying, 'welcome all three of you'. The *asura* was curious to know what this meant as he had come alone to visit the ascetic, and the ascetic told him that he was carrying inside his belly not only his wife but also a magician. Fearing that the magician might rip open his belly to make his escape, the *asura* threw up the box again and found his wife and the magician in the box, sporting merrily. The demon was so amazed at the Boddhisattva's vision – and so thankful that his life had been saved from the sword of the magician – that he let the woman go and praised the wisdom of the holy man:

O stern ascetic, thy clear vision saw
How low poor man, a woman's slave
  may sink;
As life itself tho' guarded in my maw,
The wretch did play the wanton, as I
  think.

LEFT *Stone relief illustrating the Vassantara Jataka tale; in this story of one of the Buddha's previous incarnations he was prince Vessantara, seen here giving his chariot to a Brahmin beggar.*

OVERLEAF LEFT *Stone relief depicting worshippers circumambulating a stupa; this ritual was performed by entering the east gate and walking clockwise, symbolically following the course of the sun and putting the worshipper in touch with the cosmos and the spiritual world.*

OVERLEAF RIGHT *Sections of a frieze showing the birth of the Buddha; in the centre is Queen Maya, clutching the tree above her. On the right of the picture are her aristocratic female attendants. Catching the sacred baby is the god Indra and next to him is Brahma; (Schist relief, Gandhara style, 2nd century* AD*).*

I tended her with care both day and
night,
As forest hermit cherishes a flame,
And yet she sinned, beyond all sense
of right:
To do with woman needs must end in
shame.

(Jataka: *Stories of Buddha's Former Births*, Ed. E. B. Cowell)

In other Jataka tales the Buddha is born as an animal. In one he is a monkey who lived alone on the river bank. It is comparable to an Aesop's fable where cleverness outwits force. In Indian tales it is often the crocodile or the tiger, the dangerous animals, who are depicted as fools.

THE FOUR VIRTUES

In the middle of the river was an island on which grew many fruit trees bearing mangoes, bread-fruit and other good things to eat. Each day the monkey would go to the island by jumping first onto a large rock that stuck out of the water, using it as a stepping stone to the island. He would eat his fill and then return home every evening by the same route. Now, there was a crocodile living in the river who was searching for food for his pregnant wife. He determined to catch the monkey by lying in wait for him on the rock. On his way home the monkey noticed that the rock was rather higher in the river than usual and called out 'Hi rock!' three times. There was silence, so the wise monkey called out, 'Why don't you speak to me today, friend?' The foolish crocodile, thinking that the monkey was really expecting the rock to answer shouted out, 'It's me, the crocodile, waiting to catch you and eat your heart'. The crafty monkey agreed to give himself up and told the crocodile to open his mouth to catch him when he jumped. As is well known, when crocodiles open their mouths their eyes close. So while the crocodile could not see him the monkey used him as his stepping stone, leaping onto his back and then onto the bank of the river and home. The crocodile realized how clever the monkey had been and said, 'Monkey, he that in this world possesses the four virtues overcomes his foes. And you, I think, possess all four'. (The four virtues are friendliness, compassion, joy and equanimity.) Tales like these provide endless subject matter for the sculptor and painter, particularly as no images of the Buddha were made at first and he was only symbolized by a wheel, his sandals, his stool or a Bodi-tree. The railings of the great Buddhist *stupas* at Barhut and Sanchi are teeming with the characters from these familiar tales, each one with a moral.

Muslims entered India as early as the year 711, by the same northwestern route as the ancient Aryan conquerors. In the 17th century the Mughal empire, famous for its glittering court, ruled almost all of the Indian subcontinent. Islam and Hinduism are two very different traditions and Islamic philosophy did not flourish as much on Indian soil as elsewhere. The literature of the Muslim community came more from Persian traditions. But the meeting of the two cultures did bear fruit. There were areas of common ground in discussion of monism and monotheism, in the traditions of saints, and especially in the mystic and devotional movements of both religions. Examples of a literature that is both Indian and Muslim are the medieval tales of romantic love. This 'Enchanting Story' is from the 18th-century poet Mir Hasan:

PRINCESS BADR I MUNIR

The beautiful young prince Benazir was captured by a fairy named Marhukh. She allowed him out on a

RIGHT *Lovers on a Terrace; 18th-century Mughal painting.*

magic carpet each evening on condition that if he lost his heart to another he would tell her. One night on his travels he came across a group of young women by a watercourse. In the centre of the group was the 15-year-old Princess Badr i Munir, clothed in fine and delicate fabrics and adorned with pearls and other priceless jewels. When their eyes met they were both smitten with love and fell down in a swoon. Their affair developed, assisted by Badr i Munir's closest friend Najm un Nisa, until the fairy discovered it. Furious at being deceived, she imprisoned Benazir at the bottom of a dried-up well in the middle of the desert, guarded by a jinn. When Benazir came no more to their rendezvous, Badr i Munir grew sick with love and sorrow and disappointment. She lost her appetite and wandered about distracted. Crying herself to sleep one night she dreamt of Benazir and saw his plight. Her friend Najm un Nisa decided to go in search of him. Dis-

BELOW *An Indian marriage; a painting of the Mughal school from Lucknow, 1775.*

LEFT *Eighteenth-century painting from Guler (Chandigarh Museum); in front of the pavilion where the prince and his wife lay is a pool with lotus flowers, while on the roof is a peacock, a symbol of the lover. A pair of love birds are in the trees in the foreground.*

guised as an ascetic and carrying a lute, she set off. The beauty of her playing attracted the attention of Firoz Shah, the handsome son of the king of the jinns. Her own beauty shone through her disguise and captured his heart, so he carried her off to his father's palace. She stayed at court for some time, playing the lute each evening, until the prince was hopelessly in love with her and begged her to marry him. Before she would agree to his proposal she explained her mission to him and asked for his help in finding Benazir. The king of the jinns sent fairies to discover his whereabouts and rebuked Mahrukh for forming such an attachment to a human. Finally Benazir was released from his prison and brought to the palace. Firoz Shah had a magic, flying throne, and on it he carried Najm un Nisa and Benazir back to the garden of Badr i Munir. Their reunion was sweet. Their bodies weak from the sorrow of separation and their eyes red from weeping, they talked long into the night and slept late into the morning. The following day all four of them took all the necessary steps to ensure that they might be married. The weddings were celebrated with great

LEFT *Garland seller in Old Delhi; the number of festivals in India is so great that he is kept busy throughout the year. On the tenth day of the rising moon between September and October falls the most popular of Indian festivals – Dussehra – a celebration of a great victory by Rama over the Demon King Ravana. An estimated crowd of five million gathered at Uttar Pradesh for the Hindu festival of Kumbh-Mela in 1966, possibly the greatest number of human beings ever assembled with a common purpose.*

LEFT *18th-century stone sculpture of the Buddha's first sermon.*

pomp and ceremony, thus fulfilling the heart's desire of all four lovers.

Almost every day of the year somewhere in India a festival is held. At the most popular festivals thousands of people gather to listen to stories of their favourite heroes and gods. At the *Rama-lila,* held in Delhi in the autumn, there are theatrical performances of the great battle between Rama and Ravana, the demon king of Lanka, who kidnapped Rama's wife Sita. The performance ends with the immolation of a vast paper effigy of Ravana.

Most of the dates of the calender are marked by an event that celebrates the myths and traditions of the culture. In the villages of Maharashtra, in western India, when the new harvest of rice is gathered in, the villagers dance around a heap of grains with an image of a deity on top. They play a ritualistic riddle game, one half of the dancers asking the questions and the other half responding. In this way they build up a familiar story, usually out of one of the great epics. Although Indian mythology has very ancient roots, it punctuates the rhythms of everyday life and is very much alive today.

BELOW *A princess and her ladies celebrating Diwali, the festival of lights, in a palace garden, with yogis and yoginis; (a painting of the Mughal school by Hunhar, c. 1760).*

Japanese Mythology

In January 1989, Emperor Hirohito of Japan died. The enthronement ceremony of the new emperor, Akihito, was done according to Shinto tradition, for the emperor has always been the head of Japan's national religion. But opposition parties in the Japanese democracy strongly criticized the idea of employing Shinto rituals in the ceremonies concerning the funeral and the enthronement. State Shintoism is a relatively new phenomenon, started about one-and-a-half centuries ago in order to unify Japan after the long period of feudalism. It took only a few decades for this artificial state Shintoism to get out of control, and the Emperor's position as a human-god was abused, mostly by the army, to justify the invasion of neighbouring countries. It is from Shinto that the authentic Japanese mythology comes, particularly from the Kojiki, *the 'Record of Ancient Things' (completed in the eighth century* AD*), which became a kind of statement of Shinto orthodoxy.*

Paper screen by Ogata Korin (1658–1716) decorated with pink and white plum blossoms.

Traditional Shinto, as opposed to state Shintoism, has its origin about 2,000 years ago. Shinto is Japan's primal religion and is integrated into Japan's culture. Around the 3rd century BC, a Japan consisting of a single race and a single language emerged after a long period of racial and cultural diversity (though the political unification of Japan was not completed by the imperial family until the 6th century AD). Japan's birth as a nation coincided with the start of rice growing – Japan's main industry until quite recently – and Shinto consisted of rituals to pray for a good harvest, keeping the community unified through those rituals. The fact that people were primarily considered as members of the community rather than as individuals explains Shinto's survival despite of the powerful influence of Buddhism: more than 70% of the Japanese were engaged in agriculture up to the end of the Second World War.

An agricultural life is hard work, and requires activity to be coordinated with the changing seasons. This inte-

ABOVE AND BELOW *Sections of a long scroll painting in black ink, 'Landscape for Four Seasons' by Sesshu, 1486.*

LEFT *Float decorated in the time-honoured tradition for the annual Gion festival in Kyoto.*

ABOVE *Head of Haniwa, a grave figurine, from the 6th century* AD.

LEFT *Izumo shrine, Shimane prefecture, the oldest Shinto shrine in Japan; the Shinto gods are supposed to assemble here in October each year, thus October is termed the 'godless month' elsewhere.*

gration of people's beliefs with their working lives still exists in Japanese companies today – it is a common practice to build small Shinto shrines on top of the office buildings – but modern industrial work lacks the sensitivity to nature required for rice growing. Nature and the changing seasons were not seen as romantic or beautiful, but life was lived according to the dictates of the seasons. So not surprisingly, the concepts of virtue in Shintoism are reflected in the success, or failure, of farming. The notions of purity, or clarity, and uncleanliness, or filth, are the most fundamental concepts in Shintoism; the word *kegare* is Japanese for uncleanliness, and stems from *ke* meaning a mythical power to make things grow, and *gare* meaning lacking. Together, *kegare* therefore means a lack of power to make things grow (and particularly rice), and uncleanliness is thus associated with failure to thrive.

The main record of Shinto myth and historical legend is the *Kojiki*, the Record of Ancient Things, completed in 712 AD. Divided into three books, the first covering life with the gods, the second life with Man and the gods, and the third, Man's life without the gods. It also covers the origins of the imperial clan and the leading families. The *Kojiki* has until recently been regarded as sacred. Many of its stories involve these key concepts of purity and uncleanliness.

RIGHT *Rengyoin temple was founded in 1164 and rebuilt in 1266 after a fire. It contains 1001 small figurines of Kwannon, known in China as Guanyin, the Goddess of Mercy.*

RIGHT *The warm climate of the island of Hinoshina, near Hiroshima, is particularly suited to agriculture. As in China – but even more so, under the threat of earthquake as a more common natural catastrophe – myth has much to do with controlling nature and ensuring a good harvest.*

The most popular hero in the *Kojiki* is Yamato-takeru. His story is found in Book Two, which deals with Man as he is about to depart from the world of the gods, and has the melancholic tone that characterizes so many Japanese epics:

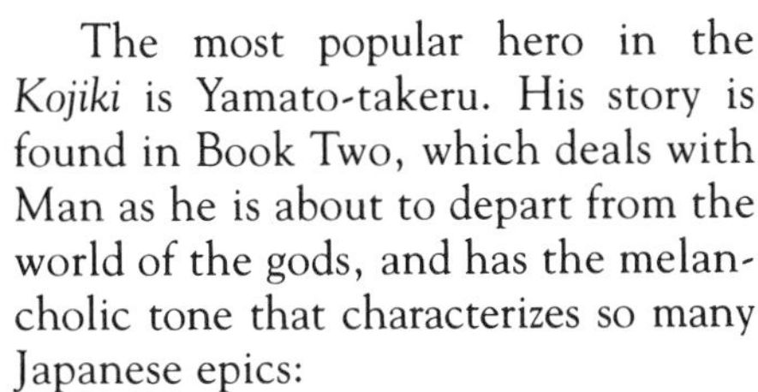

FRATRICIDE WITHOUT REMORSE

Among the many children of Emperor Keiko were the brothers Opo-usu and Wo-usu, the second of whom was later named Yamato-takeru. One day the emperor sent Opo-usu to summon two maidens who were renowned for their beauty. But instead of summoning them, Opo-usu made them his wives and sent others in their stead. When the emperor learned of his son's betrayal, he ordered Wo-usu to persuade his elder brother to come to dine with his father. Five days passed, but Opo-usu still did not come. When the emperor asked Wo-usu why his brother had not come, Wo-usu explained 'I captured him, grasped him, and crushed him, then pulled off his limbs, and wrapping them in a straw mat, I threw them away'.

This example of brute strength without any regard to morality explains why Yamato-takeru is seen as an embodiment of natural force, beyond the understanding of a mortal being. Nature brings about harvest, and at

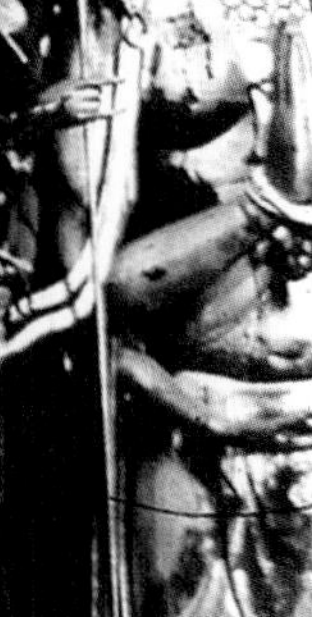

BELOW *Workers in the Yamaha factory in Hamamatsu are required to take part in daily exercises, fostering the sense of being part of a community.*

BELOW *A guardian figure at Horyuji temple at Nara, the oldest preserved temple complex in Japan and a fine example of the architecture of the Asuka period (552–645 AD).*

the same time can be utterly destructive. It is to be admired and feared.

Throughout, the style of the *Kojiki* is realistic, and often cruelly bloody. This violence is in evidence throughout the adventures of Yamato-takeru as he is sent by his father the emperor to quell both real political enemies, and also 'unruly' deities. Japan's natural sport, Sumo, is characterized by its display of sheer power. Wrestlers are often very quiet people and are expected to live simply. We can see in Sumo the same sort of admiration as that shown for the boy-hero Yamato-takeru. There are many elements of Shinto ritual in Sumo. Wrestlers throw salt before each bout to purify the ring. They use water put beside the ring to clean their mouths, symbolizing the purification of the bodies. The ring is made of packed soil inside which there are various things dedicated to gods.

CLEANSING BY FIRE

Yamato-takeru next embarked on a long journey as the emperor dispatched him to destroy rebel forces.

LEFT *A bout of sumo wrestling, which may last for a few seconds only, ends when one of the contestants touches the ground with any part of his body other than his feet. The reverence felt for the explosive power of the Sumo wrestler can be linked to the admiration of the mythical figure Yamato-takeru, master of gods and men.*

First he was sent to the west to kill two mighty brothers; when he arrived at their house he found it surrounded by rows of warriors. Yamato-takeru was so young (perhaps 15 or 16) that he could disguise himself as a young girl by combing his hair down and dressing in women's clothes. He went into the house while the feast was taking place. The brothers were very pleased to see this 'girl' and had her sit between them. Then, when the feast was at its height, Yamato-takeru seized one of the brothers by the collar and stabbed him clear through the chest. The younger brother ran, but Yamato-takeru seized him and stabbed him too.

On his return home, Yamato-takeru subdued and pacified all the mountain, river and sea deities, but it was not long before the emperor commanded

LEFT *Splashed-ink landscape by Sesshu, given by the artist to his pupil. The accompanying text explains how he went to China to learn this particular technique. The influence of China upon Japanese art and Japanese mythology is widespread.*

ABOVE *Print by Utamaro (1754–1806) of young women visiting the seashore at Ise; at New Year the sun rises between the twin rocks, joined by a straw rope that marks the boundary of the territory of the gods.*

Yamato-takeru to deal with more unrest in the east. Yamato-takeru went to his aunt Yamato-pime, complaining that he was being sent out again too soon, and without adequate protection. On his departure, Yamato-pime gave him a sword, and a bag, and said 'Should there be an emergency, open this bag'.

Yamato-takeru, after conquering his father's enemies, met a man in the land of Sagamu who deceived him, saying that an unruly deity resided in the middle of the plain. When Yamato-takeru entered the plain, the man set fire to the area, but Yamato-takeru escaped using his aunt's bag and sword. He mowed the grass with his sword, then lit a counter-fire with a flint which he found in his aunt's bag. Then he killed the man and all his clan, burning the bodies.

One of the imperial treasures that Japan's new emperor Akihito inherited from the late Hirohito is a sword. A sword is one of the symbols of the figurehead of Shintoism, because it symbolizes lightning: thunder is re-

RIGHT *The traditional dance theatre, Kabuku, which is played by men only, has been popular since the 17th century.*

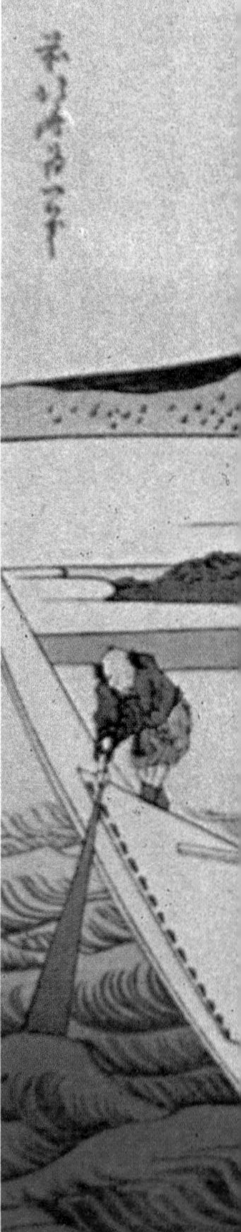

BELOW *Woodcut print by Hokusai of Tago-no-ura, in the series 'Thirty-six Views of Mount Fuji'.*

garded as promoting good harvest. The amount of thunder, and consequently rain, has most to do with the growth of rice. The idea of the gift of fire is so widespread that it would seem to be practically a part of racial memory: consider the Prometheus myth.

DEATH OF YAMATO-TAKERU

As Yamato-takeru crossed the sea, the deity of the crossing stirred up the waves, and the boat began to drift helplessly. His wife, Oto-tatibanpime, offered to sacrifice herself to the sea god in his place, and stepped out onto layers of sedge-mats, skins and silk carpet spread out on the waves. As she went down onto them, she sang:

O you, my lord, alas –
You who once, standing among the
flames
Of the burning fire, spoke my name
On the mountain-surrounded
Plain of Sagamu!

Seven days later, her comb was washed ashore. Taking this comb, they made

OVERLEAF Waves at Matsushima *by Tawaraya Sotatsu (1575–1643); ink, colour and gold on paper, Edo period.*

her tomb and place her within.

Yamato-takeru then experienced the first of the incidents that lead to his downfall. On his way back to the capital, when he was eating his rations at the foot of the pass of Asi-gara, the deity of the pass, assuming the form of a white deer, came and stood next to him. Yamato-takeru struck the deer with the leftovers from his meal, hitting the deer's eye and killing him. Then he climbed up the pass and, grieving, sighed three times: 'My wife, alas!'.

He is defeated by the deity of Mount Ibuki who causes a violent hail storm which dazes Yamato-takeru. His mind recovers a little as he rests at a spring, but because of his extreme fatigue he walks along slowly, using a staff. He proceeds across the plain of Tagi to the plain of Nobo, where he sings this song recalling his homeland:

From the direction
Of my beloved home
The clouds are rising
Next to the maiden's
Sleeping place
I left
The sabre, the sword –
Alas, that sword!

He dies. When his family come down to the plain of Nobo to construct his tomb, they also sing:

The vines of the Tokoro
Climb around
Among the rice stems,
The rice stems in the rice paddies
Bordering the tomb.

The *Kojiki* has many beautiful songs such as these which anticipate *waka*, or *haiku*, Japanese poetical forms. They are symbolic rather than descriptive, their simplicity attempting to capture emotion or instantaneous thought without using words of emotion. The above song is meant to capture the desolate feeling of people who have lost the man they loved.

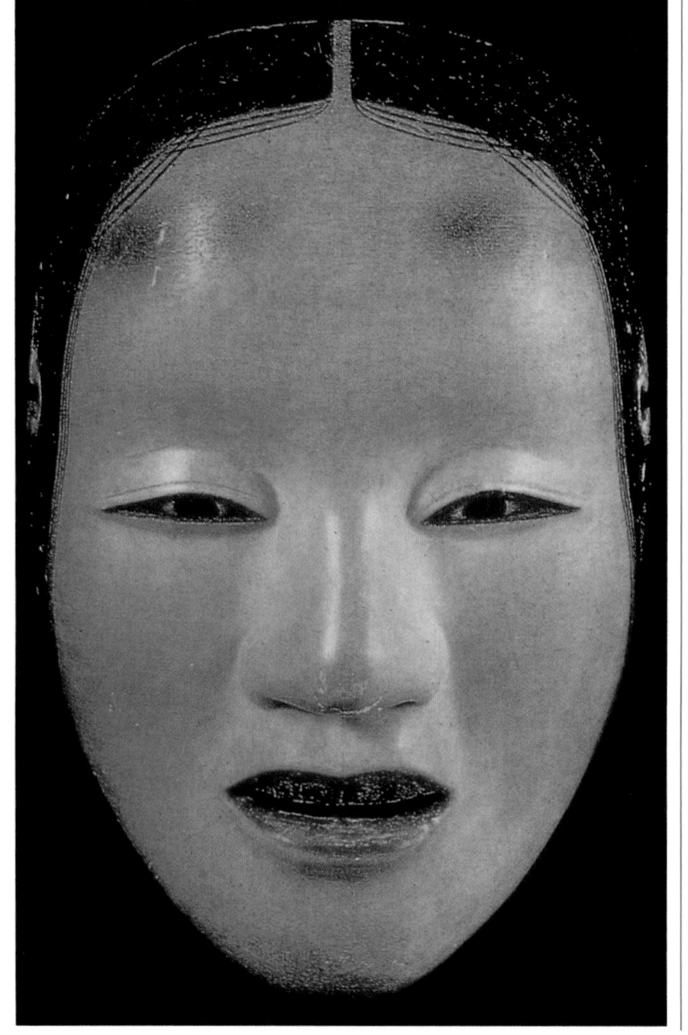

BELOW *Noh mask worn by an actor playing a middle-aged woman in the 15th-century drama* Fukei *by Tokuwaka.*

ABOVE *The puppets ir Bunraku theatre are manipulated by three people, clearly visible behind a narrow stag*

EXCLUDED FROM THE DIVINE

Transformed into a giant white bird, Yamato-takeru flew away toward the beach followed by his family:

Moving with difficulty, up to our waists
In the field of low bamboo stalks,
We cannot go through the skies
but, alas, must go by foot.

As they waded into the sea, they sang:

Going by sea, waist-deep in the water
We move forward with difficulty
Like plants growing
By a large river
We drift aimlessly
In the ocean currents.

Again, when the bird had flown to the rocky shores, they sang:

> The plover of the beach
> Does not go by the beaches
> But follows along the rocky shores

These concluding songs to the story of Yamato-takeru express the destiny of earth-bound man. The exclusion of Man from the realm of the divine, and his struggle to return, is common to many mythologies from around the world. Some authorities believe that in this tale the flight of the bird is connected to the tradition of mourners dressing as birds to sing and dance at funerals. It is either an attempt to call back the soul that has flown away, or to assist the soul in its ascent to the higher regions.

Whereas the story of Yamato-takeru deals with the story of Man, Book One of the *Kojiki* concerns itself with the creation. The cosmology of the *Kojiki* is a step-by-step evolution of the universe. There is no creation from absolute nothing by an absolute being, and the creation of the islands of Japan is described thus:

THE BIRTH OF JAPAN

Two gods, Izanagi and Izanami, were given the command to create the islands, which they did by standing on the heavenly Floating Bridge and, lowering the heavenly Jewelled Spear, stirring with it. They stirred the brine

LEFT *The Jidai festival in Kyoto includes a 2½-mile-long procession of groups dressed in costumes representing styles from the late 8th to 19th centuries, celebrating Kyoto's time as the capital.*

ABOVE *When praying at a Buddhist temple, the devout also light incense.*

with a churning sound: and when they lifted up the spear again, the brine dripping down from the tip of the spear piled up and became an island. Descending from the heavens, Izanagi and Izanami married on this island and erected a heavenly pillar and a spacious palace.

Discovering that their bodies were differently formed, Izanagi asked his spouse Izanami if she was agreeable to giving birth to the land. When she agreed, he suggested, 'Then let us, you and me, walk in a circle around this heavenly pillar and meet and join'. After several failures, they started to bear children, which are the islands of Japan.

BELOW *Noh drama began in the Heian period (8th–12th centuries), was highly developed by the 14th century, and is still very popular today.*

There have been various interpretations of this ritual of circling around the heavenly pillar. Scholars of the late Edo period (from the 18th century to the early 19th century) regarded the pillar simply as the symbol of the phallus. It clearly has links with the European maypole, which is believed to capture the vital powers latent in a tree, and also with the ancient Japanese belief that processions round tall trees are needed to summon down the deities who live in the heavens or on high mountains.

Until the scholar Motoori Norinaga discovered the importance of the *Kojiki* in the 18th century, it was regarded as far inferior to its contemporary, the *Nihon-shoki,* a history book completed in 720AD, eight years after the presentation of the *Kojiki.* The *Nihon-shoki* is in many ways more accessible than the *Kojiki* as it presents its material in a more detached way. The *Kojiki,* on the other hand, invites the readers to have strong sympathy with the myths, and does not seem to care much about the coherence and logic of the stories it includes. Norinaga, however, thought that the very simplicity and incoherence of the *Kojiki* is what its compilers intended, aiming to recreate the religious sense of ancient Japanese through a careful organization of prose and poetry. It is important to read the myths with imagination and faith, rather than looking for rational explanations to the stories.

When the *Kojiki* was written, the influence of China was starting to be apparent everywhere. The legal system, the arts and literature were strongly affected. As the influence of Buddhism spread from China and Asia in the 6th century and became the dominant belief among the aristocracy, the *Kojiki* was important in recording Japanese life before foreign influences took too great a hold. The book portrayed an image of life filled with a strong sense of the unity of Man with nature and god, and the unity between people through simple rituals. It also aimed to bring about clear self-consciousness through having a lucid image of the past to overcome the crisis of national identity, in some ways a crisis similar to the one Japan is facing now.

In the book, purity (or growth power) is exemplified by the story of Yamato-takeru. The opposite concept of *kaegare* (or pollution) is illustrated by the story of Izanami's death:

THE HEARTH OF YOMI

After giving birth to numerous islands and other features of nature

BELOW *Yakushi-nyorai (Lord of the Eastern Paradise) shown here flanked by two attendants in the Yakushiji temple in Nara. The gilt statues were blackened in a fire in 1528.*

ABOVE RIGHT *Sacred dance hall of Kasuge shrine, Nara; here the ritual Kagura dances are performed in honour of Amaterasu.*

– waterfalls, mountains, trees, herbs and the wind – Izanami died of a terrible fever. Izanagi followed her to Yomi, the land of the dead but was too late: she had already eaten at the hearth of Yomi. She asked Izanagi to wait for her patiently as she discussed with the gods whether she could return, but he could not. He threw down the comb he was wearing and set light to it, and then he entered the hall. What he saw was dreadful:

'Maggots were squirming and roaring in Izanami's corpse. In her head was Great-Thunder; in her breast was Fire-Thunder; in her belly was Black-Thunder; in her genitals was Crack-Thunder; in her right hand was Earth-Thunder; in her left foot was Sounding–Thunder; in her right foot was Reclining-Thunder. Altogether there were eight thunder deities.'

As can be seen from the above description of the land of the dead, ancient Japanese ideas about death and the afterlife contained no thought of a final judgement. The land of the dead, Yomi, is the land of filth and uncleanliness rather than that of horror or punishment. By eating from the hearth of Yomi, Izanami can no longer return to the land of the living. Norinaga considered that this was because food cooked with the fire of Yomi became impure. A simpler interpretation is that Izanami, having eaten the food of Yomi, had become a person of Yomi. The idea that one cannot return home after having eaten the food of the afterlife – or even of a foreign land – is a common one throughout the world. In the final passage of the relationship between Izanami and Izanagi, the concept of mortality for mankind is introduced. The use of peaches as a weapon is a sign of Chinese influence on the *Kojiki*. In China, peaches and peach trees have from antiquity been used to dispel demons and evil spirits. The peach is also often used as a symbol of longevity (see page 171).

DEATH COMES TO THE WORLD

Izanagi was frightened by the sight of Izanami, and he turned and fled. Shamed by his actions, Izanami sends the hags of Yomi to pursue him, but he evades them using magic tricks. When Izanagi arrived at the border between the land of the living and Yomi, he attacked his pursuers with three peaches he had found nearby. They all turned and fled. Then Izanagi said to the peaches: 'Just as you have

saved me, when any of the race of mortal men fall into painful straits and suffer in anguish, then do you save them also.'

Finally, Izanami herself came in pursuit of Izanagi. He pulled a huge boulder across the pass from Yomi to the land of the living, and Izanagi and Izanami stood facing each other on either side of the boulder. Izanami then said: 'O my beloved husband, if you do thus, I will each day strangle to death 1,000 of the populace of your country.' To this Izanagi replied: 'O my beloved spouse, if you do this, I will each day build 1,500 parturition huts' meaning that this number of people would be born.

Thus the marriage of Izanami and Izanagi brings the natural world into existence, and their separation, or 'divorce', is the beginning of mortality.

On his return to the land of the living, Izanagi rids himself of the sullying effects of his descent into the underworld by undergoing purification.

'He arrived at the plain by the river-mouth, where he took off his clothes and the articles worn on his body. As each item was flung on to the ground, a deity came into existence. And as Izanagi entered the water to wash himself, yet more gods were created.'

Izanagi's act of cleansing (*misogi*) shows how vital force can be recovered by purification. In the same way that rice growing follows a cycle in which both the land the the people become exhausted, and are then revitalized by water or a period of rest, so Izanagi regains his strength and vitality by taking off his heavy garments and immersing himself in the waters. Water is a potent symbol in many scenes of everyday life in Japan today. For example, as soon as you take a seat in a *sushi* restaurant in Tokyo, the table will be wiped with a white cloth soaked in water. This has little to do with hygiene, rather it is an act of purification before rice is eaten.

LEFT *Large hanging scroll painting of a waterfall by Maruyama Okyo (1733–1795), said to have been commissioned by an abbott who felt bereft without an actual waterfall to contemplate.*

LEFT *In order to make a wish come true the Japanese buy good luck Daruma dolls and paint in one of the eyes. If their wish is granted, they paint in the other as a sign of gratitude.*

RIGHT *To the untutored eye, it is very difficult to differentiate between Japanese and Chinese painting: these are in fact three of a set of eight album leaves attributed to the Chinese artist Gong Xian (fl. 1656–82), ink and slight colour on paper. Compare this to the Japanese paintings on pages 226 and 233. The long and complex relationship between the two countries has been both tragic and fruitful.*

Nothing evokes the feeling of clarity more for Japanese than seeing a fall of water against a mountain setting, preferably with a small shrine at the base of the waterfall.

Finally, when Izanagi washes his eyes, he brings into being three of the most important gods in the Japanese pantheon – the sun goddess, the moon god and Susano, the storm god. The brother/sister pair of Amaterasu, the sun goddess, and Tukiyomi, the moon god, are respectively responsible for day and night. Of the many stories recounted of Amaterasu, the tale of her withdrawal of labour, is very well known. Amaterasu and Susano had fallen out after Susano played a trick on the sun goddess which resulted in the destruction of her rice fields. Amaterasu retaliated by withdrawing into a cave, thus casting the world into darkness. There she stayed until a goddess, egged on by other deities, performed a riotous dance outside the cave. Unable to contain her curiosity, Amaterasu emerged and caught sight of her reflection in a mirror that the gods had suspended from a tree. Since then the world has experienced the normal cycle of day and night.

Amaterasu is supposed to be the direct ancestor of the Japanese imperial family; a mirror forms part of

BELOW *Shigisan scroll from the Kamakura period (12th–13th centuries) depicting scenes from the lives of ordinary people; agriculture, represented by the bullock, is never far away.*

the imperial regalia. The obedience that was owed to the emperor finds an echo in the veneration of the sun goddess. Amaterasu occupies a key position among the huge number of Shinto gods (by some counts, more than eight million) of which the mythological creatures known as *tengu* are amongst the most ancient.

PART HUMAN, PART BIRD

Tengu are believed to inhabit trees in mountainous areas, particularly pines and cryptomerias. Part human and part bird, they are sometimes shown wearing cloaks of feathers or leaves, and often sport a small, black hat. *Tengu* love to play tricks, although this stems more from a sense of mischief than evil. Often, however, they fail to appreciate it when the joke is on them! A boy taunted a *tengu* by claiming he was able to see into heaven by using a hollow piece of bamboo as a telescope. The *tengu,* overcome with curiosity, agreed to swap his cloak of invisibility for the stick of bamboo. When he found he had been deceived, the *tengu* took his revenge by causing the boy to fall into an icy river.

Oni are supposed to have come to Japan from China along with the Buddhist faith. They are horned devils, often of giant size, with three fingers and toes. Sometimes they also have three eyes. Whereas tengu are playful, *oni* are usually cruel, generally not very bright and often lecherous, as the following stories show:

ONI AND *KAPPAS*

Momotaro, revered for his nobility of spirit and accomplishments in battle, was born into a peach. A childless couple found the peach floating in a mountain stream, and on cutting it open, revealed a tiny baby boy. They named him Momotaro, which means 'peach child' and brought him up as their own son. When he was 15, Momotaro decided to repay his adopted parents and their neighbours for their generosity. A number of *oni* inhabited an island nearby and were making raids on the mainland to steal treasure and terrorize the population. Taking three rice cakes from his mother, Momotaro set off on his mission. On his way he met a dog, a

ABOVE Dotaku, *a mysterious bronze object, probably though not certainly a bell, now held by the Kobe City Museum. Its ritual significance or purpose can only be guessed at.*

pheasant and a monkey who each agreed to accompany him in return for a rice cake. The band of four took a boat to the island of the *oni,* where they found a number of girls being held captive after being kidnapped and raped. With the help of his companions, Momotaro launched an attack on the *oni* stronghold, and killed all the supernatural beings. The boat was then piled high with the stolen treasure and the prisoners released. Momotaro returned home in triumph, and was able to ensure that his parents lived out their lives in comfort.

Another diminutive hero is Issun Boshi, whose name means 'Little One Inch':

After many years of marriage, Issun Boshi's parents had not managed to conceive, so they prayed to the gods for a child, even one just as long as the end of a finger. The gods took them at their word, and Issun Boshi was born. At the age of 15 (a significant birthday for tiny heroes, it seems) Issun Boshi set off on a trip to Kyoto, the capital. He took with him his parents' gifts of a rice bowl, a pair of chopsticks and a needle stuck in a sheath of bamboo. He travelled by river, using the bowl as a boat and a chopstick as a punt. On arriving in the city, Issun Boshi found himself employment in the service of a noble family. He worked hard for a number of years and entered the affections of his employers. One day Issun Boshi accompanied the daughter of the house to the temple. On their way two giant oni leapt out in ambush. Issun Boshi tried to draw attention to himself, thus enabling the girl to escape. When one of the oni swallowed him, Issun Boshi drew his needle from its scabbard and began to stab the oni's stomach. He then clambered his way up the giant's gullet, stabbing with his weapon all the time. When he reached the mouth, the oni spat him out as fast as he could. The other oni lunged for Issun Boshi, but he jumped into its eye were he continued to wield his miniature sword.

As the hapless devils retreated, one of them dropped a mallet. Recognizing this as a lucky instrument, Issun Boshi and the girl struck it on the ground and made a wish. Immediately, Issun Boshi grew to normal size and was clothed in the armour of a samurai, whose attributes he had already shown himself to possess. On the couple's return, the father happily gave his permission for them to wed. Issun Boshi proved himself to be a devoted husband and brought his aged parents to Kyoto to share in his good fortune.

BELOW *Heian shrine in Kyoto; the pagoda structure is an adaptation of Chinese architecture.*

According to some, the *kappa* is a creature descended from the monkey messenger of the river god. Resembling a monkey, but with fish scales or a tortoise shell instead of fur, the child-

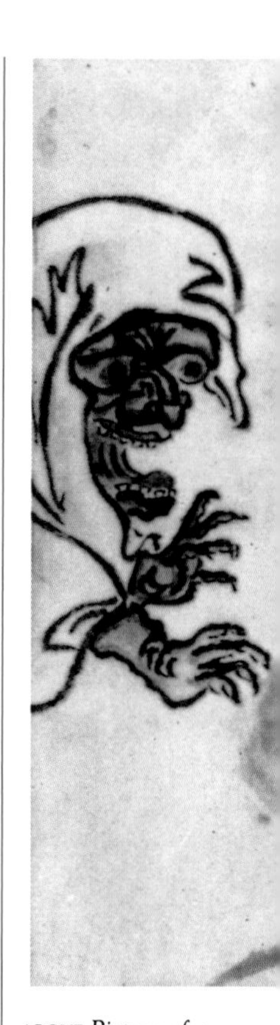

ABOVE *Picture of a* kappa *emerging from a pool; from the scroll painting* Bakemonojin, The Compendium of Ghosts *(1788).*

sized *kappa* is yellow or green in colour. They inhabit rivers, ponds and lakes and have a hollow in the top of the head in which water is carried. If this water is spilled, the *kappa* is then deprived of his magical powers. Like vampires, *kappa* feed on human blood, although they are also known to consume the blood of horses and cattle. As well as blood, *kappa* have a taste for cucumbers, and can be persuaded not to harm humans if a cucumber inscribed with the names and ages of the members of the family is thrown into the water in which they live. The ability to keep a promise is a distinguishing and appealing feature of *kappas*, as is their politeness. This is often their downfall, as when they bow down, the water spills from the indentation in the head causing their strength to disappear.

A *kappa* who resembled a small child would ask passers-by to play pull-

BELOW *Play performed at Sansen-in temple at Ohara, a mountainous area dotted with quiet villages, depicting the ancient gods and heroes.*

ABOVE *When prayers are offered to the guardian deity of children, these stone figures in a Tokyo Buddhist temple are dressed up to look like dolls.*

finger, and then drag its victims down into the pond in which it lived. A horseback rider agreed to play the game, but when their hands were locked, urged his horse into a gallop. As the water spilled from the *kappa*'s head, it begged for mercy. In return for its freedom, the *kappa* promised to teach the rider how to mend broken bones. On being released, the kappa kept its word and taught the rider all it knew. The knowledge handed over by the *kappa* was passed down through generations of the rider's family.

BUDDHIST INFLUENCE

Buddhism was introduced to Japan from Korea in the middle of the 6th century. The first, and one of the most profound texts on Buddhism, *Giso,* appeared as early as the 7th century and was written by Shotoku Taishi, a member of the imperial family who gave much support to the new religion. As is clear from the stories of the *Kojiki,* Shinto is a cult in which the spirit of every thing is worshipped, without a systematic structure or doctrine. Life after death is accepted, but early Shinto contained no moral teaching, or concept of reward or punishment after death. The term Shinto, which means 'Way of the Gods', only came into use after the introduction of Buddhism when it became necessary to differentiate between the two systems of belief.

Although there was opposition to the spread of Buddhism, by the middle of the 8th century the two religions were closely intertwined. Kobo Taishi (774–834) introduced the doctrine of Ryobu, or 'Shinto with two faces', which permitted a compromise to be reached. For the next 1,000 years, Buddhist temples would contain Shinto shrines and Shinto deities would be regarded as Buddhist guardians. Buddhist monks conducted the services at Shinto shrines (except at Izumo and Ise, where Amaterasu's shrine still exists). This happy coexistence came to an end with the beginning of the Meiji Restoration in 1868.

SOUL OF THE BUTTERFLY

This charming tale combines the Buddhist virtue of filial piety with the Shinto belief that all things, inanimate and animate, have a spirit.

A young man and woman who shared a great passion for gardening were married. They lived together in great happiness, their love for their plants only surpassed by the pleasure they took in one another's company. Late in life they had a son, who fortunately inherited his parents' interest in plants. The couple died from old age a few days apart, while their son was still a youth. The boy took over the responsibility for the garden,

ABOVE *In front of the main building, marking off the area of the gods, hangs the shrine* nawa, *which is made from rope that has been ritually purified.*

tending it with the care and devotion that he had learned from his parents. In the spring that followed their death, he observed each day two butterflies in the garden. One night he dreamed that his mother and father were wandering round their beloved garden, inspecting the plants they knew so well to see how they were faring in the boy's care. Suddenly, the old couple turned into a pair of butterflies, but continued their round of the garden, alighting on each flower in turn. The next day the pair of butterflies were still in the garden, and the boy knew that they contained the souls of his parents who were continuing to derive pleasure from their life's work.

It was during the Kamakura period (12th and 13th centuries) that a truly Japanese Buddhism emerged. Honen and his disciple Shinran were responsible for the spreading of the Jodo school among ordinary people, and can thus take credit for its immense popularity ever since. Jodo made Buddhism accessible by arguing that one could achieve enlightenment by

BELOW *A Netsuke rat, one of the 12 animals of the zodiac, another of the many examples of Japanese borrowings from China. Netsuke are exquisitely carved ornaments originally used as fasteners or brooches.*

abandoning oneself to Amida Buddha, and popular Buddhism embraced many gods, including the seven gods of fortune:

THE SEVEN GODS

Hotei can be distinguished by his enormous pot belly, which overhangs his lower garments, but western assumptions of greed would be quite wrong, however. For Hotei's protruding stomach is a symbol of a soul that has achieved serenity through Buddhism, and an indication of its owner's contentment and good nature.

The god of longevity, *Jurojin,* is always depicted with a white beard and shown in the company of a crane, tortoise or deer – which are themselves symbols of long life. He carries a staff from which hangs a scroll that contains the wisdom of the world.

Fukurokuju is easily identified by his odd appearance. He has a very long and narrow head, which is combined with a short and squat body and legs. He, also, is associated with the desirable attributes of long life and wisdom.

Daikoku is regarded as the patron of farmers. He is often shown seated on rice bales, which are sometimes being eaten away beneath him by rats. To this, Daikoku responds with his customary good humour as he is so wealthy that he can afford not to be perturbed! He carries a mallet with which he is able to grant wishes.

Another Buddhist god, who is sometimes seen as a god of wealth also, is *Bishamon.* He is always portrayed in full armour, carrying a spear in one hand and a miniature pagoda in the other – thus showing that he combines the virtues of a warrior and a missionary.

The qualities exemplified by the god *Ebisu* are those of honest toil. The patron of traders and fishermen, only the latter activity identifies him – he is usually shown holding a fishing rod and his catch, a sea bream.

ABOVE *Netsuke showing the seven gods of fortune in their ship.*

RIGHT *Ink on paper painting by the monk Hakuin (1685–1768) of Bodhidharma, founder of the Zen sect.*

The last of the seven is the goddess *Benten.* She occupies an important position among the group for she is associated with the sea. Many shrines to Benten are by the sea or on islands, and she is often portrayed riding a dragon or sea serpent. Benten is an example of the ideals of feminine deportment and accomplishment in the arts, and is often pictured playing a *biwa,* a mandolin-like instrument of which she is fond.

The Kamakura period was the heyday of Japanese chivalry, when the shoguns employed the samurai as their bodyguards. The samurai, who were not aristocrats but mostly came from farming backgrounds, were well acquainted with the harsh realities of life. They found in Zen Buddhism – which was introduced to Japan at the same time as Jodo – another route to the heart of Buddhism. The directness of Zen, 'the spiritual cult of steel', held great appeal for the samurai warriors, who had neither the time nor the inclination to undertake long study or indulge in abstract argument in order to achieve enlightenment. The

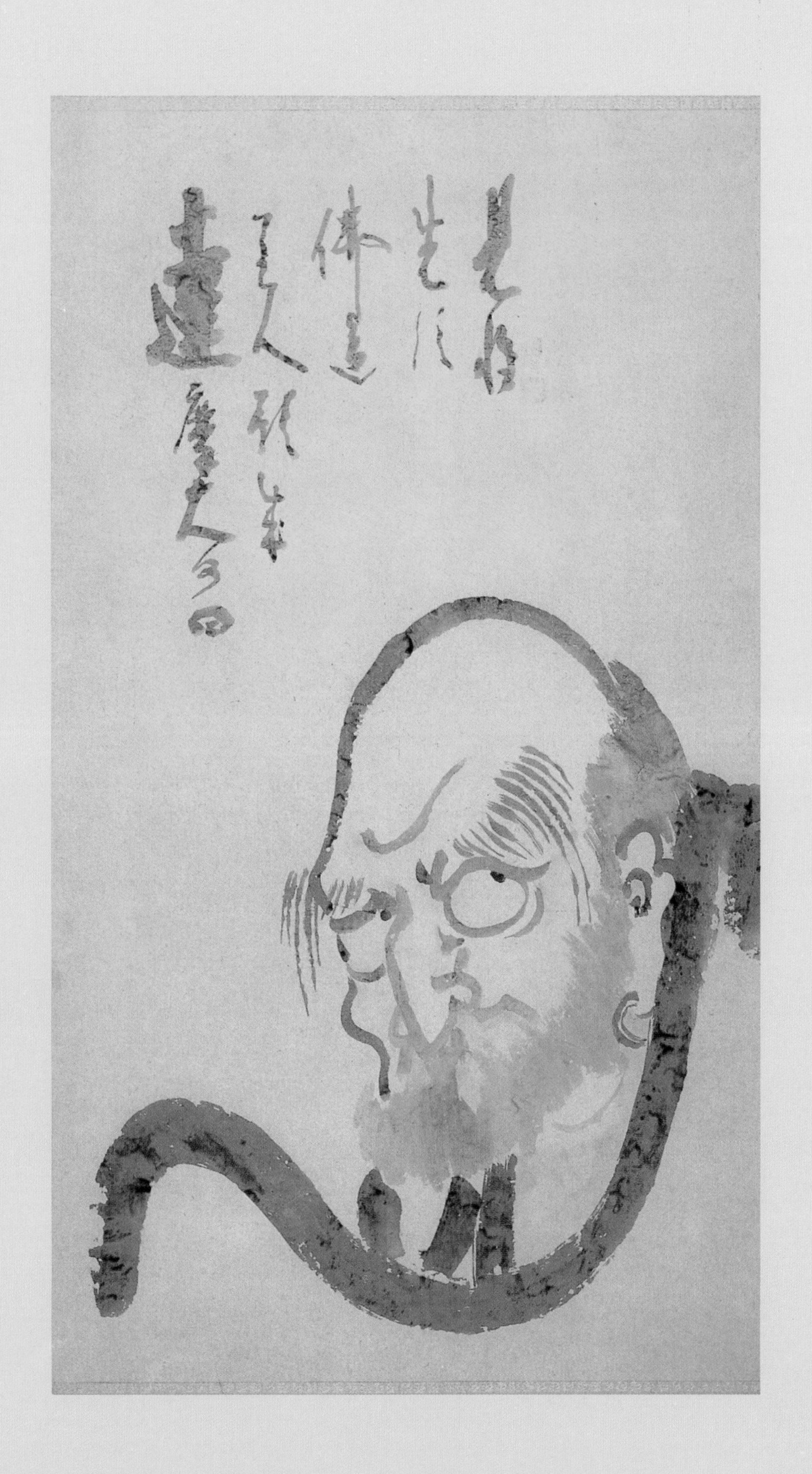

RIGHT *Pine trees, of which there are many varieties, have a particular significance in Japanese painting. Because the leaves do not fall or change colour, they have come to symbolize longevity; (ink on paper by* Tohaku Hasegawa, 1539–1616).

purpose of Zen is to move beyond the realm of the intellect. Zen rejects the use of words to explain experience as mere substitute for reality. Zen is taught through a series of short, elliptical dialogues (*mondo*) which have been described as a duel between master and pupil, another reason perhaps for their appeal to the warriors. When Joshu was asked about the fundamental principle of Buddhism, he replied, 'The cypress-tree in the courtyard in front of you'. 'You are talking of an objective symbol,' said the pupil. 'No, I am not talking of an objective symbol.' 'Then,' asked the monk again, 'What is the ultimate principle of Buddhism?' 'The cypress-tree in the courtyard in front of you,' again replied Joshu.

Zen stresses the one-ness of man and nature and herein lies the reason why it has become the dominant school of Buddhism in Japan. The myths of the *Kojiki* demonstrate that familiarity with and reverence towards the natural world that are so strong in the Japanese tradition. Not only is there no antagonism between Zen and the native Shinto sensibilities, but the different beliefs actually enhance one another. After being accepted by the samurai class, Zen started to permeate every single aspect

BELOW *View of the extensive gardens of Tofukugi temple, Kyoto.*

ABOVE *White sand and rocks laid out in the garden of the 15th-century Ryonji temple; Zen purity.*

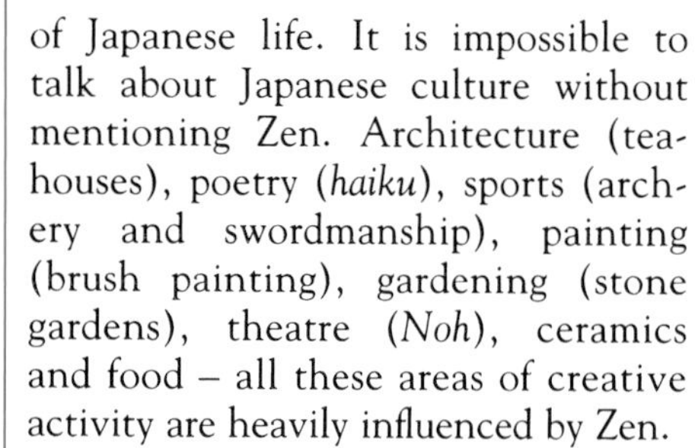

of Japanese life. It is impossible to talk about Japanese culture without mentioning Zen. Architecture (teahouses), poetry (*haiku*), sports (archery and swordmanship), painting (brush painting), gardening (stone gardens), theatre (*Noh*), ceramics and food – all these areas of creative activity are heavily influenced by Zen.

Shinto architecture gave concrete form to the concept of purity, as exemplified in the stories of the *Kojiki* and its simplicity and lack of abstraction also follow the precepts of Zen. Ise Shrine, the central shrine of Shintoism, is situated in the deep forest beside a river whose water is crystal clear. The shrine occupies a vast area. The buildings are in the shape of a rice-storage house, and all are made of bare wood, without paint or ornament, built on white pebble stones. Clear, straight lines dominate, with a few curves on the rooves. All the buildings, together with their various contents, are rebuilt every 20 years, thus ensuring that the necessary skills to make them are transferred from generation to generation. This tradition goes back to ancient times. When they are newly built, the bare wood

BELOW *Calligraphic poem from the late Heian period; the flourishing of calligraphy in Japan is also influenced by Zen Buddhism.*

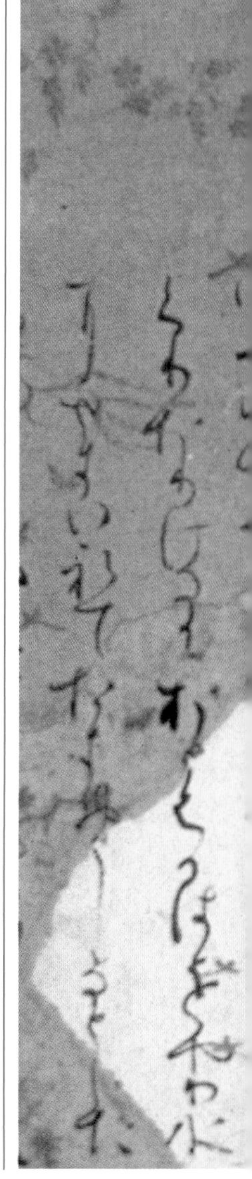

RIGHT *Miyajima (shrine island) near Hiroshima; since time immemorial, neither births nor burials nor dogs are permitted on the island.*

RIGHT *Young girl assistants, known as* Miko, *participating in Shinto ritual at Ise Grand Shrine.*

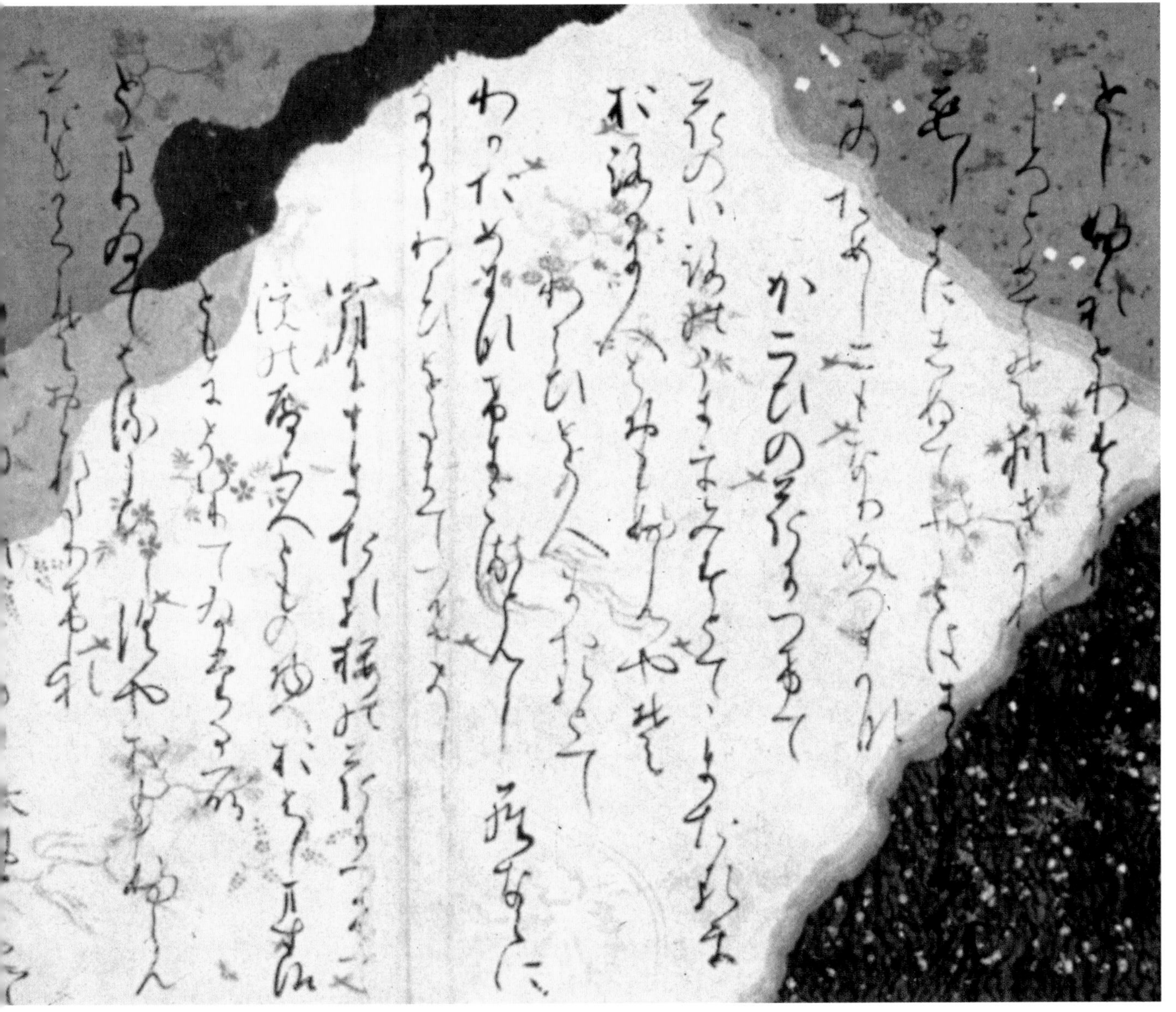

RIGHT *The Golden pavilion of Kinkakuji temple, completed in 1955, an exact replica of a 14th-century villa that was destroyed by fire.*

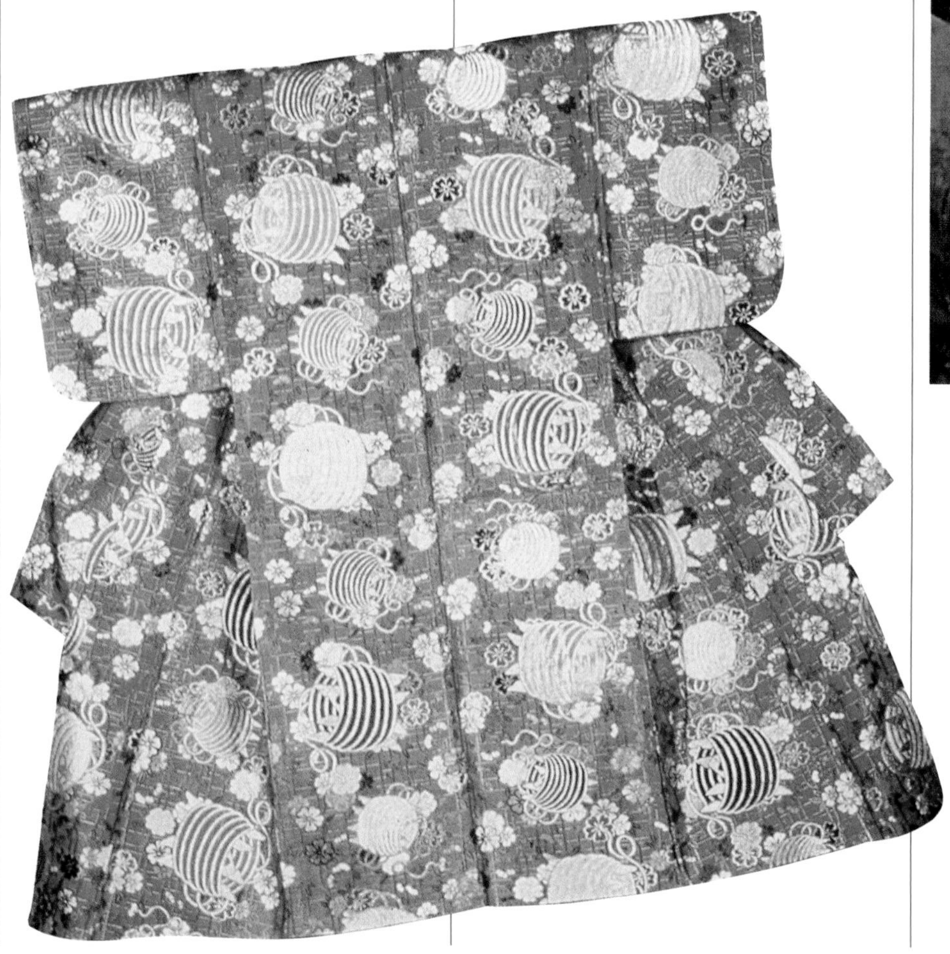

RIGHT *Jacket from a Noh costume woven in a style that imitates a Chinese technique.*

shines gold in the quiet, dark forest. The shrine shows us what an architect can express employing only purely functional lines. Ise shrine is the prototype of later Japanese architecture: Katsura imperial villa, which was made in the 17th century, has much in common with Ise shrine. This building, which was designed by Kobori Enshu, exemplifies the Japanese style of simplicity and functionality, and an intense affinity with natural form and material.

The high points for artistic activity in Japanese history – the Kamakura and Muromachi periods – gave full expression to the spirit of Zen. But the manner and form that it took harked back to ancient times, the times so lovingly recorded in the *Kojiki*: sculptures of angry Buddhist gods remind us of Yamato-takeru, and the costumes of Noh plays display elegant designs that represent the plants that grow on the mountains and blossom in the fields where deities of the *Kojiki* once lived.

ABOVE *Sliding door painting from Chisyaku-in temple, Kyoto; the contemplation of, and respect for, the natural world is central both to Shintoism and Buddhism. Shintoism, with its acceptance that every natural thing, be it a man or a plum tree, has a* kami *or spirit, encouraged the proliferation of mythical stories, and its complex relationship with Buddhism further enriched and invigorated Japanese mythology.*

Chinese figure of a thunder god.

Bibliography

CHINESE MYTHOLOGY

Chinese Mythology (Library of the World's Myths and Legends) by Anthony Christie. Newns Books, London, 1968
Dragons, Gods and Spirits from Chinese Mythology by Tao Tao Liu Saunders; illustrations by Johnny Pau. Peter Lowe: Eurobook Ltd, 1980
Classical Chinese Myths, edited and translated by Jan and Yvonne Walls; illustrations by Guo Huai-ren. Joint Publishing Co., Hong Kong, 1984
Monkey by Wu Cheng'en; translated by Arthur Waley. Unwin Paperbacks, London, 1984
Myths and Legends of China by E.T.C. Werner, London, 1922
A Dictionary of Chinese Symbols: Hidden Symbols in Chinese Life and Thought by Wolfram Eberhard. Routledge, London, 1988

INDIAN MYTHOLOGY

Seasons of Splendour – Tales, Myths and Legends of India by Madhur Jaffrey; illustrations by Michael Foreman. Pavilion Books, London, 1985
Indian Myth and Legend by Donald A. Mackenzie. The Gresham Publishing Company
Demons, Gods and Holy Men from Indian Myths and Legends by Shahrukh Husain; illustrations by Durga Prasad Das. Eurobook, 1987
The Dance of Shiva and Other Tales from India by Oroon Ghosh. Signet Classics, New York, 1965
Hindu Myths, translation and introduction by Wendy Doniger O'Flaherty. Penguin Books, New York, 1975
The Sword and the Flute by David R. Kinsley. University of California Press, Berkeley, 1977
Myths and Symbols in Indian Art and Civilization by Heinrich Zimmer. Harper Torchbooks, New York, 1962
The Indian Way by John M Koller. Macmillan Publishing Co. Inc., New York, 1982

JAPANESE MYTHOLOGY

Continuity and Change by Ichiro Hori. University of Chicago Press, 1968
At the Fountain-head of Japan by Jean Herbert. George Allen & Unwin, London, 1967
The Kami Way by Sokyo Ono. Bridgeway Press, 1962
Japanese Religion: Unity and Diversity (The Religious Life of Man Series) by Byron Earhart. Wadsworth Publishing Company, California, 1982
On Understanding Japanese Religion by Joseph M. Kitagawa. Princeton University Press, Princeton, 1987
Living by Zen by Daisetz Suzuki. Rider & Company, London, 1969
What is Zen? by D. Suzuki. The Buddhist Society, London, 1971
Zen Culture by Thomas Hoover. Routledge, London, 1977
The Kojiki, translated with an Introduction and Notes by Donald L. Philippi. University of Tokyo Press, 1968

REX
AR TV
R VS

Celtic Mythology

Introduction

OUR READING OF THE CELTS

Sad to remember, sick with years,
The swift innumerable spears,
The horsemen with their floating hair,
And bowls of barley, honey and wine,
Those merry couples dancing in tune,
And the white body that lay by mine;
But the tale, though words be lighter than air,
Must live to be old like the wandering moon.

(From *The Wanderings of Oisin* by William Yeats, 1889)

Yeats' lines provide a concise poetic summary of how aristocratic pagan Celts passed their days in hunting and fighting and their nights in feasting, dancing and love-making. It was during the feasting that the myths and legends of Celtic society were relayed by professional poets called bards; these early expressions of Celtic culture have not survived, for the simple reason that the bards relied on memory in the oral tradition. What was the subject matter and form of these early poems? The Roman writer Ammianus Marcellinus, writing in the fourth century AD, states that the Gallic Celts by that time had become civilized (he meant Romanized) but maintained their own Druidic religious philosophy and musical trad-

RIGHT **Uffington White Horse, Oxfordshire, England** *(chalk-carved figure; c. first century BC to first century AD?). There is no proven date for the carving of one of the largest pictorial works of art in the world. The taut curvilinear style, and location near an Iron-Age hill-fort, would suggest that the 111–metre (364-ft) figure was carved by the local Dobunni Celts to signify their territory. It may represent the Gaulish horse-goddess Epona as a patron deity of the Dobunni. The horse requires 'scouring' to keep it free of grass, an activity undertaken up to the last century by local people amid great festivity.*

ABOVE **Gaulish stone with Celtic inscription** *(Vieux-Poitiers, France; c. first century AD). The ancient Celtic language has not survived as literature. Our knowledge of it comes from place-names, names of tribes and kings on coins and inscriptions carved on altars or sacred stones. The letter-forms were borrowed mainly from the Latin of contemporary Romans; Greek letters were sometimes used in southern Gaul.*

itions: 'The bards celebrated the brave deeds of famous men in epic verse to the accompaniment of the sweet strains of the lyre.' Other sources as well as the later written versions of the myths themselves support Ammianus' statement, though 'epic' and 'lyre' were probably Graeco-Roman equivalents for whatever terms the Celts used. The original music and much of the epic poetry disappeared from the tradition when the myths were recorded by later Christian writers. However, some of the stories, dealing mainly with the heroic exploits of legendary Celtic warriors, have survived and make up the body of literature that we now call Celtic mythology.

Mythology can tell us many things about a society, ancient or modern. However, before we can begin to understand the nature of Celtic mythology, we must first of all deconstruct our own modern myth of the Celts. As can be seen from Yeats' early poems, during the late eighteenth and nineteenth centuries the main reference to Celtic myths was in Romantic texts: they provided a nostalgic escape from the Industrial Age back to an era ruled by 'nature' and 'magic' and peopled by heroic warriors and fair-skinned maidens. Each country's poets and painters rediscovered their own Celtic past: Ireland looked to pre-Christian legends such as the CuChulainn and Fianna (or Fenian) tales; Wales had the heroic saga of Pryderi in the *Mabinogion;* the Scottish poet James Macpherson (1736–96) forged his *Ossianic Ballads,* claiming them to be translations of a third-century Gaelic poet named Ossian; England resurrected the legends of King Arthur in works such as Tennyson's poem, *Idylls of the King.* The Romantic Age imbued the myths with their own romantic notions and often retained those elements of Christian medievalism which had become attached to the early written versions.

The Romantic vision of the 'Celtic Twilight' continues to influence our late twentieth-century perception of the Celts. We too require our dreamworlds and the word 'Celtic' conjures up mysterious moonlit landscapes with white-robed Druid priests performing strange rituals and brewing magic potions. Celtic art remains fashionable, particularly in jewellery: it has an abstract charm of its own and also signifies an attraction to an unknown past. Celtic literature weaves a similar spell: the narrator takes us from a world of seemingly real people and places into fantasy lands of fairies and monsters; his skill is such that we do not notice the transition. It is easy to be bewitched by such a culture.

We must ask whether the Celts themselves perceived their religion as a mystery and their poems as escapes from the real world. The answers are not readily forthcoming: the Celts did not write their own histories. Therefore, we have to learn about their customs and behaviour from the hands of contemporary Greek and Roman authors; although their view of the Celts was as mythical as ours, being based on the assumption that the Celts were uncivilized barbarians. Archeology has, however, confirmed some of the more extreme observations of the classical writers: the Celts do indeed appear to have performed human sacrifice and indulged in head-hunting. Archeology has also increased our knowledge of how the Celts lived, worshipped and buried their dead.

THE CELTS IN HISTORY

The earliest historical references to the Celts occur in Greek literature from around 500 BC. By this time they already appear to be inhabiting a wide geographical area, ranging from the upper reaches of the Danube in eastern Europe across to France and Spain. Archeological dating of Celtic finds

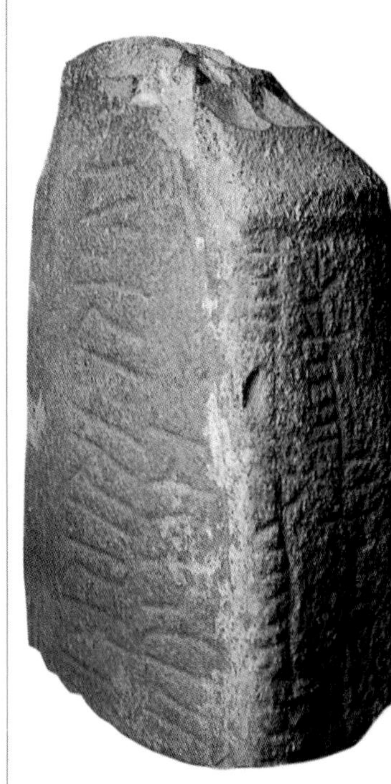

ABOVE **Irish cross-base inscribed with ogham and runic letters** *(Killaloe Church, County Clare, Ireland; c. 1000 AD). The earliest Irish writings were in ogham script and date back to about the fourth century AD. Linear letters were carved on wood or stone across a central line and were differentiated by number and length of lines. Each letter was named after a tree or plant: for example 'd' was* daur*, meaning 'oak'. In Scandinavia, runic letters were used for the Teutonic (early Germanic) language. The oghams (right) read: 'A blessing upon Thorgrimr'; the runes (left) read: 'Thorgrimr carved this cross'.*

not only confirms the histories, but also informs us of the prehistoric Celtic past. A recognizably 'proto-Celtic' culture existed around the upper Danube in 1000 BC. However, some archeologists now argue for a widespread and gradual 'Celticization' of cultures which already existed in Bronze-Age northern and western Europe: thus, 'Celtic' Britain might date back to as early as 1500 BC, when the Wessex culture had the 'heroic' social features which conform with the early Irish Celtic myths.

Soon the eastern European 'Hallstatt' Celts were exploiting iron for tools and weapons and expanding their territories, firstly across Europe towards France and the Iberian Peninsula, as the early Greek historians affirm. The Gallic tribes then made incursions into Etruscan and Roman Italy, and having almost succeeded in besieging Rome in 387 BC, finally settled in the Po valley. The Celtic culture of this period is known as 'La Tène', after a site in Switzerland which demonstrates typical features of fifth-century BC Celtic society. Many archeologists see La Tène as the first truly Celtic culture, and certainly these are the people referred to from now on as Celts by the classical historians. Their military presence in northern Italy in the fifth and fourth centuries BC is attested by Roman mythical accounts of the Gallic siege of Rome, which was apparently frustrated by the warning cackles of sacred geese; and some Etruscan funerary relief sculptures depict battles with Celtic warriors. A further Celtic expansion was directed towards south-eastern Europe, the Baltic, and western Turkey. In the fourth century BC we find Alexander the Great receiving Celtic ambassadors at his Macedonian court; and in 279 BC we hear of Celtic tribes attempting to loot the Greek sanctuary at Delphi, defied by a miraculous fall of snow sent by the god Apollo.

The Greeks distinguished between the oriental Celts, whom they called *Galatoi* (Galatians originally from Gaul), and the Celts of western Europe whom they called *Keltoi*. The Romans made a further distinction by naming the French Celts *Galli* (Gauls), and the British Celts *Belgae* (originally from what is now Belgium) and *Britanni* (Britons). Celtic Gaul became the Roman province of *Gallia* after Julius Caesar's conquests in the first century BC and Britain became Roman *Britannia* under the emperor Claudius in AD 43. Ireland was never invaded by Rome and their myths therefore tend to preserve their earlier, prehistoric Celtic culture in more detail.

Julius Caesar and other writers of the first centuries BC and AD provide us with graphic accounts of Celtic culture and customs as seen by non-Celts. The main feature which emerges is that there was little unity among them: they were divided into aristocratic tribes ruled by chieftains who appear to have been constantly fighting one another. However, it must be remembered that the Romans probably encouraged such native tribal divisions to facilitate their own invasions.

BELOW **The 'Dying Gaul'** *(Roman marble copy of Hellenistic bronze original of the second century BC). The Greek rulers of Pergamon (central Turkey) commemorated their victory over the Galatian Celts with a public monument depicting stereotypes of the defeated enemy. The Romans later copied the figures in marble, probably in celebration of their own victories in Gaul and Britain. The heroic chieftain is readily identified by his Celtic torc, moustache and bristling lime-washed hair.*

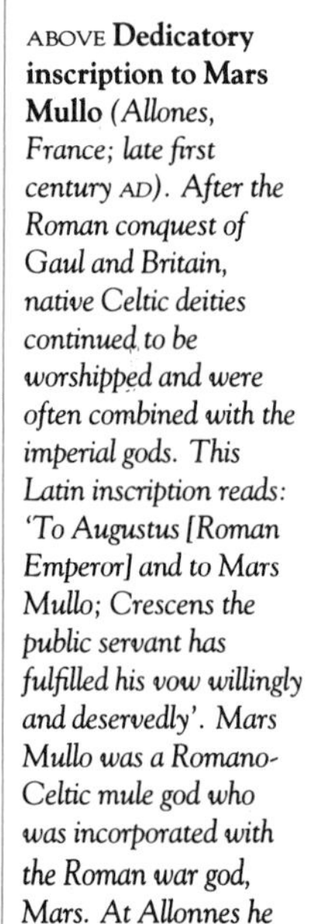

ABOVE **Dedicatory inscription to Mars Mullo** *(Allones, France; late first century AD). After the Roman conquest of Gaul and Britain, native Celtic deities continued to be worshipped and were often combined with the imperial gods. This Latin inscription reads: 'To Augustus [Roman Emperor] and to Mars Mullo; Crescens the public servant has fulfilled his vow willingly and deservedly'. Mars Mullo was a Romano-Celtic mule god who was incorporated with the Roman war god, Mars. At Allonnes he was worshipped as a healer of eye disease: Mars was often seen as a peaceful healer in conquered territories.*

ANCIENT CELTIC SOCIETY

BELOW **Roman bronze figure of Gaullish prisoner** *(probably from Umbria, Italy; c. first century AD). The prisoner wears the trousers, belted tunic and cloak of a Gaulish aristocrat: a practical outfit for horse-riding. Irish male and female aristocrats appear to have worn long linen tunics gathered at the waist with decorative belts or girdles; woollen cloaks were also worn. Social status was reflected by the relative richness of colour and embroidered decoration on both tunic and cloak. Gold and silver brooches, torcs and other body ornaments would also be worn by high aristocrats.*

Caesar gives us a reasonably objective account of Celtic behaviour and dress in the first century BC. He tells us that the Celts lived in *oppida* or townships, some of which have been identified with the three thousand or so Iron-Age hill-forts of southern Britain; similar *oppida* existed in Europe and Galatia. Archeological evidence has allowed for reconstructions of the *oppida* dwellings, such as at Butser Hill in Hampshire, England. These were generally circular houses with wooden walls and thatched roofs; the banqueting halls of the myths would appear to be rectangular, though this may have been a medieval adaptation of the original story.

The Celts were primarily a warrior society ruled by warrior kings, queens and aristocrats, and the myths tell us nothing of the lower classes. They grew corn and herded cattle and learnt the use of coinage from the Greeks and Romans. Religious rituals played an important role in maintaining the social hierarchy of chieftains and tribes; the myths often presented and reinforced the sacred power of the Druidic priests, and the bards appear to have held equal respect. Both the myths and historical accounts reflect the Celtic pride of dressing up for battle: 'The Britons dye themselves with blue woad in order to appear more terrifying in battle. They wear their hair long, and their bodies are shaven except for the head and the upper lip.' (Caesar, *Gallic War V*). Herodian, writing in the third century AD, adds: 'As they are not used to clothes, they wear iron ornaments about their waists and necks, which they consider to be both decorative and a sign of wealth . . . they tattoo their bodies with abstract patterns and all sorts of animals.' Diodorus of Sicily, a contemporary of Caesar, describes the Celts as 'tall and muscular, with pale skin and blond hair which they highlight artificially by washing it in lime-water; they gather it back from the forehead to the top of the head and down to the nape of the neck . . . therefore the hair becomes so heavy and coarse that it looks like the mane of horses.' Classical representations of Celts conform with these literary stereotypes and archeologists have found tattoos on preserved Celtic flesh.

ABOVE **Etruscans fighting Gauls** *(Etruscan alabaster funerary urn from Pieve, Italy; fourth century BC). The warriors are represented in an idealized classical Greek manner; the Greeks are distinguished from the Celts by their horses and helmets. The Etruscan language, like ancient Celtic, has only survived in brief inscriptions such as that above the scene.*

Caesar has little to say about Celtic women, except that they were 'shared between groups of ten or twelve men'. To the Romans and ourselves this would appear barbaric, but it may well imply a matriarchal system in which women had the social privilege of a number of lovers. Certainly high-ranking Celtic women enjoyed a degree of power unknown to their classical counterparts: witness the warrior queen Boudicca, who led the first-century AD rebellion against the Roman invaders. Although we must bear in mind that the Celtic myths were probably always told from a male viewpoint, the human female characters in Celtic mythology are rarely the downtrodden or faceless figures of the Greek myths, which might also suggest that, unlike in Classical Athens, free-born women formed part of the bard's audience.

THE CELTIC LANGUAGES

The pagan Celts spoke an Indo-European language which relates them in prehistory to the Greeks, Romans and Hindus. However, no record exists of the ancient languages, except brief inscriptions from the Roman period, and references in the classical authors to Celtic names. When the Celtic myths were finally written down in the early medieval period, the languages varied according to the author's country of origin: thus the Irish myths were recorded in Old Irish, but the contemporary Welsh form of the Celtic language would not have been understood by the Irish writers. It would appear that, by the time of the Roman invasion, any former cultural unity provided by a single Celtic language had disappeared: the Irish Celts were speaking 'Goidelic', while the British Celts were speaking 'Brythonic'. The Brythonic language seems to have been related to that spoken by the Gauls. Around the fifth century AD there were invasions and population movements in the western Celtic lands which led to linguistic changes: the Irish Goidelic language entered Scotland, later to become Scottish-Gaelic; the Anglo-Saxon 'English' language entered southern Britain, pushing the Brythonic language to Brittany.

THE SURVIVAL OF CELTIC MYTHOLOGY

Celtic myths were preserved in two main traditions: some were recorded by Christian writers and survive from the seventh century AD onwards while others have stayed alive in the oral folk traditions of Celtic areas. The apparent bias of the myths towards Britain and Ireland is due to the lack of surviving material from other former regions of the Celtic world, although surviving Celtic themes can often be observed in European folk-tales.

The earliest substantial survival of Irish mythology is a manuscript called the *Book of the Dun Cow*, containing versions from the CuChulainn sagas. Its Christian writer (author would be the incorrect term, implying an original creation) was a certain Maelmuri, whom historians know was murdered by Viking raiders in his cathedral at Clocmacnois in 1106. The curious title derives from a lost earlier manuscript of the seventh century AD written on cowhide (that of his pet cow!) by St Ciaran.

British mythology is now best known from the *Mabinogion* which was the title given by Lady Charlotte

ABOVE **Head of 'Medusa the Gorgon'** *(pediment of the Temple of Sulis Minerva, Bath, England; first century AD). The Greek female monster, with her snake-locks, was often used as an apotropaic figure in Greek and Roman religious contexts to 'avert the evil eye'. Here 'she' has become a 'he' complete with moustache and staring eyes in the Celtic style. Medusa's head was worn by Minerva on her breastplate to (literally!) petrify her enemies; her worship was combined with that of Sulis, the Celtic goddess of the healing waters of Bath. However, this 'Gorgon' has many unusual features, which may equally signify a Celtic sun deity, perhaps the consort of Sulis.*

Guest to her 1849 English translation of a collection of eleven Welsh tales preserved in earlier manuscripts: these are the *White Book of Rhydderch* of c1300–25 and the *Red Book of Hergest* of c1375–1425. *Mabinogi* means, broadly speaking, 'a tale of childhood': this was a mythical account of the conception, birth and early training of a Celtic hero. Lady Guest's word *Mabinogion* (which she incorrectly thought was the plural form) therefore implied that all eleven tales were of this genre. In fact only the first four 'Branches' are from an original *Mabinogi*; the other seven stories are of different genres and just happened to be included in the original manuscripts.

ABOVE **Pewter mask from culvert of Roman baths** *(Bath, England; first century AD). Many objects were thrown as offerings into the healing waters of Sulis Minerva. This may have been the face mask of a priest or priestess, held in front of the face during rituals.*

Celtic folk-tales survive in 'collected' versions recorded from the mouths of storytellers and singers by interested scholars. Unfortunately, with the advent of television in even the remotest areas of the Celtic world, the oral folk tradition is dying out. Although many of these folk-tales are simply good stories told by and for the rural community, there are some which preserve the 'high' myths and legends of the ancient Celtic ruling class.

ABOVE **Lead defixio (curse tablet) from Roman baths** *(Bath, England; first to second centuries AD). Curses were written in Latin onto lead strips which were rolled up and thrown into the spring waters; the curses invoke the goddess Sulis to bring harm to a personal enemy. Thus the Celtic goddess was believed to have harmful as well as healing powers.*

THE NATURE OF CELTIC MYTHOLOGY

The bards were priests and teachers as well as entertainers and the behaviour of their mythical and legendary characters provided living Celts, both men and women, with ideals and thus ensured the continuity of the warrior society. Recurrent themes in Celtic mythology can therefore inform us about the preoccupations of their society. A love of beauty and bodily display is evident throughout the myths: when CuChulainn goes into battle, for example, his brightly coloured clothing, glowing jewellery and bristling hair are visual symbols of his heroic status. And heroines signify their own high and leisured status by wearing their hair in time-consuming intricate plaits, and by setting off their white unweathered skin with rich jewellery.

The world of nature was an unexplained and alien place to the Celts: therefore magical happenings tend to occur outside the stronghold, for example during the hunt; talking animals and birds feature in many of the stories; and Celtic divinities often represent the forces of nature. However, there is one important religious aspect which is often overlooked when we read the Celtic myths: scholars have demonstrated that the myths of other cultures tend to be narrative 'explanations' of historically attested religious rituals. Therefore, it is most likely that some of these stories were originally mythical explanations of religious mysteries or quests. So visits to the Otherworld might reflect an original rite of passage in which Celts passed from childhood to adulthood by means of a ritual period of absence outside the community. The Druidic philosophy encouraged a belief in immortality and the myths celebrate this idea: love persists beyond the grave in the form of intertwining trees on burial mounds; heads of dead heroes retain supernatural powers. Such beliefs were a consolation to the warrior society, where the hero's greatest glory was to die in battle.

Many elements in the surviving myths appear to mirror an earlier prehistoric 'heroic age' of Celtic culture, and thus the Celts of Caesar's day probably viewed their mythical ancestors with as much romantic nostalgia as did their admirers in the nineteenth century. However the myths also contain legendary representations of real historical characters, such as the fourth-century AD Roman emperor Magnus Maximus who appears as Macsen Wledig in the *Mabinogion*. This historical example suggests that mythical figures such as Pwyll and Branwen, though unknown in history, might also have once existed in prehistory as real persons whose deeds were outstanding enough to have been preserved in both bardic poetry and folk memory.

The mythical world remained so integral a part of Celtic society that when Christianity arrived, the spoken myths could not be destroyed. Instead they were often Christianized or given Christian endings: gods became God; the Druid priests of the old religion were overcome by the Saints of the new religion. The greatest wonder of these stories is that they have survived for so many centuries and provide an enchanting window into the rich and varied past of the Celtic West. These myths are now ours, and we should read, feel and learn from them before handing them on to our children.

ABOVE **The Holy Well** *(William Orpen; tempera on canvas, 1916). The Irish symbolist artist has depicted the 'beehive' huts of a Late Celtic Arran community. The islanders are being converted to Christianity in the waters of their pagan well; Orpen's artist friend Sean Keating stands above the well, apparently unconvinced by the new religion. The deserted crofter's hut in the background and the shamefully naked 'Adam and Eve' in the centre reinforce Orpen's criticisms of cultural change in Celtic places.*

CELTIC BRITAIN & IRELAND
PICTI
CALEDONIAN CONFEDERACY
Antonine Wall
Lindisfarne
VOTADINI
SELGOVAE
DAMNONII
NOVANTAE
HADRIAN'S WALL
CARVETI
ULSTER
Emvin. Machae
CONNAUGHT
MEATH
Cruach
Kells.
Uisneach
Boyne
Tara.
Clonmacnois
Shannon
Liffey
LEINSTER
MUNSTER
Bruig Na Boinde (New Grange)
IRISH SEA
ISLE OF MAN
BRIGANTES
SETANTII
PARISI
Anglesey
DIN LLIGWY
Alderley Edge
DECEANGLI
ORDOVICES
Harlech
CORNOVII
CORITANI
Severn
DEMETAE (DYFED)
Kilpeck
DOBUNNI
Gloucester
ICENI
SILURES
CATUVELLAUNI
TRINOVANTES
Camulodunum
BRITTANY
Uffington White Horse
BELGAE
ATREBATES
Londinium
Tintagel
Glastonbury
Stonehenge
CANTIACI
DUROTRIGES
DUMNONII
Cadbury Castle
REGNENSES
Butser
Maiden Castle

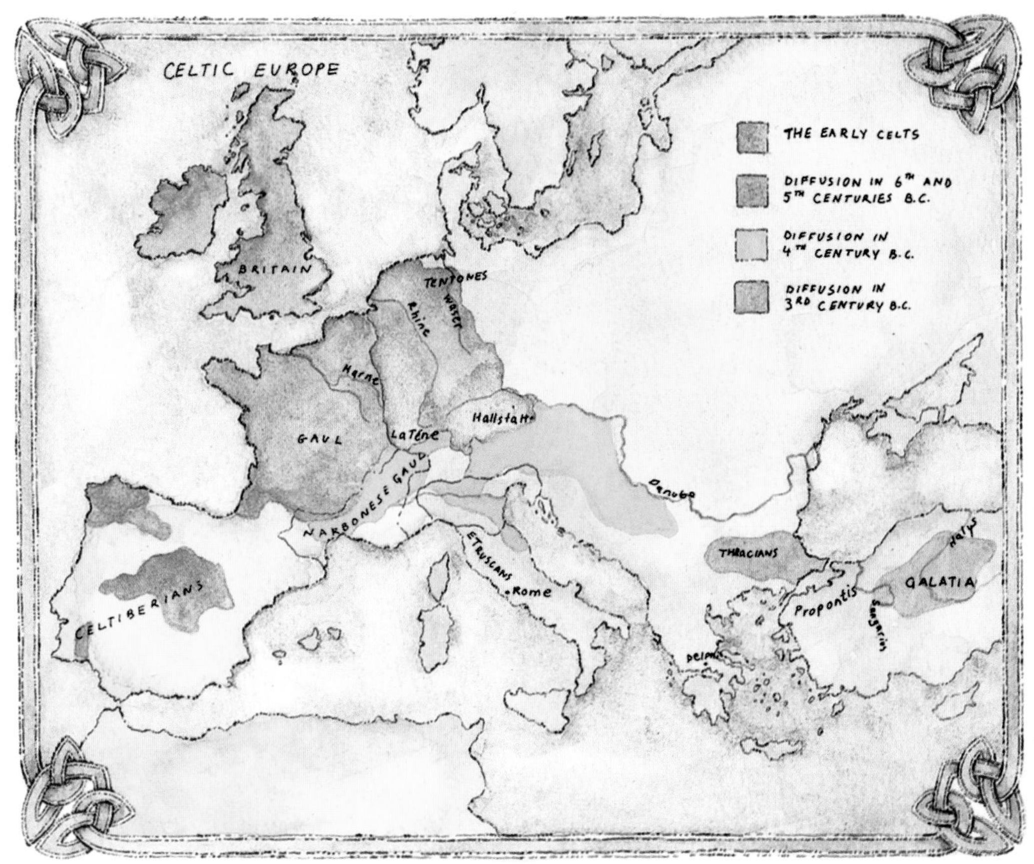
CELTIC EUROPE
THE EARLY CELTS
DIFFUSION IN 6TH AND 5TH CENTURIES B.C.
DIFFUSION IN 4TH CENTURY B.C.
DIFFUSION IN 3RD CENTURY B.C.
BRITAIN
TENTONES
Weser
Rhine
Marne
GAUL
LaTène
Hallstatt
NARBONESE GAUL
Danube
CELTIBERIANS
ETRUSCANS
Rome
THRACIANS
Halys
GALATIA
Propontis
Sangarius
Delphi

ONE

The Saga of CuChulainn

The pagan Iron-Age Celtic world of Ulster (ancient Ulaid) is graphically preserved, albeit as a mythological fantasy, in the Ulster cycle of early Irish storytelling. The young hero of the tales was CuChulainn, who bears some resemblance to the Welsh Pryderi: both births are associated with colts which the heroes later own, and both are renamed later in life. These stories served as an education for young Celtic noblemen, the vivid heroic characters providing them with models of youthful warrior behaviour. Details such as the miniature weapons and sports equipment reflect the military and athletic training of them The following extracts from the saga of CuChulainn are taken from the twelfth-century manuscript known as The Book of the Dun Cow, *the earliest surviving written version of the tales of CuChulainn and the Ulster heroes. Various themes and mythical features of the stories suggest early pagan origins, with the Celtic gods Lugh and Cu Rui appearing in human guise. As in the tale of the Welsh Pwyll, the storyteller presents his audience with an apparently 'real' ancient Celtic world of hill-forts and recognizable place-names. However, the 'fairy' world is never far away: 'real' landmarks such as New Grange burial mound (ancient Bruig na Boinde) exert their magical influence, heroes are born, and superhuman deeds are performed.*

The story begins with the appearance of strange birds wearing silver chains. Like the chains worn by the Children of Lir, these are tokens of their fairy nature, and the storyteller uses them to transport the warriors, and the audience, into the Otherworld.

THE BIRTH OF CUCHULAINN

In the days when Conchobar was King of Ulster, his chieftains noticed a flock of birds feeding on the grass of the plain by Emuin Machae, and they fed until they had laid bare the land as far as the eye could see. The warriors were bird-hunters and they set out in their chariots to pursue the birds wherever they might lead them. Dechtire drove the chariot of her brother Conchobar, and nine chariots sped across the plain after the birds. A silver chain linked each pair of birds and their flight and song was so beautiful as to enchant the Ulstermen.

Evening drew near and the Ulstermen searched for shelter for it was snowing. They were welcomed into a cottage by a man who gave them food and drink, and the Ulstermen were merry by nightfall. Their host announced that his wife was about to give birth and asked Dechtire to help. The Ulstermen brought in from the snow a pair of new–born foals and presented them to the baby boy whom Dechtire was nursing.

In the morning the Ulstermen woke to the sight of the boy and his colts, but the strange birds and the house had vanished; they were just east of the Bruig. Back to Emuin Machae they went, where the boy grew for several years until he suddenly fell ill and died. Dechtire cried from her heart for the death of her foster-son. She asked for water and a copper bowl was brought to her, but every time she raised it to her lips a little creature would spring at her mouth from the water, and every time she looked into the bowl, nothing could be seen. Dechtire's sleep was broken by a dream of the man in the phantom house. He told her that his name was Lugh son of Ethniu and that he had lured her to the house and that she was now bearing the seed of his son: the boy was to be named Setanta and given the two colts which were meant for him alone.

When the Ulstermen saw that Dechtire was with child they wondered whether the father might be Conchobar himself, for brother and sister slept side by side. Conchobar saved his embarrassment by betrothing his sister to Sualtam son of Roech. However, Dechtire was mortified at having to sleep with her husband whilst already bearing another man's child, so one night she lay alone and crushed the baby in her womb. But Dechtire soon became pregnant again by Sualtam and a son was born.

RIGHT **CuChulainn,** *(John Duncan, 1866–1945). The Dundee artist drew on the style and medievalism of the Pre-Raphaelites to create his images of the Celtic heroes of literature and folklore. His pencil drawing portrays the Irish hero with tartan cloak and late Celtic brooch. The image is seen from the front, which reflects Duncan's love of Byzantine art, while the dreamy eyes point to the influence of Rossetti and Burne-Jones. Duncan's inscription applies to both hero and artist: 'I care not though I last but a day if my name and my fame are a power forever'.*

THE BOYHOOD EXPLOITS OF CUCHULAINN (SETANTA)

Conchobar had lost the allegiance of several Ulster chieftains after he had slain the sons of Usnach. These men had gone across to Connaught on the west of Ireland. One of them, Fergus, recounted the childhood of Cuchulainn to his hosts Ailill and Medb, King and Queen of Connaught:

'He was brought up at Mag Muirthemni in the south of Ulster. One day Sualtam and Dechtire told their son of the famous boys of Emuin Machae, whom Conchobar watches at play when he is not playing the board games or drinking his way to bed. CuChulainn asked Dechtire if he could go and see the boys. "You must wait until an Ulster warrior can go with you," she replied.

'"I want to go now," said CuChulainn. "Which road must I take?"

'"Go northwards," answered his mother, "but take great care, for the route is filled with dangers."

'"I shall go anyway," said CuChulainn, and he set off with his toy weapons, a tiny spear and shield; he also took his hurley stick and ball, hoping to play a game with the boys of Emuin Machae.

'At Emuin he walked straight out onto the playing field without first asking for the protection of the other players. The boys were angry at this lack of courtesy, for we all know the rules of behaviour on the playing field. They told him to get off the field and threw their three fifties of spears at him (for they numbered one hundred and fifty): every spear stuck in the tiny shield of CuChulainn. They hurled three times fifty balls at him and each one he held to his

RIGHT **Din Lligwy settlement, Anglesey.** *The entrance (right) of this late Iron-Age (fourth century AD) circular hut faces the central courtyard of a small Celtic settlement. It consisted of two circular and seven rectangular dwellings surrounded by a limestone wall; two of these contained evidence of iron smelting in their hearths. The roofs would have been of thatch.*

chest. They threw their three times fifty hurley sticks at him, but he caught them all.

'CuChulainn was furious: the hairs on his head stood on end and sparkled with his rage. One eye he closed to the size of the eye of a needle, the other he opened to the size of a bowl. He grimaced so that you could see down his throat and his teeth gleamed from ear to ear. The moon of the great young warrior rose from his head. I myself was playing chess with Conchobar when in ran nine of the boys with CuChulainn in hot pursuit. Fifty of them already lay outside where he had struck them down. "This is not sporting," shouted Conchobar.

'"They are the bad sports," answered CuChulainn, "for I wanted to join in their games, and they tried to throw me off the playing field."

'"What is your name?" asked Conchobar.

'"I am Setanta, son of Sualtam and your sister Dechtire."

'"Why," asked Conchobar, "did you not ask for the protection of the other players?"

'"I have not been taught the rules," replied CuChulainn.

'"Then will you take protection from your uncle?" asked Conchobar.

'"I will," said CuChulainn, "but one thing I ask of you, that I be allowed to undertake the protection of the three times fifty boys." Conchobar agreed, and they all went out to the playing field and the boys whom CuChulainn had knocked to the ground arose at the sight of their new hero.'

Conall, another of the Ulster chieftains, continued the story:

'We knew the boy when we lived in Ulster, and it was a joy to watch him growing up. Soon after the episode at the playing field related by Fergus, CuChulainn was involved in more heroic adventures.

'Culann the blacksmith invited Conchobar to a feast. Not too many were to accompany the King of Ulster, for the smith had only the wealth produced by his hands and his tongs. Therefore only fifty favourite old champions were to accompany Conchobar. Before they left Emuin, the king paid a visit to the playing field to bid the boys farewell; CuChulainn was single-handedly playing the three times fifty boys, and he was winning. When they tried to fill the goal with their balls, CuChulainn defended on his own and stopped every ball. Afterwards, in the wrestling, he threw them all to the ground; yet all three times fifty of them could not pin him down. In the game of stripping, he had the clothes off the lot of them, without even losing his brooch.

'Conchobar wondered at the feats of his nephew and he asked his men whether CuChulainn would grow into a man and perform similar heroic deeds: they all agreed that this would be so. "Come with us to the feast of Culann," said Conchobar.

'"I shall finish the games", replied CuChulainn, "and follow after you."

'At the feast, Culann the smith asked his royal guest whether all were present. "Yes," answered Conchobar, forgetting his foster-son, "and we are ready to eat and drink."

'"Well then," said the smith, "let us close the doors and make merry; my dog shall guard the cattle in the

LEFT **Head of the Romano-British deity Antenociticus, from his shrine at Benwell, near Newcastle-Upon-Tyne, England** *(c. third century AD). This local Celtic god was worshipped in a small temple near a Roman military fort on Hadrian's Wall. The shrine provides evidence of the adoption of native divinities by Roman soldiers. The head is carved in the classical manner, but its Celtic features shine through in the powerfully modelled eyes and hair.*

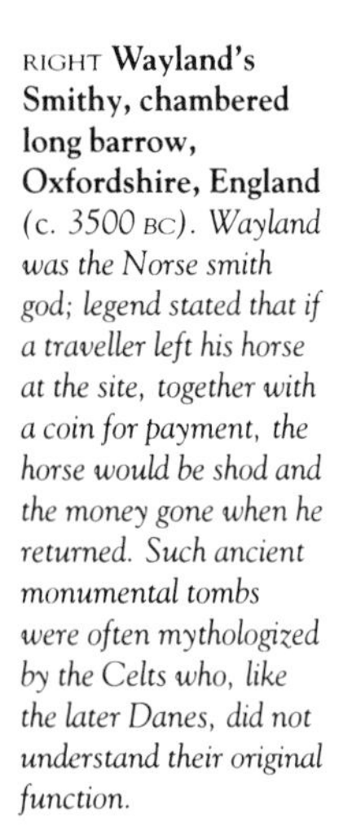
RIGHT **Wayland's Smithy, chambered long barrow, Oxfordshire, England** *(c. 3500 BC). Wayland was the Norse smith god; legend stated that if a traveller left his horse at the site, together with a coin for payment, the horse would be shod and the money gone when he returned. Such ancient monumental tombs were often mythologized by the Celts who, like the later Danes, did not understand their original function.*

fields: no man will escape him, for he requires three chains to hold him, and three men on each chain."

'Meanwhile, the boy was on his way to the feast, and to amuse himself he was throwing his ball in the air, and his hurley after it; and he was hurling his spear ahead and running to catch it before it hit the ground. As he entered the courtyard of Culann the smith, the dog went for him. The disturbance was heard by Conchobar and his men, and they watched from the windows as CuChulainn fought the dog with his bare hands. He held it by the throat and back and smashed it to pieces against a pillar. CuChulainn was taken into the house. "I am glad for your mother's sake," said Culann, "that you are alive. But that dog protected all my goods, and now I am done for."

'"Fear not," said CuChulainn; "I shall raise a puppy of similar pedigree for you, and until it is large enough to guard your property I myself shall be your watchdog."

'"Then we shall call you CuChulainn, 'The Hound of Culann', from now on," said Conall.

'Such were the exploits of a boy of six,' said Conall. 'What mighty deeds can we expect of him now that he is seventeen?'

THE FEAST OF BRICRIU

Bricriu 'Nemthenga' ('Poison-Tongue') invited Conchobar and the Ulstermen to a magnificent feast in a beautiful house designed specially for the occasion. Opposite the house Bricriu built a cottage with large glass windows so that he could see into the house, for he knew that the Ulstermen would not allow him to dine with them.

Before the feast Bricriu visited Loegaire, Conall Cernach and CuChulainn, three of the greatest heroes of Ulster, and told them of a prize which would be reserved at his feast for the champion of champions: 'You will become king of all Ireland,' Bricriu told each hero, 'if you win the champion's prize. You will receive a cauldron large enough to hold three warriors full of wine. You shall have a boar fed for seven years on milk and grain in the spring, curds and sweet milk in the summer, wheat and acorns in the autumn, and meat and soup in the winter. And you shall have a noble cow which for seven years has grazed on heather and milk, meadow-herbs and corn. And you shall have in addition one hundred large honey-cakes. This is the prize intended for you alone, for you alone are the greatest of the Ulstermen. You are to claim the prize as the feast begins.' So Bricriu tempted each hero and returned to finish the preparations for the feast.

The Ulstermen arrived on the day appointed for the feast, and each man and woman took their place in the great hall according to their rank. When all was ready the musicians began to play and Bricriu announced, 'Over there is the portion reserved for the champion. May the best man win.' And with those words he left the hall and entered his cottage.

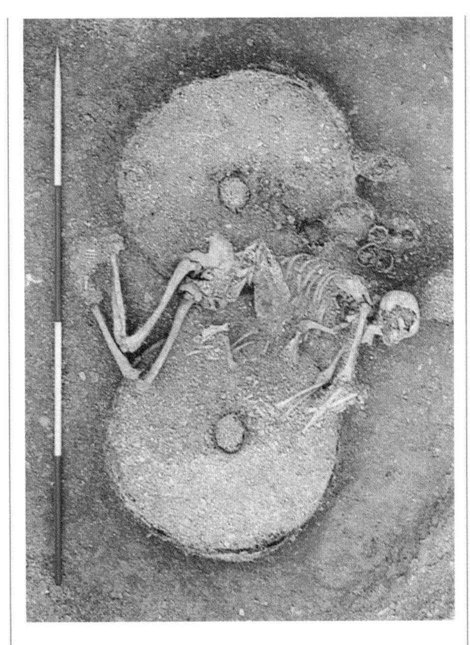

LEFT **Chariot-burial of young adult female, Wetwang, Yorkshire, England** (*c. second to first centuries BC*). *A square barrow marked the grave. The wheels and shaft can be seen alongside bronze female goods, including a mirror and work-box; a side of pork, often mentioned in mythology as 'the champion's joint', was included for the underworld meal. A similar male burial was found nearby, his Celtic warrior status signified by sword, spears and shield.*

BELOW LEFT **Handle of bronze bowl, Hallstatt, Austria** (*sixth century BC*). *An early example of Celtic metalwork. The myths abound with descriptions of such fine metal vessels at aristocratic banquets. The cow and calf are solid cast bronze and are depicted in a geometric style typical of Hallstatt art.*

As Bricriu had hoped an argument began immediately between Loegaire, Conall Cernach and CuChulainn, and soon the three warriors were fighting. Conchobar stepped between them and Senchae, who was the oldest and wisest of the Ulstermen, said, 'We should not have fighting during the feast. Tonight the portion shall be divided between all three of you, and tomorrow we shall ask Ailill, King of Connaught, to settle the dispute.' All agreed with these words of wisdom and soon the company was merry with food and wine.

Meanwhile Bricriu was scheming in his cottage as to how he might set the great women of Ulster against one another. At that moment Fedelm, wife of Loegaire, came out of the house. 'Surely,' said Bricriu, 'you are wife of the greatest hero of Ireland. If you lead the women of Ulster back into the house tonight, you will forever be first lady of Ulster.' And Bricriu made the same promise to Lendabair, wife of Conall Cernach, and to Emer, wife of CuChulainn. The time came for the women to rejoin their husbands in the hall. They started walking at a stately pace, but as the house came in sight, they walked faster and faster until soon they were hitching up their dresses and running. The Ulstermen heard the commotion and, thinking that they were being attacked, barred the doors of the hall. The women hammered on them from the outside, as each wanted to become the first lady of Ulster. CuChulainn used his great strength to lift up a wall of the house and Emer was thus able to slip into the feast and claim her prize.

The feasting continued but soon the three heroes and their wives began squabbling once more over the champion's prize. It was decided that the three should journey in their chariots to either the King of Munster, Cu Roi, son of Daire, or to Ailill and Medb, King and Queen of Connaught: one of these would settle the dispute. They raced one another westwards across the hills and plains towards Connaught and Munster, and the ground shook beneath them.

Medb heard the commotion from the citadel at Cruachu and asked her daughter Findabair to go to the gatehouse tower of the fort and describe who was coming in such great fury: 'In the first chariot I see a man with long hair: he wears it in braids and from root to tip it changes colour from brown to blood red and golden yellow.'

'That is surely Loegaire,' said Medb, 'and he will slay all in Cruachu.'

'In the next chariot stands a man with the loveliest hair: like the manes of his horses is it braided, and his face glistens with red and white hues. He wears a blue and crimson cloak, and carries a shield with bronze edge and yellow boss; in the other hand he holds a spear of burning red, and the birds swoop around him.'

'That must be Conall Cernach,' said Medb, 'and he will cut us all to pieces.'

'And the third chariot,' continued Findabair, 'is pulled by the swiftest of horses: one is grey and one is black, and they run faster than the birds and they breathe flashes of lightning. And the warrior is a sad, dark man, the most beautiful man in Ireland; I see his white breast beneath his scarlet tunic, fastened with a golden brooch; his eyes gleam with jewels of dragon-red, and his brilliant red cheeks are aflame as he leaps like a salmon above his chariot.'

'That is CuChulainn,' cried Medb, 'and we shall be ground to dust by his rage.'

Medb welcomed the heroes with a vat of water to cool them off and fifty women to attend them in their guestrooms. They then told Ailill and Medb that they had come to seek their judgement in the dispute over the prize of Bricriu; and all cursed Bricriu for his troublemaking.

RIGHT **Gold amulets from Szarazd-Regoly, Hungary** (c. 100 BC). *These fine examples of miniature Celtic metalwork are formed from embossed gold-leaf with filigree and granulated decoration. The wheel symbolized the sun god and was used in burials as a protective talisman against the forces of darkness.*

Ailill could not make his mind up about the three contestants, so Medb took the judgement upon herself: 'There is no difficulty at all in judging them,' Medb told her husband, 'for Loegaire is as different from Conall Cernach as tawny bronze is from white gold, and Conall Cernach is as different from CuChulainn as white gold is from red gold.' She summoned Loegaire: 'I consider you to be king of all Ireland,' said Medb, 'and you are to have the champion's prize; you are to return to Conchobar and the Ulstermen and show them this as a token of our choice.' And she gave him a bronze cup, its base decorated with a bird in white gold, and Loegaire drained the wine in it, and joined his fifty women in bed.

Medb then summoned Conall Cernach, and said the same to him, and gave him a white gold cup with a golden bird on its base. He too drained the wine and went to bed; his fifty women were joined by Sadb Sulbair, daughter of Ailill and Medb.

Finally she summoned CuChulainn, and Ailill joined her in judgement. To the hero was given a cup of red gold, and the bird on its base was carved from a priceless gem. 'You are champion of champions,' said the King and Queen of Connaught, 'and your wife Emer is in our opinion the first lady of Ulster. Return to Conchobar tomorrow and claim the prize.' CuChulainn was joined in bed by Princess Findabair.

Before their departure on the next morning, the heroes entertained the court with their competitions. They played the game of throwing the wheel: Loegaire only managed to reach the top of the wall of the hall; Conall Cernach hit the ridge-beam to the cheers of the youth of Connaught; but CuChulainn's throw hit the ridge-beam so hard that the wheel flew out of the roof and landed an arm's length into the ground outside. CuChulainn then took the needles from the three times fifty women, and threw them one by one into the air, so that each was threaded in the eye of the next to form a chain. He returned each needle to its owner to the cheers of the crowd that had gathered in the courtyard. The three heroes then bade farewell to Ailill and Medb and the people of the fort of Cruachu and each returned separately to Ulster.

Conall Cernach and CuChulainn were held up by various adventures and when they eventually reached

LEFT **Human head on a large bronze cauldron from Rynkeby, Denmark** *(first century* BC*). He wears the warrior torc, and his stylized features are typical of Celtic representation. Heads of oxen also decorate this cauldron, and may have signified its use as a ritual container for animal sacrifice.*

Conchobar's fort at Emuin Machae, they found the court in mourning: Loegair had arrived before them and falsely announced their deaths. The bickering which ensued was halted by Sualtam, father of CuChulainn, who called everyone in for a homecoming feast. 'Why not let another hero claim the champion's prize?' said one of the Ulstermen during the merry-making. 'After all, if any of these three had been chosen during their stay at Cruachu, he would have brought home a token as proof.' At this challenge Loegaire produced his cup and claimed Bricriu's prize. 'The prize is for me,' said Conall Cernach, taking out his cup, 'for mine is a golden cup and yours is only bronze.'

'Then I am champion of champions,' cried CuChulainn, and he showed the company the red–gold cup with its precious-stone bird.

'Ailill and Medb have judged,' shouted Conchobar and the Ulstermen. 'We award you the champion's prize.' But Loegaire and Conall Cernach refused to acknowledge the decision and accused CuChulainn of bribing Ailill and Medb. Out came the swords once more. Conchobar stopped the fight and Senchae the Wise pronounced that the three should go to Cu Roi of Munster for his final judgement.

When they reached the fort of Cu Roi, they found that he was away from home, but Blathnat his wife had been instructed to wine and dine them until her husband's return. After dinner Blathnat told the three that each night one of them must take the night-watch, according to Cu Roi's bidding. That night was the turn of Loegaire, for he was the eldest. The moment the sun had set, they felt the fort revolve like a water-wheel for Cu Roi put a spell on it every night, so that no enemy might find its entrance gate after dark.

Loegaire stood watch while the others slept. As it began to get light, a giant emerged from the ocean in the west. Though he was far away, the giant seemed to Loegaire as tall as the sky. As he advanced, Loegaire noticed huge tree trunks in his fists, which he hurled at Loegaire. They missed their target and the raging giant picked Loegaire up like a baby in his fist and crushed him as if between two mill-stones. The giant dropped Loegaire over the walls of Cu Roi. When the others found his half-dead body, they thought he had tried to leap the walls as a challenge to the other men.

On the following night it was the turn of Conall Cernach to watch and the same giant caused the same injuries that had befallen Loegaire. The next night was for CuChulainn and it was an evil night, for it had been prophesied that a monster from the lake beneath the citadel would devour all who dwelt there. Just before sunrise there was a great thrashing of water which startled CuChulainn who was half asleep. He looked over the walls and saw the monster, who rose high above the lake. It turned its head and attacked the fort, opening its huge mouth to swallow hut after hut. CuChulainn leapt high into the air, thrusting his arm down the beast's throat and tearing out its heart.

BELOW **Maiden Castle hillfort, Dorset, England** *(c. 300 BC). The stronghold of the Durotriges Celtic tribe has a long and complex building history, dating from around 2500 BC, but only reaching its present size in the Celtic period. The remarkable winding approach to the main entrance proved of little defence when the Romans stormed the fort in the first century AD. The site continued thereafter as a religious centre: a circular timber temple was rebuilt in stone together with a square stone temple in the fourth century AD.*

The hero hardly had time to rest before he too saw the giant rising from the ocean. The giant threw his tree trunks and CuChulainn threw his spear: all missed their targets. The giant then tried to grasp CuChulainn in his fist, but CuChulainn was too quick, and he performed his salmon leap and circled the giant with his sword. 'I'll give you anything, if you spare my life,' said the giant. 'I want the champion's prize and Emer to be first lady of Ulster,' said CuChulainn. 'Granted!' called the giant as he disappeared into the morning mists.

ABOVE **Celtic god on outer panel of the Gundestrup Cauldron, Denmark** *(first century BC). This gilt-silver cauldron was found in a bog in Denmark, outside the boundaries of the Celtic world; but its mythological images are undoubtedly Celtic. Here, a colossal god demonstrates his power over men holding wild boars. The boar and pig were sacred animals, often used for important sacrifices; and were also employed as warrior symbols in the form of helmet crests.*

Cu Roi returned the next day and heard about the great deeds of CuChulainn. He accordingly granted him the prize of champions and the three heroes of Ulster set off for home. And once more Loegaire and Conall Cernach refused CuChulainn the prize, but CuChulainn was weary of the contest and the matter was allowed to rest.

Some time later, Conchobar and the Ulstermen were about to dine at Emuin Machae when a hideous ogre appeared at the door and challenged them to the game of beheading. The three great heroes were absent and Muinremur accepted the challenge. 'The rules are these,' cried the giant, 'you cut my head off tonight and I cut off yours tomorrow.'

'Fair enough!' laughed Muinremur, who had no intention of keeping his side of the bargain with the foolish ogre. The ogre laid his head on the chopping block and Muinremur sliced off his head with an axe. To the surprise of them all, the ogre arose, took his head and walked off, saying that he would be back the next day. The following evening he returned but Muinremur was nowhere to be seen. The ogre protested at the outrage and another warrior agreed to make the same bargain. On the following night that warrior also kept out of the way of the ogre. This happened for three nights and on the fourth night many people gathered in the court to witness the marvel. CuChulainn was present and the ogre challenged him to the game of beheading. CuChulainn not only knocked his head off with one blow but he also smashed it to bits on the floor. Even so the ogre arose, picked up the pieces and left. The following evening the ogre returned, knowing that CuChulainn was a hero who kept his word. 'Where is the hero CuChulainn?' asked the ogre.

'I shall not hide from the likes of you,' answered CuChulainn.

'You sound worried,' said the ogre, 'but at least you have kept your word.' CuChulainn laid his neck on the block and the ogre raised his axe; everybody gasped and turned away. As he brought the axe down, the ogre turned the blade so that only the haft caught CuChulainn on the neck.

'Now rise up, CuChulainn!' cried the ogre, 'for of all the heroes in Ulster and indeed in the whole of Ireland, you are the greatest in terms of valour and honour. You are champion of champions and the prize of Bricriu is for you alone. Your wife Emer is the first lady of Ulster. And if any of you dispute this fact, your days will be numbered.' With these words the ogre left the room, but as he left he was transformed into Cu Roi, son of Daire, and thus ensured that his judgement of the three heroes was to be final.

BELOW **The Death of CuChulainn** *(bronze sculpture by Oliver Sheppard, The General Post Office, Dublin, Ireland; erected after the 1916 Easter Uprising). The Irish hero was eventually mortally wounded by a spear thrown by his enemy Lugaid. In his desire to die upright and fighting he lashed himself to a stone pillar. Lugaid only dared to approach when the crow settled on his shoulder, signifying death. The head of the hero was buried beneath a mound at Tara. This public memorial symbolizes those who have died in the fight for Irish independence.*

Celtic Art

The eye-catching quality of Celtic art reflects a society which placed great importance on visual displays of its wealth. The style is at its most characteristic in the abstract curvilinear patterns used as ornamentation on a wide range of objects. The early Celtic craftsmen established a basic repertoire of attractive decorative patterns. These patterns, though to our modern eyes 'abstract' and therefore without obvious meaning, must have provided the ancient Celts with a powerful visual sign of cultural identity: the same patterns are found throughout the Celtic world.

The remarkable resilience of this decorative style to external changes in Celtic culture can be gauged by its survival through time. The unmistakable taut, curving

ABOVE **Cernunnos and beasts** *(inner plate on the Gundestrup Cauldron, Denmark; first century* BC*). A rare example of figurative art from the La Tène period. The silver cauldron had thin gold foil applied over its exterior scenes. The silverworking techniques were learnt from the eastern Celts; the images were carved into metal or bone dies, and the bronze plate was then hammered into the dies from behind (repoussé); further details were then chased onto the surface with punches and engraving tools. The scenes and mythical characters are Celtic: Cernunnos the antlered god appears with stag, boar, bull, ram-horned snake and La Tène style torc.*

lines of Celtic art can be traced in an unbroken tradition from the eighth century BC with the early 'Hallstatt' culture in eastern Europe. The style appeared in Britain in the third century BC, with the 'La Tène' culture and survived some fourteen hundred years through to the Norman conquests. Various chronological changes in the basic style as well as regional variations have been identified by art historians. The style never completely disappeared from artistic production in those areas which retained a strong sense of their Celtic past. Ireland and Scotland have been particularly successful in reviving the art at different times of their post-Norman history, and nineteenth-and twentieth-century metalworkers have continued to find a market for Celtic jewellery designs.

The Celtic craftsmen seem to have left storytelling to the poets, and there is little that can be called 'narrative' in Celtic art. In place of the representation of heroic adventures found for example in ancient Greek art, the Celtic artists attracted the eye with what were often highly intricate interwoven linear forms: these forms range from simple threaded lines through to complex fantasies drawn from the natural world. When human or animal forms do appear, the naturalistic representations of Classical western art are avoided, and nature is interpreted in a strikingly stylized, even distorted manner.

The fantastical and sometimes bizarre forms of this art should be seen in the overall context of Celtic culture. The sheer time and skill involved in creating such complex forms in stone, wood and metal provided the tribal leaders with visible signs of their dominant position in Celtic society. The wealthy men and women who wore and handled these art objects also commissioned the storytellers, and the myths themselves rely on a similar interweaving of plots and sub-plots to hold the listeners' attention; likewise, mythical narratives are peppered with marvellous incidents and occasional shocks. The mysteries of Druidic religious ritual were at the core of Celtic thought, and this also must have affected the artistic tendency to avoid direct images of gods and men.

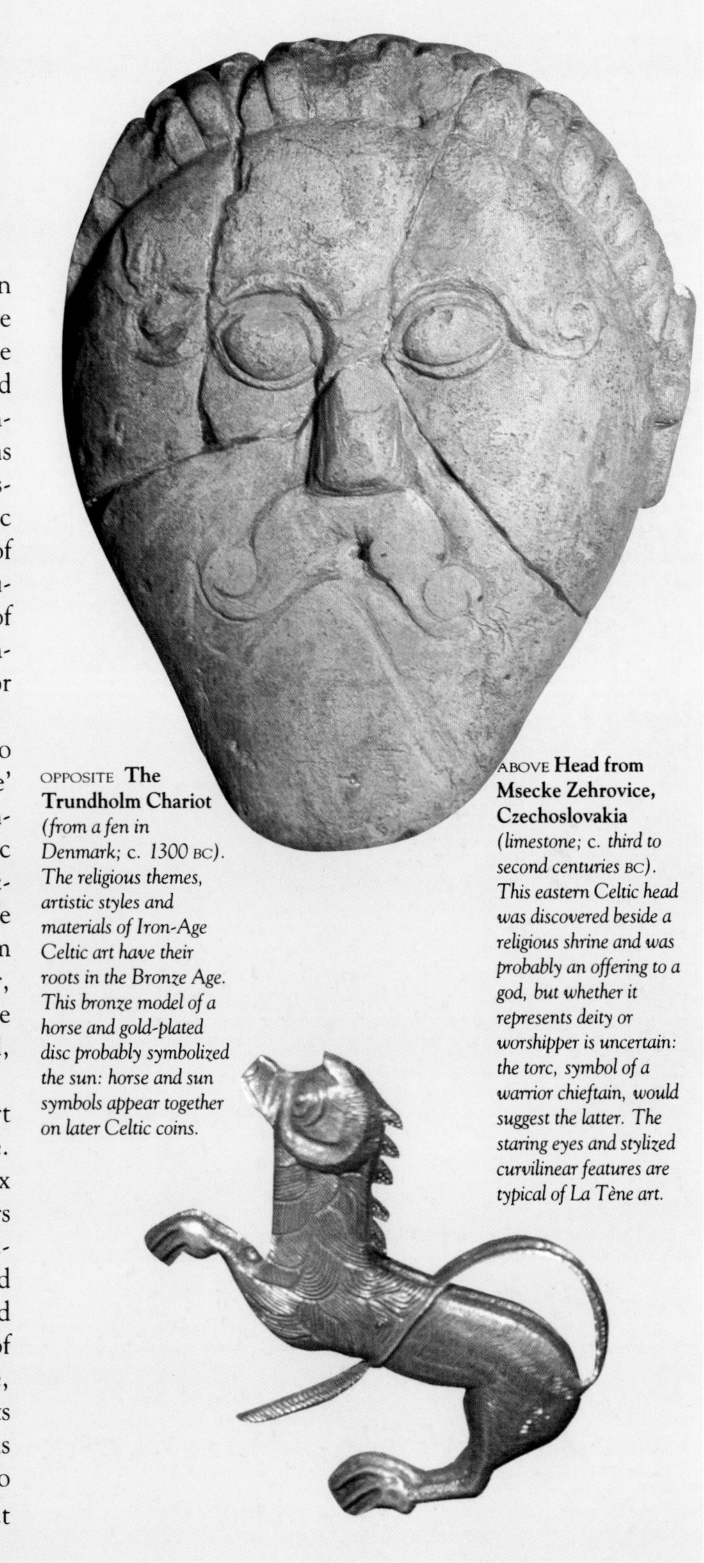

OPPOSITE **The Trundholm Chariot** *(from a fen in Denmark;* c. *1300* BC*). The religious themes, artistic styles and materials of Iron-Age Celtic art have their roots in the Bronze Age. This bronze model of a horse and gold-plated disc probably symbolized the sun: horse and sun symbols appear together on later Celtic coins.*

ABOVE **Head from Msecke Zehrovice, Czechoslovakia** *(limestone;* c. *third to second centuries* BC*). This eastern Celtic head was discovered beside a religious shrine and was probably an offering to a god, but whether it represents deity or worshipper is uncertain: the torc, symbol of a warrior chieftain, would suggest the latter. The staring eyes and stylized curvilinear features are typical of La Tène art.*

ABOVE LEFT **Electrum torc** *(from Snettisham, Norfolk, England; first century* BC*). Eight twisted wires make up each of the eight main strands; these were soldered onto the terminals, which were decorated with curving La Tène style ornaments. The British artists developed an increasingly insular version of the continental style.*

BELOW LEFT **Irish silver penannular brooch** *(seventh century* AD*). This type of brooch was exported from pre-Roman Celtic Britain to Ireland. By the early medieval period the Irish Celts were making their own extremely rich examples.*

LEFT **Base of the Cross of Cong** *(County Mayo, Ireland; bronze and oak; twelfth century). The Viking invaders influenced Late Celtic Irish art with its interweaving tendrils and dragons. The use of a beast to support the cross symbolizes the triumph of Christianity over 'nature'. The cross was made for the High King of Ireland, Turlough O Conna.*

RIGHT **Horse mask** *(from Stanwick, Yorkshire, England; first century* AD*). This bronze fitting was one of a number of horse trappings from the Celtic tribal centre of the Brigantes, destroyed by the invading Romans. The unnaturalistic features are typical of this period.*

LEFT **South door of the Church of St Mary and St David, Kilpeck, near Hereford, England** *(twelfth century). A rare example of Late Celtic art in medieval England. Interlacing tendrils, dragons and warriors decorate the columns. The door was restored in the nineteenth century with Celtic revival ironwork.*

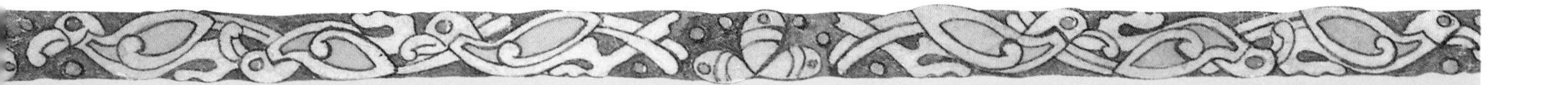

The pagan Celts took their most treasured possessions into the grave and the finest examples of Celtic art appear in aristocratic tombs. Clothing accessories for both men and women, such as brooches, neck collars, torques and armlets, were of rich metals. Gold, silver or bronze were cast in flat moulds bearing Celtic designs or the metal was simply twisted and sometimes plaited to create more complex forms; some torques consisted of hollow tubes. Colour was provided by enamel inlays. Bronze hand-mirrors have been found mainly in women's graves, their backs incised with Celtic designs. Finely decorated metal horse-tackle, drinking bowls, swords, shields and helmets reflect the fighting and feasting of the myths and female as well as male chariot-burials provide evidence of the strong position of women in the Celtic warrior society. Celtic art also manifested itself in stone carvings connected with tombs and religious sites, but the most monumental expressions of the style are the huge figures carved into the chalk of downland hills: these have been interpreted as religious images or tribal emblems.

The work of Celtic craftsmen under Roman rule kept the artistic tradition alive: Celtic and Roman artistic styles can often be identified in the same art object. The Romans never penetrated Ireland and it is perhaps ironic that the 'golden age' of Celtic art occurred not under the patronage of pagan chieftains but within a Christian context. New metalworking techniques of filigree and granulation were learnt by the Irish artists in the seventh century AD. The old pagan interlaced designs now appeared on objects of Christian ritual – crosses, chalices and patens for Communion; reliquaries for the bones of saints; bishops' crooks as signs of the new spiritual leaders; and decorative letter-headings in Christian manuscripts. The richest Celtic brooches are also from this late period.

The most recent revivals of Celtic visual art occurred mainly in the works of late nineteenth-century Scottish painters such as John Duncan. They incorporated the old Celtic patterns into the clothing and furniture of scenes from the Celtic myths. These artists tended to romanticize the myths, according to the taste of their day. In the more recent Celtic revival, the artwork of the Devon painter Alan Lee has provided new romantic evocations of the ancient Celtic world in his book-illustrations of Welsh and Arthurian myths. Lee, like Duncan, has drawn on the decorative patterns of earlier Celtic artists to imbue his more realistic images with an authentic Celtic flavour.

LEFT **The Riders of the Sidhe** *(John Duncan; tempera on canvas, 1911). The Sidhe (Shee) ride out on Celtic Beltaine (May-Eve), to usher in the Summer. The Daoine Sidhe were the Irish version of British fairies, ancient heroes and deities who lived in the Sidhe or 'hollow hills' of the Otherworld. Duncan said that he could hear 'fairy music' as he painted. Duncan gives Celtic authenticity to his late Romantic images: horse-masks and trappings, and cup, sword and shield are all drawn from ancient examples.*

TWO

The Story of Deirdre of The Sorrows

This is one of the most popular stories in the oral tradition, and several versions of it were written down between the ninth and the nineteenth centuries. This is a slight adaptation of a version recorded from a Scottish Gaelic oral source in 1887, and is therefore in a 'folk' rather than a 'literary' style. The earlier Irish accounts gave Conchobar (Connachar) as Deirdre's father — presumably this relationship was considered too incestuous and altered in later versions — and the old prophet was Conchobar's Druid, Cathbad. The lovely Deirdre's Lament is from an early Irish account, and the story incorporates pagan divinities which would have been excized by Christianization. The names here are in their Scottish forms: Ferchar mac Ro, for example, would be Fergus mac Roigh in an Irish version. In the early collections of Celtic literature, this is one of the Three Most Sorrowful Tales of Erin (which also include The Children of Lir and The Children of Turireann). It is an episode (probably an evening session in an elaborated oral recital) from a larger hero-tale and deals with the theme of the outcast. The detail of the intertwining lovers' trees may be compared to other love stories, including a version of Tristan and Isolt. A particularly Celtic feature is the powerful female characterization of the heroine Deirdre, including her wooing of the hero rather than waiting for his advances. Early cultural links between Scotland and Ireland are reflected in the story.

ABOVE **The mountainous Atlantic coast of Ireland.** *Landscape description was an essential skill for the Celtic bards: by locating the heroic activities of mythical characters within a recognizable world, myth became reality.*

Malcolm Harper and his wife lived in a remote corner of Ireland; they wanted a child dearly. They had made offerings to the fertility goddesses but had little hope of success now that they were approaching old age. Unknown to them, however, their prayers were to be answered. An old man who could see what they could not see visited them with a message from the gods: 'You will have a daughter,' he promised, 'but she will be the cause of more bloodshed than this island has ever witnessed. Three men, all of them heroes, will lose their heads because of this woman, your daughter.'

By the end of the same year, a daughter was born but the mother was not even allowed a glimpse of her. Malcolm took the baby from the house and visited a childless woman who lived in their village. 'You can have the child,' said the father, 'but I want her out of this place, where no other living person will ever set eyes on her.' They travelled for three days until they reached the high mountains. On a mountain peak they dug a hole and covered it with a roof of mud and wood: here the foster-mother and baby girl made their home. Malcolm named his daughter Deirdre and departed.

The first sixteen years of Deirdre's life were spent in this humble bothy, which soon became part of the landscape, a green mound touching the blue sky. She saw no one but her foster-mother, who taught her everything that she knew about the flowers and birds which lived around them in the sunlight and the stars which visited them at night. Deirdre, unsullied by the greed and lusts of others, thus grew into a fair young woman. Indeed she was the fairest in Ireland, and if any man had looked into her face, she would have blushed fiery red. Her keeper, now an old woman, in obedience to Malcom made certain that this would never happen, leaving her in the bothy whenever she ventured into the valley for provisions.

In the white winters, kings and noblemen hunted wild boar and stag on the wooded slopes of the mountains. Deirdre would hear their screaming horns and feel the terror of the deer as it bellowed at the rising moon. Her keeper told her that these were the wild hunters of Cernunnos,

ABOVE **The horned god Cernunnos** *(Romano-Celtic relief sculpture on the Tiberian Sailors' Pillar, Paris, France; first century AD). The god of wild beasts is in human form with the ears and antlers of a stag: from each antler hangs a torc, symbol of the Celtic warrior class. Cernunnos was popular in Gaul, but there are very few references to him in Irish and British art and mythology, although he appears later as the antler-horned Herne the Hunter.*

wandering the night sky when the moon was at its brightest. It was on such a night that the moon lost herself behind a mass of black thunderclouds. A hunter lost his dogs and companions, and found shelter from the gale beside the green mound. Cold and exhausted he lay down and was soon fast asleep. In his sleep he dreamed of fairies dancing and making music within the mound.

'Let me in before I die of the cold night,' the hunter cried out.

Deirdre heard his voice above the storm. 'There is someone out there,' she said to her keeper.

'Go back to sleep,' replied the old woman. 'It is the sound of birds who have lost their homes in the wind.'

'You yourself once said that we should give lost creatures a home,' replied Deirdre. 'I am going to let a lost bird in.'

She drew the bolt and the hunter entered. Deirdre, avoiding his steady gaze, led him to a seat beside the hearth and brought him food and clear spring water. It was the old woman who broke the silence: 'You are a lucky man to find shelter on such a night. In return you can keep quiet about what you have seen.'

'A fair enough request for saving my life,' said the hunter, 'but by your two hands and the hands of your father and his father, I know men who would take this lovely girl from you were they to set eyes on her.'

'And what men are these?' said Deirdre, ever interested in knowing the unknown.

'I will tell you since you ask,' said the hunter. 'Naois, the son of Uisnech, and his brothers, Allen and Arden.'

'What do they look like,' hesitated Deirdre, 'if we were to see them, that is?'

'You could not mistake them,' answered the hunter. 'Their skin is as white as the swan against the ripples of a dark lake, their hair is as black as the raven's wing against the bright sky, they have cheeks like the blood of the brindled red calf, and they can run and leap like deer on the mountain slopes or the salmon in the raging torrent. And Naois is the tallest man in the land of Erin.'

'No more of this,' cried the old woman. 'It is time for you to be gone, and by the sun and the light, I wish that you had not come to this place!'

The hunter left and went straightaway to the court of King Connachar of Ulster to tell him that he had found the fairest girl in Ireland and that he would take him to where she lived.

BELOW **Human and animal warriors** *(bronze matrix for making decorative helmet plaques; from Torslunda, Sweden; eighth century AD). Shape-shifting from human into animal form is a regular feature of Celtic mythology, particularly among the gods.*

It was on a May morning, before the birds had started singing and with the dew still heavy on the spring flowers, that the King of Ulster set out with his friends and the hunter to track down Deirdre in her green mound on the mountain. It was a long journey over rocky terrain and soon the spring had gone out of the step of even the youngest among them. As they approached the place the hunter called a halt. 'There is the bothy where dwells the loveliest girl in Erin, but you can complete the journey without me; I have no wish to see the old woman again.'

Connachar and his kinsmen approached the mound and knocked at the door. 'It would take the command of a king', called the old woman from within, 'for me to open the door. So tell me who you are.'

'I am Connachar, King of Ulster.' The old woman opened the door and they all crowded into the bothy.

The king looked at Deirdre and saw the girl of his dreams and felt great love for her; but Deirdre, though she blushed a fiery red at his gaze, did not see the man of her dreams. She was raised onto the shoulders of one of Connachar's heroes and was taken with her foster-mother to the court of Ulster.

Connachar told Deirdre of his great love for her and that he desired her in marriage. To the king's surprise the girl replied: 'Allow me a year and a day, and then ask me again.' 'A year and a day I grant you,' said Connachar, 'but only if you promise that you will indeed be my wife on that day.' Deirdre promised, though her heart remained silent. Connachar was content and surrounded his future wife with noble girls and, realizing that she was uneducated, provided her with a teacher. It was not long before this wild girl of the mountains was transformed into a lady fit for a king: but her heart was not in it.

It was summertime and Deirdre was sitting with her new friends on a hillock behind the castle. It was her favourite place, for from it she could see the distant mountains and imagine the birds and flowers around the old bothy. Into her daydream stepped three men making their way along the dusty track which led to the castle gates. As they passed beneath the hillock Deirdre recognized them from the portraits that the hunter had painted in her mind: these were surely the sons of Uisnech. And Deirdre felt for Naois, the tallest of the three, what Connachar had felt for her. Leaving her attendants behind, she ran down the hill in headlong pursuit of the men.

BELOW **The Turoe Stone, County Galway, Ireland** (c. *first century* BC). *The shape suggests a sacred fertility stone: it is similar to the World-Navel stone in ancient Greek Delphi. The carved decoration with its curvilinear stylized foliage is typical of Irish La Tène art.*

RIGHT **Round tower at Clonmacnois monastic settlement, Ireland** (*c. tenth century* AD). *This Christian settlement was vulnerable to Viking boats sailing up the River Shannon: such defensive towers were typical of the early Celtic Christians in Ireland. It was here that the* Book of the Dun Cow, *a rich and early manuscript of Irish myths, was written on the hide of a pet cow.*

Allen and Arden had heard of Deirdre's beauty, and had in mind that their elder brother Naois might take her for his own wife: after all, she was as yet unmarried. It was dusk and they were hurrying to reach Connachar's court before nightfall. Deirdre, whose fleet foot was hindered by her courtly dress and shoes, called out after them in despair: 'Naois, son of Uisnech, how can you go without me?' The hero stopped in his tracks. 'What was that cry so harsh and yet so melodious?' 'It is the sound of the swans on Connachar's lakes. We must be near his castle,' replied the brothers. But Naois the hero recognized the voice of a woman in distress and turned to see Deirdre behind him. Deirdre, knowing her loved one to be the man who stood before her and forgetting her new courtly manners, stepped forward and placed three kisses on Naois' brow and one kiss each for Allen and Arden. Suddenly aware of what she was doing, Deirdre blushed a fiery red, but it was gone as quickly as the aspen quivers by the stream. To Naois she was fairer than the fairest vision.

Realizing the strife that this love would cause between himself and Connachar, his uncle's son, Naois took Deirdre on his shoulders and made his way out of Ulster. The three brothers took Deirdre across the sea to Alba, which some men call Scotland. They built a tower beside Loch Ness and were happy together hunting the deer of the mountain slopes and the salmon of the raging torrent.

The day finally arrived when Deirdre had pledged her hand in marriage to Connachar. The King of Ulster could not believe that the woman he loved so well would not return to honour her promise. She did not come. Connachar decided to avenge himself by taking her from Naois, whom he did not consider to be her rightful husband. Therefore he planned a splendid feast to which all the great kings and nobles of Erin would be invited; his uncle, Ferchar mac Ro, was sent off to Alba to give word of the feast to the sons of Uisnech; 'Tell them', said Connachar, 'that I shall not sleep again if they refuse my invitation.'

Ferchar mac Ro and his three sons sailed to Alba and soon reached the tower by Loch Ness. They were warmly welcomed by Naois who asked Ferchar for the news from Erin. 'A great feast is planned by the King of Ulster,' answered Ferchar, 'and the king has vowed by the forces of earth, heaven and the westward-travelling sun that he will not rest unless the sons of his father's brother Uisnech join the celebrations.'

'We accept Connachar's invitation,' said Naois.

Deirdre could see what the invitation really meant and tried to persuade Naois to remain in Alba. Knowing that words alone would not temper her husband's pride at being invited to such a feast of heroes, Deirdre broke into song:

'I had a dream, O Naois, son
of Uisnech,
A dream for you to read.
On the warm south wind
flew three white doves
Soaring over the sea,
Bearing in their beaks what
every child loves,
Sweet nectar from the
humble bee.

'I had a dream, O Naois, son
of Uisnech,
A dream for you to read.
On the warm south wind
flew three grey hawks
Soaring across the sea,
Bearing in their beaks three
bloody torques
That meant the earth to me.'

And Naois sang:

'I read only the dreams of the
fearful night,
In the morning they fade to
dust, Deirdre,
In the morning they fade
away.'

'And if we fail to accept the invitation from the great Irish king, we shall be an enemy to Erin forever,' added Naois.

Ferchar mac Ro was unaware of Connachar's grudge, and he pledged: 'If anyone should harm the sons of Uisnech, I, Ferchar, and my three heroic sons will fight to the death to defend you.'

Deirdre's sorrows began on the day they set sail for Erin: standing on the stern of the wooden ship she sang her farewell to Scotland:

ABOVE **Celtic bronze torc from Dumfriesshire, Scotland** (c. *first century* AD). *Classical writers tell us that torcs were worn in battle by otherwise naked Celtic warriors. The taut abstract designs are found on many types of object in La Tène art.*

'Across the waves I see you,
Alba,
Slipping away from me,
I cry for your woods and quiet
lakes
But my place is beside the
one I love,
My heart is beside my Naois.'

And the sons of Ferchar sang:

'We weigh the anchor, hoist
the sail,
And make towards the ocean
deep,
In two days' time, come wind
and gale,
Onto Erin's white shore we'll
leap, we'll leap,
Onto Erin's white shore we
shall leap.'

When they had arrived in Ireland, Ferchar sent a messenger to tell Connachar that the sons of Uisnech had accepted his invitation to the feast. Connachar was not ready for them, and asked them to wait for a day or two in a house reserved for important guests. That evening, wondering whether Deirdre was still the same fair girl that he had taken a year ago from the bothy, Connachar sent for Gelban Grednach, the Prince of Lochlin: 'Pay a visit to the sons of Uisnech, Gelban, and bring me word as to whether my Deirdre has the same fair skin as when she left Erin. If she has altered, then let the son of Uisnech keep her; but if she is still the woman of my dreams, then I shall have her back by the sword's point and the blade's edge.'

Gelban, known for his charm and cheerfulness, walked down to the house where the sons of Uisnech and Deirdre were lodging with the three sons of Ferchar mac Ro: Daring Drop, Hardy Holly and Fiallan the Fair were their names. He did not bother to knock at the door, but peeped at Deirdre through a hole in the door. Deirdre, conscious of the man's gaze, blushed a fiery red as was her wont. The effect was not lost on Naois who, realizing that a man must be staring at his wife through the peephole, picked up a dice from the gaming table and threw it hard at the small hole: his aim was sure, and cheerful Gelban the Charmer returned to Connachar minus an eye.

'You left the court charming and cheerful as ever, yet you return as cheerless Gelban the Charmless,' said the King of Ulster. 'Well, is my Deirdre as fair as when I last saw her?'

'I lost an eye through gazing at her in admiration,' replied Gelban, 'and would have remained to look at her with my other eye, but pulled myself away from the fair vision in order to report back to you.'

'Is she still so fair?' said Connachar. 'Three hundred of my bravest heroes shall take her from the house, killing those that are with her.'

LEFT **Bronze shield from the River Thames at Battersea, London, England** *(c. first century AD). Such fine objects appear to have been deliberately thrown into rivers by Celtic warrior aristocrats as votive offerings to the water gods. The shield has curvilinear La Tène designs which become abstract faces in the central roundel. Colour was provided by applied red glass.*

RIGHT **The Druids: Bringing in the Mistletoe** *(by George Henry and EA Hornel; 1890). The late nineteenth century saw attempts at revival of Celtic art and language in Scotland: this was one of the first 'revival' paintings. The ancient literary source for this monthly ritual is Pliny the Elder: he relates that on the sixth day of the moon (seen rising above the hill), the Druids climbed a sacred oak and cut off the mistletoe with a golden sickle (held by the leading figure); two bulls were sacrificed. The Druids wear rediscovered Celtic and Pictish jewellery. A year later the two artists painted* The Star in the East *as a Christian counterpart: Christ's birthday fell at the pagan winter solstice, which is the setting for* The Druids.

Naois and Deirdre heard the three hundred approaching and the brave sons of Uisnech armed themselves for the attack. The sons of Ferchar mac Ro stopped them from leaving the house: 'This is our fight,' they cried. 'Before our father left for Alba he made us swear that we would defend you from any danger.' What a fine sight they made as they went to battle: the most handsome of men, with beautiful auburn hair and shining bronze armour engraved with fierce lions and eagles, slinking snakes and leaping tigers. Three-thirds of the army sent against them fell in the fighting.

Connachar came running out: 'Who are you men who can kill three hundred of my greatest heroes with such ease?'

'We are the sons of Ferchar mac Ro,' they replied.

Connachar was desperate: 'You and your kinsmen shall have great rewards if you join my army this night,' he bargained.

'We shall have none of it,' countered the three brothers, 'for we would rather return to our father recounting deeds of heroism than accept your faithless gifts. We have seen you turn on the sons of Uisnech and they are as close to you by birth as we are. Why should we expect different treatment?' And the three glorious heroes, tall and handsome with their auburn locks shining from the heat of the battle went back into the house: 'Now we must leave you,' they told Deirdre and the sons of Uisnech, 'for we have to tell our father that we have done our duty.' And away they went into the night.

With the dawn twilight Deirdre and Naois, Allen and Arden decided that they too must return to Alba. The King of Ulster had his spies and he soon heard that the party was on the road. Connachar sent for his Druid, a great magician called Duanan Gacha. 'All the money that I have spent on your training in the art of magic will be of no avail if these men leave Erin now,' said the king.

RIGHT **Deirdre of the Sorrows** *(black chalk by John Duncan, 1866–1945). The Scottish poet Fiona Macleod (in reality William Sharp) explored the tragedy of Deirdre in her play* The House of Usna, *performed at The Globe, London, in 1900. Duncan's drawing is undated, but many of his images are drawn from the same repertoire as the poet, providing the visual matter of the Scottish Celtic revival. The artist had a pool of Celtic designs which he incorporated into his images to give them an authentic flavour.*

'With my command over nature, I can easily call a halt to their journey,' replied the Druid, and he blocked their path with an impenetrable forest. But the sons of Uisnech were practised in hunting the boar, and walked straight through, with Deirdre holding the hand of Naois.

'So much for that!' cried the king. 'I have no power over them.'

'Let us see if they find my next trick so simple,' said the Druid, and he placed a grey sea before them where the green plain was a moment before. The heroes stripped and with their clothes tied round their necks swam the obstacle; Deirdre travelled on the shoulders of Naois.

'So much for that!' cried Connachar. 'I have no power over them.'

'Here is one that they cannot possibly overcome,' said Duanan Gacha, and he solidified the grey sea into rocks with the poison of adders on their sharp edges. 'I am weary of this,' cried Arden, and the great-hearted Naois took his brother on his shoulders together with Deirdre. Arden was soon dead but Naois would not drop his brother in enemy territory. Allen was the next to fall and Naois took him on his back too. It was not long before he felt Allen's grip fail and, seeing both his brothers dead, Naois no longer cared if he lived or died: his heart burst as he sighed the bitter sigh of death.

'Success!' cried the Druid. 'I have destroyed the sons of Uisnech as you bid me, and you can now take your wife whom I have left unharmed.'

'Your education was worthwhile after all,' replied Connachar: 'Now clear the plain of your magic and let me see my Deirdre.' Duanan Gacha Druid did as he was told and the company of Ulster looked down on the plain. There they saw the three sons of Uisnech laid out on the green meadow side by side, and above them the bending figure of Deirdre, showering her loved ones with her tears and lamentations:

'O Naois, my most beautiful warrior, flower of all men; my lover who once stood so tall and powerful; my man of the shining blue eyes, dearly loved by his wife; I shall never forget the sound of your voice when we first met in the woods of Erin: as clear and true as spring water it was. From this moment I am unable to eat, drink or raise a smile to the world once so lovely. May my heart not break today, for the sea-tides of our everyday sorrows are strong, but I am sorrow itself, O Connachar.' And she looked towards the king who had brought this about.

The people of Ulster were watching and they asked their king what was to be done with the bodies of the three heroes. Connachar ordered that a burial pit should be dug and the brothers laid to rest beside one another. Deirdre remained there while the grave was being dug, encouraging the diggers to make the pit larger than was necessary. The sons of Uisnech were lowered into the grave and Deirdre sang her elegy:

> 'May Arden and Allen
>   together lie,
> As they stood together in life;
> May Naois make room for his
>   love Deirdre,
> In death she remains his
>   wife.'

Deirdre leapt into the grave as the salmon leaps in the raging torrent or as the deer bound on the mountain slopes; she placed herself beside Naois, son of Uisnech, and hand in hand they lay together in death. But Connachar's love for Deirdre also lay beyond death and he had her body lifted and buried on the opposite bank of the loch.

When the company departed into the twilight, a mountain fir sprouted from Deirdre's tomb and a second from the tomb of Naois; they grew towards one another, entwining themselves in a lover's knot above the still waters. They were cut down by the king, but they grew again.

BELOW **'Ossian's Grave': a neolithic grave above Glen Aan, County Antrim, Ireland** (c. *2500* BC). *The monumental stone graves of earlier cultures were revered as sacred by the Celts. The attribution of this grave to the Irish hero 'Ossian' (Oisin) was probably made under the influence of James Macpherson's spurious eighteenth-century* Gaelic Romances of the Bard Ossian.

THREE

The Fate of The Children of Lir: One of The Three Sorrowful Tales of Erin

This is one of the Three Sorrowful Tales of Erin; the other two are Deirdre of the Sorrows and The Children of Tuireann. It is not certain how ancient The Children of Lir tale is, as the earliest surviving written accounts date from as late as the eighteenth century, and are heavily Christianized. I have altered the Christian ending in which the children are transformed back to human form and baptized before they die, although this episode might have existed in a pagan version where the swan-children are in a fairy world of perpetual youth: the silver chains linking the swan-children are the tokens of their fairy status, and once removed they re-enter the human world. The Christian version would have taken the myth with its pagan elements and altered the ending to demonstrate the triumph of the new religion.

The surviving pagan Celtic themes seen here include the jealous stepmother and the inviolable nature of swans, both of which are popular themes in Irish folk-tales. The interwoven verses were a feature of the Celtic storytellers and were probably sung.

LEFT **Dolmen at Kilcloney, County Donegal, Ireland** (c. 2000 BC). *The dolmen (or cromlech) type of prehistoric tomb was originally covered with an earth mound. Many folk-tales surround these structures which, like other Neolithic and Bronze-Age sites, were often reused, misinterpreted or mythologized by later Celts.*

The five kings of Ireland gathered together one day to elect one great king of Erin from among themselves. Their nobles chose Dearg, son of Daghda, for the reason that he was the eldest son of a highly respected Druid. King Lir, however, left the Gathering of the Kings in anger, for he himself had expected the high kingship. The remaining kings wanted to ride after him and wound him with sword and spear on account of his treachery, but Dearg restrained them. 'In order to maintain the peace,' he said, 'we shall make him our kinsman, sending him word that he may select as a wife one of the three beautiful daughters of Oilell of Aran, my own foster-children.

Messengers were sent to the Hill of the White Field where King Lir kept his court. He accepted the offer and the following day set off with fifty chariots for the Lake of the Red Eye near Killaloe. King Dearg was waiting there for him together with the three daughters of Oilell: 'Take whichever maiden you desire,' said Dearg.

'I cannot decide which of them is the most beautiful,' replied Lir, 'therefore I shall have the eldest, for she is the noblest.'

'The maiden Ove is the eldest of the three, and she is yours if you so desire,' said Dearg.

Lir rode back to the Hill of the White Field with Ove as his bride. Not long after a daughter and son were born together; Fingula and Aod were their names. Two more sons followed, Fiachra and Conn, but their birth brought the sad death of Ove. Now Lir had dearly loved his wife, and his heart would have broken had he not felt an equal love for his four children.

When he heard the news King Dearg felt much grief for Lir, and sent messengers to offer him Oifa, the sister of Ove, as a second wife. They were married and lived together happily for some time. But Oifa became jealous of the children, who were great favourites with everyone. So she took them out in her chariot with wicked intent. Fingula resisted, for on

RIGHT **The Children of Lir** *(bronze sculpture by Oisin Kelly, the Garden of Remembrance, Phoenix Park, Dublin; erected in 1966 to commemorate the 1916 Easter Rising). The sculptor has depicted the moment of metamorphosis from human to animal form as a visual mythological metaphor of political liberation.*

the previous night she had dreamt terrible things about her stepmother; but her fate was sealed, and into the chariot she went.

The five riders arrived at the Lake of the Oaks. 'I shall give you whatever you most desire in the world,' cried Oifa to the people dwelling there, if you kill the four children of Lir.' But the people would have nothing to do with her. Then she told the children to go for a swim in the lake and cast a spell upon them with a wand once given her by a Druid. And as she pointed the wand, she sang the spell over the waters and threw silver chains around the children's necks:

'Into the waters wild, royal
offspring of Lir!
Forever more your cries will
be lost among the birds.'

Immediately the four children began to sprout downy feathers and soon they had turned into beautiful swans of purest white. And Fingula sang:

'We know you for what you
are, witch woman!
You have the power to make
us swim the lake,
Yet we shall take our rest on
land when we choose;
We shall be soothed, but you
shall be scolded.
For though now you see us on
the waves,
Our spirits are on their way
home.'

'Lift the magic curse which you have laid upon us,' cried Fingula. 'Never!' Oifa laughed. 'Not until Lairgnen of Connaught marries Deoch of Munster, and southern woman is united with northern man. For nine hundred years you are to sail the lakes and rivers of Erin and no one will be able to lift my magic. One thing I grant you: the speech of man you are to keep, and no man or animal will prove equal to your poignant singing.' This last she granted out of sudden remorse; then she sang:

ABOVE **Silver torc from Trichtingen, Germany** (*c. second century* BC). *Decorated in a more linear, Eastern style, the bull-head terminals are symbols of the strength and virility of the Celtic warrior.*

'So off with you now, young
children of Lir,
From this time hence wild
winds will mock you
Only to cease when Deoch
and Lairgnen are wed,
And you swimming in the
northwest of red Erin.

'My treacherous sword has
pierced the heart of Lir,
Though in battle he be a
great champion,
Yet the sword which enters
him,
Is no victory to my wounded
heart.'

Oifa rode on to the Hall of King Dearg. 'Where', asked the courtiers, 'are the children of Lir?'

'King Lir does not trust them in the Hall of Dearg,' she replied. Dearg was suspicious of Oifa, and sent messengers to the court of Lir to ask after the children. 'But are they not at the Hall of Dearg with Oifa?' asked Lir.

'No,' they replied, 'and Oifa told us that you were unwilling to let them stay with Dearg.'

Lir, troubled by the news, set off with his chariots for the Lake of the Red Eye, where his children were at that time. The swans heralded his approach and Fingula sang:

RIGHT **Figurative corbels on exterior of Kilpeck Church, near Hereford, England** *(twelfth century). The sculptors who decorated the church represented Christian saints in the interior but portrayed a number of figures from the pagan Celtic repertoire on the outside, thus defining the Christian and pagan spaces. The pagan fertility deity (above), Sheela-na-gig (Irish for 'Sheelagh of the Breasts'), is probably apotropaic, being used to ward off the 'evil eye'. The gaping animal head (below) performs the same function. The large, staring eyes and wedge-shaped noses are traditional in Celtic representation.*

'Our greetings to the
company of horsemen
Drawing near to the Lake of
the Red Eye,
Are these not men of magic
and might
Seeking us out on the waves?

'Then make for the shore,
brothers Aod,
Fiachra and beautiful Conn,
For these are no strange
horsemen
But our father King Lir and
his men.'

Lir heard the wonderful human voices of the swans and asked their names. 'We are the children of Lir,' they cried. 'Our stepmother has cast a cruel spell on us, as you can all see, and the spell cannot be lifted until the wedding of Lairgnen and Deoch.'

The swans sang their wild and woeful ballads, and Lir and his company wept and raged until the swans at last flew away. Thereupon Lir made his way to the Hall of Dearg and told him of his second wife's treachery. 'What creature', Dearg asked Oifa, 'would you least like to be in this world of shapes and forms?'

'Why,' she answered, 'anyone would hate to be transformed into a demon of the air.'

ABOVE **'Flesh-hook' from County Antrim, Ireland** *(c. sixth century BC). The birds (geese?) are represented in the taut geometric style of Hallstatt art. The function of the object is debatable: water-birds and geese often appear in Celtic art and myth in both sacred and warrior contexts. Therefore such decorations would be apt on banquet or ritual equipment.*

OPPOSITE **The Children of Lir** *(tempera by John Duncan, 1866–1945). Duncan depicts the children meeting on the Rock of the Seals during the storm. Is this the moment of their return to human form (with the coming of Christianity), or has Duncan simply depicted them in different stages of swan/human form for narrative reasons? Their expressions denote the approach of something both fearful and wonderful.*

'Then become one,' said Dearg, and he pointed his own Druid's wand at Oifa. Immediately her face became demonic and her sharp wings took her away into the air to remain an air-demon until the end of time.

The children of Lir sang their songs of sadness to the clans who dwelt around the Lake of the Red Eye until they felt that the time had come to depart. Fingula sang to the people of Dearg and Lir as they stood on the shores of the lake:

'Fare thee well, Dearg our
king,
You who have mastered the
art of the Druids!
And fare thee well, dear
father of ours,
King Lir of the Hill of the
White Field!

'We are off to live out our
final days
Far away from the dwellings
of men.
We shall swim in the flowing
tides of the Moyle,
Our feathers all bitter and
salty.

'Till that day when Deoch
joins Lairgnen,
Let us fly my brothers who
once had red cheeks;
From the Lake of the Red Eye
we travel;
In sorrow we fly from our
loved ones.'

They flew away, high into the sky and out of sight, and took no rest until they reached the Moyle, the water which lies between Erin and Alba. And the people of Erin were so upset at the departure of the swan-children that a law was made banning the killing of swans.

The children found themselves cold and alone with a great storm brewing. Fingula suggested that they agree on a meeting place in case they lost one another in the tempest. 'Let us gather', said her brothers, 'at the Rock of the Seals.' And the lightning and thunder cracked at their words and the children of Lir were thrown apart on the raging deep. When at last it had died down Fingula sang:

'I wish I had died in the
waters wild
For my wings have turned to
ice.
My brothers three, come
back again
And hide once more beneath
my wings.
But I know that this can
never be
Till dead men rise from their
graves!'

She made her way to the Rock of the Seals and two of her brothers appeared, Conn and Fiachra, their feathers heavy with the salt thrown up by the stormy seas. Fingula cradled them under her wings: 'If only our brother Aod were here with us,' she

BELOW LEFT **Din Lligwy, Anglesey, Wales** *(c. fourth century AD). A well-preserved native British settlement from the late Roman period. The old Celtic cultural traditions survived in such remote areas, the circular and rectangular huts contrasting vividly with the contemporary luxurious Roman villas of southern England.*

cried, 'then we would be so happy.' Aod arrived with his head and feathers dry and preened. Fingula tucked him under her breast with Conn and Fiachra under each wing and she sang:

'The magical spells of a
wicked woman
Have sent us into the
northern seas,
Transformed by our
stepmother are we
Into magical forms of swans.

'And now our bath is the
water's edge
In the salty foam of the
breaking waves,
And the only ale we drink at
the feast
Is the salty draught of the
deep blue sea.'

One fine day a troop of gleaming white horses came galloping up and the swan-children recognized the two sons of Dearg. 'The king, our father,' they said, 'and indeed your own father Lir, are alive and well, but they have not been happy since you flew away from the Lake of the Red Eye.' Fingula then sang of their lot:

'There is meat and drink in
the court tonight,
In the court of Lir is
rejoicing.
But what has become of the
children of Lir?
Our beds are our feathers,
Our food is the white sand,
Our wine is the deep blue sea.
Beneath my feathers rest
Fiachra and Conn
Under my wings they sail on
the Moyle,
And beneath my breast lies
Aod dear,
Together we lie in our feather
bed.

The sons of Dearg returned and told of what they had seen and the beautiful song that they had heard.

The flowing waters of the Moyle carried the children of Lir to the Bay of Erris where they remained until the fated day when they were to return to the Hill of the White Field. And there they found everything in a state of desolation; only nettles remained where once stood the high walls of dwellings. Three times they cried out their grief. Then Fingula sang:

'How sad it is for me to see
My father's fallen halls:
Here once were dogs and
hunting hounds,
Here women laughed with
gallant knights,

'Here once was heard the
clash of cups
Of horn and wood in merry
feasts,
Now all I see is desolation
My father long since dead
and gone.

'And we his children have
wandered for years,
And felt the cruel blast of
freezing winds;
But the harshest blow of all
has come:
To return at last to an empty
home.'

The swans then flew to the lovely Isles of the West. At that time the prophecy of Fingula's song had come true: Deoch the Princess of Munster had promised to marry Lairgnen Prince of Connaught. But Deoch would not be wed until her prince had brought her the wonderful swans. Lairgnen found them swimming happily on the Lake of the Birds; he rowed out to them and removed their silver chains. In an instant they became human again, but the boys had aged into bony old men and young Fingula was now a bent and scrawny old woman. They died within the hour and were laid to rest as they had been in life: Fiachra and Conn on either side of Fingula, with Aod at her breast.

RIGHT **Bronze-Age grave on Shovel Down, Dartmoor, England** (c. *1000* BC). *The upland areas of western Britain provide the best surviving evidence of the Celtic landscape. Here there are Iron-Age farms and field boundaries, outside of which are the stone-circles and burial mounds of the preceding Bronze Age.*

Celtic Storytellers

ABOVE **Beard-pullers and beasts from the Book of Kells** *(Irish; eighth to ninth centuries AD). The Christian scribes illustrated their texts with motifs and styles from the pagan Celtic past. The interlacing forms of human and animal figures symbolize the bestiality of man and nature in the eyes of the new religion.*

Our knowledge of the early pagan Celtic poets comes mainly from the recorded observations of their Greek and Roman contemporaries. Diodorus of Sicily, writing in the first century BC, tells us that among the Gallic Celts were 'lyric poets called bards, who accompany their songs with instruments similar to lyres: these songs include praise-poems and satires' (Book V, 31). This suggests that the bards played an important social role: they would be hired to write poems praising their patrons, but also to pour scorn on the patron's enemies.

The bards referred to by Diodorus did not record their poems in writing as did their classical counterparts, but passed them down from teacher to pupil in the manner of prehistoric Greek poetry. And like those early Greek poets, the bard was considered to be a kind of priest, passing religious mysteries on to future generations. This may account for the many 'unexplainable' aspects of the myths. Diodorus tells us in the same passage that they 'converse with few words and in riddles, mainly using obscure hints to refer to things and saying one word when they mean another; and they tend to use superlatives to boost their own achievements and put down those of others.'

The surviving Celtic myths themselves can also tell us about the status of the poets. In the story of the *Dream of Rhonabwy* in the *Mabinogion*, a poet sings a song of praise which can only be understood by other poets. In the medieval period there were highly paid and socially respected bards employed in the houses of the surviving Celtic nobility. There were also wandering minstrels who usually received small payments for their songs, but who certainly helped to keep the oral tradition alive by carrying the poems across Britain and Europe. It was in this period also that the first written versions of the myths were made, although since the scribes were usually monks, the stories were often heavily Christianized.

Finally there were the storytellers, who since time immemorial have told both heroic myths and folk-tales wherever there were people to listen, round the domestic hearth or in a corner of the pub. They still exist in the remoter Celtic areas and their feats of memory are legendary. A

fisherman in Barra is recorded as saying that when he was a boy he listened to the same storyteller every night for 15 years and that he hardly ever repeated a story.

The 'high' bardic tradition has survived in the annual Welsh Eisteddfod meetings, but there is also an attempt to revive it in less formal surroundings. The British singer and harpist Robin Williamson performs and records the Celtic hero-tales in spoken and sung poetry to the accompaniment of his 'Celtic' harp and the Breton artist Alan Stivell similarly recreates the Celtic myths of Britanny. The Celtic storytelling tradition is therefore still very much alive for those who wish to experience it.

ABOVE LEFT **Robin Williamson** *The Scottish songwriter and storyteller often accompanies his singing on the Welsh harp. A founder member of the Incredible String Band in the 1960s, more recently he has created sung and spoken versions of Celtic myths and legends. He has also written music and lyrics for a play of the* Mabinogion *and musical accompaniments for a television history of Wales.*

ABOVE RIGHT **A scribe writing a book** *(Anglo-Saxon ivory). Monastic scribes were the only literate men with the time and ability to record the oral Celtic myths in written form.*

FOUR

The Art of Description in Celtic Mythology

Celtic storytellers were experts in the vivid description of imaginary worlds, fantastic animals and superhuman characters. Bright colours and meticulous details of landscape, human appearance and dress are the main characteristics of Celtic descriptive passages, mirroring a similar manifestation of rich colour and detail found in the Celtic visual arts. Descriptions of women tend to be highly voyeuristic and unrealistic, reflecting the male gender of the storyteller, and for the same reason, storytellers glamourized the warrior aspects of their male characters.

ABOVE **The Atlantic coast and the Ring of Kerry mountains, Ireland.** *Mild winters encourage continual vegetation and pasturage throughout the year here; Mediterranean trees grow in some parts. Kerry was on the prehistoric migration and trade routes and has many surviving remains of its ancient past. It is easy to see how such landscapes could be mythologized into paradises.*

FANTASY LANDSCAPE: THE DISCOVERY OF PARADISE ON EARTH

The storm was over and the wind blew gently now; the sea-warriors hoisted their sail and the boat took in less water. A stillness fell upon the wide ocean, the waves were smoothed and it was bright and calm. Birds of different kinds never seen before filled the air round about with their singing. A land of graceful shape and fair shores came into view ahead of them; the sailors rejoiced at the sight of it. They sailed closer and entered a beautiful estuary, its green breasts hanging above silver-pebbled beaches, and in the clear waters the splendid deep purple of the handsome salmon flashed; and they looked about them and were pleased by the lovely streams running through woods tinged with purple.

Tadhg the Irish Prince of Munster stood at the bow and addressed his men: 'This is surely the island of our dreams, my fighting men; it is blessed with fruit and all things most lovely; we shall make for the beach, haul up the boat and give it time enough to dry out after its storm-battering.' Twenty stout warriors went on ahead with Tadhg, leaving twenty behind to guard the boat; and the wonder of it was that though they had come through wind and hard rain and the extremes of cold and hunger, they felt no desire for food and the camp fire

ABOVE **Bronze belt hook from the German Tyrol** *(fourth century BC). Early La Tène artists preferred running tendril patterns; here 'dragons' (or stylized horses, perhaps?) and human figures are depicted within such a fantasy pattern. Whatever the subject matter, it appears to symbolize the power of man (or god?) over beast, and would therefore have been fitting decoration for the aristocratic warrior.*

in that place. It was enough and more than enough to breathe in the incense of the trees, glowing with purple flowers about them.

Tadhg led them into the wood beside their path and they soon came to an orchard of glorious purple-fringed apple trees and oaks with leaves of lovely hue and hazels teeming with nuts of bright yellow. 'What a wonderful thing occurs to me,' said Tadhg to his warriors. 'It is winter back home, yet summer reigns here.'

There was indeed no end to the lovely places they discovered in that land. Leaving the orchard, they came upon a wood without shadows, with round purple berries the size of men's heads giving off wonderful scents; and the birds that fed on the berries made the men blink and look again, for they were white birds with purple heads and golden beaks. They sang the songs of minstrels as they ate their fill of the berries, and their music was plaintive and yet so soothing, that it would have lulled wounded warriors to sleep . . .

Anonymous Irish author of the fourteenth or fifteenth century

FANTASY WOMAN: A VISION OF ETAIN THE FAIRY

The men could see a woman beside the spring. In her hand glinted a comb of silver with decorative work in gold and she was about to wash her hair in a bowl of beaten silver with reddish-purple gems glittering on its rim and on its sides four inlaid golden birds could be seen as she turned the bowl. The woman wore the fleece of a fine shaggy sheep dyed purple, and on the shoulders of this cloak were silver brooches worked in twisted filigree with golden ornament. Beneath the cloak she wore, stiff yet smooth, a tunic of green silk with a long hood, embroidered with reddish-gold thread; they could see the interlacing of exotic animals worked into the tunic in gold and silver running over her breasts, shoulders and shoulder blades. The gold gleamed in the sunlight against its green silken background.

Her golden-blond hair was arranged in two long tresses; each tress was made up of four plaits, and at the end of each plait hung a bead. To some men her hair was the colour of the yellow flag iris which grows by summer water; others thought it like ruddy polished gold.

ABOVE **Spring nymphs from the Roman fort at High Rochester, Northumberland, England** *(stone relief sculpture; third century* AD*). Many dedications to a Celtic water deity named Coventina have been found in northern England. This relief may portray a Roman goddess (Venus or Diana, disturbed while bathing) or it could also represent Coventina: classical iconography was often borrowed for Celtic deities. The original context is not known: it was reused in a water-tank at the fort.*

She began to untie her hair for washing, her arms reaching out from the openings in her dress. The arms were straight yet soft, their tops as white as a fall of night snow before the sun rises; the skin of her face was clear and her cheeks blushed red like the foxglove on the moor. Like the black beetle's wings were her eyebrows; like a spray of pearls were her teeth; like the brilliant blue starry flowers of borage were her eyes; of bright red vermilion were her lips. Her soft, smooth shoulders stood high and white; of the purest white were her fingers, long and slender as were her arms; and long, slender and soft as pliable wool were her white sides, like the foam on the wavecrest. Smooth, shiny and sleek were her warm white thighs; her small, firm knees were white and rounded; white shins she had, short and straight. She stood straight and even on her heels, which looked lovely from behind; if a straight rule were placed along her feet, no fault would be found, unless the skin or flesh were made to bulge by pressing too hard.

The bright blush of the rising moon glimmered in her noble face; her smooth forehead was high and dignified; the beams of eroticism shone from her royal eyes; her cheeks bore the dimples of her sport which flushed now with a purple as red as the blood of the frisky calf and now the white brilliance of snow. Her voice was noble and gentle; she walked as befits a queen, stepping steadily and stately. She was the most perfect woman in the world to behold, as fair and lovely as they could ever hope to see; the men agreed that she must have been a fairy . . .

Anonymous Irish author of the ninth century

FANTASY MEN: SOME HEROES FROM THE COURT OF KING ARTHUR

Morfran son of Tegid, was so ugly that he was thought to be an evil demon; therefore he was avoided in Arthur's last battle at Camlan. He was as hairy as a stag. Sandde Angel-Face was also left unharmed at that battle, but for a different reason: he was so beautiful that he was thought to be a heavenly angel.

BELOW LEFT **Bronze armlet from Pitkelloney, Tayside, Scotland** *(c. first century* BC*). This massive piece of warrior ornament was originally polished and shining like all other Celtic bronze objects, with additional colour provided by red and yellow enamel inlay.*

There were three men, all sons of Erim, best known for their magical speed. Henbeddestr could run faster than any other man, even when they were on horseback; Henwas the Winged could run faster over even the shortest distance than any man or four-footed beast; and Scilti the Nimble-footed was often sent as a messenger by Arthur, for he would

ABOVE **Bronze helmet with decorated neck-guard** *(British; first century AD). The Celtic warrior's helmet was often highly decorated depending on his rank. This is a relatively restrained example with decoration in the taut curvilinear La Tène style: however, the holes on the crown might have held a plume or other fixture. Artistic representations of Celtic warriors depict them wearing animal crests, such as birds or boars; horned helmets were also worn.*

not bother with roads, but take the shortest route, touching the tree-tops and skipping the bog-rushes on the mountain slopes. Scilti was so light of foot that he never once bent or broke the rushes that he stepped on.

Teithi the Elder, son of Gwynham, who barely escaped when his lands were covered by the sea, had come to Arthur's court. Some magic curse was on his knife, so that no haft could be found to fit it; and therefore he lived a life of disease and misery, and died of it.

Drem the son of Dremidydd had eyes that could see the gnat in the rising sun's light as far away as Penn Blathon in Scotland from Cellig Wig in Cornwall.

Cynyr of the Beautiful Beard — some say that Cei was his son — once said to his wife, 'If there is anything of me in your son, my girl, he will be touched by a magic which removes the warmth from his heart and makes him headstrong. He will have other magical abilities: no one, from in front or behind him, will ever be able to see what he is carrying, however large or small it is; he, more than anyone, will be able to face fire and water; he will be the most loyal page and court official.

Then there was Gwallgoig, who used to keep whole towns awake with his bodily requirements when he was staying overnight: no one could sleep.

Osla of the Great Knife, who carried a short broad weapon at his side, used to be a boon to Arthur whenever he came to a torrent with his army. Osla's knife in its sheath would be placed across the narrowest point above the raging stream so that a bridge was formed broad enough to take the army of the three lands of Britain and its three offshore islands (England, Wales and Scotland, Anglesey, the Isle of Man and the Isle of Wight).

Gilla Stag-Legs was the champion of Ireland at long-jump: three hundred acres were his in one bound.

There were three more great heroes: Sol, who could stand on one foot for a day; Gwaddn Osol, who could level a mountain by standing upon it; and Gwaddn of the Bonfire, a boon to Arthur when his armies encountered woody obstacles: the sparks from his metal-studded soles were as large as pieces of red-hot iron drawn out of the forge.

There were the two great eaters, Hir Erwm and Hir Atrwm. On feasting days they would get their supplies by raiding three hundred towns. Then they would eat till noon and drink into the night; they would not stop eating in bed but would bite off the heads of the rats. When invited to another man's feast they would polish off the meat, be it lean or fat, hot or cold, sweet or sour, fresh or salted. Another eater was Huarwar, son of Halwn, who only smiled when he was

LEFT **Horned warrior from Roman coastal fort, Maryport, Cumbria, England** *(Romano-British). This naïve and roughly incised image represents a naked horned warrior with shield and spear. His virility is symbolized by the horns and erect phallus: a straightforward image of the male fighter ready for battle. Although crudely carved, the frontal staring face and wedge-shaped nose are in the high Celtic style.*

full. One of the Three Great Plagues of the West Country was caused by his demands to be given his fill from Arthur as a present.

There were a number of curious heroes. Sugn, son of Sugnedudd, had the ability to suck up the sea from beneath as many as three hundred ships, leaving only the dry sea-bed; he used to get red-hot heartburn. Cachamwri, one of Arthur's serving men, could work his way through a barn containing the crops of thirty ploughed fields: he would thresh around with his iron flail until the wooden posts, rafters and cross-beams were lying in as many bits on the floor as there were oats. When Gwefl son of Gwastad had the sulks, his lower lip would hang down to his navel and he would pull the upper lip over his head for a cap. The beard of Uchdryd Cross-Beard was so long that he had to throw its bristly red strands across the fifty rafters of Arthur's hall when he came to visit him.

RIGHT **Neolithic burial cairns in the Loughcrew Hills, County Meath, Ireland** *(c. 2500–2000 BC). Most of the prehistoric graves we see today have had their original earth mounds weathered away. These well-preserved examples allow us to understand the frequent mythological Celtic view of them as 'fairy castles'.*

Others had wonderful senses. You could have buried Clust, son of Clust-feinad seven fathoms underground, but he would still have heard an ant getting up in the morning fifty miles away. Medr, son of Medredydd could stand at Celli Wig in Cornwall and shoot through the legs of a wren standing at Esgeir Oerfel in Ireland. Gwiawn, 'Eye of the Cat', could cut the lid from a gnat's eye without damaging the eye.

Cei, whom I have already mentioned, was able to hold his breath underwater for nine days and nine nights; his sword-cut could be cured by no doctor; he could extend his height to look out over trees; his body-heat was such that, when it was pouring with rain, whatever he was holding would stay dry; and when his companions were freezing he was the kindling to light their fire.

Anonymous Welsh author of the tenth century

FAIRY LANDSCAPE: THE WOMAN FROM THE LAND OF EVERLASTING LIFE

Two warriors were walking up on Uisnech: Conn of the Hundred Battles and his red–haired son Connla, one of the Fianna, the hundred and fifty fearless chiefs who led Ireland in the wars. Over the hill came a woman, strikingly dressed so as to make the young Connla exclaim, 'Where did you come from, woman?'

'From Tir Na mBeo, the Lands of the Living,' she replied, 'and not of your world, for there you will find no men looking for a fight, and no one dies. We feast without servants, and bear no grudges. See there,' the woman pointed to a barrow on the ridge. 'That is where we live, and some call us the fairy hill folk.'

'Who is that you're speaking to?' cried Conn, for he could not see the strange woman. She answered for the dumbstruck Connla, 'I am young, beautiful and of high family; and I shall never grow old and die. I have fallen in love with your red-haired son and offer him a place in the court of King Boadhagh, who has known no weeping since he came to power in the Plain of Delights. So are you coming, Connla the Redhead, with the jewels of your torque glinting in your eyes of candle flame? You shall have a crown of gold!'

Conn turned to his Druid, Corann, and said, 'I cannot fight the magic of this woman, for all the battles I have won since I became king. You have the power of song. Use your skills, Corann, against these unseen forces which will take my handsome son from me.' The learned Druid sang his magical song, and no one saw or heard the weird woman as she wandered off, leaving only an apple in her young man's hand.

For a month Connla could not drink or eat, except of his apple; and yet there beside his bed was the apple, untouched. Connla secretly yearned to see the strange woman again.

It happened on the plain of Archommin. He was with his father, who would not let him out of sight, yet she appeared from nowhere, saying: 'I see Connla seated on a high throne, surrounded by the dead, and waiting to join them. Come to the Land of the Living, before it is too late. All the time the immortals are watching you from the hill, waiting for you to join them.'

Conn heard the voice and called for his Druid: 'You have let her evil tongue off the leash, Corann!' 'No!' shouted the woman. 'It is your Druid who is the evil one. One day a good man will step ashore and rid our land of such black magicians.'

ABOVE **Sunset beach at Harlech, Wales.** *In the distance are the hills of the Lleyn Peninsula, some of which bear evidence of Celtic occupation. This area is rich in ancient remains: it was protected by the mountains of Snowdonia from over-exposure to the Romans and later invaders, yet it invited contact with prehistoric Mediterranean and Irish cultures. A perfect setting for the tale of Branwen in the* Mabinogion, *with its Welsh and Irish topography.*

Conn saw that his son was being taken in by the woman's words. 'I can't help it!' cried Connla. 'I love my own people dearly, but my longing for this woman overcomes me.'

The woman spoke once more: 'You long to ride the wave of your desire and tear yourself free from your people. In my boat of crystal we might have reached the fairy hill of King Boadhagh. That is now impossible; but look, in the setting sun I can see another land for you. It is far distant, but we can be there by nightfall. All who travel to that land are made happy: only girls and women live there.'

Connla leapt into the crystal boat. Conn and his warriors watched the two rowing into the sunset until their eyes could no longer make them out. They were never seen again.

Anonymous Irish author of the eighth century

FIVE

Pwyll, The Prince of Dyfed

The story of Pwyll is the first of the 'Four Branches' (or portions) of the Welsh Mabinogion *collection and was probably first written down in the eleventh century. The* Mabinogion *deals with the birth and childhood of Pryderi, and this self-contained tale based on the hero Pwyll was probably once just the beginning of a complete saga dealing with the life and death of the hero Pryderi.*

This relatively late, written version of the myth has lost little of its early pagan quality. The writer was not tempted to alter the powerful simplicity of his characters and reduce them to mythical 'types'. We are immediately plunged into a world where reality and myth intermingle: human characters with earthly passions encounter Otherworld and Underworld characters; one moment we are in a recognizable Welsh landscape, the next we are in a magical country. It is the Celtic storyteller's gift that he can take us in and out of these worlds without us noticing.

The mythological themes include the fathering of an earthly hero by a god; the false slandering of the hero's mother; and the linking of the hero's birth with the birth of a colt (as in the CuChulainn saga). The story is punctuated by hunting, banqueting and love-making, reflecting the preoccupations of the early Celtic chieftains for whom these wonderful tales were composed.

Pwyll ruled the seven cantrefs of Dyfed in the southwestern part of Wales, a land of high sea-cliffs and inland mountains. One day, while he was holding court at Arberth, he felt like going on a hunt in the woods of Glyn Cuch, where the hunting was good. When evening came he set out, stopping the night at Pen Llwyn Diarwya. Before dawn he was up and out with his dogs, loosing them at Glyn Cuch. Pwyll blew on his hunting horn and was off into the woods after his dogs; soon those that were with him were left far behind.

Pwyll followed the yelping of his hounds, but began to hear the cries of another pack mingling with his own. In a few moments he was at the edge of a clearing in the woods, and from the other side of the clearing a stag appeared, chased by the alien pack into the open ground. The hunter's gaze was diverted from the handsome stag to the dogs that brought it down: they were gleaming white in colour, with ears of glowing red. Pwyll entered the clearing and put the strange hounds to flight, so that his own might have their fill of the dead stag.

BELOW RIGHT **Cocidius as Silvanus, the Roman hunter deity** *(jasper seal-stone from Wall, near Hadrian's Wall, Northumberland, England; second to fourth centuries* AD*). Cocidius was a native Celtic hunter god, whose worship was taken up by Roman soldiers defending northern England. As no iconography existed for the Celtic god, the invaders depicted him as his Roman counterpart, the woodlander Silvanus: he is in hunting tunic with bow, quiver and hunting dog, and holds a captured hare; the tree may be the alder, sacred to the god. Silvanus/Cocidius signified the wild, uncultivated aspects of nature, and was therefore a fitting god for soldiers living so far from civilization.*

ABOVE **Thracian rider god on a gilt-silver helmet from Rumania** *(c. fourth century* BC*). Thracians, like the Celts, were considered hostile barbarians by the Greeks and Romans. Their culture was also one of aristocratic warriors in which the horse and rider symbolized hero or god.*

While all this was happening, the master of the strange hounds approached the clearing on a tall steed; and the horse was dapple-grey and the rider was in hunting clothes of similar hue, a horn hanging from his neck. He rode up to Pwyll and addressed him thus: 'Chieftain of Dyfed, I know who you are, but I refuse to offer my greetings.'

'Maybe your own rank', answered the prince, 'is such as to make that unnecessary.'

'My rank', the stranger answered, 'has nothing to do with it.'

'Chieftain,' said Pwyll, 'then where lies the problem?'

'May the gods hear me,' replied the horseman. 'It lies in your own lack of courtesy and breeding.'

'In what way have I been discourteous towards you, chieftain?'

'Why,' he answered, 'I have never met a man so impolite that he can bait his own hounds on a stag brought to the ground by another man's pack. That shows complete lack of courtesy, and, though I do not seek revenge, I shall make sure that you lose your honour to the tune of a hundred such stags.'

'Chieftain,' replied Pwyll, 'I have wronged you and will win back your favour.'

'How do you mean to do that?' asked the horseman.

'It depends on your rank,' said the prince. 'Tell me who you are.'

'I wear the king's crown in my own land.'

'My greetings then towards you,' said Pwyll, 'but what land is that?'

'My name is Arawn and I am King of the Underworld, which you mortals call Annwn.'

'My Lord,' cried Pwyll, 'then how shall I recover your good favour?'

'In this manner. Another king rules down in Annwn. His name is Hafgan and he makes repeated incursions on my territory. Get rid of him and you will win back my favour.'

'Tell me how,' said Pwyll, 'and I shall gladly do as you bid.'

'You will be joined to me by an oath of friendship,' explained the King of Annwn, 'and I shall disguise you as myself. You will rule in my place in the Underworld, and sleep with the fairest lady imaginable; and neither she nor others of my court will know that it is not me. We shall meet again at this trysting-place in a year and a day.'

I agree to that,' said the prince, 'but how do I find King Hafgan?'

'One year from tonight,' answered the king, 'I have arranged a tryst with him at the ford yonder. You must come to that place looking like me, and you are to hit him with one fatal blow; and however much he entreats you to hit him again, hold yourself back, for if you hit him a second time he will be back fighting me again the next morning.'

'I agree to that,' said Pwyll, 'but what will become of my own kingdom of Dyfed?'

'I shall rule in your stead, and nobody will know the difference between us.'

'Well,' said Pwyll, 'I had better be on my way.'

'I shall be your guide, so that your path will be free of obstacles until we reach my kingdom.' And Arawn and Pwyll descended into Annwn.

'This is my kingdom,' said Arawn, 'and my court is yonder. Go ahead now, all within will recognize you.'

Pwyll walked into the courtyard; on all sides were grand halls and sleeping-quarters; he entered the great hall and was surrrounded by squires who helped him off with his hunting boots. In came two knights who removed his hunting clothes and dressed him in a silken gown brocaded with gold. The hall was soon filled with a throng of handsome people: there were warriors with their pages, all fitted out with the finest armour; and there among them, dressed in a silken gown brocaded with gold was the fairest lady imaginable, the Queen of Annwn. The company washed their hands and sat at table, with the queen and the earl sitting on either side of the Prince of Dyfed.

Pwyll talked with the queen; she was of graceful temperament and the least affected and most eloquent of all the women he had ever spoken with. They wined and dined the evening

ABOVE **Teutonic gilt-bronze brooch from Denmark** (c. 500 AD). *The Teutonic tribes were probably originally close to the Celts of Eastern Europe; by the historical period (the time of the first written records) the two had become separate cultures. Similarities of style and subject matter can be seen in this brooch, with its decorative spirals, frontal wide-eyed faces and monster/human oppositions.*

away to the sounds of minstrels and drinking-songs. Pwyll had never in his life seen such a profusion of fine foods and drinks served in golden bejewelled cups and dishes.

When the time came for bed, Pwyll turned his back on the queen and remained silent until the morning, when they continued to speak with the gentle friendliness of the evening before; and however tender they were to one another by day, every night of the year was as cold as the first.

Pwyll filled this year with the hunt and the feast, enjoying the company and affection of his court, until at last the night arrived for his tryst with the rival king. That man had also remembered the appointment and as King Hafgan approached the ford of Glyn Cuch with his knights, a man on horseback stood on the opposite side of the river and addressed the company: 'Gentlemen, pay attention to what I say. This tryst is between the two men who claim the kingdom of Annwn as their own. The fight is for them alone, and you must stand watch.'

The two kings rode into the ford. Pwyll, King Arawn's substitute, was the first to strike: the blow fell on the central boss of Hafgan's shield which was shattered as was the king's armour behind it. Hafgan was fatally wounded by this single blow and was hanging the length of his arm and spear out of his horse's saddle. 'Chieftain,' he gasped, 'you have no right to kill me; I have not challenged you in any way, and I know no reason why you should wish for my death. But by the gods, now that you have mortally wounded me, put an end to me with a second blow.'

'Chieftain,' replied Pwyll, 'I may come to regret what I have done. You must find another to finish you: I will not do it.'

'Carry me away from this place,' said Hafgan to his knights, 'I can no longer be your king, for my death has at last been accomplished.'

'And gentle knights,' added he who was acting on behalf of Arawn, 'take my advice and consider whether you are now my vassals.'

'Lord Arawn,' said the knights in unison, 'every man of us shall obey you as the sole king of Annwn.'

'Good,' replied Pwyll, 'I shall receive the submissive, and may the arrogant be humbled by the sword.'

The knights rendered homage to their new king and by noon of the following day the two old kingdoms of Annwn were in one man's power. It was now a year and a day since his first meeting with King Arawn and Pwyll made his way to the tryst at the clearing in Glyn Cuch. Arawn welcomed him: 'I have heard what you have done for me; may the gods reward you for keeping your oath of friendship.'

'Yes indeed,' said the prince, 'and when you return to your own land you will see the proof of what I have done in your name.'

'May the gods reward you,' said the king, 'for what you have accomplished on my behalf.'

ABOVE **Bronze shield-boss from the River Thames at Wandsworth, London, England** *(second to first centuries BC). The Celtic La Tène style is evident in this rich votive offering to the water gods by a warrior aristocrat: the taut curvilinear foliate patterns are imperceptibly combined with bird forms. The repoussé designs were hammered from behind the bronze plate; fine details were then engraved onto some of the resulting shapes to give them texture.*

RIGHT **Dragon Hill, Uffington, Oxfordshire, England.** *This distinctive hill lies close to the monumental chalk-cut White Horse on the side of the Ridgeway, an ancient track rich in prehistoric and Celtic remains and legends. A legend tells of Saint George killing the dragon on the summit: no grass can grow where its magic blood was spilled, hence the bare chalky patch. Saint George was originally a pagan smith god who also slew dragons: the new religion transformed him into a saintly Christian soldier.*

King Arawn returned the Prince of Dyfed to his proper appearance and took back his own from Pwyll. He rejoiced greatly on his way back to Annwn, for he had missed his warriors and court. They received him with the customary politeness since they were unaware of his absence. Yet the king spent the day in feasting and drinking, and spoke all day and evening to his wife and nobles. Weary of the day's feasting, at last they retired to their beds.

Arawn continued the evening's conversation in bed with his wife and, not having slept with her for a year, made love to her with great passion. She lay awake in the afterglow wondering at his sudden erotic fervour after a year of coldness. 'Why', asked her husband, 'have you gone quiet?'

'Why', she answered, 'do you ask me that after a year of quietness?'

'But', said he, 'we have always been close in bed.'

'I swear', said she, 'that for a year and a day we have neither spoken nor even faced one another in bed.'

That made Arawn think: 'By the gods,' he said to himself, 'my new comrade is an honourable man indeed.' And then he spoke the truth to his wife: 'My lady, do not blame me for what I am about to tell you.' And Arawn recounted his adventures in the Land of the Living. 'May the gods hear me,' said she, 'when I say that you have great influence over your friend for him to resist sensual pleasures and keep his faith.'

Meanwhile Pwyll had returned to his own lands in Dyfed and had made inquiries into what his subjects thought about his government over the past year. 'My lord,' they all replied, 'we have never known you to be so affable, lovable and generous.'

'By the gods,' he said, 'you should be thanking the man who really was with you. A year and a day ago . . .' And Pwyll told them his story. When he had finished his men said, 'Well, my lord, we have the gods to thank for such a friendship; but you will not grudge us the good that has been accomplished this year?'

'By the gods, of course not,' replied the Prince of Dyfed.

From that day onwards the two leaders continued to grow in friendship. They sent one another heartfelt gifts for the hunt: fine falcons, hounds and horses. Pwyll was greatly honoured by the people of Dyfed for what he had achieved during his year in Annwn; indeed, they considered that his bravery in uniting the two realms was such as to deserve a higher title than Prince of Dyfed: from that day onwards Pwyll, Chief of Annwn, was his name.

Some time later Pwyll was at his court at Arberth enjoying a great feast. After the first course, he felt like walking to the top of a mound, called Gorsedd Arberth, which towered up behind the court buildings. One of his courtiers warned him, 'It is said that if a man of noble birth takes his seat on top of the mound of Gorsedd Arberth, he will either come away covered with wounds, or else he will have seen something wonderful.'

'No one can harm me when I have so many of my men around me,' Pwyll replied, 'but I should like to see this wonderful thing.'

Pwyll and his men climbed the mound of Gorsedd Arberth, sat down, and waited. A lady appeared on the road beneath the mound. She rode a large pearly white steed, and was draped in silk brocaded with gold. The horse strode solemnly past the mound and Pwyll addressed his men: 'Do any of you recognize the rider?' None of them answered. 'Then one of you must go and ask her who she is.' One of the men ran down the mound, but at the roadside she had disappeared. He set off after her, but the faster he ran the greater the distance between them. He gave up and returned to Pwyll: 'Lord Chief of Annwn,' said the man, 'it is pointless to follow her on foot.' 'Then,' replied Pwyll, 'take the swiftest horse from the stables and catch her up.'

The man galloped away but though his horse was fast and he used his spurs and whip, the lady receded from his view as before. The man returned to Pwyll: 'Lord,' he said, 'there is no faster horse in Dyfed. We waste our time in following after her.' 'Yes,' replied Pwyll, 'magic is the only explanation.'

On the following day they held another feast. After the first course Pwyll once again decided on a walk to the top of Gorsedd Arberth. A swift horse was taken with them. They had just taken their seats on the mound when the lady appeared once more, wearing the same dress and riding the

ABOVE **The goddess Epona on horseback.** *This Celtic deity was the patroness of horses. The Roman cavalry adopted her as their own protective goddess, and this sculpture is carved in a classical style. She may be linked with the mythical Rhiannon in the story of Pwyll: both are Underworld figures. In her right hand she holds what resembles a rose-garland, offered to her by worshippers.*

BELOW **Rhiannon** *(watercolour by Alan Lee; 1981). Alan Lee's illustrations for the* Mabinogion *combine Celtic decorative features with Romantic medievalist images. A pervading tone of dark sepia produces a misty 'Dark Age' atmosphere in the paintings, which is broken only occasionally by the unfading colours of precious stone jewels, metals or dyes. This wonderful mixture of styles is a perfect visual counterpart to the various cultural layers imposed onto the myths over the centuries. Here, Rhiannon appears as a medieval Arthurian princess looking back at her pursuers. Her birds were harbingers of the Otherworld and their singing at Harlech in the tale of Branwen suspends earthly time.*

same horse. 'Look there,' cried Pwyll, 'Yesterday's rider. Now one of you, take the horse and go after her!' The lady was just at the foot of the mound riding, as before, at a solemn pace; one of the men started off after her at a moderate canter. But still he could not catch her up, even though he broke into a gallop. Indeed the harder he drove his horse, the further she was from him. He gave up the chase and returned to Pwyll at the mound. 'Lord,' he said, 'you saw how hard I rode.' 'I saw,' answered Pwyll; 'there is no point in trying to catch her. But by the gods, there is some reason for her journey here, if only we could break her resolve to avoid us. Let us all return to the court.'

That night was spent in drinking and singing. On the following day after dinner Pwyll said, 'Everyone who was on the mound with me yesterday is to accompany me there once more.' And he told his stable-groom to saddle his horse and bring his spurs. Up Gorsedd Arberth they went and they sat down. The lady came into view, in the same silken gold dress and on the same pearly white horse. After her rode Pwyll, but the faster he galloped the further she was from him. Soon he was riding as fast as he had ever ridden in his life, but he saw that he followed her in vain. So he called after her: 'Lady, for the sake of the man you most love, wait for me.'

'I am glad to do so,' she replied, 'and my horse wishes that you had made the request long ago.' She waited for Pwyll and, drawing aside her head-dress, fixed him with her eyes and spoke with him.

'Lady,' asked Pwyll, 'where are you coming from and going to?'

'I go my own way,' she answered, 'and I am pleased to meet you.' Pwyll thought that he had never seen a lady or maiden fairer than the one who was before him.

'Lady,' he asked, 'I would gladly know what you are doing in these parts.'

'Then I shall tell you,' she said; 'it is you I come to see. My name is Rhiannon daughter of Hefeydd the Elder, and he has pledged me in marriage to a man I despise. For my part I will marry no man save yourself. This is the reason for my journey here.' 'My answer to you, by the gods,' said Pwyll, 'is that there is no maiden or lady in the world that I would rather marry.' 'Then let us make a tryst,' she said. 'A year from now at the court of my father Hefeydd a feast shall be prepared for you.' 'I shall be there,' said Pwyll. They went their separate ways and Pwyll changed the subject whenever his men questioned him about her.

A year later Pwyll set off with a hundred men. They rode to Hefeydd's court and were given a great welcome. At dinner Pwyll sat at the top of the table, with Rhiannon and her father on either side of him. They had finished the meat and were beginning their drinking-songs, when a striking young man with reddish-blond hair entered the hall. 'The gods welcome to you,' called out Pwyll to the man,

LEFT **Bronze fittings on a wooden bucket from Aylesford, Kent, England** *(first century BC). The helmeted head on the handle mount suggests that the bucket was used in a warrior ritual. The wide-eyed and angular facial features are typical of La Tène art, as are the spiralling patterns on the hoop.*

for he looked of royal blood. 'Please be seated.' 'I shall not,' replied the man, 'unless you grant me what I am here for.' 'You shall have what you desire,' said Pwyll. 'Why did you give such an answer?' cried Rhiannon too late. 'He must keep his word,' said the stranger, 'in the presence of such nobles.' 'What is it you want, friend?' asked Pwyll. 'You are feasting,' he replied 'and shall sleep tonight with the lady I most love, and I am here to take your place.'

Pwyll was struck dumb by the stranger's words, and Rhiannon upbraided him for his stupidity: 'This is Gwawl son of Clud, the man who wishes to marry me against my will, and now you must let him have me or you will be dishonoured.' Pwyll did not know what to say. 'You must let him have me,' continued Rhiannon, 'and I shall make sure that he does not have me.'

'How can that be?' asked Pwyll in bewilderment.

'You can remain for the night's feasting, and I shall make a tryst with Gwawl: I shall promise to sleep with him in a year's time, but you are to come to the trysting place with a hundred knights. Leave them in the orchard by the court. Enter the hall in rags and ask him to fill this small bag with food: I shall put a spell on it so that it can never be filled up. When he asks whether it will ever be full, you must answer: 'Only if the greatest in the kingdom presses the food in with his feet.' And when he has his feet in the bag you are to pull it over his head and tie it; then you must blow your hunting-horn as a signal for your hundred riders to take the court.'

'Lord,' interruptd Gwawl, 'I am waiting for your answer.' 'You may take what is in my power to give,' said Pwyll. 'But these men of Dyfed,' added Rhiannon, 'are here as my guests, and they will enjoy the night's feasting. In one year's time I shall

prepare a feast for you, and then you may sleep with me.' Each chieftain returned to his own court.

When the year was up Gwawl son of Clud came for his feast at Hefeydd's court. Pwyll Chief of Annwn also came, dressed in beggar's clothing as Rhiannon had told him. At the height of the merrymaking, he entered the hall. 'May the gods be good to you and make you prosper,' called out Gwawl. 'The same to you sire,' replied Pwyll, 'and I should like to make a request.' 'So long as it is reasonable,' said Gwawl, 'you shall have what you ask.' 'Will you fill this small bag with food for me to keep the wolves from my door?' 'A humble request,' said he, and he called for the servants to fill the bag to the brim. They could not fill it and Gwawl asked: 'Will the bag ever be full?' 'Only', said Pwyll, 'if the greatest man in the kingdom presses the food in with his feet.' 'Go on then, my man of valour,' said Rhiannon to Gwawl. And Gwawl had no sooner stepped into the bag than it was up over his head and its thongs were knotted. Pwyll shed his rags and blew his horn. The hundred knights who had hidden in the orchard were soon in the court; as each man entered the hall he smacked the bag and asked, 'What have we here?' 'A badger,' the others cried. And in this manner was first played the game of Badger in the Bag.

Inside the bag Gwawl protested: 'This is no honourable death for me, to be battered to death in a bag.' 'He is right,' added Hefeydd the Elder. 'I accept what you say,' said Pwyll, 'but what must I do with him?' 'This is what you must do,' said Rhiannon. 'The court poets and suitors are now at your command if Gwawl will make them over to you; and you must make him swear that he will not seek revenge for this night's events.' 'I swear,' called Gwawl, and he was let

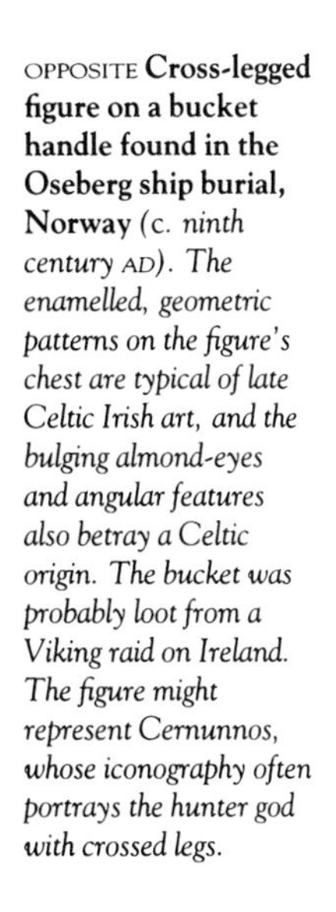

OPPOSITE **Cross-legged figure on a bucket handle found in the Oseberg ship burial, Norway** *(c. ninth century AD). The enamelled, geometric patterns on the figure's chest are typical of late Celtic Irish art, and the bulging almond-eyes and angular features also betray a Celtic origin. The bucket was probably loot from a Viking raid on Ireland. The figure might represent Cernunnos, whose iconography often portrays the hunter god with crossed legs.*

LEFT **Late Bronze-Age sacrificial well at Moen, Denmark** *(c. 800–400 BC). The stylistic similarities in the art of non-Celtic northern Europe points to cultural connections during the Bronze Age. The well held votive bronze vessels and ornaments as well as animal sacrifices. There were also remains of joints of meat in an alder trunk.*

out of the bag. 'Rhiannon has laid down the terms,' said Pwyll, 'and you must keep them.' 'All I want', said Gwawl, 'is to go home and take a bath for my bruises; my warriors can stay here as hostages.' And Gwawl limped away. The night was spent in food and drink, each seated as he had sat a year earlier. Later, Rhiannon and Pwyll went to their bed and enjoyed one another.

The next day Pwyll gave a feast for the court poets and suitors and all were content. At the end of the meal Pwyll addressed old Hefeydd: 'Lord, with your permission I should like to return to Dyfed tomorrow.' 'That is allowed,' said Hefeydd, 'but give Rhiannon good notice of when you would like her to follow you.' 'Lord,' answered Pwyll, 'I should like her to accompany me.' 'Is that so?' asked Hefeydd. 'Yes, by the gods,' said Pwyll, 'that is the way I shall have it.'

In the morning they set out for the court of Arberth in Dyfed. A warm welcome awaited them. A feast was prepared and all the most important lords and ladies in the kingdom were present. Pwyll sent each one off with a gift to remember him by: some took brooches, some rings, and some took jewels. Pwyll and Rhiannon brought prosperity to Dyfed over the next two years.

In the third year of their reign, the leading men of Dyfed summoned Pwyll to a place called Preseleu and counselled him to take another wife, since Rhiannon had not produced a child. Pwyll persuaded them to be patient for one more year.

Before the year was out, a baby was born to Rhiannon and Pwyll at the court of Arberth. Six women were called in to watch the boy's first night with Rhiannon; but by midnight they were all asleep, and when the cock crew they awoke to find the baby gone. 'What are we do to?' the women cried, 'for Rhiannon will blame us.' One of them answered: 'Look here, there is a hound in the corner with pups; let us kill the pups and scatter their bones in Rhiannon's

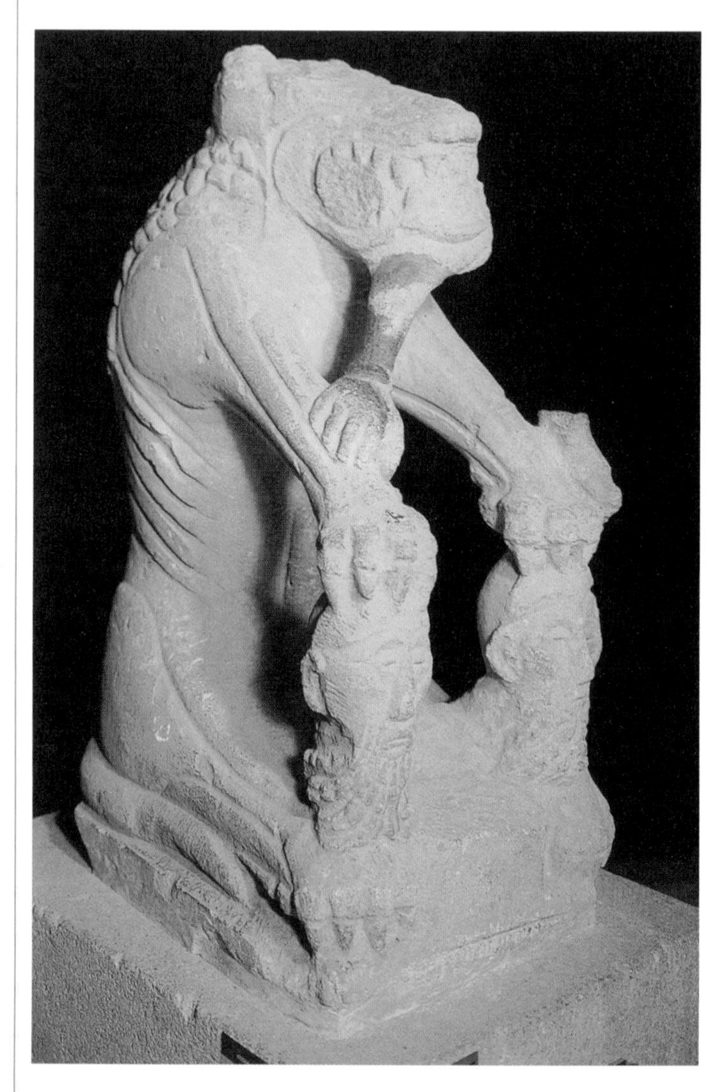

RIGHT **The 'Monster of Noves', Bouches-du-Rhône, France** (*c. fourth century* BC). *Monsters devouring human bodies symbolized the triumph of death and the Otherworld over the Earth's living creatures. A victim's limb protrudes from this Gallic monster's jaws and his claws clasp severed heads, which were often taken in battle by Celtic warriors and used later for ritual purposes. The erect phallus symbolizes the Celtic religious connection between fertility and death, a theme which is present in the myths.*

BELOW **The 'Druid's Stone', Dartmoor, England.** *The hole in the rock was formed by the continuous action of running water over many centuries. A local legend refers to the stone as a place of Druid baptism: the initiate would be passed through the hole into the stream below. Many such legends survive as 'explanations' of natural and man-made curiosities in the landscape.*

lap and smear her with the blood; all six of us will swear that she has killed her own baby.'

As the sun rose Rhiannon woke up and asked for her son. 'Lady,' replied the women, 'we tried to stop you, but see, you have battered your baby to death in the middle of the night.' 'You know that you are making this up,' answered Rhiannon, 'but I shall not harm you if you tell me the truth.' But the women kept to their story, and although Pwyll trusted Rhiannon's word, the Druids gave her a punishment: she was to sit outside the court by the horse-mounting block for seven years, and offer to carry in any man who would let her. Few allowed her to do this, but in this manner she spent most of that year.

In those days Teyrnon Twryf Liant ruled Gwent Is-Coed. He was the finest of men. He owned a mare more beautiful than any in the kingdom. Every year on the eve of May, the mare would foal, but no one had ever seen her colt. 'This May-eve,' said Teyrnon to his wife, 'I shall sit up and watch and find out who or what is taking our colts.' He had the mare brought into his room and in the middle of the night a colt was born: it was a handsome colt, large and already standing where it was born. Teyrnon was just remarking what a fine colt it was when all of a sudden there was a crash: a giant claw came through the window and grabbed the colt's mane. In a flash Teyrnon had drawn his sword and lopped off the monstrous arm at the elbow. There

was a great scream from the courtyard and Teyrnon rushed out but could see nothing in the darkness. Remembering that he had left the door open behind him he gave up his pursuit and ran back to his room. In the doorway was a baby boy in swaddling-clothes, wrapped in a gold brocaded silk sheet.

Teyrnon took the boy into his wife's room. 'My lady,' he called, 'are you asleep?' 'I was', she replied 'before you came in.' And Teyrnon told her what had happened in the night and that he had a noble son for her. 'I shall pretend that he is our own child, since we have never had one,' she said. The boy was taken to the holy stone and baptized by a Druid. He was named Gwri of the Golden Hair, for his head was ablaze with gold. By the end of the year Gwri was already walking confidently about the court like a three-year-old. After two years he was more like a boy of six. And before he was four he was already arguing with the stable-hands to let him take their horses to water. Teyrnon's wife recalled the handsome colt that was born on the night the boy appeared and she had it broken in for Gwri to ride.

In the meantime they heard the news concerning Rhiannon and her punishment. Teyrnon Twryf Liant wondered at the story, for it had happened on the same May-eve that the boy had been found. Teyrnon had often been amazed at the striking resemblance between the foundling and Pwyll Chief of Annwn, and he now realized the truth. His wife agreed that their Gwri of the Golden Hair should be sent to Rhiannon: 'We shall gain three things by doing this,' she said. 'Rhiannon's gratitude for releasing her from her punishment; Pwyll's favour for looking after the boy and educating him; and, moreover, should the boy grow into a hero, he shall be our foster-son and do good deeds for us.'

The following day saw Teyrnon and two of his knights riding towards Arberth. Gwri rode beside them on the handsome colt. As they approached the court a woman called to them from the horse-mounting block: 'Let me take you both the rest of your journey on my back, for I killed my son in my sleep with my own hands.' 'None of us will go on your back,' said Teyrnon, 'but we shall walk beside you.'

The hall was filled with sounds of great rejoicing at the homecoming of Rhiannon's son. Pwyll and Rhiannon placed Teyrnon between them at table; on the other side of Pwyll sat Teyrnon's two knights with the boy between them. After dinner the drinking began and each told their own wonderful tale. Teyrnon told of the mare and the foundling boy, and everyone present saw the features of Pwyll in the boy's countenance.

'If this really is my own son,' cried Rhiannon, 'I shall be delivered of my care.' 'This phrase of yours shall be his name,' said Pendaran of Dyfed, 'Pryderi, for that means 'Care' in our Celtic speech!' 'Though Gwri of the Golden Hair is also a fitting name,' said Pwyll, 'it is most fitting that he has the name his mother cried when she heard that he was safe: Pryderi, son of Pwyll Chief of Annwn.' Teyrnon Twryf Liant and his wife were praised by the assembly and Pwyll and Rhiannon offered them gifts of fine horses, hounds and jewels: but Teyrnon Twryf Liant refused them all and went back home content with the praise.

Pwyll and Rhiannon placed Pryderi in the care of the noble Pendaran of Dyfed. Pwyll grew old and died and Pryderi grew into a handsome hero and was loved by the people of the seven cantrefs of Dyfed. His conquests took in the three cantrefs of Ystrad Tywi and the four of Ceredigiawn: these are the seven cantrefs of Seisyllwch. And one day Pryderi son of Pwyll Chief of Annwn married Cifga, daughter of Gwyn Gohoyw, son of Gloyw Wallt Lydan, son of Casnar Wledig: these were sons of the high kings of this island.

Here ends the first branch of the *Mabinogion.*

LEFT **Gold Thracian helmet from Cotofenesti, Romania** *(c. 400 BC). The warrior aristocrats of Thrace, like their Celtic neighbours, wore finely decorated armour of precious metal to display their social status. The cheek-flaps of this unusually rich helmet depict men confronting monsters, a typically Celtic motif signifying power and bravery.*

Archeology and Celtic Sites

Ancient writers began to refer to the Celtic civilization from the fifth century BC onwards. These literary accounts by Greek and Roman authors present an external and generally biased view of Celtic society which needs to be balanced by the objective research of modern archeology. Scientific excavation of physical Celtic remains can often tell us more about the Celts than the witness and hearsay of the classical authors. However, because of the lack of Celtic literary sources and the fragmentary nature of the material evidence (there is no Celtic 'Pompeii'), archeological controversies abound. The recent discovery of a peat-preserved man in Lindow Moss, near Manchester, England, has led to various opinions concerning his identity, ranging from executed criminal to murdered aristocrat or Druidic sacrifice. Likewise, opinions vary as to the exact function of Iron-Age hill-forts: were they permanent villages or temporary shelters?

These problems of interpretation were highlighted in the excavation of an archeological site at Hayling Island, Hampshire, England. In 1975–76, excellent weather conditions for the discovery of new archeological remains occurred, as due to drought crops growing over buried walls received less water than usual and became stunted (these variations in height appear as darker areas or 'crop-marks' when seen from above). Aerial photographs of Hayling Island in 1976 revealed a rectangular walled enclosure some 40 sq m/48 sq yd surrounding a circular structure. Early this century archeologists had interpreted the site as a Roman villa with a fish-pond at its centre, a most unusual plan which was further called into question by certain features in the aerial photographs. New excavations were undertaken between 1976 and 1981, and as the modern layer of topsoil was gradually removed and various investigatory trenches were dug, further clues as to the history and function of the site were brought to light.

The circular structure was found to have had two quite different building periods. The earliest had post-holes sunk

LEFT **Excavating the Hayling Island Celtic temple.** *The site was systematically stripped in order to recover every available piece of evidence, however small: a coin or a fragment of pottery can provide crucial dating and other information, such as of trade patterns. The polythene sheeting sealed moisture in the unexcavated area, so that soil colour variations were retained: these provided pointers to the sub-surface remains.*

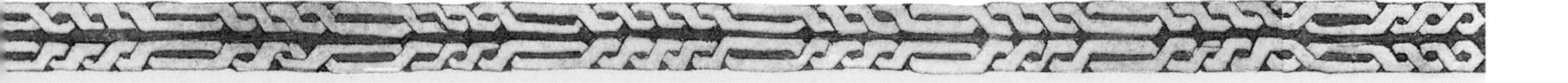

OPPOSITE **Aerial photograph of Romano-Celtic temple site, Hayling Island, Hampshire, England in June 1976.** *The rectangular boundary and circular temple were clearly visible as crop-marks during the severe drought of 1976. Many other British sites were revealed by the dry weather that year.*

LEFT **Foundations of the circular temple, Hayling Island.** *The stone foundations of the Roman building can be seen surrounding the gullies of the earlier British structure. The radial sliced wedges are archeological trenches which gradually revealed the various layers of the building's history. The central pit was possibly for holding a ritual stone or sacred wooden post or 'totem pole'.*

LEFT **Bent spear from the Hayling Island site.** *The rectangular courtyard contained votive burials of intentionally damaged military equipment, including spearheads, swords and chariot equipment. These suggest that the cult activity was in honour of a warrior god. Pig and sheep bones provided evidence of animal sacrifice.*

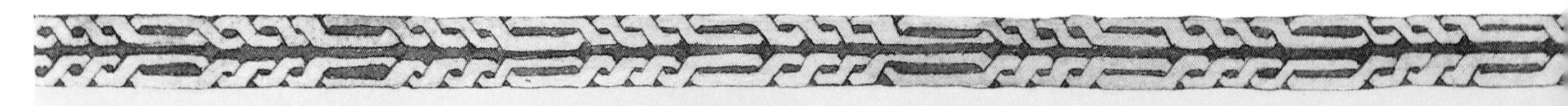

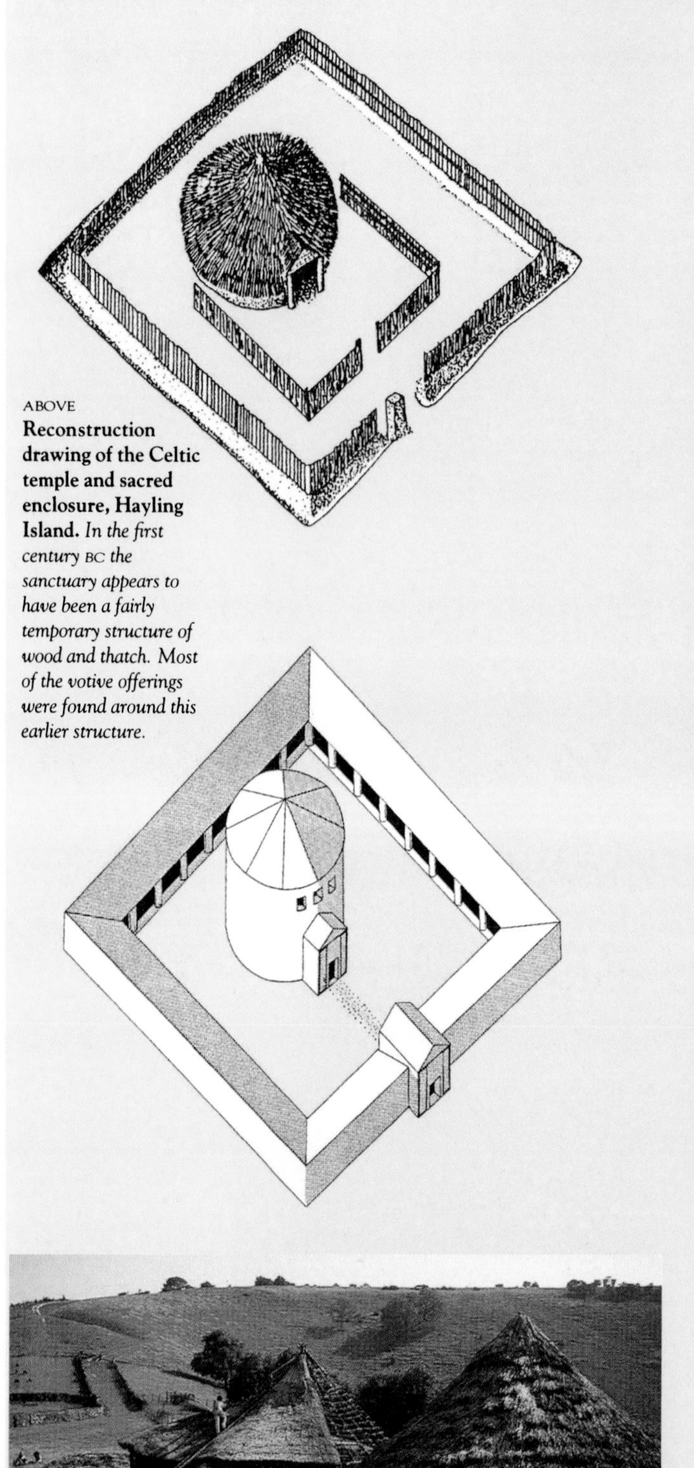

ABOVE
Reconstruction drawing of the Celtic temple and sacred enclosure, Hayling Island. *In the first century* BC *the sanctuary appears to have been a fairly temporary structure of wood and thatch. Most of the votive offerings were found around this earlier structure.*

into an inner circular gully with two larger post-holes at the entrance suggesting that the original building was a typical Celtic 'roundhouse' dwelling, probably roofed with thatch and with a doorway on its eastern side. However, excavations in the surrounding courtyard revealed the true function and approximate date of this early structure. The finds included votive offerings often grouped around burnt areas: sheep and pig bones; Celtic coins (dating the first building and subsequent ritual activity to around 50 BC onwards); horse equipment; and weapons.

All this material evidence suggested that the 'round-house' was actually a Celtic temple, typically orientated towards the rising sun, in use during the period of early Roman contact. Contemporary literary sources help to explain the wider context of the discoveries. Julius Caesar tells us (*Gallic War*, Book VI, 17) that the Celtic Gauls used to bring piles of booty from the battlefield to their sacred places, where they would dedicate them to a war god and accompany the ritual with animal sacrifice. Among the Hayling Island votive weapons were spearheads, intentionally bent during the rituals to signify the defeated enemy. The sanctuary was in a region of Celtic inter-tribal warfare until the Roman invasion, so there was ample opportunity for such military victory dedications.

Far from being destroyed after the Roman invasion in AD 43, this potent architectural symbol of Celtic religion was added to; a second building was put up by the Romans soon after the Claudian invasion. It was a larger and more permanent stone version of the Celtic temple, and apparently even more imposing. The width and depth of the surviving foundations suggest a high tower surrounded, like many other Romano-Celtic temples, by a covered portico. Roof tiles and eye-catching red wall-plaster were found which would have covered the temple's exterior, and an entrance porch had been built. There was no evidence to identify the deity, but a similar site in Gaul included an inscription to the Romano-Celtic war god, Mars Mullo.

It is interesting that there were far fewer votive offerings from the Roman period, suggesting that the site was now intended as a symbol of the dominant Romano-Celtic culture rather than as a place for native British religious ritual. This important evidence from Hayling Island not only confirms Celtic religious architecture and ritual, but also indicates the apparent continuation of Celtic religious activity during Roman domination.

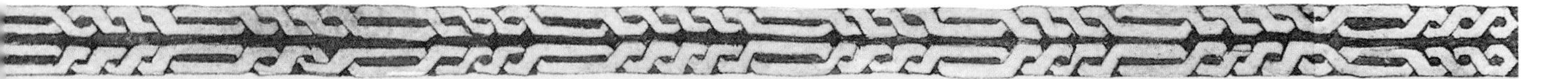

OPPOSITE
Reconstruction drawing of the Romano-Celtic temple and sacred enclosure, Hayling Island. *After the Roman invasion of southern Britain in* AD *43, the temple and sanctuary were rebuilt in more durable materials. The new buildings were larger and more impressive, but the ritual activities around the temple virtually ceased.*

OPPOSITE BELOW
Reconstructing Iron-Age huts at Butser Hill, Hampshire, England. *Archeology has provided evidence of sizes, shapes and materials used in building Celtic dwellings. The original Hayling Island temple probably looked like one of these roundhouses. Butser Ancient Farm has also launched experiments with Celtic farm animals, crops, cooking and pottery methods.*

LEFT **Temple of Vesunna (?), Perigueux, Dordogne, France** *(late first to third centuries* AD*). This rare survival of a Romano-Celtic temple gives some idea of the probable appearance of the second Hayling Island temple. The Gallic building was originally 24 metres (79 ft) high and (unlike Hayling Island) had an ambulatory: the holes for its roof beams can be seen 11 metres (36 ft) up. It too was orientated eastwards and had a larger galleried portico.*

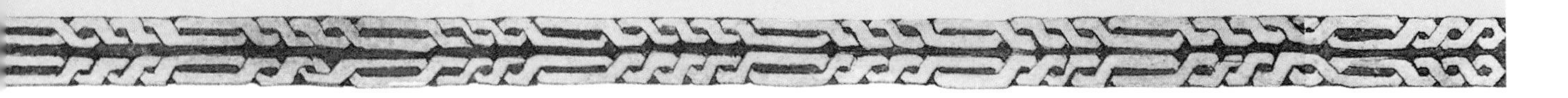

SIX

The Story of Branwen, Daughter of Llŷr

This is the second of the 'Four Branches' of the Mabinogion. *It hardly mentions Pryderi, and the oral tradition has evidently ousted the original 'childhood exploits' of Pryderi which would be expected in this part of his saga, and has replaced them with the exploits of the children of Llŷr. The Irish settings and mythical themes (the cauldron and the house built for Bendigeidfran for example) would suggest that an Irish storyteller intruded on the original Welsh saga of Pryderi at some stage of the oral tradition.*

The grandfather of the children of Llŷr is named as Beli and probably refers to the god Belinus, a Celtic solar deity and legendary King of Britain. The mythological theme of the 'falsely slandered wife' (as with Rhiannon in the tale of Pwyll) recurs in this story. Here it is used as the trigger for revenge and war, reminding the reader of the Greek legend of Helen and the Trojan war. The 'iron-house' in which the giants are nearly killed reflects the pagan Celtic Iron-Age origin of the story, and while some scholars have suggested that it is a mythical version of human sacrifices practised by the Celts, others see it as the kiln used by the enamellers of Celtic jewellery. The Celtic religious notion of water as a supernatural dwelling is present here, seen in the lake from which the giants emerge.

RIGHT **The coast at Harlech, Wales.** *This west-facing stretch of the north-west coast of Wales provides the ideal setting for the tale of Branwen: shallow beaches provided landing-places for ancient ships, while the mountainous hinterland encouraged the building of strongholds, from prehistoric camps to medieval castles.*

The two sons of Llŷr, Bendigeidfran and Manawydan, were sitting on the rock of Harddlech (Harlech) which towers above the Irish Sea. Bendigeidfran was king of the Island of Britain and was staying at one of his courts at Harddlech in Ardudwy, on the north-west coast of Wales below the high mountains of Snowdonia. Beside them on the rock sat the two sons of Euroswydd, Nisien and Efnisien: the four men had the same mother, Penarddun, daughter of Beli, son of Mynogan. And when the sons of Llŷr were angry with one another, Nisien would be their peacemaker, but when they were on the best of terms, Efnisien would be sure to make trouble.

From the rock they saw thirteen ships come sailing from the south of Ireland; the wind was behind them and they approached the Welsh coast with great speed. 'Those ships', said King Bendigeidfran, 'are making for our shores. Let every man in the court arm himself and run down to discover their intentions.' The men went down to the beach and saw that the ships were finely fitted out with beautiful flags of brocaded silk. One of the ships moved ahead of the rest and they saw a shield held up above the deck with its point to the sky as a symbol of peaceful intent.

Small boats brought some of the strangers towards the rock where the king was seated. 'May the gods make you prosper,' he called from above. 'You are welcome. But tell me, who commands these ships?'

'My Lord,' they shouted back, 'they belong to the King of Ireland, Matholwch, and he is here with us.'

'Does he want to come ashore?' said Bendigeidfran.

'Not unless he succeeds in his mission,' answered the Irishmen.

'And what mission is that?' asked Bendigeidfran.

'My lord, our king would be your ally; he asks for the hand of your sister Branwen in marriage and thus to form a mighty union between Ireland and the Island of the Powerful.'

'Well, bring him ashore then,' said Bendigeidfran, 'and we shall discuss the matter.'

The Irish king and his men came ashore and made welcome that evening at the crowded court. The next morning Branwen was promised to Matholwch: she was one of the Three Matriarchs of the island, and the most beautiful woman in the world. It was decided that they should all journey to Aberffraw, Matholwch with his ships and Bendigeidfran by land; there the Irish king would sleep with the daughter of King Llŷr.

They all met at Aberffraw and entered a great tent for the feast, for Bendigeidfran was too large for any house. On either side of the King of the Island of the Powerful sat his brother Manawydan, son of Llŷr, and Matholwch; and next to the King of Ireland sat Branwen, the daughter of Llŷr. And when they had tired of talking, drinking and singing, they went to bed and Matholwch slept with Branwen.

Matholwch heard the news from his men. 'Your property', said one, 'has been harmed and harm will come to yourself.'

'But why', said Matholwch 'should they wish to do this to me when they have just given me such a lady of high rank and beauty?'

'Whatever the cause,' said another, 'the effects are plain to see. You must return to your ships.' And so the King of Ireland prepared to sail back to his own land.

ABOVE **The Gundestrup Cauldron, Denmark** *(first century BC). On this silver inner panel of the gilt-silver ritual vessel, the artist depicted warriors going into battle, preceded by a ram-horned snake. The figures on the right blow carnyxes, or war-trumpets; some of the warriors have bird and boar crests, or horns, on their helmets; on the left, a god dips a human sacrifice into a bucket.*

On the next day the men of Ireland were given billets for their horses and grooms on the land between the court and the sea. Efnisien, the troublemaking half-brother of Bendigeidfran, saw the billets and asked whom the horses belonged to. 'Why,' said the grooms, 'these are Matholwch, the King of Ireland's horses.'

'Will you tell me, then,' asked Efnisien, 'what they are doing here?'

'Why, our Irish king is on a visit to sleep with your sister Branwen, and the horses are his.'

'How dare they do such a thing to my sister without first asking me,' said Efnisien. 'I have never been so insulted in my whole life.' And he cut the horses' lips back to their teeth, their ears to their heads, their tails to their backs, and when he managed to catch hold of their eyelids he tore them from the bone. The horses were maimed beyond repair.

LEFT **Iberian bronze female figurine, from Aust-on-Severn, Gloucestershire, England** (c. *fourth to third centuries BC). Similar objects are known to have been made in Spain. The glass-eyed figure was probably imported from Iberia along the trade-routes of the Atlantic coast.*

When Bendigeidfran discovered that his royal guest was making ready to leave the court without giving polite notice, he sent messengers after him to question his motive. 'Is that not obvious?' replied Matholwch. 'I am amazed to have first been offered Branwen, the royal daughter of Llŷr who is, after all, one of the Three Matriarchs of the Island of Britain, and then to have received such outrageous insults as these.'

'No man in the court of Bendigeidfran committed this act, at least not with his authority.'

'I wish I might believe you,' said Matholwch, 'but the insult stands.'

The messengers reported Matholwch's words to Bendigeidfran. 'We must not allow him to leave in anger,' said the king. 'Brother Manawydan, take messengers and offer him the finest replacements for his injured horses; take him also this silver staff and golden plate and tell him that I know that my half-brother committed this crime, and that it would be difficult to punish him with death. Let him come and discuss peace on his own terms.'

Matholwch and his men accepted the offer and that night another great feast was prepared in a tent as before. Bendigeidfran noticed the change of heart in his new ally and decided to improve his peace-offerings: 'You are to have a cauldron of magical strength: for if one of your men is killed, and you throw him into the cauldron that evening, by the morning he will have revived to perfect health except that he will have lost the power of speech.' And Matholwch was exceedingly pleased with the new gift.

The next day Matholwch received new horses from the surrounding territories and once more they sat together at dinner. 'Tell me,' said Matholwch, 'how did this cauldron come into your possession?'

'Well,' replied Bendigeidfran, 'it was brought to me from Ireland by Llasar Llaes Gyfnewid and his wife Cymidei Cymeinfoll. You must know the story of how they fled from the white-hot House of Iron, for this escapade took place in your own island.'

'Yes, lord,' said Matholwch, 'and I can complete it for you. One day I was out hunting on a mound which overlooks the Lake of the Cauldron. I saw a reddish-blond man emerging from the lake carrying a cauldron; he was huge and monstrous and was accompanied by a woman twice the size of him. They came towards me and I greeted them. The man addressed me, saying, "This woman is going to conceive a son at the end of a month and a fortnight, and the son will be born fully armed and ready for battle." I took the pair of them into my care. For a year they behaved themselves, but the following year they began to cause disturbances in the land, molesting both ladies and gentlemen. Soon everyone hated them and a petition was raised for me to destroy the pair. This was not easy because both of them were so huge and strong. Therefore blacksmiths came from all over Ireland and built an iron house. The monstrous pair were tempted in with plenty of food and drink. And when they were drunk a great fire was lit around the house of iron, but they escaped through the wall with a mighty shoulder-charge. Presumably they then came across the sea to you with the cauldron?'

ABOVE **The Gundestrup Cauldron, Denmark** *(first century BC). This interior silver panel represents a divinity and warrior grappling with a wheel. The wheel is a solar symbol in Celtic art, and it is interesting that griffins are also depicted as these were Greek monsters associated with the sun-god Apollo. The Celtic god could be any one of a number of sky divinities.*

'No,' said Bendigeidfran, 'I shall tell you how the cauldron came to me. I allowed the pair to go where they please on my island, for wherever they went they built grand fortresses for my warriors.'

It was a feast of great joyfulness, and the kings talked well into the night. The following day Matholwch set out with Branwen for Ireland; they sailed from Aber Menei in their thirteen ships. There was much rejoicing in Ireland at their return, and every noble man and lady who visited the king brought Branwen some lovely brooch or ring or perhaps a royal jewel from their own treasure. Branwen was a favourite with everyone, and that year she bore a son who was named Gwern, son of Matholwch. He was sent away for a fine education.

BELOW **Gilt-silver brooch from Ardagh, County Limerick, Ireland** *(*c. *eighth century* AD*). The meticulous golden filigree and granular decoration of this late Celtic penannular brooch would have signified a high degree of wealth and social status in the wearer.*

But as it became known how Matholwch had been insulted during his visit to Wales, there was a change of spirit in Ireland. Soon even those close to him were demanding revenge and Branwen was forcibly put in the kitchens to cook for the court, and to have her ears boxed daily by the butcher when he had finished with the meat. 'And you must refuse permission', added his men, 'to any ship wishing to travel to Wales. And likewise you must take prisoner any who come from there.'

Meanwhile, Branwen trained a starling and taught it to speak so that it might talk of the insults she was suffering in Ireland. She tied a letter under its wings and sent it off across the sea to her home, where at last it found Bendigeidfran at his court of Caer Seint in Arfon. It landed on his shoulder and spread its wings so that all might see the letter. They realized that the bird was tame and the letter was read aloud to the court. When Bendigeidfran learnt of his sister Branwen's unhappiness he gathered a great army from the whole island and they decided to make war on Ireland. Seven lords were left behind at Edeirnon to guard the realm, and for this reason the town became known as Seith Marchawg ('Seven Riders'). The chief of them was Cradawg, son of Brân.

Bendigeidfran set off with the gathered armies of Britain and he himself waded across the sea, for in those times the water was deep but not wide. On the hills above the coast of Ireland the swineherds saw a marvellous sight and came to tell Matholwch: 'We have seen marvels today,' they said, 'for across the sea we have seen a forest and beside it a mountain, where there was neither forest nor mountain before; and what is more, they are moving towards Ireland.'

Matholwch was baffled by the report and sent messengers to ask Branwen if she could explain the phenomenon. 'I am no lady as you call me,' she replied, 'but I know what this marvel is. The forest is a fleet of ships and the mountain is my brother Bendigeidfran, for he will come by wading as there is no ship big enough to hold him.'

'But,' said the men, 'we also saw a ridge on the mountain with two lakes on either side.'

'My brother's angry eyes on either side of his nose,' laughed Branwen.

Matholwch called on all the armies of Ireland to come and take counsel, and they decided to retreat across the River Llinon (Shannon or Liffey) and break down its bridge, for the river was full of rocks which would obstruct the British boats.

ABOVE **Branwen** *(watercolour by Alan Lee; 1981). Branwen sends her starling to Wales bearing the message of her dishonour at the hands of the Irish. On the frame, Alan Lee has depicted the Welsh fleet sailing across the Irish Sea; the eyes and arms of Bendigeidfran can be seen above and to the sides of the main painting.*

Bendigeidfran and his fleet arrived at the river. 'How can we cross over this river?' asked his men. 'There is no bridge,' answered Bendigeidfran, 'so I as your chief shall be a bridge for you.' (That was the first saying of this well-known proverb.) He lay across the river and the armies passed across him.

The Irish armies sent messengers to offer the kingdom of Ireland to Branwen's boy Gwern, son of Matholwch: 'This is to repair the wrong that Matholwch has committed to you and your sister,' said the messengers. 'It is up to you to decide what will become of Matholwch.'

'I am rather inclined to become King of Ireland myself,' answered Bendigeidfran, 'unless you come up with better terms than that.'

The messengers returned to Matholwch and told him to think of a better offer. 'What do you all suggest?' said Matholwch.

'Well,' they replied, 'he has never been able to find a house large enough to hold his great body. So we suggest that you have such a house built, and that half of it should contain Bendigeidfran and his men and the other half is for yourself and all of us.'

Bendigeidfran accepted the offer on Branwen's advice. The house was indeed built, but the men of Ireland had planned a trick. On all the pillars of the house they fixed pegs, and from every peg was hung a sack, and in every sack they hid an armed warrior. Efnisien entered the house and immediately questioned one of the Irish as to the contents of the bags: 'What is in this one?' he asked and squeezed it hard. 'Only flour, friend,' answered the Irishman. Efnisien asked the same question and received the same answer of all two hundred bags; he squeezed one so hard that the man inside was crushed to death.

The men of both islands entered the hall and Gwern, son of Branwen, was invested as the new king. He greeted Bendigeidfran and Manawydan, the sons of Llŷr; Nisien, son of Euroswydd called him over, and the boy went as a willing friend. But he would not approach Efnisien. 'Why does the boy avoid me?' said Efnisien; 'after all, I am his uncle.' Bendigeidfran sent him across to Efnisien, who cried: 'May the gods witness the atrocity I am about to commit.' And he took hold of the new boy king and threw him head-first into the great fire. When she saw her dying son, Branwen in her despair tried to jump into the fire with him, but her brother Bendigeidfran held her back, protecting her with his shield in the fight that followed.

ABOVE **Clapper bridge over the Waller Brook, Dartmoor, England.** *These primitive bridges are believed to date back to the Saxon period. The area is rich in Bronze- and Iron-Age settlements and the Celts would also have had to cross these streams; their bridges were probably of wood.*

Many warriors died that night. The Irish took the magic cauldron and built a fire beneath it, casting their dead into it until it was full: the next morning they would be as good as new, save that their power of speech would be gone forever. Efnisien realized that the cauldron was not for the dead of the Island of the Mighty: 'May the gods hear me in my distress,' he cried, 'for I have led so many of my countrymen to their deaths. I shall win back my honour and redeem the Island of the Mighty from defeat.' He lay down unseen among the Irish dead and was thrown into the cauldron by two survivors.

LEFT **Bull-headed terminal of iron firedog, Capel Garmon, Denbigh, Wales** *(c. first century BC). One of a pair used to support roasting spits over a fire, the bull was a Celtic symbol of virility and would have been a fitting decoration at a warrior banquet.*

Once inside he pushed hard against the sides of the cauldron: it broke in four pieces and his heart burst with it.

Efnisien's deed brought but small assistance to the Island of the Mighty. Bendigeidfran's foot had been wounded by a poisoned spear and only seven of his men survived: these were Manawydan; Pryderi; Glifieu, son of Taran; Taliesin; Ynawg; Gruddieu, son of Muriel; and Heilyn, son of Gwyn the Old.

Bendigeidfran ordered his men to cut off his head: 'Take it to the White Mount in London,' he said, 'and bury it there facing France. Your journey will take some time. Rest at Harddlech for seven years of feasting; the birds of Rhiannon will sing to you and my head shall be as good company as it was when it sat on my shoulders. Your next resting place will be for eighty years at Gwales in Penfro. The sign for departure will be the opening of the door which looks across Aber Henfelen towards Cornwall; from that moment you must not rest until my head is buried in London. Now cross the sea to Wales.'

His head was cut off and the seven crossed over to the other side, Branwen and the head of Bendigeidfran with them. They landed at Aber Alaw in Talebolion. Branwen looked back across the sea to Ireland and at her own Island of the Mighty. 'Pity that I was ever born,' she cried, 'for I am the cause of the destruction of these two fine islands!' She sighed to the heavens and her heart was broken. She was buried by her companions in a four-sided tomb on the banks of the River Alaw.

The seven men carried the head to Harddlech. On the road they met a group of travellers. 'Any news?' asked Manawydan.

'None,' they replied, 'except that Caswallawn, son of Beli, has conquered the Island of the Mighty and now wears the crown in London.'

'Then what has happened to the seven men we left behind as guardians under the leadership of Cradawg, son of Brân?'

'Six of the men were killed by a sword without an owner: Caswallawn held the sword, but wore a magic cloak to make him invisible. Caswallawn would not kill his nephew Cradawg, but his heart was broken by what he saw. Cradawg became one of the 'three men whose hearts were broken by despair'. One young man, Pendaran Dyfed, fled into the woods.'

They reached Harddlech where they feasted for seven years. While they were eating and drinking, three birds sang them a song lovelier than any they had ever heard; and though the birds hovered far out to sea, their song was clear within the hall.

After seven years they made for Gwales in Penfro, where they were entertained in a fine royal castle which towered above the sea. The hall had three doors, two of which stood open. 'We must not open the third door,' said Manawydan, 'for it looks towards Cornwall.' The eighty

RIGHT **Wooden figure from Ralagan, County Cavan, Ireland** *(c. first century BC). Before they learnt stone-carving techniques from the Greeks and Romans, the Celts used carved wooden images as representations of deities and/or worshippers. This male figure originally had an attached phallus and may have been a fertility god.*

years were spent without cares in joyful feasting, for they did not age and the head of Bendigeidfran was as cheerful as it had been in life. This feasting was called the Gathering of the Wondrous Head. The earlier feasting in Ireland was called the Gathering of Branwen and Matholwch.

One day, when the eighty years were up, Heilyn, son of Gwyn opened the third door and the company looked out across Aber Henfelen towards Cornwall. The memory of the loved ones lost in battles came flooding back and they mourned the loss of their chief Bendigeidfran. From that moment they did not rest until the head was safely buried on the White Mount of London. That deed was one of the Three Happy Hidings, although one day it would become one of the Three Unhappy Findings, for no plague could cross the sea until the head was found.

This ends the adventures of the men who travelled from Ireland, but those who stayed in Ireland fared worse. No one survived the battle except five women who were hidden in a cave deep in the wild countryside. Each woman carried a son inside her, and when those five sons were born, they grew into fine youths with a desire for marriage. Each son married one of the five mothers, and the land was divided into five and ruled by each. This is how the five provinces of Ireland came into being. They returned to the sites of the earlier battles and found plenty of gold and silver, enough to make them very rich.

Here ends this branch of the *Mabinogion*: we have heard of the insult to Branwen, one of the Three Unhappy Blows on the Island of the Mighty; and of the Gathering of Bendigeidfran, when the armies of one hundred and fifty-four districts crossed the sea to Ireland to avenge the insult to Branwen; we have heard of the seven years feasting at Harddlech and the songbirds of Rhiannon; and we have heard of the eighty-year Gathering of the Wondrous Head.

The Arthurian Legends

In general, the kings, queens and heroes of the Celtic myths are not otherwise known in history, although exceptions occur in the Welsh *Mabinogion*. Cassivellaunus, for example, appears in history as the Belgic chieftain who led the defence of Celtic Britain during Julius Caesar's second Roman invasion in 54 BC: in myth he becomes Caswallawn, the King of Britain, in the tale of *Branwen*. The tendency for myth to ignore the historical realities of time and space can be seen in the placing of Caswallawn in London, which was founded over 100 years after Cassivellaunus fought Caesar. Such inconsistencies between fact and fiction are unavoidable when real men and women become legendary heroes and heroines, and nowhere is this more apparent than in the Arthurian legends.

The earliest mythical tales of King Arthur and his court to appear were probably written in Welsh in the tenth century: the story of *Culhwch and Olwen* is certainly one of the first. In that story we are presented with a pagan Celtic world with quite different social codes to the later Arthurian legends. The poems of the twelfth-century writer Chrétien de Troyes provide the earliest versions of Arthurian romance – the polished medieval conventions of courtly love are epitomized in Lancelot's love for Queen Guinevere; brash warriors of Celtic tradition are transformed into handsome knights; and heroic quests for elusive Druidic tokens become Christian pilgrimages in search of the Holy Grail. Many other medieval Arthurian romances followed and the tales of King Arthur and his Knights of the Round Table were soon well known throughout Europe. Gradually, these loosely connected stories were bound together into 'complete' versions as the quests of various knights were woven around the central heroic figure of Arthur himself, and what were originally non-Arthurian romances, such as *Tristan and Isolt*, were also incorporated.

The late medieval popularity of the Arthurian legends is demonstrated by the fact that Sir Thomas Malory's prose version, *Le Morte d'Arthur* (1485), was one of the earliest

LEFT **Merlin as a stag** *(medieval manuscript; Bodleian Library, Oxford, England). Merlin had the Celtic sage's ability to shape-shift. The transformation into a stag is in the pagan tradition of horned warriors and gods such as Cernunnos: the stag signified powerful animal strength.*

RIGHT **King Arthur riding a goat** *(mosaic from Otranto Cathedral, Italy; twelfth century). The British hero is found in medieval art from all over Europe. Here he is identified in Latin as 'Rex Arturus' in a southern Italian mosaic which incorporates both biblical and pagan figures.*

ABOVE **The Failure of Sir Gawaine** *(Edward Burne-Jones [1833–1898]; wool and silk woven on cotton warp, 1895–6). Burne-Jones was influenced both thematically and stylistically by the medievalism of the Victorian Pre-Raphaelites, of which he was a late member. In the last decade of his life his interest in Malory was revived and he created a series of tapestry designs for his industrialist patrons on the Grail theme. Here Sir Gawaine and Sir Uwain are refused entrance to the Chapel of the Holy Grail because of their sinful natures. The treatment of space and natural detail is intentionally medieval.*

printed works in English. The mythical Arthur fell from favour during the seventeenth century and the Age of Reason, however, but late eighteenth- and nineteenth-century Romantic writers of both prose and poetry revived the medieval Arthurian romances, culminating in the Victorian period with Lord Alfred Tennyson's poem, *Idylls of the King*. The music world also explored the romances; the German composer Wagner found large audiences for his Romantic Arthurian operas *Lohengrin, Parsifal* and *Tristan and Isolde*. The twentieth century has kept the tradition alive in music, film, art and literature with novels by TH White, Rosemary Sutcliffe, Mary Stewart and Alan

Garner being just a few of the many works which have dealt with the Arthurian legends, directly or indirectly.

The 'real' historical Arthur has been almost entirely transformed by the romantic legends of the medieval and modern periods. Early accounts of the man, as found in the ninth-century *History of the Britons* and the twelfth-century Geoffrey of Monmouth's *History of the Kings of Britain*, are dubious since their historical 'facts' are extremely questionable. However, cautious use of these sources together with the mythical 'evidence' point to a famous Celtic Romano-British warrior, fighting for a Britain left defenceless by the departure of the Roman legions in the early fifth century. Arthur's enemies probably included the Celtic Picts and Scots, but his major battles would seem to have been against the non-Celtic Anglo-Saxons. The mythical hero-worship in court poetry and folklore of such a patriotic figurehead would have been compounded by the lack of contemporary written literature.

Geoffrey of Monmouth's 'mythical history' began in earnest the tradition of associating episodes from the Arthurian legend with real topographical locations. The most famous of these is Tintagel Castle in Cornwall, which since medieval times has been referred to as the legendary birthplace of Arthur. The highly dramatic setting must have inspired early medieval romantic interpretations, and in return the legendary associations with ancient kings would have encouraged the building of the thirteenth-century castle by the earls of Cornwall. More recently, 'Merlin's Cave' at Tintagel was named after the Arthurian magician for the benefit of late nineteenth-century tourism, and a Victorian lead-mining tunnel became 'King Arthur's Mine'.

Until recently, Tintagel 'island' was believed to have been a monastery, lacking any signs of possible Arthurian connections. But a fire in the 1980s revealed further features and finds which showed it to have been an important community in the late Roman period. More excitingly from the Arthurian point of view, the site appears to have developed into a powerful post-Roman stronghold and centre of trade in the fifth and sixth centuries. However, a separate medieval folk tradition presented Tintagel as the palace of the legendary King Mark of Cornwall with its Tristan and Isolt associations. Such is the power of myth and legend to impose itself on landscapes.

ABOVE **The Four Queens Find Lancelot Sleeping** *(Frank Cadogan Cowper [1877–1958]; oil on canvas, 1954). Cowper was one of the last British painters to be influenced by the Pre-Raphaelites. Even in this late work their influence can be seen in the choice of medieval subject and late Romantic style. The scene is from Malory's* Morte d'Arthur: *four British queens find the Arthurian hero asleep beneath an apple tree. The sorceress Morgan le Fay attempts to make him take one as a lover, but he remains faithful to Guinevere. Cowper contemporizes the subject by portraying the queens as 1950s starlets admiring a film star.*

SEVEN

Culhwch and Olwen

The following tale of Culhwch and Olwen is one of the best known stories from the Mabinogion *collection and one of the earliest tales in which King Arthur appears. References to iron and blacksmiths suggest a Celtic Iron-Age setting for the story; in which case it takes place in the cultural period of the 'genuine' Arthur. The hunt for a fabulous boar is a feature of the heroic myths of many cultures, as is the setting of impossible tasks by a tyrannical king in order to win a bride. Typical Celtic themes include the jealous stepmother, age-old talking animals and the freeing of a prisoner, subjects equally popular in folk–tales. Also of a particularly Celtic nature are the colourful descriptions of the attributes of Culhwch and Olwen.*

The story is rich in British mythical characters, the most significant of whom is Mabon, the Celtic God of Youth. Culhwch's quest to free the ancient god might suggest that the original myth reflected a serious religious ritual, which involved the symbolic rediscovery of a lost god. However, by the medieval period such original mythical meanings would have become lost beneath the breathtaking excitement of the surface narrative.

Culhwch's birth was followed by the death of his mother. But before she died she made the king, her husband Celyddon Wledig, swear that he would not take another wife until a wild rose-bush with a pair of blossoms appeared on her grave. Several years later the flowering bush appeared and Celyddon married King Doged's widow. She immediately told her stepson, Culhwch, that he would marry no other woman than Olwen of the court of Arthur.

Culhwch therefore rode to the court of King Arthur, who was a cousin. How impressed were Arthur and his nobles when the youth rode into their courtyard! His horse was a beautiful grey, covered with a square purple cloth, a golden apple embroidered on each corner; the bridle and saddle, stirrups and shoes were of gold. The horse's hooves cast up the soil as it cantered, as though four swallows were ever around the youth's head. In each hand Culhwch held a silver spear, at his thigh was a sword of gold, its blade inlaid with a cross the colour of lightning, and alongside him trotted a pair of brindled greyhounds, their breasts gleaming white, with ruby-studded collars. The onlookers were amazed to see the blades of grass untouched by their passage, so light of foot was the horse.

Arthur welcomed the handsome stranger and offered him a high seat at the evening banquet. 'Sir, I come not for food and drink,' said Culhwch, 'but to ask a favour from you.'

'You will receive anything on earth or from sea which lies under wind, rain and sun,' replied Arthur, 'except for my ships, sword, shield, cloak and spear, or the hand of my Queen Guinevere.'

'Then I ask for Olwen, daughter of Yspaddaden,' said Culhwch.

'I have never heard of this woman,' said Arthur, 'but my men will search for her for one year, until when you will stay as my guest.'

A year later the men returned with nothing. 'You have failed to grant me my sole request,' said Culhwch, 'and I shall leave this place with a part of your honour.'

'How dare you insult our king?' cried Cei (Kay). 'Come with us and see for yourself that the woman is nowhere to be found.' Cei was one of the wonderful heroes of Arthur's court. He could hold his breath for nine days and nights under water; a wound from his sword could never be healed; and he could grow in an instant to the height of a tree.

Arthur selected Cei and several other heroes to accompany Culhwch on his quest. With them went Bedwyr (Bedivere) the One-Handed: no other man in the kingdom save Arthur himself could outrun him, his spear had the power of nine spears, and his single hand had the strength of three warriors on the battlefield. Kynthelig, the guide, went with them also; and Gwalchmai (Gawain), nephew and heir to Arthur, who had never returned from a quest unfulfilled; and Menw who could cast a magic spell over the party to make them disappear in hostile places. Gwrhyr went also, for he could speak the language of men and animals.

The heroes rode through the mountains for many days until they came to a great open plain. In the far distance they saw a magnificent castle, but although they rode straight towards it, several days passed before it began to loom above them. Outside the castle they found a giant shepherd with flocks of sheep which stretched to the horizon. They told the herdsman, whose name was Custennin, of their quest, but the giant warned them off, saying that no man had ever left the castle alive. They offered him a gold ring in return for information about Olwen, and he sent them to his wife who dwelt in a cottage beside the castle. The woman came running out to greet them, and went to embrace Cei, who quickly picked up a log from the woodpile and thrust it between the woman's arms to take his place; afterwards, the log fell to the ground, twisted and broken.

RIGHT **Kilhwych, the King's Son** *(tempera on wood by Arthur Joseph Gaskin, 1862–1928). Gaskin's interest in the early Italian painters is evident in his use of tempera paint as well as in the curious perspective and flat forms seen here. This style was intentionally medieval, as was his choice of Arthurian subjects: Culhwch appears as a courtly huntsman from the Age of Chivalry. The great contrast between the finely attired prince and the homespun clothes of the whipper-in may reflect Gaskin's Socialist leanings.*

'What an affectionate greeting!' said Cei. 'If that log had been me, no one would ever have hugged me again.'

They entered the cottage and the strange woman gave them dinner. Afterwards they asked her about Olwen. 'The girl comes here every seven days to bathe and wash her clothes,' said the old woman, 'but you must swear not to do her any harm, for she is the fairest maiden in the kingdom.' And Olwen walked in. She wore a silken robe the colour of flaming fire with a collar of reddish gold, set with rubies and emeralds. Her hair was more golden than yellow broom flowers, and her skin was whiter than foam on the wave-crest. The fingers on her hands were fairer than the wood anemones that grow beside the spring. Her eyes glanced and gleamed like those of the falcon. Like the downy breast of the swan were her breasts, her cheeks were like red roses, and all who saw her felt great love for her. White three-leaved flowers sprang up in her footsteps, which led to her being named Olwen, meaning 'White Track'.

Culhwch told her of his love for her since he had heard her lovely name in childhood, and Olwen returned his love but told him that he must perform the tasks set by her father Yspaddaden, if he was to win her hand. Thereupon Olwen took Culhwch and his companies up to the castle and introduced them to Yspaddaden Pencawr, her royal father. 'Lift up the skin which has fallen over my eyes,' said Yspaddaden, 'so that I might see what kind of man desires to be my son-in-law.'

When Yspaddaden had seen Culhwch, he sent the group away after they had been promised an answer by the next morning; but as they walked off, the old king threw a poisoned dart at their backs. Bedwyr heard it whistling through the air, caught it, and hurled it back at Yspaddaden, catching him on the knee. 'Is that the way for a son-in-law to treat me?' cried the king. 'I shall have an eternal limp because of his discourtesy.'

The warriors returned to the cottage of Custennin the Giant, and the next day visited Yspaddaden for his decision. 'I must ask the permission of the four great-grandparents of Olwen,' said the king, but as they walked away he threw a second dart at them; this time it was Menw who returned the iron dart to its owner, piercing his breast. 'A curse on such an ungentlemanly son-in-law,' cried Yspaddaden. 'I shall never climb the hill again without a pain in my chest.'

On the following day the warriors once more sought an audience with Yspaddaden, and again he threw a dart at their backs. Culhwch caught it in the air and in a second the dart was through the eye of Yspaddaden and out the back of his head. 'I shall never see the same again,' said the king, 'due to the insolence of a son-in-law. A curse on the smith who forged the iron darts.' They sat down together to eat, and Yspaddaden turned to Cylhwch and said: 'So it is you who wishes for the hand of my daughter. Firstly you must swear never to unjustly harm me. Secondly you must bring to me whatever I ask of you. Only then shall my daughter be yours.'

'Make your request,' answered Culhwch.

'My hair and beard have not been cut for years,' said Yspaddaden, 'and the only comb, razor and scissors which will do the job are between the ears of the monstrous boar, Twrch Trwyth. Fetch me those implements and my daughter is yours. One word of advice I give you: enlist the help of Mabon the Hunter. Only he can hunt the boar with his dog Drudwyn; but no one has seen him since he was stolen from his mother when only three days old. You must find his kinsman Eidoel, who might be able to tell you where Mabon now dwells.'

Culhwch and the warriors of Arthur set out on the next stage of his quest. They soon found Eidoel who took them to seek the advice of an enchanted bird, the Ousel of Cilgwri. Gwrhyr, who knew the speech of birds, asked, 'Tell us where we can find Mabon, who was stolen from between the wall and his mother when only three nights in the world?'

'There was once', said the bird, 'a smith's anvil in this place, and I have pecked it for many years to reduce it to the size of a nut. But I swear that in all that time I have never heard of this Mabon. However, there is a race of beasts born long before my time; I shall take you to them.'

RIGHT **The 'Drosten' Stone** *(Pictish cross-slab from St Vigeans, Scotland; ninth century* AD*). The late Celtic art of the Picts continued earlier themes and styles. On the shaft of this Christian cross are the age-old subjects of mastery of animal over animal, and man over beast: an eagle clutches a salmon, while a hunter shoots at a wild boar. The spiralling lines of both the decorative and representational figures are continuing Celtic elements, expressed in a vigorous and naïve manner by the Pictish sculptors.*

The Ousel of Cilgwri thereupon led them to the Stag of Redynvre. 'We come to you, great stag,' said Gwrhyr, 'for we know of no animal older than you, and therefore perhaps you might know where we can find Mabon the Hunter.'

'There was once a great plain in this place,' replied the stag, 'and nothing grew on it save an oak sapling; that oak I have watched grow into a huge tree of one hundred branches, and I have watched it decay until now you see only a withered stump before you; and never in all that time have I heard of Mabon. But I shall take you to an even older creature than I,' and the Stag of Redynvre led them to the Owl of Cwm Cawlwyd.

'I would tell you if I knew,' said the owl to Gwrhyr, 'but when I first came to this broad valley it was a narrow wooded glen; a race of men were born who uprooted every tree. Since then two more woods have grown, and even so I have not heard of the man you are seeking. But let me take you to the oldest animal in the world, the Eagle of Gwern Abwy.'

'Many ages have passed since I came here,' said the eagle to Gwrhyr, 'and this rock was then so high that I could peck at the stars in the night; but now it is a span in height. But in all that time I have never heard mention of this Mabon. However, many years ago I was soaring above Llyn Llyw looking for food, and I spotted a salmon. I dived to catch it but it took me down into the depths and I scarcely managed to escape him. I returned to the lake with other eagles and he made his peace with me; I removed fifty fisherman's harpoons from his back as a sign of friendship. He must be older than I am, and I shall take you to where he lives in Llyn Llyw.'

The Eagle of Gwern Abwy led them to the Salmon of Llyn Llyw. 'I have come to visit you, old friend,' said the eagle, 'because these men are from the court of Arthur and they seek Mabon, the man who was snatched from between the wall and his mother when only three days old.'

'I can tell you this,' replied the salmon; 'with the turn of the tide I swim upstream as far as Gloucester, and there I find such evils; two of you must ride up with me on my back to witness what I see.' Cei and Gwrhyr volunteered and the salmon took them in leaps and dashes up to the city of Gloucester, where they heard loud cries from the castle dungeon beside the river.

'Who is it,' called Gwrhyr, 'that cries so mournfully from within this stone prison?'

'It is I, Mabon, the son of Modron!' was the reply.

LEFT **Olwen** *(watercolour by Alan Lee; 1981). Olwen is here depicted in the midst of nature, associated with the Celtic Otherworld. The side frames show the warriors of Arthur's court banqueting as they discuss Culhwch's request for the hand of the unknown Olwen; in the base-frame, warriors ride out in search of the giant's daughter.*

ABOVE **Bronze boar from Bata, Hungary** *(second century BC). The wild boar remained a symbol of the warrior's ferocity throughout the pagan Celtic period. This figurine may have been worn as a helmet crest. The raised dorsal bristles symbolize the animal's aggression: in the myths, the hair of Celtic warriors similarly stands on end when they go into battle, and historians refer to the use of lime to make it bristle.*

The warriors returned to Arthur, who assembled his whole army to besiege the castle at Gloucester. During the battle Cei and Gwrhyr entered the dungeon from the river and rescued Mabon on the back of the salmon, and thereupon, Arthur called upon all the warriors of the islands of Britain to accompany them on the hunt for the boar, Twrch Trwyth. At that time it was living in Ireland with seven young pigs. The dogs were loosed upon the boar and they chased him until they reached the sea, a fifth of Ireland lain to waste behind them. Twrch Trwyth swam the sea to Wales, and Arthur and his companions followed boar and hounds to dry land. As the hunt progressed through Wales, one by one the seven pigs were killed, although the boar also killed many of Arthur's champions.

They came at last to the River Severn and the boar was about to swim across it to Cornwall when Mabon, son of Modron appeared. He rode at the boar and skilfully snatched the razor from between its ears. Cei likewise took the scissors, but the beast turned into the river estuary with the comb still safely lodged in the hair of its neck. It was on the shores of Cornwall that the comb was finally taken after a great struggle, and Twrch Trwyth disappeared into the deep sea, never to be seen again.

The warriors returned to the castle of Yspaddaden and cursed the king for the deaths he had caused. The king's beard was shaved right down to the bone.

'Is that a close enough shave?' asked Culhwch.

'It is,' said Yspaddaden, 'and my daughter is yours. But you would never have won her without help from Arthur for I would not have given her up of my own free will; and so I die as I lose her.'

In this way did Culhwch meet and take to wife Olwen, the daughter of Yspaddaden Pencawr.

OPPOSITE **Warriors with boar-crested helmets** *(bronze matrix for making decorative helmet plaques, from Torslunda, Sweden; eighth century AD). Cultural links between pre-Viking Scandinavia and the Celts are reflected in similar warrior aristocracies wearing similar armour: such boar crests are found in representations of Celtic warriors.*

RIGHT **'Maponus' head from Corbridge, Northumberland, England** *(c. second to fourth centuries AD). The stone head has a hollow carved in its crown for libations. Maponus was the divine Youth of northern Britain.*

Celtic Religion

Our understanding of Celtic religion is hindered, perhaps more than any other aspect of the Celtic world, by the lack of written sources and the difficulties involved in interpreting archeological evidence. These problems are increased by the secret nature of many Celtic religious cults, which was in part due to the great political respect commanded by Celtic priests and their consequent elitism.

Therefore we have to turn to the limited observations of ancient non-Celtic authors, whose writings are biased by their view of the Celts as primitive barbarians. The Greek Diodorus of Sicily, writing his 'mythical history' in the first century BC, refers (Book V, 31) to the high social status and learning of the Celtic Druids: 'Those men called by us philosophers and theologians are held in great honour by them; they call them "Druids" . . . and no sacrifice may be performed without a Druid present . . . for only they speak the language of the gods.' This Druidic control of religious affairs accounts for the many occasions in myth when they are consulted by clan-chiefs and kings – like ancient Greek oracles, they were able to influence political decisions. Julius Caesar tells us in his *Gallic War* (Book VI, 13–18) that the Druidic system originated in Britain and was exported to Gaul. He too refers to their great authority in Celtic society not only in religion, but also in educational and legal affairs, adding that their privileges included exemption from military service and taxation. Students of Druidic religion had to 'learn many verses by heart, sometimes for a period of 20 years. It is considered sacrilege to put their teachings into writing.' Celtic religion was thus *intended* to be mysterious and exclusive.

RIGHT **Pagan Celtic stone figures** *(Boa Island, Lough Erne, County Fermanagh, Ireland; c. fifth to seventh centuries AD). The double-sided figures stand in a Christian graveyard but retain the stylized, staring features of pagan Celtic images.*

The importance of prophets in Celtic religion was also recorded by Diodorus: 'These men predict the future by observing the flight and calls of birds, and by the sacrifice of holy animals: all orders of society are in their power . . . and in very important matters they prepare a human victim, plunging a dagger into his chest; by observing the way his limbs convulse as he falls and the gushing of his blood, they are able to read the future.' Recent archeology has provided evidence to support such statements made by Greek and Roman writers that the Celts practised human

RIGHT **Reconstructed portal to a Celtic shrine** *(Roquepertuse, Bouches-du-Rhône, France; third to second centuries BC). Niches in the columns contained the human skulls of fit young men, probably head-hunted in battle; a stone bird stood on the cross-beam.*

sacrifice. Excavations in the 1980s of a sacred Gallic site at Ribemont in Picardy, France, revealed pits filled with human bones, the thigh bones purposefully arranged into right-angled patterns. This sanctuary was levelled by Julius Caesar during his conquest of Gaul. The body of 'Lindow Man', recently discovered in a Cheshire peat bog (now in the British Museum in London), might also have been the victim of Druidic sacrifice.

The names of Celtic deities are known from references in later myths and from religious inscriptions of the Roman period in Gaul and Britain. However, there are several reasons why their natures and mythical 'biographies' remain elusive compared to the many surviving divine stories of other ancient cultures. Celtic artists rarely produced anthropomorphic (human) images before they came under Greek influence during the 'La Tène' period (between the third and the first centuries BC). Therefore the relatively late artistic representations of Celtic divinities, produced by artists trained in the Graeco-Roman style, are not very helpful in telling us about original Celtic perceptions of their gods. Likewise it is difficult to unravel information about pagan religious ritual from Celtic literature as Christian writers would later have adapted or omitted any blatant pagan elements. However, some scholars have argued that the underlying structures of many of the myths reflect their original significance in Druidic religious rituals, with the texts containing many significant pagan details.

Celtic divinities as well as religious rituals became intermingled with their Graeco-Roman counterparts during the period of Roman domination. Mercury, a god of merchants and 'inventor of all the arts', found his Celtic equivalent in Lugh, who in Irish mythology is called 'skilled in all the arts'. Animal gods were important in Celtic religion, and Epona, particularly revered as a horse goddess, was even worshipped by the Romano-British cavalry. Cernunnos ('the horned one') is connected not only with the stag, but with bulls, rams and other powerful male animals. Both hunter and protector of animals, Cernunnos has persisted in British folk traditions as Herne the Hunter.

Celtic goddesses and gods represented the elemental forces of nature, and according to classical writers, their shrines tended to be in secluded groves. Many of these sacred sites must have disappeared, and our knowledge of ritual activities is mainly limited to the monumentalized religious sanctuaries of the Roman period. Although absolute evidence is lacking, Druidic religious rituals probably also took place at pre-Celtic monuments such as stone circles. The Celtic religious year revolved around the control of the seasons and nature by sun and moon, and topographical 'focuses' of worship were ordained. Thus the Irish Druids met at Visnech, the 'navel' of Ireland, and Stonehenge in the south of England may also have been such a centre.

ABOVE **St Bride** *(John Duncan; tempera on canvas, 1913). The pagan Celtic goddess Brigit was daughter of Dagda, one of the original Irish gods, the Tuatha de Danaan. Around* AD *450 she was transformed into the Christian St Brigit, founder of the first nunnery at Kildare. A Scottish legend tells of her travelling from Iona to Bethlehem and returning with the baby Jesus. Duncan portrays her equally as the pagan bringer of Spring, being carried by angels across the Sound of Iona.*

The Celtic year was divided into summer and winter. Summer began on the first of May, after the feast of Beltain on May-Eve. During this festival in honour of 'the fire of Bel' (Irish Bile was an ancient god of life and death), domestic fires were extinguished and rekindled from a new Druidic fire. Winter began on the first of November, preceded by the feast of Samhain (our Hallowe'en) when, in Ireland, the Sidhe (fairies of the Otherworld) were believed to be abroad signalling the time of the dead.

EIGHT

Tristan and Isolt

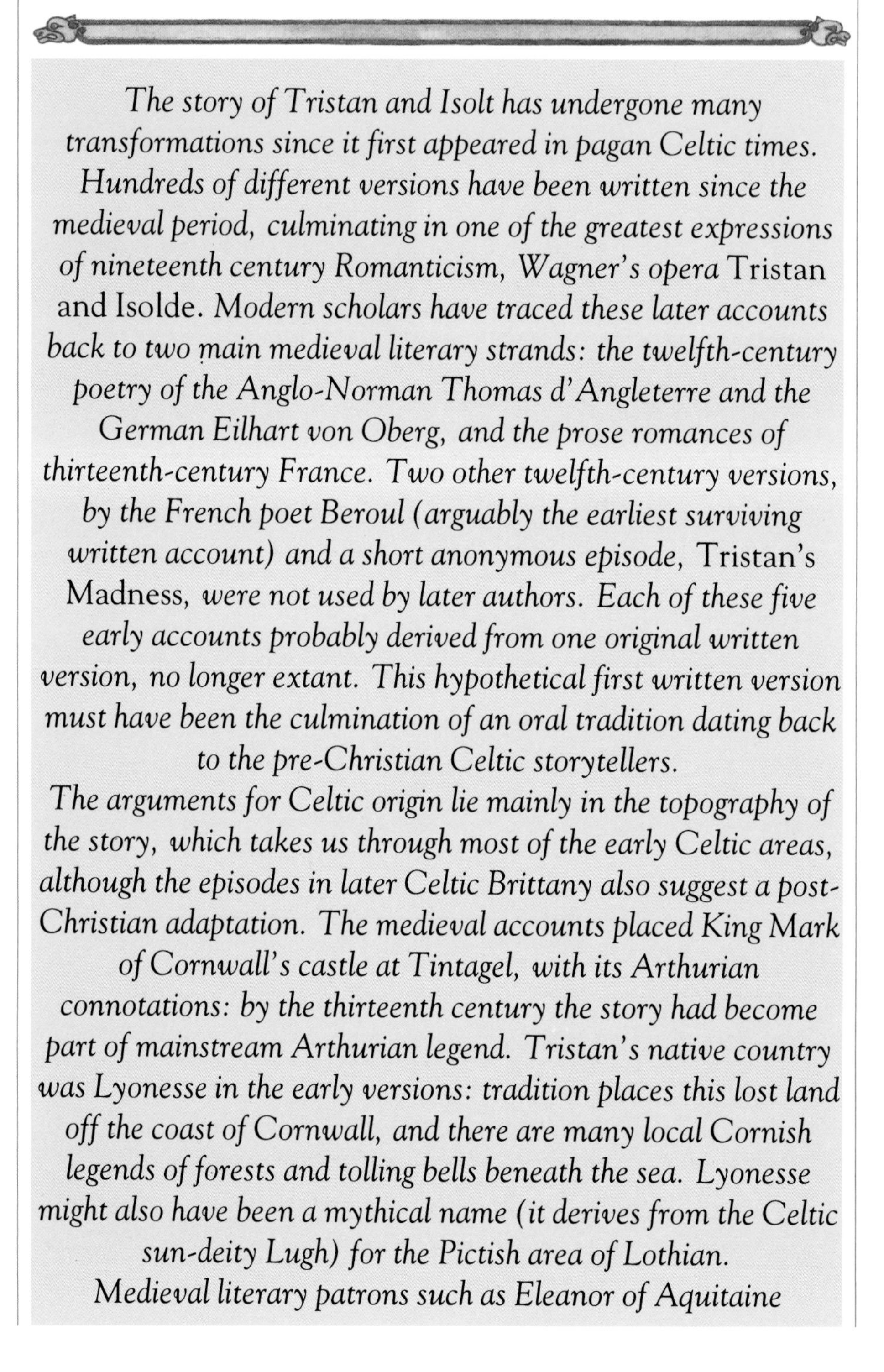

The story of Tristan and Isolt has undergone many transformations since it first appeared in pagan Celtic times. Hundreds of different versions have been written since the medieval period, culminating in one of the greatest expressions of nineteenth century Romanticism, Wagner's opera Tristan and Isolde. *Modern scholars have traced these later accounts back to two main medieval literary strands: the twelfth-century poetry of the Anglo-Norman Thomas d'Angleterre and the German Eilhart von Oberg, and the prose romances of thirteenth-century France. Two other twelfth-century versions, by the French poet Beroul (arguably the earliest surviving written account) and a short anonymous episode,* Tristan's Madness, *were not used by later authors. Each of these five early accounts probably derived from one original written version, no longer extant. This hypothetical first written version must have been the culmination of an oral tradition dating back to the pre-Christian Celtic storytellers.*

The arguments for Celtic origin lie mainly in the topography of the story, which takes us through most of the early Celtic areas, although the episodes in later Celtic Brittany also suggest a post-Christian adaptation. The medieval accounts placed King Mark of Cornwall's castle at Tintagel, with its Arthurian connotations: by the thirteenth century the story had become part of mainstream Arthurian legend. Tristan's native country was Lyonesse in the early versions: tradition places this lost land off the coast of Cornwall, and there are many local Cornish legends of forests and tolling bells beneath the sea. Lyonesse might also have been a mythical name (it derives from the Celtic sun-deity Lugh) for the Pictish area of Lothian.

Medieval literary patrons such as Eleanor of Aquitaine

RIGHT **Tintagel Castle, Cornwall, England.** *Remains of the thirteenth-century castle can be seen overlooking the high cliffs (centre right). The modern bridge from mainland to island is also visible (bottom left).*

encouraged their 'troubadours' to produce new versions of the old love stories which would both emphasize the contemporary ideology of 'courtly love', as well as bring them into line with current religious attitudes. The trend for 'medieval revivals' seen in nineteenth-century Europe inspired Romantic interpretations of the rediscovered poems. Wagner's main source was the German poem of Gottfried von Strassburg (c.1210), but the story had personal relevance to Wagner in reflecting his own love affair with his best friend's wife, Mathilde Wesendonck. Tennyson and other Victorian poets also produced versions of the story.

The underlying pagan Celtic nature of the story has never been lost: it is difficult to entirely Christianize or tame a story which deals with an adulterous love affair. Many even believe that the love potion was a post-Christian addition which provided an excuse for the lovers' sinful behaviour. However, it would seem likely that this is a Christian interpretation *of an original Celtic feature as magical devices are common in Celtic mythology and reflect Druidic religious ritual. Ironically, the monks of Lindisfarne Priory still make a love potion from a secret recipe!*

The upbringing and heroic adventures of Tristan recall the deeds of the Irish CuChulainn and the Welsh Pryderi. Likewise, the strong and uncompromising characterization of Isolt and indeed the basic plot itself are paralleled in the stories of Irish Deirdre and Welsh Branwen. There is no 'authentic' version of Tristan and Isolt: major details of the plot differ from one account to another and the driving motives of the main characters vary according to the intentions of poet and audience. Some of the better known episodes are here incorporated into a prose version, omitting the blatantly Christian and medieval elements. However, some medieval French troubadour lays are included to enhance the narrative in the Celtic manner.

King Mark was ruler of Cornwall and dwelt in a fort at Tintagel, an impregnable stronghold on a high rocky promontory overlooking the Irish Sea. Cornwall was at war with Ireland and Mark's ally, Rivalin of Lothian, sailed down from Scotland to join in the struggle. As a sign of gratitude, Mark allowed Rivalin to return to Lothian with his sister as a wife. She died while giving birth to a son who, born in the midst of sorrow, was named Tristan.

Tristan was educated by Gorvenal, a wise and trusted member of Rivalin's court; the boy learnt all the arts of fighting and diplomacy, hunting and swimming. One day, when Tristan was sitting on the cliffs playing his harp to the sea birds, Gorvenal saw that the boy was ready: 'Young Tristan,' he said, 'I have taught you everything I know, and it is time for you to see what lies beyond the bounds of Lothian.'

'But where shall I go?' asked Tristan.

'To where the winds blow you and to where your heart guides you.'

And Tristan, with his tutor Gorvenal as companion, sailed to the land of his mother in Cornwall. As they approached Tintagel Fort, Tristan turned to his men: 'None of you', he said, 'are to tell these noble people who I am. For if I am to be received by them, it must be out of respect for my behaviour and not my royal title.'

King Mark welcomed them honourably into his fort, and that evening invited them to the banquet. Once the wine was flowing he turned to his guests: 'Strangers,' he said, 'tell us who you are and from where you have come.'

ABOVE **Ornamented 'Q', the first letter of the Latin version of St Luke's Gospel** *(illuminated manuscript of the Gospels, Lindisfarne, Northumbria, England; c. 698 AD). Christian monks working in Celtic areas often ornamented their Christian manuscripts in a Celtic style; pagan monsters and human figures often appear among the interwoven patterns. The use of expensive colours such as gold and silver meant that the material value of these spiritual texts increased the likelihood of Viking raids on the monasteries.*

LEFT **Aerial view of Tintagel, Cornwall, England.** *The Lower Ward of the thirteenth-century castle is visible on the mainland (centre left). A modern bridge leads to a steep cliff-path which climbs up to the castle's Island Ward. On the summit of the Island are remains of the medieval Christian chapel. Archeologists have found evidence of an earlier, wealthy post-Roman stronghold on the Island contemporary with the 'Arthurian' Age, c. 450–600 AD). Local medieval legends associated the site with the birth of Arthur, while others saw it as King Mark's castle and the setting for tales of Tristan and Isolt.*

'We come from the north,' answered Tristan, 'and our fathers are merchants; but none of us has a heart for trading, and so we offer ourselves as warriors in your service.' Tristan then made music and the whole room fell quiet at the plaintive melodies of his harp.

'You shall stay here gladly,' said King Mark.

For over a year Tristan and his men from Lothian remained at Tintagel. The war with Ireland had ended with a treaty in which Mark had promised to send annual tribute to the King of Ireland. With the arrival of the warriors of Lothian Mark decided to refuse the payments, which consisted of the enslavement of young Cornish boys and girls, and thus came the chance that Tristan was waiting for to prove himself to the king.

FAR RIGHT **Door column of the Church of St Mary and St David, Kilpeck, near Hereford, England** *(twelfth century AD). Late Celtic warriors are interlaced with dragons in the pagan decorations of the Church exterior.*

RIGHT **Stone head** *(Salzburg, Austria; c. first century BC to first century AD). The Celts believed heads to contain magical properties: the heads of the enemy were greatly valued as battle-prizes and there are many mythical references to powerful heads. Carved stone heads probably had similar ritual significance.*

A new champion had emerged in Ireland; he was Morholt, brother of the Irish queen and a great warrior. Tristan was the first to see Morholt's ship sailing towards Tintagel and he knew what he was coming for. Morholt beached his ship and sent a message to the king demanding the tribute. 'He shall not have it', said Tristan, 'without a fight.' As there were no other volunteers to meet Morholt in single combat, Mark agreed to Tristan's request to do so with a promise that he would be raised to the nobility of Cornwall if he succeeded.

Morholt accepted the challenge but on condition that his adversary was of equal royal bearing to himself.

Tristan could no longer conceal his real identity from the court of Tintagel: 'I am the son of King Rivalin of Lothian,' he said, 'and nephew to King Mark of Cornwall.' King Mark was at once happy and sad that this fine young man was his sister's son, and yet he was to risk his life for Cornwall. Tristan, however, would not be dissuaded and it was agreed that the fight would take place on a small island opposite Tintagel.

At dawn on the appointed day, Tristan rowed out towards the island, and seeing Morholt's boat drawn up on the beach, he abandoned his own and waded ashore. Morholt was clearly puzzled by this behaviour: 'Why did you push your boat out to sea?' he asked.

'Only one of us will be leaving this island today,' answered Tristan, drawing his sword and striking the first blow.

The sea birds were the only witnesses to the long and bloody battle. The final blow was struck by Tristan: his sword smashed through Morholt's helmet, splitting his skull. Morholt was taken from the island in the Irish ship, while Tristan rowed the small boat back to Tintagel where there was much rejoicing that night. But Tristan was strangely troubled: his sword had splintered and a small fragment was missing.

Morholt died on the sea voyage home and there was great mourning in Ireland for the death of their hero. The king's daughter, whose name was Isolt, had been taught the magic properties of herbs by her mother. While attempting to revive Morholt with her craft, she extracted a piece of sharp metal from his fractured head. She wrapped it in silk knowing that one day she would discover the sword from which it came: on that day she would avenge her uncle.

Tristan had suffered a small wound from Morholt's spear, but did not realise at first that it had been dipped in one of the poisons brewed by Isolt of Ireland. The wound began to fester and soon no one would approach Tristan's room for the stench. Tristan knew that the antidote for the poison lay somewhere across the sea and he had himself pushed out into the ocean where he drifted for many days. Manannan the Sea God watched over him and blew his boat gently towards Ireland. When the land came into view Tristan took up his harp and sang. The people of Dublin were amazed at the sight of the boat without a pilot. As it drew nearer they heard the soft sounds of a sweet harp playing and a voice singing. The music enchanted them and they drew the boat ashore and carried the wounded minstrel, who called himself Tantris, to the court. There he was tended by the maids of Princess Isolt and cured by her herbs: but the two never met before it came time for Tristan to return to Cornwall.

LEFT **Iron-Age settlement, Chysauster, Cornwall, England** *(c. first century BC to third century AD). The well-preserved remains of nine 'courtyard houses' at Chysauster reveal a stone-paved passage leading into an open courtyard, off which open several small rooms. Originally with thatched roofs, the houses had drains and terraced gardens.*

ABOVE **Warrior fights monster** *(bronze matrix for making decorative helmet plaques, from Torslunda, Sweden; eighth century* AD*). The Teutonic warriors of pre-Viking Sweden, like their Celtic neighbours, decorated their helmets with scenes of power. Here, a warrior with axe confronts a wild beast.*

In Cornwall, he had long been given up for dead and great was the rejoicing at his homecoming; but there were some in Mark's court who were jealous of the affection which the foreigner Tristan had inspired in their king, and they planned to find Mark a wife, in the hope that a son would be born and inherit Cornwall. The king was aware of their schemes and one day found a reason for putting off the marriage for ever. It was early summer and Mark was sitting by a window looking out to sea. The swallows were swooping low over the cliffs and one of them dropped a ruddy golden thread into his lap. Mark ran it through his fingers and realized that it was a woman's hair. At the feast that evening Mark held up the long fair hair: 'Many of you,' he said, 'wish to see me married; but I shall marry no one except the owner of this hair. There will be great rewards for the man who discovers her and brings her back to Cornwall.'

'I killed Morholt for you,' said Tristan, 'and I shall find you a wife.'

Tristan set sail from Tintagel with his friends and Manannan blew up a great storm which shipwrecked them on the coast near Dublin. The men of Lothian disguised themselves as merchants and stood around in the markets listening out for clues to the owner of the golden hair; but the news was not of women but of dragons. The countryside around Dublin was being devastated by a fire-breathing monster and the King of Ireland had offered the hand of his daughter Isolt to the man who brought him evidence of the creature's death. Tristan instinctively set out to find the dragon, following the scorched earth towards its lair, where he sat and waited for the monster's return.

Tristan was gazing at the full moon when against it appeared the black shadow of the dragon. The air grew hot as it approached and Tristan caught sight of it in the moonlight as it flew towards the den. It was a white dragon with huge flapping wings and a long pointed rail; along its spine ran a line of poisonous thorns and its teeth gleamed razor-sharp. Tristan confronted the monster which roared and shot out billows of white smoke from its nostrils, enshrouding him in a mist. Tristan could see nothing until suddenly the clouds were broken by the dragon's opening jaws. Tristan's reactions were fast and he plunged his spear into its throat, performed the salmon leap onto its neck and reached over to slice off the dragon's poisonous forked tongue. He put the tongue inside his stocking and set off for Dublin; but the warmth of his body drew out the poison and Tristan collapsed on the path which led to the dragon's lair.

The Irish king's steward, who secretly lusted after Isolt, had been watching the whole battle from a tree; he hacked off the dragon's head and took it to the King, claiming his prize. Isolt shrank at the thought of marrying this man, who was considered a liar and coward by many in the court. Therefore she went with her mother and Brangaine, her maidservant, to the dragon's lair; there they found Tristan unconscious, with the forked tongue in his hand, and they carried him between them back to the court. Brangaine then recognized him as Tantris, the minstrel they had tended months earlier, and Tristan continued to hide his true identity.

It was several weeks before Tristan began to recover with the help of Isolt's herbs. Isolt had become increasingly attracted to this stranger, who even on his sick-bed played the harp so beautifully. It seemed curious to her that such a minstrel should also be a valiant fighter, and she hoped in her heart of hearts that he would survive the dragon's poison and claim her as his prize.

The day came for him to leave his bed and while he was bathing Isolt cleaned his armour. The notch on his sword caught her notice and she ran to her room to find the silk-wrapped

LEFT **Gaullish prisoner** (c. *first century* BC). *This Roman bronze depicts the Celt as a stereotyped heroic enemy, hands tied behind back. Trousers were favoured by Celtic chieftains from the Hallstatt period onwards, whereas Irish aristocrats wore knee-length tunics and cloaks. Aristocratic Celtic women also wore tunics and cloaks.*

John Dunca
1912

LEFT **Tristan and Isolde** *(tempera on canvas by John Duncan; 1912). In the manner of the Pre-Raphaelites, the Dundee artist has here used the white priming of the canvas to produce a gleaming, jewel-like image of the two lovers. He chose the turning-point of the story, with the two unknowingly about to drink the magic love-potion. Celtic patterns are employed to give authentic details of dress and wood-carving. Duncan married a woman who had found a cup in a well in Glastonbury and claimed it to be the Arthurian Grail. He believed that profound and beautiful art can only be produced in circumstances of unrequited love, one of the main themes of the Tristan myth.*

splinter which not so long ago she had removed from her uncle's head: the piece perfectly fitted the notch in the minstrel's sword. At that moment Isolt's feelings of love for Tristan turned to hatred. 'So at last the gods have brought you to me,' she said to him. 'You are the man who slew my uncle Morholt. On that mournful day when I realized that my herbs had no power over death, I swore that one day I would have my revenge.'

'I killed Morholt in single combat,' said Tristan, 'and on behalf of my king. There was no treachery in your uncle's death, but treachery will triumph if you kill me, for then you must marry the steward who lays claim to the dragon-slaying. I am the only man who can prove him false.' And Isolt stormed out of the room, and neither of them could sleep that night.

The next day the court gathered to hear the steward make his official claim to Isolt. 'It was no easy task,' he said holding up the dragon's head, 'but I suffered no wounds and will defend you equally well when the next monster arrives.'

'You are that lying monster,' cried Isolt, 'and here is the man who truly killed the dragon.' Tristan was led into the hall.

'Prove it!' spat the steward.

'This coward has the head,' said Tristan, 'but I have the deadly tongue. I am Tristan, royal nephew of the King of Cornwall. I was sent here to find the owner of this golden hair, and I think that in killing the dragon, I have found her.' And Tristan held up the dragon's tongue in one hand and the hair in the other. Every man and woman present gasped, for the tongue was hideous and the hair beautiful: and every head turned from the cowering steward to the Princess Isolt.

'Your king shall have Isolt as his queen,' said the Irish king, 'and let this marriage bind a peace between our two countries.' The day before they left for Cornwall, Isolt's mother gave a powerful love potion to Brangaine: 'You are to slip half of this into the King of Cornwall's wine, and half into my daughter's on their wedding night. It will surely bind them together in love.'

The ship sailed out of Dublin harbour and Isolt stood at the stern and watched the sun setting in reds and golds over her land as it slipped away from her. For two days the sea was whipped up by the storm chariots of Manannan the Sea God; by the third day the winds had died away and the ship was strangely becalmed. The sun beat down on Tristan and Isolt as they played a board game to pass away the time: Isolt still would not speak to Tristan. She called Brangaine to fetch them a refreshing herbal drink from her travelling-chest. They drank, as was the custom, from the same bowl; and as they drank the winds blew and the sail filled, the waves lashed and the salt spray was in their hair. Their hands touched as they passed the bowl from one to the

ABOVE **Fight of the Red and White Dragons** *(The St Alban's Chronicle, Lambeth Palace Library, London, England; fifteenth century AD). The fifth-century AD British leader of history, Vortigern, had become a semi-mythical character by the time of the twelfth-century author, Geoffrey of Monmouth. He recounts a traditional tale concerning a prophetic vision of two fighting dragons. The manuscript illustration seen here depicts Ambrosius (the Arthurian Merlin) explaining the meaning to Vortigern: the red dragon (representing Celtic Britain) defeats the white one (the invading Saxons).*

other, at first shyly and then with the full passion that the draught inspired: for Brangaine had mistakenly served them with the love potion.

The ship arrived at Tintagel and King Mark was highly pleased with Isolt. But it was not Isolt that he slept with on their wedding night. Tristan realized that the King would discover that he was not the first to make love to Isolt: therefore he persuaded Brangaine to slip into the marriage bed the moment the lights were extinguished. Thus began the many deceits that were to lead eventually to the discovery of Tristan and Isolt's secret love, for the lovers could not keep away from one another, try as they might. Both Tristan and Isolt felt much guilt, for each of them felt great affection towards Mark, but the love potion's magic was intended to last for three years and it was too strong for them to resist.

Those that had always been jealous of Tristan now found a way of putting him out of favour. It was not difficult for them to arouse the king's suspicions for Tristan and Isolt were ever flirting across the table at banquets. One man in particular, Andret, who had a secret desire for Isolt, hoped that one day the lovers would be discovered. The rumours grew and Mark expelled Tristan from the court. Even so, Tristan and Isolt could not be parted. There was a spring in the orchard outside the walls of Tintagel which flowed as a stream into the fort; Tristan would hide up a tree in the orchard and throw summer flowers or twigs in winter into the stream as a sign to Isolt that he was waiting for her. Andret asked a Druid to determine from the stars whether the two were still seeing one another. The Druid saw it all in the night sky: the orchard, the flowers in the stream and Isolt slipping out of the fort.

One day the Druid predicted that a lover's tryst was to take place while the king was out hunting the wild boar that night. Andret therefore schemed to bring the king back home earlier than expected at the following dawn. Tristan and Isolt met among the night-scented flowers of the orchard while Brangaine kept watch as usual from the tower above Isolt's chamber. As the first glimmers

BELOW **Bronze boar statuette** *(Hounslow, Middlesex, England; first century* BC *to first century* AD*). The figure was found together with other boars and a wheel, which were perhaps votive offerings to a sun god at a Celtic shrine. Like other Celtic boars, its dorsal spine is emphasized: the animal was a symbol of virility, which was signified in myth and reality by the warrior's bristling hair.*

of dawn were touching the starry sky Brangaine sang:

'God of light which makes
things true and clear,
Please be faithful and help my
companions,
For I have not seen them
since twilight
And before long will it be
dawn.

'Fine companions, whether
you sleep or are waking,
Sleep no more, my masters, if
you please.
For in the eastern sky the star
ascends
Which heralds the day which
I knew would come,
And before long will it be
dawn.

'Fine companions, my song is
calling you,
Sleep no more, for I hear the
bird singing
As it looks for the day
amongst the thickets.
And I fear that the jealous
man is after you,
And before long will it be
dawn.'

Tristan returned her song:

'Beautiful sweet companion,
so rich is this place,
That I wish that it would
never be dawn or day.
For the woman I hold in my
arms
Is the most beautiful ever
born of a mother,
And that is why I care so
little
For the jealous fool and the
dawn . . .'

Tristan's song was interrupted by King Mark and his warriors, who had crept into the orchard guided by Andret. The two lovers were bound and immediately their punishment was pronounced: Tristan and Isolt were to be burnt in a pit of flaming branches. On their way to the place of death, Tristan was allowed to make an offering of appeasement to the angry gods on a sacred rock above the sea. 'Save yourself!' cried Isolt. 'If you live then I shall also live in death.' And Tristan leapt into the sea; so high was the cliff that all who saw him jump considered him dead. The only sound was the crying of sea gulls.

'A fine sacrifice to Manannan the Sea God,' said Mark, and Isolt was taken to the death-pit. A group of diseased men who lived in the woods surrounding Tintagel approached the place. 'Since Queen Isolt is to die anyway,' said one of them, his face

ABOVE **Distant view of the headland at Tintagel, Cornwall, England.** *The legendary birthplace of King Arthur was also believed in local folklore to have been the fortress of King Mark. Tintagel was its medieval name, meaning 'The Fortress of the Constriction' and taken from the Celtic words* din *(fort) and* tag *(obstruct or construct). An apt description for the dramatic manner in which the Island meets the mainland.*

hideously pock-marked, 'why not give her to us for our pleasure. She will soon be dead, and her death will appease the evil demons who bring disease to your lands.' And Isolt was unbound and taken away.

Tristan had survived his plunge into the sea and lay in ambush for the captors of Isolt as they took her away to the woods. He had no difficulty in saving her from them, and Tristan and Isolt lived as outlaws in the woods for many months. The effects of the love potion, which had been brewed to last for three years, were wearing off: they had shared a beautiful dream and were waking into a world of harsh reality. Their love for one another became real, but so did their strong sense of remorse for having wounded the heart of King Mark. Tristan decided that he must leave Cornwall for Brittany; and Isolt returned to Tintagel and swore an oath of loyalty to her husband. Soon Isolt saw from her tower a small boat sailing southwards along the coast; and she knew that she would never see Tristan alive again.

Tristan landed in Brittany with his companion Gorvenal, and they offered themselves as warriors to the local king, whose name was Hoel. Tristan, who no longer cared whether he lived or died, immediately proved his courage in battle against a neighbouring tribe. That evening at the victory banquet, King Hoel stood up and announced: 'Today I have seen a new hero who is quite reckless in battle; as a reward I offer him my daughter, Isolt of the White Hands, as a wife.' Tristan was now as reckless in his drinking as he was at fighting. He looked at Isolt of the White Hands who had blushed the colour of the foxglove on the moor, reminding him of another Isolt. That night they slept together, but Tristan could not bring himself to make love to a distant heart. His excuse was that he was suffering from an old wound.

Isolt of the White Hands tolerated her husband's lack of interest and even began to joke about it with her maidservants. One day she was out hunting with her brother Kaherdin; as they were jumping a fence the mud splashed up and spattered her thighs: 'Why!' she laughed, 'even the mud is more interested in me than my husband.' And that evening Kaherdin questioned Tristan and discovered the real reason for his coldness; Tristan swore Kaherdin to silence by promising that he would make every effort to forget his former love.

The following day brought a surprise attack on Hoel's fort and Tristan was badly wounded. Isolt of the White Hands did not have the potent herbal cures of Isolt the Fair (as the men of Brittany called the Cornish queen). Tristan, realizing that he was going to die unless Isolt herself came to him, gave a message to Gorvenal to take to Cornwall: 'Tell the men of Cornwall that I am dying of a poisoned wound, and that only Queen Isolt can cure me. Go in my boat and if you return with Isolt, hoist the white sail, but if she will not come, then let the sail be black.' Isolt of the White Hands overheard the message and at last knew where Tristan's absent heart lay.

Several days later Tristan had become very weak and was on the threshold of the Underworld; suddenly he heard the watchmen of King Hoel's fort shouting that a boat was in view. 'What colour is the sail?' he asked his Breton wife. Isolt of the White Hands felt the jealousy well up inside her: 'It is black, my lord,' she replied. Tristan's heart burst within him as Isolt the Fair and King Mark came running into his room. Isolt stood above her dead lover and, hearing the sounds of his harp in her memory, sang:

'The sun is shining, clear and
fair,
And I can hear the sweet
song of birds;
All around me they sing in
the thickets
And their songs are new.

BELOW **Head of the Celtic god Coriosolites** *(bronze coin from Brittany; first century BC). The Celts borrowed the idea of coinage from the Greeks and Romans; local kings portrayed themselves on the coins, together with symbols of their trade and wealth on the reverse, such as ears of corn or horses. This Gallic coin depicts a local god, with fashionable Celtic warrior hairstyle: note the chain with a severed head attached hanging from his hair. Diodorus refers to the Celtic custom of taking heads as proof of valour in battle, and such heads were sometimes offered to warrior gods.*

RIGHT **Gold boat model** *(from Broighter, County Derry, Ireland; first century BC). This miniature boat, complete with benches, mast and oars, was part of a hoard of gold jewellery and may have been an offering to a water deity such as the Irish sea god, Manannan.*

'I see my own death coming,
And I sing a lay which will be
held most dear,
And will not fail to touch
lovers,
For it is love which makes me
long to die.

'Tristan, my friend, friend,
friend,
Here is my heart which I
entrusted
To your love; not a good
place for it,
and now it will die by your
sword.

'Tristan, my friend, friend,
friend,
Even though the gods despise
my desire,
My soul shall dwell in your
spirit,
In the lands of the blessed or
in the Underworld.'

Falling on Tristan's sword, Isolt followed him to the Underworld, and thus did the lovers return in death to King Mark's fort at Tintagel. They were buried in two mounds, side by side, and the intertwining branches of two trees grew from their graves.

NINE

Folktales and Songs From Around the Celtic World

CORNWALL

Cornwall was a stronghold of Romano-Celtic culture until the Saxon invasions and not surprisingly it is the birthplace of many Arthurian legends, including that of Tristan and Isolt. Until recently, the river Tamar was regarded by the Cornish people as a cultural boundary between the Cornish and the English. The Cornish language was related to Breton, but was extinct by the nineteenth century. However, Cornish folk-singers such as Brenda Wooton have kept the poetic language alive, and recently there have been attempts at revival. This poem appeared in the Cornish language in the seventeenth century. It originates in an earlier English folk song. Strawberry water was once a favourite skin toner. The bold replies of the girl continue the Celtic mythological tradition of feminine pride.

LEFT **Alderley Edge, Cheshire, England.** *Arthurian myths and legend are present in most areas of Celtic Britain. At Alderley Edge, local legend and folklore tells of a king and his warriors who sleep in a cave beneath the hill: one day they will be awakened to defend us against invaders. Such legends occur elsewhere in Britain and Europe and are often associated with Arthur. The summit of Alderley Edge commands a sweeping view of the Cheshire Plain, where the peat-preserved body of a murdered or sacrificed Celt was recently discovered in Lindow Moss.*

'Where lies your path,
lovely girl,' he said,
'with your flaxen locks, and
your face so pale?'
'I go to the spring, kind sir,'
said she,
'with strawberry leaves, I'll
never fail.'

'May I come too, lovely girl,'
he said,
'with your flaxen locks, and
your face so pale?'
'If that is your wish, kind
sir,' said she,
'with strawberry leaves, I'll
never fail.'

'And what if I lay you on the
grass,
with your flaxen locks, and
your face so pale?'
'I'll rise up again, kind sir,'
said she,
'with strawberry leaves, I'll
never fail.'

'And what if you find
yourself with child,
with your flaxen locks, and
your face so pale?'
'I'll carry that child, kind
sir,' said she,
'with strawberry leaves, I'll
never fail.'

'What man will be there to
hold the child,
with your flaxen locks, and
your face so pale?'
'You'll be the father, kind
sir,' said she,
'with strawberry leaves, I'll
never fail.'

'With what will you clothe
this child of yours,
with your flaxen locks, and
your face so pale?'
'From the father's thread,
kind sir,' said she,
'with strawberry leaves, I'll
never fail.'

ABOVE **Restaurant signboard, Alderley Edge, Cheshire, England.** *Legend tells of a farmer who is travelling to the market to sell a white mare. He is waylaid on the Edge by a strangely dressed man who offers to buy the mare. The farmer refuses, expecting a better price in the market. To his surprise, no one buys the horse, but on the way home the wizard reappears and the farmer accepts his offer. The wizard takes him into the hill and shows him the sleeping knights, one of whom was lacking a horse. The farmer receives magic jewels as payment. The story was retold in* The Weirdstone of Brisingamen *by Alan Garner.*

THE ISLE OF MAN

The island's position in the Irish Sea between Ireland and Scotland has ensured it a place in Celtic mythology and tradition. It may have been considered one of the Isles of the Blessed, as was the island of Arran, ruled by the archaic Irish God of the Sea, Manannan (another child of Lir). The Manx language, closely related to Scottish Gaelic, was considered extinct by the 1950s, but there have been recent attempts at revival. An oral traditon of law, which might reflect original Druidic practice, had precedence, until recently, over written laws. Post-Celtic man was governed by Vikings until Scottish rule began in the thirteenth century. The following Manx folk–song has Christian references, but its themes of love vows, curses and powerful natural elements are those of Celtic mythology.

I first met my truelove at the Christmas ceilidh; we sat while the fiddler played and began our courting.

For seven whole years we met and made love, and her unfaithful tongue swore that she would never leave me.

On the Sunday before Ash Wednesday I visited by truelove; she placed her hands over mine and swore she would marry only me.

I came home in ecstasy, everything was roses; on the Wednesday I heard she had married another.

I cursed her for courting me for so long a time; when she found she had no love for me she should have said so.

But I cannot speak wickedly of her or call for bad luck; may she make her new friends glad, though love has a made a fool of me.

No one knew about our love save the old walnut tree; it cannot speak for me though it knows my lover false.

On St Patrick's Day I shall visit the fair in my young man's clothes, I'll walk right by her, pretending not to notice.

At the fair I'll take my pick from all the best girls; but she has no second chance with her deceitful new husband.

I walked the long winding road and grew weary of the slopes, but whenever I rested I thought of my love.

I wish that the wind would bring me news of my love; I wish she would cross the steep highlands to greet me and meet me by the shore.

How happily I would run to the shore if she were there; how happily my hand would make a pillow for her hair.

I wish that the sea would run dry and let me have my way; but the white snows of Greenland will sooner turn the red of roses before I forget my truelove.

LEFT **Madron Well, Cornwall, England.** *Sources of water were revered by the Celts for their religious powers, and many of these sacred springs and wells continued to be visited for spiritual healing in the Christian era, often dedicated to saints. Madron was also the site of a baptistry. Sick people still drink these waters and hang votive rags on the surrounding trees.*

BRITTANY

In the fifth century, several noble Welsh families fled the Saxon invasion of their country and landed in France. The area later became known as 'Little Britain' or Brittany. The Bretons brought their Celtic language and mythology with them, but many of their stories have been lost owing to the French government's past ban on speaking Breton. Only folk-tales and songs have survived in the Breton tongue: the Breton singer and harpist, Alan Stivell, has led the recent revival. The following traditional ballad contains a reference to the Virgin Mary, but the common ancient Celtic theme of the sea as a setting for miraculous tales involving women is present in the song. It was collected from the singing of Janet ar Gall of Kerarborn in 1849.

It was the first of November when the English reached Dourduff.
They beached at Dourduff and snatched a young girl.
They snatched a lovely maiden and took her to their ship.
Her name was Marivonnik and she came from Plougasnou.
As they carried her away, she cried at her father's door:

'Fare thee well dear mother and father, for I'll never see you more.
'Fare thee well dear brother and sister, for we'll never meet on earth.
'Fare thee well kinsmen and friends, for I'll never see your world again.'
And young Marivonnik wept, with no one there to comfort her.
No one was there to comfort her save the big Englishman, he comforted her.
'Do not cry, my Marivonnik, your life is not at risk;
'Your life is not at risk, but I cannot save your honour.'
'Sir Englishman, my honour

means more to me than all your ships at sea;
'Tell me then, shall I lose my honour to more than you alone?'
'To me and to my cabin boy, and to the sailors if they want you.
'To my sailors if they want you, every one hundred and one.'
'Tell me then, Sir Englishman, may I walk with you on the bridge?'
'You may walk up on the bridge, but take care not to drown.'
Young Marivonnik cried, whilst walking on the deck:
'Help me, Mary Virgin, shall I end it all by drowning?
'It is for you, dear Virgin Mary, so as not to offend you.
'If I fall in the sea, then drowned I shall be; if I stay I shall be killed.'
Young Marivonnik was guided by the Virgin and dived into the sea.
She was brought back to the surface by a small fish.
The big Englishman then called out to his sailormen:
'Sailors, sailors, rescue her and five hundred crowns are yours!'
And later that day he told young Marivonnik:
'You should not have done this, Marivonnik, for you were to be my wife.'

WALES

The Welsh language has survived in education and broadcasting, though what chance it stands against the English and American mass-media remains to be seen. The Mabinogion *and Arthurian legends have survived in folk–tales as well as in high literature. The following story appears in the* Journey Through Wales *by the twelfth–century churchman, Giraldus Cambrensis. In that Christianized version, Elidor is training to be a monk and runs away from his harsh teachers: I have omitted the Christian elements. The modern English author Alan Garner sets the story in Manchester where the escape is from urban squalor. The theme of the visit to the fairy world is one of the commonest in Celtic mythology. Such myths also provided the Celts with an 'explanation' for the great tomb mounds of the earlier Bronze–Age culture. The 'yellow ball' in this story is a fairy flower in other versions, all of which contain the feature of the fairy rule that you may not take anything back with you to the mortal world.*

Elidor was a young boy who was fed up with life. One day on the way to school he turned around and made his way to the woods. He wandered along the river in a dream and soon found himself at the entrance to a cave. Two little people came running out and said: 'Why don't you come inside and have some fun? Our world is happier than yours!'

Elidor did not stop to think, but followed them into the cave and found himself in a dark passageway which became narrower and lower until he was squeezing through on all fours. Just as he was beginning to panic the tunnel opened out into another cavern; they made for the light at the entrance and Elidor emerged into a world which he had only ever seen in paintings and dreams. It was an idyllic landscape with flowery meadows running down to lazy rivers; and yet there was something wrong too — Elidor looked up and saw that, although the world was bright, there was a mist hanging over everything so that neither sun, moon nor stars would shine.

Elidor was led before the king who asked who he was and from where he had come. The king was rather confused by the boy's answers and waved

RIGHT **Snowdonia.** *The highland region of north-west Wales has proved a difficult obstacle for Roman and English invaders. Many Welsh myths are located in the region, which provides a dramatic backdrop of lakes, streams and mountains.*

LEFT **A Spirit or Sidhe in a Landscape** *(oil on board by George William Russell, 1867–1935). The Irish artist's play* Deirdre *was performed in Dublin in 1902, and he is best known as a poet of works based on Celtic mythology. As a painter he tended to concentrate on a particular theme during a particular period. Between 1900–1905 he produced a series of images of Celtic spirits in landscape settings.*

him away saying, 'You will remain here as a playmate for my son.' That afternoon, if indeed it was afternoon, Elidor stood back and watched the little people as they played. They were finely proportioned and most had long fair hair. Their riding was on horses the size of greyhounds, but they did not hunt for they did not eat meat, preferring milk flavoured with saffron. In their conversations they ridiculed Elidor's people for their lives of violence and deceit, yet they did not have any religious beliefs.

Elidor grew homesick and the king allowed him a visit to his mother on condition that he returned. The little people led him back into the cavern, through the cramped tunnel which became wider and higher, until they reached the cave by the river. Here Elidor left his tiny companions and returned to his mother's house. She asked him where he had been and begged him not to leave home again, but he told her of his promise to the king. Thus Elidor spent his time divided between the ordinary world and the land of the little people.

One day Elidor told his mother of the brilliant yellow balls that they played with in the other place. His mother asked him to bring one home for she was poor and thought that they must be golden. So the next time Elidor was playing with the little people he took one of the balls and ran off with it into the cavern, through the widening passage and back to his mother. But just as he entered the house a tiny foot tripped him up and he dropped his treasure. He turned just in time to see the two little people scowl at him and run off with the ball.

The following day Elidor went into the woods and walked along the river to the cave, but he could no longer find it. Many years later he would walk along the river with his own children and tell them again and again the story of the little people.

SCOTLAND

The original Celtic inhabitants of Scotland north of the rivers Forth and Clyde were known by the fourth century as Picti ('Painted Ones'). The Picts were probably given this nickname by the Roman soldiers guarding Hadrian's Wall to describe their tattooed bodies. Archeologists have found tattoos on preserved Celtic flesh and ancient writers tell us that they painted their bodies. The Scotti ('Irishmen') came to Argyll from the kingdom of Dalriada in Antrim, Ireland, bringing their Irish Gaelic language to Scotland. In the ninth century the Scots took over the Pictish areas and it is their Gaelic language which still survives in parts of the Highlands and Hebrides. The land of Scotland features in many of the ancient Irish myths and legends and the Scottish folk-tales and local legends which have survived are mainly from the later Gaelic tradition. The following folk–tale looks back to the ancient period.

RIGHT **Horseman drinking** *(Pictish stone from Invergowrie, near Dundee, Scotland; c. ninth century AD). The native Celtic Picts were probably a continuation of the Caledonian tribes who resisted the Roman invasion. Together with the intrusive Irish Scotti, they invaded the Roman territory of northern Britain in the fourth and fifth centuries AD. The Pictish Kingdom controlled northern Britain between the sixth and ninth centuries, and eventually joined with the Scotti in the formation of Scotland. Horses were status symbols in all Celtic societies; here, the rider drinks from a horn which, with its eagle-headed terminal, is a further symbol of power.*

Some say that the Picts knew the recipe for the brewing of heather-ale. The secret was passed down from father to son for many centuries, but was finally lost when the Scots invaded the Pictish kingdom in the ninth century. The story goes as follows. The Scots loved the heather-ale which they imported from the Picts, and they longed to have the secret recipe. The family who guarded the recipe lived in the Mull of Galloway in the far west of the Pictish kingdom. One day father and son were captured in battle and the Scots had them brought out onto the open moor high up above the sea where the purple heather used for the famous brew was growing all around them. The Scots demanded the recipe, threatening and torturing the old man and his young son until they were on the point of death.

The sea-gulls were mewing as dusk began to fall. 'I shall tell you what you want to know,' spoke the old man at last, 'but only on condition that you first kill my son, so that he does not have the pain of witnessing his father bring dishonour and shame to our people.' The weary Scots raised a cry of victory and the boy was put to the sword. 'Now, old man,' they said, 'tell us the recipe.'

'Ha!' said the father, 'do you really think I would tell a Scot the secret of heather-ale? My son was about to divulge the recipe, for he still had many years to live and would not readily give up this beautiful world of sea-birds, high cliffs and the sounds of the foaming sea. Therefore he had to die; and the secret of heather-ale dies with him, for you will never have it from me!'

The Scottish chieftain was furious. 'Take him,' he cried, 'and hurl him from the highest cliff. Let him be smashed to pieces on the sharp rocks below, and may the sea mourn him forever more with her salty tears.'

Thus the old man died, and now shares the secret of heather-ale with the sea.

IRELAND

For historical reasons the Celtic tradition has survived better in Ireland than in any of the other Celtic areas. Modern Irish Gaelic is a close descendant of the ancient Celtic language; it is still spoken in the southwest and was recognized as an official language by the Republic of Ireland in 1921. Many Celtic myths and legends have come down to us in Irish, and the Irish folk-tale tradition is equally strong. The following traditional ballad was first sung at the time of the mass emigrations to America by young Irish men and women seeking work after the Great Famine of the 1840s. This relatively modern song is addressed to the legendary heroes of Ireland, a typical use of myth to conjure up a distant Golden Age. The emigrations themselves have now become legendary and the mythical power of the song remains relevant in a country still affected by emigration; it was recently recorded in 1983 by the Irish band Planxty.

RIGHT **Christy Moore.** *The Irish singer/songwriter continues the tradition of the Celtic bards by heroizing the modern freedom-fighters of Ireland and Central America. He has sung with the Irish folk group Planxty as well as with Moving Hearts, one of the earliest bands to combine folk, rock and jazz styles. Here he is playing the Irish bodhran, a hand-held drum.*

You brave Irish heroes
wherever you be,
I pray stand a moment and
listen to me,
Your sons and fair daughters
are now going away,
And thousands are sailing to
Americay.

So good luck to those people
and safe may they land,
They are leaving their
country for a far distant
strand,
They are leaving old Ireland,
no longer can stay,
And thousands are sailing to
Americay.

The night before leaving they
are bidding goodbye,
And it's early next morning
their heart gives a sigh,
They do kiss their mothers
and then they will say
'Farewell, dear old father, we
must now go away.'

Their friends and relations
and neighbours also,
When the trunks are all
packed up, all ready to go,
O the tears from their eyes
they fall down like the
rain,
And the horses are prancing,
going off for the train.

So good luck to those people
and safe may they land,
They are leaving their
country for a far distant
strand,
They are leaving old Ireland,
no longer can stay,
And thousands are sailing to
Americay.

When they reach the station,
you will hear their last cry,
With handkerchiefs waving
and bidding goodbye,
Their hearts will be breaking
on leaving the shore,
'Farewell, dear old Ireland,
will we ne'er see you
more?'

O I pity the mother that rears
up the child,
And likewise the father who
labours and toils,
To try to support them he
will work night and day,
And when they are older they
will go away.

So good luck to those people
and safe may they land,
They are leaving their
country for a far distant
strand,
They are leaving old Ireland,
no longer can stay,
And thousands are sailing to
Americay.

ENGLAND

In spite of the various invasions of England from the Roman times onwards, there are still folk memories of the Celtic past when the Brythonic language was spoken. England has a good number of pagan Celtic folk-customs, from the corn dolly to Morris Dancing. Un-Christianized Arthurian legends have persisted in local folklore and many English folk–songs appear to stem back to a pagan Celtic origin.

The 'high' subject matter of the following ballad suggests that it was composed for the court, but the colloquial language points to its later transformation into folk-song. The court bards were travellers and their songs were often heard by rich and poor alike. The song contains typical Celtic themes: the wife from across the sea and the problems of cultural integration. The use of magic spells to forestall a royal birth has its counterpart in the Greek myth of Herakles, where a similarly jealous but divine wife sends the goddess of childbirth

ABOVE **Corn-dolly seller, Lyme Regis, Dorset, England.** *The Celts relied heavily on agriculture, and many sacrificial rituals were linked to the continuing fertility of the land. Until recently, the last sheaves of corn during harvest used to be plaited into figures or talismans which contained the spirits of the corn. The associated religious ritual died long ago, but the dollies survive as a country craft; they are still widely believed to bring 'good luck'. This craftsman is making a selection of pagan and Christian motifs including horseshoes and crosses.*

to delay the birth of her husband's mortal son: the delay allows a rival prince to be born first and thus to claim the throne over Herakles. What we would now term 'witchcraft' was originally Celtic pagan religious lore and ritual, suppressed by Christianity. The tying of complex magical knots has its counterpart in the interwoven forms of Celtic art. The repetitions originate in the oral tradition but also increase the ritual atmosphere of the piece.

The song was recorded by a pioneer in the English folk-song revival, Martin Carthy, who sings it to the tune of a traditional Breton drinking-song, Son ar Chistr (Song of Cider), *which has itself been recorded by Alan Stivell. The tune was apparently composed in 1930 by a Breton piper who is now a Paris tramp. Such borrowings of tunes and changes of fortune must also have been present in the life and work of the ancient Celtic bards.*

King Willy he's sailed over
the raging foam,
He's wooed a wife and he's
brought her home.
He wooed her for her long
golden hair,
His mother wrought her a
mighty care:
And a weary spell she's laid
on her,
She be with child full long
and many's the year,
But her child she would never
bear.
And in her bower she lies in
pain,
King Willy at her bedhead he
do stand
As down his cheeks the
salten tears do run.

King Willy back to his
mother he did run,
And he's gone there as a
begging son.
He says: 'My truelove has this
fine noble steed
'The like of which you ne'er
did see:
'At every part of this horse's
mane
'There's hanging fifty silver

BELOW **Martin Carthy.** *The English solo singer and guitarist also performs with the Watersons, Dave Swarbrick, and John Kirkpatrick, all of them pioneers in the revival of English folk song and dance. His songs range from the collected folk material of the Celtic fairy and British historical past to the contemporary lyrics of Leon Rosselson, on subjects such as Britain's war with Argentina over the Falkland Islands.*

RIGHT **The 'Swearing Stone'** *(Castledermot Churchyard, County Kildare, Ireland). Folk memory carries traditions from the Celtic past, and prehistoric standing stones were probably used in pagan healing and fertility rites. This would explain why the Christians gave them evil names such as the 'Devil's Arrows', but their original sacred properties have survived in local superstitions: this one is still employed in the binding of oaths.*

bells and ten,
'There's hanging fifty bells and ten.
'This goodly gift shall be your own,
'If back to my own truelove you'll turn again
'That she might bear her baby son.'

'O but child, she will never lighter be,
'Nor from sickness will she e'er be free;
'But she will die and she will turn to clay,
'And you will wed with another maid.'
And sighing, says this weary man,
As back to his own truelove he's gone again:
'I wish my life was at an end.'

King Willy back to his mother he did run
And he's gone there as a begging son.
He says: 'My truelove has this fine golden girdle,
'Set with jewels all about the middle.
'At every part of this girdle's hem
'There's hanging fifty bells and ten
'There's hanging fifty silver bells and ten,
'This goodly gift shall be your own,
'If back to my own truelove you'll turn again
'That she might bear her baby son.'

'Oh but child, she will never lighter be,
'Nor from sickness will she e'er be free;
'But she will die and she will turn to clay,
'And you will wed with another maid.'
And sighing, says this weary man,

As back to his own truelove
he's gone again:
'I wish my life was at an end.'

Well up and spoke his noble
queen;
And she has told King Willy
of a plan
How she might bear her baby
son.
She says: 'You must go, get
you down to the market
place,
'And you must buy you a loaf
of wax;
'And you must shape it as a
babe that is to nurse
'And you must make two eyes
of glass.
'Ask your mother to the
christening day,
'And you must stand there
close as you can be,
'That you might hear what
she do say."

King Willy, he's gone down
to the market place,
and he has bought him a loaf
of wax;
And he has shaped it as a
babe that is to nurse,
And he has made two eyes of
glass.
He asked his mother to the
christening day,
And he has stood there close
as he could be,
That he might hear what she
did say.
And how she stormed and
how she swore:
She's spied the babe where no
babe could be before,
She's spied the babe where
none could be before.

She says: 'Who was it undid
the nine witch-knots,
'Braided in amongst this
lady's locks?
'And who was it who took
out the combs of care,
'Braided in amongst this
lady's hair?

LEFT **Green Man: capital of door column of the Church of St Mary and St David, Kilpeck, near Hereford, England** *(twelfth century AD). The pagan fertility god was used to 'scare away the evil eye' in many medieval Christian churches. His staring eyes and the tendrils emerging from his mouth demonstrate the continuing stylistic traditions of Celtic art.*

'And who was it slew the
master kid,
'That ran and slept all
beneath this lady's bed,
'That ran and slept all
beneath her bed?
'And who was it unlaced her
left shoe?
'And who was it that let her
lighter be,
'That she might bear her
baby boy?'

And it was Willy who undid
the nine witch-knots,
Braided in amongst this lady's
locks.
And it was Willy who took
out the combs of care,
Braided in amongst this lady's
hair.
And it was Willy the master
kid did slay,
And it was Willy who
unlaced her left-foot shoe,
And he has let her lighter be.
And she has poured out a
baby son,
And prayed to the blessings
that be them upon,
And prayed to the blessings
them upon.

FURTHER READING

MYTHS, LEGENDS AND FOLKTALES

Most of the following translations and versions are readily available in paperback:

Barber, R (ed), *The Arthurian Legends* (Woodbridge and Wolfeboro, 1979)
Beroul, *The Romance of Tristan* (trans. A S Fedrick; Harmondsworth, 1970)
A Celtic Miscellany (trans. K H Jackson; Harmondsworth, 1971)
Early Irish Myths and Sagas (trans. J Gantz; Harmondsworth, 1981)
Gottfried von Strassburg, *Tristan* (trans. A T Hatto; Harmondsworth, 1960)
The Mabinogion (trans. G Jones and T Jones; illustrated by Alan Lee; Hendrik-Ido-Ambacht, 1982)
The Mabinogion (trans. J Gantz; Harmondsworth, 1976)
Malory, *Le Morte d'Arthur* (Harmondsworth, 1969)
Rolleston, T W, *Myths and Legends of the Celtic Race* (London, 1985)
Scott, M, *Irish Folk and Fairy Tales Omnibus* (Harmondsworth, 1989)
The Tain (trans. T Kinsella; Dublin 1969 and London 1970)
Williamson, R, *The Craneskin Bag: Celtic Stories and Poems* (Edinburgh, 1989)
Wilson, B K, *Scottish Folk-Tales and Legends* (Oxford, 1954)

SUITABLE FOR YOUNGER READERS

Jacobs, J (ed), *Celtic Fairy Tales* (London, 1970)
Cooper, S, *The Dark is Rising Sequence* (London 1984)
Dickinson, P, *Merlin Dreams* (illustrated by Alan Lee; London, 1988)
Garner, A, *Elidor* (London, 1965); *The Weirdstone of Brisingamen* (London, 1960); *The Moon of Gomrath* (London, 1963); *The Owl Service* (London, 1967); *Red Shift* (London, 1973)

INTERPRETATION

The following modern studies of Celtic Mythology are also of interest:

Matthews, C, *Mabon and the Mysteries of Britain: An Exploration of the Mabinogion* (London, 1987)
Matthews, J & C, *The Aquarian Guide to British and Irish Mythology* (Wellingborough, 1988)
Rutherford, W, *Celtic Mythology* (Wellingborough, 1987)
Senior, M, *Myths of Britain* (London, 1979)

VARIANT SPELLINGS AND PRONUNCIATION GUIDE

Spellings of Celtic names are inconsistent from source to source. Anglicizations are generally attempts to reproduce the sound rather than the spelling of the words. Here is a selected list of characters and places with some of their variant spellings. Pronunciations are given only for major figures.

PRONUNCIATION KEY:

[´] = before stressed syllable; [ch] = ch in Scottish 'loch'; [ou] = Welsh aw as ou in 'out'; [th] = Welsh dd as th in 'there'; [tl] = Welsh ll as tl in 'little'; [oo] = Welsh w as oo in 'cook'; Welsh u and y = i as in 'pill'; Stresses generally come on the penultimate syllable.

MYTHOLOGICAL GROUPS

(A) Arthurian; (I) Irish; (S) Scottish; (W) Welsh

Ailill [´ailitl] (I)
Albain/Albion/Britain
Allen (S) / Ainle (I)
Aod/Aed [id] (I)
Arden (S) / Ardan (I)
Bedwyr [´bedwir] (W) / Bedivere (A)
Bendigeidfran [bendi´gaydfran] / Bran the Blessed (W)
Branwen [´branoowen] (W)
Bricriu [´brikru] (I)
Brigit/Brigit/Bride (I) (S)
Caswallawn [kas´watloun] (W) / Cassivellaunos
Cathbad [´kafuv] (I)
Cei/Cai/Kay/Keu [kai] (A)
Conchobar mac Nessa [´konchovor] (I) / Connachar [conn´acher] (S)
Connla/Conle [´konlle] (I)
CuChulainn/Cú Chulaind [ku´chulinn] (I)
Culhwch [´kilhooch] (W)
Custennin [küs´tenhin] (W)
Dearg [´dayarg] (I)
Deirdriu [´derrdru] / Deirdre [´derrdri] (I)
Efnissien [ev´nissien] (W)
Erin/Ireland
Etain/Édaín [´edain] (I)
Ferchar [´ferchar] (S) / Fergus (I)
Fingula/Fionnuala
Gwalchmai [goo´alchmai] (W) / Gawain (A)
Gwrhyr [´goohrir] (W)
Harddlech/Harlech [´harthlech] (W)
Isolt/Iseult/Yseult/Isolde (A)
Llŷr [tleer] (W)
Manannan [´mannernan] (I)
Manawydan [man´ouithan] (W)
Matholwch [math´olooch] (W)
Medb/Medhbh/Maeve [methv] (I)
Naoisi/Naois [´noisi] (I)
Oifa/Aoife [´ifer] (I)
Ove/Aobh [´iver] (I)
Pryderi [pri´deri] (W)
Pwyll [´pooitl] (W)
Rhiannon [hri´annon] (W)
Sidhe [shee] (I)
Sualtam [´suerllterm] (I)
Twrch Trwyth [toorch´trooeeth] (W)
Uisnech/Usnach [´usnerch] (I)
Yspaddaden [usba´thaden] (W)

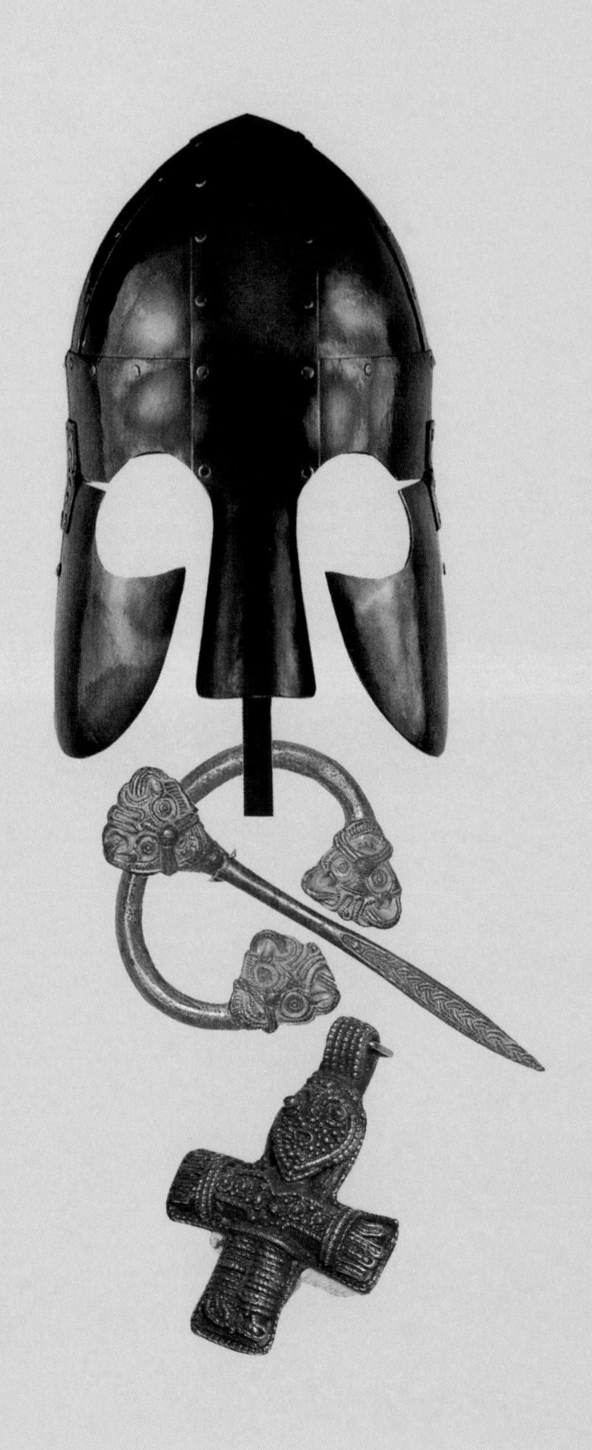

Viking Mythology

INTRODUCTION

Viking mythology is Norse mythology, and Norse mythology is in turn the best recorded version of Teutonic mythology. It seems fitting that the main records we have of the Viking myths come from an outpost, Iceland.

The Vikings were a Teutonic people who established themselves in Scandinavia between the late 8th century and the middle of the 11th century. They were characterized by a mixture of great chivalry and barbaric cruelty. They pillaged the eastern coastline of mainland Britain, killing men and children and raping women – who were then in their turn killed. The methods of slaughtering peasant fisherfolk were disgusting – but then we have to remember that this was a fairly disgusting age. Around this time the Galwegian warriors, on the west of Scotland, were enjoying the sport of impaling babies. The difference between the Vikings and such savages as the Galwegians was that the former had built up for themselves some kind of philosophical construct to account for their actions; their mythology gave them a way whereby they could justify the most bestial behaviour. Their gods dictated that men should be almost inhumanly brave in death, and so it was a token of respect to a defeated foe to give him the maximum latitude to display his bravery. In this respect the Vikings did, though, show a great deal of honesty: should one of their number be submitted to similar tortures it was expected of him that he should bear them without undue complaint, and should bear no grudge into the afterlife against his tormentors. The whole ethical system bears a great resemblance to that of the school playground – except that the bullies (the Vikings) were encouraged rather than discouraged by the teachers (the gods) in their acts of brutality.

TOP RIGHT *Danish Iron Age grave of a woman. The large silver brooch bears a runic inscription; the silver coin near to the necklace is the coin to pay for entry into the afterlife – the Scandinavian equivalent of 'Charon's penny'.*

BOTTOM RIGHT *A fifth-century horned god, gold, from Gallehus, Denmark.*

At first sight it seems that there is very little to recommend the Viking people: their civilization was based on war, looting, aggression, rape and other crimes that make the average modern human being blench. The truth was, though, that these crimes made most of the members of the Viking culture blench, too. They were content that the warriors should travel far afield to terrorize distant lands – after all, if innocents are going to be massacred, your priorities are that you shouldn't be one of them and that the persecution should be happening as far away as possible, so that you have no direct experience of it.

However, even the most warlike of the Vikings did pay lip-service to an ethical system. Most of the tenets of this system bore little resemblance to the modern commandments: in one poem Odin gives advice about how not to be cheated or to do self-evidently stupid things. For our 'Thou shalt not commit adultery', for example, we have Odin's advice that adultery's all right as long as you don't get caught by the jealous spouse and as long as you don't whisper any dangerous secrets into the ear of your lover in a moment of passion.

But however much we may have doubts about this ethical code we have to acknowledge that it was *there*. The contemporaneous Celts seem to have had a much more rigorous scheme of ethical behaviour, but they could be equally cruel. The Christian peoples, whose own mythology affected that of the Vikings, had a far more benign system of ethics yet used it as justification to burn or fry people alive. Greek morality, never too delectable in the first place, was perverted by the Romans into an ethical system so repulsive that words fail us.

And so we return to the Vikings. They lived in lands which were not particularly hospitable to life – the summers were short and the winters long, and always the glaciers in the north seemed threatening. They tried to explain the things they saw around them. The crashing of thunder must be Thor throwing his mighty hammer, Miölnir, at the frost giants. The cracking of the glaciers must be the cries of the frost giants themselves. The rainbow must surely be a bridge between the land of the gods and the land of the mortals.

TOP RIGHT *A Danish bronze plaque of a horse dating from about* AD 400–800.

It is hard to assess the overall impact of the Vikings on our modern culture; at best it was minimal. However, the mythology which the Norse people have left us – even if in only the most fragmented form – has had a powerful affect on our imaginations. JRR Tolkien's *The Lord of the Rings* owes a great deal to it; then there is Alan Garner's *The Weirdstone of Brisingamen*. Jack Yeovil's long story 'The Ignorant Armies' is based very directly on the legend of Valhalla. My own series of novels, *The Legends of Lone Wolf*, written in conjunction with Joe Dever, draw extensively on the Viking mythology – and, in doing so, are typical of the genre called 'fighting fantasy'. The list of modern fiction based on Norse mythology is long.

MIDDLE RIGHT *A Norwegian plate, in gold, from the fifth century.*

In this book I have attempted to tell all of the significant tales. The overall chronology of the mythology is problematical; the details of many of the legends equally so. I have attempted to make the whole system of stories as self-consistent as possible, although I've pointed out instances where the task has proved completely impossible. I am reassured by the fact that every other writer on the subject has found similar difficulties. Viking mythology is not a single continuous story; instead it is a set of stories – many of them very good ones – that relate to each other only with difficulty.

JG

BOTTOM RIGHT *Twelfth-century gilt panel from Jutland, purporting to show the baptism around 960 of the Viking king, Harald Bluetooth, by Bishop Poppo.*

ONE

Guide to Gods, Goddesses and Others

Norse mythology is very complex and its surviving sources are not always as clear as they could be. Some people may therefore disagree with the way in which, in this chapter, I have classified the various important figures from the legends; one person's mortal could be another person's god or giant or dwarf.

LEFT *Eighth-century Swedish bronze matrix used for making helmet decorations. The boar's head on the helmet indicates that these warriors were dedicated to the cult of Frey, whose boar was called Hildisvin.*

GODS AND GODDESSES

LEFT *Eleventh-century gravestone from the cemetery at Ed, Uppland, Sweden. The runic inscription begins: 'Thorsten caused this monument to be made in memory of Sven, his father . . .' Of course, this wasn't the Thorsten who featured among the Norse heroes.*

AEGIR, HLER The god of the sea. *See* Chapter 3.

BALDER A beautiful and gentle god, slain inadvertently by his brother Hoder (*q.v.*) as a result of Loki's trickery. *See* Chapter 3.

BOLWERK One of the pseudonyms used by Odin (*q.v.*) for his adventures among mortals.

BRAGI The god of music, poetry and eloquence, the son of Odin and Gunnlod (*q.v.*), the giantess whom he had seduced. Bragi married Idun (*q.v.*). Odin carved runes on his tongue and gave him the job of composing songs to honour the gods and the dead heroes in Valhalla.

DELLINGER (Delling) The god of dawn and the third husband of Night (*q.v.*). Their son was Dag (*q.v.*).

EIRA (Eyra) One of the attendants of Frigga and also the goddess of medicine. To the Norse the medical deity was naturally female (unlike, for example, the Greek god Asclepius) since by their tradition only women practised medicine.

FJORGYN (Erda, Jörd) The earth goddess and one of Odin's three wives. She and Odin combined to produce Thor (*q.v.*).

FORSETI The god of justice and truth, son of Balder and Nanna (*q.q.v.*). As soon as he became known to the other gods of Asgard he was honoured; they gave him the hall Glitnir which had a silver roof supported on pillars of gold. Forseti had the ability to talk so eloquently that foes would make peace; if they didn't, Forseti would strike them dead.

FREY (Freyr, Fro) One of the Vanir race of gods. The son of Njord (*q.v.*), Frey came to Asgard as a hostage along with his father and his sister Freya (*q.v.*). All three liked it so much there that they stayed. Frey was a fertility god – as, indeed, were the other named Vanir. *See* Chapter 3.

FREYA (Freyja) The goddess of sex and, later, also of war and death – a curious juxtaposition of responsibilities. One of the Vanir, she came to Asgard as a hostage accompanied by her father Njord and her brother Frey (*q.q.v.*). She married the God Od, who deserted her; thereafter she divided her time between mourning his absence and being promiscuous. In the German version of the Teutonic myth she is identified with Frigga (*q.v.*). *See* Chapter 3.

FRIDLEEF One of the pseudonyms used by Frey (*q.v.*) for his adventures among mortals.

FRIGGA (Bertha, Frigg, Holda, Nerthus, Wode) The most important goddess of Asgard; one of the three wives of Odin and the mother of Balder and Hoder (*q.q.v.*). She was the principal goddess of fertility. Ve (*q.v.*) and Vili are reputed to have slept with her, and the same has been said of Ull (*q.v.*). There has been a certain amount of confusion between her and Freya (*q.v.*), to the extent that in the German version of the Teutonic myth the two of them were regarded as the same deity. *See* Chapter 3.

RIGHT *Eighteenth-century illustration of Hermod riding down to Hel on Sleipnir in his attempt to rescue Balder.*

FULLA A goddess who acted as Frigga's attendant and messenger; she was a fertility goddess.

GANGRAD One of the pseudonyms used by Odin (*q.v.*) for his adventures among mortals.

GEFJON (Gefion) A goddess who served as one of Frigga's attendants. She slept with Gylfi (*q.v.*), king of Sweden, and was consequently allowed by him to claim as much of his nation as she could plough within a 24-hour period. She fetched four huge oxen, who were the four sons she had borne to a giant, and within the requisite 24 hours wrenched free a colossal area of Sweden, which her sons towed out to sea. The tract of land is now the island known as Zealand; the hole in Sweden was soon filled up with water, becoming Lake Malaren. We are told by most of the sources that this is an explanation of why Zealand is exactly the same shape as Malaren; unfortunately, a swift check with a map of Scandinavia shows that the two share no resemblance whatsoever, and are of vastly different sizes.

GERSEMI One of Freya's and Od's two daughters.

GNA (Liod) A servant of Frigga (*q.v.*) who acted as the great goddess's messenger. Perhaps her most significant mission was to bring the apple of fertility to the mortal Rerir (*q.v.*).

GRIMNIR One of the pseudonyms used by Odin (*q.v.*) for his adventures among mortals.

HEIMDALL A somewhat puzzling god born from nine giantess mothers simultaneously (*see* Wave Maidens). As Riger he wandered around Midgard impregnating women to found the serf, peasant and warrior races. He was the guardian of the rainbow bridge Bifrost. *See* Chapter 3.

HEL A goddess or a monster, a daughter of Loki and Angrboda (*q.q.v.*), who ruled over Niflheim. Opinions differed over whether she was alive or dead. After the death of the god Balder she was asked by Hermod if she would simply allow the much-loved god to leave her premises; her response was that she didn't think that Balder was nearly as much-loved as all that. She was similarly unsympathetic when Bragi turned up hoping to recover Idun. Ull, in his role as god of winter, was supposed to spend a couple of months each year as Hel's lover. Some versions of the mythology say that one of the Norns, Skuld, was the same person as Hel. She and her ghostly army will support the other gods at Ragnarok, after which her domain will be consumed by flames.

HERMOD (Irmin) The son of Odin and Frigga (*q.q.v.*). He welcomed the heroes to Valhalla and otherwise acted as the equivalent of the Greek god Hermes. His most spectacular errand was to Hel (*q.v.*) in an effort to recover the god Balder (*q.v.*); *see* Chapter 3.

HLER According to a version of the Creation myth, one of the first gods. *See* Kari.

HLIN A goddess who attended Frigga (*q.v.*). She was the goddess of consolation and very beautiful; she kissed away mourners' tears, relieved grief and heard the prayers of mortals, passing them on to Frigga with recommendations that she answer them.

ABOVE *A pair of dragons depicted on a carved stone from Öland, Sweden.*

HNOSS One of Freya's and Od's two daughters.

HODER (Hod, Hodur) The twin brother of Balder. Because of Loki's trickery, Hoder unwittingly slew Balder and was therefore condemned to death; the justice involved is dubious, to say the very least. In due course Hoder was killed by Vali (*q.v.*), specially bred for the task.

HOENIR (Honir) There are two versions of the story about the earliest gods. In one Odin and his brothers Ve (*q.v.*) and Vili gave to humanity the gifts the species has. The alternative is that Odin's first brothers were Hoenir and Loki (*q.v.*). According to this version Hoenir gave to humanity the gifts of motion and the senses.

IDUN The goddess of spring and of immortal youth. She was the daughter of the dwarf Ivald and the wife of the god Bragi (*q.q.v.*). *See* Chapter 3.

KARI According to some versions of the Creation myth (*see* Chapter 2) the sons of the giant Ymir (*q.v.*) were Hler (the sea), Kari (the air) and Loki or Lodur (fire). These three gods gave birth to the giants or monsters Beli, Fenris, Grendel, Gymir, Hel, Mimir, Thiassi and Thrym (*q.q.v.*).

KVASIR A somewhat enigmatic figure, in that it is uncertain whether he was a god or merely a supernatural being. If a god, he was probably one of the Vanir, but with an admixture of Aesir. He was brought into existence at the end of the war between the Aesir and the Vanir; as a token of the truce all the gods spat into a ceremonial vase, and from their spittle they generated Kvasir. He became renowned for wisdom and virtue, and was consequently murdered in his sleep by two dwarfs called Fialar and Galar, who wished to take his wisdom for the benefit of the dwarf race. They drained his blood into three containers (a kettle or cauldron called Odhroerir and two bowls called Boden and Son), mixed it with honey and fermented it to produce a brew that had the startling effect, when drunk, of turning the drinker into a poet. We've all come across drinks like this. The murderous pair later disposed of the giant Gilling (*q.v.*) and his wife, and as a consequence were forced by the giant Suttung (*q.v.*) to hand over the mead they had brewed. Suttung's daughter Gunnlod (*q.v.*) was put in charge of guarding the mead, but Odin seduced her and, in her passion, she allowed him to drain all three vessels. As soon as he had done so, Odin turned himself into an eagle and flew back to Asgard. Suttung, realizing at last what had been going on, likewise turned himself into an eagle and flew off in pursuit. Odin just made it to Asgard, where the other gods had laid out all kinds of jars and pots to take the blood of Kvasir, which Odin dutifully vomited up. Some of the mead, however, had been leaked by Odin during his flight to Asgard, which is one of the reasons why the mortals of Midgard could on occasion spout fine poetry. The other reason was that, when in a generous mood, Odin would give a dose of the mead to a mortal.

LODUR According to one version of the Creation myth, Odin's brothers were Hoenir (*q.v.*) and Lodur; these three gave humanity its life. Lodur's contributions were blood and a healthy complexion. Lodur can be equated with Loki (*q.v.*).

LOFN An attendant of Frigga. A beautiful maiden, Lofn had the responsibility for easing the path of true love.

LOKI The 'wizard of lies' and in many ways the most interesting of all the gods of Asgard. Loki was related to Odin, but the exact nature of the relationship is muddled. He came to Asgard either as of right or because Odin entered into a blood-brotherhood with him. *See* Chapter 3; *see also* Thokk (giantess).

MAGNI A son of Thor and the giantess Iarnsaxa (*q.q.v.*). He rescued his father after the latter's duel with the giant Hrungnir (*q.v.*). After

LEFT *Tenth-century cross shaft from Sockburn, County Durham, Britain, showing a mounted figure with a bird on his shoulder. This almost certainly represents Odin, only one of his ravens being visible. The figure below may be a valkyrie.*

Ragnarok Magni and his brother Modi will possess Thor's hammer Miölnir.

MIMIR The wisest god of all the Aesir; he – or, at least, his head – guarded a spring (Mimir's Well) at the base of Yggdrasil (*q.v.*). There is some confusion concerning his decapitation, but it seems that he and Hoenir were sent by the Aesir to the Vanir as hostages to protect the truce agreed between the two families of gods. The Vanir did not like Hoenir so they killed Mimir – an explanation so illogical that one cannot believe it even of the gods. It is possible that he was the creator of the sword Miming (*q.v.*). Odin made a habit of consulting Mimir's head on occasions when he was stuck for advice; in some versions it is reported that Odin's loss of one eye came about because he had to give it to Mimir's head as down payment for this counselling service.

RIGHT *Detail from a copy of the Cannin Casket (dated about* AD *1000) now in the National Museum, Copenhagen, Denmark.*

MODI A son of Thor and the giantess Iarnsaxa (*q.q.v.*). After Ragnarok he and his brother Modi will possess Thor's hammer Miölnir.

NANNA The wife of Balder (*q.v.*).

NERTHUS (Hlodin) The wife of Njord (*q.v.*); a goddess often equated with Frigga (*q.v.*). *See* Chapter 3.

NJORD The father of Frey and Freya; one of the Vanir; a god of the sea who slowly attained ascendance over the Aesir sea-god Aegir (*q.v.*). He was the husband of both the giantess Skadi and the goddess Nerthus (*q.q.v.*).

NORNS The three goddesses concerned with destiny; called Skuld ('Being'), Urd ('Fate') and Verdandi ('Necessity'), they were obviously closely related in concept to the Fates of Greek mythology. They sprinkled Yggdrasil (*q.v.*) with holy water every day so that it would stay in tiptop condition. They were also keen weavers, producing webs of great vastness but haphazard design, as if they didn't know what the outcome of their weaving was likely to be. Two of the sisters, Urd (who was incredibly old) and Verdandi (who was young and lovely in a sort of rock-jawed way), were generally pretty friendly towards mortals, but Skuld was swift to take offence over the most trivial slight or perceived slight – *see*, for example, the story of Nornagesta (*q.v.*). Skuld also had a habit of ripping up the webs of the three sisters when they were nearly finished.

NOTT The goddess of night; daughter of the giant Norvi (*q.v.*). She had three lovers/husbands: Naglfari (*q.v.*), to whom she bore Aud (*q.v.*); Annar (*q.v.*), who gave her the daughter Erda (*q.v.*); and Dellinger (*q.v.*), whose son by her was called Dag (*q.v.*).

OD (Odur) The first husband of Freya (*q.v.*). She loved him madly but he was a god with a roving heart; he departed in search of mortal bimbos. Freya spent the rest of eternity in a confusing mix of mourning and copulation.

ODIN (Wodan, Woden, Wotan) The son of Börr and Bestla (*q.q.v.*) and the father of Thor, Balder, Hoder, Tyr, Bragi, Heimdall, Ull, Vidar, Hermod and Vali (*q.q.v.*). His wives were Fjorgyn, Frigga and Rind (*q.q.v.*). He was the chief god in the Norse pantheon. One of his frequent habits was to roam around Midgard in human guise seducing and impregnating women; many mortals were therefore able to trace their ancestry back to Odin rather than to travelling salesmen. *See* Chapter 3.

RAN The wife of Aegir (*q.v.*), and like him associated with the sea. She had a net which she used to drag down drowning people. *See* Chapter 3.

RIGER One of the pseudonyms used by Heimdall (*q.v.*) for his adventures among mortals.

RIND (Rinda) A goddess mentioned only as the third wife of Odin, and who gave birth to his son Vali (*q.v.*). She was by all accounts frigid, being the goddess of the frozen soil. There is some confusion between her and the mortal Rind (*q.v.*), daughter of King Billing; it is possible that the two were originally the same character.

SAGA A mistress of Odin whom the god visited for a daily drink at her hall, Sokvabek (*q.v.*).

SATAERE The Teutonic god of agriculture, possibly one of the many personae of Loki (*q.v.*).

BELOW *Nineteenth-century book illustration of the chained Loki tended by his faithful wife Sigyn.*

SIF The goddess who married Thor and bore his stepson (by Odin) Ull (*q.q.v.*). She was exceptionally proud of her golden hair, so Loki (*q.v.*) cut it all off while she slept. *See* Chapter 3.

SIGYN The third wife of Loki (*q.v.*) and the one who was unremittingly faithful to him; she bore his mortal sons Narve and Vali (*q.q.v.*). Even after Loki had been thrown out of Asgard because of his crimes Sigyn remained loyal to him. *See* Chapter 3.

SKULD One of the Norns (*q.v.*).

SNOTRA One of Frigga's attendants and also the omniscient goddess of virtue.

SUMMER One of the early gods. He was loved by all except Winter (*q.v.*).

SVASUD A beautiful and gentle god whose son was Summer (*q.v.*).

SYN A goddess who guarded the door of Frigga's palace against unwelcome visitors. Once she had decided to refuse someone entry there was no possibility of changing her mind, and appeals to higher authority were fruitless. She was therefore responsible for all trials and tribunals among mortals.

THOR The son of Odin and Fjorgyn (*q.q.v.*). Thor was associated with thunder, the sky, fertility and the law. Armed with his hammer and his girdle of strength, he had a simple way of righting wrongs: if it moves, kill it. The other gods – notably Loki (*q.v.*) – took advantage of Thor's simplicity on numerous occasions. *See* Chapter 3.

TYR The god of war; son of Frigga by either Odin or the giant Hymir (*q.q.v.*). He was generally regarded as the bravest of all the gods. When the Aesir were preparing to bind Fenris using the chain called Gleipnir (*q.q.v.*), the giant wolf refused to submit unless one of the gods put his arm in the wolf's mouth as a guarantee. Tyr volunteered and thereby lost his right hand.

ABOVE *Nineteenth-century book illustration showing Tyr, the bravest of all the gods.*

RIGHT *Nineteenth-century book illustration showing Ull, the god of winter, hunting, archery, death and skiing.*

ULL (Holler, Oller, Uller, Vulder) The god of winter, hunting, archery, death and skiing; a son of Sif, stepson of Thor and maybe husband of the giantess Skadi (*q.q.v.*). Ull, possibly a lover of Frigga, was regarded as the next most important god after Odin but never attained great popularity because of the frigid season with which he was associated. Some versions of Norse mythology tell how each year, in the summer, Ull is forced to spend some months in Hel so that Odin, in his guise as the god of summer, can govern the weather. The Aurora Borealis was believed to be Ull putting on a visual display.

URD (Urdr, Wurd) One of the Norns (*q.v.*).

VAK One of the pseudonyms used by Odin (*q.v.*) for his adventures among mortals.

VALI The son of Odin and Rind (*q.v.*). This god was conceived deliberately to avenge the death of Balder. He is not to be confused with the Vali who was the son of Loki and Sigyn (*q.q.v.*). *See* Chapter 3.

VALTAM One of the pseudonyms used by Odin (*q.v.*) for his adventures among mortals.

VARA One of Frigga's attendants. Vara was responsible for the keeping of oaths, the punishment of perjurers and rewarding people who kept their word despite any adversity.

VASUD The father of Vindsval and grandfather of Winter (*q.q.v.*). By all accounts Vasud was a very unfriendly god.

VE One of the three sons of Borr and grandsons of the giant Ymir, the other two being Odin and Vili. The three killed their grandfather and out of his body created Midgard, the world of mortals. According to some legends, Odin once spent so long away from Asgard, journeying in the mortal world, that Ve and Vili took over both the throne and Frigga – apparently without any objections on her part.

VECHA One of the pseudonyms used by Odin (*q.v.*) for his adventures among mortals.

VERDANDI One of the Norns (*q.v.*).

VIDAR The son born to Odin and the giantess Grid (*q.q.v.*). He will slay Fenris (*q.v.*), survive Ragnarok and avenge the death of Odin.

VILI *see* Ve.

VJOFN One of Frigga's attendants. Vjofn's responsibilities to the mortal world focused on conciliation: she strove to keep the peace, bring quarrelling spouses to concord and bend the hardest of hearts to love. Her role seems somewhat paradoxical, given the Vikings' penchant for glorifying warfare.

VÖR One of Frigga's attendants. Her name meant 'faith', and she had full knowledge of the future.

WINTER The vile enemy of the god Summer (*q.v.*); son of Vindsval and grandson of Vasud (*q.q.v.*).

WYRD The mother of the Norns (*q.v.*).

GIANTS AND GIANTESSES

ANGRBODA The mother of Loki's hideous children Hel, Jormungand and Fenris (*q.q.v.*).

BAUGI The brother of Suttung (*q.v.*). This giant employed Odin as a labourer when the god was on his way to Suttung's hall intent on stealing the mead of poetry.

BELI One of the descendants of Kari (*q.v.*). The same name was given to the brother of Gerda (*q.v.*) who lost his life in an attack on Frey.

BERGELMIR (Farbauti) The only giant who survived the deluge caused by the blood of the murdered giant Ymir (*q.v.*). According to some versions of Norse mythology, Bergelmir was the father of Loki (*q.v.*), the mother being Laufeia (*q.v.*).

BESTLA The wife of Börr (*q.v.*) and mother of Odin, Ve and Vili (*q.q.v.*).

BOLTHORN The father of Bestla (*q.v.*).

FENIA A giantess who, along with Menia (*q.v.*), was unlucky enough to be enslaved by Frodi, king of Denmark (*q.v.*).

GEIRROD A would-be vanquisher of Thor. Geirrod captured Loki (who was in the guise of a falcon) and forced him to promise to deliver Thor to his hall. *See* Chapter 3.

GERDA A frost giantess of spectacular beauty often associated with the Aurora Borealis; she became the wife of the god Frey (*q.v.*).

GIALP The name of one of the Wave Maidens (*q.v.*) and also of a daughter of Geirrod (*q.v.*).

GILLING A victim of the murderous dwarfs Fialar (*q.v.*) and Galar. Gilling was drowned, but there are different accounts as to how the pair effected this. One version has it that they came across him sleeping on a riverside and simply rolled him into the water; another says that they sent him fishing in a leaky vessel; a third says that they took him fishing, capsized the boat in the knowledge that he couldn't swim, and rowed home with a merry song on their lips. Gilling's wife was understandably a bit upset by all this, so the dwarfs dropped a millstone on her head, to fatal effect. Gilling's son was Suttung (*q.v.*).

ABOVE *Nineteenth-century book illustration showing the giantess Gunnlod in the process of being seduced by Odin, whose aim was to gain from her the mead of poetry.*

GREIP The name of both a daughter of Geirrod (*q.v.*) and one of the Wave Maidens (*q.v.*); *see also* Gialp.

GRENDEL According to one version of the myths, a sea giant descended from Ymir (*q.v.*). Grendel hit the heights in Old English myth through being slain by the hero Beowulf.

GRID A giantess who gave a night's lodging to Thor and Loki as they travelled towards the hall of the giant Geirrod (*q.v.*). After Loki had fallen asleep, Grid told a drunken Thor that Geirrod was planning to kill him and that he was foolish to make the journey without his hammer and his girdle of strength. She gave him gloves made of iron, a replacement girdle of strength, and an unbreakable staff. On another occasion she seems to have given her son, the god Vidar (*q.v.*; the father was Odin), a massive shoe made out of either leather or iron.

GUNNLOD The daughter of Suttung (*q.v.*), seduced by Odin in order to gain the mead of poetry. The result of their coupling was Bragi (*q.v.*).

GYMIR The father of Gerda (*q.v.*); he has also been equated with the son of Aegir (*q.v.*) and with Aegir himself.

HRAESVELGR A giant whose name means 'corpse-eater'. He sat in the far north in the guise of an eagle; the cold winds from there were the result of him flapping his wings.

HRUNGNIR The strongest of all the giants. He reckoned that his horse Gullfaxi could outrace Odin's steed Sleipnir, and proposed a race. *See* Chapter 3.

HRYM The steersman who will be at the helm of the frost giants' ship when they war with the Aesir during Ragnarok.

BELOW *The giant Hymir (on the right) out on a fishing expedition with the god Thor, who is attempting to catch Jormungand, the World Serpent. This is a fragment from the tenth-century cross found at Gosforth, Cumbria, Britain. With a little imagination we can work out that the bait Thor is using is the head of an ox.*

HYMIR An elderly giant who was unfortunate enough to own an extremely large cauldron. The god Aegir (*q.v.*) was honest enough to admit to the other Aesir that his own cauldron was not really big enough to brew sufficient quantities of ale for them to get drunk; Thor announced at once that he and Tyr would go and find a cauldron of suitable dimensions. They ended up at the hall of Hymir; the giant was less than delighted by his guests but treated them hospitably, his mask of politeness staying in place even when Thor scoffed two out of the three oxen Hymir had slain in their honour.

The following day Thor behaved very badly even by his own standards. He and Hymir decided to go fishing together; when the giant suggested that Thor should go and find some bait, the god slew Hymir's biggest bull, Himinbrioter, in order to put its head on his hook. Thor then rowed their boat far out to sea and caught the World Serpent, Jormungand (*q.v.*); he was just about to despatch the beast when Hymir, terrified, cut the line. Thor hit the giant with his hammer, knocking him overboard, but Hymir swam to shore and met Thor there amicably. The two of them then breakfasted on a couple of whales Hymir had caught; after the repast the giant challenged the god to smash his beaker. Thor threw the vessel at everything in sight but without success; finally he shattered it by throwing it at Hymir's forehead, the only available substance stronger than the beaker itself.

Hymir then told Thor and Tyr that they could have the cauldron; Tyr was unable to lift it, and even Thor could do so only with difficulty. As the gods were leaving Hymir summoned his fellow frost giants and suggested that a bit of deicide might be fun. They attacked Thor and Tyr, but Thor killed them all with his hammer. (Since Hymir had been courteous and hospitable up to this point we must suspect that the attack on the gods was a later invention, devised solely

ABOVE *A superb animal head, probably from the bow of a Viking longship, discovered during recent dredging of the River Scheldt, Belgium.*

to give an excuse for the slaughter.) The two gods then triumphantly returned with the cauldron to the hall of Aegir.

HYNDLA A giant enchantress. Freya's lover Ottar (*q.v.*) was in dispute with another hero, Angantyr (*q.v.*), over a piece of property. The Thing (*q.v.*) had decreed that whichever of the two men could show the more distinguished lineage would win the lawsuit. Freya turned Ottar into the likeness of a boar which she called Hildisvini and rode to Hyndla's dwelling. She persuaded the giantess to trace Ottar's ancestry back for many generations and to give him a draught of a magical brew so that he would remember all the details. Ottar was able to recite his lineage in its entirety. Angantyr was not so assisted and therefore lost the case.

HYRROKIN A giantess who launched Balder's great funeral boat, *Ringhorn*. She travelled about on a wolf, using serpents for reins.

IARNSAXA (Jarnsaxa) The name of a mistress of Thor and also of one of the Wave Maidens (*q.v.*). Magni and Modi (*q.q.v.*) were Thor's sons by the former.

MENIA A giantess who, along with Fenia (*q.v.*), was unlucky enough to be enslaved by Frodi, king of Denmark (*q.v.*).

MUNDILFARI The father of Mani and Sol (*q.q.v.*).

NORVI (Narvi) The mother of Night (*q.v.*).

SENJEMAND A giant who fell in love with a mortal maiden called Juternajesta (*q.v.*); she rejected him out of hand, on the grounds that he was far too old and repulsive. Senjemand was made a little unhappy by this, and decided to kill her. From a distance of 80 miles he loosed off an arrow at her. The arrow would have killed her had it not been for the intervention of one of Juternajesta's other admirers, the giant Torge, who threw his vast hat in the air to intercept the missile. Senjemand saddled his horse to flee, fearing that Torge would exact terrible revenge for the attempted murder, but just then the Sun rose and transformed Senjemand, the arrow and the hat into stone.

SKADI A giantess, daughter of Thiassi. For a time she was married to the god Njord. *See* Chapter 3.

SKRYMIR A disguise adopted by Utgard-Loki (*q.v.*).

SKRYMSLI A giant who defeated a peasant at chess and thereby won the ownership of the peasant's son. The peasant called upon Odin, Hoenir and Loki for assistance, the latter saving the boy's life. *See* Chapter 3.

SURT (Surtr) A flame giant who guarded the realm called Muspell (*q.v.*); at Ragnarok he will slay Frey and then set all the world alight.

SUTTUNG The son of Gilling (*q.v.*). Suttung discovered that the evil dwarfs Fialar (*q.v.*) and Galar had murdered both of his parents, and threatened to drown them. To save their lives the dwarfs gave him the mead of poetry, which they had brewed out of honey and the blood of the god Kvasir (*q.v.*). Suttung was very proud of this coup, and told the world about it. Odin, as a mortal called Bolwerk, callously seduced Suttung's daughter Gunnlod (*q.v.*) so that she allowed him to drink the mead.

THIASSI (Thiazi) A giant who kidnapped the goddess Idun (*q.v.*) and her apples. *See* Chapter 3.

THOKK (Thok) A giantess who refused to obey the Aesir's command that all living things should weep for the death of Balder (*q.v.*) so that he might be returned from Hel. The general assumption is that Thokk was actually Loki (*q.v.*) in disguise.

THRUD The daughter of Thor and Sif (*q.q.v.*). The dwarf Alvis (*q.v.*) sought her hand in marriage, and she was not unwilling to accept his proposal; the rest of the Aesir gave their approval to the marriage. However, Thor was not so keen. He expressed contempt for the dwarf's diminutive stature and demanded that Alvis prove that, if not a physical giant, he was at least an intellectual one. Thor then hurled tricky questions at the unfortunate dwarf, hour after hour, until the new day broke. Dwarfs were turned to stone by daylight, and this is exactly what happened to the unfortunate Alvis. So much for Thrud's notions of romance.

THRUDGELMIR A six-headed giant born in the dawn of time from the feet of Ymir (*q.v.*); Thrudgelmir in turn produced Bergelmir (*q.v.*).

THRYM Son of Kari (*q.v.*); a giant who stole Thor's hammer and told Loki that it would be returned only on the condition that Freya marry him – for once the goddess declined to offer herself. *See* Chapter 3.

TORGE *see* Senjemand.

UTGARD-LOKI The ruler of Utgard; Thor, Loki, Thialfi and Roskva (*q.q.v.*) went to visit him. *See* Chapter 3.

VAFTHRUDNIR A clever giant who was challenged by Odin (in mortal guise as Gangrad) to a battle of wits; the loser would forfeit his head. Odin answered all the giant's questions correctly, and the giant answered all of Odin's likewise except for the last of them, which was to repeat the words Odin had whispered into the ear of his dead son Balder. The giant immediately realized that no one could answer this question except Odin himself and that the god had tricked him. According to the legend Vafthrudnir announced that the contest had been honourable and willingly surrendered his head.

WADE The father of Völund (*q.v.*), according to Anglo-Saxon and Danish myth.

WAVE MAIDENS There is some confusion about the legend of the nine Wave Maidens – Atla, Augeia, Aurgiafa, Egia, Gialp, Greip, Iarnsaxa, Sindur and Ulfrun – but they seem to have been giantesses and the daughters of the sea-god Aegir. According to one version, Odin was strolling along the shore during one of his frequent sojourns in Midgard when he saw these huge and beautiful women playing in the shallows. The deed followed the impulse, and as a result all nine of them combined to give birth in due course to the god Heimdall (*q.v.*). There is a very similar legend in Irish history. Ruad Rigdonson was sailing from Ireland to Norway with a little fleet of three ships when suddenly all progress ceased. He dived down to see what was happening and found that three giant women were clinging to the rear of each ship. They refused to let him go until he had slept with each of them for a night in their home beneath the sea. He then continued to Norway, promising to stop off for another bout on his way home. However, after seven years in Norway he decided to break his promise and went straight back to Ireland. The furious giantesses pursued him but his ships were too swift, and so in revenge they cut off his child's head and hurled it after him.

It seems certain that these are two different versions of the same tale, with the major difference that in the Irish telling the child is not a god and fails to survive. In addition, the matter of Heimdall's father is uncertain, and various hybrid forms of the legend are to be found.

YMIR (Fornjotnr, Orgelmir) The primaeval giant; *see* Chapter 2.

ABOVE *Detail of the woodcarving found on the remains of the longship used for the floating funeral pyre at Oseberg.*

DWARFS

ALFRIGG One of the four dwarfs who manufactured the Brisingamen (*q.v.*) and enjoyed a night of sex with Freya.

Two renditions of the dragon Fafnir being slain by Sigurd: the one BELOW is a detail from a twelfth- or thirteenth-century wooden portal at Hylestad Church, Setesdal, Norway; the one OPPOSITE LEFT is a detail from a tenth-century Viking carving found at Jurby, Isle of Man, Britain.

ALVIS Dwarf who was unlucky enough to fall in love with Thor's daughter, the giantess Thrud (*q.v.*).

ANDVARI A king of the dwarfs whom Loki robbed of all his gold, including a cursed golden ring that brought devastation to the family of Hreidmar (*q.v.*).

AUSTRI The dwarf who supposedly supported the celestial vault at the east.

BERLING One of the four dwarfs who manufactured the Brisingamen (*q.v.*) and enjoyed a night of sex with Freya.

BROCK (Brokk) A dwarf who won a very important bet with Loki. *See* Chapter 3.

DAIN A dwarf briefly mentioned as a master smith.

DVALIN One of the four dwarfs who manufactured the Brisingamen (*q.v.*) and enjoyed a night of sex with Freya. He seems also to have been the dwarf whom Loki commissioned to spin the goddess Sif a new head of hair as well as to make the spear, Gungnir, and the collapsible ship, Skidbladnir (*q.q.v.*).

FAFNIR The son of Hreidmar and the brother of Otter and Regin (*q.q.v.*). Loki killed Otter, and so the three dwarfs determined to kill Odin, Hoenir and Loki. However, Odin told the dwarfs that Loki hadn't realized that Otter was anything other than an animal, and pleaded for their lives. Hreidmar said that the three gods could live if they filled the skin of the dead Otter with gold; Loki was sent off to fetch sufficient quantities of the metal, leaving Odin and Hoenir as hostages.

Loki stole all of the gold belonging to the dwarf Andvari and brought it back to Hreidmar's home; he omitted to mention to the dwarfs that on one piece of it, a ring, there was a curse that would afflict whoever came to be its owner. The gold was sufficient to fill Otter's pelt and even to cover it. Hreidmar said that he was satisfied and so Loki told him about the curse; Hreidmar was not impressed. This

ABOVE *Detail from an eighth-century stela at Lillbjärs, Sweden, showing an early version of the Viking longship.*

was a mistake on his part, because the curse soon came into operation; Fafnir killed Hreidmar and drove Regin into exile; during this period of exile Regin taught humanity a great deal of technology while Fafnir was transformed into an avaricious dragon. Fafnir was in due coure killed by the hero Sigurd (*q.v.*).

FIALAR (Fjalar) One of the two dwarfs who murdered Kvasir, Gilling (*q.q.v.*) and Gilling's wife.

GALAR One of the two dwarfs who murdered Kvasir, Gilling (*q.q.v.*) and Gilling's wife.

GRERR One of the four dwarfs who manufactured the Brisingamen (*q.v.*) and enjoyed a night of sex with Freya.

HREIDMAR The father of Fafnir (*q.v.*).

IVALD A first-rate blacksmith; the father of Dvalin and of the goddess Idun.

LIT A dwarf murdered by Thor during the cremation of Balder and Nanna.

NABBI A dwarf briefly mentioned as a master smith.

NORDRI The dwarf who supposedly supported the celestial vault at the north.

OTTER A dwarf who took the form of an otter and was slain by Loki; a brother of Fafnir (*q.v.*).

REGIN A brother of Fafnir (*q.v.*). There is some confusion between him and a human called Regin (*q.v.*), who was Sigurd's tutor.

SINDRI (Eitri) The brother of Brock (*q.v.*).

SUDRI The dwarf who supposedly supported the celestial vault at the south.

WESTRI The dwarf who supposedly supported the celestial vault at the west.

VALKYRIES

ALVIT One of the three sisters raped by Egil, Slagfinn and Völund (*q.q.v.*). The other two sisters were Olrun and Svanhvit.

BRUNHILD (Brynhild, Brynhildr) A valkyrie who loved Sigurd (*q.v.*). When he decided to separate from her and be with Gudrun instead, she had him murdered by Guttorm (*q.v.*). Gunnar (*q.v.*), her husband, buried her beside Sigurd. *See* Chapter 4.

GUDRUN A valkyrie who saw Helgi's prowess in battle and fell in love with him; soon after they were wed. It wasn't long before Helgi (*q.v.*) was murdered by Dag (*q.v.*), and so Gudrun looked around for another husband, eventually settling on the hero Sigurd (*q.v.*). Later she was pressured into marrying Atli (*q.v.*), which she didn't enjoy at all. *See* Chapter 4.

OLRUN *See* Alvit.

SVANHVIT *See* Alvit.

SWANHILD The daughter of Gudrun (*q.v.*). *See* Chapter 4.

OTHER PROPER NAMES

AFI A mortal whose wife, Amma (*q.v.*), gave birth to Karl (*q.v.*), the progenitor of the race of peasants.

AGNAR The elder son of Hrauding (*q.v.*). He and his brother Geirrod (*q.v.*), while children, caught the fancy of Odin and Frigga who, disguised as mortals, spent some time with them on an island. When the boys returned home, Geirrod leapt suddenly from their boat and pushed it and Agnar out to sea. Geirrod succeeded to his father's throne. Years later Odin determined to visit King Geirrod as a mortal (taking the name Grímnir) to prove to Frigga that the man was good at heart. Frigga, however, warned Geirrod to look out for

RIGHT *Nineteenth-century book illustration showing Odin being tormented between two fires at the palace of King Geirrod.*

the visiting stranger, telling him that he was an evil sorcerer. Geirrod did not treat Grimnir well: he had him tied up and placed between two fires whose flames lapped at him, roasting him. Agnar, however, had earlier sneaked into his brother's court, working there as a humble servant; he took pity on Grimnir and gave him some ale. Grimnir, revived, sang a prophecy of Geirrod's imminent death by his own sword; then his bonds vanished, the fires went out, and Odin stood before Geirrod in his full glory. Geirrod had drawn his sword to attack the stranger who had uttered such a dire prophecy; when Odin revealed himself the king was so startled that he tripped and fell on the weapon, killing himself. Odin rewarded Agnar with the throne and a promise that prosperity would be his.

Geirrod's son was likewise called Agnar, and this has led to some confusion of the legend. An alternative version is that Agnar the brother survived a harum-scarum ocean voyage after Geirrod had pushed him out to sea, and eked out a bestial existence in a faraway land. It was therefore Agnar the son who took pity on Grimnir and acceded to the throne.

AI A mortal whose wife, Edda (*q.v.*), gave birth to Thrall (*q.v.*) and hence started the race of serfs.

ALFHEIM That part of Asgard (*q.v.*) where the light elves dwelled.

ALSVIDER One of the horses that pulled the chariot conveying the Moon.

ALSVIN One of the horses that pulled the chariot containing the Sun.

AMMA The wife of Afi and the mother of Karl (*q.q.v.*). Nine months after the god Heimdall had stayed a few nights with Afi and Amma she gave birth to a son called Karl (*q.v.*). She thereby became the ancestress of the race of peasants.

ANDHRIMNIR The cook in Valhalla; he spent all his time cooking the boar Saehrimnir to supply dead warriors with food.

ABOVE *Detail from a tenth-century Danish neck-yoke for a pair of horses.*

ANDVARANAUT The ring of the dwarf Andvari (*q.v.*).

ANGANTYR A hero who lost a case against Ottar (*q.v.*).

ANGURVADEL The magic sword of Viking (*q.v.*).

ANNAR The second husband of Night. He sired her daughter, Earth.

ARVAKR One of the horses that pulled the Sun's chariot across the sky.

ASEGEIR The twelve wise men who decided to unify the Vikings. They set off in a small ship and found themselves blown hither and thither. They made an appeal to the god Forseti (*q.v.*), after which they noticed that there was a thirteenth passenger on board; this person took the helm and steered them towards an island, where he created a spring. A lecture was delivered and then Forseti disappeared. From this time on, the island (Heligoland) was immune from attacks by the Vikings.

ASGARD The home of the Aesir.

ASKR The first man.

ASLAUG The daughter of Sigurd and Brunhild (*q.q.v.*). At the age of three the child was orphaned: Brunhild's father concealed her within a harp. A peasant couple broke open the harp and found the child within; they assumed that she was a mute because she refused to speak. However, she spoke willingly to a passing Viking, Ragnar Lodbrog, and became his wife.

ATLÉ A warrior who challenged Frithiof (*q.v.*).

ATLI A brother of Brunhild (*q.v.*) and king of the Huns; thanks to a magic potion he ended up as the husband of Gudrun (*q.v.*). Gudrun did not like her husband, who was parsimonious to the *n*th degree; she nevertheless managed to bear two sons by him, Erp and Eitel, both of whom she killed. Atli was responsible for the deaths of both Gunnar and Högni (*q.q.v.*), two of Gudrun's brothers, so it's hardly surprising that the marriage was less than totally happy.

AUD The offspring of Night and her first husband Naglfari (*q.q.v.*).

AUDHUMLA (Audumla) A sacred cow. From the four teats of her udder came four streams of milk that nourished the primaeval giant Ymir (*q.v.*). Ymir was satiated by the milk but then the cow looked around for different sustenance, settling on an iceberg whose salty outer coating she licked away with her rough tongue. The cow kept on licking the iceberg until it melted to leave Buri (*q.v.*), the forefather of the gods.

BALMUNG The sword of Sigmund (*q.v.*), fashioned by Völund (*q.v.*).

BELDEGG A son of Odin who became king of West Saxony.

BELÉ Usurped heir to the throne of the kingdom of Sogn.

BELI The brother of Gerda (*q.v.*). He made the foolish mistake of attacking Frey; the god, lacking his sword, slew him with a nearby antler.

BEYGGVIR (Byggvir) One of Frey's servants. He was Beyla's husband.

BEYLA One of Frey's servants. She was Beyggvir's wife.

BIFROST (Asa-Bridge, Asabru) The bridge linking Midgard to Asgard, guarded by the god Heimdall. Built of fire, air and water, it took the form of the rainbow.

ABOVE *Patterns of stones at Lindholm Løje, Denmark, trace out the shapes of longships, commemorating Viking burials there.*

BIL The waning Moon; a sister of Hiuki and companion of Mani (*q.q.v.*). According to some versions, Mani took the two children up from Earth because of their father's cruelty – he'd demanded that they act as water-bearers all night long. There may be some link with Jack and Jill.

BILLING The king of the Ruthenes and father of Rind (*q.v.*).

BILSKIRNIR Thor's palace in Asgard.

BJÖRN A friend and confidant of Frithiof (*q.v.*).

BLODUGHOFI Frey's horse.

BODEN One of the bowls into which the dwarfs Fialar (*q.v.*) and Galar drained the blood of the god Kvasir, whom they had murdered.

BODVILD Daughter of the king of Sweden, Nidud (*q.v.*). Nidud took Völund (*q.v.*) prisoner, hamstrung him and stole all his property. *See* Chapter 5.

BORGHILD A princess by whom Sigmund (*q.v.*) had two sons, Hamond and Helgi. Sinfiotli (*q.v.*), Sigmund's son by Signy (*q.v.*), killed Borghild's brother in a brawl and so Borghild poisoned him. After Sinfiotli's death Sigmund realized that there was something amiss in the marriage and so divorced her.

BÖRR (Bor) The son of Buri (*q.v.*) and the father of the gods Odin, Ve and Vili.

BRANSTOCK An oak tree that stood in the centre of the hall of Volsung (*q.v.*). At the wedding feast of Siggeir and Volsung's daughter Signy (*q.q.v.*) a stranger suddenly appeared and thrust a sword into the Branstock; whoever could pull the sword out could have it, the stranger said, and it would bring him victory in every battle. Siggeir had a try, but without success, and Volsung's nine eldest sons likewise failed miserably. It was left to the youngest son, Sigmund (*q.v.*), to do the deed. It was because of Siggeir's jealousy about this that the feud sprang up between him and the line of Volsung.

BREIDABLIK Balder's hall in Asgard.

BRIMER (Brimir, Okolnir, Okolnur) One of the halls that will exist after Ragnarok. Here the giants will at last be able to enjoy warmth, for there will be no such thing as cold. Even if there were, the giants wouldn't mind because one of the other delights of Brimer will be endless supplies of strong drink.

BRISINGAMEN An ornament, generally assumed to be a necklace, manufactured by the four dwarfs Alfrigg, Berling, Dvalin and Grerr. Freya came across the smithy of the four while wandering in Svartalfheim and instantly lusted to possess the Brisingamen; the dwarfs instantly lusted after her, and soon a contract was agreed whereby she could have the ornament in return for spending a night of passion with each of them. Loki told Odin, who commanded him to take the necklace away from Freya. In order to regain it Freya, hitherto only the goddess of sex, had to take on the additional portfolios of war and death.

BROCKEN (Blocksberg) The highest peak of the Harz mountains in East Germany. Here the witch-followers of Freya danced on Walpurgisnacht.

BURI The forefather of the gods, brought into existence when the sacred cow Audhumla (*q.v.*) licked an iceberg.

DAG Day; son of Nott by her third husband Dellinger (*q.q.v.*). He travelled daily across the sky, his chariot pulled by the horse Skinfaxi, whose shining mane lit up the world.

DAG The sole survivor of the family of Hunding (*q.v.*) after they had made the foolish mistake of doing battle with Sigmund's sons Sinfiotli and Helgi (*q.q.v.*). Dag bought his life by promising not to avenge the death of his kin, but he betrayed the oath and murdered Helgi.

BELOW *The Lindisfarne Stone, from Northumbria, Britain, showing seven warriors usually thought to be Vikings. It is generally believed that the carving commemorates the first Viking attack on the Holy Island around* AD *793.*

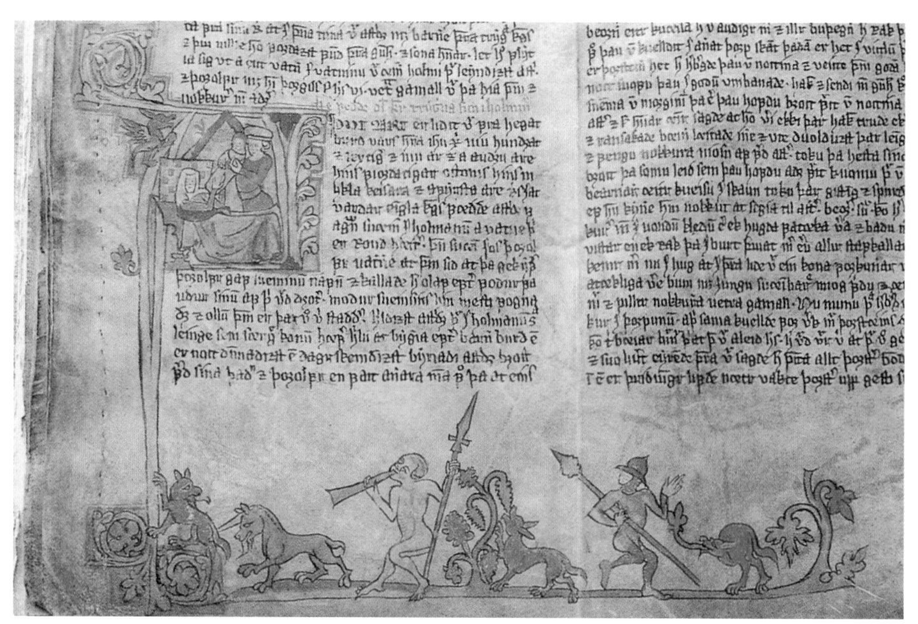

LEFT & RIGHT *A detail from an Icelandic manuscript copy of the* Flateyjarbok, *part of the Poetic Edda.*

DAIN One of the four stags dwelling on Yggdrasil.

DRAUPNIR A gold ring owned by Odin. Every ninth night it spawned eight exactly similar rings.

DROMA The second chain produced by the gods in their attempts to bind Fenris.

DUNEYR One of the four stags dwelling on Yggdrasil.

DURATHOR One of the four stags dwelling on Yggdrasil.

DVALIN One of the four stags dwelling on Yggdrasil. Also the name of a dwarf (*q,v.*).

EARTH The daughter of Norvi; her father was Annar (*q.q.v.*).

ECKHARDT A bosom friend of Tannhäuser (*q.v.*).

EDDA A mortal, the mother of Thrall (*q.v.*) and the ancestress of the race of serfs. The god Heimdall stayed a few nights with Edda and her husband Ai, and nine months later Thrall was born.

EDDAS Two anthologies of Norse legends, the Prose Edda and the Poetic Edda, of which the more important is the former. The Prose Edda was compiled by the Icelandic writer Snorri Sturluson (1178-1241). It is in four parts: a Prologue, 'The Deluding of Gylfi' (*q.v.*), 'Poetic Diction' and 'List of Metres'. The Poetic Edda was compiled about 1270 – i.e., some while later – and is often confusingly called the Elder Edda.

EGIL A brother of Völund (*q.v.*).

EGLIMI King of the Orkney Islands and the father of Hiordis (*q.v.*), the last wife of Sigmund (*q.v.*).

EINHERIAR (Einherjar) The slain warriors who were brought to Valhalla (*q.v.*), there to battle during the day and feast the night away. They will continue this curiously masochistic practice until Ragnarok.

EINMYRIA One of Loki's two daughters by Glut (*q.v.*).

EISA One of Loki's two daughters by Glut (*q.v.*).

EITEL A son of Atli and Gudrun (*q.q.v.*).

ELDE (Eldir) A servant to the god Aegir (*q.v.*).

ELDHRIMNIR The cauldron in Valhalla in which the boar Saehrimnir (*q.v.*) was cooked daily.

ELF (Elb, Helferich, Helfrat) A water sprite whose name was given to

ABOVE *Part of the carving in whalebone on the early-eighteenth-century Franks Casket, now in the British Museum, showing Egil fighting off attackers.*

the Elbe River; in certain Teutonic mythologies Elf is regarded as a god. Also, a Viking who married Hiordis after the death of Sigmund and became the stepfather of Sigurd (*q.q.v.*).

ELLI The name of the old woman with whom the god Thor unsuccessfully wrestled during his excursion to Utgard (*q.v.*). Afterwards the giant Utgard-Loki (*q.v.*) explained that Thor hadn't had a chance since Elli was really old age, who can be resisted by no mortal.

ELLIDA The magical dragon ship given by the god Aegir to Viking (*q.q.v.*).

ELVIDNER The hall of the goddess Hel (*q.v.*).

EMBLA The first woman; the sons of Borr created her from an elm tree.

ERMENRICH King of Gothland, a mortal who married the Valkyrie Swanhild (*q.v.*).

ERNA The wife of Jarl (*q.v.*).

ERP A son of Atli and Gudrun (*q.q.v.*).

ESBERN SNARE A lover of Helva (*q.v.*). He wanted to marry Helva and consequently struck a bargain with a troll to the effect that, as soon as the troll had built a church, Esbern should either name the builder or lose his eyes and heart. Luckily Helva helped, naming the troll as 'Fine' (*q.v.*).

FADIR (Fathir) Husband of Modir (*q.v.*), the ancestress of the warrior race.

FAFNIR (dragon) *see under* DWARFS.

FENRIS (Fenrir) Son of the god Loki and the giantess Angrboda (*q.q.v.*). This child took the form of an enormous wolf and became steadily more threatening to the gods. They tried to fetter the beast using the chains Laeding, Droma and (with success) Gleipnir. *See* Chapter 3.

FENSALIR Frigga's hall in Asgard.

FIMBULVETR (Fimbul-Winter) The three-year winter that will be inflicted upon the world immediately before Ragnarok.

FINE The troll who hoped to slaughter Esbern Snare (*q.v.*).

FIOLNIR (Fjolnir) The son of Frey and Gerda (*q.q.v.*).

FOLKVANG Freya's hall in Asgard.

FREKI One of the two wolves owned by the god Odin.

FREYGERDA A mortal woman who married the god Frey (*q.v.*) in his guise as Fridleef after he had rescued her from the attentions of a dragon. She bore their son Frodi (*q.v.*).

FRITHIOF A Norse hero, son of Thorsten and Ingeborg (*q.q.v.*). *See* Chapter 5.

FRODI The son of the god Frey and the mortal Freygerda (*q.q.v.*); he is recorded in Norse mythology as a pacifist king of Denmark who ruled about the time of Christ.

FUNFENG One of the two main servants of the god Aegir; the other was Elde (*q.v.*).

GAMBANTEIN Hermod's magical wand.

GARM A dog at the gate of Hel, chained in the cave Gnipa. When Ragnarok occurs this dog and the god Tyr (*q.v.*) will battle to their mutual death.

GELGIA The end of the chain with which the Aesir finally succeeded in tethering Fenris (*q.v.*).

GERI One of the wolves that accompanied Odin.

GIALLAR The bridge over the Giöll River (*q.v.*). Guarded by Modgud (*q.v.*), this represented the boundary between the mortal world and Niflheim (*q.v.*).

GIALLAR-HORN (Gjall) The trumpet possessed by the god Heimdall (*q.v.*).

GIMLI The hall which, after Ragnarok, will be populated by the surviving gods.

GINNUNGAGAP The primaeval abyss between Muspell and Niflheim (*q.q.v.*). According to the legends, this abyss was so deep that no mortal eye could see to its bottom.

GIOLL The rock to which the Aesir bound Fenris (*q.v.*).

GIÖLL RIVER The boundary of Niflheim (*q.v.*).

GIUKI King of the Nibelungs, husband of Queen Grimhild and father of Gunnar, Guttorm and Hogni (sons) and Gudrun (daughter); the last married Sigurd (*q.v.*).

GLADSHEIM A hall where the Aesir met in council.

GLAUMVOR Second wife of Gunnar (*q.v.*).

GLEIPNIR The third chain used by the Aesir in their attempts to fetter Fenris (*q.v.*).

GLEN The husband of Sol (*q.v.*).

GLITNIR The hall of the god Forseti (*q.v.*) in Asgard.

LEFT *Details of the stern of the Oseberg longship.*

GLUT The first wife of Loki and mother of Einmyria and Eisa (*q.q.v.*).

GNIPA (Gnippahellir) A cave by the entrance to Niflheim (*q.v.*) in which the dog Garm (*q.v.*) dwelled.

GREYFELL (Grane) The horse belonging to Sigurd (*q.v.*).

GRIMHILD Queen of the Nibelungs, husband of Guiki, and a devious sorceress. It was thanks to her machinations that Sigurd married Gudrun (*q.q.v.*) bigamously and Gunnar married Brunhild (*q.v.*) equally bigamously.

GRIPIR The stable master to Elf (*q.v.*). He gave a prophecy to Sigurd (*q.v.*) of the hero's major future life events and death.

GROA *See* Orvandil.

GUDRUN The name of both a Valkyrie (*q.v.*) and of a mortal (daughter of Giuki and Grimhild – *q.q.v.*) who was married successively to Sigurd (bigamously, through no fault of her own; their daughter was Swanhild) and Atli (*q.q.v.*). *See* Chapter 4.

GULL-TOP Horse belonging to the god Heimdall (*q.v.*).

GULLFAXI Horse belonging to the giant Hrungnir (*q.v.*). The animal was given by Thor to his son Magni (*q.v.*), who freed the god after he had been crushed to the ground by Hrungnir's corpse.

GULLINBURSTI A vast boar made by the dwarfs Brock and Sindri (*q.q.v.*). The beast eventually became the property of the god Frey.

GULLINKAMBI A cock living in Valhalla, where its crow awakened the Einherjar each morning so that they could resume their battling. The cock will also crow to forewarn the Aesir of the onset of Ragnarok.

GUNGNIR A magical spear commissioned by Loki from the dwarf Dvalin (*q.v.*) as a present to placate Thor and Sif.

GUNGTHIOF Brother of Hunthiof and son of Frithiof (*q.q.v.*).

GUNNAR (Gundicarius) Eldest son of Giuki and Grimhild (*q.q.v.*); he became the husband of the Valkyrie Brunhild (*q.v.*) through his mother's sorcery.

GUTTORM A son of Giuki and Grimhild (*q.q.v.*) who was the unhappy recipient of one of his mother's magic potions and consequently killed Sigurd (*q.v.*) and the latter's baby by Gudrun (*q.v.*). In his dying seconds Sigurd slew Guttorm.

GYLFI A king of Sweden who permitted Odin to build a city in his country. In another story Gylfi disguised himself as a wayfarer, Gangleri, and journeyed to Odin's hall in Asgard. There he conversed with three mysterious creatures – Har, Iafnhar and Thridi – who described to him the fundamentals of Norse mythology in considerable detail.

ABOVE *Detail of an early-twelfth-century wallhanging in Baldishol Stave Church, Norway, showing a Viking warrior on horseback. The resemblance between this image and that of a Norman – like William the Conqueror – is no coincidence: the name 'Norman' is a version of 'Norsemen', indicating where these conquerors of Normandy originated.*

HAGAL The foster-father of Sigmund's son Helgi (*q.v.*).

HAKON The father of Thora (*q.v.*).

HALFDAN Son of Belé and a close friend of Viking (*q.q.v.*).

HAM One of two witches (the other was called Heid) summoned up by Helgé to interfere with a voyage of Frithiof (*q.q.v.*). Frithiof cut up his golden armlet and gave an equal portion to each of his crew so that they would have something with which to propitiate the goddess Ran (*q.v.*); then he was able to control his ship, Ellida, sufficiently to make mincemeat out of the two witches and the whale upon which they were riding the seas.

HAMDIR A son of Gudrun (*q.v.*) by her third husband, Jonakur.

HAMOND A son of Sigmund and Borghild (*q.q.v.*).

HAR One of the three mysterious beings seen by Gylfi (*q.v.*) at the gate of Odin's hall.

HATI One of the wolves – the other was Sköll (*q.v.*) – that pursued the Sun and Moon across the sky. The name means 'hatred'. Just before Ragnarok Hati will finally succeed in devouring the Moon.

HÁVAMÁL (High Song) A long poem by Odin in which the god set out a code of practice for the Norse.

HEID *See* Ham.

HEIDRUN The goat in Valhalla that produced an endless supply of mead for the dead heroes.

HEIME The son of Völund (*q.v.*) and owner of the sword Miming, made for him by his father.

HEL The realm of the dead in Niflheim (*q.v.*). Either it took its name from the goddess Hel (*q.v.*) or she was named after it when presiding over it. There are many tales of individuals sojourning in Hel, the most notable being the god Balder (*q.v.*); readers are referred to the index.

HELGÉ One of the sons of Belé (*q.v.*); the other was Halfdan (*q.v.*). He refused to let his sister Ingeborg marry Frithiof (*q.v.*) but eventually allowed her to be betrothed to Sigurd Ring (*q.v.*).

HELGI A son of Sigmund and Borghild (*q.q.v.*). He was fostered out to Hagal (*q.v.*); he became a lover of the Valkyrie Gudrun (*q.v.*) but was then slain by the treacherous Hunding Dag (*q.v.*).

HERVOR A daughter of Angantyr (*q.v.*). She raised him from the dead in order to recover the sword Tyrfing (*q.v.*).

HIALLI An unfortunate murdered in place of Högni (*q.v.*).

HILDING The foster-father of Frithiof and Ingeborg (*q.q.v.*).

HIMINBIORG (Himinbjorg) The hall in Asgard of the god Heimdall (*q.v.*).

HIMINBRIOTER (Himinhrjot) A huge ox owned by the giant Hymir (*q.v.*). Thor killed it and used its head as fishbait.

HIORDIS Daughter of Eglimi and, in his later years, a wife of Sigmund (*q.v.*). Lygni (*q.v.*) was so upset that Sigmund's suit should be preferred to his own that he raised an army to take revenge.

HIUKI The waxing Moon; the brother of Bil (*q.v.*) and companion of Mani (*q.v.*).

HLESEY The island near to which the gods Aegir and Ran (*q.q.v.*) lived. The name comes from Aegir's alternative name Hler.

HLIDSKIALF The high throne of Odin from which he could see all over the nine worlds.

HLORA A foster-parent of Thor, whose other foster-parent was Vingnir. Together, Vingnir and Hlora constituted sheet lightning. The god was grateful enough to them both to use as his own alternative names Hlorridi and Vingthor.

HNOSS A daughter of Freya and Od; their other daughter was Gersemi (*q.v.*).

HOFVARPNIR The horse of the goddess Gna (*q.v.*).

HÖGNI A son of Giuki and Grimhild (*q.q.v.*). He and his brother Gunnar (*q.v.*) were the only two to know where the Nibelung hoard had been hidden. When Atli (*q.v.*) tortured Gunnar to find out its location, the latter refused to tell him until he was brought the heart of Högni, saying that he had sworn to keep the information secret so long as his brother was alive. Atli's soldiers brought the heart of a ne'er-do-well, Hialli, pretending that it was Högni's, but Gunnar saw that the heart trembled at his gaze and refused to believe that it was his brother's. So next time the soldiers brought the real thing, which, believe it or not, Gunnar recognized for what it was. Gunnar then told Atli that, since his brother was now dead, only he, Gunnar, knew where the treasure was hidden, and he wasn't telling. So Atli had him thrown into a pit full of venomous serpents, one of which (in some versions said to be Atli's mother in disguise) ended his life.

HRAUDING The father of the youths Agnar and Geirrod (*q.q.v.*) to whom Odin and Frigga took a fancy.

HRIMFAXI The horse of Nott (*q.v.*).

HUGI The boy against whom Thialfi (*q.v.*) was matched in races when Thor was visiting the giant Utgard-Loki (*q.v.*). Hugi won by miles. Later the giant confessed to Thor and his companions that Hugi was actually 'thought' in disguise; Thialfi had lost the races because, of course, nothing physical can run as fast as thought.

RIGHT *Bronze metalwork from a Swedish Viking grave, possibly from the tenth century, apparently showing Thor fishing for Jormungand, the World Serpent.*

HUGIN One of Odin's ravens; the other was Munin.

HUNDING A noble who was infuriated by the impertinence of Helgi (*q.v.*) and consequently waged war against him.

HUNTHIOF Brother of Gungthiof and son of Frithiof (*q.q.v.*).

HUNVOR A Swedish princess rescued and married by Viking (*q.v.*).

HVERGELMIR The cauldron in Niflheim next to which there was one of the roots of Yggdrasil (*q.v.*).

IAFN-HAR One of the three mysterious beings with whom Gylfi (*q.v.*) had a discussion.

IARN-GREIPER The glove belonging to the god Thor.

IDAVOLD (Idavoll) A plain in Asgard.

IFING The river running around the edge of Idavold (*q.v.*).

INGEBORG A daughter of Belé (*q.v.*) whom Frithiof (*q.v.*) married. The same name was given to a wife of Halfdan and a wife of Thorsten (*q.q.v.*).

JARL Like Thrall and Karl (*q.q.v.*) before him, Jarl was the offspring born of one of Heimdall's illicit unions, this time with Modir (*q.v.*); he became the ancestor of the warrior race.

JORMUNGAND (Iörmungandr, Midgardsormr, World Serpent) The serpent who was the child of the god Loki and the goddess Angrbodr. This snake surrounds Midgard, biting on its own tail to complete the circle.

JOTUNHEIM The land of the giants.

JUTERNAJESTA A beautiful girl with whom the giant Senjemand (*q.v.*) fell in love.

KARL The son of an illicit union between the god Heimdall and the mortal Amma (*q.q.v.*); the progenitor, with his wife Snor, of the race of peasants.

KNEFRUD (Wingi) A servant of Atli (*q.v.*) who was supposed to kill the Nibelungs.

KONUR The first king of Denmark, direct descendant of Jarl (*q.v.*).

LAEDING The first chain that the gods produced in their attempts to bind Fenris.

LANDVIDI The hall of the god Vidar (*q.v.*).

LAUFEIA (Nal) The putative mother of the god Loki (*q.v.*).

LEIPTER One of the icy rivers that flowed away from the cauldron Hvergelmir (*q.v.*). On the banks of this river oaths were sworn.

LERAD (Laerad) The uppe branch of Yggdrasil (*q.v.*); alternatively, another name for the great tree itself.

LIF The man who'll survive Ragnarok and father humanity thereafter. His wife will be Lifthrasir.

LIFTHRASIR The woman who'll survive Ragnarok and mother humanity thereafter. Her husband will be Lif. It's interesting that, in the science fiction of the 1950s and 1960s, there were countless tales about the last two survivors of nuclear war (or some other genocidal event) who were by astonishing coincidence always called Adam and Eve, and who would always be able to procreate to produce our successors. Clearly the idea that there's some great catastrophe up ahead, and that humanity as a whole will be saved because of a pair of survivors, is very deeply ingrained in our collective subconscious.

LOGI (Fire) The cook in the hall of the giant Utgard-Loki (*q.v.*). He was entered in an eating race with the god Loki and won by a long way. Later Utgard-Loki confessed that Logi was in reality fire, which devours things more swiftly than any mortal can.

LORELEI A lovely young woman

BELOW *Bronze and gilt brooch found in a Viking grave in Norway.*

seated upon the St Goar Rock on the Rhine River. She sang a sweet song that enchanted many a mariner to his death.

LORRIDE One of the daughters of Thor.

LYGNI A king who wanted to marry Hiordis (*q.v.*) but was rejected by her in favour of Sigmund (*q.v.*); he therefore raised an army and fought a battle with Sigmund's supporters in which the hero was slain.

MAELSTROM The primaeval whirlpool.

MANAGARM A wolf who was the child of Iarnsaxa; the father was Fenris (*q.q.v.*).

MANI The Moon.

MANNIGFUAL A vast ship owned by the giants, according to a Frisian tradition. Its size can be assessed from the fact that youths instructed to scale the masts were old men by the time they returned!

MEGINGIÖRD The belt of Thor.

MIDGARD (Manaheim) The world inhabited by human beings.

MIMING A sword made by Völund (*q.v.*) for his son Heime; an alternative version is that it was made by the god Mimir (*q.v.*).

MIÖLNIR The hammer belonging to Thor (*q.v.*). It was forged by the dwarfs Brock and Sindri (*q.q.v.*).

MODGUD A grim, skeletal woman who guarded the bridge over the river Giöll (*q.v.*).

MODIR (Mothir) The wife of Fadir and, thanks to a visit from Heimdall, the mother of Jarl (*q.q.v.*). Modir was therefore the progenitor of the warrior race.

MOKERKIALFI (Mist Calf, Mokkurkalfi) A mock giant made out of clay by the giant Hrungnir (*q.v.*) to battle with Thialfi (*q.v.*).

MUNIN One of Odin's ravens; the other was Hugin.

LEFT *A dress fastener dating from the Viking period. It is bronze and gilt.*

MUSPELL The realm of fire, involved in the Creation (*see* Chapter 2). At Ragnarok the giant occupants of Muspell will emerge, led by the realm's guardian, Surt (*q.v.*), to do battle with the gods.

MYSINGER The Viking leader responsible for murdering Frodi (*q.v.*).

NAGLFARI The first husband of Night (*q.v.*); their child was Aud (*q.v.*).

NARVE (Narvi) The mother of Night (*q.v.*).

NASTROND The part of the realm of Hel (*q.v.*) in which stood the hall to which the wicked went after death. Here the dragon Nidhug (*q.v.*) chewed up their corpses.

NIDHUG A voracious dragon that chewed up the corpses of evil-doers after their death as well as (presumably for roughage) gnawing at the roots of Yggdrasil.

NIDUD A king of Sweden who came across Völund (*q.v.*) while the latter was sleeping, took him prisoner, stole all his property, then hamstrung him and set him to work in a smithy forging weapons and ornaments. *See* Chapter 5.

NIFLHEIM A land of darkness and freezing mist in which lay one of Yggdrasil's roots as well as the region of Hel.

NIGHT (Nott) The daughter of the giant Norvi. She had three husbands: Naglfari, Annar and Delling.

NINE WORLDS The worlds that constituted the whole of creation. It is hard to produce a definitive list of them, because of confusion in the legends. Muspell is mentioned in the Prose Edda as the first of all the worlds, yet cannot easily be fitted into the Norse cosmogony. Hel can be considered either as a world or (probably more correctly) as a part of Niflheim – or even, come to that, as just another name for Niflheim!

The worlds existed on three levels, down through all of which Yggdrasil (*q.v.*) penetrated and in each of which it had a root. The bottom-most level contained Hel and Niflheim (or Hel/Niflheim); the middle level contained Jotunheim (the land of giants), Midgard (the middle world or land of mortals), Nidavellir (the land of dwarfs) and Svartalfheim (land of dark elves); the top level contained Alfheim (land of light elves), Vanaheim (land of the Vanir) and, in utmost splendour, Asgard, the home of the gods.

NIP The father of the goddess Nanna (*q.v.*).

NJORFE A foe and then bosom friend of Viking and Halfdan (*q.q.v.*). His sons and Viking's sons were less keen on the paternal friendship. *See* Chapter 5.

NÖATÛN The hall of the god Njord (*q.v.*).

NORNAGESTA A bard who possessed the gift of youth. This was because, at his birth, someone insulted Skuld (*q.v.*), one of the Norns; she furiously said that the babe would live only as long as it took for a bedside candle to burn down. There was a deal of mourning until one of the other Norns had the wit simply to put the candle out. Nornagesta carried it with him wherever he went. At the age of 300 he was forced to become a Christian by Olaf Tryggvesson and, to prove that the conversion was not just lip-service, to light the candle-stub. This he did and, when it burnt out, he dropped down dead.

The legend is slightly curious, because it must have originated some time after the Norse had become Christians; yet its clear moral is that people should stick to the old, heathen religion. Maybe it came into existence as a rumour spread by the die-hards who resented the coming of the new religion?

RIGHT *Part of a belt-buckle found in a sixth-century chief's grave at Aker, Norway. The work was done in silver and gilt together with niello, gold and garnets.*

OD-HROERIR One of the containers into which the dwarfs Fialar and Galar drained the blood of Kvasir (*q.q.v.*).

ORVANDIL (Aurvandil) Either the son or the husband of Groa (*q.v.*), the sorceress summoned by Thor to try to get the whetstone out of his head after his duel with the giant Hrungnir (*q.v.*). Groa had assumed that her son/husband was long-dead, but as she chanted her spells to loosen the stone from Thor's forehead the god became so pleased with her that he decided to cheer her up by telling her that her loved one was very much alive, thanks to the good actions of none other than himself, Thor. The god had gone to the land of the frost giants to recover Orvandil, putting him in a basket to carry him home. Unfortunately Orvandil had persisted in sticking a toe out through the wicker of the basket, and this toe had frozen solid; Thor had therefore snapped it off and thrown it up into the sky, where it became a star. Thor took Groa to show her the star as proof of his tale, and she was so excited that she forgot where she had got to in her spells. She lost a job but, we assume, regained her son/husband; Thor was left with a stone embedded in his forehead.

OTTAR A hero who disputed a piece of property with Angantyr. Ottar was lucky enough to get assistance from Freya, and so won the legal argument. For more details, *see* the entry on the giantess Hyndla.

RAGNAR LODBROG Son-in-law of Brunhild and Sigurd through his marriage to their daughter Aslaug (*q.q.v.*).

RAGNAROK The final battle during which the gods will succumb to the forces of evil. *See* Chapter 6.

RANDWER The son of Ermenrich (*q.v.*). He was falsely accused of making love with Swanhild (*q.v.*), and so his father condemned them both to death.

RATATOSK A loquacious squirrel living in Yggdrasil (*q.v.*). Ratatosk spent all its time rushing up and down to relay to the eagle at the top of the tree and the dragon Nidhug (*q.v.*) at its bottom to tell them both the latest insult each had uttered about the other. This squirrel, the object of contempt among the Norse, was obviously the precursor of tabloid journalism.

RATI An auger owned by Odin (*q.v.*).

RIGHT *Sigurd slays his tutor Regin – a carving from Starkirba Church, Norway. Or was it his tutor? There was also a dwarfish Regin, a brother of Otter, and the coincidence of names has caused some confusion in the legends.*

REGIN A very wise man who was appointed by Elf (*q.v.*) to be the tutor of Sigurd (*q.v.*). There is some confusion between this Regin and one of the brothers of the dwarf Fafnir (*q.v.*); often the two are conflated.

RERIR The son and heir of Sigi (*q.v.*). Rerir and his wife were not blessed with a son to inherit the throne until Frigga decided to have compassion on them. She sent her messenger, the goddess Gna, to Rerir with a magic apple which he shared with his wife. Perhaps it was the vitamin C, but nine months later Volsung (*q.v.*) was born to them. They died while the boy was still an infant.

RIND The daughter of King Billing. Odin attempted to seduce her, and later described her in contemptuous terms because she had declined the offer. There is some confusion between her and the goddess Rind (*q.v.*) who became Odin's mistress and gave birth to the god Vali (*q.v.*).

RING A son of Viking (*q.v.*).

RINGHORN The longship on which the god Balder and his wife Nanna (*q.q.v.*) were cremated.

ROSKVA The sister of Thialfi (*q.v.*) and, like him, forced to become a servant of Thor.

ROSSTHIOF A Finnish magician who used his magic to pull travellers into his realm so that he could kill them and take all their treasure. He was also able to read the future, but didn't like doing so. He was captured by Hermod (*q.v.*) and forced to predict that a son of Odin would be murdered but avenged by another son of Odin; these sons were, respectively, Balder and Vali (*q.q.v.*).

SAEHRIMNIR A boar slain daily by the cook Andhrimnir (*q.v.*) and boiled in the cauldron Eldhrimnir to feed the dead warriors in Valhalla; no matter how much they stuffed themselves, the meat of the boar was always sufficient – and the beast returned to life in time to be slaughtered again the next morning.

ABOVE *Tenth-century Viking axe, inlaid with silver, from Mammen, Denmark.*

SAEMING A son of Odin who became a king.

SESSRYMNIR The hall of the goddess Freya (*q.v.*).

SIBICH A dishonest man who told Ermenrich (*q.v.*) that his son Randwer (*q.v.*) had been making love with Swanhild (*q.v.*). The accusation was false but nevertheless Ermenrich had Swanhild and Randwer put to death.

SIEGFRIED *see* Sigurd.

SIGGEIR King of the Goths and Volsungs and cuckolded husband of Signy (*q.v.*). He made the mistake of getting Sigmund and Sinfiotli (*q.q.v.*) angry, and paid with his life.

SIGI Emperor of the Huns and father of Rerir (*q.v.*). Sigi, a son of Odin, seems to have been a rather nasty piece of work, murdering a hunting companion for having killed more game than he had. He was in extreme old age when he was assassinated by members of his wife's family.

SIGMUND A hero of the Vikings. *See* Chapter 5.

SIGNY Twin sister of Sigmund (*q.v.*) and wife of Siggeir. She was keen that her sons should grow up to become great warriors, and so she sent her firstborn to Sigmund to be tested for courage. The boy failed the test; Sigmund, one of life's sterner dominies, killed him. Signy's second son likewise failed the test but was let off with a caution. She had never been particularly fond of Siggeir, who had committed the heinous crime of killing her father, Volsung (*q.v.*), as well as nine of her ten brothers, and so now she concluded that her sons by him were all going to be as foppish as the first two. What she needed was a son with the pure blood of Volsung flowing in his veins. She therefore took the form of a beautiful young witch and had three nights of lusty incest with Sigmund. The result was Sinfiotli (*q.v.*).

SIGURD (Siegfried) A hero of the Vikings. *See* Chapter 5.

SIGURD RING King of Ringric who wanted to marry Ingeborg (*q.v.*); he achieved his goal and also extracted a yearly tribute from Helgé and Halfdan (*q.q.v.*).

SINFIOTLI The eldest son of Sigmund (*q.v.*); his mother was Sigmund's sister Signy (*q.v.*). Sinfiotli was from the start a brave child, unlike his two elder halfbrothers whom Signy had borne to her husband, Siggeir (*q.v.*): his mother tested his courage by sewing his clothes directly onto his skin and then ripping them away, to which the young hero responded with a merry laugh. Sinfiotli and Sigmund had many adventures together. In one of these they transformed themselves into wolves and savaged everything in sight. They found this such fun that they started savaging each other, and Sinfiotli was killed. Luckily a passing raven gave Sigmund a magic leaf with which he was able to restore his son to life. Sinfiotli later killed the two youngest children of Siggeir and Signy, at Signy's behest. For this murder both he and Sigmund were justifiably sentenced by Siggeir to be buried alive, but Signy delivered Sigmund's magic sword to Sinfiotli and he was able to hack out an exit from their tomb. The pair went to Siggeir's hall and burnt alive all of the men there; the women they allowed to flee – with the exception of Signy, who had decided she didn't want to go on living: just before her death she broke it to Sigmund that Sinfiotli was in fact his son. Sigmund then married Borghild (*q.v.*) who killed Sinfiotli by poison.

SKIDBLADNIR A magical ship commissioned by Loki from the dwarf Dvalin (*q.v.*) as a present to placate Thor and Sif.

SKINFAXI The horse pulling the chariot of Dag (*q.v.*).

SKIOLD A king of Denmark who was in theory one of the sons of the god Odin (*q.v.*); he married Gefjon (*q.v.*).

ABOVE *Asbyrgi, a rock in Iceland supposed to have been a hoofmark made by Sleipnir.*

RIGHT *Eighth-century Swedish stela from Tjängvide, showing Odin's eight-legged steed Sleipnir.*

SKIRNIR A servant of the god Frey (*q.v.*); thanks to the efforts of Skirnir, Frey was able to marry the giantess Gerda (*q.v.*).

SKÖLL The wolf that pursued the Sun. Just before Ragnarok this wolf will succeed in catching the Sun and eating it.

SLAGFINN A brother of Völund (*q.v.*); he raped a Valkyrie.

SLEIPNIR The eight-legged horse belonging to Odin (*q.v.*). In contradiction to common sense, this horse ran very swiftly; you would have expected it to fall over its own extranumery legs. The god Hermod (*q.v.*) was allowed to ride him on occasion; Loki (*q.v.*) was probably its father or even mother – *see* Chapter 3.

SNOR The wife of Karl (*q.v.*).

SOKVABEK (Sokkvabekk) The hall of the goddess Saga (*q.v.*).

SOL The Sun.

SON One of the bowls into which the dwarfs Fialar (*q.v.*) and Galar drained the blood of the god Kvasir, whom they had murdered.

SÖRLI A son of the Valkyrie Gudrun by Jonakur (*q.q.v.*).

SOTÉ A pirate who stole an armlet forged by Völund (*q.v.*).

SVADILFARE (Svadilfari) A horse that helped to put walls around Asgard and, thanks to Loki, sired Sleipnir (*q.v.*).

SVALIN A shield that protected the world from the harshest of the Sun's rays.

SVARTALFHEIM The realm in which lived the dark elves.

SVASUD The father of Summer.

TANNGNIOSTR A goat belonging to Thor; the name means 'tooth cracker'.

TANNGRISNR A goat belonging to Thor; the name means 'tooth gnasher'.

TANNHÄUSER A Teutonic hero who was, apparently, ensnared physically by the goddess Holda, or Frigga (*q.v.*); he found this great fun at the time but then went off to ask absolution from the pope. The pope said that worshippers of heathen gods should accept whatever they were given (in other words, eternal hell-fire) and that Tannhäuser would be forgiven only when the pope's holy staff bore fruit – an impossibility, because the staff was made of dead wood. Tannhäuser was a bit depressed by all this, and so decided to return to Holda's embrace. Three days later the pope's staff began to produce green buds, and a message was sent urgently to Tannhäuser saying that, after all, he was forgiven. Unfortunately the message arrived too late, so Tannhäuser was condemned to spend the rest of eternity making passionate love with Holda.

THIALFI The son of a peasant who, along with his sister Roskva (*q.v.*), was conscripted as a slave by Thor. The boy proved to be one of the more significant members of the Norse pantheon.

THING The Thing was (and still is) a Scandinavian public assembly or law court.

THIR (Thyr) The wife of Thrall (*q.v.*).

THORA Daughter of Hakon and wife of Elf (*q.q.v.*).

THORER Son of Viking and brother of Thorsten (*q.q.v.*).

THORSTEN A hero of the Vikings; a son of Viking and brother of Thorer. *See* Chapter 5.

THRALL The son born of an illicit union between the god Heimdall and the mortal Edda (*q.q.v.*). Thrall was not the most attractive of men but he stirred the heart of Thir (who was not the most attractive of women); they succeeded in giving birth to the race of serfs or thralls.

THRIDI One of the three creatures that spoke with Gylfi (*q.v.*).

THRUDHEIM (Thrudvang) The realm of Asgard in which Thor lived.

TYRFING A magical sword created by the dwarfs and owned by Angantyr (*q.v.*).

UNDINES Friendly female water spirits; they were the Norse equivalents of mermaids.

URD (Urdr) The fountain of the three Norns (*q.v.*).

UTGARD A place in Jotunheim ruled over by Utgard-Loki (*q.v.*).

VALASKIALF (Valaskjalf) Odin's hall in Asgard.

VALHALLA The hall to which warriors went after being slain.

VALI Not to be confused with the god Vali (*q.v.*), this was the son of Loki and Sigyn (*q.q.v.*). He killed his brother Narve (*q.v.*).

VANAHEIM The realm in which lived the Vanir.

VEDFOLNIR The falcon that sat between the eyes of the eagle atop Yggdrasil (*q.v.*) and saw everything that happened in the nine worlds, reporting each event to the gods.

VIGRID The plain in Asgard on which Ragnarok (*q.v.*) will take place.

VIKING A hero of the Vikings. *See* Chapter 5.

VINDSAL The father of Winter and the son of Vasud (*q.q.v.*).

VINGNIR Husband of Hlora (*q.v.*).

VINGOLF A hall in Asgard; here the goddesses met and conversed.

VOLSUNG The father of Sigmund and Signy (*q.q.v.*). He became the king of the Huns after the death of his father Rerir (*q.v.*); he had ten sons and one daughter, Signy (*q.v.*), whose twin brother was Sigmund. *See* Chapter 5.

VÖLUND (Wayland, Weland) The smith captured and hamstrung by Nidud (*q.v.*). *See* Chapter 5.

VON A river that flowed from the mouth of Fenris (*q.v.*).

WALPURGISNACHT The eve of May 1. According to Teutonic myth, on this night the witches associated with the cult of Frey dance on the Brocken (*q.v.*).

YDALIR Hall in Asgard of the god Ull (*q.v.*).

YGGDRASIL (Yggdrasill) The World Tree, an ash that linked all of the nine worlds. It was created by All-father not long after he had created the human race. It had three enormous roots; one in Asgard, one in Midgard and one in Niflheim. It was a haven for wildlife. On its topmost branch, which overshadowed Odin's own hall in Asgard, there rested an eagle between whose eyes sat a falcon called Vedfolnir; a goat called Heidrun wandered about the tree's branches; four stags – Dain, Duneyr, Durathor and Dvalin – did likewise. The dragon Nidhug (*q.v.*) chewed away at the tree's roots. A squirrel called Ratatosk (*q.v.*) ran up and down the tree telling lies about the things the eagle and the dragon had said about each other.

BELOW *The Viking–Christian cross at Gosforth, Cumbria, Britain. The carving at the base of the cross is thought to represent Yggdrasil.*

TWO

The Creation

In the beginning there was nothing. No, not quite nothing. There was an endless space and a god called Allfather (often confusingly identified with Odin) who was invisible and who had existed for ever. He had eleven other names, ranging from Spear-shaker to Gelding to Ruler of Weather. The huge abyss of emptiness was called Ginnungagap. Long before the Earth was created, there came to exist Yggdrasil, the World Tree, an ash that would link all of the nine worlds.

Under one of its roots, to the south, there was a realm called Muspell, which was so hot that anyone who did not live there would be consumed by the heat; it was guarded by a giant called Surt who was armed with a burning sword. This was a place of fire: embers from it floated down into Ginnungagap. Under another root, to the north, there was a realm called Niflheim, a land of mist and darkness; directly beneath this great root was Hvergelmir, a bubbling cauldron that supplied the waters for twelve huge rivers. In the cauldron there was also a repellent dragon called Nidhug that gnawed away at the roots of the great tree; when it and its wormlike allies succeed in killing the tree, the world will come to an end. The waters of the rivers pouring from Hvergelmir flowed torrentially into Ginnungagap and, as they fell into the frigid void, became great blocks of ice.

Far down, at the base of Ginnungagap, the embers from Muspell dropped onto these piles of ice so that great clouds of steam arose. The steam turned into rime, which progressively filled up Ginnungagap. To the north, near Niflheim, there were gales and a neverending drizzle of cold rain; to the south, near Muspell, the glowing embers lit up the sky as they met the ascending rime. The result was that the centre of the rising surface became a temperate ocean, This was incarnated in the form of an evil giant called Ymir – the first of the ice giants.

The thawing of the rime created also a cow, Audhumla. Her udder gave out four streams of milk, and from these Ymir was able to gain sustenance. The cow licked blocks of salty ice so that, on the first day, the hair of a being appeared; her licking on the second day revealed the head of the being; her licking on the third exposed the entire body of this being, Buri. In the meantime Ymir had been sleeping, and as he slept he sweated; from the sweat of his left armpit were born the first man and the first woman (but see below). Ymir's legs copulated with each other to produce a six-headed giant called Thrudgelmir, who in due course gave birth to Bergelmir, the direct ancestor of the frost giants.

Buri became the forefather of the gods. He had a son, Börr, and the two of them immediately began to battle against the evil giants. The battle lasted for a longer time than human beings can reckon, but then Börr married a giantess called Bestla and sired three great sons – Odin, Vili and Ve.

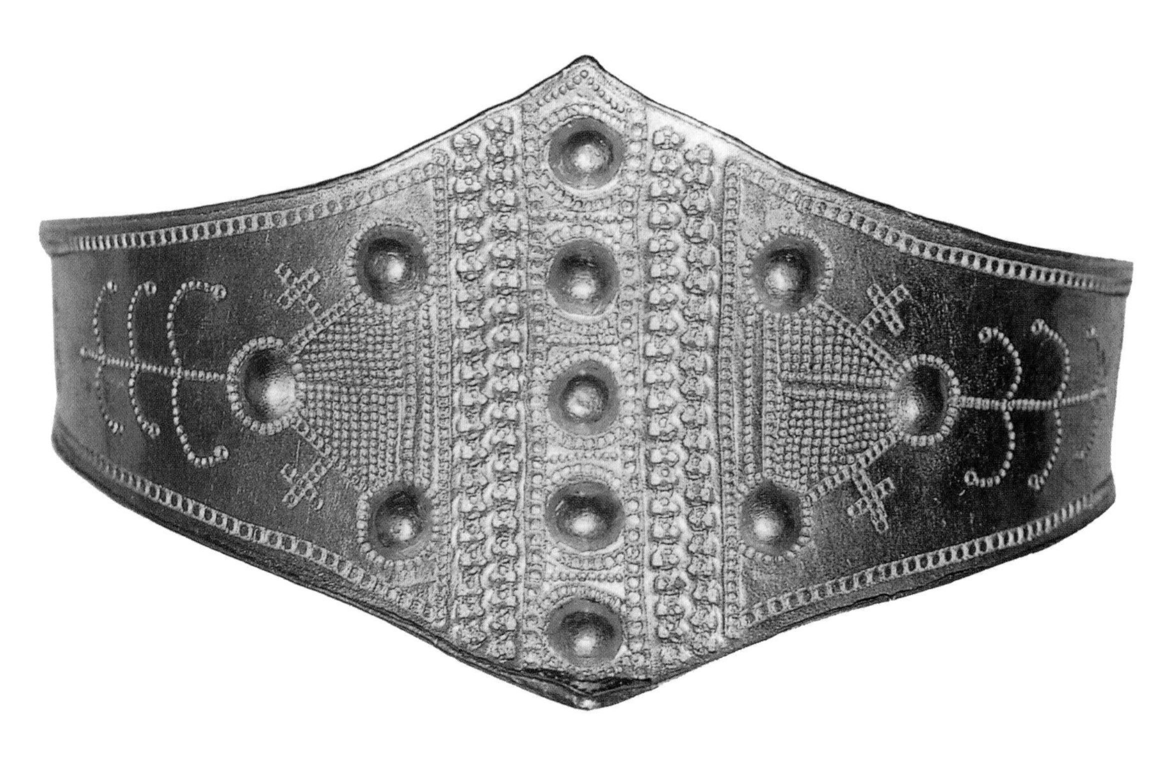

BELOW *A ninth or tenth-century golden arm-ring from Råbylille, Denmark, whose decoration consists of symbols of Yggdrasil.*

These three leapt into battle alongside their father, so that soon Ymir was slain. All the giants were drowned in the flood of Ymir's blood except Bergelmir and his mate; these two fled in a longship to a place called Jotunheim, where they bred. The frost giants who descended from Bergelmir and his wife perhaps understandably regarded the gods ever after as their natural foes – even though, on occasion, members of the two factions could exhibit amity.

Odin, Vili and Ve were left with Ymir's corpse, presumably wondering what to do with it. They tugged it out across Ginnungagap and started to chop it up to make the various parts of the physical world. Our world of mortals, Midgard, they manufactured from Ymir's flesh; the giant's blood they used for the oceans and his unbroken bones for the mountains. His broken bones, his teeth and bits of his jaws became the cliffs, rocks and stones of the world. His skull they made into the dome of the sky; to keep it aloft they created four dwarfs (Austri, Nordri, Sudri and Westri), corresponding to the four cardinal points, who supported it. His brains became the clouds. They used the embers from Muspell to create the light that illuminates both heaven and the Earth; they also made the stars and the planets. The three gods then created the first human beings (but see above) out of a pair of trees they discovered: Odin's contributions to these people were life and spirit, Vili's mobility and intelligence, and Ve's the senses.

The first man was called Ask (meaning ash tree) and the first woman Embla (meaning, possibly, elm). Right in the middle of what had now become the world the gods built Asgard: the gods are still living there, and will do so until Ragnarok.

The brightest of the embers from Muspell were given special names and special prominence: they were the Moon (Mani) and the Sun (Sol). These two beings were set by the three gods into chariots that were designed to cross the sky. (An alternative version is that the Moon and Sun were the son and daughter, respectively, of a man called Mundilfari; Sun's husband was a man named Glen or Glaur. The gods were outraged by Mundilfari's impertinence in calling his children by the names of the heavenly lights they had created, and so snatched away the gleaming children to drive the chariots of the Moon and the Sun. It is these children that we see as bright lights in the sky.) The two horses drawing Sol's chariot, Arvakr and Alsvin, had to be protected from Sol's great heat: they were endowed with cooling devices plus the shielding of another device called Svalin. The horse that drew Mani's chariot was called Alsvider. Mani had two attendants, children he snatched up from the ground while they were collecting water from a well. They were called Hiuki and Bil, and represented the waxing and waning Moon.

RIGHT *The earliest known Norse crucifix, dating from the tenth century and discovered in a grave at Birka in Sweden. It is silver gilt.*

A giant called Norvi had had a daughter called Nott, or Night. She, in turn, had children by three husbands: Aud was her son by her first husband, Naglfari; Fjorgyn (Jörd; Earth) was her daughter by her second husband, Annar; Dag (Day), an astoundingly beautiful and radiant youth, was her son by her third husband, Dellinger, the god of dawn, a relation of Odin, Vili and Ve. These three gods gave Nott a chariot in which she could circle the heavens; it was drawn by a horse called Hrimfaxi. Later, when they saw the beauty of Dag, they gave him a chariot as well; its horse was Skinfaxi. The mane of Skinfaxi gives off a brilliant light which serves to illuminate the world.

Mani precedes Sol across the sky, but Sol is always in a hurry to catch up. This is because Sol is being pursued by a wolf called Sköll. Mani is likewise being chased by a wolf, Hati. From time to time the wolves succeed in catching their prey, so that the light of the Sun or the Moon is blotted out; however, people on Earth can make enough noise to scare the wolves away and restore the light. In the end, though – just before Ragnarok – the wolves will finally triumph.

The gods appointed various other guardians. The responsibility for the changing of the seasons was divided between Winter and Summer. Winter was the grandson of the god Vasud – the frigid wind – and the son of Vindsval, neither of whom were the sort of progenitor you'd particularly want to meet up a dark alley. Winter took on their nastier characteristics and therefore unreasoningly loathed Summer, who was a son of a benign and lovely god called Svasud. Less important guardians of the regularity of passing time were Noon, Afternoon, Evening, Midnight, Morning and Forenoon.

The three original gods had something of a problem. While they'd been reducing Ymir's body to its constituent parts they'd noticed that the flesh of the giant's body had been crawling with maggots. The gods decided to be merciful to these creatures. They gave them a subhuman form, the nature of which depended upon their spiritual characteristics. Those whose ethics were questionable became dwarfs: they were condemned to live underground, knowing that if they came out into the open during the day they would be instantly turned to stone. (Dwarfs could also be called dark elves, gnomes, kobolds or trolls; whatever the name, they were banished to Svartalfaheim.) The maggots that were considered ideologically sound became fairies and light elves. They had a much better time of it, being given the lovely realm of Alfheim, which was halfway between Heaven and Earth; from here they could flit down to Earth whenever they wanted. Neither of these two classes of being could be considered as human: normally they were deadly enemies, but on occasion they could be friendly towards mortals or gods.

The gods then created their own realm, Asgard, and the realm of mortals, Midgard. All of the worlds were still connected by the trunk of the great ash tree Yggdrasil, whose roots lay in Asgard, Jotunheim and Niflheim. Its topmost bough, Lerad, had perched on it an eagle between whose eyes sat a hawk called Vedfolnir; it was the duty of Vedfolnir to look down over all of Heaven, Earth and Niflheim and report what was happening there. Yggdrasil had other infesting fauna. Aside from Nidhug, chewing at the tree's roots, there were the four deer – Dain, Duneyr, Durathor and Dvalin – that roamed among its branches: the dew dripping from their antlers came together to form the world's rivers. Then there was a squirrel called Ratatosk: it spent its time running up and down the great tree's trunk exchanging malicious gossip between the eagle and the dragon, hoping to make them declare war on each other. The Norns had the daily task of sprinkling water from a blessed well called Urdar down over the branches of Yggdrasil, so that the great tree was constantly refreshed; the water falling from the lower branches became bees' honey.

RIGHT *Part of the animal head recovered from the ship used for a funeral pyre at Oseberg.*

RIGHT *Nineteenth-century book illustration showing King Gylfi contemplating Asgard. The conversation which the king had at the gates of Asgard, as recorded in the Prose Edda, is one of our major sources of the Norse myths.*

The family of gods sired by Odin and his brothers was called the Aesir. But there was also another family of older gods, the Vanir, fertility gods whose powers were generally related to those of the wind and the sea; they lived in Vanaheim. Very early on there was a war between the Aesir and the Vanir. The result was a stalemate, and so hostages were exchanged. The Vanir sent Njord to Asgard with his two children, Frey and Freya, and the Aesir sent Mimir and Hoenir, a brother of Odin, to Vanaheim. This disposition of gods seems to have suited everybody, because Frey and Freya became important members of the Norse pantheon, while Hoenir will be one of the very few lucky enough to survive Ragnarok.

Asgard

Asgard was the home of the gods. It was built by Odin and the other gods and goddesses in the very early days. Mortals were unable to see this realm because the plain on which it was sited, Idawold (or Idavoll), floated far above the Earth. A river called Ifing separated Idawald from the rest of the world: its waters were distinguished by the fact that they never froze.

However, there was a link between our mortal Earth and Asgard – the magical bridge called Bifrost, which be equated with the rainbow: its colours were born of fire, water and the air. The gods were able to use this bridge to travel up from and down to Midgard, the world of human beings. One difficulty the gods faced was that their weight might shatter Bifrost: the god Thor therefore eschewed the bridge altogether, while the others trod warily. At the Midgard end of the bridge stood the god Heimdall clutching a horn: every time the gods entered or left Asgard, Heimdall would sound a quiet note on this instrument. When Ragnarok happens he'll sound a loud and savage blast to signify the end of the world.

Asgard was furnished with several halls belonging to the major gods and goddesses. Freya's hall, for example, was called Folkvang; Forseti's was Glitnir; Gladsheim was one of Odin's halls, and was equipped with twelve thrones where the major gods sat in council. Another feature of Asgard was Hlidskialf, the great throne of Odin. From here the great god – or Frigga, because she was allowed to sit on Hlidskialf as well – could see everything that was happening in all of the worlds.

THREE

Tales of Gods and Goddesses

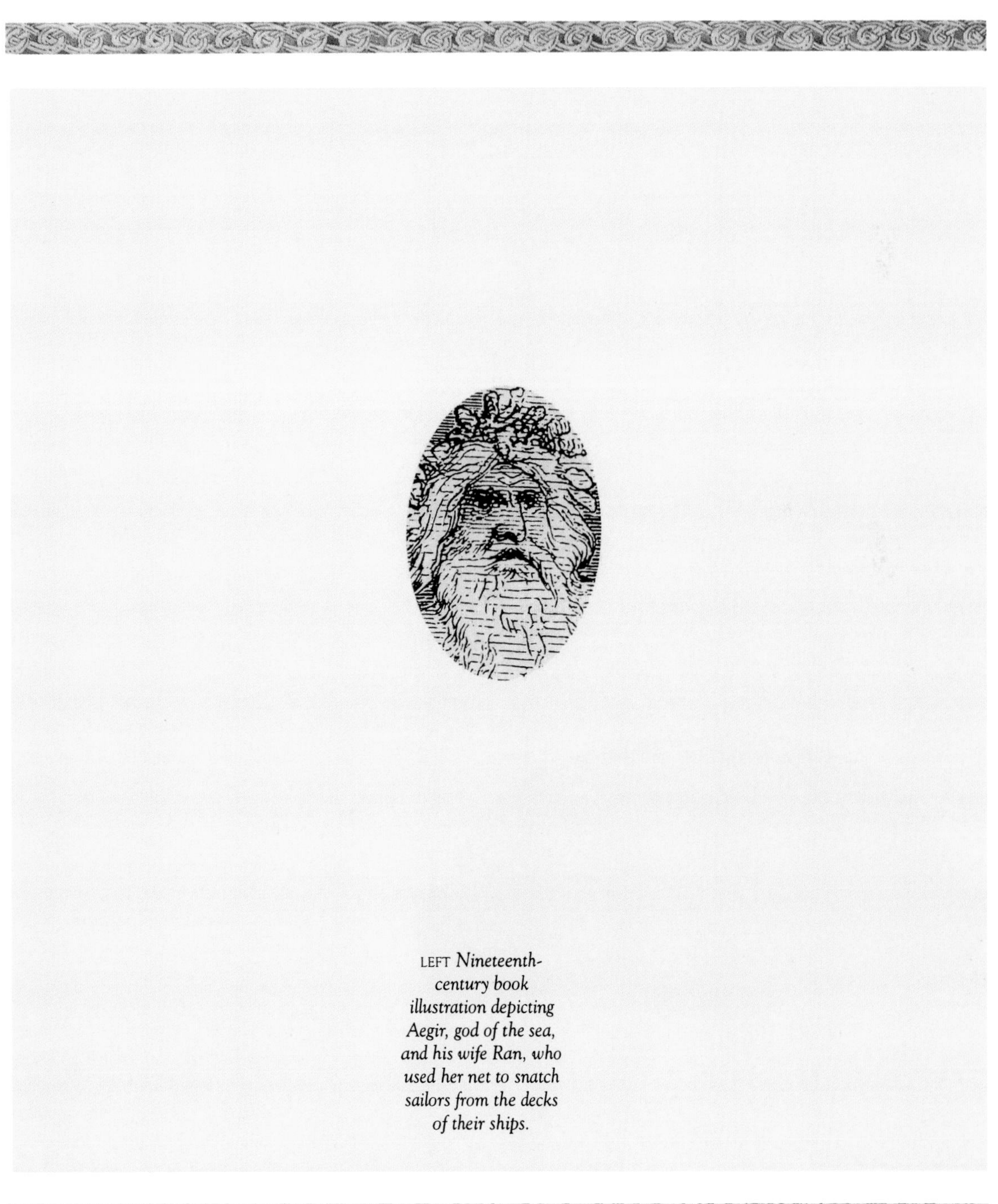

LEFT *Nineteenth-century book illustration depicting Aegir, god of the sea, and his wife Ran, who used her net to snatch sailors from the decks of their ships.*

AEGIR AND NJORD

BELOW *Viking sword pommel found in Sweden and now in the National Museum of Antiquities, Stockholm. This could date from about the tenth century.*

RIGHT *Nineteenth-century book ilillustration representing Njord and Skadi on their way from Asgard to Noatûn after their honeymoon.*

Both Aegir and Njord were gods of the sea; the former was one of the Aesir (if not a member of an even earlier family of gods) and the latter one of the Vanir. In the early days the Norse worshipped Aegir and nodded their heads towards Njord; later they worshipped Njord and barely remembered Aegir as a separate god. During this time the stories of Aegir and Njord became inextricably mixed up with each other. Since the sea was so important to the Vikings, the whole process represented a fairly significant turnaround.

Aegir lived in a hall beneath the sea near the island of Hlesey. He shared the hall with his wife-sister, Ran. Much hated, Ran was the goddess of death for all who perished at sea. Her task was to use a net to haul men from the decks of ships to a watery grave in the hall she shared with her husband-brother. One legend has it that mariners might reappear at their own funeral feasts if Ran had welcomed them to the seafloor with especial enthusiasm. And, even for those less fortunate, her welcome was not necessarily unfriendly: in her seafloor hall the mead flowed as freely as it did at Valhalla, and couches were set out to receive the bodies of the drowned. Sailors who went overboard bearing gold were particularly well received; Ran loved gold, and used its gleam to illuminate the submarine hall. Ran and Aegir had nine beautiful giantess daughters, the Wave Maidens, with whom Odin mated to produce (from all the mothers simultaneously) the god Heimdall.

Aegir himself was one of the brothers of Loki and Kari. He, too, seems to have been unpopular among the Vikings, because of his perceived delight in swooping over the tops of the waves to capsize ships and seize their crews.

Once Aegir and Ran were relaxing in their hall when Thor and Tyr burst in. The gods of Asgard had run out of mead: Thor demanded that Aegir and Ran should swiftly do some brewing to end this shortage. Aegir was not best pleased by Thor's demand, but said that he would try his hardest if Thor could only produce a cauldron or kettle large enough for Aegir to brew sufficient of the stuff. The god replied that this would be no problem, and Tyr chipped in to mention that his father, the giant Hymir, possessed a suitably huge cauldron. Thor and Tyr went to the home of Hymir but found that he wasn't there; instead there were two women. One of these was Tyr's grandmother, now transmuted into a hag with 900 heads. The other was Tyr's mother, and was lovely; she brought the two gods mugs of ale and suggested that, after they'd drunk it, they should conceal themselves under a pair of Hymir's cauldrons; she warned them that his glance was so powerful that it could kill. Almost immediately afterwards, Hymir entered his hall, looking around with a venomous gaze; all of the rafters split except, fortunately, the one that had been supporting the cauldrons hanging over the two gods. Hymir welcomed his visitors and gave them food, killing three cows, two of which Thor ate. The giant was

somewhat upset by this, and told Thor that the following morning they would go fishing together, using their own bait. Thor responded by chopping of the head of one of Hymir's cattle, Himinibrioter, to use as a bait.

The god and the giant rowed out to sea. Thor was looking for the Midgard Snake (Jormungand), and frequently he dipped his fingers beneath the boat to search for it. Even though he had the bull's head, the god was unsuccessful; Hymir, on the other hand, fetched up two whales. Then Thor caught the Midgard Snake, stretching his feet against the base of the ship. His feet went right through, and the giant panicked: he cut the line so that the snake sank back to the depths of the ocean.

Thor, infuriated, hit Hymir with his hammer. The giant was fortunately unharmed and the two of them waded ashore: Thor carried the boat they had been sailing in while the giant carried his two whales. They shared the whales for breakfast. Then the god attempted to prove his strength by throwing a pewter beaker against the giant's forehead. Hymir, impressed by this demonstration, told Thor that he could take away the cauldron. This was how Aegir gained a cauldron large enough to brew mead for all the gods.

Another tale of Aegir concerns the banquet he offered to the gods, whom he invited down to his hall at the bottom of the sea. The gods accepted the invitation happily, but regretted the absence from the feast of Balder. Loki, who had used Hodur to murder Balder, was likewise absent but then, to the gods' dismay, appeared. He took pleasure in slandering them all, Sif in particular.

Njord started off as one of the Vanir; he was brought, along with his children Frey and Freya, to Asgard as a hostage at the end of the war between the Aesir and the Vanir. Like Aegir he was a sea god; his special responsibilities were the sea near to the shore and the wind off the sea, as well as fishing and trade. From his hall, Nôatûn, he worked to calm the tempests created far out at sea by Aegir. Despite the fact that their responsibilities differed, Njord in due course took over the Vikings' allegiance from Aegir – aside from anything else, he was seen as a much more beneficent god than Aegir, even though later he was regarded as responsible for storms at sea, as Aegir had been. He was also thought of as being very handsome, a quality that was never widely attributed to Aegir.

The first wife of Njord was Nerthus; some myths equate Nerthus with Frigga, but this cannot have been true because Nerthus was one of the Vanir. Once Njord came to Asgard he had to look around for a new wife. His prayers were answered when, one day, a young giantess called Skadi arrived in Asgard from her home in Thrymheim. Her father had been the giant Thiassi (see Chapter 1), who had been responsible for kidnapping the goddess Idun; the gods had slain Thiassi after Loki had succeeded in rescuing Idun, and now Skadi wanted some form of reparation. She can be regarded as the Norse equivalent of the Greek Diana: she was associated with hunting and winter. She was also very lovely – but vengeful for the death of her father. The Aesir admitted that she had a valid cause, and offered to give her gold, but she was so furious that she demanded a life in return for the life of her father. The Aesir would have been in trouble had it not been for Loki, who capered and danced (at one point tying his scrotum to a goat) until the giantess's features melted into a smile; the gods then took advantage of her mellowness, pointing to the constellation which they had created from her father's eyes. They added that, rather than kill one of them, she could instead select from among their number a husband – provided that she would be willing to do so through examination of their naked feet alone. (The chronology of these events in Asgard is given in a different order in different sources.) Perhaps there had been a lot of mead flowing, but she agreed to this condition and looked around for the prettiest pair of feet she could see. And there was a pair of sumptuously formed feet! She assumed they must belong to Balder, the fairest of all the gods, whom she had earlier seen and taken a fancy to. To her horror she discovered that in fact she had selected Njord, and so they had to be married.

In fact, she and Njord had a fine honeymoon in Asgard; all of the Aesir went out of their way to make her feel honoured. Afterwards Njord took her back to Nôatûn – where the trouble started. Although the couple were still fond of each other, Skadi couldn't tolerate the sound of the breakers, the screams of the gulls and the harsh cries of the seals. She told Njord that she would never have another good night's sleep again unless he took her back to Thrymheim. He was so entranced by her that he readily agreed that they could spend nine nights out of every dozen (or nine months of each year – sources differ) there, returning to Nôatûn only for the other three. Unfortunately, he soon came to detest Thrymheim because he was kept awake each night by the din of the frequent avalanches, the whistle of the wind through the pine trees, the crashing of waterfalls, the crackling of the ice and the howling of the wolves.

Njord and Skadi – equated with the summer and the winter – put up with their privations for some time, she spending the three months of summer by the sea and he remaining with her for the other nine months in her home in the mountains. Eventually, though, they agreed that neither of them could put up with the situation much longer, and so they amicably agreed to separate. Long after, Skadi gave birth to Saeming, the first king of Norway; the father was supposed to have been Odin.

BALDER

Balder was the most beautiful of all the gods. He was a son of Odin and Frigga. His twin brother was Hoder but, while Balder, the god of light, was radiantly handsome, poor Hoder, the god of darkness, was blind and gloomy. Nevertheless, the two brothers were deeply devoted to each other, living together in Balder's hall, Breidablik, along with Balder's wife Nanna.

Balder had runes carved on his tongue – indeed, he could read all runes. He was also a master of herbal medicine, and he could see the future – except, that is, for the truth about his own fate. As he walked Asgard, loved by mortals and gods alike, he talked of his dreams, which were always of the best. But then his demeanour began to change: he walked slumpedly and defeatedly, and the light vanished from his eyes. When the gods asked why this was he explained that his dreams had now become nightmares bearing with them a presentiment of some terrible fate awaiting him. Balder's mother and father took his fears seriously, and Frigga determined to do something to ensure her son's safety. She accordingly elicited from every object in the world – animals, plants, stones, ores, everything – a promise that they would not harm Balder. The only thing whose promise was not given was the mistletoe but, as the goddess's minions pointed out, this plant was too soft, young and puny to do the great Balder any serious harm.

The gods then, on several occasions, had fun in Gladsheim by testing Balder's new-found invulnerability. They threw rocks at him, fired arrows at him, struck at him with axes and swords – nothing had any effect, and there was much hilarity. One god, though, was not so pleased. This was Loki, who for long had been jealous of Balder's popularity. He schemed the radiant god's downfall. Knowing that Frigga had given Balder his apparently complete invulnerability, he nevertheless suspected that there might be a loophole. He therefore changed himself into the form of an old woman and came to Frigga where she sat spinning in her hall. It didn't take him long to discover from the goddess that the mistletoe had failed to be enlisted to her cause.

Loki swiftly left her and went to find a bunch of mistletoe. He stripped away most of the berries and branches to leave one that was long and straight; this he sharpened at one end. He then went to the place where the gods were enjoying themselves throwing objects harmlessly at Balder. Loki's eyes fastened on Hoder, who was doing his

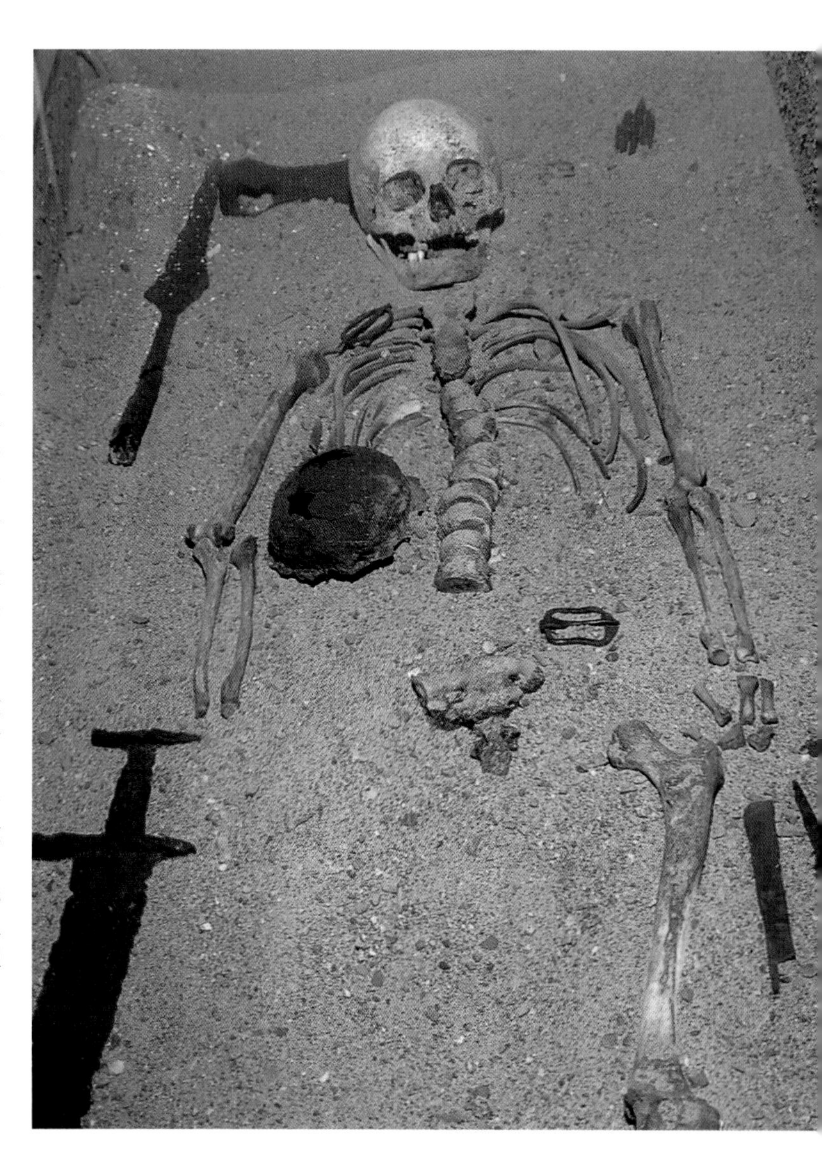

BELOW *To be granted a funeral pyre was a great honour among the Vikings: a lesser honour for a warrior was to be buried alongside his weaponry. Here we see a reconstruction of a grave believed to date from about the tenth century.*

best to join in the fun – but with little success, because of his blindness. He went up to Hoder and offered to help him by guiding his hand if he wanted to throw an object – like this sharpened stick that Loki just happened to have with him. Like a fool Hoder agreed to this plan, threw the dart of mistletoe and killed his brother.

Earlier, Odin, worried like Frigga about Balder's future, had travelled to Hel to consult a prophetess. The prophetess had been interred in the grim otherland for many long years, and was unwilling to stir herself. However, Odin – pretending to be a mortal called Vegtam – used runes and magic spells to force her to answer his questions. He pointed around them to where the denizens of Hel were preparing a feast, and asked who the feast was to be in honour of; she responded that it was being readied to welcome Balder, who would soon be slain by his brother Hoder. Odin was grief-stricken, but found the time to press the prophetess into telling him who would avenge Balder's death. She told him that this would be the task of Vali, a god who would be born to Odin and the earth-goddess Rind. Odin then asked the prophetess a further question: would anyone refuse to weep at Balder's death? She immediately guessed that the person speaking to her had foreknowledge of the future and must therefore be Odin, so she refused to answer this last question and descended once more to her grave. Greatly saddened, Odin returned to Asgard, where he was reassured to discover that Frigga – or so she thought – had extracted the promise of all things not to harm Balder.

When the dart of mistletoe killed Balder the gods were horrified. They could see all too well who had been guilty of the crime – Loki – but at the same time their cruel code dictated that it was Hoder who should die to avenge his brother's death. Nevertheless, it was taboo to shed blood in Gladsheim, and so there was nothing they could immediately do. Frigga, however, was less concerned with vengeance than with the possibility that Balder might – just possibly – be restored to life. She asked the assembled company if there were anyone there who might risk great peril and travel to Hel to ask the goddess of death if there was any way that she might be bribed into releasing Balder back to the land of the living. There was an embarrassingly long silence at this, because the journey to Hel was by no means a pleasant one, but, eventually, when Frigga promised that the brave volunteer would be considered by herself and Odin to be the dearest of all the Aesir, Hermod stepped forward to say that he would perform the task. Soon he was on his way, Odin having lent him his eight-footed horse Sleipnir for the journey.

Once Hermod had departed, it was the duty of the gods to create Balder's funeral pyre, for which they used his ship, Ringhorn, and vast quantities of wood cut from a nearby forest. The gods each added to the pyre their most treasured possessions. In Odin's case this was his ring called Draupnir. As he added it to the pyre he also whispered some words into the dead Balder's ear, but none of the other gods were near enough to hear what those words were.

The preparation of Balder's pyre was too much for the god's wife, Nanna. She collapsed and died, and so was put on Ringhorn beside her husband, to share his fiery fate.

Unfortunately, the gods had loaded Ringhorn so enthusiastically with precious objects that they found themselves incapable of launching the ship. Luckily the mountain giants, who had been watching the whole proceedings, stepped in to offer help. They told the gods that one of their number, a giantess called Hyrrokin, was so strong that she would be able to shove the ship from shore unaided. When the giantess was summoned, she arrived riding an enormous wolf, the pacification of which took the company some while. The Hyrrokin put her shoulder to Ringhorn and with a single heave managed to launch it: the rollers down

RIGHT *Hermod, his initial plea to Hel having failed, bids farewell to Balder and Nanna. At this stage Hermod was optimistic, because he believed that all the world would fulfil Hel's condition for releasing the beautiful god by weeping for him. A nineteenth-century book illustration.*

which it ran caught fire from the friction and all the worlds shook from the force of her effort. The gods staggered and Thor, for one, was so incensed by the perceived insult that he prepared to assault the giantess with his hammer; luckily the other Aesir pointed out that she had been helping them, and his anger diminished. But soon afterwards a dwarf called Lit got in Thor's way and the god responded by kicking him, still alive, to perish in the flames of the pyre.

Meanwhile Hermod was on his way to Hel, in Niflheim. Finally he crossed the bridge over the river Giöll to reach the dreaded realm, and there he was stopped by the hideous guard called Modgud. She told him that his clattering across the bridge had made more noise than a whole army of the dead who had ridden over it the day before: it seemed pretty clear to her that he was alive, and she demanded to know who he was and why he had come here. He answered her honestly, and she told him that Balder and Nanna had already arrived; she gave him directions to the gates of Hel itself. These seemed impassable at first, but Hermod spurred Sleipnir into a colossal leap, which whisked both of them safely into Hel.

BELOW *A Viking sword with a silver and gold hilt found at Dybäck, Skåne. This sword may have been either made in England (the metalwork is typical of that being produced at the time at Winchester) or made in Scandinavia but strongly influenced by the English style.*

When he came to Hel's banquet hall, Eljudnir, Hermod found Balder and Nanna. Balder sadly told him that his quest had been at least partly in vain: he was doomed to remain in this place until Ragnarok. However, there was a chance that Hermod could at least take Nanna back to Asgard. But the goddess refused, saying that she preferred to remain with her husband, come what may. Hermod then spoke with the goddess Hel, telling her that all over the nine worlds people were grieving the death of Balder; in this context, he argued, would it not be just to release the god? She thought about this for a time, and then said that she doubted that the grief was quite as universal as Hermod claimed. However, if everything everywhere, living or dead, could prove its sorrow by weeping for the death of Balder she would be prepared to let him and Nanna go. Mind you, should a single person, animal, plant or object refuse to weep, she would hold onto Balder until the end of time. This particular stricture did not much concern Hermod, who knew – or so he thought – that everything and everyone mourned Balder, and so he was happy as he made his way back to Asgard.

Frigga and the other gods sent messengers to every part of the nine worlds to inform all things of what must be done to save Balder. Soon the weeping was universal – even the vilest things of the worlds were sobbing for the loss of the light-god. There was only one dissident, a giantess called Thok. When the messengers told her what she should do she simply mocked them, saying that she'd never much cared for Balder during his life and saw no reason why Hel should not hold onto him forever. Gloomily the messengers returned to Asgard, where at once the gods realized that the news was not good. Soon they guessed that Thok had in fact been Loki in disguise.

Even though Loki had now twice, in effect, murdered Balder, it still seemed to the gods important that Balder's death be avenged by the death of Hoder. Odin therefore paid suit to Rind, a goddess of the frozen earth. She, however, was less than flattered by his attentions, perhaps feeling that it was rather insulting to her that he should merely wish to use her as breeding stock to produce Vali, the avenger of the prophecy. In the end she consented, however, and the eventual result was a baby boy who grew so rapidly from the moment of his birth that on the very first night of his life Vali came to Asgard and slew Hoder with an arrow.

FREY

Frey was one of the Vanir who came to Asgard as a hostage at the end of the struggle between the Vanir and the Aesir; he was the son of Njord and the twin brother of Freya, whom at one point he also married. He was a fertility god and the god of summer, and the cult associated with him seems to have been pretty unpleasant, involving such practices as human sacrifice. His name is often given as Freyr. He was connected with the image of the boar because of his own magical boar Gullinbursti (made by the dwarfs Sindri and Brock at Loki's request); this creature had shining bristles that lit up the world as it flew through the air. Frey also owned the ship Skidbladnir (fashioned by the dwarf Dvalin, again at Loki's request), which could fly through the air and, although large enough to carry all the gods, their horses and their equipment, could, when not in use, be folded up and put in a pocket. Another useful possession was his sword, which under its own motivation would start slaying his enemies as soon as it was drawn from its sheath. His horse was called Blodughofi. His hall was in Alfheim, the realm of the light elves.

Frey is regarded as one of the three major Norse gods – the other two being, of course, Odin and Thor – yet there are surpringly few tales about him. The most important concerns his love for a frost giantess, Gerda, the daughter of Gymir and Angrboda. Frey first caught sight of her when he was trespassing on Hlidskialf, Odin's great throne from where everything in the nine worlds was visible. Gerda was a figure of pulsating light (she is often associated with the Aurora Borealis, or Northern Lights), and Frey was instantly stricken with lust for her. For ages afterwards he pined, until Njord, worried for his son's welfare, decided to do something about it. Njord summoned his best servant, Skirnir, and told him to find out what was the matter.

Skirnir quizzed Frey and eventually got the truth out of him. The god realized only too well that the union he wanted to seek with Gerda would be unconscionable to gods and mortals alike, yet still he craved her. So he asked Skirnir to go to Gerda and attempt to woo her; the servant agreed on condition that Frey lend him his sword and his horse. He took with him also eleven of the golden apples of eternal youth as well as Odin's magic ring Draupnir.

Blodughofi bore Skirnir swiftly to Jotunheim, where he found that Gymir's hall was surrounded by curtains of coruscating flame; the servant merely spurred the horse to greater speed, and the two of them shot through the fire. They found that the hall was guarded by huge, horrific hounds, who set up such a howling that Gerda was alerted to their arrival.

BELOW *Twelfth-century tapestry from Skog Church, Hålsingland, Sweden, showing the battle between Scandinavian paganism (on the left) and the insurgent Christianity (on the right). The three figures on the left are believed to represent the gods Odin, Thor and Frey.*

She realized at once that the visitor had been sent by Frey, who had slain her brother Beli in a brawl, but politely asked him in for a horn of mead before sending him on his way. He, however, had other plans, and immediately began to urge Frey's suit – to which she responded forthrightly. Skirnir then tried to bribe her with the apples and with Draupnir, to which she replied in both cases with equal frankness. (The business with the apples, by the way, suggests a link between Gerda and the goddess Idun. It's possible that the two characters were originally one and the same.)

RIGHT *Tenth-century cross fragment found at Michael, Isle of Man, Britain, apparently showing Frey and Gerda. She is probably the birdheaded figure and he the tethered stallion.*

Skirnir abandoned the subtle approach and told her that he would chop her head off if she did not agree to obey Frey's summons. This time she told him that she wasn't scared by his threats and that her father, on getting home, would take great pleasure in taking Skirnir apart. The servant finally used his deadliest threat. Carved on his staff were runes, and he used the magical power of these to lay on her a curse so vile that she was terrified into acquiescence. Refuse and, forever afterwards, he told her, she would be devoured by lust yet remain celibate; be consumed by hunger yet find that all food tasted brackish to her; be confined by Hel's gates and forced to watch that miserable prospect, all the while knowing that she was becoming a repulsive hag. The only way to avoid this miserable fate was to accede to Frey's demands.

This she agreed to do, but said that she would not meet the god for nine nights yet. Frey somehow managed to live through this interminable time and finally the two married. Despite the shocking way in which she had been treated – the whole business, because of the threats, was essentially rape – she came to love him, bearing his child Fiolnir.

A story of the cult of Frey is worth repeating, even though probably quite apocryphal. It was the practice to carry around a carved image of the god on a cart, accompanied by a priestess, so that the faithful could make offerings and sacrifices to it and therefore ensure good harvests and fertile marriages. It is said that in the 11th century a Norwegian called Gunnar Helming found himself, for some reason, the only person near the cart – apart from the god's lovely young priestess. Helming suddenly had a Good Idea. Thereafter the people visited by the cart were astonished to discover that the wooden figure of the god had miraculously transformed itself into an apparently living young man. The god's enduring characteristic of fertility was in due course evidenced by the changing shape of the priestess. Moreover, this incarnation of the god was willing to walk among mortals and share their food and drink, so they were only too pleased to comply when he suggested that precious gems and coins might make more fitting tributes to him than their previous somewhat tedious offerings and sacrifices. Eventually the Norwegian king, Olaf Tryggvason, heard about this 'miracle', and soon afterwards the god's image became wooden once more.

ABOVE *A bronze statuette from Lunda, Sweden, of Frey. His role as a fertility god is extremely obvious.*

FREYA

To call Freya a fertility goddess is to euphemize: she was the goddess of sex. Daughter of Njord and twin sister of Frey, she was one of the three Vanir who came to Asgard as hostages at the end of the war between the Vanir and the Aesir; there is some confusion between her and Frigga. The Aesir were so enchanted by her beauty that they granted to her the realm of Folkvang and the hall Sessrymnir; this latter was so well built that it was regarded as impregnable unless the doors were opened by Freya herself. Her chariot was pulled either by her boar Hildisvini or by a number of cats. She owned a falcon coat which she could use to fly around the world in the guise of that bird. Horses were involved with her cult, for reasons, it appears, of orgiastic sex. Besides her role in terms of sex and beauty she had a somewhat grimmer aspect, because she often led parties of Valkyries down to fetch the dead from battlefields, bringing them back to her hall so that they could enjoy all the benefits of the afterlife.

Her first husband was called Od (or Odur), but he deserted her, and thereafter she wept golden tears of grief at all opportunities – such as there were, for her life thereafter was one of unbridled promiscuity. Counting her various conquests is a fraught matter, but we can list her brother Frey (it's possible that the two of them were originally a single god, and that the tale of their sexual relations represents an explanation of the way that, by the time the Eddas were being written, they had become two), Odin and other gods, a man called Ottar (*see* Chapter 1), not to mention four very important dwarfs – see below. When, at his *flyting*, Loki cast certain doubts upon her virtue, it is hard not to agree with his accusations. The gods were not alone in looking on her with a merry grin: the giant Hrungnir, during his bet with Odin, admitted that, while he'd prefer Sif, he'd be quite happy to make do with Freya. She did have her standards, though: she refused to sleep with Hrungnir and likewise with the giant Thrym, even though in the case of the latter she was encouraged to do so by Loki and Thor.

Thrym had stolen Thor's hammer, which was bad news for the gods of Asgard. Loki borrowed Freya's falcon skin and flew over the world to try to ascertain who the thief might be; at last he discovered that the culprit was this rather unprepossessing giant, who said that he had buried Miölnir many miles beneath the surface of the Earth and would not surrender it until Freya had been delivered up to him as his bride. Loki thought this was a fair exchange and so, on his return to Asgard, he proposed it to Freya, seconded by Thor. Freya's fury was spectacular to behold, so the gods had to try another tack.

RIGHT *Arthur Rackham's vision of the female sex goddess Freya.*

Heimdall came up with a possible solution. He pointed out that the problem was really Thor's and Loki's, and that therefore they should have the responsibility for solving it. He suggested that Thor should dress in Freya's clothing and pretend to be her; Loki should likewise dress in female garb and act as 'Freya's' handmaiden. This the two gods rather reluctantly did, and then they journeyed in a goat-drawn chariot back to Thrym's hall.

The giant – presumably myopic – took the gods to be the beautiful women they pretended they were, and welcomed them to a wedding banquet attended by many other giants and giantesses. He was a little disconcerted when 'Freya', at dinner, demolished an ox, eight large salmon, two barrels of mead and all the sweet dishes set out, but Loki explained that this feat had come about simply because 'Freya' had been pining for Thrym for days, and hadn't been able to eat a thing. Next Thrym tried to steal a kiss from 'Freya' but was rocked backwards on his feet by the glare he received from his putative bride. Not to worry, explained Loki: that was just a burning look of passion. The giant's sister asked about the dowry but was ignored: Thrym was convinced that a night of mad ecstasy awaited him. He called for the hammer and commanded that it be placed between 'Freya's' knees as a symbol of their marriage. This was a foolish mistake, because Thor proceeded to use Miölnir to slaughter not only Thrym but also every other giant and giantess on the premises.

Freya's exploits with the four dwarfs involved her more directly. She was exploring the world one night when she came across the smithy of four dwarfs called the Brisings, or Brosings. They were in the process of making an ornament (the Brisingamen, generally assumed to have been a necklace) of such exquisite beauty that Freya could hardly believe her eyes: gems and polished metals mingled and glimmered so that it seemed almost to be liquid flame. There was nothing that the goddess would not do to possess that treasure: when the dwarfs declared that she could have it only if she spent a night of lust with each of them in turn she readily assented.

What she hadn't realized was that Loki had seen her leaving Asgard and had followed her. The wizard of lies rushed to tell Odin of her prostitution, and the king of the Aesir was furious – he longed for Freya himself, so to discover that she was disporting herself with four dwarfs hurt him grievously. At the same time, though, the bulk of his wrath was reserved for Loki, the malicious messenger bearing bad news. He told Loki that he was to steal the Brisingamen from Freya: otherwise there would be terrible punishments in store. Loki pointed out that her hall Sessrymnir could be entered only with Freya's permission, and that the command was therefore an unfair one, but Odin's only response was to become even more threatening, so Loki decided that he would do his best.

The wizard of lies had the advantage that he could change his shape at will. It took him a long time before he discovered a tiny aperture through which he could squirm his way into Sessrymnir, but in the end he managed it. There he saw the lovely form of Freya sprawled on her bed but, alas, in such a position that he was unable to reach the clasp of the Brisingamen. He fidgeted and fumbled for a while and then turned himself into a flea; lighting on Freya's breast he bit her, so that she turned over in her sleep, exposing the clasp. Loki swiftly returned to his own form and let himself out of Sessrymnir, taking the Brisingamen.

What happened next is a matter of debate. According to some versions, the god Heimdall – who could hear even grass growing – heard Loki as he was perpetrating the theft and pursued him. The two waged a battle involving considerable shape-shifting until Loki was finally persuaded that, if he valued his life, he should return the Brisingamen to Freya. An alternative is that Loki, as instructed, took the necklace to Odin, who accepted it. When, next morning, Freya discovered the loss of her treasure, she realized that the only possible culprit had to be Loki, and so she went straight to Odin to complain, saying that if he had had anything to do with the theft he was ... well, the women of the Norse myths could, as ever, be blunt. His response was not unreasonable: she was calling him a degenerate, yet had she not debased herself by whoring to the dwarfs in order to obtain the Brisingamen? He therefore charged her that, by way of punishment, she should in future adopt as part of her responsibilities the spreading of warfare and misery – otherwise he would keep the Brisingamen forever. Freya was ashamed, but agreed to the bargain: she needed the necklace almost more than she needed her life itself.

Freya, as noted, was no paragon of virtue. It might have been expected that she should have been reviled for her sexuality – especially in a primitive society, where women are commonly expected to be both chaste and willing. Yet she was one of the most important and respected members of the Norse pantheon. Possibly the Vikings recognized a sexual equality – a *fairness* in their attitudes towards the behaviour of the two different sexes – that might well be adopted by many of the 'developed' societies of today.

FRIGGA

Second wife of Odin and mother of Balder, Frigga was the most imimportant goddess in the Norse pantheon. Because of her connection with fertility, there was obviously a marked overlap between her responsibilities and those of Frey and Freya. It seems likely that all three initially had the same identity before Frigga was separated from Frey/Freya and then these two likewise became divided from each other. However, the chronology of all this is hard to establish: in some branches of Teutonic myth Frigga and Freya are regarded as identical – both, for example, have falcon skins that they can wear to fly around the nine worlds – yet Frey has his own personality. However, Frigga seems always to have been a much gentler fertility goddess than Freya: where the latter represented rampant sex and was associated with a good deal of violence, Frigga was much more associated with that aspect of fertility related to placid domesticity, conjugal happiness and maternity – she was often represented with a bunch of keys at her waist, the symbol of the good housewife. It should not be assumed, however, that she was a consistently obedient spouse: the myths suggest that, early on, she enjoyed adultery with Odin's brothers Ve and Vili and later, often enough, she would work to trick Odin in order to advance the cause of someone she preferred. Frigga's hall was called Fensalir, and she spent much of her time sitting there spinning golden thread or brightly coloured clouds.

Her parentage is something of a conundrum. According to some versions she was the daughter of Odin and the very early goddess Jörd; alternatively she was Jörd's sister, both of them being daughters of the giantess Fiorgyn. Either way, she became Odin's wife and, alone among all the other deities, was permitted to sit upon Hlidskialf, his great throne from which one could see everything that was going on in all the worlds. In addition to this shared omniscience she had also the ability to foretell the future, but she was ever loth to tell what she saw there. She was, perhaps, a little too fond of glorious attire for her own good, but that seems to have been her only notable sin.

It was a sin that could get her into trouble, though, as we discover from one tale (which bears strong resemblances to the story of Freya and the Brisingamen). Odin had had erected a statue of himself and, never modest, had placed a piece of gold inside it. Frigga was keen to have made for her by the dwarfs a magnificent necklace,

LEFT *Nineteenth-century book illustration showing Frigga with some of her handmaidens. These handmaidens were goddesses in their own right.*

and so she stole the piece of gold for the dwarfs to use. The product of their labours was of amazing beauty – so much so that Odin fell even further in love with her than he had been before. However, he was less than amused when, a little later, he discovered that it had been made from gold stolen from his statue. He immediately summoned the dwarfs and demanded that they tell him who was the thief, but they refused to betray the secret. Odin next composed runes so that the statue would be given the power of speech: it was to be placed high on a gate, and sooner or later would tell the truth of the theft to the world.

Frigga was terrified to hear of all this. She summoned her attendant Fulla and instructed the hapless servant to find some way of avoiding Odin's discovery of the crime and his subsequent wrath. Fulla soon returned in the company of a revoltingly ugly dwarf, who promised that he would stop the statue from speaking if Frigga would sleep with him. Hardly sooner said than done, and the following morning the dwarf went to the gate, magically made the guards fall into a deep sleep and shattered the statue, so that Odin would never be able to reconstitute it and discover the truth it was willing to tell.

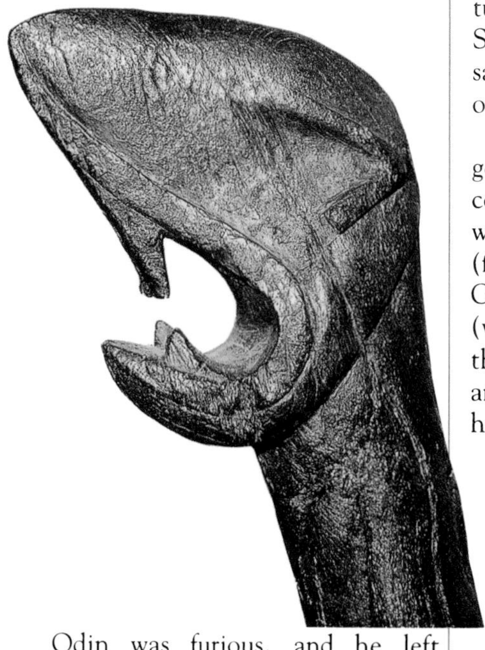

RIGHT *A superb animal head, probably from the bow of a Viking longship, discovered during recent dredging of the River Scheldt, Belgium.*

Odin was furious, and he left Asgard and his favourite wife for seven long months. During this time, perhaps assuming that Odin had abdicated his throne, Ve and Vili took power – and also, according to some sources, enjoyed Frigga's sexual favours. However, they did not have the powers of Odin, and so both Asgard and Midgard were mightily relieved when the great god returned to reassume his throne.

Frigga and Odin often walked Midgard together – although she was a much less frequent traveller than he was. A major legend of one of these ventures concerns Agnar and Geirrod (*see* Chapter 1); here Frigga successfully tricked her husband. Another tale of her wiles concerns a war between the Vandals and the Winilers – a war that the heavenly couple had watched with interest from Hlidskialf. Odin was very much on the side of the Vandals, whereas Frigga much preferred the Winilers. One night Frigga asked Odin which of the two sides would win the war on the morrow and he, evasively, said that it would be whichever he first saw. His stratagem was that, because of the direction in which his couch was turned, the first army to meet his gaze would necessarily be that of the Vandals. But he hadn't reckoned with Frigga's cunning. She simply waited until he was fast asleep and then turned his bed around the other way. Sure enough, when Odin awoke he saw the Winilers and, a man of honour, he gave them the victory.

Frigga is identified with many other goddesses in various mythologies. A complete list would be impossible: here we can note Bertha, Brechta, Eástre (from which the term 'Easter' comes), Gode, Hlodin, Holda, Horn, Nerthus (who also features in the Norse pantheon), Ostara and Wode. As the archetypal Earthmother, of course, she has parallels in almost all mythologies.

HEIMDALL

Heimdall is a somewhat enigmatic member of the Norse pantheon, in that it is unclear whether he was a member of the Aesir or of the Vanir. The identity of his father is uncertain (it was probably Odin), but his mothers were nine giantesses called the Wave Maidens (*see* Chapter 1), themselves daughters of Aegir, who together managed to produce this single son. A gynaecological mystery. Heimdall, the White God, the Golden-Toothed, had a trumpet called the Giallar-horn whose tone could be heard throughout the nine worlds; he will use it to announce the onset of Ragnarok. This instrument symbolized the crescent Moon; the god sometimes hung it on one of Yggdrasil's branches and other times put it in Mimir's well, where it lay alongside Odin's lost eye, a symbol of the full Moon. His hall in Asgard was called Himinbiorg and his horse Gull-top (Gold-tuft). He was regarded as the epitome of beauty, brightness, wisdom and goodness.

Heimdall had the task of guarding the rainbow bridge Bifrost to stop the giants attempting to invade Asgard. In order to make this job easier, the gods gave him incredibly acute senses – a sparrow falling would have sounded like a thunderclap to him, because he could hear the wool growing on a sheep's back – and the ability to require little or no sleep. In addition, along with Bragi, he welcomed heroes to Valhalla.

Clearly Heimdall shared many of the attributes of Balder. He also had, like Odin, a habit of wandering among mortals and siring children. In so doing, he started off the lines of the three different classes of human beings. The three legends involved are very much the same. In the first of them, Heimdall – pretending to be a mortal called Riger or Rig – visited a rickety old hut where a husband and wife called Ai (Great Grandfather) and Edda (Great Grandmother) lived. They invited him in for a fairly unpalatable meal, and he ended up staying with them for three nights. Each night he slept between the couple on their bed, and presumably Ai was a sound sleeper because, nine months later, Edda gave birth to Heimdall's son Thrall. The boy was not the most physically prepossessing of fellows, but he was mightily strong and was willing to work from dawn until dusk. He married a woman called Thir who was likewise a willing worker and soon they gave birth to a plentiful brood of children, who were the first members of the class of serfs.

Meanwhile Heimdall had been repeating exactly the same act elsewhere. Afi (Grandfather) and Amma (Grandmother) welcomed him for three nights in similar circumstances, although the food was somewhat better and certainly there was plenty of it. Nine months later a boy called Karl appeared; he proved to be an excellent farmer and, with his wife Snor, who was prudent and, it seems, notable for the ampleness of her bosom. Their children became the first of the peasant class.

The food was much better when Heimdall stayed three nights with Fadir (Father) and Modir (Mother); the accompanying wines were first-class, too. Perhaps for these reasons, the result of the clandestine mating, Jarl, was delicate, handsome and refined. He soon learned to use the runes and to be very good at killing people; he and his aristocratic wife Erna became the ancestors of the ruling and warrior classes. The youngest of their children was a boy called Konur or Kon, who was if anything even more remarkable than his father. He had the strength of eight men and could speak with the birds, douse fires, still the sea, blunten blades and ease troubled hearts. Unfortunately, because of the fragmented nature of the surviving manuscripts we know little more about Konur except that he, or one of his descendants, became the first king of Denmark.

BELOW *Part of a carved cross slab found at Jurby, Isle of Man, Britain, depicting Heimdall blowing his horn to summon the gods to Ragnarok.*

Heimdall's wisdom was useful to the Aesir. When the giant Thrym demanded to have Freya as his bride if he were to return Thor's hammer, it was Heimdall who proposed the plan whereby Thor and Loki travelled in female garb to Thrym's hall. In fact, he seems to have been a champion of Freya's somewhat frail virtue, because there are fragments of another myth in which he wrestled with Loki for the return to her of the Brisingamen. The two gods indulged in a battle of shape-changing (a version of which, fought between Merlin and Madam

Mim, appeared in the 1963 Disney movie *The Sword in the Stone*). Loki became a flame and Heimdall a cloud to rain on him; Loki became a polar bear and prepared to swallow the water but Heimdall became another bear and attacked him; both of them became seals and struggled in the water, with Heimdall being the eventual winner. As he will be in the very last resort: Loki, bound until Ragnarok, will eventually be slain by Heimdall, although the White God will lose his own life at the same time.

BELOW *Detail of an eighth-century stela found in Gotland, Sweden, showing a Scandinavian warrior on horseback.*

IDUN

Idun, the wife of Bragi, was the goddess of Spring and the guardian of the gods' eternal youth. This youthfulness was incorporated in the form of golden apples, which she kept in a magic basket; no matter how many apples she removed from the basket to give to the gods during their feasting there was always still the same number left. Idun reserved her apples exclusively for the gods, who therefore remained young and vigorous while all other beings grew old and died. Naturally the apples were coveted by the dwarfs and giants, and this fact led to Idun's major adventure.

Odin, Hoenir and Loki were one day wandering in the world when they became hungry. Spotting a nearby herd of cattle they promptly killed one of the beasts, made a fire and roasted it. However, when in due course they kicked away the embers of the fire and sat down to eat they discovered that the ox was hardly cooked at all. They tried again, but still without success. At that moment a huge eagle spoke to them, saying that its magic had been stopping the flames from cooking the flesh, and offering the three Aesir a deal: the eagle would remove the spell so that the gods could cook their dinner, but they were to give the bird as much to eat as it wanted. This seemed fair enough to the Aesir, and the bargain was struck.

They hadn't reckoned on the eagle's appetite. It took the shoulder joints and the rump of the ox for its own portion, leaving the gods with not very much. This drove Loki into a fury, and he picked up a branch and plunged it into the bird's back. The eagle dropped the meat and flew off, still impaled by the branch, which Loki now found his hands were stuck to. Low over the ground they flew, so that Loki was bumped and dragged along, being bruised and battered and cut and torn until he was in agony. He screamed for mercy, and finally the bird agreed that it would release him if he would promise to do something for it: lead Idun out from the safety of Asgard so that she could be captured. Loki rapidly agreed to do this and the eagle – who was in fact a giant called Thiassi in disguise – let him go.

Some while later Loki went to Idun and told her that he had discovered a grove where apples grew that were in every respect like her magic ones. Credulously she accepted his offer to lead her to this place. However, as soon as they were out of Asgard he deserted her. Thiassi, again in his guise as an eagle, swooped down from the skies and carried the goddess away to his hall, crowing that at last he had captured the gift of eternal youth. He was deeply chagrined to discover that Idun – although she had always seemed such an ineffectual goddess – refused to let him have a single apple.

It was not long before things at Asgard began to go badly wrong. The Aesir, who had initially assumed the Idun had gone away with her minstrel husband Bragi on one of his ramblings, became very worried about her, especially when they started wrinkling with age and losing their reason to senility. Odin summoned the Aesir to a conference, and when they were gathered they discovered that all were present except Loki. Even their aging brains didn't take long to work out that the wizard of lies had been up to some more of his mischief, and their suspicions were confirmed when one of the servants of Heimdall announced that, the last time he'd seen Idun, she'd been going over Bifrost with Loki.

The other gods made it plain to Loki in no uncertain manner that, unless he got them out of this mess – and quickly – his end was not going to be an enjoyable one. He therefore borrowed Freya's falcon-skin and flew off to Thiassi's hall, Thrymheim. Luckily the giant wasn't there. Loki turned Idun into a nut and, clutching her in his claws, flew back towards Asgard.

When Thiassi returned and found the goddess gone he was furious. At once he adopted the form of a huge eagle once more, and set off in hot pursuit of Loki. And so it was that, when the gods looked out from Asgard to watch for Loki's return, they saw not only the falcon but also, in chase, the great black eagle. The Aesir swiftly gathered up a great heap of fuel. As the falcon flopped exhaustedly into Asgard bearing its precious burden, they set light to the fuel so that Thiassi flew straight into a wall of flames. Burnt and stunned, the eagle crumpled to the ground, where it was swiftly despatched by the Aesir. Later, however, mellowed by a feast of apples and feeling young and fresh again, they threw Thiassi's eyes up into the sky to form a constellation, a tribute which they reckoned would placate any vengeful relatives of the dead giant. (They thought wrong. His daughter Skadi came to Asgard to demand recompense. However, she relented and instead ended up marrying Njord.)

Another legend about Idun has largely been lost to us. It seems that one day she accidentally fell into Niflheim where she went into a frozen and horrified coma. Odin sent Bragi and a couple of the other gods down there after her with some skins to warm her, but they were unable to get her to respond. In the end Bragi told the other two to leave them there, and that he would keep his wife company until she was ready to go. What happened next is, sadly, unrecorded.

LOKI

There are far more tales about Loki than about any of the other gods. The reader is referred to the index for reference to those legends involving Loki that are not discussed here.

Loki, the wizard of lies, the god of mischief and deception, is the most fascinating of all the members of the Norse pantheon, not just because of his wiles and cunning but because he shows that rarest of things in a mythological personage, character development. Although never to be trusted, in the early days he helped Odin create the world and then was useful to the other gods on countless occasions. Later his mischief took on a more malevolent nature, as when he chopped off the hair of Sif (*q.v.*). But he then became actively evil, arranging for the murder of Balder (*q.v.*) and committing other hideous crimes – as we shall see.

Loki married three times. His first wife was called Glut and she bore him the children Einmyria and Eisa; all three names refer to fire and its warmth, since in one of his aspects Loki was the charming god of the fireside, relaxation and leisure. For this reason the peasant classes maintained he was the greatest of all the gods – understandably, because the few moments of leisure they had must have been as precious as gold dust to them. The offspring of his second marriage were less pleasant. This time his wife was a giantess called Angrboda, and their children were Hel, the goddess of death, Jormungand, the World Serpent, and Fenris, the monstrous wolf who came to threaten the very existence of the gods. Loki's third wife was the beautiful Sigyn; their two children were Narvi and Vali (not to be confused with the god called Vali).

As noted, Loki could be very useful to the gods. One such instance occurred when they made a foolish promise. A giant came to Asgard and offered to build a protective wall around it. There was some haggling over his fee, but eventually the gods agreed that he could have the hand of Freya if he could complete the task within a single winter, six months – something they believed to be impossible. Their reasoning was that they could get at least part of the wall built for nothing, saving themselves a deal of hard work. They hadn't reckoned on the giant's horse, a doughty animal that was capable of performing prodigious feats of labour, never ceasing by night or day. As time passed, it began to dawn on the gods that it was very likely that the giant might indeed succeed in his task; then they realized that it was a certainty, and, not wishing to lose Freya, they turned to Loki for help. The last morning of the six months came and there were only a few stones left to be put in place. Then out from Asgard danced a sexy little mare; she whinnied suggestively at the giant's horse and then, with a swish of her tail, danced off into the forest. Suddenly the giant didn't have his equine assistant any longer, and saw that he had no chance of finishing the wall.

RIGHT *The western face of Gosforth Cross, Cumbria, Britain, which dates from the tenth century. At the bottom is the chained Loki beneath the serpent; Sigyn, above the serpent, is catching the venom in a cup. Above this scene is Odin, and at the top we see Heimdall being attacked by two dragons.*

He was dejected about having been cheated, and Thor killed him. When the mare returned to Asgard she was the proud mother of a foal, the eight-legged horse Sleipnir, which became Odin's mighty steed.

Another instance of Loki's helpfulness occurred when the giantess Skadi came to Asgard seeking vengeance for the slaying of her father Thiassi. Loki entertained her with lewd knockabout humour until she relented and became the wife of Njord (*q.v.*).

The trickster could also befriend humans. A peasant gambled on a game of chess with the giant Skrymsli: if the giant won his prize was to be the peasant's son, unless the boy could be hidden so well that he could not be found. And, of course, the giant did win. The grief-stricken peasant turned to Odin for help, and the god changed the lad into a tiny grain of wheat. However, Skrymsli immediately saw through this subterfuge, went to the field in which the boy was concealed and mowed the wheat until at last he came to the right grain. Odin snatched it from his hand at the last moment, returned the boy to his parents and then lost interest in the whole matter. Next the peasants turned to Hoenir, who transformed the boy into a tiny down feather which he placed on the breast of a swan. Again the giant saw through the trick, and would have eaten the down feather had not Hoenir puffed it away from his mouth.

Like Odin, this god then lost interest, so the peasants begged Loki to assist them. He turned the boy into a single egg in a fish's roe. Skrymsli managed to see through this ruse as well, and after some inspired angling was able to draw from the sea the very fish in which the boy was hidden. The giant was picking through the roe looking for the correct egg when Loki snatched it from his grasp and ran away with it. He turned the egg back into the boy again, and told him to flee for home but to make sure, as he did so, to pass through the boathouse where Loki, having taken precautions against failure, had rigged up a sharp spike.

ABOVE *Part of a Viking cross slab at Maughold, Isle of Man, Britain, showing Loki crouching with the stone with which he is about to kill Otter (with salmon in mouth).*

The boy did as he was told and ran off, and Skrymsli, chasing him, seriously injured himself.

Loki chopped off one of the giant's legs but almost immediately it began to join back on to Skrymsli's torso. Swiftly the god realized that there was magic at work, so he chopped off Skrymsli's other leg and this time placed flint and steel between the limb and the body, thus rendering the magic inoperative, so that the giant bled to death.

But Loki could be randomly cruel. One day he, Odin and Hoenir were out walking when Loki spotted an otter by a riverbank preparing to eat a salmon. The god threw a stone accurately and killed the animal, claiming its salmon for the trio's meal. However, this was no ordinary otter: it was Otter, one of the sons of the dwarfish king Hreidmar. So began the whole miserable business of Andvari's gold, mentioned in Chapter 1.

As we saw, Loki's children by the giantess Angrboda were Hel, Jormungand and Fenris. The marriage had been unauthorized and so he tried to keep the children hidden in a cave, but they grew very rapidly and so it wasn't very long before Odin discovered their existence. The father of the gods determined to get rid of them before they grew so large that they threatened all the world. He cast Hel into Niflheim, in which dismal realm she reigned gloomily as the goddess of death. The snake Jormungand he threw into the sea, where it grew so huge that soon it encircled the entire world and was able to swallow its own tail. Odin was rather alarmed that Loki's offspring could grow so prodigiously, and he looked at Fenris with new nervousness. Might it not be a good idea to try to educate the wolf into the ways of gentleness? He brought Fenris to Asgard.

RIGHT *Thorwald's Cross Slab, at Andreas, Isle of Man, Britain, dating from about the tenth century and showing Odin being attacked by Fenris at Ragnarok.*

The gods were terrified of the beast – all except Tyr, the god of courage, who was therefore given the task of tending him. Still Fenris continued to grow in both size and ferocity. The gods were unwilling to kill the wolf, which had been brought to Asgard as a guest, so they decided to bind him so securely that he would never be able to threaten them again. They got hold of a strong chain called Laeding and set to work. Fenris just grinned: he was confident in his own strength, so he waited until they had finished and then casually snapped the chain into a million pieces. The gods tried again with an even stronger chain, Droma, but the result was much the same, although this time Fenris had to struggle a little harder and longer.

A servant of Frey's called Skirnir was sent to ask the dwarfs to make a tether so strong that nothing could ever break it. They gave him a slender strand, Gleipnir, made out of the sound of a cat's footfall, the voice of a fish and other such intangibles. The gods told Fenris that surely, after his exploits with the chains, he couldn't be scared of embarking on this new test of his strength, but he had inherited some of his father's wiliness and looked at it suspiciously, eventually agreeing to be tied up in it only if one of the gods would put a hand in his (Fenris's) mouth as an earnest that no magic was involved. Nobody was willing to do this except Tyr, who lost his hand when the secured Fenris discovered that he had been duped.

The wolf was then placed beneath the ground, but he howled with such abandon that the gods couldn't stand the noise. To silence him the Aesir put a sword vertically in his mouth, with its point in his palate; blood flowed forth to form a great river. And so Fenris will stay until Ragnarok, when Gleipnir will be sundered and he can exact his revenge on the gods. There is an interesting parallel here with Loki's own fate, as we shall see.

RIGHT *The southern face of Gosforth Cross, Cumbria, Britain. Here we can see, at the bottom, the bound Fenris; above is Odín on horseback.*

Loki's tricks became more and more spiteful. With his lies and his habit of revealing secrets he constantly stirred the gods against each other. One of his worst tricks was the shearing of Sif's (*q.v.*) magnificent hair. It was as a result of this and his wager with Brock and Sindri that Loki suffered the agonies of having his lips stitched up. The gods' lack of sympathy for – indeed, their merriment over – his torment was probably what turned his petty maliciousness into a vindictive lust to destroy them.

Balder (*q.v.*), of course, he did destroy, and thereafter he decided that it would be prudent not to show his face in Asgard for a while. The gods were grief-stricken. In order to try to cheer them up a bit, the sea-god Aegir threw a banquet; naturally enough, Loki was not on the guest list. However, he turned up anyway, contributing to the merriment by murdering one of Aegir's servants and insulting all of the gods in the most vitriolic terms, as recorded in a riveting *flyting* ('insult poem'). Their wrath was intensified by the fact that many of the insults were all too true. Freya, for example, he labelled as a whore because she had slept with the entire male pantheon (including her own brother), uncountable dwarfs, and so on; her response was to tell him that he was lying – but for once, of course, he wasn't. The diatribe continued until Thor threatened to hammer him to death, at which he fled.

The gods decided that enough was enough: something had to be done about Loki. They decided to bind him, much as they had his son Fenris. But first, of course, there was the task of finding him.

Loki was all too well aware that the Aesir would try to track him down. Although he lived quietly in a little shack, he knew that Odin's all-seeing eyes would be able to spot him. He therefore determined that, should the gods come to seek him out, he'd jump into a nearby river and take the form of a salmon. Then he began to worry that the other Aesir might catch on to this ruse: a hook he could, as a highly intelligent salmon, avoid with ease – but what if they used a net? Most nets he would have little trouble in breaking, but perhaps they could make one especially strong ... The thought nagged away at him. He reckoned that he was the cleverest of the gods: if *he* couldn't make such a net then none of the others would be able to. In an attempt to set his mind at rest he gathered cord and set to work.

To his alarm he found that it would indeed be possible to make a net capable of catching him. He was halfway through the task when he perceived that Odin, Thor and Kvasir were approaching his shack. In a panic, he threw the half-finished net on the fire to destroy the evidence, ran off and jumped into the river.

The three vengeful gods looked around the empty shack. It seemed that Loki had left no trace of where he had gone to, but then Kvasir, the wisest of all the gods (*see* Chapter 1), spotted the stranded ashes of the burnt net. After a little thought, he realized that Loki must have turned himself into a fish, and suggested that the trio quickly weave a net and trawl the river.

The first time they threw the net Loki was able to escape: he put himself between two stones so that the net couldn't reach him. The three gods had an inkling that this might have been his stratagem, and so, next time around, they weighted the net. Loki avoided it by jumping over it against

the current, something fish had heretofore never been able to do. However, his leap was seen by the gods, and so they tried again with the weighted net. This time, as Loki jumped over it, Thor was ready and waiting and was able to catch him by the tail.

The three of them dragged him away to bind him – both as punishment for his crimes and to ensure that never again would he plague them. They took him to a deep cavern. Believing that the sins of the fathers should be visited on the children, they induced Loki's son Vali to become a wolf and rip out the throat of his other son, Narvi. From Narvi's corpse they extracted the entrails, and these they used to tie up Loki to three great rocks; as an afterthought they turned the guts into iron, to make doubly sure that Loki would be unable to escape until Ragnarok. Skadi – the giantess whom Loki had charmed so long ago – decided that his fate hadn't been nearly nasty enough. She fetched a serpent and hung it over Loki's head, so that its venom would drip, second after second, into his face for the rest of eternity – until Ragnarok. Naturally, every drop of venom caused him unspeakable pain. Sigyn, Loki's wife, was not only beautiful but also virtuous and faithful. She could have gone back to Asgard, and enjoyed the life of the gods, but instead she resigned herself to staying beside her husband for all the rest of time, catching the drips in a cup held above his face. She is still there. From time to time, however, the cup becomes filled and she has to empty it. During those moments the venom falls onto Loki's face and he screams in agony.

Come Ragnarok, the gods will regret their cruelty.

BELOW *Made from walrus ivory around 1135–1150 and found on the Isle of Lewis, Scotland, these pieces come from a Viking chess set.*

RIGHT *Nineteenth-century book illustration of Odin's wild hunt; traditionally Odin rode on eight-legged Sleipnir for this, but here we can see that the artist has omitted the extra four legs. Gales were considered to be the physical manifestations of Odin leading his wild hunt across the sky.*

ODIN

Odin is often called Allfather, which is the name of the primordial deity who initiated the Creation; in fact, in many of the legends it is assumed that the two gods are one and the same. (The roles played by both Allfather and Odin or by Allfather/Odin in the Creation are discussed in Chapter 2.) This may seem like an inconsistency in the mythology – and probably is – but we should remind ourselves that there is a parallel in Christianity, where Christ is both God and the son of God. A further resemblance to this situation is found in a legend relating how Odin, pierced by a spear, was hanged for nine days and nights from a branch of Yggdrasil as a sacrifice to himself. During this time he learned great wisdoms and invented the runes; he became the patron god of hanged men.

There are many tales in this book about Odin: the reader is referred to the index for most of them. Here we shall look at only a few.

Odin required no food, although he would partake of the gods' heavenly mead. His spear was Gungnir, which always found its mark; in addition, it had the property that any oath sworn upon it could never be broken. He owned the magical golden ring called Draupnir: every ninth night this would shed eight replicas of itself. His steed Sleipnir, a son of Loki (*q.v.*), had eight legs and could travel at colossal speed all over the nine worlds. His high throne in Asgard was called Hlidskialf, and when seated on it Odin could see everything that happened anywhere; Frigga (*q.v.*), his second wife, was allowed to sit here also. (His other two wives were Jörd and Rind.) Further information from the worlds was brought to him by his two ravens, Hugin and Munin, who flew from Asgard each morning and returned each evening. He was the master of

LEFT *Nineteenth-century book illustration depicting Odin and a group of beautiful valkyries welcoming a dead hero to Valhalla. Notice the two ravens and the two wolves.*

LEFT *From the ninth century, the skull of a woman sacrificed at a Viking ship burial at Ballyteare, Isle of Man, Britain. It can be seen that the top of her head was chopped off.*

two wolves, Freki and Geri, which he personally fed with gobbets of raw meat. He was one-eyed because he had drunk from the well of the wise god Mimir (*see* Chapter 1), and had willingly surrendered an eye for the continuing wisdom he received.

He was instrumental in starting the war between the Vanir and the Aesir. A witch called Gullveig – probably one of the Vanir – came to Asgard and explained to Odin and the other Aesir that she was consumed by the lust for gold. The Aesir were revolted by her avariciousness, and determined to put her to death; they tried this three times. The Aesir then gave up their attempts and the witch, now called Heid, was permitted to wander Asgard. (There is a possibility that Heid and Freya were really one and the same.) However, the Vanir were enraged when they heard how she had been treated, and soon it was clear that there must be conflict between the two races of gods. The war began when Odin impatiently threw his great spear at the rallied Vanir.

Odin's halls were Gladsheim, Valaskialf and Valhalla; the last of these is discussed later in this book.

The cult of Odin spread far further eastwards than one might have expected. There is no room here to discuss the matter in detail, but it is worth looking at one aspect. There are mentions in the myths of wives being killed, or killing themselves, at the funerals of their warrior husbands – the death of Nanna at the funeral of Balder (*q.v.*) is one example. This seems to have been a regular habit of the Vikings, because double graves have been found in plenty. The practice seems to have diffused eastward across Europe and Asia, and has obvious connections with the Indian ritual of *suttee*. However, as with so many aspects of cultural archaeology, it is almost impossible to work out the directions in which ideas spread.

Odin was simultaneously a wise, a kind and a cruel god, and as such he may represent human nature – for all of us can be simultaneously wise, kind and cruel.

SIF

Not a lot is known about the goddess Sif. She seems to have been a fertility goddess whose prominence had faded by the time the chroniclers were writing their tales. Thor was her second husband; to her first, an anonymous frost giant, she bore a son called Uller. Her sons by Thor were called Magni and Modi.

The reason for guessing that she was connected with fertility is that she had a mane of beautiful golden hair that reached all the way to the ground; this is taken to represent abundant corn. She was extremely proud of her hair, as was Thor, so neither of them were terribly amused when one night as she slept someone came along and cut it all off. When things like that happened in Asgard, the culprit was invariably Loki. Thor responded to the situation with his usual subtlety, and so a few moments later a battered and bloodied Loki discovered that he'd promised that somehow – anyhow – he'd get Sif a new head of hair from somewhere. No, not a wig: it had to be genuine, growing, golden hair.

Such things are not easy to procure, and Loki knew that he had no alternative but to seek aid from the master craftsmen of the nine worlds, the dwarfs of Svartalfaheim. He went to the smithy of a dwarf called Dvalin and persuaded him to make the hair. The dwarf did a miraculous job (literally: the dwarfs could use rune-magic as much as physical skill in their work) and, despite the fact that all Loki offered by way of payment was a string of empty promises, went on to create also Frey's magic ship Skidbladnir and Odin's magic spear Gungnir. Loki was amazed by the magnificence of these gifts and also by the gullibility of the dwarf, who had done so much for so little payment.

He was on his way back to Asgard when a thought struck him. If one dwarf could be so easily duped,

mightn't others be likewise? No sooner thought than tried! Instants later he was showing the three treasures to two dwarfs called Brock and Sindri (in some versions Eitri) and enthusing to them over how, surely, no dwarf could ever hope again to make anything quite as fine – in fact, the god got so carried away that he bet the two dwarfs that, if they could craft anything better, as judged by the gathered Aesir, they could chop off his head! 'All right,' said the dwarfs smugly, and it was at that moment that Loki realized he might have made a mistake.

Sindri told Brock to keep the bellows blowing consistently, without any pause whatsoever, while he himself went off to mutter the appropriate runes. As Brock worked away an insect flew in and landed on his hand, stinging him very painfully, but he didn't miss a beat. When Sindri reappeared they pulled from the forge Gullinbursti, the great magical boar that Frey would use to ride across the sky. The dwarfs set to work making the next artefact. This time while Sindri was out of the smithy chanting the runes the gadfly reappeared and stung Brock on the cheek. Once again, the doughty dwarf managed to keep up the regular pumping of the bellows – although he must have been becoming pretty suspicious about the shape-changer Loki's reputation for honest wagering. And this time the product of the forge was the magical golden ring (or armlet) Draupnir which, every ninth night, would produce eight others identical with itself; in time it was to become the property of Odin.

LEFT *Discovered in a tenth-century Swedish Viking grave – Arab coins. Clearly the Viking civilization had contacts far beyond the geographical limits we popularly assume.*

Loki realized that these two treasures were almost beyond compare and that there was a very good chance that the Aesir might prefer them to the others. This time, as Brock was pumping away, the gadfly stung him on the eyelid, so that blood ran down into the dwarf's eye. Blinded, he took his hand away from the bellows for just a moment to wipe the blood away. The object the two dwarfs then drew from the forge was the mighty hammer Miölnir, which would of course become the property of Thor. It was perfect in every respect except for the fact that its handle was perhaps just a trifle too short.

Loki and the dwarfs went to Asgard with all six of these wonderful gifts. The god was not particularly worried, because of the imperfection of Miölnir. The gifts were handed out to their various recipients, and the Aesir marvelled at all of them. Sif's golden hair, everyone agreed, was if anything more splendid than her previous mane had been. However, they pointed out that Miölnir, wielded by Thor, was the most valuable of all the gifts because it could guard them from the predations of the giants.

The gods laughed as Loki tried to bargain his way out of this one. They were still laughing when he fled from the hall. Brock begged Thor, on the honour of the Aesir, to bring the wizard of lies back so that the wager could be completed, and the huge god recognized the force of this argument. He fetched Loki and placed him in front of the others, and all waited for the execution. However, Loki had been thinking further. His head, it was true, was forfeit to Brock and Sindri, but not his neck: if the dwarfs could find some way of decapitating him without harming his neck then he would be the last to stop them.

The Aesir and the dwarfs realized that, alas, Loki had a point here (shades of *The Merchant of Venice*). But the reason the dwarfs had wanted Loki's head was to stop his mischievous lying. Brock therefore said that he would be content to sew up Loki's lips, and this he did with Sindri's magic awl. The god's agony was excruciating, and he ran from the place screaming as he tore away the thongs. The Aesir laughed all the more merrily at his discomfiture, which was perhaps unwise of them, because thereafter Loki became ever more malicious.

BELOW *At Ragnarok Thor will battle Jormungand, the World Serpent. Also in this nineteenth-century book illustration we can see Odin fighting Fenris and Frey struggling with Surt. The figure on the right is probably Tyr. In the background is Bifrost.*

THOR

The god of thunder was among the most important three in the Norse pantheon, the others being Odin (obviously) and Loki. He was responsible for the weather and crops, as well as for sea-voyages that might be affected by the weather. Interestingly, the cracking of the sky during thunderstorms was not regarded with dread by the Norse: instead, they regarded it as a sign that Thor was carrying out his responsibilities, which were, essentially, the slaughter of giants. We can wonder if, perhaps, the Scandinavians equated the crashing of thunder with the equally loud sounds of sintering glaciers, because the frost giants were of course connected with the glaciers that were so much a feature of the northern part of the Viking terrain.

As sophisticated as he was gentle, Thor was red-bearded, gluttonous and loud-voiced: his standard way of dealing with any problem was to kill anyone foolish enough to be nearby. Perhaps for this reason he has been enduringly loved. His most significant manifestation in popular culture during this century being the long-running series of his adventures published in the comics. His invincible hammer was Miölnir and his wife was the beautiful goddess Sif; it is hard to work out which of the two he loved the more, but we can guess it was the hammer. Thor, because of his violent encounter with the giant Hrungnir, will spend all of the rest of time until Ragnarok with a stone implanted in his head.

The tales of Thor's adventures can be found on many pages of this book: the reader is referred to the index. Here are a few not covered elsewhere. The story of Thor and Hrungnir and how the former got a lump of stone in his head clearly demonstrates Thor's approach to things.

It all started when Odin was out on one of his rambles around the world. Astride his eight-legged steed Sleipnir, the father of the gods came to the hall of the giant Hrungnir, generally known to be the strongest of all the giants. It was only moments later that Odin and Hrungnir agreed a wager: Sleipnir versus the giant's horse, Gullfaxi (Golden-mane) – the prize, should Odin lose, being his own head.

RIGHT *'Thor' is still very popular as a placename and personal name in Iceland and the Faeroe Islands; when linked to a placename it seems to indicate local worship of the god. This is Torshavn ('Thor's Harbour') in the Faeroes.*

Soon the two riders were spurring their steeds into action, and soon after that Odin, realizing that the giant's horse might indeed be the swifter of the two, was galloping very speedily indeed towards Asgard, where he knew Hrungnir could not follow. For his part the giant didn't notice what direction they were taking until he found himself just outside Valhalla – not the best of discoveries, for it was likely to mean that he'd lost his life. The giant was understandably furious about this deception but prepared to meet his doom; luckily the Aesir recognized that he had been rather ill done-by and, instead of killing him, invited him in for a meal.

Mead was swallowed in pints, then quarts, and then gallons; the giant followed this act by consuming whole oceans of mead. Hrungnir began to wax large on his ambition to destroy Asgard and all the gods and goddesses dwelling there, with the exception of Freya and Sif, whom he respected for something other than their minds. This caused the sort of frigid silence most of us have experienced at mortal dinner parties.

And it was at this stage that Thor came back from one of his journeys. He was incensed to discover that Hrungnir was there in the first place, and even more so that the giant was regarding his (Thor's) wife, Sif, with a certain degree of mental impropriety. The god proposed to resolve this little argument by hammering the giant's head down between his shoulderblades. The other Aesir, however, differed: they pointed out that the laws of hospitality forbade random slaughter of guests – especially those who'd had too much to drink, and whose words could therefore not be taken seriously – and so Thor had to bite his tongue as Hrungnir left. The two of them, though, agreed that three days later (by which time Hrungnir would presumably have recovered from his hangover) they would meet for a formal duel at a place called Griottunagard.

The morning after, Hrungnir realized that he had been rather foolish. He consulted some of the other giants as to how he might get out of the duel, and they told him it was impossible. However, they did point out that the formalities of the duel meant that not only did Hrungnir have to do battle with Thor, their two squires had to fight each other: surely it would be easy enough to elect a squire who could make mincemeat out of Thor's squire, Thialfi (see below). This struck Hrungnir as a good idea, and so, not wanting to leave too much to doubt in the contest between the squires, he gave orders that a nine-mile-tall clay giant called Mokerkialfi should be constructed to fight against Thialfi. Into this vast edifice the giants placed a mare's heart – a human heart would not have been sufficient – but they became nervous when they noticed that even this powerful organ was fluttering with worry.

Hrungnir had become less worried. He was vast and had a shield, club, heart and skull made of stone; his squire was even vaster and, it would seem, twice as invulnerable. The duel proved in fact to be a walkover, because Thialfi had little difficulty in slaughtering Mokerkialfi and Thor even less in killing Hrungnir. However, the giant held up his stone club in an attempt to ward off the thrown hammer of Thor; the club shattered into millions of pieces, which can now be found all over the world as fragments of flint. One of these bits of rock flew into Thor's forehead. At the time it caused the god to collapse forward into unconsciousness, but fortunately his descending hand brought down his hammer, Miölnir, on Hrungnir's head, and —— the giant died as a result.

One of the giant's legs fell over Thor. Luckily the god's son Magni strolled up and – although still aged only three – was able to remove the hugely heavy leg. Thor rewarded his son by giving him the steed Gullfaxi.

And that was the end of that adventure – except for the problem of the shard of stone in Thor's forehead. The Aesir tried everything to get it out, and finally thought they would succeed in doing so when they secured the service of a powerful sorceress called Groa. However, for reasons described in Chapter 1, even this proved of no avail.

Thor had two regular attendants: the boy Thialfi (who became important, as we've seen) and a girl, Roskva. The god gained them in a rather despicable way. He and Loki were wandering the world when the two gods decided that they would like lodging for the night. They took this from a very poor peasant couple, who produced a supper that was in no way big enough to satisfy Thor's huge appetite. The god therefore killed their only two

LEFT *Icelandic bronze statuette, dating from about the year 1000, showing Thor with his hammer.*

goats – although he told the family that, should they leave all the bones untouched and put them back into the empty skins of the animals, things would be all right in the morning. This would have been an honest enough scheme had not Loki encouraged the son of the house, Thialfi, to break one of the bones and lick out its marrow. The next day Thor touched the two heaps of skin and bones with his hammer and suddenly there were two living goats again.

LEFT *Arthur Rackham's conception of Thor, produced as one of his illustrations to Wagner's* Das Rheingold. *Wagner was retelling the older German versions of the Norse myths, and so in the opera the god is named Donner rather than Thor.*

One of them was lame, though, and this made Thor very angry – angry enough to threaten to slaughter the entire family, even though they had given him hospitality for the night. In order to spare all of their lives, the peasant offered Thor Thialfi, the culprit, and his sister Roskva as slaves for eternity. Thor accepted at once.

The gaining of these two slaves occurred during a venture of Thor's to Jotunheim, the land of the giants; the gods had become concerned that the giants were beginning to be too impertinent. Taking the two children with them, Thor and Loki quested on into Jotunheim, their destination a place called Utgard. That night they were cold and lonely, and were only too happy to discover a house where they could sleep; the house was rather strange, but they didn't mind that – all they wanted was somewhere they could sleep. However, sleep was not as easy to come by as they had hoped, because every now and then the ground trembled. Finally the two gods retreated into an annexe of the house, and there at last they were able to sleep in peace.

The reason that the ground had been shaking became obvious to them the following morning when they stumbled, bleary-eyed, out of the strangely shaped house. Nearby a giant was snoring. He almost immediately registered their less than friendly stares and awoke; he reached around him for something that he had lost during the night and soon found it. It was a glove – and also it was the oddly shaped house in which Thor and Loki had spent the night. The annexe which they had finally discovered was the thumb of the glove.

The giant told the two gods that his name was Skrymir; he, too, was on the way to Utgard, and he would gladly show them the way. He offered to share his provisions with them and they readily accepted, because they were running low on supplies. The giant showed what he meant by 'sharing' when he scooped up their pathetically thin bag and simply popped it into his own. All day long the two gods and the two children suffered the tortures of hunger as they did their best to keep up with Skrymir. Things didn't improve that evening, despite the fact that the giant tossed them his bag of provisions: even the mighty Thor was unable to get the damned thing open.

Brought to a pitch of fury by this and by Skrymir's snoring, Thor came as near to rational argument as he usually did. His first piece of witty repartee was to crash Miölnir down on Skrymir's forehead with a mighty blow; the giant responded by half-waking and enquiring if a forest leaf might have landed on his brow. Thor, ever the diplomat, waited until the giant was fast asleep once more: this time he brought his hammer down viciously on the top of Skrymir's skull. Again the giant half-awoke, this time enquiring if, perhaps, an acorn had dropped down onto his head. Questions like these did not please Thor, and so the god kept himself awake, loathing the incessant snoring, until it was nearly dawn. Then he crept across to where Skrymir was sleeping and buried Miölnir up to the very hilt in the giant's brains. The giant stirred and wondered if perhaps a bird seated in a branch above him had shat on his head.

Grey with lack of sleep, Thor roused his companions; the god was treated to a discourse from Skrymir about how he (the giant) was a veritable midget in comparison with the denizens of Utgard. Thor's temper was as sweet as might be imagined.

Thanks to Skrymir's guidance, the four of them were able to make their way to Utgard, which was where the giant Utgard-Loki lived. Rather to their surprise they found themselves welcomed by him, although he did make tactless remarks about their diminutive stature. They were heralded into a hall where countless giants and giantesses were feasting.

A challenge was soon set up between Loki and Utgard-Loki (who was, incidentally, no relation to the god). Loki avowed that he could eat more swiftly than anyone or anything in the nine worlds. The giant nodded and chuckled, and gave orders that a great trough of food should be set up the length of one of the huge tables. Loki was commanded to start eating at one end and Utgard-Loki's champion, Logi, at the other. To his astonishment Loki discovered that, when he reached the midpoint, his rival had devoured not only the food, as Loki had done, but the trough as well.

Thor felt that the honour of the Aesir had to be retrieved, and so he proposed a second contest. He told Utgard-Loki that there was no one in all the nine worlds who could swig so much mead as he could, and so he would like to suggest a drinking contest. He would drain whatever vessel the company could put in front of him. The giant immediately called for a horn of mead and, on its arrival,

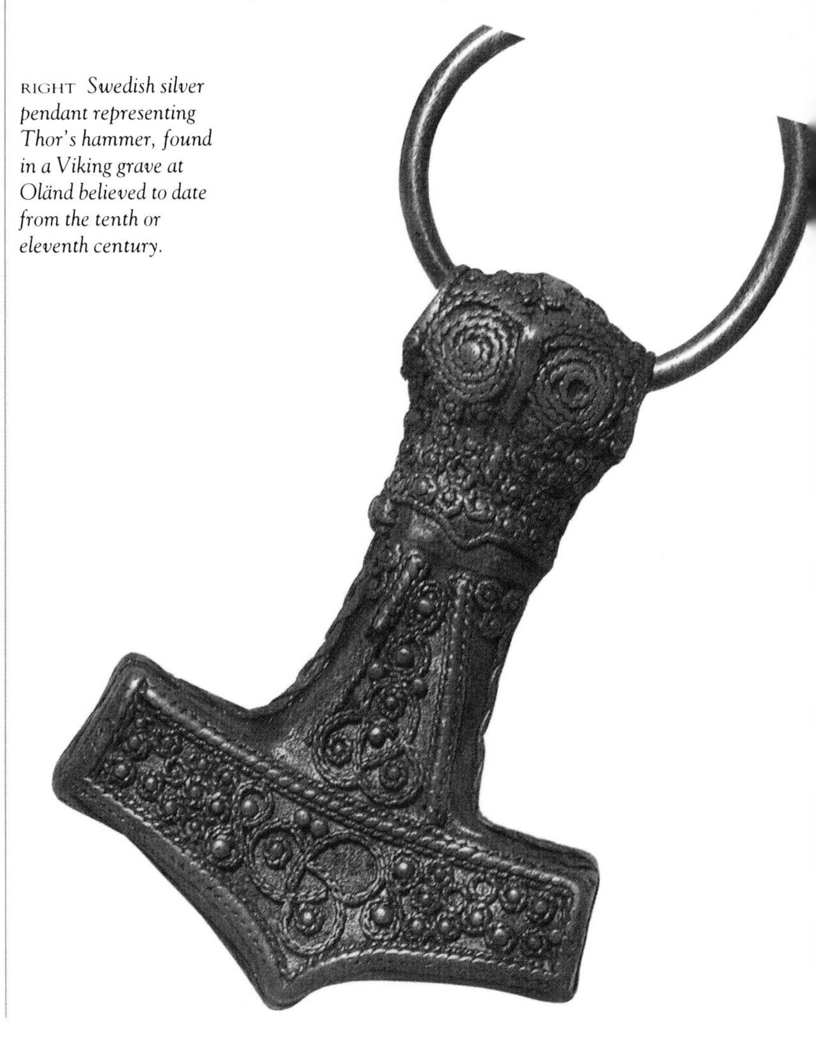

RIGHT *Swedish silver pendant representing Thor's hammer, found in a Viking grave at Öländ believed to date from the tenth or eleventh century.*

explained that in his hall modest drinkers required three draughts to finish it, reasonable tipplers a couple, and real experts only the one. Thor regarded himself as a real expert and so was surprised to find, having taken a draught so huge that he felt his head would explode, that he had hardly reduced the liquid's level at all. A second attempt made very little more difference. A third, and the horn was still almost full. Thor slumped down in defeat.

Thialfi was then asked to race. His opponent was a boy called Hugi. At his first attempt Thialfi was soundly beaten; in later attempts he found Hugi strolling back to ask if he could offer any help.

RIGHT *Danish silver amulet representing Thor's hammer and dating from perhaps the tenth century.*

Thor offered to show his huge strength, and the giant laughed. He asked the god to try to lift one of the cats of Utgard, which Thor tried with little success. 'All right,' said the giant, 'if that foe proved too much for you, why not have a try against my old nanny, Elli?' Once again Thor proved humiliatingly incapable of putting up even a decent fight. He and Loki – rather surprisingly, in view of the Aesir's disposition to cheat in these affairs – finally admitted that they had been well and truly beaten by the giant's champions. Utgard-Loki smiled and offered them a bed for the night.

The following morning the giant himself escorted the quartet away from his hall. He had to confess, he said, that in many ways he had cheated them. He had taken on the guise of the huge Skrymir and, while pretending to be asleep, had interposed a mountain between Thor's hammer-blows and himself; otherwise he would have been slain – as it was, all the mountains of the worlds showed the scars of the blows. Loki's opponent in the eating competition, Logi, had in fact been fire, than which nothing can eat faster. Thialfi's opponent in the running race, Hugi, was none other than thought – obviously nobody and nothing can hope to race against the speed of thought. The horn out of which Thor had been drinking had been connected with the wide ocean, which, plainly, even this great god could never hope to drain – although he'd managed, creditably, to cause a noticeable drop in the water level. The cat with which Thor had fought had been Jormungand, the World Serpent, which was well known to be unliftable. When Thor had been wrestling old nurse, Elli, he had had little chance because in fact she was old age: no one can hope successfully to resist old age.

Thor would have liked to have exacted vengeance for all these deceptions, and he started to whirl his hammer in preparation. However, Utgard-Loki wisely disappeared, and the thunder-god was never able thereafter to find the giant's hall.

The thunder-god had various other adventures with giants, often involving Loki. The recovery of his hammer from Thrym involved him disguising himself as Freya (*q.v.*). He destroyed Geirrod and his daughters as well as the previously amicable giant Hymir. In fact, it is curious that any of the giant race should show anything other than loathing for this god, so many of them did he slay, yet there are some examples of them being helpful to him – for example, his life would have been forfeited had it not been for the prior assistance of a giantess called Grid.

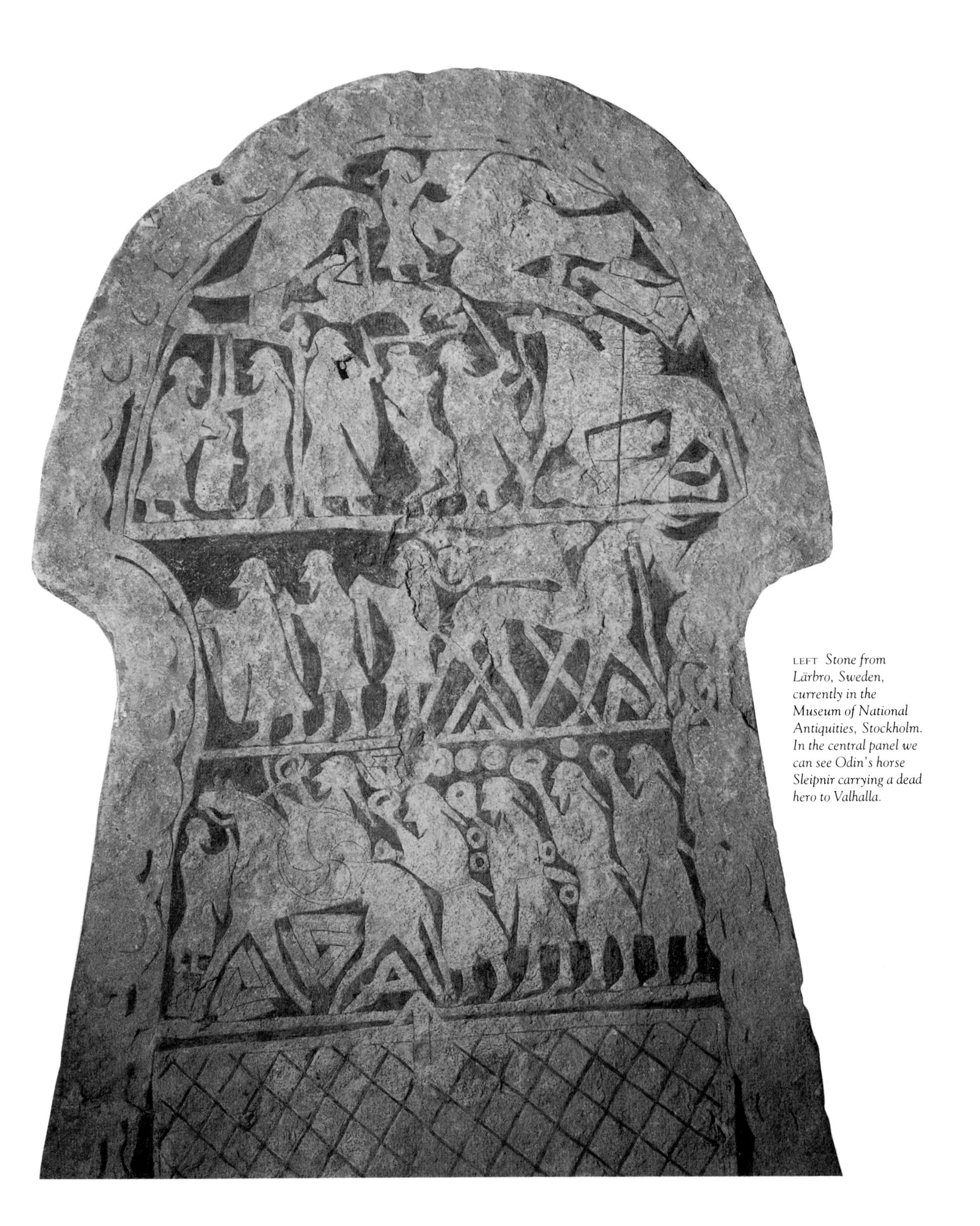

LEFT *Stone from Lärbro, Sweden, currently in the Museum of National Antiquities, Stockholm. In the central panel we can see Odin's horse Sleipnir carrying a dead hero to Valhalla.*

VALI

LEFT *Pages from a fourteenth-century Icelandic biblical text. Many of the Viking myths show signs of having been modified or extended to accommodate the influx of the Christian tradition.*

Vali, the god of eternal light, was conceived with no purpose other than to avenge the death of Balder. A dead prophetess had told Odin that he must mate with the goddess Rind to produce this child, who would grow to adulthood in a single day (quite a number of the lesser deities did this) and then, before he had either washed his face or combed his hair – as the prophetess eloquently put it – slay Hoder; for more details of this prophecy *see* the discussion of Balder earlier in this chapter.

Rind, his mother, is generally taken to have been an earth-goddess. One tale of his conception, possibly tacked on later, portrays her as a mortal – although perhaps, despite her mortal origins, she afterwards became a goddess.

The Rind in this particular tale was the only child of a king called Billing. Her father's country was being threatened by invaders and he was now too old to go to war to repel them, yet she stubbornly refused to take a husband – despite the fact that her beauty had attracted, like iron filings to a magnet, exquisitely handsome suitors from all directions. This was good news for Odin because, in order to avenge the death of Balder, the god had of necessity to sire Vali with Rind. Accordingly, one day Odin, in the guise of a mortal, turned up at Billing's palace offering his services as a military commander. The king, desperate for any help he could get, took him on immediately, and it wasn't very long before the enemies had been repulsed. The triumphant general begged Billing's permission to pay court to his daughter, and there was very little argument. From the father, that is: Rind had other ideas, and sent the grizzled soldier packing.

Odin next appeared as a smith called Rosterus. He could make the most marvellously beautiful brooches and bangles, which delighted all of the court, including Billing and Rind herself. The request for permission to woo being duly granted, the smith tried his luck. The response from Rind was painful to him, to say the least, and he was never seen again at Billing's palace.

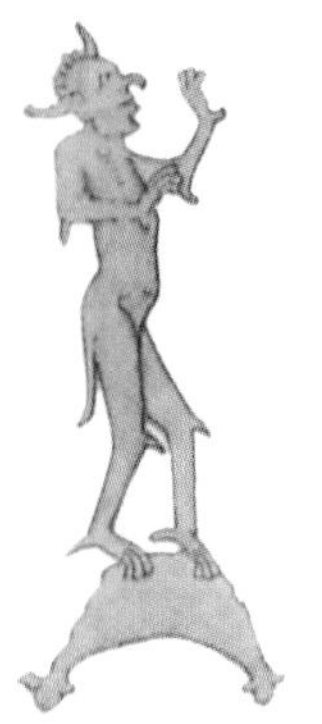

LEFT *Detail from the manuscript shown in full on the opposite page.*

The god decided that perhaps middle-aged soldiers and crinkled smiths were not quite what Rind had in mind as a future husband, so next time he turned up as a mighty-thewed warrior – but with the same result. Odin was annoyed at being constantly hit about the head and worse, and so he levelled at her a runestaff, chanting vicious magic spells. Rind collapsed at this onslaught and, by the time she'd revived, the bulky stud had gone. Even after her recovery she was witless. Billing wept for the plight of his daughter, and was much cheered when an old woman arrived at the palace announcing that she alone could bring the lass back to reality. The hag publicly tried a footbath on Rind but without success; there was no other option, she said, but that Rind be put completely under her control. Billing agreed eagerly. Now that this wish had been granted the old woman revealed that in fact she was Odin in disguise. Rind, over whom whom he had been given total mastery, had no choice but to have sex with him – and thereby Vali could be conceived. (The rape theme recurs disturbingly often in the Norse legends.)

An important point about Vali is that he will survive Ragnarok (*see* Chapter 6). He is one of the comparatively few gods who will do so.

Valhalla

Valhalla was the hall of Odin to which the warriors slaughtered in battle – the Einheriar – were brought so that they could enjoy a glorious afterlife. The word 'enjoy' is used cautiously, because few of us now would find much pleasure in the daytime activity of the Einheriar. Each morning they had to dress in their armour and then do combat in the plain before Valhalla, perhaps enjoying the lethal blows they dealt to their fellows but, presumably, suffering over and over again the agonies of the lethal blows that had been dealt by others to themselves. Each evening they were brought back to life, free from any of the mutilations they might have suffered, and came back to Valhalla to engage in feats of consuming limitless food and mead. So much did this 'lifestyle' appeal to the Vikings that, apparently, warriors who had failed to be slain during their active years would fall on their own spears in order to qualify for inclusion among the company of the Einheriar.

BELOW *A detail of an eighth-century stela from Lillbjärs, Sweden, showing a valkyrie offering a horn of mead to a slain warrior as he arrives at Valhalla.*

The boiled meat they ate came from a huge boar called Saehrimnir, and the supplies were unending because, even though the boar was slaughtered each day by Valhalla's cook, Andhrimnir, it would be reborn in time to be slaughtered again for their next meal. The mead came from the udder of Odin's goat Heidrun, who supplied more than enough for the Einheriar, who drank it from the skulls of their enemies. Presumably an additional delight of Valhalla was that no one ever suffered a hangover, because the quantities of mead drunk by the dead warriors were colossal. The servants at these gargantuan feasts were the Valkyries, sumptuous young women whose favours were, one gathers, readily available to the bold – although at the same time they remained everlastingly virginal.

BELOW *Nineteenth-century book illustration by Gaston Bussière showing a highly romanticised image of a valkyrie. In the original legends the valkyries might be beautiful and free with their favours once dead warriors had reached Valhalla, but on the battlefield they were regarded as possessed of the utmost sadistic bloodthirstiness.*

RIGHT *A romanticised vision from a nineteenth-century book of the valkyries carrying off slain heroes to Valhalla. The lowermost hero appears to have attracted the attention of a nubile valkyrie through having incurred a fatal hangover.*

RIGHT *Figures in silver from Swedish Viking graves. The one on the right, dating from an eleventh-century grave, shows a stereotyped valkyrie holding up a drinking horn. The one on the left, dating from the previous century, shows a horseman — presumably the warrior himself riding to Valhalla.*

Our modern image of the Valkyries has been coloured by performances of the operas of Richard Wagner: we think of them as objects of ridicule, buxom and garbed in a costume which goes largely unnoticed except for their precarious metal brassières. In fact, according to the Norse, they were far from that. They were beautiful and desirable, yes, and they were also unbelievably sadistic – except to the Einheriar. Assistants to Tyr, the god of war, they rode on their panting steeds – sometimes wolves – across the skies above battlefields, swooping to pluck the dead from the ground and bring them to Valhalla. Sometimes they took monstrous forms and poured rains of blood down over the land or rowed a ship across the skies through a torrent of blood. In one account they are described as seated on a battlefield weaving a tapestry from human intestines, using an arrow for a shuttle and men's heads to weigh down the ends of their gory cords.

Valkyries are connected with several of the heroes, whose wives they became. There is a great deal of evidence that the myth of their existence had some basis in reality (or perhaps the myth gave rise to the reality), and that priestesses did indeed attend Teutonic armies, including the Norse, with the responsibility of, after a battle, selecting those prisoners to be killed and choosing the manner of their death. This latter was generally not pleasant, but could be regarded as an honour conveyed by the victors upon the vanquished. One delightful tribute the Norse made to those who had been bested in battle, but who were regarded as particularly valiant foes, was the Eagle. The prisoner was held face-downwards and split open along the backbone. His ribs were then splayed outwards and his lungs dragged away to form a canopy over them. It was regarded as a particular sign of valour if the victim showed no sign of pain during all this.

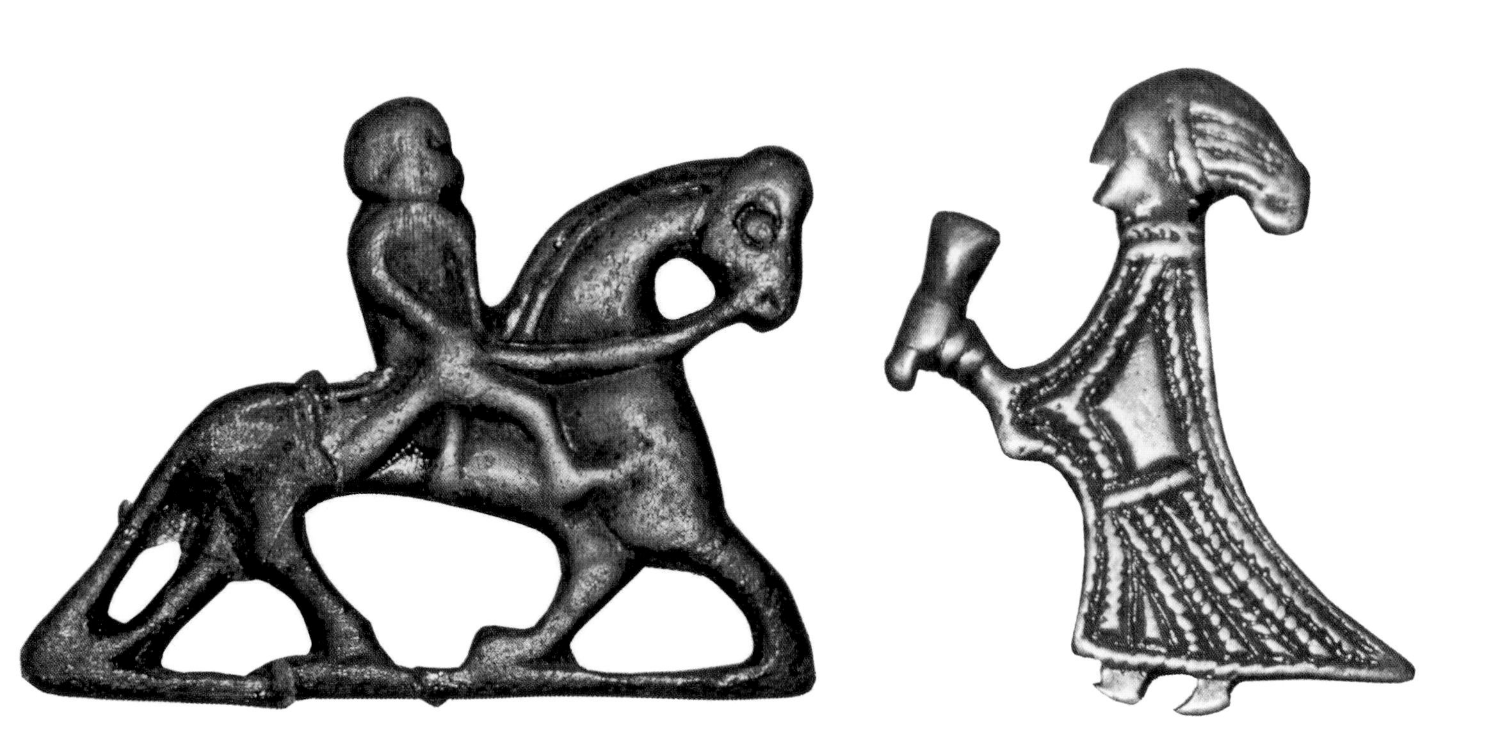

FOUR

Tales of the Valkyries

LEFT *Nineteenth-century book illustration showing Brunhild with Gunnar.*

BRUNHILD

The tale of Brunhild is a very muddled one, with several mutually incompatible strands. We shall pick our way through it as best we can.

After the hero Sigurd (*q.v.*) had stolen Fafnir's gold (*see* Chapter 1) he rode on until he came to a hall set high on a mountain. Inside it there was a beautiful woman asleep, dressed in full armour. Instinctively knowing what to do in such circumstances, Sigurd took his sword and cut away her armour, at which point she awoke and told him that her name was Brunhild and that she was a Valkyrie.

This is where the tale starts to become confused. According to the Prose Edda, Sigurd then continued on his way as if nothing had happened until he came to the palace of a king called Giuki, one of whose daughters was Gudrun (*q.v.*). (There is a version that states that Sigurd had agreed to marry Brunhild but that, after he had come to Giuki's court, Queen Grimhild determined that he should marry her daughter and so used magic to erase all memory of his earlier betrothal.) Sigurd married Gudrun and became the blood-brother of two of Giuki's sons, Gunnar and Högni. Sigurd and the two brothers went to ask a king of the Huns called Atli if he would consent to the marriage of his sister Brunhild to Gunnar. (You were forewarned that this would be difficult to unravel.) This sister lived in a hall called Hindarfiall which was surrounded by a curtain of flame; it was well known that she would not consider marriage to any man who was not prepared to ride through the flame. Gunnar's horse refused the challenge, but then Sigurd had a ready answer: he would take the shape of Gunnar and, on his own much braver steed called Grani, endure the fire to capture the hand of Brunhild on Gunnar's behalf. This he did with little difficulty. The beautiful maid took one look at him and was much in love. Sigurd, however, being an honourable man, although he slept with Brunhild did not make love with her – a fact which she must have found rather perplexing. In the morning Sigurd gave her as a wedding gift the ring that Loki had taken as part of Andvari's gold: bearing in mind that this ring was accursed, the wedding gift might perhaps have been better chosen. Then Sigurd rode back to join the two brothers and exchanged forms with Gunnar, who thereafter became Brunhild's loving husband.

There was a certain degree of tension between Brunhild and Gudrun, because both of them were essentially in love with the same man. In one instance the two of them were washing their hair in the river and conducting a boasting contest about the prowess

RIGHT *A carving on a cart recovered from a ninth-century ship burial at Vestfold, Norway, shows on the left how Gunnar met his end. He was condemned by Atli to be cast into a pit of snakes. In the pit, his hands being bound, he played on his harp using his toes, and thereby reduced all but one of the serpents to tranquility. This last serpent – Atli's mother in disguise – gave the fatal bite.*

of their respective husbands. Brunhild bragged about Gunnar's bravery in riding through the wall of flame, and Gudrun broke it to her that the man who had performed this feat had in fact been Sigurd.

Brunhild was not at all delighted to hear this news, and decided that Sigurd's deception should be avenged. She tried to persuade the brothers Gunnar and Högni to kill Sigurd, but they refused, delegating the task instead to their brother Guttorm. Guttorm lost his life while killing Sigurd and Sigurd's infant son; as Gudrun expressed her grief Brunhild laughed mockingly. Soon, however, Brunhild changed her mind: she killed herself in order to be placed on Sigurd's funeral pyre.

RIGHT *Another rendition of Gunnar in the pit of snakes, this time from a tenth-century Viking–Christian cross at Andreas, Isle of Man, Britain.*

There are many variant versions of this story. According to some, Brunhild and Sigurd did not behave quite as decorously as described above when Sigurd had come into Hindarfiall, the result being a daughter called Auslag. The child was still very young when her parents died and so was looked after by her grandfather, Giuki. However, a revolution drove him from his kingdom and he was forced to wander the world as a minstrel, bearing a harp in which was hidden his lovely granddaughter. In the end he was murdered by peasants who thought that there was gold in his harp and who were very disappointed to discover the girl-child. Because they thought she was a deaf-mute they reared her as a skivvy, not noticing that she was growing up to be an exceptionally fair young woman. At last a Viking called Ragnar Lodbrog saw her and fell in love. He had to travel away for a year, killing people in order to attain glory, but when he returned he took her as his bride – and so she became the queen of Denmark.

Another possible interpretation of the story is that Brunhild was initially a mortal. Sigurd, on his death, was clearly destined to be taken to Valhalla. Her love for him was so great that she wished to follow him there, becoming a Valkyrie – and the only

RIGHT *An illustration from FL Spence's* Rhine Legends *(1915) showing Odin and Brunhild.*

way that she could do this was to kill herself and be consumed beside him on his pyre. Yet another version of her story describes her as a king's daughter rudely plucked by Odin from the mortal world to become the leader of all the Valkyries, a position of honour that meant she became, in effect, Odin's own daughter. Obviously there is always the possibility that these legends are confusing two quite different Brunhilds, one a mortal and the other a Valkyrie. The variation of the tale rendered in Wagner's *Ring* cycle is a far later version, bearing little relation to the Norse legends.

GUDRUN

As with Brunhild, the tales of Gudrun are very confused: it is likely that they are confabulations of legends about two quite separate Gudruns, one a mortal and the other a Valkyrie. The exploits of the 'mortal Gudrun' are discussed above: she was the wife of Sigurd and, as such, was probably less poorly treated in the legends than might have been expected of the Norse, who attributed to women a great many powers and guiles, few of which were very flatteringly portrayed. Like Brunhild, Gudrun may have started off as a mortal and then been transformed into a Valkyrie.

The son of Sigmund and Borghild was called Helgi, and he was a very brave warrior. Gudrun, as she swooped over a battlefield where Helgi and Sinfiotli were fighting with the Hundings, was much taken by the young man. She accordingly descended to Earth and threw herself before him, offering her all. Helgi thanked her but, as it were, he had this battle to fight first: they could be betrothed but the consummation would have to wait a while. After the battle there was only one of the Hundings still standing – a youth called Dag, who was given his freedom on the condition that he would not seek to carry on the vendetta any longer. Dag agreed to this but then betrayed his oath and slew Helgi.

Gudrun's grief was great; not surprisingly, she laid a curse on Dag. She discovered that the dead Helgi, buried in his mound, was calling for her incessantly, and so she went to him. She found that he was still bleeding prodigiously, and he told her that this was because of her continuing grief: every time she shed a tear, he shed a matching drop of blood. From then on she kept back her tears.

BELOW *Viking period gilt brooch found in a Viking grave in Sweden. It dates from around the ninth and eleventh centuries* AD.

The loving couple were soon reunited. Helgi was gathered to Valhalla and Gudrun joined him there. He became a leader of the armies of the dead warriors, the Einheriar; she, in order to help him, returned to her role as a Valkyrie so that she could bring as many slain warriors as possible to swell the ranks of his armies.

The rest of the tale of the 'mortal Gudrun' is less edifying. While Brunhild had so graphically displayed her love for Sigurd by immolating herself upon his pyre, Gudrun was not prepared to do likewise, so she and her daughter Swanhild fled to the court of a king called Elf. His queen was Thora, and

RIGHT *Arthur Rackham's typically romantic image of Brunhild. Warlike the valkyries might be, but there is little to make us believe that the Vikings saw them as beautiful, clean-limbed maidens like this, rather, they were hideous creatures, akin to vampires or the Irish tripartite death-goddess The Morrigan, when they visited earthly battlefields to carry off the souls of the dead.*

FAR RIGHT *Detail of a cross slab found at Michael, Isle of Man, Britain, dating from the late tenth or early eleventh century; the slab is called 'Joalf's Slab'. The Viking depicted is bearing a spear and a round shield.*

RIGHT *A detail from a stone-carved cross, from Middleton, North Yorkshire, Britain, dating from about the tenth century, showing a Norse warrior laid out for burial. The cross was, of course, a Christian artefact, the burial a pagan one. This mixture of paganism with Christianity became increasingly a characteristic of the late Viking period, until eventually the new religion took over almost completely.*

soon Gudrun and Thora were close friends. However, this situation didn't last too long, because Atli, king of the Huns, was demanding to be avenged upon Gunnar; the latter, now king, was eager to avoid war and so he told Atli that he could marry his sister Gudrun. The marriage was eventually performed, much to Gudrun's disgust: she loathed Atli. In due course she murdered the sons he had sired upon her and served bits of them up to him in a banquet: their skulls were used for goblets, their blood was mixed into the wine, and the meat was their roasted hearts. Then Gudrun revealed the truth to Atli before setting fire to his palace and dying with him and his cronies in the flames.

Swanhild, Gudrun's daughter, met an equally unsavoury end. A king called Ermenrich wanted her as a wife and sent his son Randwer to fetch her. When they reached Ermenrich's palace, however, a lying and treacherous servant called Sibich claimed that, during the journey, Randwer had seduced Swanhild. At Ermenrich's order Randwer was hanged and Swanhild sentenced to be trampled to death by wild horses. Early attempts to carry out this execution failed because of Swanhild's exquisite beauty: the horses simply refused to harm her. In the end she was covered with a blanket to shield her beauty from the horses, and so she lost her life.

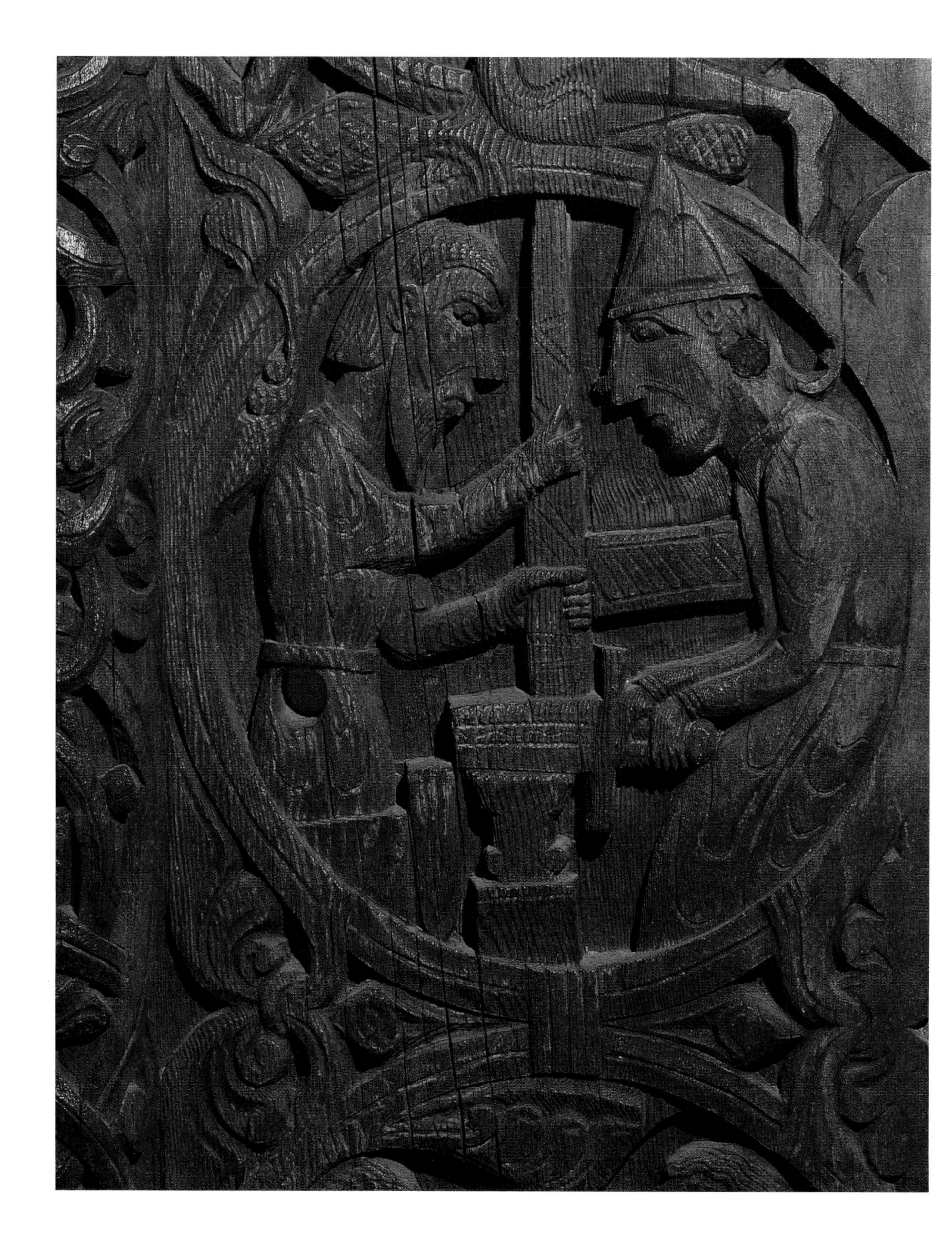

FIVE

Tales of Heroes

LEFT *Detail from a twelfth- or thirteenth-century wooden portal at Hylestad Church, Norway, showing the dwarf Regin reforging the sword Sigurd had been given by his father.*

FRITHIOF

Frithiof was the son of Thorsten (*q.v.*) and Ingeborg. Early in his life he was given out to a man called Hilding for fostering (this was a not uncommon practice among the Vikings). Hilding later became the foster-father of a girl who was also called Ingeborg; she was the daughter of Thorsten's great friend King Belé. The two children grew up together and, predictably, fell in love with each other; but Hilding forbade them to marry, pointing out that Ingeborg was a princess while Frithiof was merely the son of a hero. Frithiof took this as well as might be expected – in other words, not very.

Belé's heirs were his sons Halfdan and Helgé, neither of whom were particularly popular; Frithiof, on the other hand, was very popular indeed – even with Belé himself. After Halfdan and Helgé had taken over the throne from their father, Frithiof decided to retire from public life, although he pined for Ingeborg.

One Spring, however, Halfdan and Helgé came to visit him and they brought with them their sister. Ingeborg and Frithiof were instantly, once again, madly and passionately in love. After the royal party had left, Frithiof decided to pluck up his courage and follow them in order to beg the two kings, his former playmates, to let him marry their sister. When he came to them, sitting on their father's barrow, Helgé told him that he was not good enough for Ingeborg, being only a peasant's son; he could, however, if he wanted, become one of Helgé's bondsmen. Aroused to a level beyond mere tetchiness, Frithiof drew his sword and sliced Helgé's shield in two. Then he went home, much disgruntled.

Ingeborg was beautiful, and the news of this spread widely, so that princely suitors sent messengers from many lands. One of these was a king called Sigurd Ring, a widower of great age. Ingeborg having, of course, no voice in any of these discussions, Helgé asked various seers and seeresses whether or not there was any chance that the marriage would be successful; Halfdan, more relevantly, wondered if the old man, Sigurd Ring, would be able to – um – give Ingeborg the full joys of marriage. The limp joke came to the ears of Sigurd Ring, who became enraged and announced publicly that he planned to wage war on Halfdan and Helgé. The response of the two kings was less than heroic: they instantly sent Hilding to ask Frithiof to command their armies in an endeavour to repel the threat. Frithiof's reply was that he had been so offended by their earlier remarks that he had little interest in sorting things out for them. Halfdan and Helgé decided that their best course of action was to give in to Sigurd Ring and to give him the hand of their sister, Ingeborg.

Frithiof was not quite so sure that that was the end of the story. He discovered that Ingeborg was pining in a religious house devoted to Balder, and so he went there. It was taboo to speak in this place, but they spoke anyway, and over many days, knowing that Ingeborg's brothers were away. The brothers returned, though; to Frithiof's request that they might think about his offer to lead their armies against Sigurd Ring the two of them – notably Helgé – remarked that they were much more interested in whether or not Frithiof and Ingeborg had been talking with each other in the grove (or monastery) devoted to Balder. Helgé pressed the question: had Frithiof and Ingeborg spoken with each other? There was a long silence before Frithiof replied that, yes, he had.

His sentence was banishment. Ingeborg declined to follow him to the sunny lands he knew lay to the south; she reckoned that now her father was dead she ought to do what her brothers told her.

Helgé was not content with Frithiof's sentence of banishment: he wanted the man dead. The king there-

RIGHT *Sigmund and Signy – a nineteenth-century book illustration.*

fore summoned up a couple of witches and asked them to send a storm out to sea so that Frithiof's ship, and all on board her, should be sunk. The witches did their best, but Frithiof, chanting a merry lay, dissuaded the elements from killing him and his crew. In this way they all came to the Orkney Islands. The natives were not much pleased by this, obviously, but Frithiof defeated the berserker, Atlé, whom they sent to challenge him. Frithiof also made friends, in due course, with the king of the Orkneys, Angantyr.

After many months Frithiof came home, only to discover that his hall had been burnt to the ground on the orders of Helgé. Also, he was given the news by Hilding that Ingeborg had been married to Sigurd Ring. He carried out various acts of slaughter and then set sail for Greece, where he lived for some years. He finally returned to the court of Sigurd Ring in the guise of a beggar, a role that he maintained only as long as it took for him to kill one of the courtiers. Sigurd Ring, very decently, did not have him executed for this crime but instead asked him to doff his disguise; this Frithiof did, thereby meeting the appealing eye of Ingeborg. The hero then had too much to drink, watched with approval by Sigurd Ring. The two men became great friends, and that was the end, for a while, of Frithiof's lust for Ingeborg.

Sigurd Ring died, and at last Frithiof and Ingeborg were free to marry. Helgé accidentally killed himself. Halfdan, on the other hand, swore an oath of friendship with Frithiof, and the two men remained friends until the end of their lives.

LEFT *Reconstruction of a Viking helmet found at Middleton Cross, Yorkshire, Britain.*

SIGMUND

Sigmund was the twin brother of the beautiful woman Signy; they were the last two children of Volsung. Sigmund was the only one of all the brothers to realize that Signy didn't want to marry Siggeir, the king of the Goths; however, Odin had a similar idea and turned up for the wedding feast, throwing a sword into the heart of the Branstock, a great oak that grew up through Volsung's hall; according to Odin, whoever was able to remove the sword would become a great hero.

Siggeir, the recent groom, tried to pull the sword from the tree but without success; Volsung was no luckier. Then Sigmund's nine elder brothers had a try, all of them unsuccessfully. Finally Sigmund himself had a go, and the sword immediately slid out of its wooden scabbard; the comparison with King Arthur is very obvious.

King Siggeir offered to buy the weapon but Sigmund refused; it was at this point that the king determined to exterminate Sigmund and all of his kin, including Signy. As Siggeir slept, Signy told Volsung that her new husband was up to no good, but Volsung wouldn't believe her. A while later Volsung sent a fleet of vessels to Siggeir's kingdom; he and all of his warriors were murdered. Sigmund himself was lucky enough to escape, although he had to give up his magical sword; he and his brothers were then sentenced to death. Signy was distraught at this, and asked that the death penalty be rescinded; the result was that their sentence was commuted to being tied up to trees in the forest, there to be eaten by wild animals, while Signy was locked up in Siggeir's palace. All of the brothers died except Sigmund; this was because Signy had the idea of smearing honey on his face, so that the wild creatures of the forest licked this away rather than eating him. The beast that attacked him that night attempted a french kiss, thrusting its tongue into Sigmund's mouth; he bit back forcefully, killing it.

Signy arrived to rejoice about her brother's survival; he, for his part, went off to become a smith, operating out of a remote part of the forest.

That wasn't the end of the story, though. Signy concluded that the sons she bore by Siggeir were wimps and decided to send them to Sigmund for a bit of bracing. The test to which he put them was to knead some bread and not notice that, within the dough, there was a viper. The first son of Signy either noticed it and fled or was killed by Sigmund; the second got the same treatment. Signy despaired of the third son she might have by Siggeir, and so she decided to have one by Sigmund instead; she called on a beautiful witch, adopted her form, and slept with her brother. The resulting son was Sinfiotli. He showed himself to be better than his stepbrothers because, when baking bread, he simply baked the viper along with all the rest.

Sigmund and Sinfiotli became boon companions and soon began to rush around Scandinavia killing people, in the typical manner of heroes. In one of their adventures they became werewolves. They discovered two men sleeping and, on the wall, a pair of wolfskins. Father and son immediately donned these, wondering what it would feel like. Moments later they were werewolves that ran through the forest and ate anyone who came in their way. The two got so excited that they started to fight each other; Sigmund killed Sinfiotli. The father then watched as two weasels fought with each other; one killed the other but then restored it to life by laying on its breast a particular leaf; Sigmund followed suit and brought his son Sinfiotli back to life. The two of them realized that they'd been a bit stupid risking their lives as werewolves, and so as soon as possible they shed their skins and reverted to human form.

Sigmund and Sinfiotli now decided that they would exact their revenge on Siggeir. They went to Siggeir's hall, where they were soon discovered by two of Signy's youngest children; their mother told Sigmund to cut off the children's heads but he refused, so she did it herself.

Sigmund and Sinfiotli were captured and sentenced to death by Siggeir; their punishment was that they should be buried alive in a mound, separated by a wall. The mound was almost complete when Signy came along and threw at Sinfiotli's feet a bale of hay. He assumed that it might contain a loaf of bread, but actually it contained Sigmund's magical sword; as quick as thought Sinfiotli hacked an exit from the burial tomb.

The two heroes immediately rushed back to Volsung's hall and built up a great pile of straw all around it. They set fire to this and then stood at the gate refusing to let anyone escape but the women. An exception was Signy, whom they would have allowed out; she apparently preferred to burn alive as a penance for her infanticide and incestuous adultery.

Sigmund went on to marry the fair princess Borghild and then the equally fair princess Hiordis. Unfortunately a certain King Lygni likewise wanted to marry Hiordis; when Sigmund became the successful suitor Lygni raised an army. In the ensuing war Sigmund slew hundreds but was eventually killed himself.

Sigmund's son was the hero Sigurd (*q.v.*).

SIGURD

Hiordis was pregnant when her husband Sigmund (*q.v.*) was slain. She was lucky enough, however, to meet up with a benevolent Viking called Elf, who asked her to marry him and promised to look after her forthcoming child as if he were its real father. The child arrived and Elf gave him the name Sigurd. In the Germanic version of the legends Sigurd was called Siegfried.

Sigurd's education was entrusted to an infinitely wise man called Regin, and so the boy learned considerable wisdom – music, diplomacy, the carving of runes, smithery, warfare, etc. On attaining adulthood Sigurd was given permission to choose from his stepfather's stable any warhorse he would like. On his way to make the selection Sigurd was met by Odin, who told him that the best means of choice was to drive all of Elf's horses into a nearby river and then pick the one that retained its feet the best in the current. This Sigurd did, and as a result he gained the horse Greyfell, a descendant of Odin's horse Sleipnir.

One day Regin told him of the cursed treasure of Andvari, now guarded by the dragon Fafnir (*see* Chapter 1), and asked him if he would be willing to do battle with Fafnir in order to recover the gold and avenge the crime. Sigurd agreed, and so Regin set out to forge for him an invincible sword. His first two attempts were unsuccessful, Sigurd being able to shatter the swords by crashing them down on an anvil. Then Sigurd remembered the sword of his father, Sigmund, the fragments of which were still kept by Hiordis. From those fragments was forged a mighty blade that, when crashed down on the anvil, made great gouges in it. Regin and Sigurd then set sail for the land of the Volsungs. On the way they picked up Odin, although they didn't realize who this stranger was.

RIGHT *As Regin sleeps, Sigurd roasts the heart of the dwarfish smith's brother, who became the dragon Fafnir. This is a detail from a twelfth- or thirteenth-century carved wooden portal at Hylestad Church in Norway.*

LEFT *Details from a twelfth- or thirteenth-century wooden portal at Hylestad Church, Norway, showing the dwarf Regin reforging the sword Sigurd had been given by his father.*

RIGHT *Part of a Viking cross found at Andreas, Isle of Man, Britain. At top left we can see Sigurd roasting Fafnir's heart.*

BELOW RIGHT *The 'Waterfall of the Gods' in Iceland. According to legend, Thorsten, on being converted to Christianity about* AD *1000, threw his pagon idols over these falls.*

Sigurd killed Lygni, the killer of his father, and then moved on, with Regin, to kill Fafnir. Again Odin helped him, this time pointing out that the dragon daily used the same path in order to quench his thirst at a nearby river: all that Sigurd had to do was to lie in wait. The operation was a complete success. Regin asked Sigurd to cut out the dragon's heart, barbecue it and serve it up as a meal, and Sigurd immediately agreed to the request. During the roasting Sigurd at one stage touched the heart with his fingers to see if it were ready yet; the hot meat stung his fingers, and he put them to his lips, immediately finding that he could understand the talk of the birds. They were saying to each other that Regin planned to kill him, and that he would be best advised to kill the sage at once and himself devour the dragon's heart and blood, then to claim the treasure. This Sigurd did. He then awoke Brunhild (*q.v.*) from her timeless sleep and became her betrothed. Unfortunately, he then became enamoured of Gudrun (*q.v.*), a daughter of the king of the Nibelungs, and forgot all about Brunhild. Sigurd had kept some of Fafnir's heart, and at his wedding to Gudrun he gave her a little to eat; he also became a blood-brother of her brothers Gunnar and Högni. Gunnar determined to marry Brunhild, with the results seen in Chapter 4. Guttorm, the third son of the king of the Nibelungs, was deputed to slay Sigurd, and succeeded, although he lost his own life in doing so. Brunhild shared her one-time lover's funeral pyre.

THORSTEN

Thorsten was one of the nine sons of the hero Viking (*q.v.*) by his second marriage and a survivor of the war with the sons of Viking's great friend Njorfe. The war started when one of Njorfe's sons, during a game of ball, treacherously hit out at one of Viking's sons, who later killed him.

Thorsten became a pirate. He encountered one of the two surviving sons of Njorfe, Jokul, who seems to have been a rather unpleasant piece of work: he had killed the king of Sogn, banished the kingdom's prince, Belé, and turned the princess Ingeborg into an old hag. Jokul used evil magic in attempts to kill Thorsten, but was unsuccessful – in large part thanks to the help of the seeming hag, whom Thorsten agreed to marry in thanks for her assistance. The hero restored Belé to his rightful throne and was delighted to discover that Ingeborg was in fact a beautiful young maiden.

Thorsten, Belé and another hero called Angantyr had many adventures together. They recovered a ship called Ellida that had once been given to Viking by the god Aegir (*q.v.*). They conquered the Orkney Isles, of which Angantyr became the king, although he pledged himself to pay an annual tribute to Belé. Then Thorsten and Belé regained from a pirate called Soté a magic arm-ring that had been forged by Völund (*q.v.*).

Thorsten and Ingeborg had a son called Frithiof (*q.v.*), who himself became a hero.

VIKING

Viking was a grandson of a Norwegian king called Haloge; according to some versions of the mythology Haloge was in fact the god Loki. Whatever the truth of this, Viking was born on an island called Bornholm, in the Baltic Sea. By the time he had reached the age of 15 he was so strong and huge that rumours of him reached Sweden and in particular a princess called Hunvor. At the time Hunvor was being pestered by the attentions of a giant. Pausing only to collect from his father a magic sword called Angurvadel, Viking sailed to Sweden and did battle with the giant. He would have married Hunvor there and then but it was considered that he was too young. He therefore sailed around the North Sea for some years, being tormented by the relatives of the dead

In the whalebone carvings on the early-eighth-century Franks Casket, now in the British Museum, we find a delicious mix of Norse and Christian mythologies. RIGHT *In this section we see, on the left, Völund's smithy and, on the right, the Adoration of the Magi.*

giant and befriended by a man called Halfdan; in due course Viking married Hunvor and Halfdan married a servant of hers called Ingeborg.

Over the next few years Viking and Halfdan led raids to other countries during which they took great pleasure in slaughtering, preferably females whom they first raped. Nevertheless, they were faithful to their wives; such is the way of Norse mythology. They also made friends, after a long war, with a king called Njorfe.

Hunvor died; Viking put out their son Ring to a foster-father and then remarried. He and his new wife had nine sons; Njorfe and *his* wife had the same number. Despite the fact that their fathers had sworn all the oaths of friendship, the sons sustained a long-term antagonism between the two families. Much of the time this took an innocent enough form: as far as one can work out from the legends, the two sets of lads merely met each other on the Norse equivalent of a

football pitch. However, one of Njorfe's sons committed an overly 'cynical' foul on one of Viking's sons, so the latter killed him. This murder infuriated Viking, and thus he banished the boy; the other brothers told their father that they would follow him into exile. The eldest of these sons was Thorsten; to him Viking gave the sword Angurvadel.

Njorfe's sons were not satisfied by this, and followed Viking's sons into the faraway land where they hid. There was a great battle, with the result that only two of Viking's sons – Thorsten and Thorer – and two of Njorfe's sons – Jokul and another – survived. These two pairs swore undying hatred for each other, so Viking sent his own two sons to the court of Halfdan. Thorsten had adventures of his own, during one of which he killed Jokul.

VÖLUND

Völund is well known as Wayland or Weland the Smith; under the former name he turns up, for example, as a character in Walter Scott's novel *Kenilworth* (1821). His brothers were called Egil and Slagfinn.

One day the three brothers came across three Valkyries – Alvit, Olrun and Svanhvit – swimming in a river, and immediately raped them, having stolen the Valkyries' swan plumage so that they were no longer able to leave the Earth. For nine years the three maidens remained with their captors, but then they were able to recover their plumage and return to Valhalla. This was much mourned by the three brothers, and Egil and Slagfinn set off on a quest to see if they could rediscover their brides. Völund, however, reckoned that their search was futile, and so stayed at home.

Alvit had given him a ring, and he looked on this lovingly. A practised smith, he made 700 other rings exactly like it and tied all 701 of them up in a bundle. One day he discovered that one of the rings had been stolen and he was much cheered, believing that this meant that Alvit had returned to Earth to reclaim it and would soon come back to be his wife again.

That night, however, he was attacked and taken prisoner by the king of Sweden, Nidud, who had confiscated Alvit's ring (giving it to his daughter Bodvild) as well as Völund's magic sword. The hapless smith was incarcerated on an island, his hamstrings being cut so that he could have no hope of escape. There he was forced to labour each and every day at his forge to manufacture weapons and ornaments for the brutal king. Völund's opinion of Nidud was by this time not of the highest, and all the time he plotted escape and revenge. He made himself a pair of wings just like those Alvit had used, so that he could fly to join her in Valhalla.

Nidud brought to Völund one day the smith's magic sword, asking for it to be repaired. Völund pretended to comply, but in fact hid it and returned to Nidud an exact replica. A little afterwards he lured Nidud's sons into his smithy, slaughtered them, used their skulls to make goblets and their teeth and eyes as adornments; these he gave to the royal couple, who received them as precious gifts, little realizing their origins. Having exacted his next revenge by raping Bodvild and repossessing from her his magic ring, he donned the wings he had crafted and flew to Nidud's palace, where he enumerated loudly and at length the king's failings and sins. Nidud called for Völund's brother Egil, who was now his slave, and instructed him to shoot Völund down out of the sky; however, Völund signalled to his brother to aim his arrow at a bladder he clutched that was full of the blood of Nidud's sons. This Egil did, and Nidud assumed that his royal archer had slain the enemy, little realizing that Völund had flown.

Völund then rejoined Alvit and is still living with her and practising his craft: he will continue to do so until Ragnarok.

RIGHT *Made from walrus ivory around 1135–1150 and found on the Isle of Lewis, Scotland, this rook (castle) comes from a Viking chess set. When we think of the Vikings we envisage only mindless slaughter, but in fact they regarded chess as such a fine sport that it could have been their equivalent of football.*

SIX

Ragnarok

In this book we have concentrated to exclusion on things that have already happened – or, at least, have done so according to the Norse myths. However, the mythology encompassed also what was going to happen at some unspecified time in the future, when the gods themselves would die. Here there is a definite parallel with the Christian account, in Revelation, *of the forthcoming Apocalypse, for Ragnarok too is a final battle between the forces of good and evil. A major difference is that after Ragnarok, unlike after the Apocalypse, there will be a rebirth of both a new pantheon and all life on Earth. The German equivalent of Ragnarok is, of course, Götterdämmerung.*

LEFT *Swedish bronze matrix, dating from about the eighth century, used for fashioning plaques for Viking helmets: a man with a boar on either side. Could this represent an early version of Odin with his two wolves? Or could it symbolize the last deathly struggle at Ragnarok between Odin and Fenris?*

LEFT *Part of the Gosforth Cross, showing one of the events of Ragnarok: Odin is attacked by a winged dragon.*

What will happen at this terrible time? The first answer to the question is that the popular translation of Ragnarok as the 'twilight of the gods' is false: this is to be the *death* of the gods. It will be brought about largely because the gods tolerated the existence of the evil Loki, who, bound in the most horrific circumstances, has for long plotted their downfall.

The first sign of the onset of Ragnarok will be Fimbulvetr, a years-long savage winter when snow will constantly fall from all points of the compass. The wolves chasing the Sun and the Moon will catch up with them and devour them. Loki and Fenris, as well as Hel's dog, Garm, will succeed in breaking their bonds in order to attack the gods. Nidhug, the dragon gnawing at one of the roots of Yggdrasil, will at last succeed in severing it. The god Heimdall (*q.v.*) will sound a note on his trumpet, warning of what is imminent, and this note will be heard by all. The Aesir and the Einheriar (the dead warriors taken to Valhalla from the battlefield) will hear this blast and rally to Vigrid, where the final battle will take place. The seas will be stirred up into a frenzy, and this will trigger Jormungand, the World Serpent, into raising himself from his bed in the depths of the ocean to join in the battle.

The serpent's writhing will create huge waves, and one of these will launch a ship called Naglfari, created entirely from the nails of those of the dead whose kin have failed to cut their nails. Loki will board this ship, accompanied by a horde from the realm of Muspell. The frost giants, too, will sail in a ship to Vigrid in order to battle with the Aesir; their captain will be the giant Hrym. Hel will join the forces of evil, as will her sycophants Garm and Nidhug. Surtr, the flame giant, will come to add to Loki's army, followed by numerous of his kin. As this last army rides over Bifrost its sheer weight will shatter the rainbow bridge.

The gods will show no fear despite the strength of the armies facing them. Odin will, one last time, consult the

RIGHT *The seeress who told Odin that Ragnarok was inevitable during his sojourn into the realm of Hel is seen at the upper left of this section of a cross slab found at Jurby, Isle of Man, Britain, which dates from the tenth century.*

Norns and Mimir, and then rejoin his fellows. Then the battle will be joined.

Odin will be slain in his duel with Fenris. Surtr will kill Frey and Loki Heimdall. Tyr will die at the teeth of Garm, and Thor in a torrent of venom from the mouth of Jormungand. Vidar will tear Fenris to pieces. Surtr will set fire to Yggdrasil, thereby destroying also the halls of the gods and all of the plant-life of the Earth.

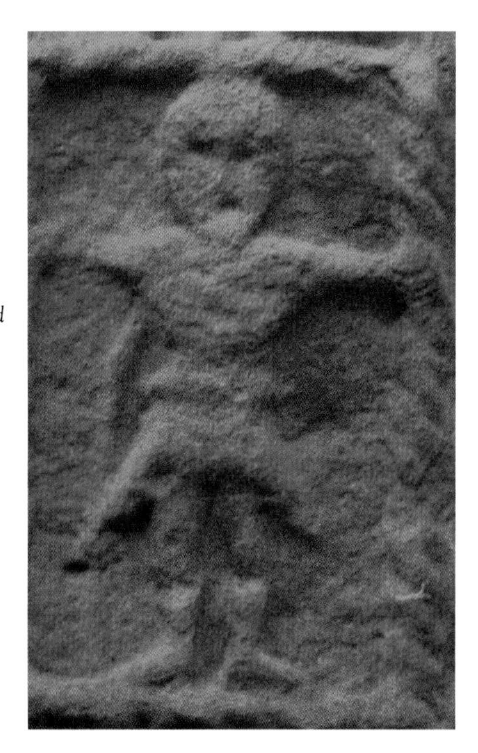

RIGHT *Three faces of the tenth-century Gosforth Cross depict scenes from Viking mythology, especially Ragnarok. The fourth (eastern) face contains an image of the Crucifixion, showing how the two mythologies had blended by this early stage.*

However, things will come into being again. A daughter of Sol will drive the chariot of the Sun, and will do so in a much better fashion than her mother had done. The first two mortals of the new race after Ragnarok will be called Lif and Lifthrasir; she and he will repopulate the Earth with their children. The gods Vali and Vidar will survive the battle, as will the sons of Thor, Magni and Modi, and the god Hoenir. Balder and Hoder will be returned to life. Christianity made its mark on Norse mythology, too, and so it is recorded that, after Ragnarok, there will be the incarnation of a god too great to be named – in other words, Jahweh.

The Truth Behind Some 'Myths'

Until a few decades ago it was assumed that the Viking myths were, without exception, nothing more than just that – myths. More recently, however, good evidence has appeared to show that some of the tales were firmly rooted in fact. The Saga of Eirik the Red tells of how this mighty warrior sailed from Scandinavia to discover a new country to the west, which he called 'Greenland' and where he founded a Viking colony around AD 985. This colony was not particularly successful, but it served as a launching post for the much more ambitious expedition of Eirik's son, Leif Eriksson, who sailed all the way across the Atlantic to found a colony, Vinland, on the eastern coast of North America. Remnants of this colony have now been found.

The Vikings also worked southwards, down to the Mediterranean, at one point – with the Irish Celts – even threatening the Roman Empire. In this context many of the 'myths' about the Vikings must be looked at very seriously indeed.

BELOW *Hjorleifshofdi, on the southern coast of Iceland, the first place where the Vikings established a settlement on that island.*

LEFT *A 1590 version of a map supposed to have been compiled by Sigurdur Stefánsson. Although the scale is lamentably awry (possibly because of copying and recopying over the centuries), it is clear that it is based on knowledge rather than guesswork.*

TOP LEFT *Reconstruction of a Viking farm at Stong, Iceland.*

BOTTOM LEFT *Interior of the Stong farm.*

RIGHT *A piece of modern sculpture at Bratahild shows representations of Viking symbols.*

RIGHT *Remains of a Viking church at Hvalsoe, Greenland.*

RIGHT *Part of the eastern coast of Newfoundland. It is on this coast that Leif Eriksson probably founded, around* AD *1000, his short-lived colony called Vinland.*

RIGHT *Dimly visible remains of a Viking settlement at Thingvellir, Iceland.*

FURTHER READING

Crossley-Holland, Kevin
The Norse Myths
London, Deutsch, 1980

Davidson, HR Ellis
Gods and Myths of Northern Europe
Harmondsworth, Penguin, 1964

Davidson, HR Ellis
Scandinavian Mythology
London, Hamlyn, revised edition 1982

Davidson, HR Ellis
The Viking Road to Byzantium
London, Allen & Unwin, 1976

Esping, Mikael
The Vikings
London, Piccolo, 1982

Green, Roger Lancelyn
Myths of the Norsemen
London, Puffin, 1970

Guerber, HA
Myths of the Norsemen
London, Harrap, 1908

Hveberg, Harald (translated Pat Shaw Iversen)
Of Gods and Giants
Oslo, Johan Grundt Tanum Forlag with the Office of Cultural Relations,
Norwegian Ministry of Foreign Affairs, 1961

Jones, Gwyn (translator and editor)
Eirik the Red and Other Icelandic Sagas
London, Oxford University Press, 1961

Sawyer, PH
The Age of the Vikings
London, Edward Arnold, second edition, 1971

Snorri Sturluson (translated by Jean I Young)
The Prose Edda
Cambridge, Bowes & Bowes, 1954

Egyptology

CHAPTER ONE

The STUDY of ANCIENT EGYPT

ABOVE: *Jean François Champollion (1790–1832) – the 'Father of Egyptology' and the decipherer of hieroglyphs.*

Although knowledge of the civilization and language of the Ancient Egyptians was lost for many centuries, their impressive monuments remained a source of amazement and curiosity to all Europeans who travelled to Egypt. Greek and Roman writers recorded their journeys and throughout medieval times pilgrims passed through Egypt on their way to the Holy Land. By the eighteenth century many travellers had published accounts of their journeys which often included detailed illustrations of the amazing things they saw. These images of Ancient Egypt appeared alien to Europeans, who were more familiar with their classical heritage. The languages of this heritage, Greek and Latin, had been maintained and its art and architecture had enjoyed fashionable revivals. The mysterious hieroglyphs, weird animal-headed gods and exotic costumes of Ancient Egypt appeared to Europeans of the past, as they do to us nowadays, very strange indeed.

The first major study of Ancient Egyptian civilization was undertaken by a group of French scholars who accompanied Napoleon's Egyptian campaign in 1798. They took with them artists to record what they saw and they eventually published a whole series of beautifully illustrated volumes called the *Description de L'Egypte*. At this time the French Army discovered a stone at a place called Rosetta which had the same text inscribed on it in Greek, hieroglyphics and another Egyptian text called Demotic. This inscription was to provide the Frenchman, Champollion, with the key to deciphering the hieroglyphs after 20 years of dedicated study. The decipherment of the script between 1822 and 1824 and the publication of the multi-volume work, the *Description de L'Egypte 1809–30,* mark the beginning of Egyptology as a separate subject.

After his success with understanding the hieroglyphs, Champollion mounted a joint expedition with an Italian called Rosellini, to record the Egyptian monuments in detail. As a result they each produced beautifully illustrated publications which, together with the *Description de L'Egypte,* did much to popularize Ancient Egypt throughout Europe. They also inspired more travellers and merchants to visit Egypt, attracted not only by eager curiosity but by the opportunity to return with antiquities which were becoming valuable. We should not forget that at this time travel to Egypt was lengthy and hazardous,

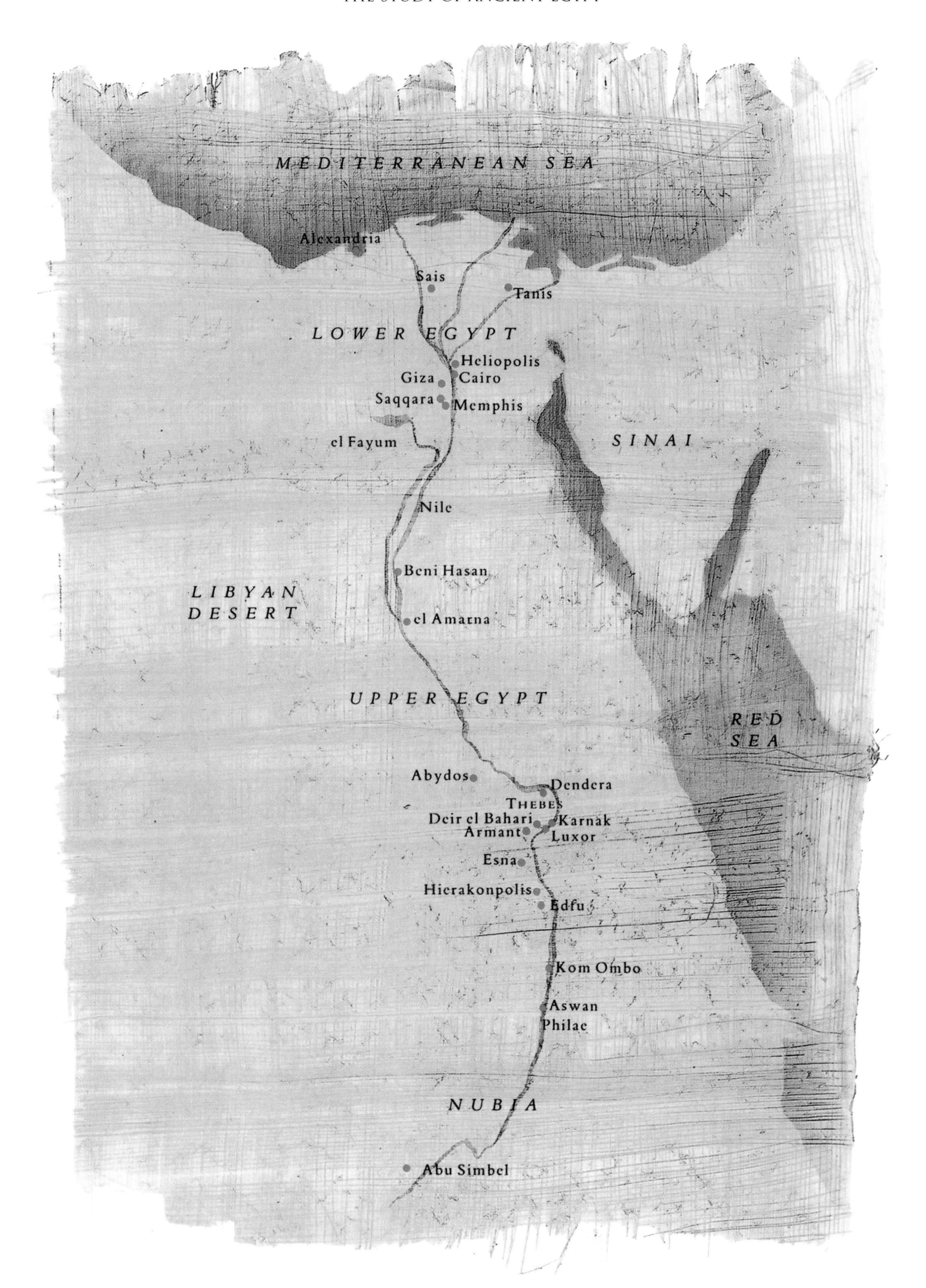
MEDITERRANEAN SEA
Alexandria
Sais
Tanis
LOWER EGYPT
Heliopolis
Giza
Cairo
Saqqara
Memphis
el Fayum
SINAI
Nile
Beni Hasan
LIBYAN
DESERT
el Amarna
UPPER EGYPT
RED
SEA
Abydos
Dendera
THEBES
Deir el Bahari
Karnak
Armant
Luxor
Esna
Hierakonpolis
Edfu
Kom Ombo
Aswan
Philae
NUBIA
Abu Simbel

ABOVE: *The Temple of Abu Simbel by Scottish artist and traveller David Roberts (1796–1864). In the 19th century many ancient monuments were covered in drifts of sand.*

the inhabitants were not particularly friendly to Europeans, while the climate and prevalence of serious diseases added to the difficulty.

The most colourful personality to be involved with Egyptology at this time was an Italian called Giovanni Belzoni. He had been a strongman performer in the London theatre and had travelled to Egypt to work as an engineer. These skills led him to become involved in the removal of a colossal bust of Ramses II which he successfully transported to the British Museum in 1818. This project was commissioned by Henry Salt, who was the British Consul in Egypt. Salt himself became a keen collector of Egyptian antiquities and his collection, with the help of Belzoni, was to form the nucleus of that of the British Museum. They were both involved in lengthy and frustrating financial negotiations with the trustees of the Museum who disputed the value of some of the sculpture. The main problem was that many people regarded Egyptian statues as greatly inferior to Classical, being merely curiosities rather than works of art. Belzoni went on to complete some successful excavations in Egypt, discovering an entrance to the Second Pyramid and the Tomb of Seti I, in the Valley of the Kings. He also travelled far south to the great temple of Abu Simbel in Nubia, which he was the first to enter since ancient times. He published a popular account of these exploits in four different languages and staged a spectacular exhibition at the Egyptian Hall in Piccadilly, in 1821.

Sir John Gardner Wilkinson is generally regarded as the founder of British Egyptology. He spent many years in Egypt copying paintings and inscriptions and mastering the ancient language. He was the first to attempt placing

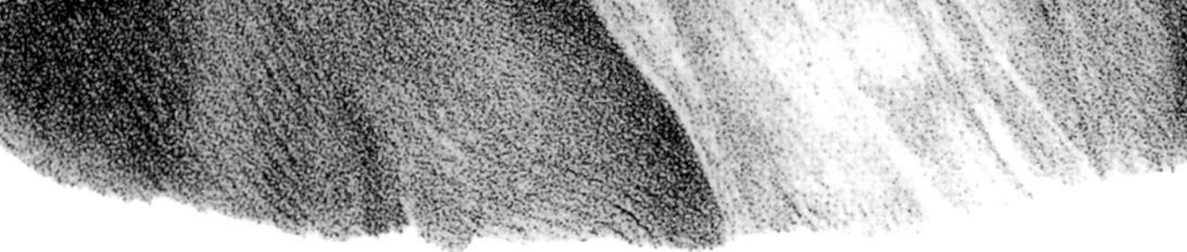

BELOW: *Giovanni Belzoni (1778–1823), an Italian excavator, explorer, and adventurer who was the most colourful character in 19th-century Egyptology.*

BELOW RIGHT: *Collection of pots from the publication* Description de l'Egypte *(1809–22) which recorded Egyptian antiquities in unprecedented detail.*

OPPOSITE PAGE: *Frontispiece from the publication* Description de l'Egypte *(1809–22) showing French soldiers among the ancient ruins.*

the royal dynasties and kings into proper date order and gave many important antiquities to the British Museum. He popularized Egyptology with his best-known book *The Manners and Customs of the Ancient Egyptians* (1837) which became the standard work on religion, daily life and culture for many years. Another key figure in Egyptology at this time was Robert Hay, who like Wilkinson was not funded by any organization. He financed a number of important expeditions resulting in detailed studies.

This essential, serious survey work eventually gained official interest and, in the 1840s, the King of Prussia financed a large-scale expedition to the Nile. This was led by the capable Karl Lepsius who secured some major antiquities for the future Berlin Museum and produced a lavish publication of 24 volumes, entitled *Denkmaeler*. This is the largest work on Egyptology ever published and is still a valuable reference work for scholars today.

Egyptologists had been largely concerned with dating and language, and excavating had been undertaken in an unscientific way. Many inscriptions and papyri were destroyed in an eager search for more attractive antiquities, while unscrupulous dealers had little regard as to how they gained access to tombs. A Frenchman, called Auguste Mariette, who was collecting antiquities for the Louvre Museum, realized the need to prevent indiscriminate looting of sites and set up an official antiquities service for the Egyptians. Mariette ensured that excavation permits were only issued to qualified scholars and went on to found the Cairo Museum. A new standard of orderly, scientific archaeology was set by W.M.F. Petrie, who excavated all over Egypt, publishing a detailed record and analysis of the finds almost every year between 1881 and 1925.

ABOVE: *W.M.F. Petrie (1853–1942), the most active archaeologist working in Egypt, who pioneered new scientific methods and produced some 1,000 publications.*

A drawing by Giovanni Belzoni (1778–1823) showing the transport of a colossal bust of Ramses II which became part of the British Museum collection. Belzoni's successful direction of the transport of such a heavy statue to England was a remarkable achievement.

RIGHT: *Portrait of Henry Salt (1780–1827), the British Consul in Egypt whose important collection of antiquities formed the basis of the British Museum's Egyptian collection. (British Museum.)*

LEFT: *Coloured drawing of painted reliefs from the tomb of Seti I by Henry Salt (1780–1827), the British Consul in Egypt. He was a keen collector, responsible for obtaining some of the British Museum's major sculptures and also a skilled amateur artist. (British Museum.)*

In the 1870s a pit was discovered at Thebes containing the mummies of most of the New Kingdom Pharaohs. These had been removed from their original tombs in antiquity by the priests and reburied to prevent their violation by tomb robbers. Archaeologists turned their attention to exploring the Valley of the Kings at Thebes to locate the original tombs. Howard Carter, a former assistant of Petrie, began excavating there in 1912 under the sponsorship of Lord Carnarvon. Eventually in 1922, he discovered the tomb of Tutankhamun, the first Pharaoh's tomb to be found virtually intact. The incredible wealth of gold and the superb artistic craftsmanship displayed

A Comparative Chronology of Ancient Egypt

Date	In Egypt	Period	Elsewhere in the World
500 AD	Last known demotic inscription Last hieroglyphic inscription Queen Zenobia of Palmyra occupies Egypt Bucolic War Alexandrian riots Death of Cleopatra	GRÆCO ROMAN PERIOD	Classical Mayan culture of Middle America Rome sacked Constantinople founded Middle Moche culture in South America Main building begins at Teotihuacan Jewish Diaspora Vesuvius engulfs Pompeii Claudian invasion of Britain
0	Temple built at Edfu Rebel native rulers at Thebes Ptolemy Lagos rules as Pharaoh Alexander the Great in Egypt Last native Pharaohs	PTOLEMAIC PERIOD DYNASTY 21–30 LATE DYNASTIC PERIOD	Birth of Christ Buddhism reaches China Julius Caesar invades Britain Destruction of Carthage Hannibal crosses Alps Start of unified Chinese Empire Death of Emperor Ashoka Alexander the Great in India Construction of Parthenon Defeat of Persians at Marathon
500 BC	Persians annex Egypt Greek colonies in Egypt Assyrian invasions Kushite kings rule Egypt Sheshonq I sacks Jerusalem Greatest power of Theban high priests		Birth of Buddha Nebuchadnezzar destroys Jerusalem Medes destroy Babylon Rise of cities in India Beginnings of Great Wall of China Rome founded First Olympic Games held Death of Solomon David rules from Jerusalem Chavin culture of South America
1000 BC	Extensive tomb robbing at Thebes Ramesses III repulses Sea Peoples Merneptah checks Libyan invasions Clashes with Hittites in Syria Tutankhamun returns to Thebes Akhenaten founds Akhetaten Luxor temple begun Tuthmosis III conquers Syria Queen Hatshepsut rules as Pharaoh	DYNASTY 18–20 NEW KINGDOM	Fall of Troy Olmec culture of Middle America Main building phase at Stonehenge Shang dynasty in China Fall of Knossos and Minoan Empire
1500 BC	First tomb in Valley of Kings Amosis expels Hyksos Thebans oppose Hyksos Hyksos seize Memphis Avaris becomes Hyksos capital Trade with Asia, Africa and Mediterranean Islands Karnak temple begun Fortresses built in Nubia New capital at Itj-tawy Mentuhotpe II reunites Egypt	DYNASTY 13–17 SECOND INTERMEDIATE PERIOD DYNASTY 11–12 MIDDLE KINGDOM	Hammurabi codifies law

A Comparative Chronology of Ancient Egypt			
Date	**In Egypt**	**Period**	**Elsewhere in the World**
2000 BC	Civil war between Thebes and Heracleopolis Pepi II reigns 94 years Unas pyramid first to contain text Sun temples at Abu Gurab Expeditions to Punt (Somalia)	DYNASTY 7–10 FIRST INTERMEDIATE PERIOD DYNASTY 3–6 OLD KINGDOM	First pottery made in Middle America Earliest smelting of iron in Middle East Indo-Europeans enter Anatolia Sargon of Agade Indus Valley Cultures of India Tablet archives at Ebla
2500 BC	Khufu builds Great Pyramid First true pyramid at Dahshur Step pyramid at Saqqara Expeditions to Sinai and Nubia Trade with Asia and tropical Africa First stone architectural elements	DYNASTY 1–2 ARCHAIC PERIOD	Royal burials at Ur
3000 BC	Invention of hieroglyphic writing Egypt united, Memphis founded Glazed composition made for first time Hard stone vessels produced Painted buff pottery	PRE DYNASTIC PERIOD NAQADA II CULTURE	First pottery made in South America Sumerians introduce writing
3500 BC	Stone vessels first produced White paint incised pottery First models of human figure Metal working practised Blacked topped red pottery first produced	NAQADA I CULTURE BADARIAN CULTURE	
4000 BC	Cereals and flax grown	EGYPTIAN STONE AGE	

ABOVE: *Howard Carter (1874–1939) and his team of archaeologists on horseback in the Valley of the Kings just before their famous discovery of Tutankhamun's tomb in 1922.*

in all this treasure attracted massive media coverage, which really captured peoples' imagination about Ancient Egypt.

Besides tombs, archaeologists excavated settlement sites in order to find out more about the Egyptians' daily life. The most important discoveries in this field have been at the ancient city of El-Amarna and the workmen's village of Deir el-Medina. At El-Amarna, a German team led by Ludwig Borchardt discovered the famous bust of Nefertiti, while excavating a sculptor's workshop. Large-scale archaeological surveys have been of great importance to Egyptology, initiated by the work of Norman de Garis Davies (1865–1941). He became the greatest copyist of Egyptian tombs and published more than 25 volumes on tombs alone, while his wife Nina made beautiful coloured reproductions of the wall-paintings. The most important work of this type to follow Davies was done by the University of Chicago who have a base at Luxor called The Chicago House. This organization, founded by James Breasted, has published an exhaustive record of the important temples at Medinet Habu and Abydos. Many specialized societies have also been founded who sponsor excavations in Egypt and publish regular journals. One of the most famous is the Egypt Exploration Society which has a distinguished history of fieldwork and offers its members a means of keeping in touch with the latest developments in Egyptological research.

Although the treasures of Tutankhamun were handed over to the Cairo Museum, the Egyptian Government has been somewhat restrictive in granting permits to excavate since their discovery. They are naturally anxious not to lose any more of their cultural heritage, and scholars and museums have found sponsorship difficult since they are not allowed to keep what they excavate. From the 1950s onwards Egyptian universities and the Egyptian antiquities organizations have themselves excavated many sites and published an increasing amount of research material. However, in the 1960s the Egyptians appealed to the world to help them save their important Nubian monuments from the flooding due to the construction of the Aswan High Dam. An International Consortium of contractors and archaeologists was set up to move the

ABOVE: *Coloured engraving from Champoillon's epic publication* Monuments de l'Égypt *(1835–47) showing Ramses II in his chariot.*

BELOW: *Coloured engraving showing a Theban tomb painting from Rosellini's publication (1832–44) which recorded Egyptian monuments in great detail.*

ABOVE: *The Pyramids of Giza (c 2,500 BC).*

LEFT: *The gold mask of Tutankhamun (c 1,350 BC).*

RIGHT: *Head of Cleopatra (c 50 BC). (British Museum.)*

huge Temple of Abu Simbel and some other monuments to higher ground.

The rescue project has inspired detailed surveys of sites under threat from the flood waters and greater interest in Nubia. Scholars now treat Nubian studies as a separate branch of Egyptology, with current research concentrating on the earliest settlements and the Kingdom of Meroe which survived into the fourth century AD.

Work in Egypt itself is only a small part of Egyptology and much has been achieved by studying collections of antiquities distributed throughout world museums. Understanding the language has always been of major importance to Egyptologists and they can learn a great deal from reading the large quantity of texts that have survived written on stone monuments, papyrus, and pottery and limestone ostraca fragments. The most useful textbook for students of the language is the famous *Egyptian Grammar* by Sir Alan Gardiner. First published in 1927, it has enabled generations of Egyptologists to study the hieroglyphic script. Great advances have been made in reading the difficult Demotic script and many texts await translation and publication. These may give us some fresh information about the Ancient Egyptians.

Nowadays, Ancient Egypt can be studied at various levels at universities, colleges, schools and adult education institutes. It can be taken as a separate degree subject or combined with Ancient History, Archaeology, Art History, Classics or Language Studies. Many museums, societies and adult education institutes also offer lecture programmes with slides, films and videos. Egypt itself is becoming increasingly popular and affordable to tourists and certain companies provide special study holidays with cruises down the Nile which have guest Egyptologists and expert guides to accompany the tours.

Modern Egyptologists have far greater study resources than their predecessors. They have dictionaries, lists of kings, and detailed site surveys to help them with their research.

BOTTOM RIGHT: *Howard Carter and Lord Carnarvon at work in the tomb of Tutankhamun in 1922.*

ABOVE: *A view of the Ramesseum, Thebes in the 19th century by Francis Frith (1822–98), one of the most notable British pioneer photographers who travelled to Egypt.*

BELOW: *A watercolour drawing by the famous archaeologist Howard Carter (1874–1939) who was also an accomplished artist from a family of painters.*

Left: *Although there are only a few obelisks still standing in Egypt, there are over 50 in the public squares of capitals in Europe and America. (David Roberts lithograph c 1846).*

Above: *August Mariette (1821–81) formed the Egyptian Antiquities service and founded the Cairo Museum. He directed many important excavations and published many books on Egyptology.*

Below: *Egyptologists at work with a computer. Modern technology has aided the study of Egyptology.*

Right: *The Tomb of Queen Nefertari – watercolor copy by Nina Davies (1881–1965). Records like these are invaluable since many tomb paintings have deteriorated greatly since their discovery.*

Study of museum collections has also greatly improved through better documentation of the artefacts on computers and detailed photographic archives. Fresh knowledge can often be gained by using the latest scientific techniques to help with dating and analysis of the material. There is greater contact between Egyptologists internationally through specialist conferences and the current popularity of loan exhibitions of Egyptian antiquities.

Ancient Egypt covered a long period of history and a vast geographical area. So much has already been achieved by Egyptologists, yet there are some periods of history and many Pharaohs that we know little or nothing about. Research on existing collections is continuing and there must be countless antiquities still to be excavated and studied.

C H A P T E R T W O

The PYRAMIDS

ABOVE: *The Pyramids of Giza.*

Many people are unaware that any other pyramids exist besides the three at Giza. There are in fact remains of about 80 pyramids in Egypt, while there are well over 100 later, less substantial ones in the Sudan. However, the superior construction, scale and accessibility to Cairo of the Giza pyramids have made them the most famous. They are the only one of the Seven Wonders of the Ancient World still surviving.

Despite many fanciful theories, these pyramids were simply tombs of the Pharaohs. They all contained sarcophagi and are situated on the West Bank of the Nile where the Egyptians traditionally buried their dead. Like all pyramids they were built in groups and were part of a vast cemetery complex. This included mortuary temples and tombs of other members of the royal family and court and numerous priests and officials. Although the Giza pyramids are unique, their perfect form developed from earlier royal tomb structures.

Until the third dynasty, the traditional form of royal tomb was a mastaba. These were mainly large rectangular, flat-topped buildings with sloping sides. Beneath them were the burial chambers and rooms cut deep into the bedrock. Usually built in mud-brick, they were like architectural forms of prehistoric burial mounds. The earliest surviving pyramid, the famous Step Pyramid, at Saqqara, was itself originally conceived as a mastaba. At some stage the plans were altered, and the pyramid grew into a series of six progressively diminishing terraces.

The Step Pyramid was built around 2,650 BC for King Djoser by his chief architect Imhotep. It is the oldest large stone building in the world and Imhotep's great achievement led him to be revered by later generations as a god of wisdom. The Step Pyramid is the major feature in a vast complex of funerary architecture. These buildings and courtyards acted as a kind of stage set for the dead king to perform his funerary rites. They are of great importance, because, being made of stone they have survived, where most earlier mud-brick structures have disintegrated. They were originally enclosed by a wall some 1,500 feet long by 900 feet wide (500 by 300 metres). In its day, the sight of this wall of shining white limestone with the pyramid rising out of it must have been a majestic spectacle. Standing on the edge of a plateau overlooking

ABOVE: *The Step Pyramid of King Djoser at Saqqara is the earliest surviving pyramid, built around 2,650 BC.*

the ancient capital of Memphis, it must have represented a great symbol of the eternal power of their God King to the Egyptians who built it. Its clean, sharp edges have since been blurred through the passage of time and its finely worked limestone casing has been plundered, yet it is still impressive rising to a height of 200 feet (60 metres). The body of King Djoser was never found and like most tombs, the pyramid had been looted in ancient times. However, two alabaster sarcophagi were discovered, one containing the body of a child, while some 30,000 stone vases were also found in the precinct.

The pyramid underwent several stages of development in the next century before the Giza pyramids. Several miles south of Saqqara, King Sneferu built the so-called 'Bent' Pyramid, which is not stepped but straight-sided, except for a curious change of angle in the middle. He built another pyramid at Maidum which seems originally to have been stepped then modified to become straight-sided. The outer courses of masonry collapsed in later times, leaving the curious structure which survives today. This has become merely a mound of sand and rubble surmounted by a tall tower which is actually the cone of the pyramid. Sneferu's son and successor was probably Khufu and he selected the imposing site at Giza to build the most perfect, impressive pyramid of all, the Great Pyramid.

The Great Pyramid in its original state rose 481 feet (160 metres) and is estimated to have contained 2,300,000 blocks of stone. Its vast size has prompted people to calculate some fascinating statistics. The area it covers is large enough to hold the cathedrals of Florence, Milan and St Peters in Rome, as well as St Pauls and Westminster Abbey in London. Napoleon estimated that the blocks of stone from the three Giza Pyramids would have been sufficient to build a wall of 10 feet (three metres) high and one foot (30 cm) thick around the whole of France. This claim was also verified by an eminent contemporary French mathematician.

The orientation of the Great Pyramid is incredibly accurate. The four sides, each of over 700 feet (230 metres) long, are aligned almost exactly on true north, south, east and

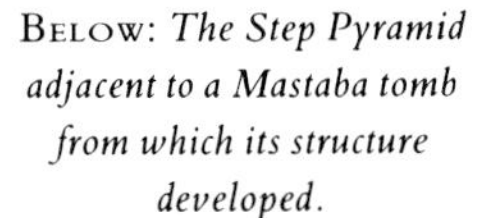

BELOW: *The Step Pyramid adjacent to a Mastaba tomb from which its structure developed.*

Above: *The Pyramids of Giza – The Great Pyramid of Khufu (far left) and the Pyramids of Khafra (centre) and Mankaura (right) – the three much smaller pyramids in front belonged to queens.*

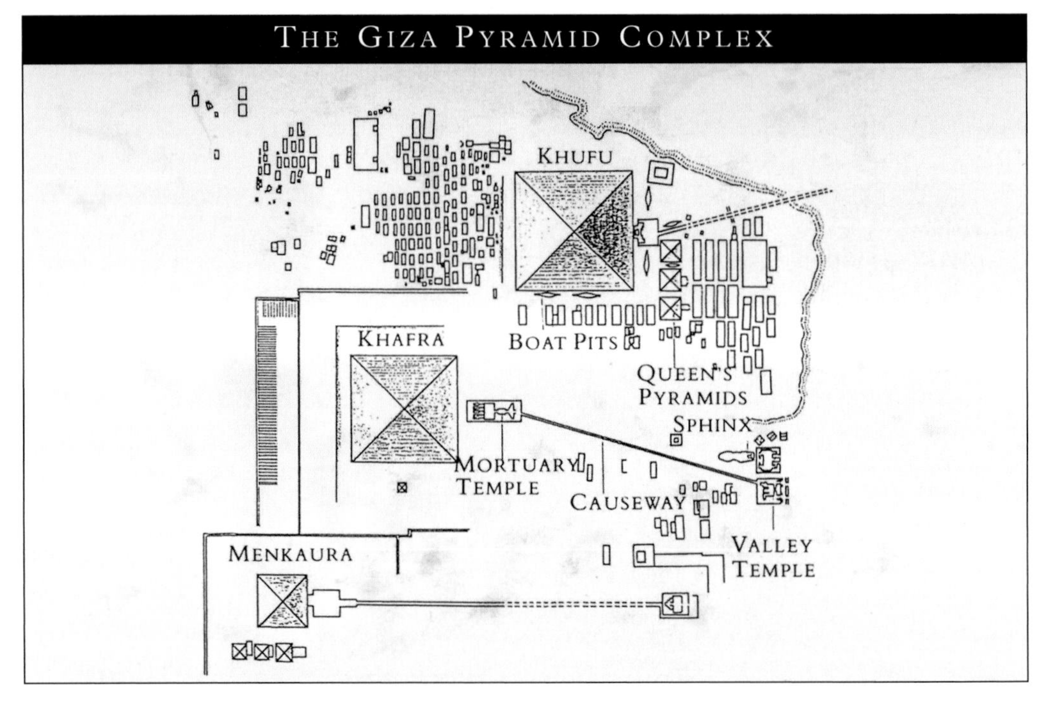

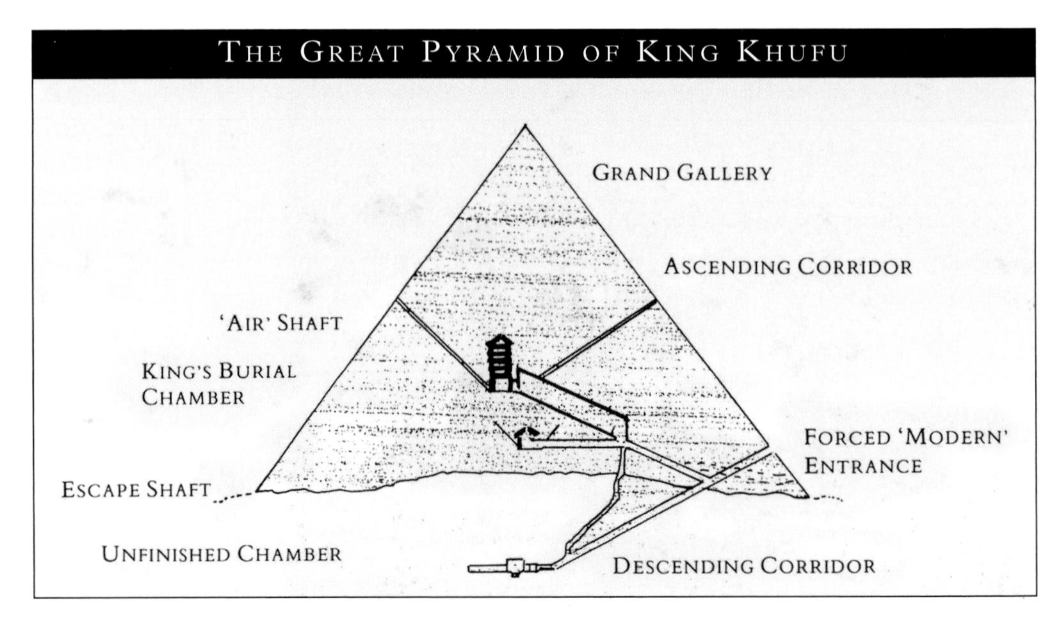

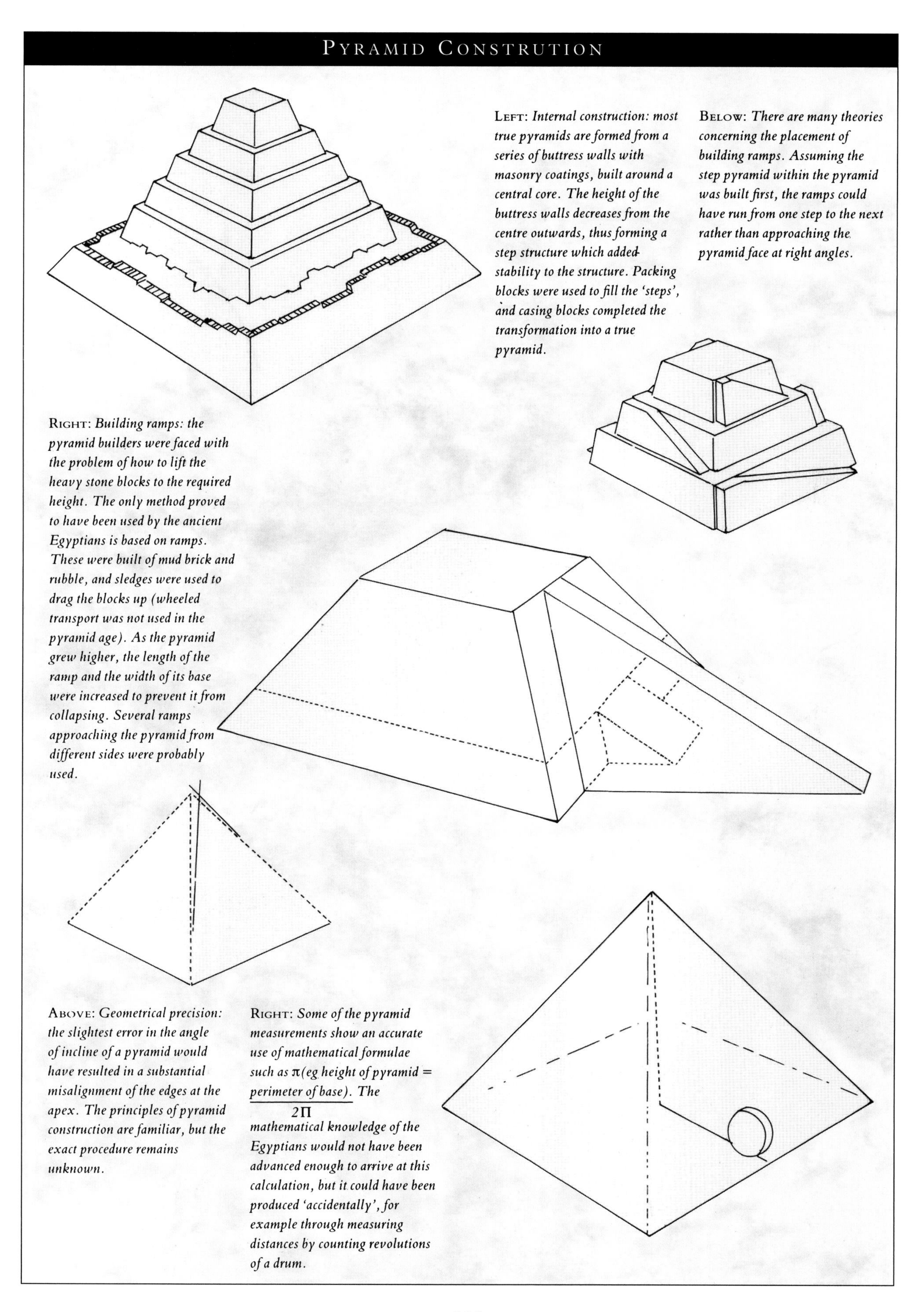

Pyramid Constrution

LEFT: *Internal construction: most true pyramids are formed from a series of buttress walls with masonry coatings, built around a central core. The height of the buttress walls decreases from the centre outwards, thus forming a step structure which added stability to the structure. Packing blocks were used to fill the 'steps', and casing blocks completed the transformation into a true pyramid.*

BELOW: *There are many theories concerning the placement of building ramps. Assuming the step pyramid within the pyramid was built first, the ramps could have run from one step to the next rather than approaching the pyramid face at right angles.*

RIGHT: *Building ramps: the pyramid builders were faced with the problem of how to lift the heavy stone blocks to the required height. The only method proved to have been used by the ancient Egyptians is based on ramps. These were built of mud brick and rubble, and sledges were used to drag the blocks up (wheeled transport was not used in the pyramid age). As the pyramid grew higher, the length of the ramp and the width of its base were increased to prevent it from collapsing. Several ramps approaching the pyramid from different sides were probably used.*

ABOVE: *Geometrical precision: the slightest error in the angle of incline of a pyramid would have resulted in a substantial misalignment of the edges at the apex. The principles of pyramid construction are familiar, but the exact procedure remains unknown.*

RIGHT: *Some of the pyramid measurements show an accurate use of mathematical formulae such as* π *(eg height of pyramid =* $\frac{\text{perimeter of base}}{2\Pi}$*). The mathematical knowledge of the Egyptians would not have been advanced enough to arrive at this calculation, but it could have been produced 'accidentally', for example through measuring distances by counting revolutions of a drum.*

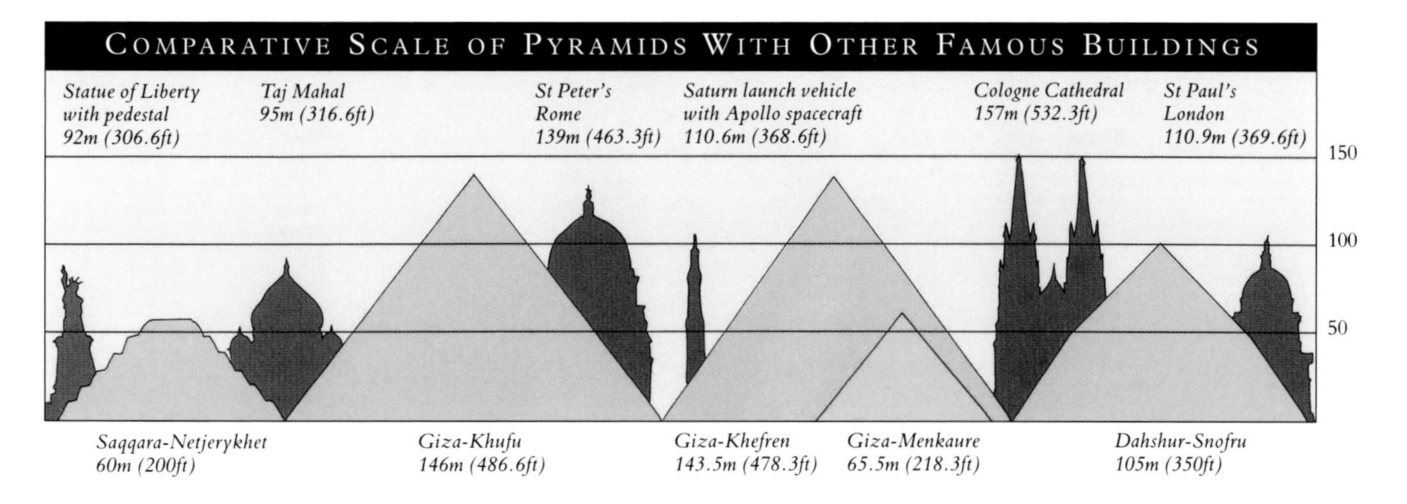

west. These alignments are so accurate that compass errors can be checked against them. This is an amazing achievement considering the magnetic compass was unknown to the Ancient Egyptians. They probably managed to obtain such accuracy by observing a northern star, rising and setting. The cardinal points, north and south, could have been established by taking measurements with a plumb line.

The millions of blocks of stone which make up the pyramid are of three main types from three sources. The great bulk of stone which forms the core is a poor quality limestone which occurs naturally in the near vicinity. Much finer white limestone casing blocks which originally covered its entire surface were mined at Tura further up the Nile. The heaviest blocks, some weighing over 50 tons, used for lining the internal chambers and passages, are made of granite quarried at Aswan some 500 miles (800 km) away. Nearly all the

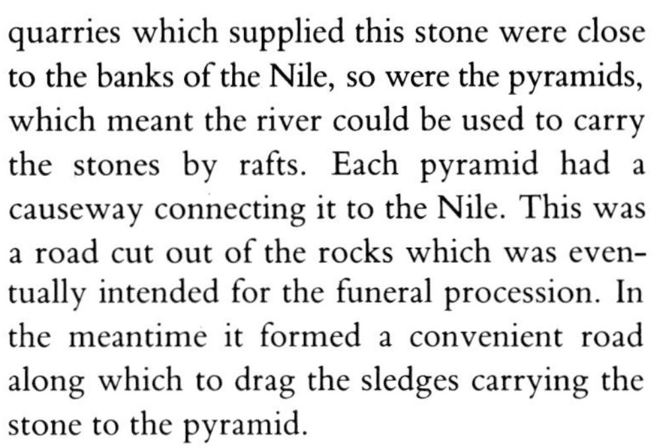

LEFT: *King Khafra, builder of the second pyramid at Giza, reflects in his proud face the supreme power of the Pharaoh in the Old Kingdom. The hawk spreading his wings protectively around the Pharaoh's head represents Horus, the god associated with kingship. (c 2540 BC.) (Cairo Museum.)*

BOTTOM: *The pyramid at Maidum represents the transitional stage of development from the step pyramid to the true pyramid. It was originally conceived as a step pyramid and subsequently modified to a true pyramid by additional casing, but the enormous pressures thus created led to its partial collapse.*

quarries which supplied this stone were close to the banks of the Nile, so were the pyramids, which meant the river could be used to carry the stones by rafts. Each pyramid had a causeway connecting it to the Nile. This was a road cut out of the rocks which was eventually intended for the funeral procession. In the meantime it formed a convenient road along which to drag the sledges carrying the stone to the pyramid.

The supply of so much stone demanded intensive quarrying. The Ancient Egyptians possessed little more than primitive copper chisels so they must have developed a specialized technique for extracting the stone. It was easier to cut the softer limestone than the hard granite. The poorer quality limestone was extracted quite easily by open-cast quarrying since it lay on the surface. However, tunnelling was required to obtain the finer Tura limestone and the granite. This was probably assisted by the application of heat and water. Wooden wedges were driven into cracks in the stone then soaked in water, causing them to expand and separate the stone. The blocks were then squared up using chisels and mallets. Copper saws were also used, perhaps with jewel chippings to assist the cutting. In order to work the granite they had to pound it with balls of an even harder stone called dolerite. Although the majority of limestone blocks which formed the core were only roughly finished, the facing stones had to be cut with great precision. Most of these have since been looted by the stonemasons of Cairo, but those which remain at the base, where sand covered them, fit so closely that the joints are almost invisible. They would have been smoothed off after they were put in place when the building of the pyramid was completed.

ABOVE: *19th-century photograph of the Sphinx, which represents King Khafra with a lion's powerful body. In the background is his pyramid tomb.*

RIGHT: *Bronze statuette of Imhotep, the architect of the earliest step pyramid at Saqqara. In later times Imhotep was worshipped as a god of wisdom. (c 600 BC.) (British Museum.)*

ABOVE: *19th-century photograph showing tourists being helped to climb the stones of the Great Pyramid. The pyramid was robbed of its fine limestone outer casing over the years and the interlocking blocks form a series of climbable, irregular steps.*

Enormous ancient waste dumps of limestone chippings from working the blocks have been discovered nearby. It has been estimated that the stone from these dumps is of an equivalent volume to over half that of the pyramids.

There is no contemporary written evidence surviving that describes how the pyramids were built. The Greek historian Herodotus, who visited Egypt in the fifth century BC, claimed that gangs of 100,000 workmen, rotating in shifts of three months each, toiled for 20 years building the Great Pyramid. Egyptologists now believe that it was built in less time by fewer men. Many people are under the false impression that the pyramids were built by slaves for a tyrannical Pharaoh. It is unlikely that the Egyptians had any slaves at this time as their society was largely composed of peasant farmers. For three months of the year, during the inundation season, the men were unable to work in the fields and would therefore be idle anyway. The concerted effort of these peasant farmers to build their Pharaoh's tomb was justified by their belief that he was a god. The Pharaoh was thought to be the Son of the Sun, who had taken human form to lead the people whom he would continue to assist in the Next World.

Peasant farmers carried out the purely physical labour but there must have been many skilled workers engaged in this vast building project. The large demand for stone would require specialist quarrymen. They worked in gangs and many stones have their names still painted on them such as 'Boat Gang', 'South Gang' and 'Enduring Gang'. The stone

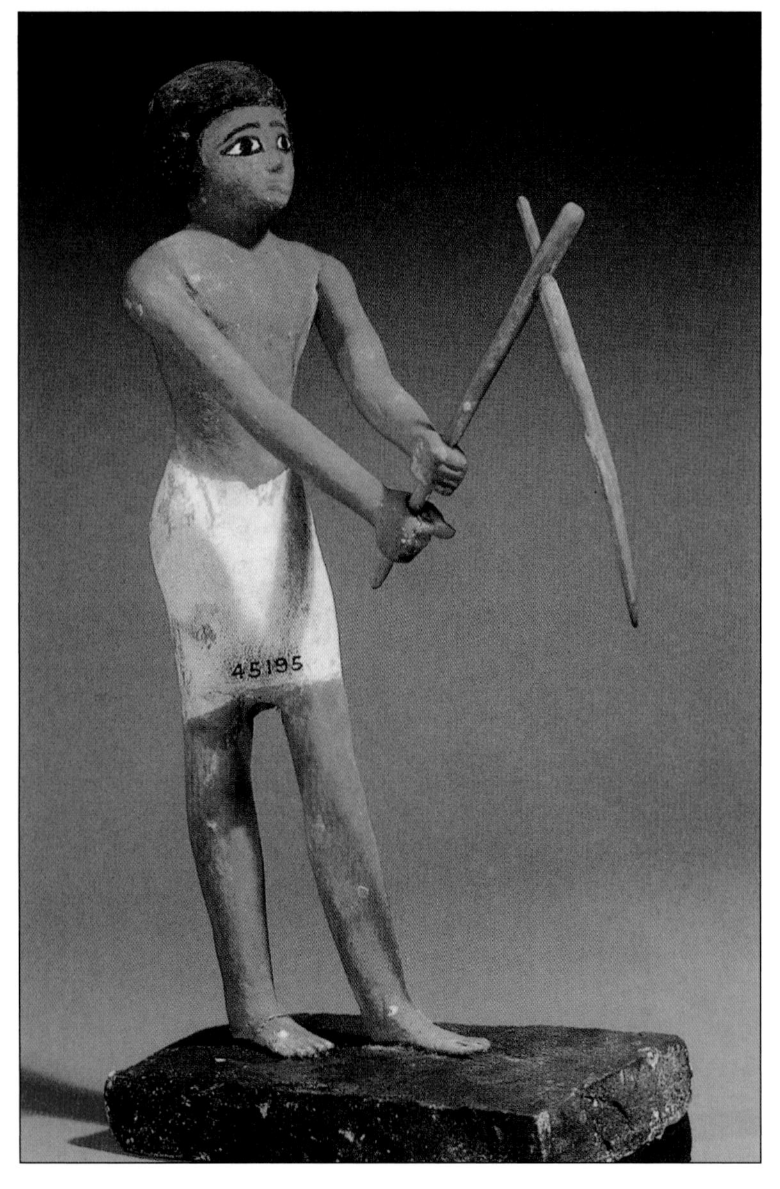

would still have to be worked into blocks and finished by stonemasons. Men with building skills would be needed to lay the blocks level and close together. The majority of the work-force was involved in moving the stone only when they couldn't work the fields, but these more specialist workers would be employed permanently on the pyramid or in the quarries. Near the Great Pyramid, barracks or lodgings for 4,000 men have been excavated. From the tools discovered there it is likely that they were occupied by builders and stonemasons working on the pyramids.

Our ideas as to how the Great Pyramid was constructed can only be based on speculation. A great deal of survey and planning work would have been necessary before any building took place. Surviving sketches of other buildings suggest that they would have made plans, and limestone models of different pyramids exist which may represent architectural planning aids. The site would need to be completely level before work commenced. They probably gauged this with accuracy by digging a trench of water around the square perimeter. Some knowledge of mathematics, geometry and astronomy would also be required for calculating the angles of the pyramid. It is certain that the various courses of stone were laid from the centre outwards since there are places where the central core blocks have been exposed beneath the casing blocks. It is also evident that they smoothed these final casing blocks from the top downwards. We do not know how the blocks were raised

ABOVE: *Aerial view of the middle pyramid of King Khafra – at the apex is the remains of the original fine stone casing.*

ABOVE: *A model of the funeral boat of King Khufu discovered in a pit near the Great Pyramid in 1951. It had been carefully dismantled into component parts after the King's funeral but has been reconstructed and is now displayed in a special museum in Giza.*

BOTTOM LEFT: *Painted wooden tomb model of an agricultural worker. (British Museum.)*

from ground level to their final position. It is likely that massive supply and construction ramps were built round the building area. The heavy blocks would have been dragged up these ramps on sleds to the working platform. The remains of ramps have been discovered at the Maidum Pyramid. They may also have used a kind of scaffolding for dressing it with limestone.

Throughout history, the huge mass of stone of the Great Pyramid has inspired people to believe that many secrets lie hidden within it. The early Christians believed the pyramids to be the granaries of Joseph, while generations of Arabs were convinced that they contained fantastic treasure. Despite various structural security measures, the burial treasure they did contain was looted when tomb robbers broke in, probably before 2000 BC. The interior of the Great Pyramid consists of an approach passage and the burial chamber itself. The slanted roof and cross-beams of granite in the burial chamber are to support the colossal weight above it. The passage leading to it is wider at the top to enable the narrower entrance to be sealed with giant plug blocks of granite. The design of the interior only appears complicated because the location of the burial chamber was changed twice during its construction. The two so-called 'ventilation shafts' may have been a symbolic means of exit for the dead king's spirit. Later pyramid texts describe the king as mounting heaven on the rays of the sun. The pyramid itself could have represented the rays of the sun shining down on earth. Perhaps it was also conceived, like the Babylonian Ziggurat, as a sort of stairway to heaven.

CHAPTER THREE

The PHARAOHS

ABOVE: *A fine early ivory standing figure of a king discovered at Abydos, probably dating from the First Dynasty c 3000 BC. The Pharaoh wears the white crown of Upper Egypt and a long robe which was worn at his jubilee. (British Museum.)*

The word Pharaoh comes from the Egyptian 'Per-aa', meaning Great House and originally referred to the palace rather than the king himself. It was used by the biblical writers and has become widely adopted since as a special word for the King of Egypt. The Pharaoh had several official titles which related to his unique status as being both god and king. He was referred to as the son of the god Ra and the name of Ra is usually mentioned within his two royal seals or cartouches, along with his personal name. He was also believed to be the incarnation of the god Horus, the son of Osiris, who in Ancient Egyptian mythology was the first King of the World.

The Pharaoh is also constantly referred to as being the Lord of the Two Lands. In early times the people of Egypt were gathered in the north and south and the unification of these two geographical regions under one Pharaoh became a primary event in Ancient Egyptian history. Although a new capital was established at Memphis, there continued to be a northern and southern centre of government administration and throughout Ancient Egyptian history there is evidence of a deep-seated awareness that the one nation had been formed out of the Two Lands. The Ancient Egyptians achieved a national unity through the Pharaoh, which brought them all the benefits of a centralized nation and enabled efficient irrigation, land reclamation and pyramid building. The Great Pyramid could only have been built by a king who exercised complete control over the economic resources of the country. The large quantities of stone, the unlimited manpower and the skill of the finest craftsmen were all at the Pharaoh's disposal. King Khufu must have been the most powerful Pharaoh at that time and his pyramid is the greatest. The decreasing size of the other two probably indicate the diminishing power of successive kings. After the collapse of royal power at the end of the Old Kingdom, the successive Pharaohs in the Middle Kingdom had to contend with the increased strength and arrogance of the provincial governors. The country was divided into a number of administrative districts called 'nomes' under these governors who had transformed their offices into hereditary principalities. Perhaps to limit their power, the Middle Kingdom kings developed a centralized hierarchy, and the royal residence was moved from Thebes

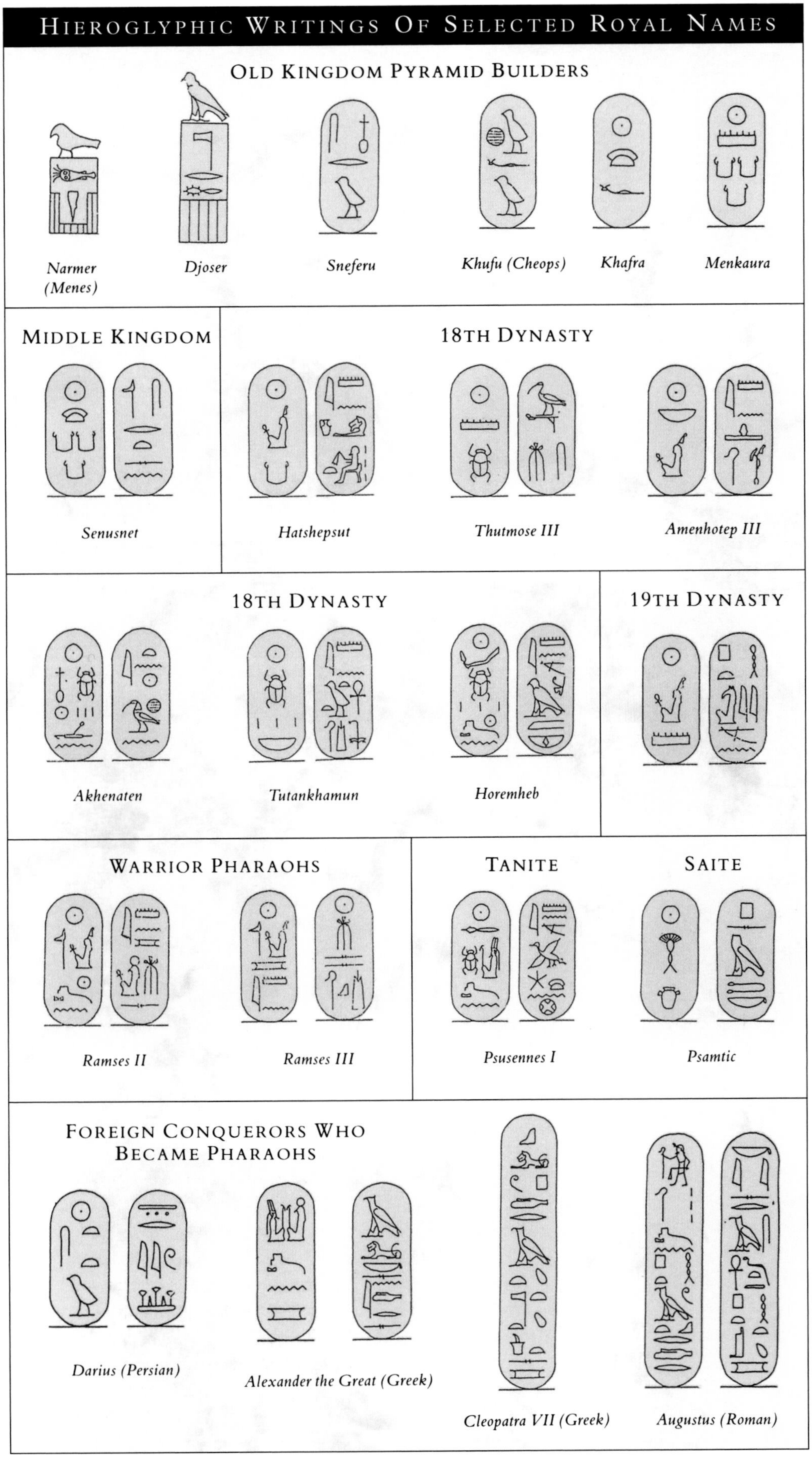

Hieroglyphic Writings Of Selected Royal Names

Old Kingdom Pyramid Builders

Narmer (Menes)

Djoser

Sneferu

Khufu (Cheops)

Khafra

Menkaura

Middle Kingdom

Senusnet

18th Dynasty

Hatshepsut

Thutmose III

Amenhotep III

18th Dynasty

Akhenaten

Tutankhamun

Horemheb

19th Dynasty

Warrior Pharaohs

Ramses II

Ramses III

Tanite

Psusennes I

Saite

Psamtic

Foreign Conquerors Who Became Pharaohs

Darius (Persian)

Alexander the Great (Greek)

Cleopatra VII (Greek)

Augustus (Roman)

to Lisht, which was a more convenient centre for ruling the whole country. These reforms enabled King Senusret III to raise a sizeable army for his Nubian campaigns, when the frontier was moved further south and was protected by a network of fortresses. In another campaign he increased the hold Egypt already had over Palestine and Syria. During the short reigns of some 70 weaker kings of the thirteenth dynasty (*c*1786–1633 BC), bureaucracy increased and the lack of a strong government enabled a group of Asiatics called the Hyksos to invade and control Egypt for some hundred years. The Hyksos immigrants introduced some important technical innovations – bronze-working, the horse and chariot, and other weapons of war such as more powerful bows.

The first Pharaohs of the New Kingdom drove out the Hyksos rulers and unified the state with a much improved economy. They went on to extend Egyptian territories into Western Asia as far as the Euphrates. The Egyptian 'Empire', which included the city states of Syria and Palestine, paid tribute but remained self-governing while Nubia was

ABOVE: *Ramses II in his chariot attacks the Hittite fortress of Dapur, in Syria – reconstruction of a painted relief from the Ramesseum, Thebes, c 1,270* BC.

administered directly by the Egyptians through an appointed Viceroy. Trade and Nubian gold produced much of the country's wealth and power in international relations and the surviving royal burial treasures display unprecedented wealth and aesthetic beauty.

The Pharaohs of the New Kingdom, and in particular those of the eighteenth dynasty, have aroused the greatest popular interest. One of the first notable Pharaohs during this period was in fact a woman, called Hatshepsut. She ruled as the dominant partner and personality in a co-regency with her nephew and stepson, the young Thutmose III. She is frequently depicted on statues and reliefs with the male attributes of royalty including the false beard. During her reign, Senenmut the chief steward assumed a position of great power as her favourite and supervised the building of her magnificent temple at Deir el Bahari in Thebes.

Thutmost III continued the policy of foreign conquest with campaigns in Palestine, Syria and Nubia. Many impressive buildings and important private tombs were created during his reign which are a sign of the economic

Above: *Queen Hatshepsut's Temple, a complex of colonnaded shrines, rises in terraces to the cliffs at Deir el Bahri.*

Below: *Standing statue of a Pharaoh from the Middle Kingdom – his thoughtful and concerned expression is characteristic of the style of portrayal during this period. (British Museum.)*

benefits of his imperialistic policy. Late in his reign he turned against the memory of Hatshepsut and ordered many of her statues and reliefs to be defaced or usurped by his own name and image. His actions were perhaps due to the Egyptian concept of kingship as being exclusively male, rather than to personal hatred of his aunt.

Under Amenhotep III, Egypt continued to be acknowledged as a superior power by her Asiatic neighbours. In Syria, the kingdom of Mitanni sent princesses as a gift of tribute to the Pharaoh and peace brought great prosperity to Egypt. There was an unprecedented output of architecture and sculpture on a grand scale during his reign, much of it of superb quality. He was succeeded by Amenhotep IV who is more commonly known by the name Akhenaten from his association with the sun cult of Aten. Akhenaten came to be regarded as the 'heretic Pharaoh' since he broke with a long-established religious tradition of worshipping many gods, choosing instead to adopt a single faith. He believed that the Aten was the universal creator of all life and its visible symbol was the rays of the sun. He became totally preoccupied with spreading his new faith and he neglected affairs of the state and military involvement. In order to disassociate himself from the powerful existing priesthood at Thebes, he built a completely new city some 200 miles (300 km) down the river at El Amarna. Here he built a palace to house his court and Amarna became the new capital and religious centre for the worship of the Aten.

Akhenaten appears to have been very interested in the arts and besides composing various hymns to the god Aten, he encouraged the development of an entirely new, more naturalistic art style. Unfortunately, very little has survived, since after his death he was proclaimed a heretic and his city was systematically destroyed and his monuments defaced. However, several pieces of royal portrait sculpture were discovered, among them the bust of Nefertiti which has come to be regarded as one of the most famous Ancient Egyptian works of art. Various diplomatic correspondence has also been discovered at Amarna which reveals the disorder within the Egyptian Empire. There are pleas for assistance from royal kingdoms under attack from the Hittites which the Pharaoh appears to have ignored.

ABOVE: *The so-called Colossi of Memnon: gigantic seated statues of the Pharaoh Amenhotep III, originally part of his mortuary temple at Thebes, c 1,400 BC. (British Museum.)*

LEFT: *Quartzite head from a statue of King Amenhotep III, c 1,400 BC. (British Museum.)*

After Akhenaten's death, the heir to the throne was Tutankhaten whose exact relationship to him has not been fully established. When Nefertiti died shortly after Akhenaten, the priests of Amun seized the opportunity to persuade the boy king to renounce his faith and reinstate the worship of the original gods at Thebes. To acknowledge this, the ending of his name was changed and he then became known as Tutankhamun. The old ways were gradually restored, and the city of Amarna was abandoned for Thebes. The usual preparations were made for the Pharaoh's tomb in the Valley of the Kings at Thebes but he died young, before its completion. It was therefore necessary to bury him in a make-shift tomb whose modesty and less obvious location caused it to be overlooked by the tomb

robbers. Although it was broken into hurriedly and with little loss early on, it remained intact for more than 3,000 years. The immense publicity the discovery of his tomb received in 1922, and the sheer wealth and beauty of the artefacts has made this historically insignificant boy king the most famous Pharaoh of all.

ABOVE: *Upper part of a large statue of Akhenaten (Cairo Museum). This is a stylized portrait of the most mysterious and individual of all the Ancient Egyptian Pharaohs.*

RIGHT: *Painted plaster bust of Queen Nefertiti. Carved in the naturalistic style used during the reign of her husband King Akhenaten, this is one of the most beautiful and famous images in Egyptian Art. c 1,365 BC. (W. Berlin Museum.)*

Tutankhamun left no heir to succeed him and an important and powerful official called Ay briefly became Pharaoh. He was followed by a successful general called Horemheb and under him all trace of the Akhenaten heresy was erased from Egyptian history. The city of Amarna was destroyed and the royal cartouches of Akhenaten and Tutankhamun were erased from the Temple records.

The first notable Pharaoh of the nineteenth dynasty (*c*1320–1200 BC) was Seti who consolidated Egyptian power in Palestine and successfully resisted the Hittites with whom he signed a peace treaty. He instigated a vast programme of building and his Temple at Abydos contains numerous superb bas-reliefs which are regarded by many as the finest examples of Egyptian Art. This style of relief sculpture was also used to decorate this tomb which is the largest and most beautiful in the Valley of the Kings. Towards the end of his reign Seti I shared his throne with his son Ramses II who became the greatest Pharaoh of all.

Ramses began his reign with a military campaign in Syria where he fought the Hittites at the notorious battle of Qadesh. There are numerous depictions of the battle on temple reliefs which show it to be a great Egyptian victory, but it is generally believed to have been an indecisive battle. Shortly after it, a truce was made, which was confirmed by marriages between Ramses and Hittite princesses, and this continued for over 50 years. Ramses may have used art as a means of propaganda and his victories over foreigners are depicted on numerous temple reliefs while he had more colossal statues than any other Pharaoh. He also usurped many existing statues by inscribing his own cartouche on them. This same cartouche is carved on every significant group of ruins in Egypt and probably half the surviving temples have additions by him. Many of these great building projects date from his early years and it appears that there was considerable economic decline towards the end of his long 66-year reign. He was nearly 100 years old when he died and was the father of about 90 children from numerous wives. Of the nine succeeding kings who have the same name, Ramses III is probably the most notable. He inherited a stable internal situation and built an impressive and beautifully decorated temple complex at Medinet Habu. He managed to defeat an attempted Libyan invasion and renewed attacks by the so-called Sea Peoples of the Mediterranean.

Throughout the New Kingdom the authority of the Pharaoh was affected by two new forces in Egypt's internal politics, the priesthood and the army. The king as the traditional protector of Egypt was assisted in police and military matters by an army. The armies of the New Kingdom were far greater and more organized than in previous times with their chariots, infantry and marines. The army was

Above: *Queen wearing a characteristic royal 'vulture' head-dress – from a drawing by Howard Carter.*

organized into four divisions of about 5,000 men each which gradually became composed of more mercenaries such as Nubians, Asiatics, Sea Peoples and Libyans. Prisoners of war could win freedom by taking up service in the Pharaoh's army and at the Battle of Qadesh, Ramses II's army included contingents of Mediterranean soldiers who had been captured in previous wars.

Although military strategy was always credited to the Pharaoh he would have consulted a War Council of officers and high state officials before embarking on a campaign. This kind of general staff would have great experience in controlling large numbers of men, which was probably why they were considered qualified to take over kingship at various times during the eighteenth dynasty when the Pharaoh had no direct heirs. Ay, Horemheb, Ramses I and Seti I had all had military training and when the country was drifting into anarchy in later periods, army officers stepped in to restore order.

By the 21st dynasty (*c*1085–945 BC) the country had become divided between two ruling houses. A group of kings established a new capital at Tanis in the Delta while much of Upper Egypt was controlled by generals who made themselves the High Priests of Thebes. A significant Pharaoh during this period was Psusennes I. The beautiful treasures from his tomb, which were discovered by Pierre Montet at Tanis in 1941, have been compared in their quality and richness to those of Tutankhamun. Political weaknesses soon led to foreign domination, first by the Libyan Kings of the 22nd dynasty, followed by the Ethiopians of Nubia in the 25th dynasty. The Pharaohs of the next dynasty established a new capital at Sais and restored order in Egypt. During this period of economic stability and greater prosperity (*c*664–525 BC) there was a rebirth of art, architecture and literature influenced by the earlier periods of Egyptian history. Some of the art of this period reached a highly stylized perfection and there was a tremendous output of fine quality small-scale sculpture.

The rule of the Saite Pharaohs was brought to a close by the Persian invasion and domination during the 27th dynasty. In 332 BC Alexander the Great conquered Egypt and his principal general, Ptolemy, set up a dynasty of Pharaohs based at Alexandria. This new city on the Mediterranean coast became a major trading centre and its famous lighthouse and library made it a Wonder of the Ancient World. The Greek domination of Egypt continued until Queen Cleopatra was defeated at the Battle of Actium in 31 BC and Egypt became a province of the Roman Empire. Through literary tradition, Cleopatra has captured popular imagination as a beautiful and scheming queen. She was the seventh Egyptian queen to bear the name of Cleopatra, and although her ancestry was Greek, she spoke the Egyptian language and shared some of their religious beliefs. Her affairs both with Julius Caesar and Mark Anthony and her final suicide were associated with her struggle to retain control of Egypt.

LEFT: *Ramses wearing the most elaborate royal crown.*

RIGHT: *The Pharaoh Amenhotep III seated on a throne and wearing the blue crown.*

ROYAR CROWNS AND REGALIA

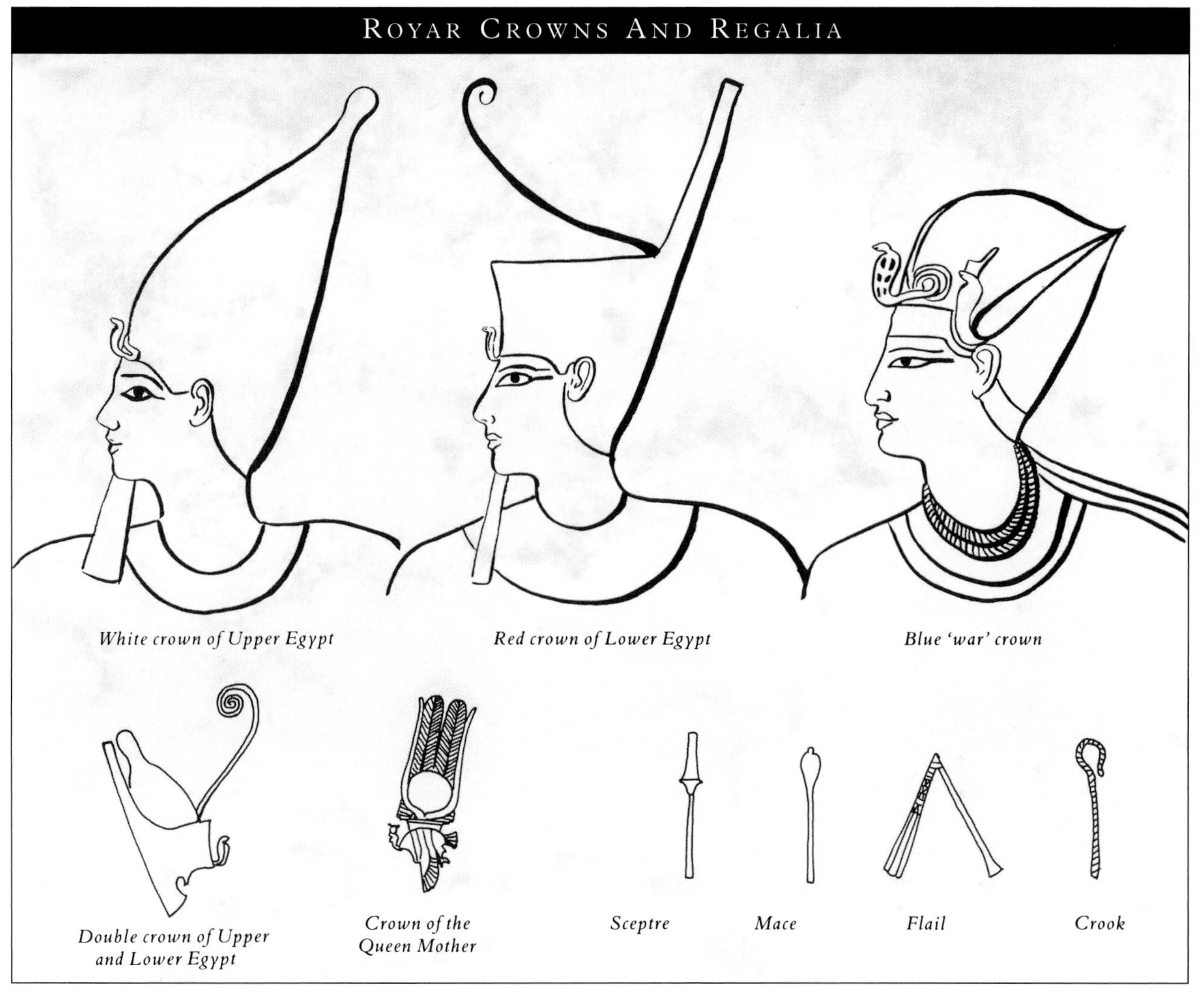

ABOVE: *Kneeling bronze figure of a Pharaoh offering two ointment jars.* c *1,420* BC.

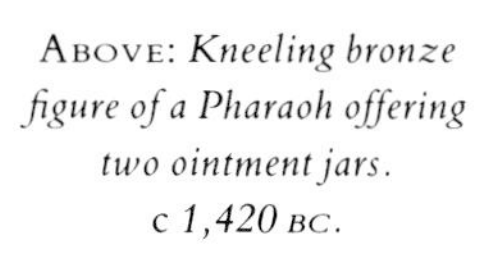

LEFT: *King Tutankhamun and his queen from the back of his gilded throne.* c *1,360* BC. *(Cairo Museum.)*

ABOVE RIGHT: *Gilded wooden figure of a king, probably Amenhotep III, wearing a plaited wig.* c *1,400* BC. *(British Museum.)*

BELOW RIGHT: *Fragmentary statue of King Akhenaten. Many statues of the 'heretic' Pharaoh were systemically broken or destroyed after he died. (British Museum.)*

ABOVE: *Scene from Tutankhamun's painted box showing the king in his chariot hunting lions. (Cairo Museum.)*

LEFT: *Upper part of a colossal statue of Ramses II.*

Cleopatra ranks with Hatshepsut and Nefertiti as one of the best-known queens of Egypt. Some of the principal queens had a powerful position in Egyptian society, second only to the Pharaoh. The king was allowed to marry several wives, but the most important was called the 'Great Wife' and her children were usually the only heirs to the throne. Queen Hatshepsut was the daughter of King Thutmose I and his 'Great Wife'. The 'Mother of the King' continued her title as wife and queen when her son became Pharaoh but she became subordinate to the new king's principal consort, the 'Great Wife'. The eldest son of the Pharaoh by this principal queen often became his heir. Intermarriage among the Egyptian royal families was not as widespread as has been claimed and was really a political union to contain power within the family and reinforce succession.

Royal pedigree was not an essential qualification for kingship in Ancient Egypt and the

divine nature of the Pharaoh's office rendered any mortal connection secondary. The king's accession to the throne was justified by his claim to be son of the sun god, Ra, rather than son of a preceding king. In taking up the very office of Pharaoh he had in effect an unquestionable right to the throne of Egypt. Ay and Horemheb had no royal pedigree, yet they each succeeded Tutankhamun and could justify their kingship through this principle. Certain foreign conquerors, notably the Macedonian Greeks, realized the benefits of depicting themselves as traditional native Pharaohs in statues and on monuments throughout Egypt. They also had their names translated and placed in the customary royal cartouche and thereby claimed their divine ancestry alongside preceding kings. They were able to gain the maximum revenue from the country that they or their predecessors had conquered by assuming this supreme position of both god and king.

RIGHT: *Head, probably of Queen Hatshepsut, carved from fine green schist, wearing a tall white crown. (British Museum.)*

CHAPTER FOUR

The GODS

ABOVE: *Silver figure of the god Ra with a falcon head and sun disc. (British Museum.)*

The gods of Ancient Egypt may appear to be strange and even frightening but to the Egyptians themselves they were an essential and comforting part of their daily life. Their apparent worship of animals should not be taken too literally since animals could be used as convenient and familiar symbols to represent the attributes of various gods. Animal heads were placed on human bodies as a means of showing gods performing various rituals and relating them to human actions. The worship of gods in the form of animals dates back to the earliest times in Egypt, and may have been motivated by man's fear of animals and their usefulness to him. These early disorganized societies viewed the natural order of the animal kingdom with awe as being symbolic of divine power. Particular animal qualities like the strength of the lion, the ferocity of the crocodile or the tender care of the cow for her young were revered and came to be associated with human ideals.

As time went on many gods came to be depicted in human form but still retained their identification with particular animals. By the late period almost every animal known to them was associated with one or more gods. Sacred creatures ranging in size from beetles to bulls were mummified and ceremonially buried. Vast animal cemeteries were created at various centres of cult worship and here people could show their devotion to a god by paying for the burial of its sacred animal. The opportunity for ordinary people to make offerings to the major gods only existed in later Egyptian history. Access to the temple interior was denied to everyone except the priesthood and only after the Middle Kingdom (*c*2000 BC) were privileged people allowed to place votive statues in the outer courtyards. In general, the images of the gods were inaccessible to the Egyptian people and any communication with them was exclusive to the Pharaoh or priests acting for him. The king was believed to be a supreme being who maintained the unity and prosperity of Egypt. The destiny of the Egyptian people was linked to that of their Pharaoh and his welfare was also theirs. Worshipping their king was a means to encourage him to intercede with other gods on their behalf.

The massive Egyptian temples were not intended for community worship like European cathedrals, and their main function was as the home of the gods. The temple with its

gateway, courts and halls was built around one small room, the sanctuary, housing the statue used by the god as its resting place. These statues did leave the temples for special religious festivals when they could be approached by ordinary people but their images were still hidden in a shrine carried on a sacred boat. Daily rituals in the temple included the washing and clothing of this divine statue and making offerings before it of incense and food. The significance of this ritual was symbolically to maintain the divine order of daily life and it does not represent blatant idol worship. In the carved reliefs in the temple, the king himself is always shown performing these rituals, but in practice they would usually have been taken over by priests. Such reliefs were usually carved with great skill and often occur even at the top of walls and columns where they could not be seen. They were not intended to beautify the building or inspire the worshippers but had an entirely magical function. In addition, the columns, ceilings and floors were all thought to have magical powers that could be invoked by rituals.

ABOVE: *The Temple was the home of the gods and needed to be of superhuman proportions. The columns of the Great Temple of Kamak are 79 feet (31.6 metres) high and 12 feet (4.8 metres) in diameter in places.*

The temple was not only seen as a symbolic representation of the world but was also built

as a model of its creation. The wavy tiers of mud brick walls surrounding the sacred precinct probably represented the primeval waters while inside the enclosure the rows of papyrus and lotus-shaped columns symbolized the earliest marsh vegetation. In Egyptian mythology, this marsh represented the first solid matter, or mound, on which the god Ra appeared and created a pair of deities, Shu and Tefnut, by masturbation or spitting. They in turn produced the sky goddess Nut, and the earth god Geb whose children were the more familiar gods Osiris, Isis, Nephthys and Set. This group of nine gods 'ennead' were worshipped at Heliopolis, and other centres had similar groups of gods. Heliopolis was also the most important centre of the cult of the sun god Ra, who was described in many texts as the creator of everything.

The sun played a central part in religious beliefs throughout Egyptian history. The sun god Ra became important as early as the second dynasty (*c*2,700 BC) and almost certainly had some connection with the building of the pyramids. By the fifth dynasty (*c*2,400 BC) Ra had become the supreme state god who was closely associated with the Pharaoh. The king took the title Son of Ra and it was

ABOVE: *Ramses II kneels before the supreme god Amen Ra in the presence of his father Seti I and the moon god Khonsu and the mother goddess Mut.*

BELOW: *Ramses II statues in the forecourt of Luxor Temple.*

RIGHT: *The god Osiris – King of the Dead, protected by falcons – from a painted coffin c 1,050 BC. (British Museum.)*

believed that after death he also joined his father Ra in heaven. Another belief was that the sun god was born every morning, aged and died, then travelled through the underworld during the night, and this was seen as the model for all regeneration. Ra was united with a minor Theban god called Amun to produce Amen-Ra who became the supreme state god in the New Kingdom. From early times Ra was also associated with the hawk god Horus and the composite god Ra-Harakhty represented Horus of the horizon.

ABOVE LEFT: *Painted wooden figure of Osiris which would have contained a rolled papyrus of the* Book of the Dead; c *1,300* BC. *(British Museum.)*

ABOVE RIGHT: *Silver and gold figure of the god Amen Ra;* c *900* BC. *(British Museum.)*

The god of the morning sun was Khepri who was identified with the beetle. The scarab-beetle was thought to have created itself from its own matter as the sun seemed to create itself each morning.

The sun is usually visible in the sky over Egypt and it is not surprising that it came to be worshipped. Towards the end of the eighteenth dynasty (*c*1280 BC) there was a religious revolution in Egypt initiated by King Amenhotep IV, better known as Akhenaten. This new religion was based on the worship of the sun as the exclusive source of all life and creation whose power was visible in the life-giving rays of the sun-disk called the Aten. Akhenaten claimed to be the sole agent or high priest of the Aten on earth which gave him the right to disperse local priesthoods and close the temples of rival deities. The temples built for the worship of the Aten were architecturally different from the usual type, being open to the sky and without a sanctuary for a divine statue. It was Amenhotep III, Akhenaten's father, who first brought Aten worship to prominence but Akhenaten ordered the complete exclusion of all the other gods. However, after Akhenaten's death the old gods were reinstated at Thebes and Akhenaten was regarded as a heretic.

An essential part of Egyptian religion was the belief in life after death and the final judgement of the individual soul. The god Osiris was both king of the dead and judge of the underworld. In Egyptian mythology Osiris was a good Pharaoh, who was murdered by his evil brother Seth, and his death was avenged by his son, Horus. Osiris was even-

ABOVE: *Khepri the scarab-beetle god, from a painted coffin c 1,050 BC. (British Museum.)*

BELOW: *King Akhenaten and Queen Nefertiti with their children. Above them is the sun disc with the rays of the sun symbolizing the god Aten which they worshipped.*

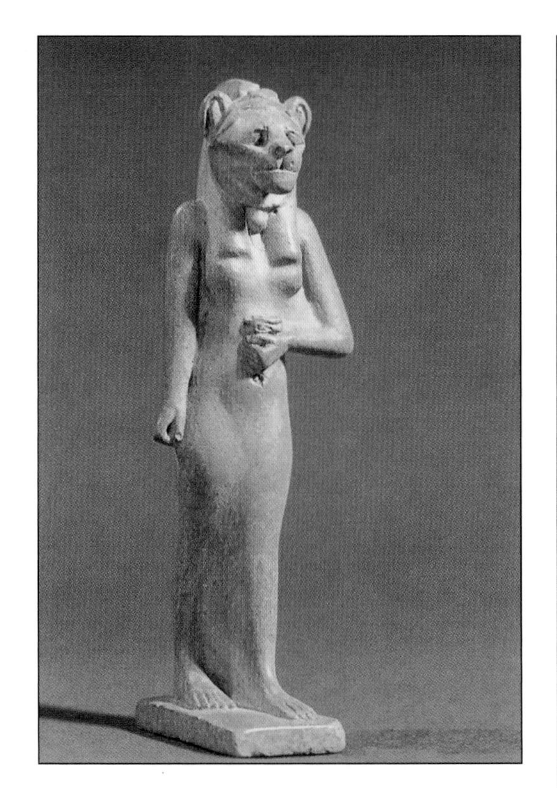

tually brought back to life, not as a human Pharaoh but as mummiform king of the underworld. Osiris had an important quality that made him more popular than the other gods. As a human king, he had experienced death and had triumphed over it and could assure his followers an eternal life. It was believed that every king would become Osiris after he died while his successor was the embodiment of Horus, his son. By the Middle Kingdom (*c*2000 BC), all worshippers of Osiris could themselves look forward to becoming an Osiris when they died and would thereby enjoy eternal life. Abydos was one of the major centres of Osiris worship and many Egyptians left inscriptions and offerings there to the god. Here they could witness the annual drama enacting the death and resurrection of Osiris, most of which took place outdoors.

Osiris was also a god of vegetation which may have been his original role. He embodied the yearly cycle of the renewal or rebirth of the land of Egypt after the Nile floods. His resurrection as king of the dead and this renewal as a vegetation god were closely linked. The wife of Osiris, Isis, represented the devoted wife and loving mother and was a very pop-

ABOVE LEFT: *Glazed figure of the lioness goddess Sekhmet. (British Museum.)*

BELOW LEFT: *This gilded bronze figure of Isis and Horus provided the universal image of a mother and child. (British Museum.)*

ABOVE RIGHT: *Bronze statuette of the Ram god Knum. (British Museum.)*

LEFT: *The Jackal god, Anubis, who was the guardian of the dead – painted relief from the tomb of Horemheb c 1,320 BC.*

ular goddess of magic who continued to be worshipped in Roman times. Osiris, Isis and Horus represented a family unit and a triad of gods. Similar groupings of three existed among many other Egyptian gods. The most notable other triads of gods were worshipped at Thebes (Amun, Mut and Khons) and Memphis (Ptah, Sekhmet and Nefertum). Osiris received general acceptance throughout Egypt and was not only a state god but also a popular god to whom ordinary people could relate.

Many other gods protected ordinary Egyptians who worshipped them in their houses. Some of the gods had no temples dedicated to them or had no place in the official temple rituals. One of the most popular of these minor gods was Bes, who was depicted as a homely, ugly dwarf god. Bes was regarded as a bringer of joy who warded off evil spirits and protected women in childbirth. The hippopotamus goddess Tauret also protected pregnant women, as did the cat goddess Bastet and the cow goddess Hathor, who were also associated with dancing and music. Representations of these household gods were used as decorative elements in the finer everyday items of the wealthy, such as beds, headrests, mirrors and cosmetic pots. Images of the gods were thought to have supernatural powers and the Egyptians wore many amulets to protect themselves. Many small faience charms were placed with their

FACING PAGE LEFT: *Kneeling bronze figure of a hawk-headed god. (British Museum.)*

FACING PAGE RIGHT: *Gilded wooden figure of the god Ptah from the tomb of Tutankhamun, c 1,350 BC.*

ABOVE LEFT: *Wooden cosmetic spoon with handle decorated with the household god Bes, c 1,300 BC. (British Museum.)*

ABOVE RIGHT: *Bronze figure of the sacred Apis Bull. (British Museum.)*

BELOW RIGHT: *Bronze statuette of the cat goddess Bartet. (British Museum.)*

mummies to protect them on their hazardous journey to the next world and their tombs contained models, statues and paintings which had a similar magical role.

It is impossible to arrange Ancient Egyptian gods into neat categories since their religious ideas were very complex. The sheer number of gods is staggering since their religion developed over a very long period of time and they did not discard old beliefs when new ones became popular. From the earliest times, there were local tribal gods in various regions of the country and some of these rose to great prominence during various periods of history. Often for political reasons, many gods were also combined together as a means of consolidating their special powers.

The belief in a divine power, as an indeterminate and impersonal force universally present in all their gods, was an essential part of Egyptian religious thought. Before gods had a particular form or were given a name the Egyptians would have worshipped the abstract concept of power. Their belief in the supernatural was closely interwoven with their daily lives, their personal relationships, their hopes and fears and their attitude to the Pharaoh's supreme authority. The day-today hazards of existence were believed to be the work of hostile powers which could be suppressed by maintaining religious cults and preserving a divine order.

CHAPTER FIVE

The MUMMIES

Mummies are the first things most people think about at the mention of Ancient Egypt, but what exactly are they and how and why were they made? Although the term 'mummy' is associated with Ancient Egypt, it is also applied to preserved bodies from many other cultures. The word itself comes from the Arabic name for 'bitumen', and was used to describe these bodies because their black appearance suggested that they had been coated in pitch. Most of the bandaged mummies that have survived date from the New Kingdom or the later half of Egyptian history. By this time, the embalming process, which had previously been reserved for royalty, became available to all who could afford it.

Why did they go to so much expense and trouble to preserve their dead? The answer is, because they believed that the survival of the body was essential for the soul to become immortal. Life after death was thought to be a re-creation of the best moments of earthly existence and so bodies were buried with their favourite possessions, a supply of food and even model labourers to do their work for them. There was nothing morbid in this life-long preoccupation with death, and gaily painted mummy cases reflect an optimism and confidence in eternal life.

The Ancient Egyptian belief in an afterlife and the development of embalming are thought to have arisen partly in response to the survival of many naturally preserved bodies from the earliest times in Egypt. In this predynastic period, the naked body was simply buried in a shallow grave in the desert.

ABOVE: *Painted wooden coffin and mummy of a Theban priestess, c 1,000* BC. *(British Museum.)*

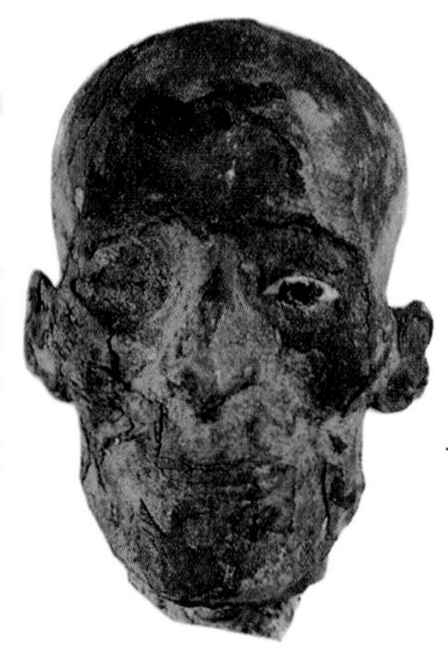

ABOVE RIGHT: *Gilded wooden inner coffin of a Theban priestess, c 1,290* BC. *(British Museum.)*

RIGHT: *Wooden shabti figure of King Amenhotep III. These figures were placed in tombs to carry out agricultural work for the deceased in the afterlife. (British Museum.)*

ABOVE: *Head of a male mummy with an inlaid eye, c 1,000* BC. *(British Museum.)*

The hot, dry sand quickly absorbed the moisture from the body and prevented decay. Some of these corpses must have been exposed by grave robbers or by shifting sands, and their discovery may have inspired later generations to believe in an afterlife. As time passed, this belief led to the need for a more dignified burial which was accompanied by an increasing amount of provisions for the next life. The tomb replaced the simple grave, but this allowed the body to come into contact with the air and decompose. From the early sand burials they must have realized that the best way of preserving a body was to dehydrate it, which prevented bacteria from breeding and causing decay.

There was a ready supply of natural sodium salts to be found in Egypt, called natron, which are an effective drying agent and mildly antiseptic. With the aid of natron, the Ancient Egyptians developed an elaborate technique of embalming which could take as long as 70 days. The first stage of this process was to remove all the internal organs except the heart. (This was left since it was thought to be the centre of human intelligence which would be required for judgement in the under-

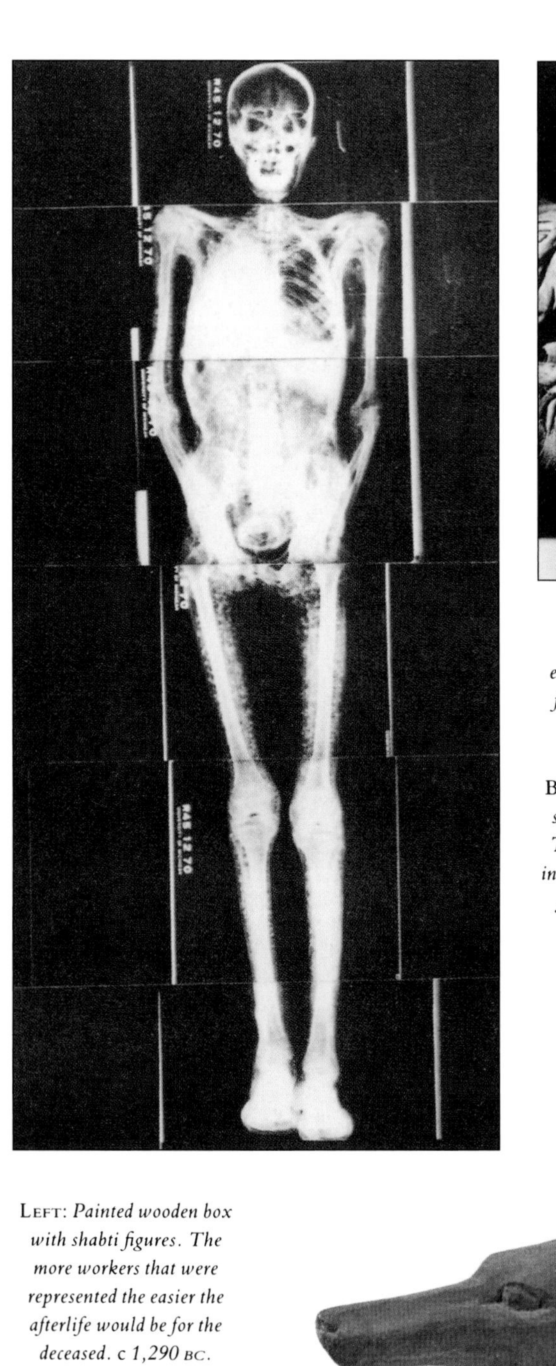

ABOVE RIGHT: *The earliest surviving mummy from the tomb of Nefer at Saqqara, c 2,400* BC.

BOTTOM: *Wooden jackal, sacred to the god Anubis. These figures were placed in the tombs to symbolically guard the dead. (British Museum.)*

world.) The other organs were dried with natron and placed in four containers called canopic jars. The empty body was then washed with palm wine and spices, and left to dry out, covered with natron salts. The dried body was packed with linen and spices to give it form again, then coated with molten resin to toughen it and make it waterproof. The mummy was then bandaged with great care since the tightness of the wrapping would help to keep the shape of the body. (A mummy was recently unwrapped which was covered in a total of three miles of three-inch-wide linen bandage, or five kilometres by 7.5 cm!)

The wrappings usually bound the arms against the body and held the legs together, although there are some mummies where the limbs were separately wrapped. Various protective amulets were distributed in the wrappings, usually in prescribed positions. An

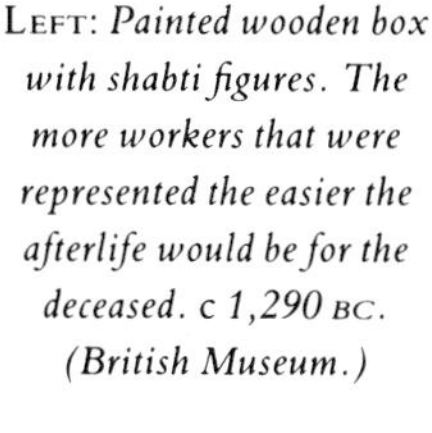

LEFT: *Painted wooden box with shabti figures. The more workers that were represented the easier the afterlife would be for the deceased.* c *1,290* BC. *(British Museum.)*

ABOVE LEFT: *X-rays of an Ancient Egyptian mummy can reveal many interesting details.*

important amulet was the heart scarab, which was placed on the chest of the mummy. It was inscribed with a religious text instructing the person's heart not to make trouble for them when weighed in the judgement before Osiris. Another popular protective amulet was the eye of Horus or 'udjat' which represented the eye of a falcon, with its characteristic markings beneath.

Although the basic function of the coffin was to protect the body from violation by animals and thieves, it was also regarded as the house of the spirit. Through the magical powers of its decoration and inscriptions it could ensure the welfare of the deceased in the afterlife. The coffin underwent various changes in shape, material and decoration throughout the long period of Ancient Egyptian history. Some of the earliest coffins were small and made of clay, basketwork or wood where the body lay in a hunched up position on its side. In the Middle Kingdom (*c*2000 BC) full-length double wooden coffins were often provided. The inner one could be made in the shape of the mummy, while the outer coffin was rectangular. On the inside this rectangular coffin was decorated with personal objects and magical texts, while on the outside it had a large pair of eyes painted in a panel by the left shoulder so that the mummy inside could look out at the world. These eyes were often painted above a representation of a doorway, through which the mummy's spirit could leave at will and have access to the rest of the tomb.

The characteristic coffins in the shape of the mummified body with an idealized face mask are mostly of New Kingdom date or later. The stereotyped faces often had a false beard to symbolize their identification with

ABOVE: *Scene showing the weighing of the mummy's heart as part of the judgement in the afterlife. From the* Book of the Dead *of the scribe Hunefer, c 1,310* BC. *(British Museum.)*

BOTTOM: *Set of limestone canopic jars for holding the internal organs of the mummy; c 1,000* BC. *(British Museum.)*

RIGHT: *Some coffins were carved from stone, like this fine basalt example made for a vizier, c 500* BC. *(British Museum.)*

29472

the dead King Osiris. The coffins were painted with a representation of the sky goddess Nut who spread her wings protectively over the lid, since she was traditionally the mother of the deceased who was associated with her godly son, Osiris. The coffins were usually made of thin planks of wood skilfully dowelled together, and the arms of the mummy were often shown carved in high relief and crossed over the chest. Painted bands of jewellery and floral collars reproduced the ornaments on the actual mummy. The head of the mummy was often enclosed in a mask of cartonnage – layers of linen stuck together and covered with a thin coat of plaster. This mask was often extended to cover the complete body and formed an ideal ground for elaborate decoration. Sometimes a painted and modelled board was placed over the body inside the coffin as an economical way of suggesting a double coffin.

In the saite period (after 600 BC) some superb hard stone mummyform coffins were made and the mummy was often covered in a bead net. By the late period many corpses were not even properly embalmed, being simply painted with pitch and wrapped with bandages. Although the vital organs were often left in the body, 'dummy' canopic jars were still provided for them which had a purely symbolic function. By Graeco-Roman times the idealized face mask was often replaced with a more realistic portrait painted on a wooden panel while the bandages were arranged in intricate geometric patterns.

Few royal coffins have survived but the evidence is that they were of gilded wood, inlaid with stones and glass paste. Surviving intact examples are the three-nested coffins of Tutankhamun. They were enclosed in a rectangular stone sarcophagus decorated inside and out with funeral gods in painted relief. One of the finest stone sarcophagi is that of King Seti I, which is of white calcite inlaid with rows of funerary figures in blue paste. The kings of the 21st and 22nd dynasties from Tanis (*c*950 BC) were buried in mummiform coffins of silver and gilded wood, two of them with silver hawks' heads.

The mummy's eternal dwelling place was the tomb. The type of tomb varied according to the period, the area and the owner's social status. We should not forget that the vast majority of poor Ancient Egyptians would have had a simple burial in the desert with

ABOVE: *Elaborately bandaged mummy of a calf, c 30 BC. The Egyptians mummified many of their sacred animals. (British Museum.)*

BOTTOM: *A finely carved wooden face from a coffin with inlaid eyes of lapis lazuli and glass. (British Museum.)*

LEFT: *Gilded mummy mask made from cartonnage, a material composed of linen or papyrus coated in plaster. (British Museum.)*

few possessions. The tombs of the privileged who could afford a more elaborate burial were either built of stone and brick or cut out of the solid rock. They all generally consist of two main parts, the burial chamber and the funerary chapel. The Old Kingdom tombs had a false door which served as a magical entrance through which the spirit of the deceased could pass from the burial chamber on the western side of the tomb into the chapel on the east. Here the spirit could partake of the offerings of food and drink provided by the relatives or priests. In the carved reliefs on the walls of the tomb, scenes of farming, hunting, fishing, baking and brewing ensured that provisions for the deceased would be continually available. As time went on these were supplemented by representational models and a large variety of personal possessions. The royal tombs in the Valley of the Kings at Thebes were completely closed with entrance stairs to four passages or corridors, a hall and a burial chamber. These all had a symbolic significance in the journey of the spirit in the afterlife.

This journey of the spirit is recorded in detail on papyri which were often placed in tombs from the New Kingdom onwards. These religious writings are known as Books of the Dead which were copies of earlier Old Kingdom stone inscriptions called the Pyramid Texts. The principal magical function of these writings was to secure for the deceased a satisfactory afterlife and to give him the power to leave his tomb when necessary. They include painted depictions of Anubis the god of mummification and show the final judgement before Osiris, the king of the dead. The mummy's personality or spirit is identified with the Ba-Bird which is portrayed as a human-headed bird hovering over the mummy.

ABOVE: *The tomb of Queen Nefertari, wife of Ramses II, is probably the most beautifully painted Ancient Egyptian tomb; c 1,250* BC.

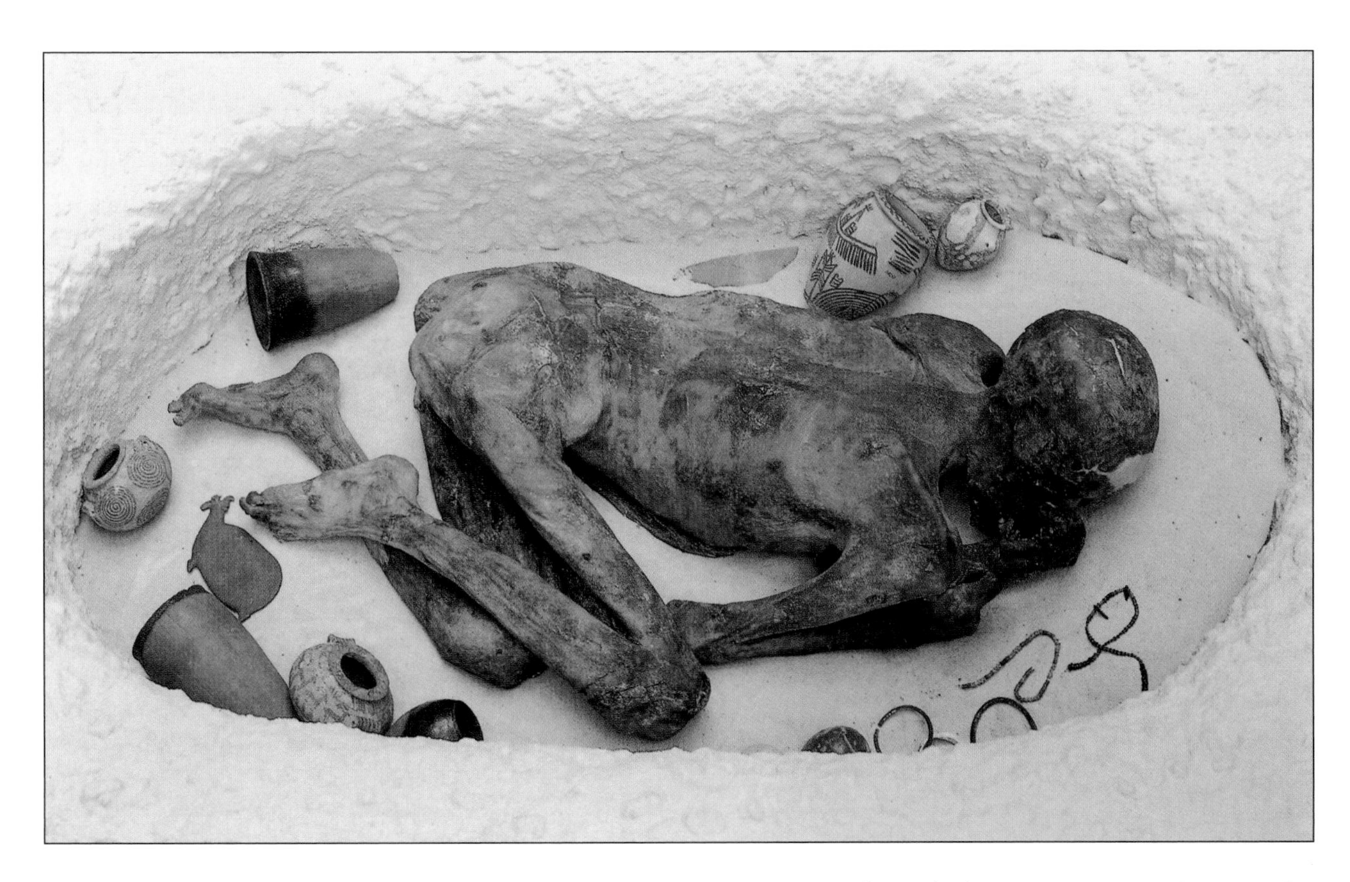

The royal tombs in the Valleys of the Kings and Queens at Thebes, were located continuously in ancient times. In order to prevent further violation, the mummies were removed secretly by the Theban priests and most of them were hidden in a deep shaft in the cliff face. Although they were eventually discovered by local villagers in the last century, who began to profit from the discovery, they were rescued by the Egyptian Antiquities Service. When they were finally transported to Cairo for the museum in 1881, the customs officer at the city gates levied a duty on them, classifying them as dried fish!

Most of the hundreds of mummies distributed throughout the world in museums and collections date from the late periods when entire families were buried together in communal catacombs. Richly painted religious scenes on these coffins replaced the need for individual tombs. From the time that mummies acquired a market value, these tombs, where the mummies were stacked, were ransacked by villagers living near the Theban cemeteries. In the sixteenth century mummies were thought to have special healing properties and many were ground up to make medicines. In order to meet the rising demand for this thriving business, fake mummies were produced using the corpses of executed criminals. In the last century, mummies were also ground up to be used as a brown artists' pigment and sold in tubes labelled 'mummy'. The Ancient Egyptians also mummified all manner of sacred animals, which were placed in special sanctuaries beneath temples and vast quantities of these have survived. At the turn of the century some 300,000 cat mummies were shipped to Liverpool, to be turned into fertilizer and sold for £4 ($7) a ton!

The unwrapping and autopsy of mummies in various institutions continues to be carried out by leading medical specialists using the latest techniques and equipment. Powerful electron microscopes, forensic tests and x-rays can often reveal the diseases that the Ancient Egyptians suffered from, their cause of death and their diet. Examination of the teeth of mummies can indicate what foods they ate and there is evidence that they practised dentistry. Some teeth have been found to contain a form of mineral cement or have been bound together with fine gold wire. By detecting blood groups and hereditary traits from royal mummies it is also possible to identify particular family connections. Establishing the age of certain kings at the time of death can also help specialists to verify the dates of various dynasties or important events in Egyptian history.

ABOVE LEFT: *Wooden coffin decorated with bands of inscription which include a prayer for food offerings. At the head end, two painted eyes enable the mummy to see out above a painted false door through which his spirit could pass. c 2,000 BC. (British Museum.)*

ABOVE: *The body of a man preserved naturally by the hot dry sand in which he was buried. The heat of the sand absorbed the moisture without which bacteria cannot breed and cause decay. Ironically this humble form of burial preserved the body far better than the most elaborate tombs and costly embalming techniques. c 3,200 BC. (British Museum.)*

CHAPTER SIX

EGYPTIAN LIFE

ABOVE: *Painted wooden model of a woman carrying a tray of cakes. (British Museum.)*

Much can be learnt about Ancient Egyptian life from the everyday items and wall-paintings to be found in their tombs. They believed that these representations of work and pleasure would assist them in the afterlife. Many tombs and temples have survived from ancient times because they were made of stone. Few houses remain since they were built from perishable materials, like mud-brick which collapsed when it was old, and is now used as a fertilizer. Many towns and villages continued to be inhabited throughout history until modern times and houses were frequently rebuilt and the material recycled. Many modern Egyptian villages probably resemble the ancient ones quite closely in their construction and way of life. Occasionally, settlements were completely abandoned, and excavating them can tell us a great deal about the daily life of the ordinary people. The two most notable sites of this kind are King Akhenaten's city at El-Amarna and the village of the workmen who built the tombs in the Valley of the Kings at Deir el-Medina. This village grew over four centuries. Rectangular walls originally enclosed the streets and houses which were laid out in a regular pattern. The individual houses were roughly the same size except for the larger houses of the foremen.

A typical house had three main rooms, with a yard, which acted as a kitchen, and two cellars for storage. There were often niches set into the walls for religious stone inscriptions, images of household gods or busts of family ancestors. Many houses came to be modified to suit individual needs or activities and some included work-rooms and shops. At El-Amarna, the finer houses had two floors and basement store rooms. They might also have a reception hall, kitchen and servants' quarters, while some even had bathrooms and lavatories. A number of walled houses had an enclosed garden with a fish pond and shady trees. Furniture consisted of beds, small tables, stools and wooden storage chests for utensils and jewellery. Hangings, mats and textiles decorated the inner rooms. Like many African peoples, the Egyptians used headrests instead of pillows for sleeping on. Many of these have survived made from either wood, ivory or stone, and they consist of a curved neckpiece set on top of a pillar which sits on an oblong base. They had lamps which were simple bowls of pottery or

stone containing oil and a wick. They also used pottery torches which could be set into brackets on the wall. Kitchens and cellars had clay ovens and large storage jars for wine, oil and grain.

The workmen who lived at Deir el-Medina were stonemasons, plasterers, sculptors, draughtsmen, painters and carpenters. The valley contains the remains of their houses, tombs, chapels, rest houses and domestic rubbish. Many written documents have been discovered there which deal with the progress of the work and there is even the earliest record of a strike when there was a delay in paying their wages. The men would have worked for eight days out of ten living in huts above the Valley of the Kings and returning to the village for their two days of rest. Attendance registers have survived and we know that absenteeism was common. Days were lost through brewing beer, drinking, and building houses, and there were also many religious holidays. Their wages were paid in wheat, fish, vegetables, cosmetic oils, wood for fuel, pottery and clothing. They used each other's skills to construct highly decorated tombs for themselves and there were many opportunities to undertake private commissions from wealthy Thebans.

Many legal documents have survived from Deir el-Medina concerning crimes and judgements, inheritances, and business transactions. The Ancient Egyptians had a legal system of courts and magistrates and they had a wide range of punishments which included forced labour camps. They had a type of police force, distinct from the army, who often used trained dogs. There existed a system of giving evidence under oath and documents often contain signatures of witnesses. Documents were legalized by affixing a seal and deposited at a record office or temple. The Ancient Egyptians had schools, but these would have been for training future scribes and officials intended for the priesthood or the civil administration who were exclusively male. The royal family had special tutors, and ordinary people were educated at home. The father traditionally handed down advice and professional secrets to his son relating to his trade or craft. Craftsmen, like officials, had an apprenticeship system.

Technical skill was greatly admired but there was no distinction between artists and craftsmen and therefore art is generally anonymous. Craftsmen were employed by the king or the temple officials and their achievement and skill using simple tools is remarkable.

ABOVE: *From a wall painting in a Theban tomb showing jewellers and carpenters at work.*

ABOVE: *Painted wooden model of breadmakers, c 2,000 BC. (British Museum.)*

ABOVE LEFT: *Painted wooden model of a man ploughing. (British Museum.)*

ABOVE RIGHT: *Painted wooden model of a woman carrying a tray of cakes. (British Museum.)*

Their most impressive achievements were in sculpture, both in the round and in carved relief. They also mastered the technique of making fine stone vessels from an early date. The precision of their carpentry was also very fine and wood was joined by dovetailing, mitres, mortice-and-tenon joints and dowels. Inlay and veneer were common forms of decoration and the Egyptians were the first to use plywood. Their tools, which would have been copper, included axes, saws, adzes, chisels and drills. The wood, much of which

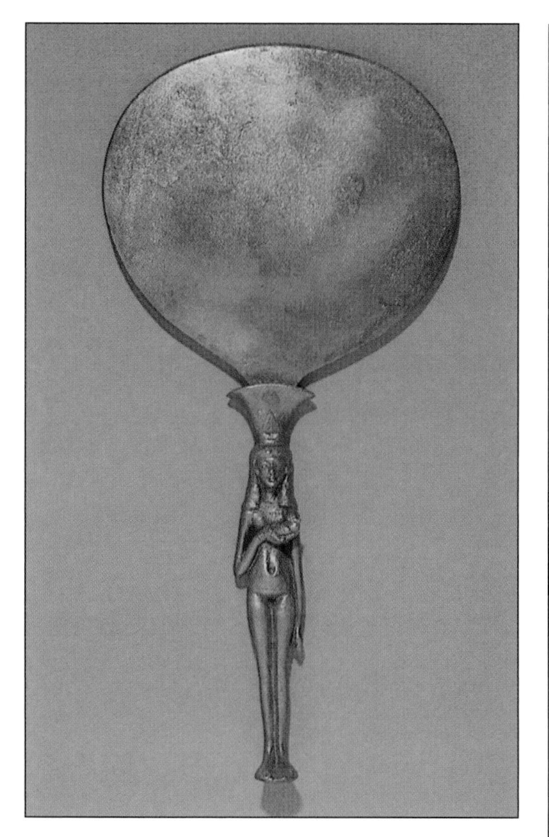

ABOVE LEFT: *Bronze mirror which would originally have been highly polished. (British Museum.)*

ABOVE RIGHT: *Ladies' vanity box containing a selection of cosmetics vessels, toilet objects and pair of sandals. (British Museum.)*

was imported, was mainly cedar, sycamore, acacia, ebony and palmwood. Metal workers and jewellers show a high degree of skill in using techniques like chasing, engraving, embossing, inlaying, filigree work and enamelling. They could beat gold into leaf as fine as 0.005 mm, and gemstones and beads of small sizes were bored with precision using a bow drill. Copper was smelted using a type of bellows and bronze was cast by the lost-wax process. These materials were essential for making tools, weapons, ritual utensils and religious statuettes.

Another characteristic Egyptian craft technique was the manufacture of glass and glazed ware. Faience ware, usually of blue-green or turquoise glaze, was produced in vast quantities, often from moulds. The Egyptians could also produce linen of outstanding quality and a shawl discovered in Tutankhamun's tomb is made of the finest linen known. Textile experts have estimated that it must have taken about 3,000 hours to make or nine months of eleven-hour days. Allied to weaving was the manufacture of mats, baskets and rope using reed, flax, papyrus, palm fibre and grass. Countless baskets and pottery have survived which were the standard household container.

The majority of the population were engaged in working on the land and their labour was conscripted for irrigation systems or royal building projects. This conscription was for everyone, but privileged officials could avoid it by paying someone else to work on their behalf. Foreign prisoners-of-war and criminals were also used in gangs for heavier work like stone quarrying. Conscripted workers received no payment for their services, only subsistence. Even the poorest peasant labourers and domestic servants were not slaves in the usual sense of the word. All Egyptians had legal rights and could own or dispose of their possessions. There was no system of citizenship or slavery, as clearly defined in Greece and Rome. Egyptian society never produced a true middle class and the social structure was a hierarchy of officials where everyone ultimately served the Pharaoh who was the embodiment of the state.

In addition to cereals, flax was grown in great quantities, to be spun into thread and finally woven into linen. Large herds of cattle

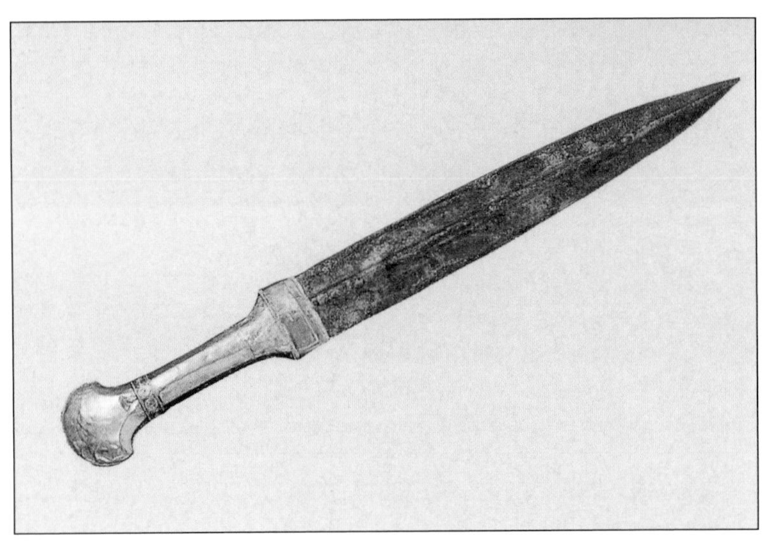

ABOVE: *The workmen's village at Deir el-Medina.*

ABOVE LEFT: *Gold handled dagger. (British Museum.)*

ABOVE RIGHT: *A man and his wife with a tray of food offerings and wine in storage jars.*

were reared and cows dragged the plough and provided milk. Other livestock kept included sheep, pigs and donkeys. Surplus agricultural produce and linen were exported by the royal government who controlled trade. In country markets barter or exchange was the means of trade. The Ancient Egyptians managed without coinage during their long history. They had a system of valuing provisions and manufactured articles in various units equivalent to fixed amounts of gold, silver or copper. Payments could be made in given weights or rings of the metal itself (unlike coins, these pieces had no official markings as a guarantee of value), or commodities like produce or livestock.

The family was at the heart of Egyptian society and early marriage and parenthood were encouraged. Many marriages would have been arranged but the romantic nature of surviving love poetry suggests that there was some freedom of choice. Marriage tended to be within the same social group, and family unions between uncle and niece or cousins were common. The words 'brother' and 'sister' were often used merely as terms of endearment in their writings and have led to a misconception that the Egyptians committed

Left: *A finely carved limestone statue of a man and his wife, showing the complexity of their wigs. (British Museum.)*

Bottom left: *Painted limestone statue of a seated woman showing a typical style of dress. (British Museum.)*

Bottom right: *Blue-glazed drinking-cup in the form of a lotus. (British Museum.)*

incest. There was no religious or civil marriage ceremony although there were family parties and festivities to celebrate the occasion. Marriage was a private legal agreement, and a contract established the right of both parties to maintenance and possessions. There was consequently an equality between men and women in their common opportunity to own, manage and receive property. If there was a divorce, the rights of the wife were protected equally with those of her husband. In some periods of Egyptian history even a woman who committed adultery still had certain rights to maintenance from her former husband. In spite of the formal legal contract of marriage with the facility for divorce, marriages were not usually short-lived or lacking in affection. Many statues and wall-paintings show married couples displaying gestures of affection for each other and their surviving literature often suggests sincere emotional ties.

Many tomb paintings depict large feasts of food which had a magical function and give a misleading impression that they had endless supplies of surplus food. The average Egyptian peasant probably lived on a few rolls of bread, a pot of beer and some onions. The staple food was always bread and by the time of the New Kingdom there were as many as 40 different varieties. The shapes of the loaves varied: some were oval, some round while others were conical. Different flours and honey, milk and eggs were sometimes added. Meat included beef, goat, mutton, pork, goose and pigeon. However, meat would not keep in the hot climate and had to be consumed rapidly, so for most people it would only be eaten on religious feast days. Fish was eaten more frequently particularly among the people living around the marshes.

Besides the cereals from which bread was made, farming provided many varieties of vegetables which included leeks, onions, garlic and cucumbers. Figs, dates, pomegranates and grapes were among the quantities of fruit available. Farms provided milk and milk products and they hatched eggs artificially. Honey played a large part in their diet as a sugar substitute and it was produced from bee-keeping. Beer was the most popular drink and it was prepared from barley which was ground and kneaded to make a dough and lightly baked like bread. This bread was then soaked in water, perhaps with the addition of dates for sweetening. After fermenting, the liquid was strained from the dough into a pot. They also made wine and various

ABOVE: *Group of female musicians playing a harp, lute, flutes and lyre.*

ABOVE LEFT: *Man picking grapes to make wine; from a Theban tomb painting.*

BELOW LEFT: *Wooden box inlaid with coloured ivory and a selection of typical Egyptian jewellery and amulets. (British Museum.)*

regions were noted for their quality. It was stored in pottery jars and had a label noting its origin, maker and date. There were many accounts of drunkenness especially after excessive banquets and parties.

We know a lot about the clothing the Ancient Egyptians wore since it is depicted in countless sculptures and paintings. Many examples of the actual clothing have also been discovered amongst other tomb artefacts. A large number of textiles were found in Tutankhamun's tomb which included over a hundred loin cloths and about 30 gloves or chariot driving gauntlets. The world's earliest surviving dress made of stitched linen, was discovered at Tarkhan in Egypt and dates from 2,800 BC. White linen was the standard material for clothing as it was cool and light to wear. Garments were often carefully pleated and they were draped around the body rather than tailored, with minimum stitching. Simple ankle-length sheath dresses were worn. In the New Kingdom they were often more pleated and fringes became popular. Women also sometimes wore an elegant heavily pleated, fringed robe over this dress. Men usually wore a short kilt, made from a rectangular piece of linen folded round the body and tied or fastened at the waist. This was sometimes starched at the front to form an apron, or pleated. Occasionally they would wear a cloak in the cooler weather. Working men wore only a loincloth while children are often depicted naked. The wealthy had a type of laundry service with meticulous methods of washing and pleating, and numerous laundry lists and marks on clothing have survived. Sandals were worn made from woven reed, grass or leather sometimes upturned like Turkish slippers.

Elaborate and colourful jewellery contrasted well with the usually plain garments. Jewellery was worn both for personal adornment and as a protection against evil. The most characteristic form of jewellery was the collar which was composed of numerous strings of beads using attractive stones like carnelian, jaspar and lapis lazuli. Armlets, bracelets and anklets were worn while finger rings often included seals. In the New Kingdom, both men and women had pierced ears and a wide variety of earrings and ear studs survive. There are many hairstyles depicted in sculpture and wall-paintings with fashions varying according to the period. Men usually wore a rounded hairstyle that followed the line of their heads. They were generally clean-shaven and razors were used from the earliest times in Egypt. The priests shaved their heads as did the wealthier men and women who wore wigs. These were mainly of human hair with some vegetable-fibre padding. Some wigs have survived that are composed of an intricate assortment of curls and plaits sometimes with attached bead ornaments.

The Egyptians were very fond of cosmetics and men, women and children used facial make-up called kohl to create a dark line round the eyes. Besides being decorative, kohl protected the eyes against infection and stopped the glare of the sun. Red ochre was used to colour the cheeks and probably as lipstick, while henna was used as a hair colourant. Countless bronze mirrors have survived (which would originally have been highly polished) and a large variety of cosmetic vessels, spoons and applicators. Medical papyri mention recipes for creams and oils to keep

LEFT: *A tomb figure wearing an elaborately pleated garment and plaited wig. (British Museum.)*

BELOW: *A fine quality stood made of ebony and ivory with a leather covered seat. (British Museum.)*

ABOVE: *Pottery tomb model of a house with a window and a roof which acts as a wind-vent to catch the breeze. In the forecourt are various provisions. c 1,900* BC. *(British Museum.)*

ABOVE: *A banquet scene with musicians and dancers and jars of wine. On their heads the women wear incense cones to perfume their wigs and garments. From a Theban tomb painting; c 1,400 BC. (British Museum.)*

BELOW: *A man and his wife playing the board game senet – from a papyrus, c 1,250 BC. (British Museum.)*

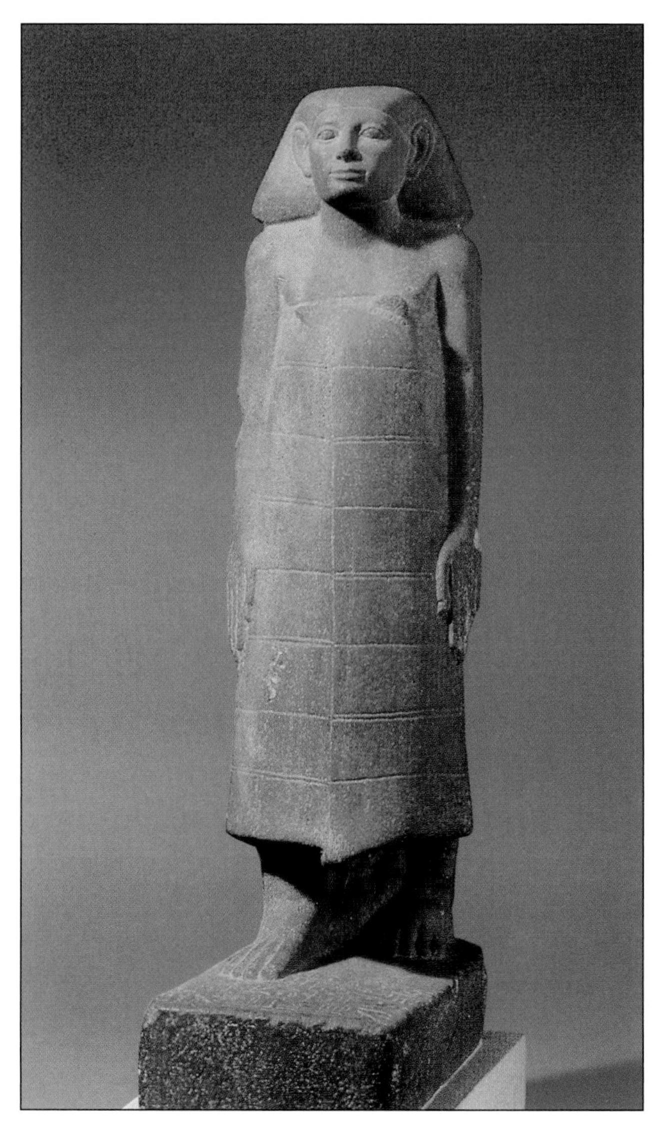

ABOVE LEFT: *Woman wearing a dress of the style worn by officials and dignitaries at the end of the Middle Kingdom. This statue is carved from quartzite, one of the hardest stones to be worked by the Egyptians. (British Museum.)*

ABOVE RIGHT: *A man with food offerings which include a goat, a hare and tray of ostrich eggs.*

the skin soft and supple after exposure to the hot Egyptian sun. Perfumes, some of which took months to prepare, were popular and were also worn by men during certain festivals. A popular form of incense cone was worn by women on top of the head at banquets to perfume the wig and garments.

The Egyptians depicted many of their favourite pastimes in their tombs because they wanted to enjoy them forever in the afterlife. Hunting was popular among the nobility and the wealthy. Athletic games and sports were often group activities and these included wrestling, boxing, stave-fighting, ball games, gymnastics and acrobatics. Many paintings have survived of banqueting scenes where acrobats and dancers performed. The pirouette and some other ballet movements were known to the Ancient Egyptians, and dancing with rhythmic accompaniment from clapping, cymbals, sistra, bells and chanting was also popular at religious festivals. Music was an essential accompaniment to dance but was also practised in its own right. The harp and the flute were used, together with various wind instruments with and without reeds, made from wood or metal. Probably the earliest known account of a full orchestra performing a concert dates from *c*250 BC. This was at a festival for the Pharaoh Ptolemy II, where 600 musicians played simultaneously.

The Egyptians also played board games. The most popular game was called 'Senet' and many highly decorative boards with counters have survived, usually made of wood and ivory. Some boards have an alternative game on the other side which was called 'Twenty Squares'. There were also games called 'Serpent' and 'Dog and the Jackal'. Children amused themselves with a variety of toys which included balls, tops, dolls and figures of animals with movable parts.

CHAPTER SEVEN

The NILE

ABOVE: *Sunset on the Nile.*

The Nile flows for over 4,000 miles (6,500 km) and is the longest river in the World. It is formed from two great streams, the Blue Nile, which rises in Ethiopia, and the White Nile, which rises in Uganda. They join at Khartoum to become the main river which runs north through the desert to the Mediterranean Sea. Along its course the river is interrupted at six points by rapids or cataracts, and the first of these, near Aswan, marks the Nile's entry into Egypt proper. For the last hundred odd miles (160 km), the river fans out in tributaries over the marshy flats of the delta. This northern region of Egypt, which includes the Delta, is known as Lower Egypt. The part to the south of it, called Upper Egypt, is quite different geographically. Here the land is drier and the river is bordered on both sides by cliffs.

Every year the main stream of the Nile, charged with torrential Ethiopian rainfall, traditionally distributed its water over Egypt. When the water receded it left behind a layer of fertile silt. The Ancient Egyptians called this the 'black land' to distinguish it from the 'red land' of the desert. The Nile gave them prosperity as the desert that it runs through provided security and protection from invasion. The contrast between these two geographical features affected the mental attitudes of the people who depended on them. They believed that the Nile was the centre of the world and the most important highway separating east from west. In the cycle of the Nile flood they could sense the continuity of life. By contrast, the desert was considered the home of the dead and a place for burial. Since the sun went down in the west, the desolate desert areas on the west bank were chosen for building their cemeteries. In Egyptian mythology the Nile was like the River Styx of the Greeks, where the soul was ferried from the east to west bank. In their creation mythology, the first living matter could be likened to the fresh land deposited after the flood. The Egyptians called their country 'the gift of the Nile' and the annual flood was seen as the arrival of the Nile god, Hapy.

If the annual flood of the Nile was too high, the spreading river could destroy the surrounding villages. If it was too low there was less agricultural land available for food crops. If this low flood was repeated for several consecutive years, famine resulted. The Nile made the Egyptians from the start an

Above: *Fowling in the marshes – from a Theban tomb painting,* c 1,400 BC.

Below: *The River Temple of Philae.*

agricultural nation, and their need to organize themselves around the river's yearly cycle was crucial to the growth of their civilization. From the earliest times they managed to determine the seasons of the year by the behaviour of the Nile and developed the first working calendar of 365 days divided into 12 months. They had three seasons called 'akhet', 'peret' and 'shemu'. The season of inundation (akhet) began around August, and by November the water had receded enough to plant crops. The final season of 'shemu' represented the drought which lasted from about March to August when the crops could be harvested.

They built dykes to prevent the river from flooding the settlements on the mounds which stood out like islands when the Nile flooded the valley. They also laid out a network of reservoirs and canals to contain the water when the flood receded. This was difficult work and the land had to be reclaimed by levelling the mounds and filling up the depressions in the ground. The water was

ABOVE: *Geese from a wall painting at Maidum, c 2,500 BC.*

MIDDLE: *Sunset on the Nile.*

BOTTOM: *After the construction of the Aswan High Dam, the River Temple of Philae had to be moved to another island – an amazing feat of organisation.*

directed into artificial canals which ran through the provincial settlements. These canals had to be dug and cleared and the courses planned to irrigate evenly as many fields as possisble. The flood water contained in reservoirs or large dug-out basins was fed into irrigation channels by simple, yet effective water-raising mechanisms. The introduction of the 'shaduf' in the New Kingdom greatly lightened the labour and is still used in Egypt nowadays. The shaduf consisted of a bucket on a pole, which was lowered into the water and then raised again by a heavy counterweight on the other end of the pole. At the end of the summer, holes were made in the dykes at the highest points, and when the required amount of muddy water had flowed through the opening was plugged. When the water had been absorbed, work could begin and the seed was sown.

The building and maintenance of the dykes, reservoirs and canals went on continuously and demanded a large labour force which was enrolled by a conscription system. (In the Old Kingdom this large organized labour force could undertake pyramid building during the inundation season.) In order to ensure the development of irrigation and land reclamation Egypt was divided into a number of administrative provinces called 'names'. When there was political crisis, the maintenance of the system of water supply became disorganized and in a short time the complete

ABOVE: *Fishing on the Nile with a draw net, from a Theban tomb painting; c 1,250* BC.

MIDDLE: *Model boat under sail. On the prow a man tests the depth of the water while the large oar is used for steering. c 1,800* BC*. (British Museum.)*

BELOW: *Colourful glass fish used as a cosmetic vessel; c1,800* BC*. (British Museum.)*

economy of the country would break down. In a land of virtually no rain, irrigation alone made it possible for crops to grow and people to live. In order to help combat the consequences of a poor flood, grain could be stored up against a bad year or succession of bad years, as in the biblical story of Joseph. They also built gauges to measure the rise of the river and eventually sited these 'Nilometers' further south in order to predict the economic repercussions as early as possible.

The Nile also formed a perfect artery of communication and, unlike transport by land, it was cheap and quick, since all the cities and

TOP: *Ship under full sail from a Theban tomb painting; c2,250 BC.*

ABOVE: *Transporting cattle by boat; from a Theban tomb painting.*

RIGHT: *Black granite statue of Hapy, god of the abundant Nile. (British Museum.)*

towns were easily accessible by boat. Even allowing for all hazards, the Nile is not a particularly formidable river, and nowadays the main leisurely tours of Egypt are on cruise-boats. All the necessary water power is provided by the current and the wind. The current can provide enough power to drift down-river, while the wind blowing from the north can be harnessed to sail upstream. The earliest record of a ship under sail is depicted on an Egyptian pot which dates from about 3,200 BC. The Egyptians pioneered the development of river craft and there were

Above: *In ancient times, the Nile was the natural habitat of the hippopotamus. Although associated with the gods, this creature was also hunted with harpoons.*

Left: *Model funeral boat which would have carried the deceased on their final journey on the Nile to their tomb; c 1,900* BC. *[British Museum.]*

many different types built for various functions. Agricultural produce, troops, cattle, wood, stone and funeral processions were all carried on the Nile and its canals. The dockyards could launch ships some 200 feet (70 m) long, made of either native wood or conifers from Lebanon. Complete ships, models, detailed drawings and a technical vocabulary specifying the various types of boat, with lists of their equipment, have survived. The Ancient Egyptian language itself contains many nautical metaphors and going south was expressed as 'going upstream'.

The land around the Nile delta was particularly fertile and the marshland was teeming with wild life. Large areas of the marsh came to be carefully preserved for hunting, cattle-raising, wild fruits and fishing. Fishing was a prosperous occupation and those who lived on the edge of the marshes were organized into

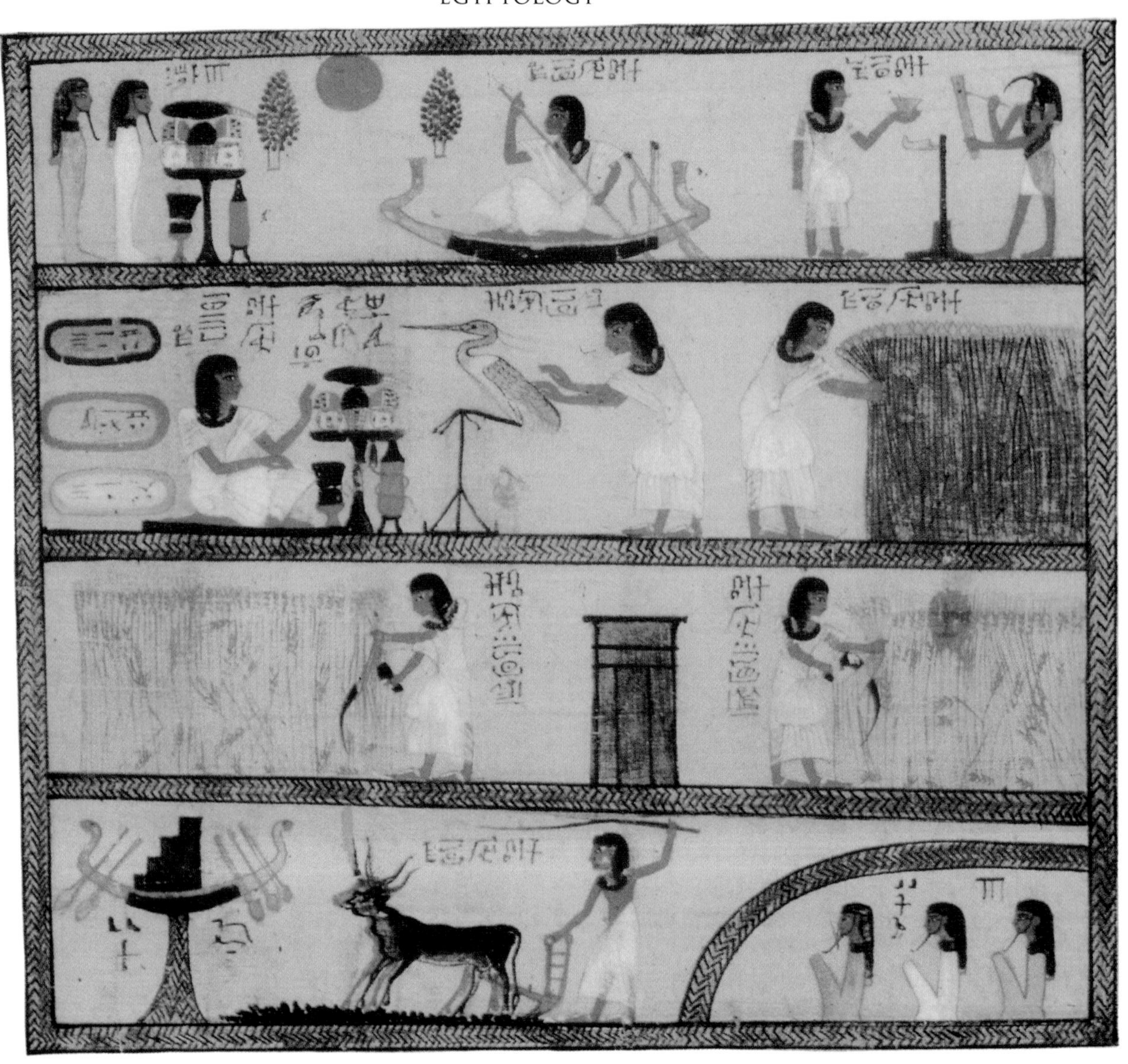

ABOVE: *Papyrus painting showing the harvesting of flax from which linen was made; c 1,350 BC. (British Museum.)*

teams for fishing. The most effective method was to drag a great trawl-net between two boats and bring it to the bank. However, some fish were the sacred animals of certain local districts where it was forbidden to eat them. The Egyptians were probably the first to regard fishing as a sport as well as a source of food. A sketch has survived which depicts a nobleman fishing from a tank with a rod and line. Harpooning and fowling with a throw stick were also popular sports for the wealthy.

The Nile was also the natural habitat of the hippopotamus and the crocodile and, although they both became associated with gods, the hippopotamus was hunted with harpoons. The beautiful temple at Kom Ombo was dedicated to Sobek, the crocodile god and it is recorded that in 10BC at Lake Moeris, Egyptian priests had a sacred crocodile which they tamed and fed with cakes and honey wine. Neither the hippopotamus nor the crocodile are to be found in the Egyptian river nowadays, as they have moved further south, deep into the Sudan.

In the extensive marshy areas of the Nile, the papyrus plant rooted in the mud rose to a great height and spread in dense thickets. The papyrus reed was the raw material of Egyptian paper making. Papyrus paper was made by cutting thin strips of pith (the spongy tissue in the stem of each reed) and arranging them on a flat stone. The papyrus was then beaten with wooden mallets until natural juice, acting like glue, bound the strips together. Then single sheets were pasted into one long roll. The Egyptians are known to have used papyrus as early as the first dynasty (*c*3,100 BC). Papyrus became an expensive government monopoly in later times and its cultivation was eventually restricted to one particular region. Papyrus no longer grows naturally in Egypt and much of the thriving tourist trade in paintings claimed to be painted on 'papy-

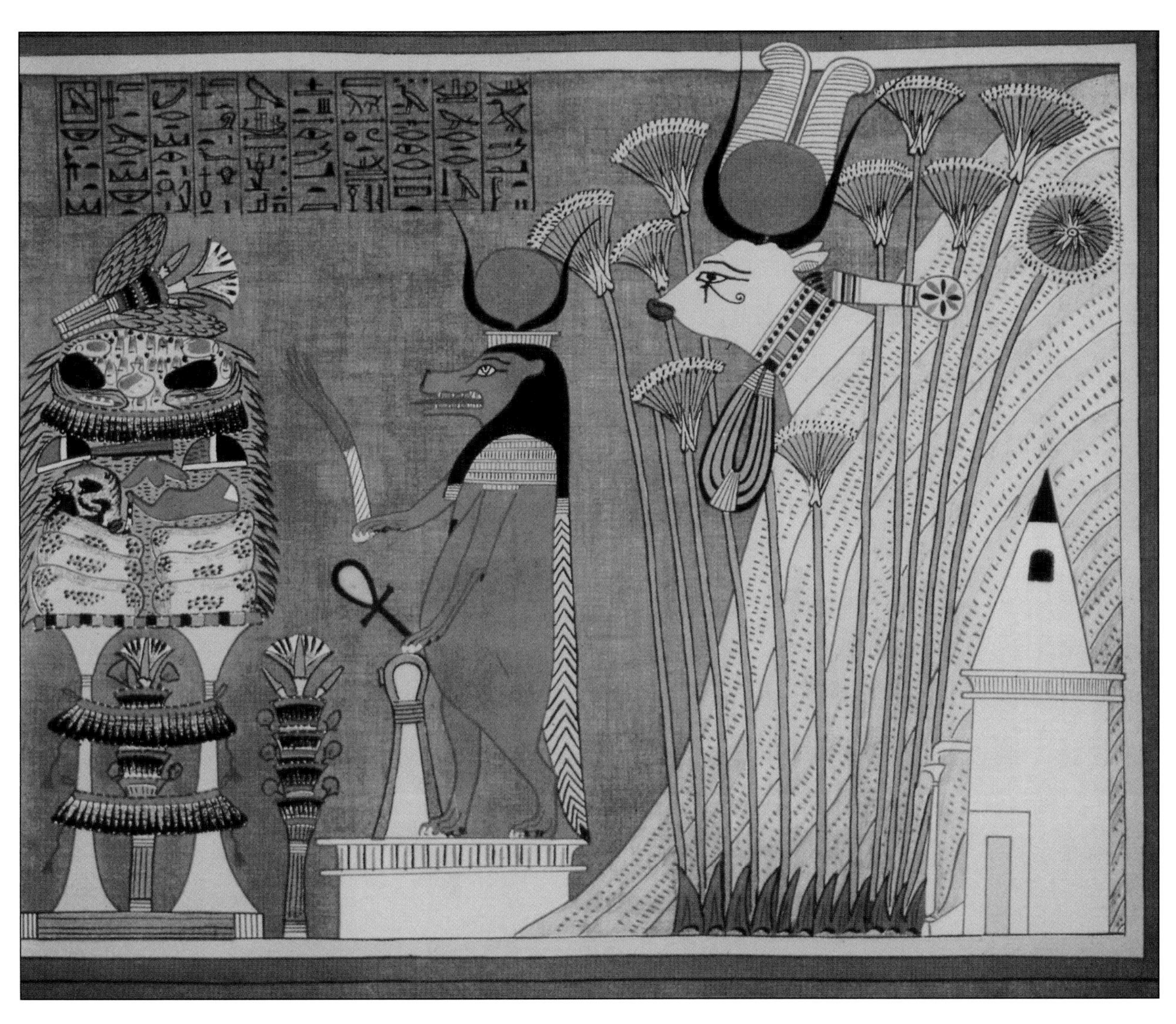

ABOVE: *Papyrus painting showing a cow emerging from a thicket of papyrus which grew to a great height by the Nile. (British Museum.)*

BELOW: *Travel brochures from the 1920s. Since the major ancient sites are easily accessible from the river, the Nile Cruise has become the most leisurely and luxurious way to tour Egypt.*

Left: *Woman carrying papyrus – the classic flowering plant of Lower Egypt.*

Right: *Pharaoh carrying a bouquet of sacred lotus flowers which symbolized rebirth and were an emblem of Upper Egypt.*

rus' is often done on a substitute paper of banana skin composition.

The Greek historian, Herodotus, claimed that the first Pharaoh, Menes, had the plain of Memphis drained, in order to build a new capital there, and thereby altered the course of the Nile. There is also evidence of an immense reservoir constructed in the Faiyum region, 66 square miles (100 sq km) in area that had vast dykes and sluices. Nowadays the colossal Aswan High Dam built between 1960 and 1970, with its own immense reservoir, has ended the traditional annual flood cycle of the River Nile. The immense reservoir, Lake Nasser, created by the dam, submerged whole villages and has required the resettlement of tens of thousands of people. Many important ancient remains have been lost but over 20 monuments were rescued with assistance on an international scale. The most impressive salvage operation was at Abu Simbel, where the vast rock temples were cut into 30-ton blocks and then reassembled at an identical site above the level of the lake. Similarly, the beautiful temples of Philae were painstakingly transferred stone by stone to a nearby island, safe from the floodwaters of the Nile.

CHAPTER EIGHT

The HIEROGLYPHS

ABOVE: *Painted limestone statuette of a royal scribe; c1,500 BC. (British Museum.)*

When looking at hieroglyphs we have a natural tendency to view each sign as a representation of a letter, since our written language is dependent upon an alphabet. The idea of an alphabet is something which occurred very late in the history of writing, and the reduction of all the possible sounds and combinations to a written system of some 20 signs took mankind a long time to accomplish. Each hieroglyphic sign does not represent a letter and does not always represent a word. Besides being pictorial indications of the meaning of words (ideograms), hieroglyphic signs also convey sounds in one, two, or three consonants (phonograms). Writing based solely on picture signs would be impractical since a complete vocabulary would require thousands of signs. It would be difficult to express clearly and without ambiguity, words for things not easily pictured, and this was probably why signs with a sound value (phonograms) were also necessary. The purely pictorial signs or ideograms could be used at the end of a word to indicate that word's precise meaning – a useful system in the absence of punctuation.

Ancient Egyptian is the second oldest recorded language. Only Sumerian is believed to be slightly earlier. The first hieroglyphs can be dated to approximately 3,100 BC while the latest are almost three and a half thousand years later (*c* AD 394). It could be claimed that the written language has survived in total for nearly 5,000 years since its final form is still used during Coptic religious services. A small number of Ancient Egyptian words have even found their way into the modern English vocabulary (eg 'oasis'). Egyptologists have identified five stages in the development of the language: The Old (*c*2650–2135 BC). the Middle (*c*2135–1785 BC) and Late (*c*1550–700 BC), Demotic (*c*700 BC – AD 500) and finally Coptic. This last stage began in the third century AD and continued until the Middle Ages when it was replaced by Arabic as the spoken Egyptian language.

Hieroglyphic writing was a highly developed system by which everything, even grammatical forms, could be expressed. Hieroglyphs can be read from right to left, from left to right and also vertically from top to bottom, according to the composition of the picture. A hieroglyphic inscription was traditionally arranged in columns. Later it was written in horizontal lines and the heads

of the signs were always turned towards the beginning of the sentence. The sequence is continuous, without punctuation marks or spaces to indicate divisions between words. Egyptian grammar is completely different from that of European languages and cannot be reduced to a series of simple rules. Mastery of the language takes much concerted study. There are over 6,000 documented hieroglyphs covering the whole period during which the scripts were used, although the majority of these were developed for religious reasons in the Graeco-Roman period. In general, about 700 were in standard use at any one time.

A striking feature of hieroglyphic writing is its absence of vowels. Egyptologists use the vowels 'e' and 'a' where necessary to communicate the language verbally. There are 24 hieroglyphic signs, each representing a consonant, which loosely correspond to the sounds of our modern alphabet. Egyptologists transliterate hieroglyphic sound values into our modern alphabetic characters to enable pronunciation, but the words would

ABOVE: *Papyrus with a hymn to the god Ra from the* Book of the Dead. *Hieroglyphs came to be used almost exclusively for religious and magical texts.* c *1,050* BC. *(British Museum.)*

Above: The Rosetta stone consists of three scripts – hieroglyphs at the top, demotic in the middle, and Greek at the bottom. It is a decree by all the priests of Egypt in favour of the reigning King, Ptolemy V. (British Museum.)

THE ALPHABET IN HIEROGLYPHS
B
Foot
D
Hand
F
Horned Viper
G
Jar Stand
H
Aerial View of Hut
H
Twisted Flax
I
Flowering Reed
J
Similar to Snake
K
Basket
M
Owl
N
Water
P
Stool
Q
Similar to Hill Slope
R
Mouth
S
Folded Cloth
SH
Pool
T
Loaf
TSH
Tethering Rope
W
Quail Chick
Z
Similar to Door Bolt

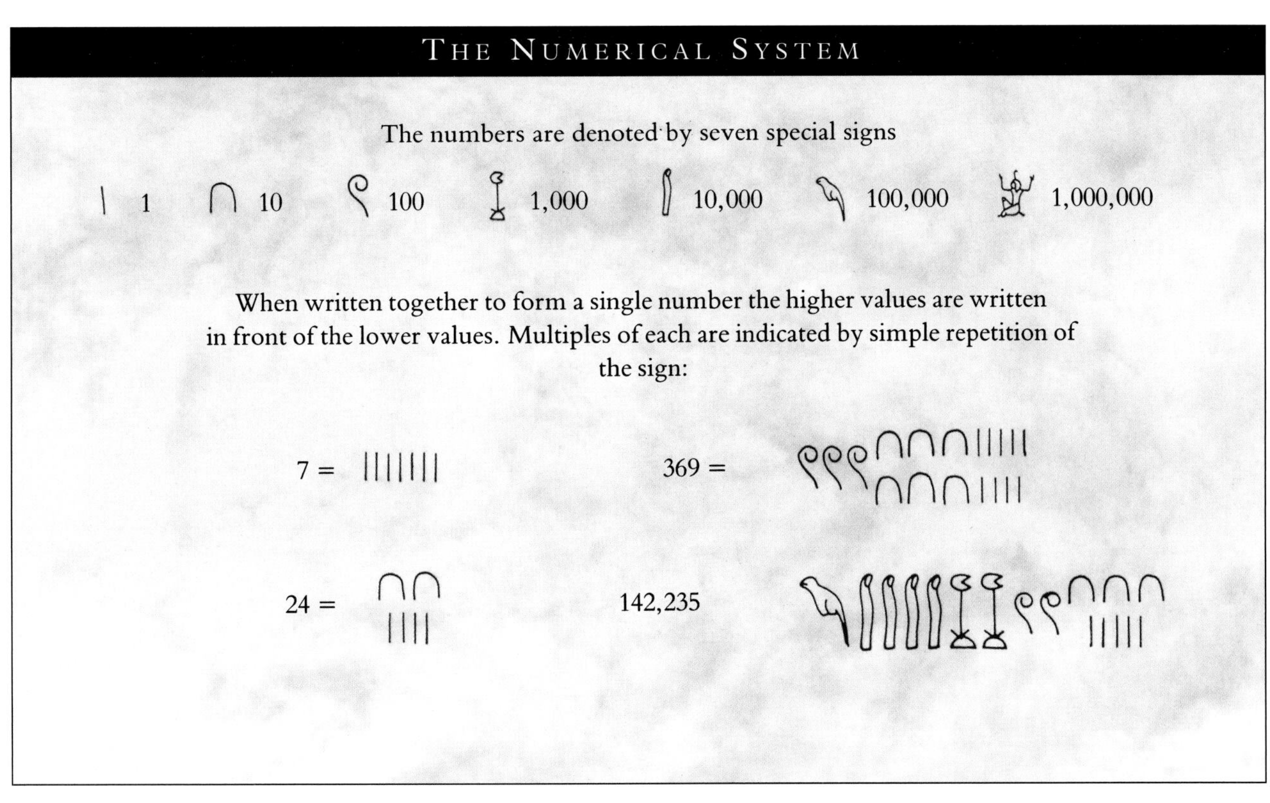
THE NUMERICAL SYSTEM
The numbers are denoted by seven special signs
1
10
100
1,000
10,000
100,000
1,000,000
When written together to form a single number the higher values are written in front of the lower values. Multiples of each are indicated by simple repetition of the sign:
7 =
369 =
24 =
142,235

not have sounded the same way in ancient times. This system of Egyptian alphabetic signs was not generally used for complete words until Graeco-Roman times when various royal names were transcribed into hieroglyphs. It has been claimed that certain hieroglyphs eventually found their way into our own alphabet via Protosinaitic, Phoenician, Greek and Latin.

Hieroglyphs are usually associated with stone inscriptions and the word itself is actually derived from the Greek 'ta hieroglyphica' meaning 'the sacred carved letters'. The signs of the script are largely pictorial in character and the majority of the signs are recognizable pictures of natural or manmade objects. The best examples of the script have an intrinsic beauty of line and colour which some claim to be the most beautiful writing ever designed. It was more than just a writing system and the Egyptians themselves referred to it as the 'writing of the divine words'. Like the representations in their art, the script was endowed with religious or magical significance. The name of a person inscribed in hieroglyphs was believed to embody his unique identity. If the representation lacked a name, it had no means of continued existence in the afterlife. Therefore, many kings' and gods' names

LEFT: *Painted limestone statue of a scribe in the traditional cross-legged pose with his papyrus scroll unfolded in the lap. (Cairo Museum.)*

ABOVE LEFT: *Two common carved stone hieroglyphs representing the sedge plant, symbol of Upper Egypt, and the bee symbol of Lower Egypt. (British Museum.)*

ABOVE: *Painted limestone relief depicting Thoth, the ibis-headed god of writing. (British Museum.)*

LEFT: *Faience book-label probably originally attached to a box of papyri in the Royal Library at El Amarna; c 1,380 BC. (British Museum.)*

BELOW: *Limestone tablet inscribed with hieroglyphs with a mallet and copper chisels. (British Museum.)*

were defaced or erased from monuments by later Pharaohs with conflicting ideals. Similarly, existing inscriptions and statues could be taken over and claimed by carving the new royal name on them.

Hieroglyphs were not suitable for writing quickly so they were developed into a more stylized, fluent script called hieratic. This became the standard administrative and business script and was also used to record documents of a literary, scientific and religious nature. It was particularly suitable for writing on papyrus or fragments of pottery and limestone called ostraca. The text was usually written with a brush or a sharpened reed in black ink, while red ink was sometimes used to highlight special sections. The name hieratic

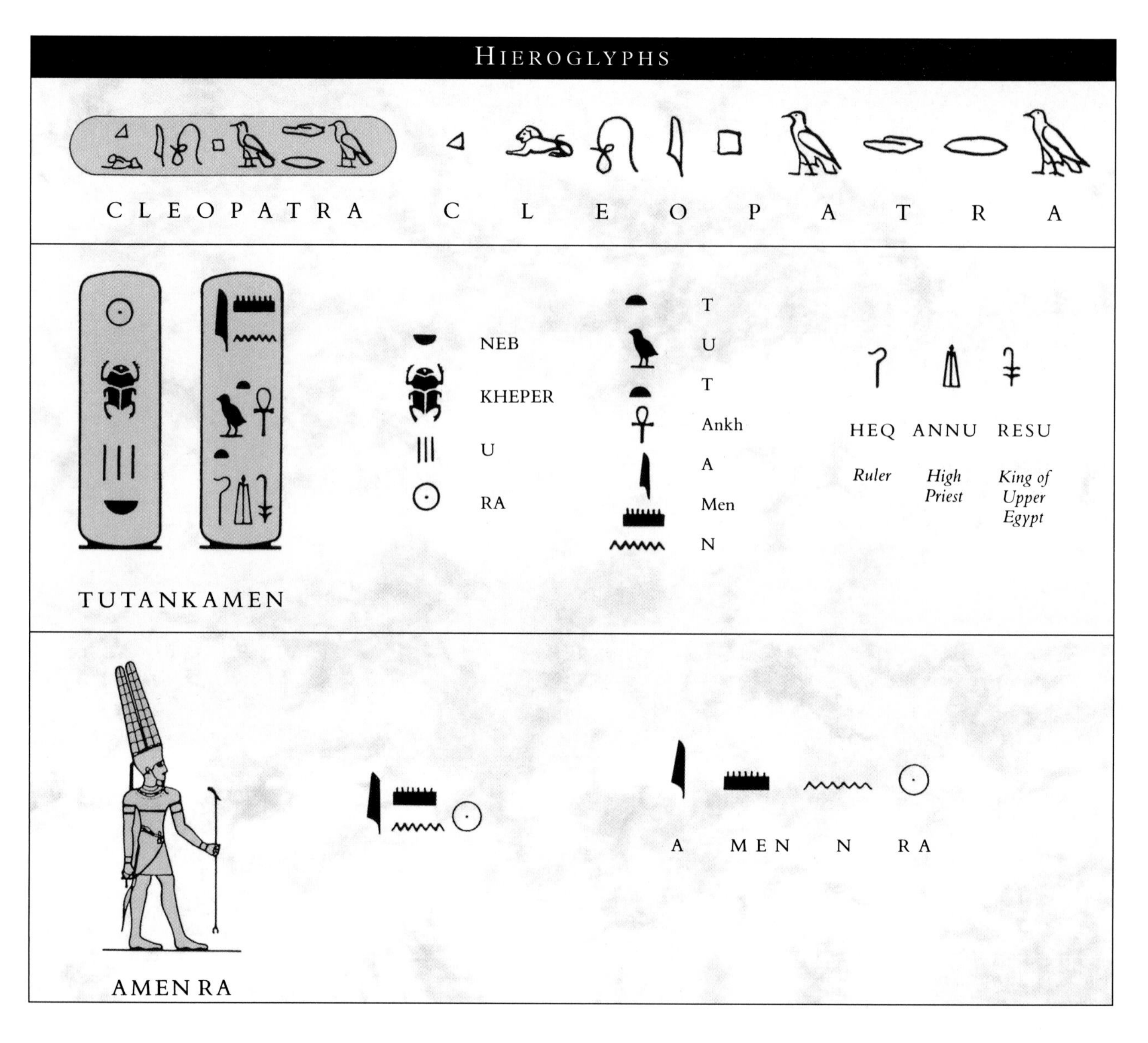

comes from the Greek 'hieratika' meaning 'priestly'. This was because, by the Late Period when the Greeks visited Egypt, its use had become confined to religious documents and demotic had replaced it as the main 'business' script. The name demotic comes from the Greek 'demotika' meaning 'popular' and this refers to its day-to-day writing function. From the Prolemaic period it was also used for literary compositions as well as scientific and religious texts.

Although writing played an important part in Ancient Egyptian society it is unlikely that literacy can have been widespread among the population. The production of writing and direct access to it was confined to an educated elite, consisting of royalty, state officials and scribes. The professional scribe was a central figure in every aspect of the country's administration – civil, military and religious. When an illiterate person needed a document to be read or written he would need to pay for the services of a scribe. It traditionally took a scribe some 12 years to learn and write the 700 or so hieroglyphs in common use by the New Kingdom and study started at the age of four. Many ancient school exercises have survived (complete with the teacher's corrections), and these were often copies of 'Egyptian Classics' in the hieratic text.

In Egypt's Roman and Christian period, the Coptic script developed as the other native scripts declined. The word 'copt' is derived from the Arabic 'gubti' a corruption of the Greek word for Egypt. It was used by the Arabs in the seventh century to denote the native inhabitants of the country. Coptic consists of 24 letters of the Greek alphabet combined with six demotic characters. The development of this standard form of the alphabet,

Above right: *Painted limestone relief inscribed with the names and titles of various pharaohs. (British Museum.)*

Facing page left: *Granite squatting statue. This characteristic 'block' form was ideally suited for inscribing long texts. (British Museum.)*

Facing page right: *Papyrus concerned with mathematical problems and their solutions; c1,570 BC. (British Museum.)*

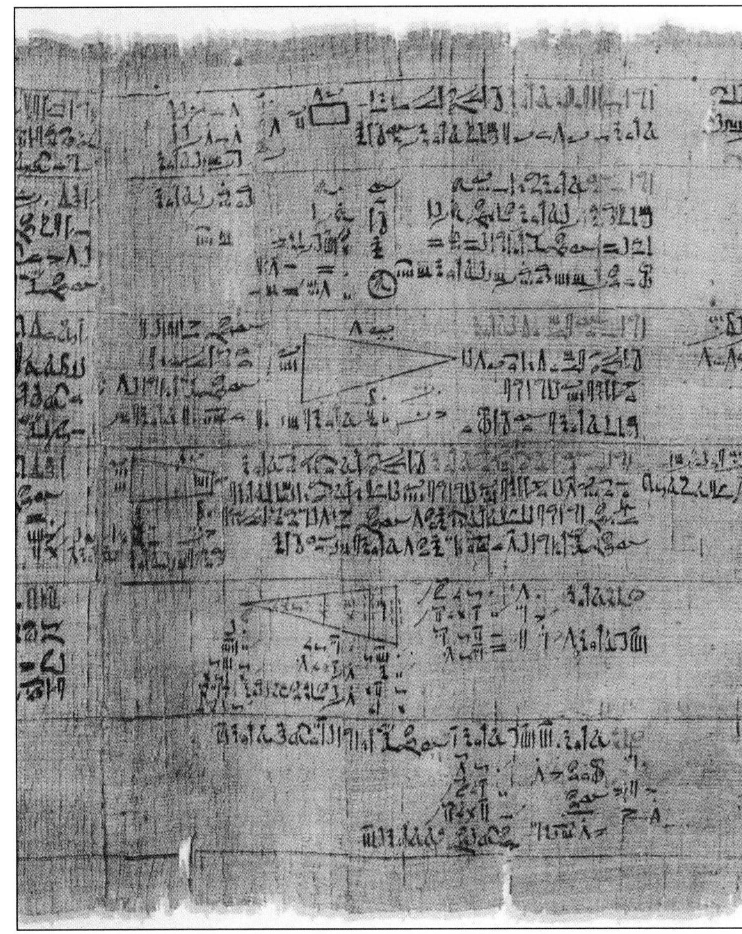

which was well established by the fourth century AD, is closely associated with the spread of Christianity in Egypt. In its earliest form, Coptic was used to write native magical texts and it was not initially devised for translating the gospels. Since it is still spoken in Coptic religious services some people believe it could reveal clues to the pronunciation of the original Ancient Egyptian language, although the links may have become too distant with the passage of time.

The art of reading hieroglyphs was lost for centuries and it was a Frenchman called Jean-Francois Champollion (1790–1832) who became the first to decipher them in full. The most important key to this forgotten writing was the famous Rosetta stone discovered in 1799 which had a bilingual text. This was a decree of the Pharaoh Prolemy V written in Ancient Greek (a known language) and two Ancient Egyptian scripts, demotic and hieroglyphic. Comparing these scripts and making use of his excellent knowledge of Coptic, Champollion studied copies of other hieroglyphic inscriptions. After considerable research he was able to recognize not only some of the letters of the hieroglyphic alphabet but also a range of other hieroglyphs from royal

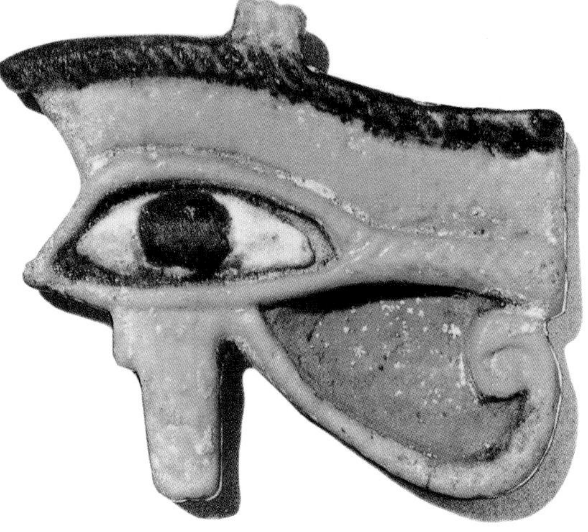

LEFT: *Copy of a temple relief from Abydos showing the typical composition with its careful balance between the figures and hieroglyphs.*

ABOVE: *Isis greets Ramses III and his son; from a Theban tomb painting, c 1,1150 BC. This shows the arrangement of columns of hieroglyphs with a pictorial composition.*

ABOVE LEFT: *Faience amulet derived from the sacred eye of Horus hieroglyph. (British Museum.)*

RIGHT: *Faience amulet derived from the falcon hieroglyph. (British Museum.)*

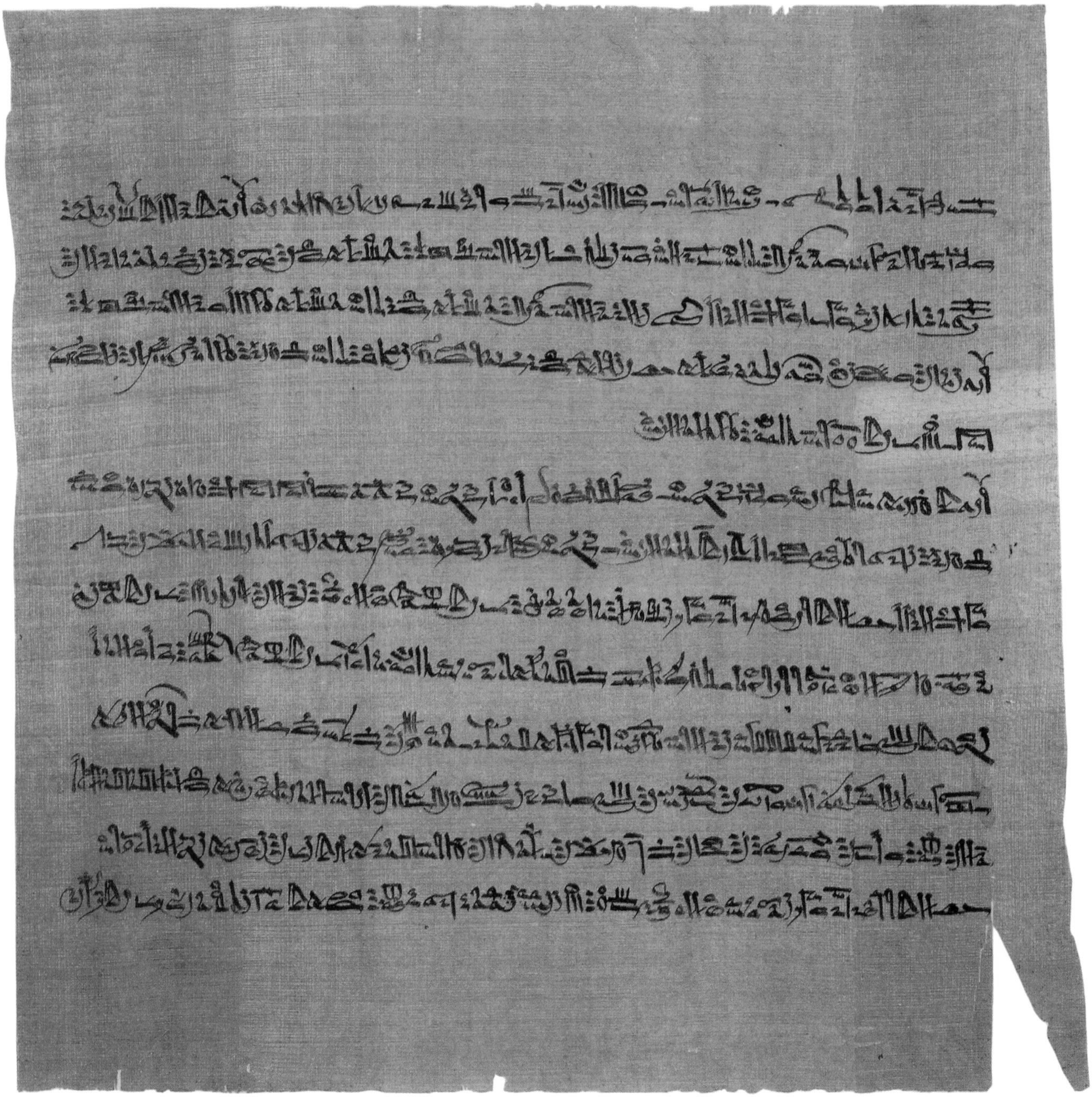

cartouches. He managed to decipher 79 different royal names, of which he recognized and tabulated all the letters one by one. Then, using the 'alphabet', all the letters of which he had progressively recovered, he managed to identify words. In only a couple of years he compiled a dictionary and grammar. Although the readings of kings' names provided the key to the writing system, it would not have led to an understanding of the Egyptian language without the assistance of Coptic. In studying the Rosetta stone text, Champollion's knowledge of Coptic enabled him to work out the phonetic values of particular hieroglyphic signs while his understanding of the Greek text helped him to identify the pictorial characters.

With a knowledge of the language we are now able to translate the countless ancient writings that have survived. The wisdom texts were the most highly regarded and oldest writings, and were popular throughout Egyptian history. They often contain moral codes and represent a high level of thinking. Besides religious literature and business records the Ancient Egyptian writings include subjects as varied as poetry, medicine and mathematics.

ABOVE: *The hieratic script in a particularly fine hand from 'The Great Harris Papyrus', the longest papyrus known. (British Museum.)*

ABOVE RIGHT: *The papyrus of the scribe Ani, one of the finest examples of the Egyptian Book of the Dead. (British Museum.)*

RIGHT: *Painted hieroglyphs on a Middle Kingdom coffin. (British Museum.)*

CHAPTER NINE

The INFLUENCE of ANCIENT EGYPT

ABOVE: Alethe – Priestess of Isis *by Edwin Lond (1829–91). Such 19th-century oil paintings reflect an idealistic romantic image of Ancient Egypt.*

The impressive monuments and fascinating artefacts are today's visible evidence of Egypt's past glory. However, many invisible aspects of our modern civilization have their origins in Ancient Egypt. Their ideas were spread to Europe via the Greeks and the Romans, whose own culture drew heavily on this legacy, and who were impressed by the achievements of a civilization so much older than their own. Ancient Egypt has become increasingly distant, mysterious and fascinating ever since. It has also become a potent vehicle for escapism which has inspired art, novels, crime fiction, science fiction, epic and horror movies. In addition many people develop a quest to discover some hidden or secret knowledge in Ancient Egypt and devise complex theories on the construction and purpose of the pyramids. The Ancient Egyptians themselves never went out of their way to spread their culture and religion to the rest of the world, and their influence took place by force of circumstance.

Trade helped to spread Egyptian culture throughout the ancient world. The Egyptians needed wood, metals, and semi-precious stones while their monopoly on African products, particularly gold, attracted countless foreigners. Ideas and technical knowledge travelled with produce. Cultural interchange between Africa, Asia and the Mediterranean countries increased during certain periods of invasion and conquest. The Phoenicians, who were sea-faring traders, borrowed and adapted many Egyptian architectural and artistic elements and spread them throughout the Mediterranean to mainland Greece.

The early Greek writers who travelled to Egypt themselves acknowledged the influence of Egypt on Greek principles of architecture and geometry. The earliest, archaic Greek sculpture reflects both the pose (with the left foot forward) and the proportions of that of Egypt. Before Socrates, followers of Pythagoras came to Egypt to complete their studies of geometry, astronomy and theology, and Egyptian story-telling was also an important influence on the development of the Hellenistic novel. In addition, some aspects of Ancient Greek religion can be traced to Egypt. The Greeks were also inspired by Egyptian medical science, and Egyptian doctors were employed by the Hittites and the Persians.

Scholars have attempted to demonstrate the development of our alphabet from hiero-

glyphic signs, and certain concepts of Egyptian law may also have come down to us. However, perhaps the greatest Ancient Egyptian legacy has been their calendar which was adopted by the Romans and formed the basis of our Gregorian calendar.

The Romans, like the Greeks before them, absorbed many native religious beliefs after they conquered Egypt. They adopted Egyptian burial practices, developing a sophisticated embalming technique and style of funerary portraiture. Many Egyptian gods were also worshipped although their true nature was often totally misunderstood. The Romans imported many Egyptian statues and made many, often spurious, copies of them. Obelisks stood in the Temple of Isis and in the circuses in Rome. Since Rome became the most important city in the Classical and Christian world, the Roman selection and interpretation of Egyptian forms strongly influenced the way the rest of Europe viewed Ancient Egypt. Consequently, the knowledge handed down to Medieval and Renaissance

ABOVE: Israel in Egypt *by Sir Edward Poynter (1836–1919).*

BELOW: The Finding of Moses *by Sir Lawrence Alma Tadema (1836–1912). Biblical subjects provided artists with an excuse for indulging in fanciful visions of Ancient Egypt.*

Europe was largely governed by what interested classical and Byzantine scholars.

The Bible has provided the only point of access to Ancient Egypt for many Christians over the centuries and it is inevitably coloured by certain prejudices. The Old Testament gives a general impression of the Egyptians as a powerful pagan state oppressing a weaker and devout nomadic people. The Jews like many nomadic people were attracted to Egypt's land of plenty and when they left they must have taken with them many native Egyptian ideas. Egyptian hymns and wisdom literature were known in Canaan from the time of the New Kingdom, and they influenced certain Old Testament writings. Meanwhile, Solomon may well have been inspired by the efficiency of Egyptian bureaucracy when organizing the Jewish kingdom.

It is often demonstrated that Christian religion contains many practices and images which had their roots in pagan Egypt. This is quite understandable since during the formative years of Christianity, the religious rituals inherited from the Romans were already steeped in Egyptian traditions. When the powerful Roman Empire officially adopted

ABOVE: Sandstorm in the Desert *by David Roberts (1796–1864), who visited Egypt in 1839. He sketched many monuments and his drawings were published in a famous series of lithographs.*

BELOW: *Bronze figure of the god Horus as a Roman soldier. The Romans adapted many Egyptian gods into their own culture without fully understanding their original religious function. (British Museum.)*

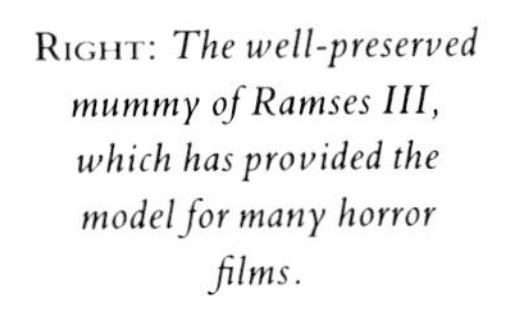

RIGHT: *The well-preserved mummy of Ramses III, which has provided the model for many horror films.*

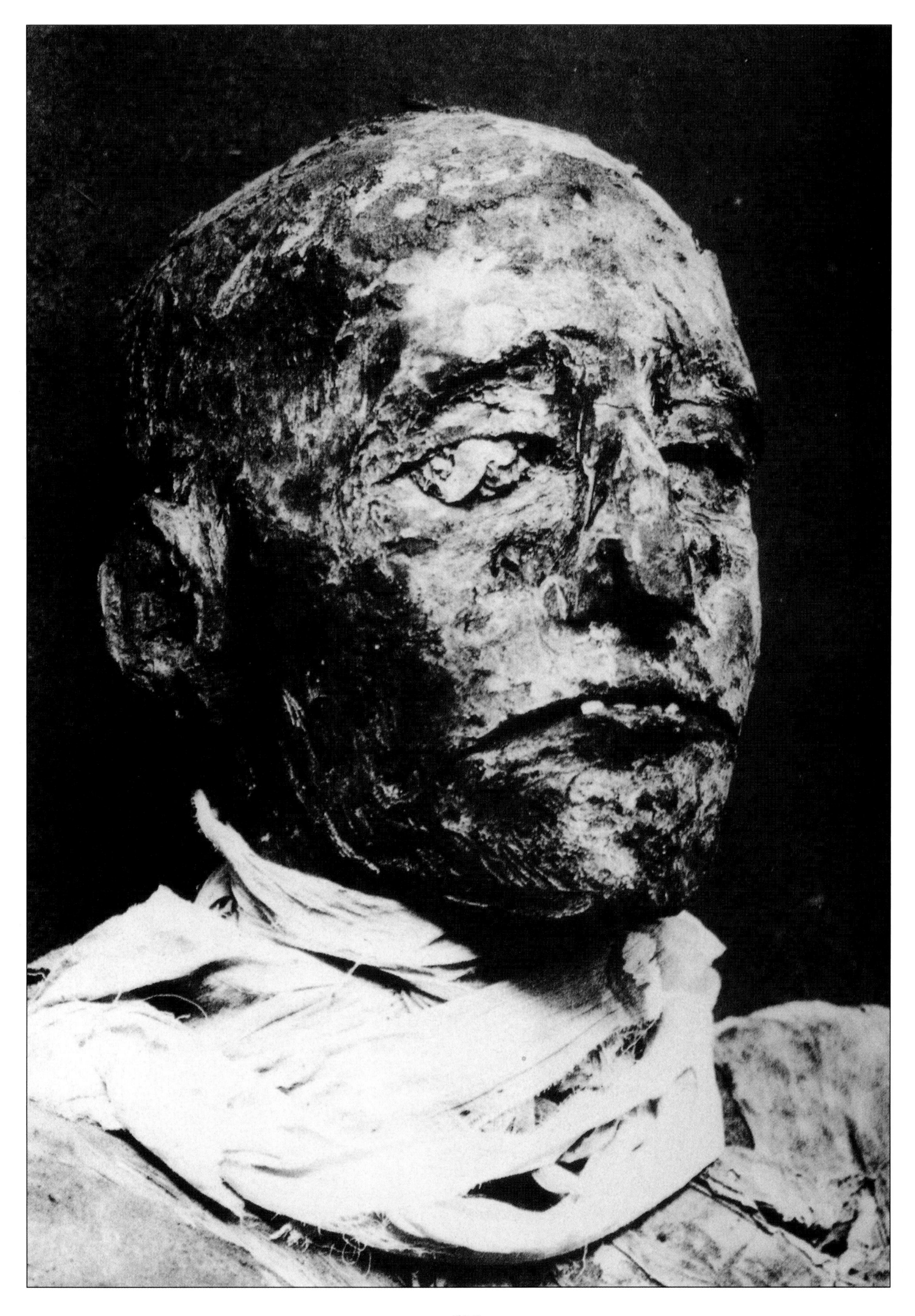

LEFT: *Painted fresco in a Coptic Church. The early Christian Church in Egypt borrowed many elements from the ancient 'pagan' heritage and the Ancient Egyptian language is still spoken today during the services.*

RIGHT: *Mummy of a Roman boy. The Romans adopted the native Egyptian burial customs and added naturalistic portraits to them. (British Museum.)*

the new Christian religion it embraced many existing concepts and images. In particular, the cult of Isis, so strong in the early Roman Empire, could have provided a prototype image of the Virgin and Child through the many representations of Isis suckling Horus. It is recorded that an original ancient statue of Isis survived in a French church until the sixteenth century, while in a different French church the birth of Isis continues to be celebrated nowadays. The popular representation of Christ triumphant over harmful beasts bears a striking resemblance to the image of Horus triumphant over the crocodile. Many similar parallels can be drawn between the portrayal of certain Christian saints and Egyptian gods while holy attributes like the halo, crook and the idea of winged men as angels have Egyptian precedents. The central Christian emblem, the cross, is often represented on early Coptic monuments as the Egyptian Ankh sign of life and is still clearly present on medieval tomb stones in the Balkans. Many subconscious Egyptian elements would have been conveyed by the bishops from Egypt who were highly influential at the early church councils in Rome.

Egyptian literature also influenced many famous Eastern folklore tales like Sinbad and Ali Baba, while many ancient phrases and sayings probably survive in modern Egypt and the rest of Africa. Certain Ancient Egyptian techniques and ritual practices have survived among the central African peoples, probably via the later Ethiopian kingdom of Meroe. In modern Egypt, although the influence of Islamic culture has been considerable, many age-old customs have survived. In the countryside, the Shaduf is still used to water the fields, as depicted in ancient times, and many aspects of village life have change little. Some boundaries have altered little and certain ancient place names have remained virtually the same. At Luxor a sacred barque is carried in honour of an Islamic saint very much as it would have been for the god Amun in ancient times. Many superstitions have also survived, such as leaving food or burning incense for dead relatives. There is also a fear of the 'evil eye', and charms are still kept as protection against evil.

FAR RIGHT: *19th-century painted bronze candlestick in the Egyptian style.*

Ancient Egypt has continued to be a source of inspiration for mystics and followers of the occult. The hermetic creed, alchemy and astrology probably originated from Alexan-

dria which became a major cultural and trading centre in the ancient world. It was here that many Ancient Egyptian, Greek and Near Eastern ideas and beliefs merged together. Hermetic writings popularized the notion that Egyptians possessed true and pure wisdom. Although astrology arrived late in Egyptian history, probably from Western Asia, there are many depictions of stars, constellations and maps of the sky which have been mistaken for true zodiacs by mystics. The Egyptians did have a system of determining lucky and unlucky influences of the day, as in modern daily horoscopes, which however, had no connection with the 12 signs of the zodiac. The lucky or unlucky character of the day was derived from mythological events which had taken place on these particular days. In Egyptian literature there was also a belief that certain numbers had a magical significance, and this may have found its way into our modern superstition for lucky and unlucky numbers.

The earliest tale about a magician is in the 'Westcar' papyrus which dates from *c*1700 BC, and many psychics, fortune-tellers and palmists call themselves by Egyptian names or claim to be reincarnated Egyptian priests

ABOVE: *19th-century porcelain plate decorated with lotus flowers in the Egyptian style.*

RIGHT: Feeding the Sacred Ibis Birds in the Halls of Karnak *by Sir Edward Poynter (1836–1919). Such engravings popularized the Egyptian style.*

or priestesses. The strange animal-headed gods, mysterious hieroglyphic writing, sacred amulets and funerary beliefs of the Ancient Egyptians provide excellent subject matter for clairvoyants and psychic writers. It is even rumoured that they sell genuine powdered mummy in a New York pharmacy for use in occult magic potions.

The Ancient Egyptian influence on the occult is reinforced by many tales of the 'mummy's curse' which continue to capture public imagination. The earliest record of a ghost story involving a mummy was written in France in 1699. 'The Mummy' together with 'Dracula' and 'Frankenstein' prove that the theme has remained ever-popular for horror movies. Ancient Egypt's connection with the occult was publicized when the so-called 'Curse of Tutankhamun' was claimed by the press to be responsible for the death of Lord Carnarvon. Carnarvon, the expedition's sponsor who had a history of ill-health, died from an infected mosquito bite shortly after the tomb's discovery. However, those wishing to support the superstition about his death never pointed out that the man mainly responsible for the famous find, Howard Carter, lived until well into his sixties. *The*

J A TREGLOWN & SONS
STUDIO TWO

ABOVE: *Silver salt dish, c 1840s, decorated in the Egyptian Revival style.*

LEFT: *Colossal bas-relief from a modern DIY centre building in Kensington, London, which reflects the vogue for Egyptian revival architecture in the 1990s.*

FACING PAGE: *The Egyptian House, Penzance. Built in the 1830s, this structure represents the Egyptian Revival style in architecture.*

Times had been granted the exclusive reporting rights on the tomb's discovery, and its rival newspapers, having no story to report, were forced to invent one. This was how the mythical 'curse' was born.

In addition to influencing the occult sciences, Ancient Egypt has continued to inspire Western art through its exotic and romantic associations. In the nineteenth century a number of European painters succeeded in producing some highly imaginative reconstructions of Ancient Egypt. This was in response to a general taste for Middle-Eastern subjects at the time, and many artists travelled all over the Islamic world. The subject matter of their paintings inevitably included turbanned Arabs, bustling bazaars, camels, palm-trees and mildly pornographic harem scenes. The pyramids and the ancient ruins of Egypt were part of this romantic ideal and are often depicted in exaggerated perspective with dramatic sunsets. These elements of the fantastic, exotic and erotic were part of many artists' fanciful visions of Ancient Egypt. Their remarkable attention to detail was a reflection of contemporary Orientalist and Pre-Raphaelite ideals. Many artists must have visited museums in order to make accurate

ABOVE: *Sphinx car mascot from a 1920s car reflects the popularity of Egyptian motifs following the discovery of Tutankhamun's tomb.*

LEFT: *Verdi's epic opera* Aida *continues to be staged as a lavish spectacle and perpetuates the myth of Egypt's ancient splendour.*

studies of original ancient artefacts. The Bible also provided Ancient Egyptian themes for paintings which are frequently charged with considerable sentiment and melodrama. Many of these images became popularized through engravings in contemporary family Bibles and children's scripture books.

For the decorative arts and architecture, Ancient Egyptian motifs provided a variation on the fashionable neo-Classical style. This is often called the 'Egyptian Revival' and it was popular in France and England throughout the Napoleonic War, with its Egyptian connection. However, the Egyptian elements were stylized to suit contemporary taste, and the figures took on a rounder, plumper style reminiscent of the Ancient Graeco-Roman Egyptian style. 'Egyptianizing' was also a feature of English and French furniture of the Regency and Empire periods and was applied to other items like clocks, candelabra and porcelain. This mixture of Egyptian and Classical forms was also used in buildings as varied as mills, law-courts, masonic lodges and cemeteries. By the 1850s, the inclusion of an Egyptian court in the Great Exhibition in London showed that Ancient Egypt had captured British public imagination, reflecting the Victorian taste for ornament and decoration.

In the twentieth century, the artistic interpretation of Ancient Egypt has become less cluttered and elaborate and more 'modern'. The lofty, spacious and geometric character of Egyptian forms are more in tune with modern taste than the Classical style. The discovery of Tutankhamun's tomb in the 1920s was a major influence of a new design movement called Art Deco. Many Egyptian forms were stylized and incorporated into contemporary architecture, furniture, sculpture and graphic art. Ancient Egypt also had a big influence on the newly formed movie industry which was generated from Hollywood. The design of many cinema façades was inspired by Egyptian temple architecture and helped to enhance the whole fantasy world of movies. Meanwhile, Ancient Egyptian themes provided the perfect vehicle for escapist epics like *Land of the Pharaohs, The Ten Commandments* and *Cleopatra* which had huge sets with casts of thousands. This grand vision of Egypt's ancient splendour is similarly captured in the world of opera by Verdi's spectacular *Aida*.

Modern artists continue to be inspired by Ancient Egypt and highly original talents like Pablo Picasso and Henry Moore both acknowledged its influence on their formative work. In recent years architects have taken a renewed interest in Egypt and forms such as the pyramid, continue to be stylishly applied to many public and commercial buildings. The Egyptian style is so ancient that it appears modern, and as we progress into the future, so does our knowledge of civilized man's most distant past become more relevant.

Left: *A Greek period bronze statuette of the god Amen Ra shows how Egyptian forms were misrepresented by later cultures. (British Museum.)*

The Romans

INTRODUCTION

The Roman Empire died out nearly 1,500 years ago but, unlike other civilizations in the world which have been long forgotten, the legacy of the Romans is still with us today. The very word 'Romans' covered many races across a vast empire, and did not just refer to people living in Rome. In this book we have given an account of the history and a description of life in the Roman world from its beginnings in 753 BC to the emergence of the Byzantine Empire in the east, over 1,000 years later.

Chapter 1 describes the founding of Rome, the seven kings of Rome, and the development of the Republic and its early history. Chapter 2 describes the end of the Republic and the beginning of the Empire after the power struggles of Pompey the Great, Julius Caesar, Antony and finally Octavian who became the Emperor Augustus in 27 BC. The development of the early years of the Empire is outlined, including the conquest of land from Scotland to Syria. Later on, the Empire was split into two parts, East and West, and Constantine I chose what is now Istanbul as his capital city.

For those interested in military affairs, Chapter 3 describes the Roman army, its weapons, armour, forts and frontiers. This is followed by six chapters on aspects of the social and everyday life of the Roman world, including towns, water supply, countryside villas, slavery, entertainment, crafts and industries, roads and transport, ships, gods and temples. The final chapter takes up the history of the Roman Empire from the time of Constantine I to the collapse of the Western Empire and its reconquest by the Byzantine Empire. Finally, we look at how evidence of Roman civilization, from small statues to whole towns, has survived to the present day (although now rapidly being destroyed by modern development), and how the legacy of the Romans influences everyone's lives.

RIGHT A shop in Ostia near Rome which prepared and sold food.

OPPOSITE The impressive Pont du Gard was part of the aqueduct serving Nîmes in southern Gaul, at the point where it crossed the River Gard. It was built on a series of arches, and the lower part was widened in the 18th century to take road traffic.

CHAPTER ONE

The RISE of ROME

"Rome was not built in a day."

(ANONYMOUS, MEDIEVAL PROVERB)

THE FOUNDATION OF ROME

Rome was not built in a day, nor did it fall overnight. Rome rose from a small village to become a powerful, wealthy city-state controlling a vast empire. Although the empire collapsed, its legacy survives today, one and a half thousand years later.

According to ancient tradition, Rome was founded in 753 BC, but its origins were much disputed even by Roman historians. As there were no early written records documenting Rome's origins, the history of this time is a mixture of legend, mythology and fact. In the 5th century BC, Greek historians wrote that Rome was founded by the Trojan hero Aeneas. He was a mythological figure (the son of Venus by Anchises) who was supposed to have fled to Italy after the sack of Troy (which occurred in the 12th century BC).

Another explanation was that the twins Romulus and Remus were abandoned as children on the banks of the River Tiber. They were saved and suckled by a she-wolf, and then rescued by a shepherd who brought them up on the left bank of the river. It was there, on the Palatine Hill, that Romulus later founded the city of Rome, having killed his brother Remus in a quarrel.

As there were insufficient women in Rome, Romulus arranged for women to be abducted from the nearby Sabine tribe (an incident often referred to as "the rape of the Sabine women"). He also chose one hundred 'fathers' (*patres*) to advise him, a group which developed into the first Senate or ruling council. The descendants of these men were known as patricians and represented the leading families of Rome. Gradually, the legends became conflated and Romulus came to be regarded as a direct descendant of Aeneas.

Early on in Rome's history, the Greeks were establishing colonies in southern Italy to facilitate trade in the area. There were also many other different peoples and tribes throughout Italy, with numerous languages and dialects being spoken. The inhabitants of Rome mainly spoke Latin and, as Rome eventually gained control of Italy, the use of Latin became widespread.

ABOVE According to legend, the twins Romulus and Remus were abandoned as children on the banks of the River Tiber. They were saved and suckled by a she-wolf, and in 753 BC Romulus founded the city of Rome.

LEFT The city of Rome developed from a cluster of small villages. The forum is situated on former marshland which was drained in the time of Tarquin I.

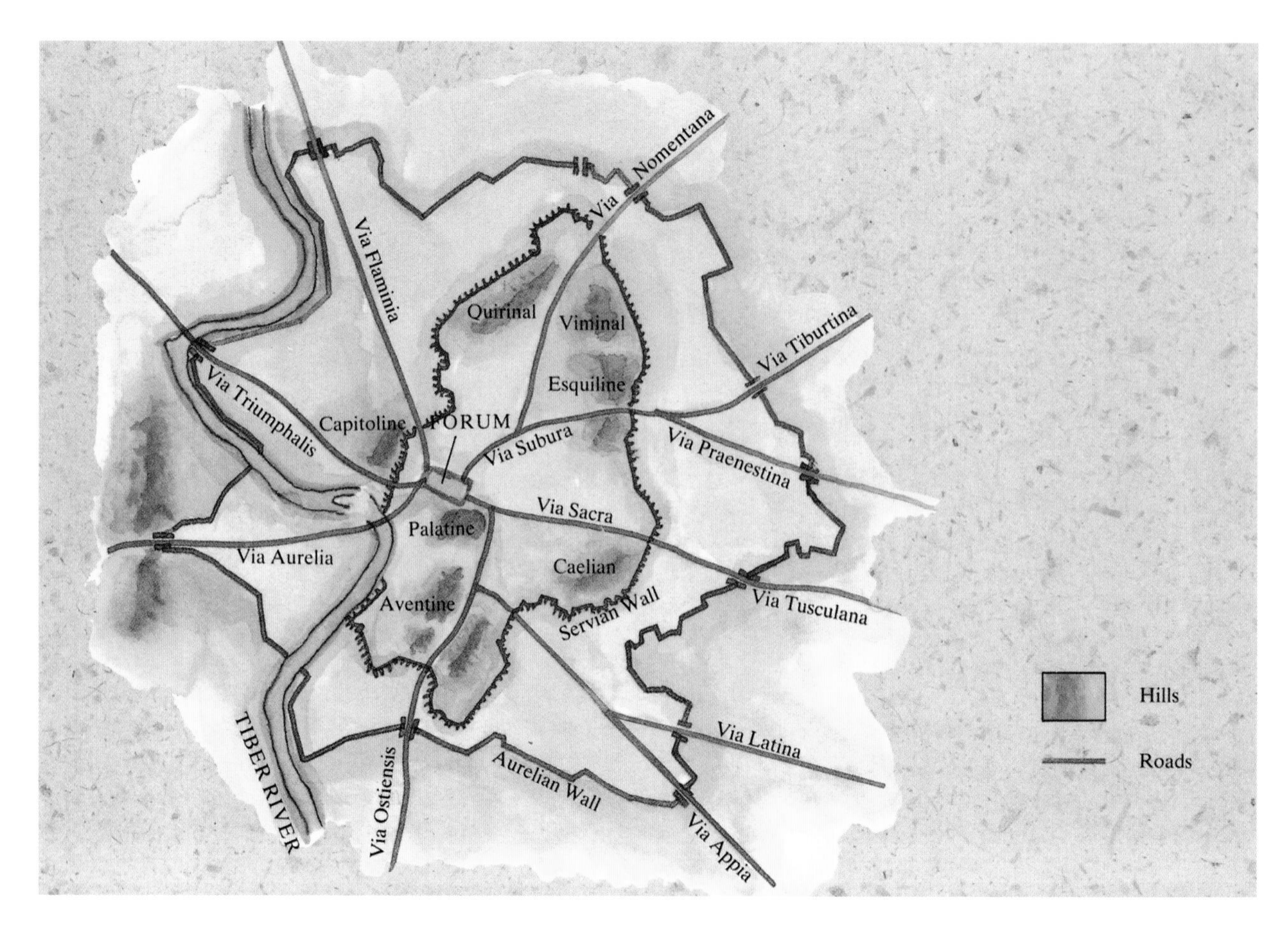

ABOVE The city of Rome in the imperial period with the seven hills which it first occupied.

The city of Rome occupied the seven hills and the intervening valleys near the mouth of the River Tiber, in the territory known then as Latium. Archaeological evidence from this area suggests that from the 10th century BC (in the latter part of the Bronze Age), there was small-scale occupation in villages of wooden huts perched on the hilltops, with cemeteries in the marshy valleys below. From about 900 BC (in the Iron Age), these village settlements expanded and their cemeteries had some rich graves which indicate a developing social structure to match. By the late 7th century BC there were some extremely rich grave goods left behind.

From around 640 BC, many towns were established by different tribes in Latium but Rome became pre-eminent. By the late 7th century BC, Rome's various hilltop villages had merged into a single settlement and occupation had spread into the marshy valleys which were by then being drained. By the beginning of the 6th century BC, Rome had become an urbanized settlement, possessing masonry structures such as temples, sanctuaries and defensive walls. There was also a public square laid out on former marshland in an area which was later to become the Forum. All this building work has been credited to the initiative of Tarquin I who ruled from 616 to 579 BC.

The Seven Kings

Including the legendary figure Romulus, there were seven kings of Rome. Much of the history of the kings was related by the Roman historian Livy (59 BC – AD 17), writing some 600 years after these events took place, and is therefore a mixture of fact and folklore. The kings were not hereditary but were chosen by the Senate. Initially, they were of Latin or Sabine extraction, until 616 BC when Tarquin I became the first of three Etruscan kings. The Etruscan tribe had controlled much of central and northern Italy from the 8th century BC, and had established many cities. Although Rome accepted the Etruscans as kings, the city did not come under Etruscan domination; nevertheless, it was greatly influenced by Etruscan civilization, particularly in architecture and art. From the time of Tarquin I, the appearance of Rome was transformed by a great deal of building work initiated by him.

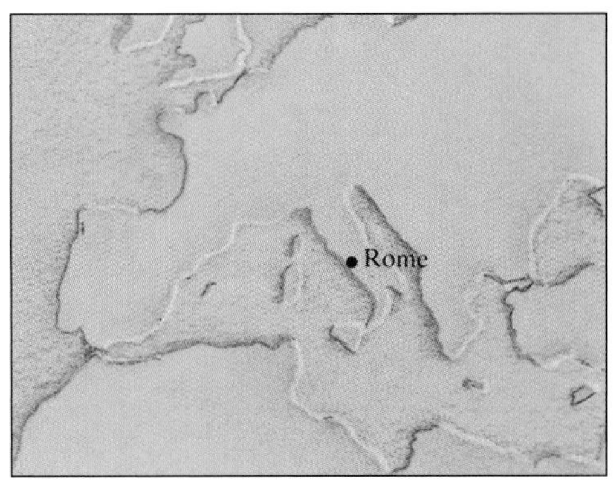

THE EARLY REPUBLIC

In 509 BC, when the tyrannical king Tarquin the Proud was expelled due to his immense unpopularity, the monarchy ended and the Republic was born. The kings were replaced by two magistrates, initially called praetors and later consuls, elected annually from members of the Senate. In addition, there were various other hierarchical categories of leadership which underwent constant modification throughout the Republic. One major innovation occurred in 494 BC, when the plebeians (the urban poor) reacted against their oppression and debt, and established a system of officers called tribunes to act on their behalf.

Rome at first dominated the surrounding Latin cities, and in 509 BC there was a treaty between Rome and Carthage (now in Tunisia) affording protection to these cities. Carthage was the main city of the Phoenicians (originally from what is now the Lebanon). They had settled in this part of North Africa and became a powerful seafaring nation. The Latin tribes subsequently entered into conflict with Rome and a lengthy military struggle began which Rome won in 499 BC. A treaty was signed leading to the establishment of the Latin League, and a joint army was created. Further hostilities with other tribes in Italy continued to erupt throughout the 5th century BC, including war with the Etruscan city of Veii situated about 9 miles (15km) north of Rome. During this war Veii was besieged for 10 years until 396 BC, when it was captured and destroyed. Rome's territory was consequently greatly increased.

ROME'S EARLIEST RULERS

753 BC	Foundation of Rome
753–715 BC	Romulus
715–673 BC	Numa Pompilius (Sabine)
673–641 BC	Tullus Hostilius (Latin)
641–616 BC	Ancus Marcius (Sabine)
616–579 BC	L. Tarquinius Priscus, Tarquin I (Etruscan)
579–534 BC	Servius Tullius (Etruscan)
534–509 BC	L. Tarquinius Superbus, Tarquin II or Tarquin the Proud (Etruscan)
509 BC	Foundation of the Republic

ABOVE At times of crisis throughout Roman history, strong men appeared to take charge of the destiny of the state. Caracalla became sole emperor from 211–217 AD after he murdered his brother Geta (see p.629).

TOP RIGHT Rome occupied a central, strategic position in the Italian peninsula. Surrounded by hostile tribes, it was early Roman policy to either conquer them or win them over as allies.

THE INVASION OF THE GAULS

During the 5th century BC, the Gauls (Celtic peoples who inhabited Gaul, now modern-

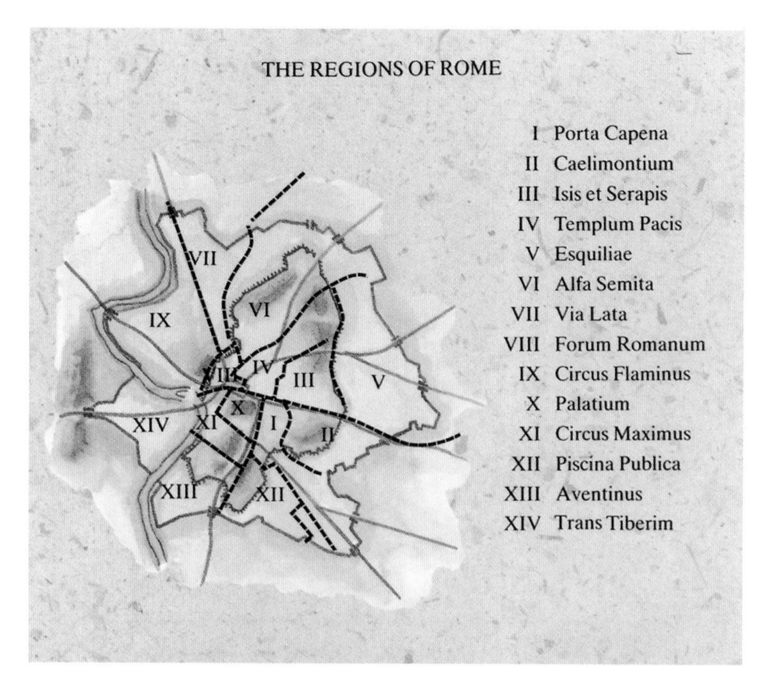

ABOVE TOP Augustus divided the city of Rome into four administrative districts. The earlier and later walls around Rome are shown here as well.

ABOVE A model of Rome in the imperial period, with the River Tiber below, the Colosseum top left, and the Circus Maximus in the centre.

day France and part of Germany) were pushing across the Alps into Italy in search of new homelands, and in 391 BC a force of 30,000 Gauls crossed the Apennines. In July of the following year the Roman army, which attempted to stop the invasions, was routed and the Gauls entered Rome with no resistance. The city was sacked but the Capitol (the citadel and religious centre) held out for seven months. Although the Gauls then left Rome with their plundered goods, it took another two centuries for them to be totally removed from northern Italy. There is in fact very little archaeological evidence for this disaster, suggesting that it may have been exaggerated by the Roman historians who later recorded the incident.

The rebuilding of Rome began almost immediately after the sacking of the city. From 378 BC a massive new defensive wall – the Servian Wall – was constructed, and it apparently partly followed the line of an earlier city wall constructed by King Servius Tullius in the 6th century BC.

The Conquest of Italy

After the setback of the Gaulish invasion, Rome again became increasingly involved in its neighbours' affairs by assisting some tribes in fighting against others. Throughout the next century there was a series of conflicts with opponents in Italy, in particular with the Samnite tribe to the south who were eventually forced to become allies of Rome in 290 BC. From controlling a small area around the city, Rome came to dominate much of Italy in its bid for power, wealth and stability.

In the late 4th and early 3rd centuries BC, the Romans became much influenced by Greek culture, including architecture, religion and the arts. It was about this time that the Roman state first issued silver coins which were modelled on the coinage of the south Italian Greek cities. By the beginning of the 3rd century BC, the Greek cities in southern Italy were in decline, and Rome came to the assistance of some of those being harassed by the nearby Lucanian tribe. The Greek city of Tarentum (now Tarento) regarded this as a threat to its own independence and appealed to King Pyrrhus of Epirus for assistance. Pyrrhus intially achieved a number of victories over the Romans, but sustained heavy losses (hence the term 'Pyrrhic victory') and in 275 BC he was eventually defeated. For the Greeks to be defeated by the Romans was unprecedented, and Rome consequently pressed home this victory and took control of the southern Italian peninsula.

Rome's conquest of Italy involved incorporating its defeated enemies as Roman citizens or half-citizens, or compelling them to become allies. Large areas of territory were annexed and colonies founded which were settled mainly by the urban poor. The system of alliances and dependencies created by the Romans during the conquest of the Italian peninsula became known as the Roman Confederacy.

By 260 BC the tribes of central and southern Italy had lost their independence. The cultural and linguistic differences in the Italian peninsula gradually disappeared and Latin became the common language. A network of military roads linking the Latin colonies accelerated this process of Romanization.

THE PUNIC WARS

The First Punic War began in 264 BC, so-called because it was fought against the Phoenicians (Carthaginians) who were called 'Poeni' by the Romans, from which the English term 'Punic' is derived. This marked the first conflict overseas and, until then, Rome had possessed little naval power because the seas of the western Mediterranean were controlled by Greece and by Carthage. Rome had previously entered into treaties with Carthage but, following a minor incident in Sicily, subsequently waged a lengthy and costly conflict with the Carthaginians. In order to fight them effectively, Rome was forced to increase vastly the size of its own naval fleet. Even so, the war dragged on for 23 years until 241 BC when the Romans finally won a decisive naval victory off the western coast of Sicily, the battle of the 'Aegates Islands'. The Cartha ginians agreed to give up all claim to Sicily and thereafter Rome gained control of Sardinia and Corsica as well. Both sides suffered huge losses in the war, and it is calculated that the Romans alone lost over 100,000 men and 500 warships.

The Second Punic War began only four years later when Carthage attempted to reassert itself by securing land in Spain. The Romans did not come into direct conflict with Carthage until 219 BC when General Hannibal continued to enlarge Carthaginian territory by attacking the town of Saguntum (now Sagunto), an ally of Rome on the Mediterranean coast. Before Rome could take retaliatory action, Hannibal marched out of Spain and made his famous trek across the Alps with elephants and a huge force of infantry and cavalry. He marched into Italy in 218 BC, and over the next two years inflicted a series of defeats on the Roman army, culminating in the battle of Cannae when at least 30,000 Romans lost their lives.

Despite these victories by Hannibal, most of Rome's allies tended to remain loyal, and Hannibal was eventually forced to leave Italy. In 203 BC he returned to North Africa but was defeated by the Romans at Zama (now in Tunisia) and was driven into exile and subsequently to suicide. As punishment, Carthage

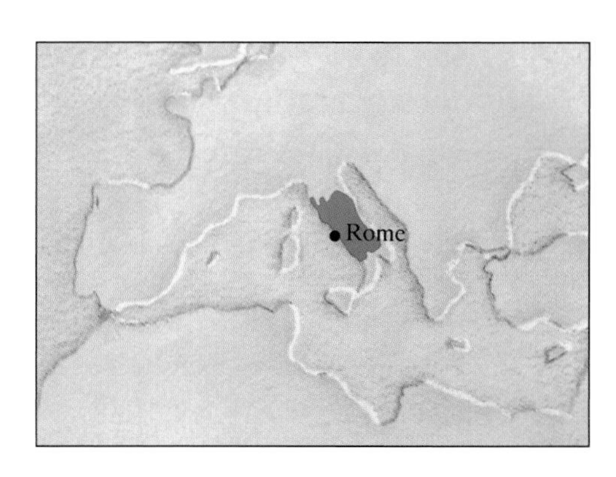

RIGHT By the 3rd century BC Rome's territory covered much of Italy.

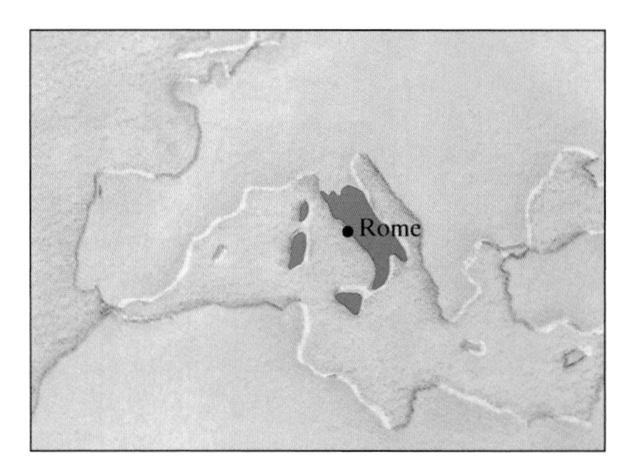

RIGHT After the First Punic War, Rome was in control of Sardinia, Corsica, Sicily and much of the Italian peninsula.

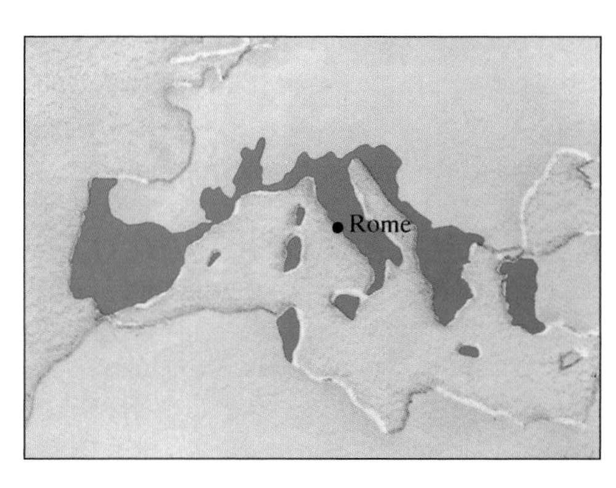

RIGHT Rome's territory had expanded considerably by the late 2nd century BC and extended from Portugal to Asia Minor.

was made to pay a massive indemnity, to destroy its fleet, and to give up all overseas territory. Thus Rome gained control of what is now south-west and eastern Spain, which was then divided into two provinces, Hispania Ulterior and Hispania Citerior. The few towns and tribes in Italy which had supported Hannibal were also punished.

The Third Punic War broke out when Rome intervened in a dispute between Carthage and Rome's friend and ally, King Masinissa of Numidia (now part of Algeria and Tunisia, and whose Latin name was derived from the Greek *nomades* or nomads). The Roman Senate was persuaded to destroy Carthage and sent a force which, after besieging the city for two years, attacked it and razed it to the ground in 146 BC. The territory belonging to Carthage became the new

Roman province known as Africa (situated today in North Africa).

The Campaigns in Northern Italy

Meanwhile, by the late 3rd century BC, those Gauls who lived in northern Italy were becoming restless. They were particularly provoked by being evicted from their land which was then allotted to Roman citizens. In 225 BC a huge Gaulish army crossed the Apennines, but was defeated by the Romans at Telamon (now Talamone), and the Gauls were forced back across the mountains. The Roman army then advanced into the Po Valley and began to take over large parts of the borders of Italy and France (an area known to the Romans as Gallia Cisalpina, usually referred to as Cisalpine Gaul). In 218 BC a large colony was established at Placentia (Piacenza) and another at Cremona in northern Italy.

The process of integrating Cisalpine Gaul with Roman Italy was halted by Hannibal's invasion, but military action in this area was resumed in 203 BC. Most of the Gaulish tribes here were defeated over the next twenty years, and Roman colonies were set up.

Greece and Macedonia

Alexander the Great died in 323 BC and his vast empire was fragmented into competing states ruled by his generals. By 275 BC three main kingdoms had emerged – Egypt under Ptolemy; Greece and the Aegean under Antigonus Gonatas; Asia Minor, Syria and the east under Seleucus. A new Greek kingdom with its capital at Pergamum was subsequently formed out of Seleucid territory in western Turkey, and was ruled by the Attalids.

In 229–228 BC Rome attacked the pirates operating along the Illyrian coast (now Yugoslavia); this campaign is known as the First Illyrian War. Macedonia (now mainly northern Greece) supported the pirates and became an enemy of Rome when the pirates' stronghold was destroyed in a second campaign in 221–219 BC (the Second Illyrian War). From 202 BC Philip V, King of Macedonia, began to take control of other areas of Greece and so, two years later, a Roman force was sent against him. This successful campaign forced Philip to confine his activities to Macedonia. At this time, Rome preferred a policy of indirect rule in the Greek east, leaving the territory as a network of theoretically independent 'client states', and so in 196 BC the Romans withdrew from Greece. In the same year, though, the Seleucid king of Asia Minor, Antiochus III, invaded Greece. A Roman force was sent back, and in 191 BC it won a victory at the famous pass of Thermopylae, driving Antiochus out of Greece. The Romans then invaded what is now Turkey and defeated Antiochus III at Magnesia in 190 BC.

In 171 BC Rome went to war against Macedonia, which was becoming an increasingly

ABOVE Following Rome's victory in the Third Punic War, much of North Africa became a new province. It soon became an important agricultural state, supplying Rome with much-needed grain. This mosaic from Tunisia depicts a villa surrounded by fowl and trees.

powerful state. Perseus (son of Philip V who had died eight years earlier) was eventually defeated in 168 BC at the battle of Pydna where his army was virtually destroyed. Macedonia was then split into four self-governing territories but, after an uprising in 148 BC, Rome annexed Macedonia as a province. A further revolt which followed in the southern peninsula of Greece (Achaea) was also suppressed, and its territory was made part of the new province. As an example to the rest of the empire, the city of Corinth was destroyed and its citizens sold into slavery in 146 BC, the same year in which Carthage was razed to the ground.

From the late 3rd century BC, the kingdom of Pergamum (now in western Turkey) had been an important ally of Rome. When Attalus III, the last king of Pergamum, died in 133 BC, he bequeathed his kingdom to Rome and five years later it became the province known as Asia. In less than 150 years from the beginning of the First Punic War, Rome's territory had expanded to incorporate parts of modern Northern Africa, Spain, Greece and Turkey.

LEFT Due to an uprising in southern Greece, the city of Corinth was destroyed in 146 BC as an example to the rest of the empire, and its citizens were sold into slavery. A Roman colony was founded on the site a century later.

CHAPTER TWO

CONQUEST *and* CONSOLIDATION

"Render therefore unto Caesar
the things which are Caesar's."

(ST MATTHEW'S GOSPEL, 22:21)

ABOVE The end of the 2nd century BC was a bleak period in Rome's fortunes, and in 105 BC a Roman army was annihilated at Arausio (now Orange) in southern Gaul, where this arch was constructed over a century later when Rome was again in the ascendant.

THE END OF THE REPUBLIC

By the late 2nd century BC, serious disturbances were occurring throughout Italy, due mainly to the worsening plight of the rural and urban poor. In 133 BC Tiberius Gracchus, who had been elected a tribune, initiated land reforms, including the resettling of dispossessed peasants on allotments of land. Intense opposition was aroused in many quarters to his proposals, and when he announced his intention to stand for a second tribunate, he was killed in the subsequent riots, with many of his supporters. Further unrest followed, and his brother Gaius Gracchus was elected a tribune in 123 and 122 BC. He introduced wide-ranging economic and legislative reforms but gradually lost popularity. In 121 BC he was declared a public enemy by the Senate and, soon after, he and 3,000 of his supporters were put to death.

Towards the end of the 2nd century BC, the military generals rose to power and this resulted in decades of civil strife. After the destruction of Corinth and Carthage in 146 BC there was a collapse in the stability of the Roman political way of life, with hostility and turmoil in all parts of the Empire. Furthermore, Rome began to suffer a series of humiliating military defeats – in 105 BC an army was annihilated at Arausio (now Orange in France) by Germanic tribes advancing towards Italy. At that moment, the State of Rome was faced with extinction.

Gaius Marius (155–86 BC) had been elected consul in 108 BC and his first major task was to lead the war against the Numidians in North Africa, whom he defeated in 105 BC, the same year as the disaster at Arausio. To achieve military success Marius completely reformed the army, whose soldiers then began to owe allegiance to their commanders rather than to the State. This allowed the military commanders to use the armies for their own political ambitions, and eventually led to various civil wars. After the North African campaign, Marius was appointed to save Italy from the Germanic tribes, and his forces defeated the Teutones at Aquae Sextiae (now Aix-en-Provence) in 102 BC and the Cimbri at Vercellae (now Vercelli) the following year.

There was increasing unrest amongst the inhabitants of Italy, resentful at being exploited by Rome. As a result, an armed revolt broke out in 91 BC which is known as the Social War (from *socii,* allies). Within two years the war was largely over, Roman citizenship having been granted to many of Italy's inhabitants in 90 BC. This gave them greater participation in politics, including an opportunity to enter the Senate.

In 88 BC Lucius Cornelius Sulla (137–78 BC) was elected consul. He was asked to lead an army in the eastern Mediterranean to suppress Mithridates VI, King of Pontus (an area around the Black Sea), who had been provoked into invading the province of Asia, had massacred Roman citizens, and afterwards invaded Greece and the Aegean islands. Sulla's appointment led to much bitter conflict between him and Marius and their supporters. For three years from 87 BC Sulla campaigned in the east and, although Marius died in 86 BC, civil war still broke out between their supporters three years later. On his return from the east, Sulla was forced to march on Rome to oppose the supporters of Marius, where he carried out a purge of his opponents in which thousands are supposed to have died. Sulla had himself been appointed dictator in 81 BC, and passed a series of laws; he retired the following year and died in 78 BC.

Julius Caesar

Above Julius Caesar became dictator after the defeat of Pompey the Great in 48 BC. Four years later he was assassinated on the Ides of March, and has been immortalized in William Shakespeare's play Julius Caesar.

The First Triumvirate

One of the generals to emerge during Sulla's period of power was Gnaeus Pompeius (later called Magnus, or Pompey the Great). He was the most powerful general of the 70s and 60s BC, and, in his own lifetime, was compared with Alexander the Great. He achieved particular military success in Spain in the 70s, and in 71 BC helped Crassus to put down the slave revolt of Spartacus in Italy. Pompey stood for the office of consul with Crassus in the following year, although he was not legally qualified to do so. Three years later he managed to clear the seas around Italy of the pirates who had been preying on shipping and coastal settlements. In the east, Mithridates was again active and Pompey took control of campaigns there for four years, conquering Anatolia (part of Turkey) and Syria, thereby acquiring much new territory for Rome. He advanced as far as Jerusalem, and returned to Rome in 62 BC with enormous quantities of booty.

During Pompey's absence in the east, Crassus and Caesar built up their own political positions. They proposed a bill to give land to the poor and to Pompey's veterans, but this was opposed by the Senate. Together with Pompey, Crassus and Caesar formed a private alliance in 60 BC, known as the First Triumvirate; this was a power base enabling their political wishes to be fulfilled. Marcus Licinius Crassus (115–53 BC) was a wealthy, unscrupulous politician who had been consul with Pompey in 70 BC. He went to Syria in 54 BC, but was killed the following year in a disastrous defeat by the Parthians (a tribe who occupied modern-day Iran) at the battle of Carrhae (now Harran in eastern Turkey).

Gaius Julius Caesar (100–44 BC) belonged

Right Legionary soldiers being addressed by their Emperor. Standard-bearers wearing animal skins are holding the standards. The soldiers are wearing either segmented plate armour or overlapping scale armour and are holding javelins.

Conquest Of Egypt

Above The defeat of Antony and Cleopatra by Octavian led to Egypt becoming a Roman province. People from this area were settled at Nemausus (Nîmes) in southern Gaul, and this was celebrated at the time by coins featuring a crocodile chained to a palm tree. This is still used as a civic symbol at Nîmes today, as shown on this brass plaque.

to a patrician family which allegedly traced its roots back to Aeneas. After the dictatorship of Sulla, Caesar had sought popularity by associating himself with Pompey and Crassus. With their support, he became consul for 59 BC and, as he needed military success, he persuaded the Senate to give him command of Cisalpine Gaul and also Gallia Narbonensis (an area of southern France) for five years. He then achieved considerable military success in Gaul and Britain.

In 56 BC the triumvirate alliance was renewed, but two years later Pompey's wife Julia (Caesar's daughter) died. This caused the already weakened alliance to split further, and it ceased to exist when Crassus died. Meanwhile, in Rome, there was civil disorder but Pompey, who was made sole consul in 52 BC, restored order. Fear of Caesar's increasing power through his military successes led the Senate, in 49 BC, to vote that he should relinquish his command, and so on 11 January of that year Caesar invaded Italy, beginning a civil war. Pompey did not confront Caesar but withdrew to the east, to be defeated by Caesar the following year at Pharsalus (now Pharsala) in Greece. After escaping to Egypt, Pompey was murdered, and Caesar suppressed all other opposition. He became dictator, but four years later in 44 BC was assassinated on the Ides of March (15 March), which led to renewed civil war.

The Second Triumvirate

When Caesar was assassinated, the official Heads of State were Marcus Antonius (Mark Antony) and Marcus Aemilius Lepidus. However, in his will Caesar had nominated his great-nephew Octavian as his heir, who then assumed the name of Caesar as a way of advancing his career. Octavian (Gaius Julius Caesar Octavianus) returned to Rome on Caesar's death to be welcomed by supporters of Caesar. When Antony went to Cisalpine Gaul in 43 BC, the Senate was persuaded that his aim was to become dictator. Octavian was therefore sent against him together with the two consuls, and Antony was defeated in two battles near Mutina (now Modena) in northern Italy, but the two consuls were killed. Octavian then demanded the office of consul, which the Senate refused, and so he marched on Rome with his army and took it by force. Meanwhile, Lepidus, who had control of seven legions in Gallia Narbonensis, joined forces with Antony. Octavian decided to meet Antony and Lepidus, and they were reconciled, forming the Second Triumvirate in 43 BC, this time a legal dictatorship which was created for five years.

The following year, Lepidus served as consul while Antony and Octavian went to war in the east against their opponents Brutus and Cassius. Numerous political murders followed. In 40 BC Lepidus was given charge of Africa, Octavian the West, and Antony the East. Lepidus made an unsuccessful bid for power four years later and, although his life was spared, his political career was finished.

During his campaigns in the east, Antony suffered several disasters in Armenia in 36 BC. He also became increasingly involved with Cleopatra, Queen of Egypt, and Octavian used this as propaganda against him. The Triumvirate was not renewed when it expired and, two years later in 31 BC when Antony was deprived of his powers by the Senate, Octavian obtained a mandate to go to war against Cleopatra. He followed Antony and Cleopatra to Greece, defeating Antony in a naval battle off Actium. Antony fled with Cleopatra to Egypt but, pursued by Octavian, they committed suicide there in 30 BC.

Octavian claimed to have restored the Republic in 27 BC, but in reality he was left in sole charge of the Roman world which by then had grown into an empire. Up until the battle of Actium, Rome had been close to anarchy, but in a few years Octavian restored stability and undertook fundamental reforms which were to remain more or less intact for 300 years. He gave land to thousands of soldiers and removed the army from the political scene. In 19 BC Augustus (the name he had assumed) was granted consular power for life. He died 32 years later, aged 77, in AD 14.

The Emperors

Augustus ruled as emperor from 27 BC to AD 14, and one aspect of his 41-year reign was the vast programme of public building that he initiated. According to the Roman writer Suetonius, Augustus claimed to have found Rome a city of bricks but left it a city of marble. Since Augustus' first two choices of successor died during his lifetime, he forced Tiberius, his stepson from his third marriage to Livia, to divorce his wife Vipsania Agrippina in 12 BC and marry Augustus' daughter Julia instead.

On Augustus' death Tiberius was accepted as his successor by the Senate, thereby setting the precedent of dynastic inheritance. Up to the mid-3rd century, there was a series of stable dynasties punctuated by occasional civil wars, but in the 3rd century there was a

BELOW A sardonyx cameo portraying Augustus. He became the first emperor of the Roman world after a period of civil war which ended in the defeat of Antony and Cleopatra. The gold chain was added to the cameo in the Middle Ages.

LEFT Augustus originally wanted his grandsons Gaius and Lucius Caesar to be his successors, but they died prematurely. This mausoleum to commemorate them was built at Glanum, in southern Gaul.

rapid succession of emperors, and it was only after the rise of Constantine I, the Great, in the early 4th century that stability with dynastic succession was restored. Much is known of the lives of the emperors through Roman and Greek historians, but a great deal of their writing is coloured by bias and exaggeration, leading to misconceptions and uncertainties about the various reigns.

Tiberius' reign was relatively well-run and stable in its earlier years, but it became notorious for its period of terror. Tiberius spent the last ten years of his life in voluntary seclusion on the island of Capri, and his death in 37 was greeted with joy. His successor was his great-nephew Gaius, nicknamed Caligula – Little Boots – because of the little soldier's boots he wore as a child. He led an unbalanced reign, believing himself to be a god, and was assassinated after only four years as emperor. Tiberius Claudius Nero Germanicus (usually called Claudius) succeeded Caligula in 41, and is best known for the invasion of Britain that he undertook two years later. There are widely varying opinions about his reign, some considering him to have been weak-willed, ruled by his advisers and family, and others that he reigned with

RIGHT Claudius (41–54) became emperor after Caligula was assassinated, and he was responsible for the invasion of Britain in 43. He is particularly well-known because of Robert Graves' book I, Claudius.

LEFT A 19th-century portrayal of the invasion of Britain in 43 under the Emperor Claudius. The Roman army has landed on the seashore, and the legionary standard-bearer calls on his colleagues to follow. The exact point of landing is much disputed by historians.

particular adroitness. Claudius died in 54, allegedly having eaten poisoned mushrooms administered by his wife Agrippina in order to promote her son Nero as emperor.

Nero's reign degenerated into cruelty and tyranny, and he may even have been responsible for his mother's murder. While he was emperor there was a serious rebellion in Britain led by Queen Boudicca who was eventually defeated, and a more prolonged and serious rebellion in Judaea, eventually put down by Titus. When a great fire at Rome in 64 was blamed on Nero (because it was thought that he wanted to build himself a vast new capital in the ruins), he tried to hold the Christians responsible, and increased his persecution of this unpopular new sect. The fire was so devastating that only four out of Rome's fourteen districts survived intact, leading to a massive rebuilding programme by Nero, including the 'Golden House', a huge urban villa for himself, the construction of which caused much resentment.

In the spring of 68, a Gallic senator Julius Vindex, then a governor in Gaul, stirred up a revolt against Nero, and persuaded the elderly governor of Spain, Servicius Sulpicius Galba, to be proclaimed emperor. This drove Nero to commit suicide in June 68 at the age of 32. A few months later in 69, Aulus Vitellius, who had been sent by Galba to take command of Lower Germany, was proclaimed emperor by his troops stationed there. Soon afterwards, Otho was proclaimed emperor by the Praetorian Guard at Rome, and Galba was murdered, but Vitellius, with his forces, marched against Otho, who committed suicide in April 69. In the east, the armies of Flavius Vespasianus (Vespasian) proclaimed him emperor. Vespasian defeated and killed Vitellius and became emperor, thus ending the chaotic 'year of the four emperors' and founding the Flavian dynasty. His 10-year rule marked a new period of stability in the Roman Empire.

Vespasian's son Titus succeeded in 79, the same year in which the volcano Vesuvius erupted and destroyed the towns of Pompeii and Herculanium in southern Italy. A few years earlier, Titus had undertaken ruthless military campaigns against the Jews in Judaea, and in 70 he captured Jerusalem and destroyed its temple. As an emperor, Titus was popular, but died through ill-health after only two years' reign at the age of 41, and his

Left Nero (54–68) committed suicide at the age of 32 after a reign which degenerated into cruelty and tyranny. While he was emperor, there was a devastating fire at Rome which was blamed on him.

LEFT Trajan's Column in Rome has a spiral frieze depicting the campaign against Dacia. Here soldiers are constructing a camp from blocks of turf. The Empire reached its greatest extent under the Emperor Trajan.

younger brother Domitian became emperor.

During Domitian's reign, the administration of most of the provinces functioned well, but towards the end of his lifetime he became increasingly autocratic and tended to ignore the role of the Senate. He was particularly notorious for his serious persecutions of the Christians and Jews. He was murdered in 96, apparently in a plot involving his wife. The elderly and respected senator Nerva was chosen as emperor by the Senate. As he had no son, Nerva appointed Marcus Ulpius Trajanus (Trajan) as his successor and established the tradition of appointment by merit. Shortly afterwards, in 98, Nerva died and Trajan assumed the leadership, reigning until his own death 19 years later. Under Trajan, the Empire expanded to its greatest extent, from Scotland to Africa, and from Portugal to Syria. His most important campaign was against Dacia (an area to the north of the River Danube roughly equivalent to modern-day Romania). His triumph was celebrated on a spiral frieze on the commemorative column still standing in Rome and known as Trajan's Column.

Hadrian, also from Spain (from a town called Italica, north of Seville), had been adopted as Trajan's successor and assumed power in 117. To consolidate Trajan's con-

quests he abandoned some of the latter's annexations. During his 21-year reign, Hadrian travelled extensively around the Empire, and during a visit to Britain in 122 he authorized the construction of what is now known as Hadrian's Wall across northern England. In 138 Antoninus Pius became emperor, and in the latter years of his life ruled jointly with Marcus Aurelius, his adopted son. On Pius' death in 161, Marcus Aurelius reigned jointly with his adoptive brother Lucius Verus for eight years until Verus died. Rather than appoint the most suitable person for his successor as had happened since the time of Nerva, Marcus Aurelius nominated

LEFT Hadrian (117–138) travelled extensively round the Empire during his reign, and did much to consolidate the frontier zones. He was a great admirer of Greek culture and had wide academic and artistic interests. Hadrian was responsible for the construction of an extensive villa at Tivoli near Rome.

ABOVE Commodus (180–193) was the son of Marcus Aurelius and was not a popular emperor, being eventually assassinated after several previous attempts on his life.

LEFT The Roman Empire at its greatest extent under Trajan.

FAR LEFT The latrines at Housesteads fort, Hadrian's Wall. During a visit to Britain in 122, the Emperor Hadrian authorized the construction of a wall across northern England as a means of defending the frontier. There was a series of forts such as the one at Housesteads. The two rows of wooden seats of the latrines are missing, but the drainage channels beneath can be seen.

his own son Commodus, and ruled jointly with him for three years. During his reign, Barbarians (a Greek term adopted by the Romans) began to break through the northern frontiers.

Commodus succeeded as sole emperor when Marcus Aurelius died in 180, and this marked the turning point of Rome's fortunes. Until then the Roman world was fairly prosperous and relatively at peace, but it was about to collapse into anarchy. Commodus became extremely unpopular in Rome and, after several attempts on his life, he was assassinated in 193. His successor was Publius Helvius Pertinax, a military officer, who was murdered by the Praetorian Guard after only three months and replaced by the senator Didius Julianus. He in turn was ousted by force by Septimius Severus who marched on Rome with his army and took control of the city. For the next few years Severus was involved in conflicts with his rivals until he defeated Clodius Albinus near Lyon in 196.

Septimius Severus came from Leptis Magna in north Africa (now Libya) and spoke Latin with a noticeable foreign accent; the

rulers of the Roman Empire now rarely came from Rome itself. Septimius Severus embarked on generous building programmes, especially at his native city. From 209 he campaigned against the Picts in Britain, but died in York two years later. His sons Geta and Caracalla succeeded him, but Caracalla soon murdered Geta to become sole ruler. One of Caracalla's main actions was to confer citizenship on all free-born men of the empire in a constitution of 212. This was mainly a fiscal measure, since it increased the numbers of people in the empire liable to taxation.

In 217 Caracalla was murdered by his Praetorian Prefect Macrinus who then became emperor, but was himself replaced the following year by Elagabalus. After his murder in 222, Elagabalus' cousin Severus Alexander assumed power, but was also murdered in 235 by the troops who had become disillusioned. His death brought to an end the dynasty of the Severans and marked the beginning of anarchy which was to last for 50 years.

A succession of emperors followed, nearly all of whom met violent deaths in war or conspiracy. The appointment of Diocletian as emperor by the Praetorian Guard in 284 brought an end to this chaos, and the system of administration and government was totally overhauled. Two years later Diocletian made the Empire into a Tetrarchy (four-man rule) led by two *Augusti* (co-emperors) – himself in the east and Maximian in the west. Two *Caesars* (below the rank of *Augusti*) completed the Tetrarchy; these were younger men who would succeed the *Augusti* in due course, and in turn appoint their own *Caesars*. Despite the economic reforms, Diocletian's reign saw a worsening economic situation with chronic inflation and a devalued currency. In 305 Diocletian and Maximian abdicated, bringing an end to the First Tetrarchy.

There followed a period of confusion, but by the early 4th century the old system of the Tetrarchy was restored, with Licinius ruling the east and Constantine the west, each supported by Caesars. In 313, Constantine and Licinius issued a declaration of freedom to worship (the Edict of Milan), which marked the conversion of the Roman Empire to Christianity. Constantine himself became the first emperor to convert to Christianity. At first the emperors managed to rule peacefully together, but from 316 Constantine began to win territory from Licinius and defeated him in 324. Constantine (Flavius Valerius Constantinus, or Constantine the Great) then received the submission of the city of Byzantium (or Constantinople as it was renamed, now Istanbul), and chose it as his new capital. He built a new city there and ruled as sole *Augustus* until his death in 337. The centre of the Roman world had shifted from Rome to the east, and it became a Greek-speaking Christian empire. The old pagan Latin-speaking Roman world with its centre at Rome was now eclipsed.

LEFT Septimius Severus (193–211) gained the position of emperor by force after the assassination of Commodus. He was a native of North Africa, and is said to have spoken Latin with a noticeable foreign accent.

OPPOSITE PAGE The Emperor Septimius Severus was from Leptis Magna in North Africa. He undertook generous programmes of building, especially in his native city. This theatre at Leptis Magna, though, was built in the 1st–2nd century by another Punic nobleman, Annobal Rufus.

LEFT The tetrarchy or 'four-man rule' of the Empire initiated by the Emperor Diocletian is embodied in this porphyry sculpture representing the four rulers. It was originally looted from Constantinople and taken to Venice, where it is now set into the wall of the cathedral of San Marco.

CHAPTER THREE

SOLDIER *and* CIVILIAN

Veni, vidi, vici – 'I came, I saw, I conquered'

(SUETONIUS, *DIVUS JULIUS*, 37, 2)

THE HOME GUARD

Rome's success in expanding and consolidating its vast Empire depended very much on the army. This became a highly disciplined, well-trained, organized and well-equipped force, using increasingly sophisticated techniques of warfare. However, in the earliest days of the Republic, the army consisted of nothing more than, literally, a 'home guard' – a militia of footsoldiers with a variety of weapons. Private citizens who owned property (mainly the peasantry) were expected to take up arms as volunteers when the need arose. By owning property, they were deemed to have a material interest in protecting the State and, at this stage, there was no need for a permanent army. Men were called up in an emergency and were obliged to provide their own arms and armour. They were paid little more than expenses for their services and were discharged when the emergency was over. Units of seamen were recruited and disbanded in the same way. A pair of consuls was appointed annually to command the army, a quite inefficient method of leadership.

In the early days of Rome, warfare on a massive scale was rare, but gradually the role of the army changed as more territory in Italy was taken over, and the tactics of warfare changed. The richest citizens served in the cavalry, the next wealthiest in the infantry, and the poorest citizens in the navy. The decision to build a network of military roads enabled Rome to undertake its conquest of neighbouring states and others further afield with greater efficiency. A peak came when the Romans defeated King Pyrrhus of Epirus in 275 BC since up to that time the Greeks had been a dominant military force. During the First Punic War Rome rapidly adapted to naval warfare and, despite some severe losses, eventually achieved success.

For the early Republic there are two important descriptions of the Roman army, one written by the Roman historian Livy and the other by the Greek historian Polybius. Livy, who was writing at the time of Augustus, described the army of the 4th century BC, while Polybius wrote about events from 220 BC to 146 BC, although not all of his work has survived.

ARMY REFORMS

Overseas expeditions became very unpopular with the soldiers because they were unwilling to leave home for long periods. The severe disruption to the peasant farmers and the number of casualties they suffered meant that the land was neglected. Small farms were amalgamated into larger estates so that the number of small landowners with a property qualification declined. This decline was also accelerated by the general exodus of people to the towns and so, despite the land reforms of the Gracchi, there was a severe shortage of recruits in the 2nd century BC. Minor reforms of the army took place, but Marius threw recruitment open to Roman citizens without property; as a result, a volunteer force

BELOW A legionary soldier and a horn-blower. The soldier is wearing segmented plate armour and has a helmet and a sword, while the horn-blower wears mail armour.

ABOVE A mosaic showing a warship with its oars, rigging and boarding plank. The Romans copied Greek and Carthaginian ships, but to compensate for their lack of naval skill they developed a boarding plank with a long iron spike mounted on the prow of the ship. This plank could be dropped on an enemy ship, and the Roman soldiers could fight their way on board.

began to be recruited from the urban poor seeking a career. Instead of being a part-time army, a standing army of full-time professional soldiers was created who signed on for 16 to 20 years. The pay of these legions was raised so that the soldiers could afford to provide their own armour and weapons to a consistent standard, and the soldiers now owed their loyalty to their commanders and not to the State.

Reforms continued so that under Julius Caesar the army had become a highly efficient and professional body. At the end of the civil war in 31 BC, Octavian (Augustus) had several armies under his control, comprising some 60 legions. He therefore decided to rationalize the army, retaining 28 legions (150,000 men) and disbanding the rest. As a result, over 100,000 veterans were settled in colonies, some of which were new foundations. Augustus was also left with 700 warships, out of which he created a permanent navy. As the empire developed and more provinces were acquired, the legions consisted of fewer Italian citizens and more nationalities from outside Italy, resulting in a very cosmopolitan Roman army.

Auxiliary troops were recruited from non-citizens to assist the legions, and initially served in their own areas. They continued to use their own language, were commanded by their own leaders, and used the type of weaponry to which they were traditionally accustomed. From the time of Augustus, auxiliaries numbered 150,000 men and became an integral part of the army. They were no longer allowed to serve in the area from which they were recruited in order to minimize the risk of local revolts.

Due to Augustus' rationalization, the army was now a peacetime force, with its main function being to police new provinces and to defend frontiers. The emperor retained control of *imperium* over provinces in which military units were based, and the Senate was able to select governors for the other provinces. This division of the Empire into imperial and senatorial provinces was an

attempt to keep the soldiers loyal, and they were expected to swear an oath of allegiance to the emperor.

The Praetorian Guard probably came into being as the personal bodyguard of Scipio Aemilianus in the 2nd century BC. It was commanded by a prefect and consisted of nine cohorts, each of 500 to 1,000 men. Only three cohorts were garrisoned in Rome, the others being spread throughout Italy but rarely in the provinces. The Praetorian Guard was an élite force whose soldiers served for 16 years and were paid far more than ordinary legionaries. From time to time, the Guard was involved in the assassination and selection of emperors until it was disbanded by Constantine I.

The upheavals of the 3rd and 4th centuries did much to change the army, and it became more of a mobile force instead of being in permanent garrisons along the frontiers. Army units were placed in cities to defend them against attack as it was no longer possible to defend all the frontier lines (the *limes*). After the defeat at Adrianople in 378, Rome had to rely increasingly on the uncertain loyalties of the 'federati' or mercenaries.

The Legions

A legion consisted of about 5,500 highly trained and professional soldiers recruited from Roman citizens. Legionaries served for 25 or 26 years and their pay and conditions were far better than those of auxiliaries. They were not supposed to marry but this regulation was relaxed at the end of the 2nd century.

Each legion was commanded by a legatus, assisted by six military tribunes, and they were all semi-professional soldiers in various stages of their political careers. The *praefectus castrorum* (prefect) was a fully professional officer responsible for the general administration and also for engineering. Below him were 60 centurions (responsible for training and discipline) as well as specialist officers such as surveyors and doctors.

A legion was divided into ten cohorts of 480 men which were in turn divided into six

LEFT Legionary soldiers wearing segmented plate armour and helmets. They are carrying large curved shields and javelins with iron tips and wooden shafts.

ABOVE An auxiliary cavalryman's helmet constructed of bronze and iron dating from the 1st century. This helmet was found near Ely in Cambridgeshire, England.

ABOVE This frieze dating to the 1st century BC shows a battle between Roman and Celtic cavalrymen. A Celtic horse has fallen and has thrown its rider. It is portrayed wearing a saddle with four pommels, a style which was adopted by the Romans.

centuries of 80 men. Within each century there were ten groups of eight men (*contubernia* who shared a tent while on the march or else a pair of barrack rooms. During the Flavian period, the first cohort was almost doubled in size so that it had five centuries of 160 men,while cohorts 2 to 10 each had 480 men. Each century was commanded by a centurion, the most senior of whom was with the First Cohort and was known as the *primus pilus.* Below the centurions, the main officers were called the *principales* and included the standard bearers (*signiferi*).

During the Empire there were usually no more than 28 legions, based mainly along the frontiers. In Republican times, legions were given serial numbers (I, II, III and so on) as they were recruited. After the Civil War, several legions shared the same number, and so they were also given nicknames, such as II *Adiutrix Pia Fidelis*. If a legion was destroyed, disgraced or disbanded, its number was never used again.

THE AUXILIARY UNITS

The auxiliary units were recruited from non-citizens in the provinces to provide specialist skills and additional help for the legions. Auxiliaries served for 25 years, and were composed of either infantry units (*cohortes peditatae*), cavalry units (*alae*), or part-mounted infantry (*cohortes equitatae*). Each *ala* or cohort had 500 men (*quingenaria*) or sometimes 1000 men (*milliaria*).

A cavalry unit was commanded by a prefect and was divided into 16 troops (*turmae*). Each *turma* had about 30 or 40 men and came under the command of a decurion. An infantry cohort was commanded by a prefect and was split into centuries under the command of centurions. The auxiliary units were originally under the leadership of their own native leaders, but this changed during the Empire.

By the end of the 1st century, the auxiliary units had become part of the established regular army, and there was a need to recruit more irregular troops from the frontier zones to make up infantry units (*numeri*) and cavalry units (*cunei*).

THE NAVY

Augustus maintained a professional standing navy which was based very much on the Greek navy, even down to using Greek terminology.

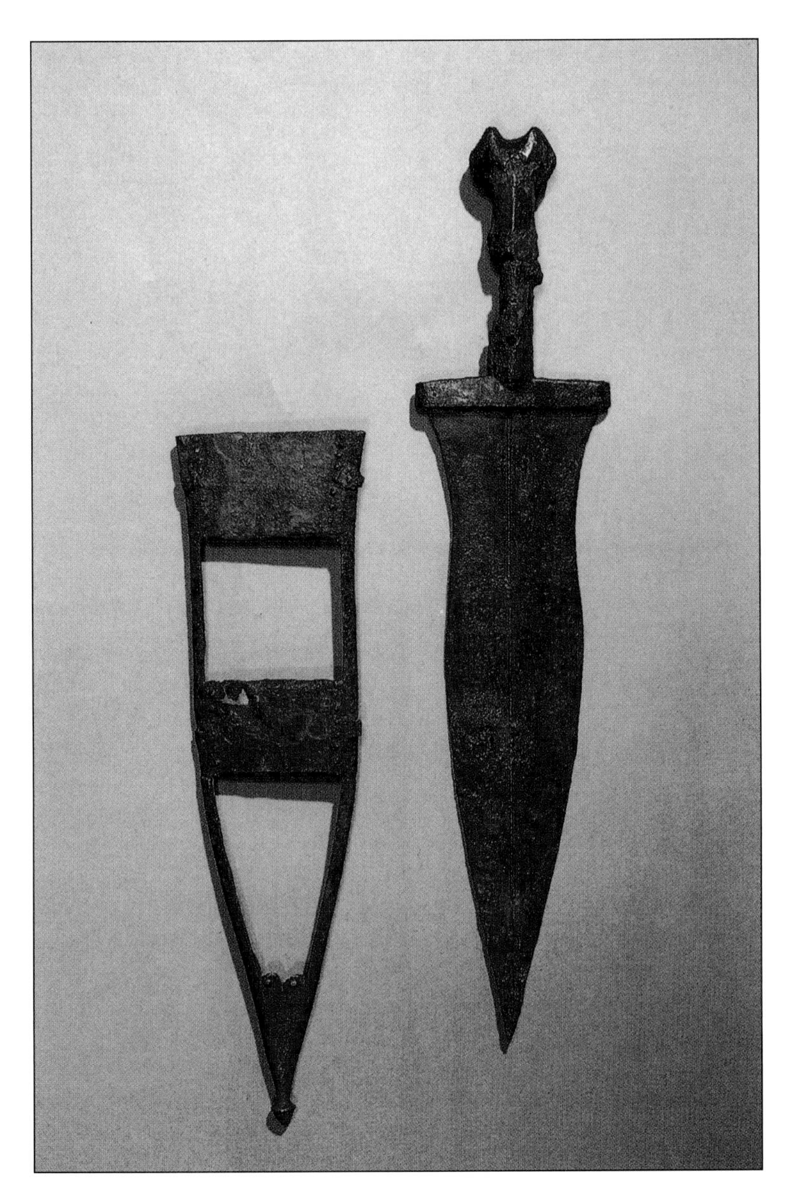

ABOVE
An iron dagger (right) with the iron framework of its scabbard (left), found in London. The dagger was known as a 'pugio', and the scabbard (originally covered in leather or wood) would have been attached to a soldier's belt.

There were three main naval bases, at Misenum (now Miseno) in the Bay of Naples, at Ravenna (now silted up and inshore), and at Forum Julii (now Fréjus in southern France), although the latter base was gradually run down. Augustus subsequently added two fleets for Egypt and Syria, and later on there was a fleet based at Gesoriacum (Boulogne) in northern France for the conquest of Britain in the 1st century. There were also subsidiary fleets on the Rhine, Danube and the Black Sea. The navy was always regarded as an inferior foreign entity and was therefore treated as an auxiliary force. Prefects commanded the imperial fleets, while individual ships were commanded by trierarchs. Ships known as quinqueremes and quadriremes were used, but in the imperial period the trireme was the most common type of warship.

ARMS AND ARMOUR

The equipment used and worn by legionaries was remarkably standard throughout the Empire and there must have been centres for the mass production of equipment. Legionaries wore a linen undergarment under a knee-length, short-sleeved linen tunic. In colder climates, they were allowed to wear leather trousers. Their sandals had very thick leather soles, reinforced with iron hobnails, and were fastened by leather thongs wound halfway up the shin, into which wool or fur could be bound in cold weather.

The early body armour consisted of reinforced leather jerkins or mail shirts of small iron rings, but by the time of Tiberius all the legionaries wore segmented plate armour made of metal strips and plates. This was later replaced by overlapping scale and mail armour. Helmets underwent constant modification from the Republic onwards. The early helmets were usually of bronze, the later ones of iron, and they had a projecting guard at the back to protect the neck. The officers were distinguished by their more elaborate uniforms.

Early legionary shields were oval in shape but in the 1st century they became rectangular, although curved to fit the body. A legionary shield (*scutum*) was made of thin sheets of wood glued together and bound round the edges with wrought iron or bronze. The centre was hollowed out for the hand grip which was protected by a metal boss. The outer surface of the shield was covered with leather on which were fastened decorative bronze plates. Weapons for attack included the *pilum* or javelin, two of which were carried by each man. The pilum was 7 ft (213 cm) long, the top 3 ft (91 cm) being of iron. The sword (*gladius*) was a double-edged weapon about 2 ft (61 cm) long and 2 in (5 cm) wide. Carried in a scabbard attached to a belt on the right-hand side of the body, it was a stabbing rather than a slashing weapon and designed for use in close fighting. The scabbard was usually made of wood and leather held together by bronze. On the left-hand side of the body there was a dagger (*pugio*) in a bronze or iron scabbard suspended from another belt. Daggers seem to have been withdrawn from the legionary armoury by the end of the 1st century.

Legionaries also carried other equipment, including a pickaxe, saw, basket and chain, all used in their duties of building camps, and so on. Within the legions the standard-bearers (*signiferi*) were responsible for the legionary standards. These were a distinctive part of army life, being a religious symbol as well as acting as a flag and a rallying point in battles. Loss of the standard was tantamount to disgrace, and could bring about the disbandment of the unit. The standard-bearers wore animal skins over their uniform following an old Celtic practice. In addition to the standards, musical instruments were used to give signals, and these included a type of trumpet and a large curved horn.

There is no standard version of the weaponry of the auxiliaries, as they used and wore the traditional native equipment and armour to which they were accustomed. Some auxiliaries wore no armour, while others (including cavalrymen) wore mail armour or scale armour (rows of overlapping metal scales sewn onto a linen or leather undergarment) as well as helmets. Their shields were usually oval in shape. In the early Empire, horses had no armour, although they did from the time of Hadrian, and the saddle also appeared in the early Empire. The cavalrymen in particular had elaborate parade equipment for themselves and their horses. The infantry used the short sword (*gladius*) as its main weapon, while the cavalry had a longer sword (*spatha*) and an oval or hexagonal flat shield. Specialist units of archers were largely recruited from the eastern provinces.

By the time of Julius Caesar, the Roman army was adept at siege tactics, employing many methods and weapons including battering rams, large catapults to throw heavy rocks, and ballista to fire iron bolts. Only legionaries were allowed to use artillery.

Forts and Camps

When on campaign, the Roman army normally constructed an enclosure or camp for each overnight stop. The camp was surrounded by a ditch and small rampart with a palisade of sharpened stakes on the top. Inside the camp were rows of leather tents, each of which could house eight men (a *contubernium*). The next day the tent could be rolled up and carried by mule, and the stakes of the palisade were pulled up for re-use elsewhere. The layout of the camps was fairly standard, a playing card shape, but apart from the ditch, very little archaeological evidence survives on such sites and they are often only recognized from aerial photographs. In Republican times, troops were sometimes kept in semi-permanent camps with tents throughout the winter.

Forts were constructed to house troops on a more permanent basis, usually close to or on frontiers. Sites were chosen for their strategic positions and acted as bases for further campaigns and as garrisons for protecting the frontiers. A 'fort' usually housed auxiliary troops or a combined auxiliary and legionary force, while the term 'fortress' was reserved for permanent establishments for a full legion. Information about camps and forts comes from excavated archaeological evidence and from relief sculptures (such as on Trajan's Column). Several classical authors also wrote in detail about military matters, and some Roman military documents have actually survived (such as discharge documents inscribed on pairs of bronze plates). A few were written on papyrus, mainly from Egyptian sites, which was used there for the everyday paperwork of the army, and there are wooden writing tablets which give an insight into routine army life. (A large quantity of these has been found at Vindolanda, near Hadrian's Wall.)

Both the legionary fortresses and the auxiliary forts of the early empire had a very similar layout, although the forts were on a much smaller scale. A fortress occupied an area of about 20 hectares (50 acres), while a fort varied from about 1 to 2.5 hectares (2½ to 6 acres), depending on the type of unit. Forts were very similar, although not identical, right across the empire, and generally they had the same basic street layout.

Above A model of a large catapult used for hurling rocks and stones as part of the artillery used in sieges.

A ROMAN FORT

ABOVE An aerial view of Housesteads fort on Hadrian's Wall, which was used by auxiliaries. Some of the excavated buildings are visible including the praetorium, principia, granary, hospital and barracks.

1 Principia
2 Praetorium
3 Granary
4 Hospital
5 Barracks
6 Latrines
7 Rampart

ABOVE Hadrian's Wall across northern England was part of the defensive frontier initiated by the Emperor Hadrian. It consisted of a stone wall (turf in places) with forts, milecastles and turrets. Similar frontier systems existed elsewhere in the Empire.

PREVIOUS PAGES A reconstruction of the fort at London by Alan Sorrell. The infantrymen and cavalrymen are marching towards the headquarters building, while construction work takes place on their right. In the distance are the ramparts which surround the fort.

The earlier forts were constructed of timber, with ramparts of timber and earth, while later forts were constructed at least partially of stone. They were rectangular in shape with rounded corners ('playing card'), and had four gateways, one in each side. Surrounding the fort were one or more ditches (*fossae*), usually V-shaped with a shallow slot at the bottom. Access to the gates was either by wooden bridges or by earthen causeways across the ditches. The ditches were usually 10–12 ft (300–366 cm) wide at the top and 6–8 ft (185–245 cm) deep. The rampart (*vallum*) inside the ditches was the main barrier; this was usually constructed of upcast material from the ditches on a wooden or stone foundation, and was faced with timber and with turf stacked like bricks to give additional strength and stability. From the 2nd century, stone walls or façades began to be used for ramparts. The gateways had timber towers (later replaced by stone structures) with large reinforced timber doors. There were also corner and interval towers, which in the early Empire did not project beyond the line of the ramparts, but projected internally. The main function of the towers was for the deployment of artillery.

In the centre of the fort, opposite the junction of the two main streets, was the *principia* or headquarters building, the administrative and religious focus of the fort. It was usually a complex of buildings around a courtyard, similar to a civic forum and basilica, and included storerooms, offices, and the shrine (*sacellum*), beneath which was a strong room. The *praetorium* was a spacious residence for the commanding officer, and there were also separate buildings for other officers. Most of the fort was taken up by the soldiers' barracks, which consisted of narrow rectangular buildings fronted by a verandah and divided into a series of rooms with a larger room at one end for officers' (centurions') quarters. Each original tent-party (*contubernium*) of eight men shared a pair of rooms, one for storing equipment and one for sleeping. The men did their own cooking and eating there, since no centralized canteen was provided. Bread, however, was baked in ovens which were located just inside the rampart to minimize the risk of fire. Grain was stored in large granaries (*horrea*) built with a raised floor to give adequate ventilation below and within the building and prevent deterioration of the grain.

Other buildings included workshops, stables and a hospital. The hospital (*valetudinarium*) was usually in a quieter part of the fort, and the army itself was in the forefront of Roman medicine. Considerable measures were taken to ensure an effective medical service, and hygiene was an important factor, with a good water supply and drainage system, including latrines and bath-houses. In a legionary fortress, the bath-house tended to occupy a central position, while in the forts it was often situated in an external annex. The bath-house consisted of a series of rooms of varying temperatures, and provided a social function as well. The amphitheatre, used for entertainment, and probably also for weapon training and parades, was always situated outside forts.

Permanent forts and fortresses invariably led to a sizeable civilian community (*vicus*) growing up outside the fortifications, providing a variety of services.

ABOVE The town of Arausio (Orange) in southern Gaul was founded as a colony for veterans in the late 1st century BC. This is a view of the remains of buildings to the west of the theatre, possibly a gymnasium or even an earlier theatre, as well as a large temple with vaults beneath.

RIGHT Part of the unique marble inscription showing the system of centuriation in and around the early colony of Arausio (Orange) in southern Gaul.

FRONTIERS

The idea of frontiers did not evolve until the early Roman Empire, when a distinction was made between Roman and non-Roman territory. In many provinces there were natural boundaries, such as a river or the desert. Rome's most serious problems, though, were along its northern boundaries, and the main way of controlling these frontiers was by a system of forts, watchtowers and signal stations.

In Britain, the Emperor Hadrian initiated the building of a human-made barrier of stone and turf, incorporating forts, milecastles and turrets, and now known as Hadrian's Wall. This defensive scheme underwent many modifications, and moved even further north to a new physical barrier in Scotland. This time a turf wall with forts was built, known as the Antonine Wall. A similar frontier system was also developed from the North Sea, along the Rhine and Danube, to the Black Sea and, with other frontiers, is called the *limes*. Along the Rhine and Danube there was a series of forts, watchtowers and signal stations integrated with legionary fortresses. The stretch between the two rivers (from south of Bonn to a point near Regensburg) was defended in a similar way and reinforced by a ditch and palisade, later to be replaced in some sections by a stone wall. In the end, though, this barrier was to prove ineffective against the invading Germanic tribes who overwhelmed the empire.

RETIREMENT

After serving their term in the army, the soldiers were given their discharge and referred to as veterans. Particularly from the time of Augustus, discharge from the army was much better organized and paid for by the state. Auxiliaries were granted citizenship, and proof of the grant was inscribed on a pair of bronze sheets, a diploma, many of which have been found. They received no land, but tended to stay in the country in which they had served.

Legionary veterans were given a cash payment, although in the early Empire they were also given the choice of a grant of land, and were often settled as groups in colonies. Probably in order to ensure that the colonists had control of the surrounding land as well, a system of centuriation was undertaken whereby a large area of countryside was divided into squares owned by the colonists. A unique discovery at Orange in France, founded as a colony for veterans, was the marble fragments of an inscribed plan of the centuriation. This layout is often fossilized in the countryside today, particularly in southern Gaul and Italy, and can be easily recognized in aerial photographs.

CHAPTER FOUR

TOWN HOUSES *and* TENEMENTS

"When in Rome, live as the Romans do."

(ST AMBROSE, 337–397)

ABOVE In the Mediterranean area, towns had existed long before the spread of Roman influence and domination. Glanum in southern Gaul was a Greek town which came under Roman jurisdiction, and so gradually acquired the appearance of a Roman town. It was attacked by Germanic invaders in about 270 and became deserted.

THE FIRST TOWNS

In the Mediterranean area, the presence of towns was not new. Greece had for long been a society of city-states, and from the 10th century BC had established colonies as far afield as southern France, southern Italy and Asia Minor. Further east there were oasis towns and caravan cities such as Gerasa (now Jerash in Jordan) and Palmyra (in Syria), while in North Africa the Phoenicians had established successful colonies, as at Carthage (now in Tunisia). In such places, the old native towns were gradually subject to Roman influence and settlement and were sometimes even given a new lease of life. They developed into truly prosperous Roman cities, resulting in a uniformity of appearance right across much of the Empire.

In many parts of the Roman Empire, particularly in areas such as northern Gaul and Britain, cities as such had not previously existed. There had been tribal centres, often situated on hilltops, but although some of these provided a few similar functions, they bore little resemblance to a Roman town. In these areas, the impact of urbanization was dramatic, and it is surprising that these towns became established within a relatively short space of time. In some areas, former tribal capitals became the new towns, controlling a similar administrative district, although they usually moved to a more convenient position away from hilltops. In the northern areas of the Empire, the number of towns remained far fewer than in southern regions such as Italy, which had over 400 Roman towns.

Some new towns developed from deliberate foundations of colonies for veterans, including Colchester in England which was established as a colony in 49 on the site of the former legionary fortress. Other veterans were settled in or near existing towns, as at Pompeii in Italy. Many towns grew up for economic reasons, such as those along trade routes or next to forts, and they often managed to survive even when the army moved on.

TOWN PLANNING

The early towns invariably grew up in a haphazard, unplanned manner, of which Rome itself is a prime example, but new towns became subject to the Greek concept of town planning. From the 1st century BC almost

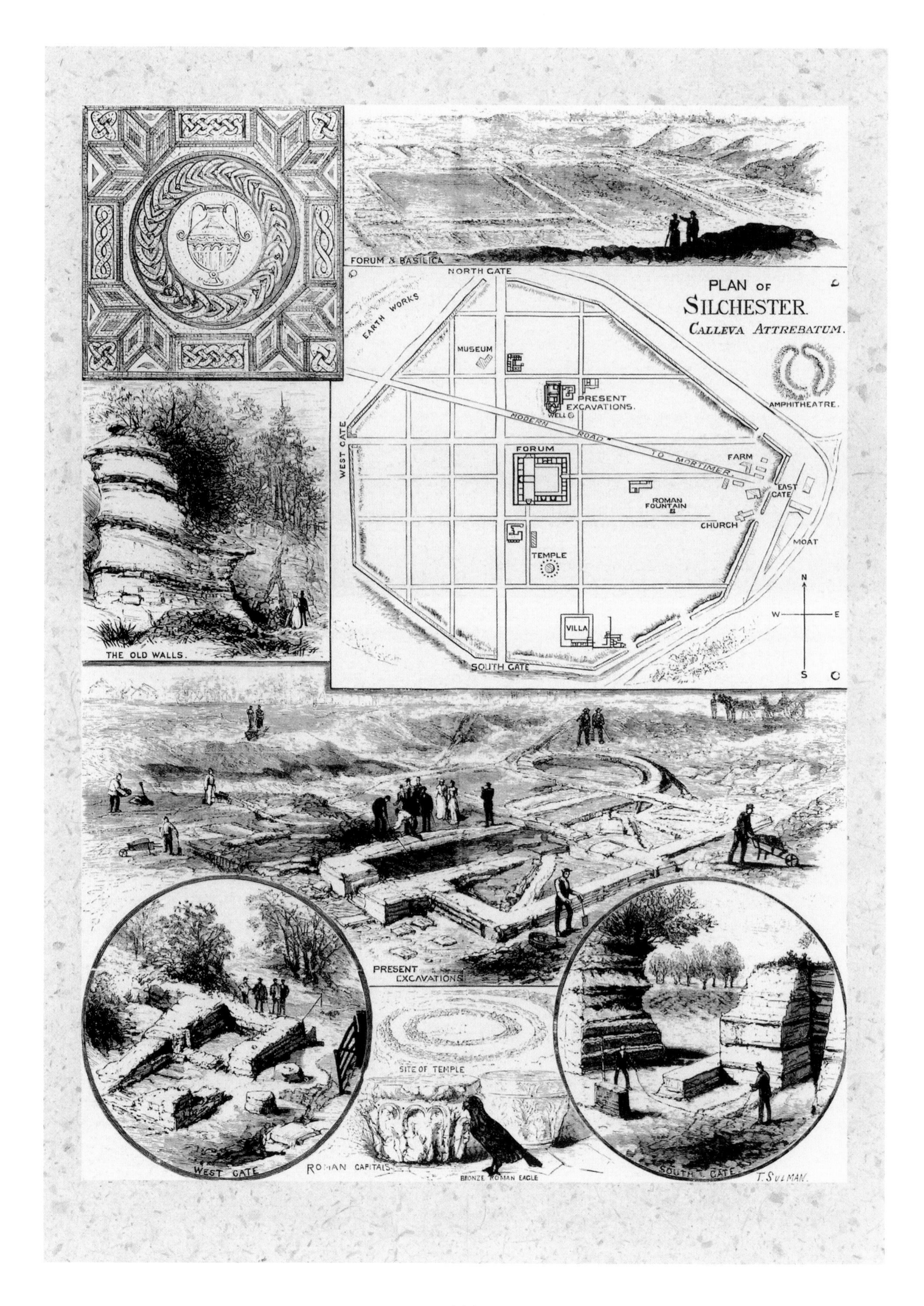
FORUM & BASILICA
PLAN OF
SILCHESTER
CALLEVA ATTREBATUM.
NORTH GATE
EARTH WORKS
MUSEUM
PRESENT
EXCAVATIONS.
WELL
AMPHITHEATRE.
WEST GATE
MODERN ROAD TO MORTIMER.
FORUM
FARM
EAST
GATE
ROMAN
FOUNTAIN
CHURCH
MOAT
TEMPLE
N
W
E
S
VILLA
SOUTH GATE
THE OLD WALLS.
PRESENT
EXCAVATIONS
SITE OF TEMPLE
WEST GATE
ROMAN CAPITALS
BRONZE ROMAN EAGLE
SOUTH GATE
T. SULMAN.

every new colony was planned on a grid system resembling the layout of a fort, while existing towns such as Palmyra retained their irregular plan, but grew in size. The population of towns varied considerably, but by Caesar's time Rome is thought to have had a population of a million.

Over the years many towns were endowed with fine buildings by imperial and private benefactors, the latter usually in an attempt to advance their political careers or enhance their prestige. The period from the Flavian to the Severan emperors was particularly prosperous for towns. Much of the architecture was influenced by Greek building techniques and styles, especially in the design of theatres and basilicas. In the 3rd century BC, though, a revolutionary technique of building completely changed methods of construction and influenced architectural design. This was the use of concrete, which was employed in conjunction with the arch (which had never been fully exploited by the Greeks), so that vast new building complexes could be constructed. This in turn led to the development of the barrel vault, which was a particular feature of the roofs of bath-houses.

ABOVE A reconstruction by Ronald Embleton of the forum at London, with a basilica on the far side and offices and colonnaded walkways on the other three sides. The open square is being used as a market.

OPPOSITE PAGE New towns such as Silchester in England were laid out on a grid plan similar to that of forts, with the forum occupying the position of the principia in a fort. The site was extensively excavated in the 19th century, without the benefit of modern techniques.

PUBLIC BUILDINGS

Apart from bath-houses, the public buildings in a town often included an amphitheatre, theatre, circus, forum, and temples, as well as other amenities and structures such as aqueducts, sewers and latrines. A town could also have its status enhanced by the provision of town walls (although these were subsequently erected for defensive purposes) and also by monumental arches. The Romans built these to commemorate various events, particularly at the entrances to provincial towns as an expression of civic pride. Such arches were frequently built to mark the foundation of the town and the exploits of the veterans settling there, and they could be either free-standing or built into the town walls.

The forum was the civic centre, used for administration, trade and as a meeting place. In the Republic they tended to be irregularly shaped un-enclosed areas, but subsequently they were surrounded by offices, colonnaded walks, and an aisled building known as the basilica. In Britain they usually had colonnades on three sides and a basilica on the fourth side, resembling the army headquarters

Left The 'Hunting Baths' on the outskirts of Leptis Magna in North Africa. They survived virtually intact beneath the sand dunes. Inside a wall painting depicting hunting scenes suggests that the baths were owned by a company of hunters who provided wild animals for use in amphitheatres.

(*principia*) of a fort. There was sometimes a *cryptoporticus* beneath the forum, as at Arles in France. This was a series of underground passageways, possibly used as a meeting place, as storerooms, or even as barracks to house the public slaves of the town.

A forum could act as a market place, but some towns had purpose-built markets, the most ambitious being Trajan's Market in Rome, a vast complex of markets, libraries, a forum and a basilica overlooking Trajan's Column. Most shops in towns were open-fronted, many with goods and food being made on the premises in full public view. Traders could also operate from street stalls, which often caused great congestion.

Public baths (run by the state or by private companies) did not become common in the early towns until the 1st century BC, but most towns came to possess at least one public bath building. They were very much linked with the provision of water from aqueducts. The four main rooms were the undressing room (*apodyterium*), the cold room (*frigidarium*), the warm room (*tepidarium*) and the hot room (*caldarium*), but more sophisticated establishments had cold plunge baths, a very hot sweating room, exercise rooms, courtyards and covered walks. The source of heat for early baths was a charcoal brazier, but by the 1st century BC a system of underfloor heating (hypocaust) was used. Bathing establishments were a social focus of the city and became extremely popular; by the 4th century there were nearly 1,000 establishments in Rome itself. The practice of mixed bathing was forbidden in a decree by Hadrian in the 2nd century, and where separate facilities were not available, the sessions for men and women had to be split, with women bathing in the morning.

The Water Supply

An adequate water supply was essential for town life, and in the early towns water was taken from wells and springs, but with a rising population this system rapidly became inadequate. The first known aqueduct at Rome dates from the 4th century BC, and a system of aqueducts soon supplied many towns throughout the Empire. Many aqueducts consisted of simple channels dug into the ground, as well as underground wood, terracotta or lead pipes. The most imposing method of water supply, though, was the overground aqueducts supported on arches, the first one being built in Rome in the 2nd century BC. Some 300 years later, ten main aqueducts were supplying Rome with water.

The overground aqueducts sometimes had to cross steep gorges and travel through hillsides in tunnels. The gradient of the masonry conduits had to be carefully controlled, and the engineering and surveying of aqueducts

Distribution Of Water

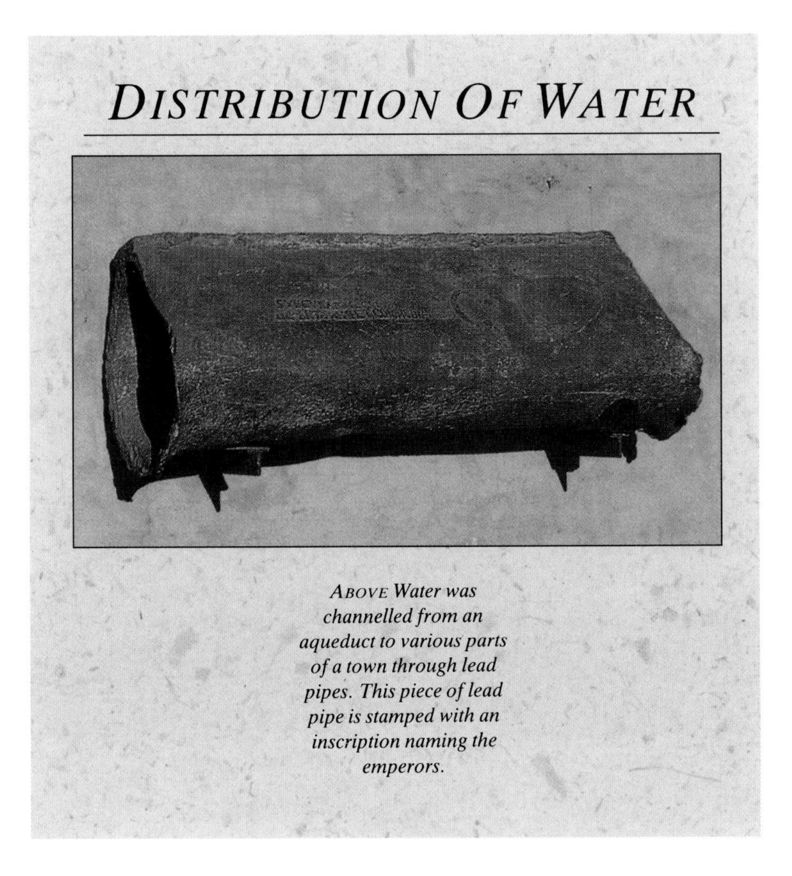

Above Water was channelled from an aqueduct to various parts of a town through lead pipes. This piece of lead pipe is stamped with an inscription naming the emperors.

was very precise. Once built, they only required routine cleaning and maintenance; at Segovia in Spain the aqueduct is still in working order. The top of the channel on overground aqueducts was sealed to prevent evaporation and contamination, and yet the channel had to be sufficiently large to enable repairs and cleaning to be carried out. One aqueduct serving Nîmes (in France) was partly in a channel, partly in a tunnel, and partly on low arches, and crossed the River Gard on a huge bridge known today as the Pont du Gard. The bridge was 1542 ft (470 m) long and 161 ft (49 m) high, and is the highest surviving bridge structure from the Roman world. It was built in the late 1st century BC and ran for 31 miles (50 km), with a flow of 1,059,300 cubic feet (30,000 cubic metres) of water per day. This aqueduct is still an impressive sight.

Once in the towns, the water was distributed in lead, terracotta or timber pipes to the various baths, public fountains and rich private houses – only a few homes could afford piped water. In Nîmes, the circular distribution settling tank at the end of the aqueduct still survives. From this, large lead pipes carried water to various parts of the town.

With such a quantity of water coming into the towns in aqueducts, and no system of controlling or stopping the flow, an efficient drainage system was essential. The drainage system could consist of substantial masonry sewers or timber-lined drains. The public latrines, usually flushed by water from the baths, often had a series of seats in a row, and it appears that there were no inhibitions in sitting alongside other people.

Domestic Houses

Town houses could be very luxurious, with a central hall (*atrium*) opening on to a colonnaded courtyard or garden. Such houses had a variety of rooms, some including a bath suite, and there is evidence of upper storeys. The houses were decorated with fine mosaics, wall paintings, sculptures, and an elaborate range of furniture, and some had glazed windows as well.

Conversely, most of the population lived in far more humble dwellings. In 4th-century catalogues about Rome, only 1,790 of the sole-family type of residence were recorded, but there were 46,000 tenement blocks, each inhabited by many families. The urban poor mostly lived in these badly constructed buildings, which were prone to gross overcrowding, collapse, fire and epidemics, as well as ever-rising rents. Eventually, a height limit of 60 ft (20 metres) was imposed on tenement blocks, along with improved building regulations to prevent collapse and the spread of fire.

In the northern empire, tenement blocks were unusual, and instead the poor lived in small rows of timber houses, sometimes incorporating shops which fronted on to the streets. For most people, towns were extremely cramped, dirty and noisy places, both day and night – in Rome, for example, carts were only allowed to pass through the streets at night. Juvenal, the satirist, writing in Rome at the end of the 1st century AD, noted that 'in this city, sleep comes only to the wealthy'.

Rich and Poor

Society was rigorously stratified by wealth and by law, and so there was a huge disparity between rich and poor, free citizens, non-citizens and slaves. Most of the written and archaeological evidence originates from the wealthier classes, who included senators, knights and magistrates. The poorer classes – citizens and non-citizens – made up a large proportion of the population. Women, al-

LEFT The covered channel of an aqueduct had to be large enough for a person to carry out repairs and cleaning. Some of the covering slabs are missing from this channel at the Pont du Gard, which is at a height of 151 ft (49 m) above the river.

RIGHT In the town, the aqueduct would usually terminate in a settling tank from which numerous pipes distributed the water to various parts of the town. This example still survives at Nîmes in southern France, and the holes for the lead pipes can be seen.

RIGHT Public latrines consisted of one or more rows of seats over a drain which was usually flushed by water from the baths. The channel in front was for cleaning the sponges on sticks used for personal hygiene. There seem to have been no concerns about privacy.

Housing For The Poor

Above A model of a substantial tenement block at the port of Ostia near Rome. They were lived in by the poor, and were usually badly constructed and prone to collapse and fire.

though possessing some rights, including ownership of property, tended to play a role defined and determined by the rights assigned to them by men.

In the 1st century, slaves represented up to one third of the urban population. They were employed extensively in a variety of ways, such as in the building and maintenance of roads and aqueducts, as domestic servants (often an educated Greek slave acting as a tutor), as factory workers and as gladiators and prostitutes. Wealthy private households might own numerous slaves. The treatment of slaves varied considerably depending on their owners; many were subject to brutality, even though the Roman economy depended on slaves.

The majority of people in the towns spent their day working to earn money to support their families, with only a few wealthy people living off their investments. Many small manufacturing trades were carried out in towns, although heavier industries were usually sited outside. Small shops and stalls sold food and other goods and services, while many workers were employed in the docks or as porters in the markets. There was plenty of entertainment, including circuses, amphitheatres, and theatres. In times of crises the towns themselves, particularly those with defensive walls, could act as places of refuge. In general, towns were noisy, dirty, bustling, crowded places but, despite all the activity, most towns depended directly on agriculture for their wealth and for food supply. In contrast to many modern towns, Roman towns were an integral part of the surrounding countryside.

CHAPTER FIVE

COTTAGES *and* COUNTRY HOUSES

'Friends, Romans, countrymen'

(WILLIAM SHAKESPEARE, *JULIUS CAESAR*, ACT III, Sc. ii, 79)

The Demise of the Peasant

The very first villages of Rome were farming villages, and in the early Republic there were many peasant farmers in Italy who were ready to take up arms to defend their land. However, this duty became too burdensome and, after the Punic Wars, many families were no longer able to work their land, which had been neglected after so many years of military campaigning. Debts were incurred, farms were sold, and the dispossessed peasants flocked to the towns to add to the increasing numbers of urban poor. In the meantime, the rich, who had profited from the wars, bought up large tracts of land, replacing the small landholdings with large estates (*latifundia*), which they ran as absentee landlords, a situation which was never substantially improved even with subsequent land reforms.

Apart from wealthy speculators, the peasants were also dispossessed by colonies of veterans who were granted land on their discharge from the army. The land was often divided into regular units, a system known as centuriation, and the resulting pattern of fields is fossilized in many areas today. It is particularly noticeable on aerial photographs in Northern Italy around the Po Valley.

Above Most slaves died without leaving any trace, but Junius is remembered in this mosaic. He was obviously a slave who worked indoors.

Slavery

The large estates (*latifundia*) were worked by slaves, in plentiful supply following each military victory. *Latifundia* spread to the provinces, although they were probably not as common there as in Italy, and there is some evidence for the use of slaves in the provinces as well. Slavery was not an innovation; many of the northern Celtic tribes, such as those in Britain, had previously traded in slaves with Rome.

Most slaves died without leaving any trace of their existence. On farms especially, their treatment could be quite harsh and in the 2nd century BC there were two slave revolts in Sicily. Soon afterwards, the final and biggest slave revolt in antiquity took place under

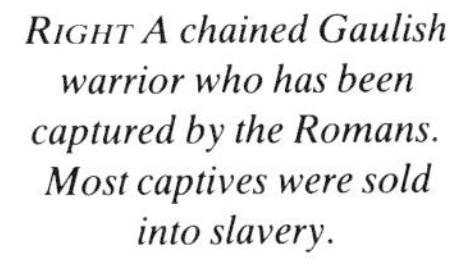

Right A chained Gaulish warrior who has been captured by the Romans. Most captives were sold into slavery.

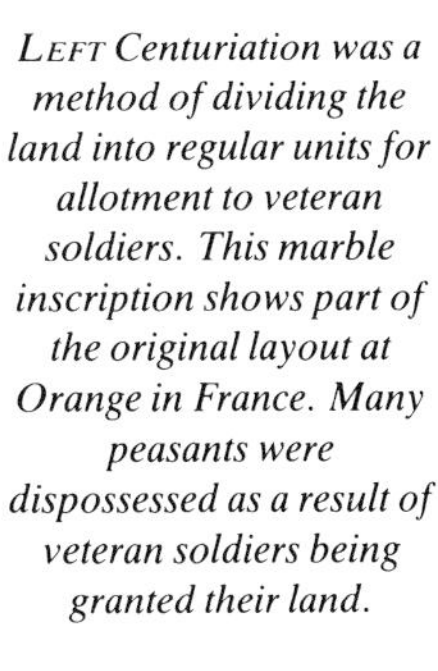

Left Centuriation was a method of dividing the land into regular units for allotment to veteran soldiers. This marble inscription shows part of the original layout at Orange in France. Many peasants were dispossessed as a result of veteran soldiers being granted their land.

ABOVE A rural scene from a wall painting in the villa of Agrippa Postumus at Boscotrecase near Pompeii.

ABOVE Much information about villas and agriculture can be obtained from mosaics. This one shows a large 4th-century estate in Tunisia, with the villa buildings and bath-house in the centre, surrounded by agricultural activity throughout the four seasons.

the leadership of Spartacus, a gladiator. In 73 BC he escaped and assembled a force of fugitives on Mount Vesuvius, eventually forming an army of tens of thousands of slaves. For two years they wandered throughout Italy, pillaging and plundering, until they were eventually defeated by the Roman army under Crassus. Following this defeat, over 6,000 captured slaves were crucified along the Appian Way, the road leading from Rome to Capua.

THE GROWTH OF THE VILLAS

Villas began to appear in the provinces from the 1st century BC, and in many areas the villa system did not go out of use for 500 years. It extended right across the Empire, from Britain to the Sahara, in diverse geographical areas. Like other aspects of Roman life, it is difficult to generalize about villas, but they had much more in common with the great country houses and plantations of 18th and 19th century Europe and America than with the more humble and utilitarian types of farming establishment.

In Italy and elsewhere, the native population that continued to farm the land gradually adopted Roman styles of living. There is evidence that Roman types of housing and furnishing were in such demand that huge debts were incurred to pay for them. The poorer farmers rented small farms and homesteads, while the more wealthy farmers lived in what are termed 'villas' – large farming estates with domestic buildings often decorated with mosaics and wall paintings, and displaying other signs of Roman influence. It used to be thought that all villas in the provinces were owned and lived in by Romans who had moved there from Italy. Except possibly for a few of the very large villas, the builders and owners of the provincial villas were probably natives, although their names are rarely recorded.

Villas were more common in the northern provinces, and examples in northern Gaul were often very extensive. Some villas clustered around towns and were used as country retreats within easy reach of the towns by their wealthy owners. A few villas were associated with industry rather than with agriculture.

The information we have about villas comes from archaeological excavations and aerial photography. Villas were sometimes represented in art, usually in wall paintings and mosaics (especially mosaics from North Africa), and ancient authors also wrote about

ABOVE A reconstruction of a Roman kitchen. In the far corner is an oven, and stored in the kitchen are pottery vessels including amphorae, metal strainers, a quernstone, and glass bottles.

agriculture and villa buildings. Marcus Porcius Cato, writing in the first half of the 2nd century BC, described how to run one of the large new estates with slaves in his book *De Agri Cultura (On Agriculture)*. Place-names can often give clues to the existence of a villa – 'Ville Rouge' in France, for example, may indicate past discoveries of Roman tiles from a villa. Place-names of original Roman estates can also survive, or at least be traced in early medieval documents.

THE APPEARANCE OF THE VILLAS

The villa buildings were usually quite different from anything else previously seen in the provinces; places like Britain took rather longer to incorporate Roman features than some of the Mediterranean provinces. Even so, the early villas with their simple rectangular timber buildings divided into rooms and adorned with mosaics, wall paintings and tiled roofs were very different from the circular wattle and daub huts with thatched roofs common in Britain before the Roman invasion.

The more prosperous villas had various features such as glazed windows, tiled roofs, mosaics, plastered and painted walls, underfloor heating, and bath-houses. Mosaics were mainly used for floors and were made from thousands of tiny cubes (*tessellae*), usually of stone, tile, glass fragments and pottery, forming either a simple pattern or a more complex scene, such as one from Greek or Roman mythology. Decorated walls were usually covered in two or three layers of plaster and then the outline of a design would be sketched or scratched on the surface. The painting could then be done in a wide range of colours.

In colder climates, rooms could be heated by charcoal braziers, but the development of underfloor heating (hypocausts), like that used in bath-houses, provided a more efficient form of heating. Hot air from a furnace passed through the air space beneath the floor, with gases and heat escaping through flues in the walls. The floor was usually sup-

Hypocaust Heating

LEFT These stacks of tiles supported a floor as part of the system of underfloor heating in one room of the villa. The hot air circulated beneath the floor.

ported on stacks of tiles or stone, or else the hot air circulated through stone-lined channels beneath the floor. This system of heating was usually only employed in a small proportion of ground-floor rooms.

Agriculture

The type of agriculture carried out depended very much on the geographical region. From the late Republic methods of agriculture improved, although vast technological changes never took place, probably because of the reliance on cheap labour. Italy was initially fairly self-sufficient and even exported quantities of wine as far afield as Britain. For a time, olive and vine production was illegal elsewhere in order to safeguard Italy's interests and to ensure that other regions concentrated on the production of cereals which could be imported for the inhabitants of Rome.

As increasing numbers of people moved to Rome, its huge population needed more food. Under Roman rule, North Africa became immensely productive, with its agriculture supported by sophisticated irrigation systems. As in Italy, estates became very large and grain was their major product, with Africa and Egypt especially supplying two-thirds of Rome's needs. By the 2nd century wine and olive oil exports from North Africa became important as well, and the distinctive and durable remains of the olive presses have enabled olive-growing areas to be mapped and have provided evidence of the thousands of small farms and villas which grew olives.

RIGHT A mosaic floor depicting the treading of grapes for the manufacture of wine.

ABOVE Towards the end of the Roman period in North Africa, many thousand acres of land went out of agricultural use due to the failure to maintain the water irrigation systems like that shown here in a mosaic from Tunisia.

In the northern provinces, where olives and vines could not be cultivated, livestock rearing was important as well as cereals and market gardening.

Farming in these areas was improved by a more efficient type of plough, by improvements in tools, including large two-handled scythes, and by the use of corn-drying ovens. These ovens have often been found on villa sites, along with a range of other outbuildings such as barns and smithies.

Surplus produce in the Roman period could be much more easily transported with the improved communication system, and the increased taxes and levies may initially, at least, have stimulated agricultural production throughout the Empire.

AGRICULTURE DECLINE

In the 3rd century there was economic collapse within the Empire and invasion from beyond the frontiers, and therefore a consequent reduction in the production of manufactured goods and agriculture. Land was left uncultivated and farms were abandoned. For some of the peasant population, life was so difficult in the 3rd century that they took to brigandage, often joining groups of Germanic tribespeople. The name *Bagaudae* appears in the late 3rd century to describe these people. There is evidence of decay and destruction in most villa sites of this period, and a general lowering of standards in areas away from the frontiers, but from the 4th century there was a recovery, although hardly ever matching the previous prosperity. In some areas, the

ABOVE The stone relief from a Roman sarcophagus depicts two women bathing a baby.

troubles in the 3rd century led to a complete collapse of the villa system.

The situation in Britain was somewhat different because during the 3rd century there was a recession rather than abandonment and destruction. Instead of a modest recovery, there was a considerable increase in prosperity in the late 3rd and 4th centuries, with new villas being built and existing ones enlarged. There is some evidence for immigration by Gaulish landowners seeking refuge from the troubles. Towards the end of the 4th century villa buildings in Britain declined and were largely abandoned, and many villas elsewhere failed to survive beyond the Roman period. Likewise, many areas went out of agricultural use, such as in North Africa where thousands of acres of arable land were lost in the 5th century as a result of the failure to maintain the water irrigation systems.

Life Expectancy

No matter where people lived, in towns or the countryside, social and economic factors affected both longevity and the quality of life. The infant mortality rate was high, and most working-class people died between the ages of 35 and 50; many people did not live beyond their 20s and 30s. Girls often married in their early teens and could be grandmothers by the age of 30. Inevitably, the wealthier classes had a better chance of living longer. The Emperor Tiberius, for example, was 79 when he died, but on the whole living to what is nowadays considered to be an advanced age was most unusual.

CHAPTER SIX

GAMES *and* GATHERINGS

'Hail Emperor, those about to die salute you'

(SUETONIUS, *CLAUDIUS*, 21)

ABOVE The playing of knucklebones was a favourite game with men and women.

PRIVATE ENTERTAINMENT

As in any society, the Romans spent their leisure hours in a variety of ways. In Roman art children are portrayed playing traditional games like hide-and-seek and leap-frog, and are also seen accompanied by their pets. Various toys have been found including dolls made of wood, bone, baked clay and cloth, although it is not always possible to be certain if miniature carvings (such as animals) were toys or votive offerings to a god. Board games were also played, probably by children and adults alike, and gambling and dicing became widespread pursuits throughout the empire. Boards divided into squares have been found, as well as counters (usually made of bone, baked clay or glass) and quantities of bone dice with a series of incised circles on each side. Loaded dice have also been found, showing that not everyone played fair. The playing of knucklebones was also a favourite game.

People of all social classes spent time at the baths and this became a recreational activity. Another form of private entertainment was eating and drinking, which for the poorer classes usually meant frequenting the numerous local taverns. These were undoubtedly of varying reputation, and could also be used as gaming houses. At Pompeii, over 100 taverns have been identified, several functioning as brothels as well, with unsettled accounts still marked on the walls.

The wealthy had the money and facilities for private entertaining, from modest dinner parties to lavish banquets. These are a common topic in the contemporary literature which has therefore given much information about details such as food, after-dinner entertainment and difficult guests. Many

BELOW An antiquarian painting showing a hunting scene on a mosaic from a villa at East Coker in Somerset. The two hunters with spears are carrying home a doe hung on a pole.

Musical Entertainment

Above Music was a minor form of entertainment in the Roman period. It was used particularly as an accompaniment to other types of entertainment in theatres and amphitheatres. This 1st century mosiac by Dioscurides portrays a scene from a comedy.

recipes have survived in a cookery book supposed to have been written by the gourmet Apicius in the 1st century. Hunting and fishing added welcome variety to the Roman diet.

Most Romans ate three meals a day, with the main meal being in the early evening. It is likely that the urban poor mainly ate a type of porridge made from boiled wheat, or else bread (if they had an oven for baking). There was a variety of other foods, including meat, cheese, vegetables, nuts, shellfish and fruit, many available only to the wealthier classes. Information about food is obtained from literary sources, art (such as mosaics) and archaeological excavations, where even the pips of different fruit can be identified. One of the most popular ingredients in Roman cooking was a fish sauce called *garum* or *liquamen*, which was widely traded and usually transported in *amphorae* (large pottery jars with a rounded or pointed bottom).

Below The poet Virgil (centre) was responsible for some of the greatest works of Latin literature. He is portrayed writing the Aeneid, *flanked by two muses.*

ABOVE The theatre at the town of Orange in France is typical of Roman-style theatres, with seats surrounding an orchestra, a stage, and a back wall (scaena). A statue of Augustus looks down upon the scene.

LITERATURE AND MUSIC

After-dinner entertainment could often include discussion and recitation of literature. Latin literature began in the 3rd century BC, with comedies written in verse by Plautus. These, like those written by Terence in the 160s BC, were based on earlier Greek comedies. Latin literature developed during the Republic, and among its greatest works were those of Virgil, Horace and Ovid in the Augustan age. Very little drama was written, but accounts of history became popular in the early Empire. At first poets were considered to be of a low status, but there was a shift in attitude towards poetry in the late Republic, and poets began to live by patronage, offering their patrons a chance of immortality. The reading aloud of literary works took place at private functions and also at recitations; it was, nevertheless, a pastime confined to a minority of educated people. Most literature was recorded with pen and ink on papyrus or parchment. Copies of works were laboriously made by hand, and yet many cities had one or more libraries.

Music played a minor part in recreation, and it was not as highly regarded as it had been by the Greeks. Most musical instruments were played to accompany public games and religious rites, and to act as signals in the army. Several types of wind, string and percussion instruments are known, and even a hydraulic organ was developed, but there is very little evidence of the type of music played. Only a few examples have been found of the *odeum*, a small permanently roofed theatre specifically for musical performances and recitations.

PUBLIC GAMES

Roman society was bound up in religious festivals which included public games, but gra-

Above
A mosaic from the 'Room of the Ten Girls' in the 3rd-century villa at Piazza Armerina, Sicily, shows female acrobats and dancers wearing black bikinis, possibly made of leather.

dually the religious significance of the games was lost although the games continued to be held regularly. In the mid-4th century BC, games only lasted one day a year, but this increased to several days and by the late Republic, 17 days in the year were devoted to them. In the 1st century BC private games were initiated by military leaders to celebrate personal military victories, and these became so lavish that the distinction between private and official games was hardly discernible.

The emperors continued this tradition of games as it was a means of obtaining popular support and of controlling the activities of the urban masses. Like subsidized food, the games were soon regarded as a right and, according to Juvenal, the populace was only interested in *panem et circenses* – bread and circuses. Colossal sums of public and private money were spent on the games and each of the emperors attempted to outdo his predecessor. The number of official celebrations increased, reaching 135 by the end of the 2nd century, and 176 by the 4th century. In addition, there were special celebrations such as the one for Trajan's victory over the Dacians, with the games lasting for over 100 days. Most people worked for a living but nevertheless found some time to attend the games.

Three types of mass entertainment emerged – gladiatorial combats in amphitheatres, chariot races in circuses, and performances in the theatre and odeum. The events had their origins in Etruscan funerary rites and in

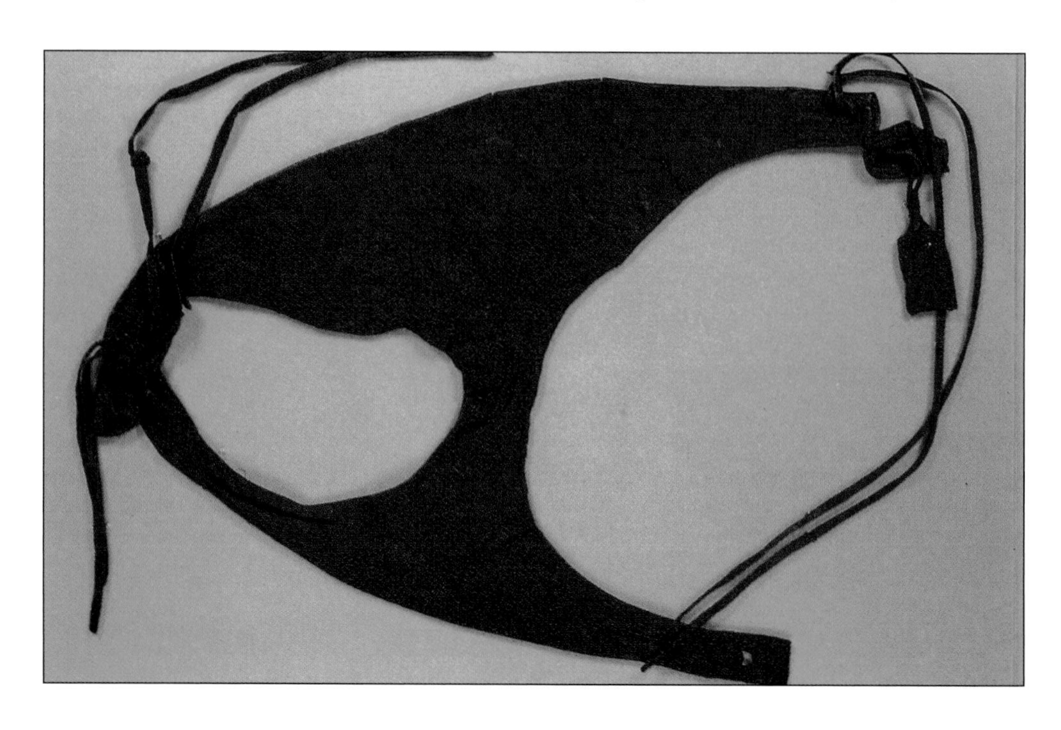

Right Although very similar in design to those worn in the mosaic above, these trunks are over a hundred years older and are perhaps the oldest example of bikini wear yet found. Surprisingly these trunks were not found in the warmer climes of Rome or Greece, but in a 1st-century well in London. The original hip measurement of the wearer has been calculated as approximately 31 inches (79 cm).

ABOVE Actors in their masks about to perform in a theatrical production.

Greek theatre but became significantly modified to satisfy the demands of the Roman populace, and were often of a sadistic nature.

In imperial times, Greek sports were included in the public games, and emperors tried to revive the glory of the Olympic Games which had waned after the Roman conquest of Greece. Few Romans themselves took part in this type of sporting activity, but in the 1st to 3rd centuries the Games did take place once more at Olympia, and similar events were staged in Italy. Nero went to Greece in 67 to compete in the national festivals, and such was his influence that he returned with 1,808 first prizes including prizes from the Olympic Games!

THEATRES

Under Greek influence, theatrical performances (*ludi scaenici*) became popular from the 2nd century BC, although the Greek tradition of theatre died out. Up to the end of the Republic, performances were produced in improvised wooden buildings which were dismantled afterwards. Permanent theatres began to be constructed, consisting of an auditorium with curved rows of seats rising in tiers, an arena or orchestra, a raised stage, and elaborate stage buildings behind. The theatre was usually unroofed, but could be protected from the weather by awnings.

Theatrical performances of Greek tragedies and comedies were popular with the educated social classes. No women were allowed on stage, and so actors wore masks to distinguish clearly their various roles, male or female. However, the few plays that seem to have been written by Roman authors were intended to be read aloud to a small audience rather than for actual theatrical productions.

Most of the public preferred less taxing entertainment, and from the 1st century BC pantomime and mime became popular, but still usually with mythological themes. In pantomimes the actors mimed their roles, accompanied by music, singing, dancing and elaborate visual effects so that the production was similar to an extravagant ballet. In mime the actors had speaking parts. Women were allowed to take part in mime and pantomime, and these events degenerated into extremely popular, vulgar and tasteless shows.

The Amphitheatre

Above Amphitheatres could be substantial stone structures, requiring a great deal of labour and engineering skill in their construction.

Amphitheatres

The amphitheatre was an oval arena surrounded by tiers of seats. It probably originated in Campania, with one of the earliest being at Pompeii. Some were associated with military forts and Rome's earliest stone amphitheatre was built in 29 BC. By the 2nd century few towns in the western provinces and North Africa were without an amphitheatre. While some were fairly simply built, with seats set into banks of earth, others were very elaborate stone structures. Five amphitheatres were built in Rome, the largest being the Colosseum (properly called the Flavian amphitheatre) which could accommodate 50,000 spectators. Below the arena floor was a complex system of underground passages and rooms for the gladiators and wild animals, as well as machinery which enabled the scenery of the arena to be changed. There was also an intricate water system for converting the arena into a lake for naval battles (*naumachia*). Like the theatre, admission to the amphitheatre was free.

One of the most popular forms of entertainment was the gladiatorial combat – a fight for life between two gladiators. This type of performance dated back to Etruscan times and often accompanied the death of a chieftain. In Rome, the earliest recorded perfor-

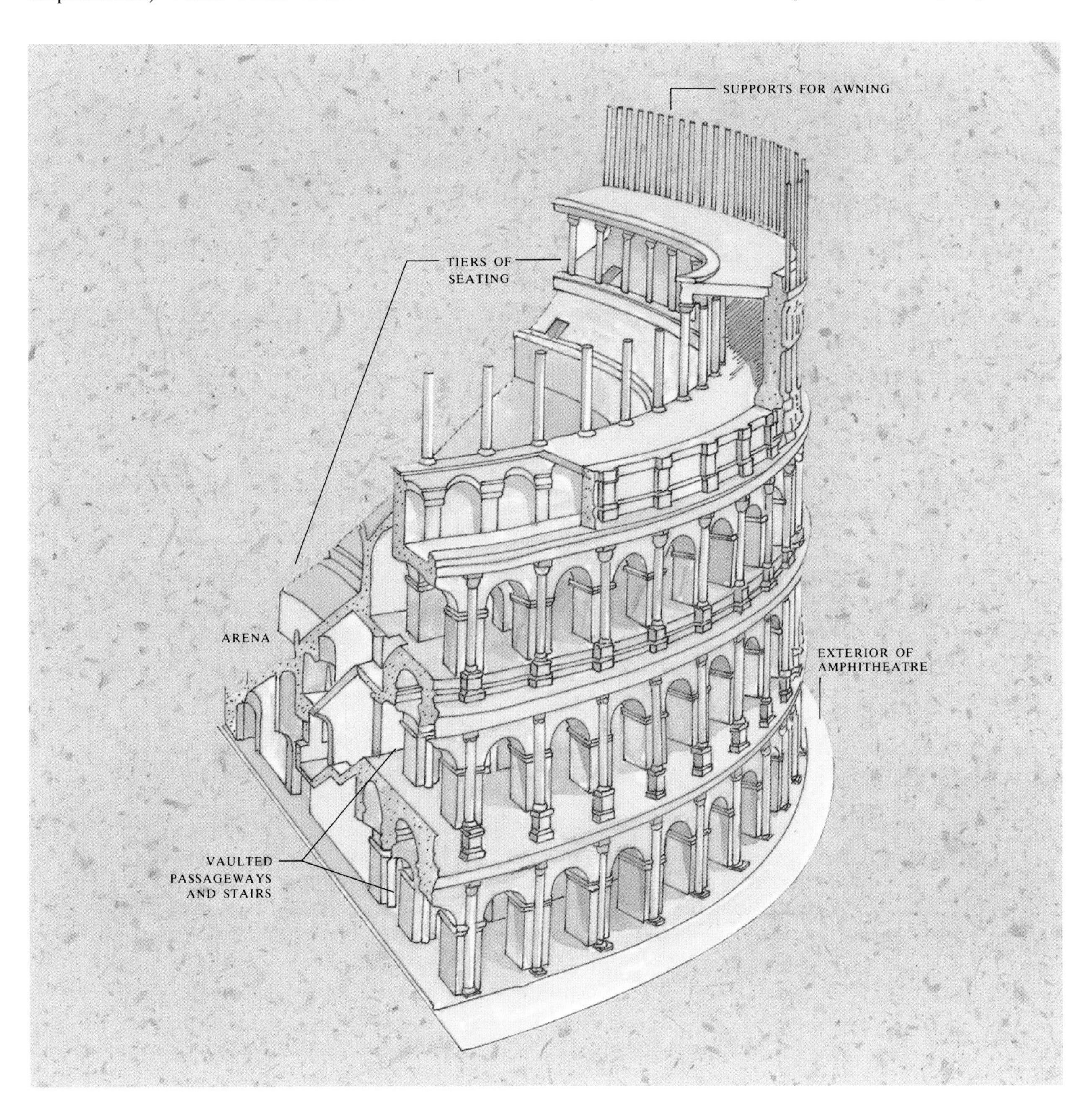

A cut-away view through an amphitheatre showing the complex system of arches, vaults, staircases and passages.

RIGHT A riot taking place between the inhabitants of Pompeii and visitors from Nuceria during games at the amphitheatre. This incident is actually recorded in Roman history, and led to the closure of the amphitheatre for several years. This wall painting also shows awnings in use at the amphitheatre.

mance was at the funeral of a nobleman in 264 BC. By the 1st century BC these contests had lost their ritual significance and had become spectacles of entertainment, with slaves being made to fight as gladiators since their lives were considered to be of no value.

Gladiatorial training schools were set up and owned by military leaders; Caesar owned a school of 5,000 gladiators. In the 1st century the schools came under state control, removing the danger of them becoming personal armies. As well as trainers, the schools employed numerous other specialists including doctors, and at any one time they could offer the services of thousands of gladiators, mostly slaves. The gladiators were housed in barracks at the schools and trained in various modes of fighting. The type of fighting was based on different native methods using national weapons; particularly favoured were the *retiarii* (net fighters) who used a net to catch their opponents and a trident or dagger to kill them.

The gladiatorial games were not part of the public games (*ludi*) but were called *munera* (duties or obligations) because of the original duty of honouring the dead with such displays. The number of contests grew

ABOVE A fragmentary mosaic from Tunisia showing a chariot race in action, with the chariots going anti-clockwise round the spina. The audience watches the entertainment from the raised seating of the circus.

rapidly, and in 65 BC Julius Caesar arranged a contest between 320 pairs of gladiators. Hundreds of thousands of gladiators must have lost their lives, although successful fighters could win much popularity and their freedom.

Games using animals (*venationes*) were based on the hunt and became very popular. *Bestiarii* were gladiators who hunted and fought wild animals on foot, and were armed with bows and arrows, although cavalry hunters were sometimes used. The animals used included bears, lions, tigers, panthers, rhinoceroses, leopards, elephants and wild bulls. Bull fights were introduced from Thessaly where they had featured in religious festivals, and bull fighting today is sometimes staged in restored Roman amphitheatres. Animals were also set against each other, such as an elephant against a bear, and the technical apparatus of the arena allowed spectacular stage sets to be used, into which the animals were let loose.

A large trade grew up with frontier provinces and beyond (particularly with Africa), to provide the exotic animals needed for the games. Hunters trapped the animals in pits or drove them into nets or enclosures, and the captured animals were transported in wooden crates with sliding doors, carried on poles by the hunter. They were then transferred to carts pulled by oxen and taken by boat to their final destination. These scenes are sometimes represented on mosaics, as at the Piazza Armerina in Sicily. The carnage of animals reached massive proportions. During Nero's reign, 400 bears and 300 lions were killed on a single occasion; during the inauguration of the Colosseum, in 80, some 9,000 animals are said to have been killed.

In addition to the slaughter of animals for entertainment, there were also well-trained animals which gave circus-like performances, often accompanied by music, which was an important feature of the games. Musicians amused the audience during intervals and announced and accompanied the different spectacles.

The morning of the games was originally reserved for fights with wild animals, midday for executions, and the afternoon for gladiatorial contests, but the divisions became less

RIGHT Romans frequently removed obelisks from Egypt for use as markers in circuses. This one at Arles in France was originally part of the spina of the circus, but in 1675 during the reign of Louis XIV it was set up on a monumental pedestal in the centre of a fountain.

distinct. As well as being victims, animals were also used as executioners of criminals and of enemies of the state (including Jews and Christians) who were condemned to die by animals (*ad bestias*). Methods of killing animals and criminals were ingenious and few people in Rome condemned these spectacles which today most people would find abhorrent.

CIRCUSES

Chariot racing was the oldest and most popular sport in the Roman world. Circus games (*ludi circenses*) were of Etruscan origin and the earliest ones in Rome consisted of chariot races and boxing matches. In the early 2nd century BC, Greek athletics and wrestling entered the games, but it was chariot racing that became the foremost entertainment.

According to Roman legend, the first chariot racing event was arranged by Romulus soon after he founded Rome in 753 BC. He invited the men of the neighbouring Sabine tribe to attend, and while they were engrossed in the games, the women were abducted. The first Etruscan king, Tarquinius Priscus, had a sports ground prepared in the centre of Rome, which was later replaced by the Circus Maximus. In 221 BC the Circus Flaminius was also constructed, and by the 3rd century there were eight tracks in the vicinity of Rome and many more throughout the empire. No circuses have been positively identified in Britain, but chariot racing could take place wherever there was a suitable flat area, with a nearby hillside for spectators.

In Rome and other cities the circuses consisted of a long racetrack flanked by tiers of seats. There were two long parallel sides and rounded ends, the seats being either of stone or built into the sloping hillsides. A low wall (*spina*) ran down the centre of the track, preventing head-on collisions, and there were markers at each end. Some of the circuses were colossal structures – the Circus Maximus at Rome could seat 250,000 spectators.

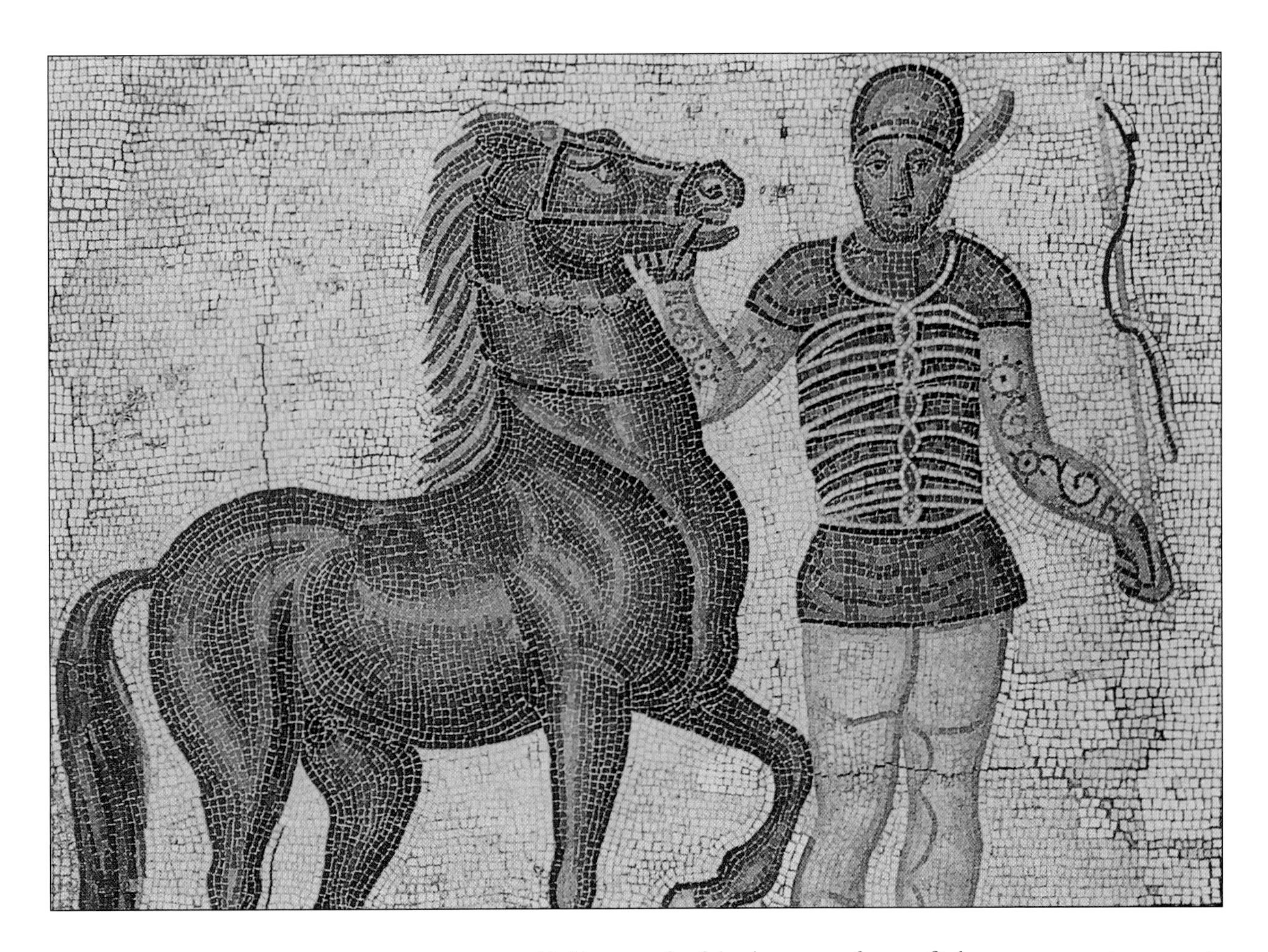

ABOVE A charioteer and his horse belonging to the popular green faction at Rome.

The charioteers were originally of the equestrian class and, although chariots were no longer used for military purposes in the ancient world, driving them remained a socially exclusive activity which could only be demonstrated at religious festivals. Gradually chariot racing lost its religious significance, charioteers became professional performers, but chariot racing remained popular with all social groups. Artistic equestrianism (such as leaping from one horse to another) was also included in the circus entertainment, but never horse racing.

Successful charioteers acquired great fame and wealth, and the names of some of them and their horses still survive on mosaics, glassware and relief sculptures. Chariots were normally drawn by four horses, although two or more could be used. The wooden chariots were lightweight and easily broken. As the races became more varied and dramatic, the most difficult part was at the turning posts where collisions frequently occurred, leading to the deaths of charioteers and horses alike.

Chariot racing was a very expensive and highly organized business run for profit by private enterprises. In Rome there were four racing factions distinguished by their colours – the reds, whites, blues and greens. The charioteers wore the colours of their stables and the greens and blues became the favourites at Rome. There was much rivalry in cities between the different factions and their supporters, which led to frequent outbursts of violence.

END OF THE GAMES

During the 4th century, restrictions were put on the games and they were eventually banned. By the end of the century, the imperial gladiatorial schools had closed down and gladiatorial combats ceased at this time in the Eastern Empire and in the 5th century in the west. Combats with animals seem to have continued in both parts of the empire until the 6th century but public athletics, including the Olympic Games, were banned. Chariot racing disappeared in the West, but it continued in the East for another 1,000 years throughout the Byzantine Empire and into the Middle Ages.

CHAPTER SEVEN

COMMERCE *and* CRAFT

"At Rome, all things can be had at a price."

(JUVENAL, *SATIRES*, iii, 183)

ABOVE Fragments of wooden writing tablets and iron writing implements (styli)*. Everyday business transactions could be done by writing on a layer of wax on the wooden tablet.*

THE PEOPLE AT WORK

Most of the information about the working population in Roman society is derived from representations in art, such as mosaics, wall paintings and sculptured reliefs, particularly those funerary monuments depicting scenes of everyday business life. There are also references in graffiti to various trades, especially the political slogans found on the walls at Pompeii such as 'the barbers want Trebius as *aedile*' (magistrate). Another source of knowledge about crafts and trades within the (magistrate) empire is in the Edict on Maximum Prices published in 301 by Diocletian in an attempt to control prices. The Edict was impossible to enforce, but nevertheless gives useful information on prices, goods and the standard of living. Much information about industry and trade can also be obtained from archaeological excavations, and in particular from the study of finds – both the finished goods and the waste materials.

There are very few references to labourers and craftworkers in the literary sources because they had a low status and did not themselves leave behind written evidence about their everyday lives. There are, however, records of business transactions, usually written on papyri or on waxed, wooden writing tablets. Within the working classes there were divisions between slaves, freedpeople, free citizens and non-citizens, although it is not usually obvious to us which group carried out the different types of work. Most businesses were probably small family-run concerns employing a few slaves and apprentices. In addition to the manufacturers of goods, there were also many traders active throughout the Empire, some of whom were organized in large trading companies or guilds. Traders had a much greater opportunity of acquiring wealth than the craftworkers, and private individuals who had enough capital to make loans could participate in money-lending.

ROMAN JEWELLERY

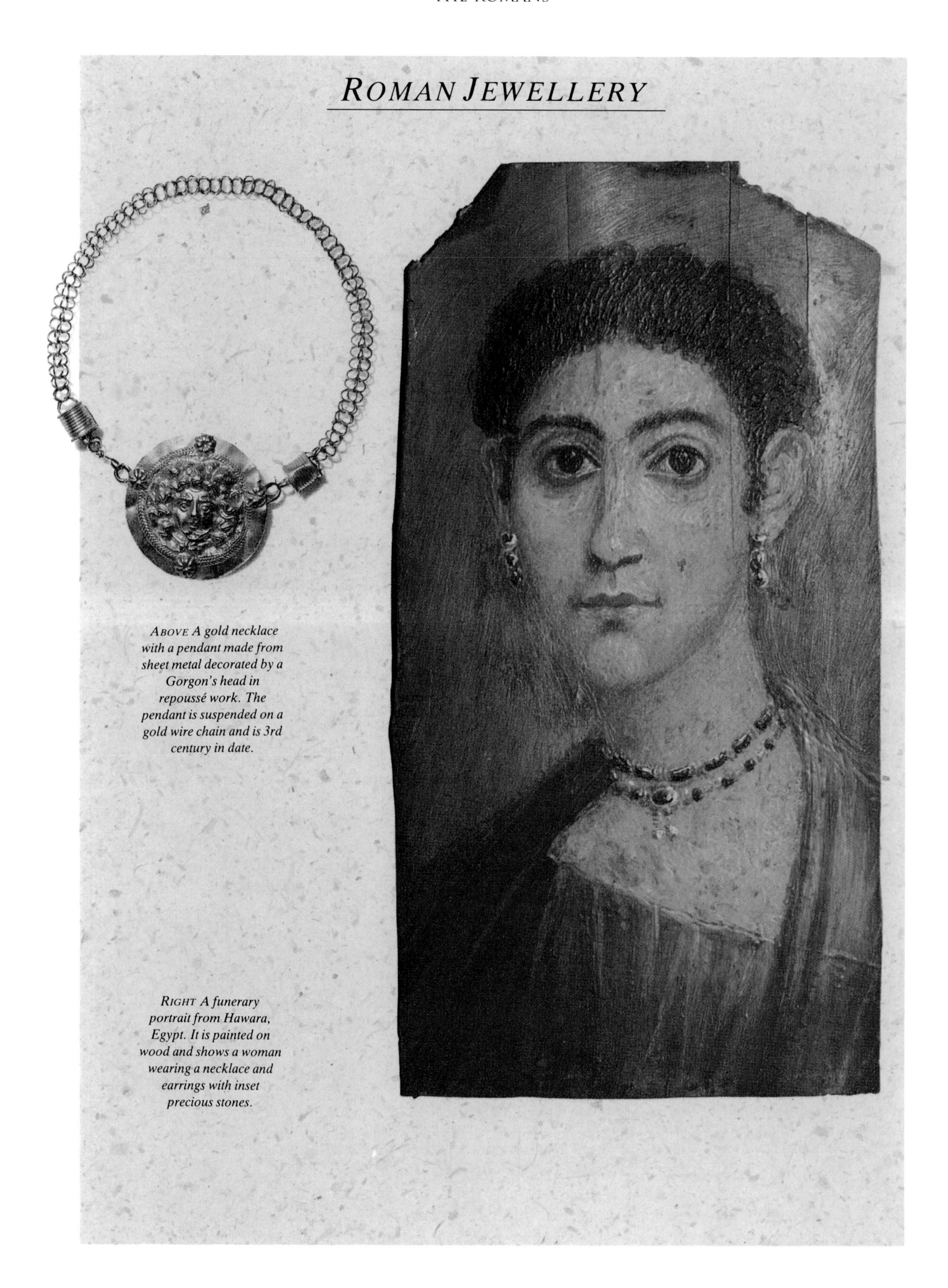

ABOVE A gold necklace with a pendant made from sheet metal decorated by a Gorgon's head in repoussé work. The pendant is suspended on a gold wire chain and is 3rd century in date.

RIGHT A funerary portrait from Hawara, Egypt. It is painted on wood and shows a woman wearing a necklace and earrings with inset precious stones.

Towns became manufacturing centres, and processed and used the raw materials brought in from the agricultural estates (such as wool, hides, timber, and produce), and from the rural industrial centres (such as stone from the quarries). The most important industry was probably the manufacturing and selling of food and drink, but a vast range of crafts was also carried out.

GOLD

Most mining establishments came under the direct control of the State within the Empire, and gold-mining could be on quite a large scale, as in southern Spain. The gold-bearing ore was extracted from the rock and smelted, and the resulting liquid gold poured into moulds to form ingots. While much of the gold went to the State for official use, such as for coins, some of it was bought by goldsmiths. Their main product was jewellery made from sheet metal, wire, or cast metal. Sheet gold was formed by hammering an ingot on an anvil until it was sufficiently thin. Only a little jewellery was made by casting, as the sheet method used a lot less metal and was therefore cheaper. Wire was normally made by twisting a strip of metal and rolling it between plates of stone or bronze. It was used mainly for ornamental chains and objects such as rings and earrings, also for filigree work. Much gold jewellery was decorated with coloured stone and glass inlays.

SILVER

One of the major silver-producing areas was Spain, where silver was mined along with lead. Silver nearly always occurs in a lead ore called galena, and in order to extract the silver, the lead ore was heated to around 1,000°C (1,800°F), a process known as cupellation. Very little silver jewellery was made, the main products being coins and silver plate. Silversmiths produced quantities of eating and drinking vessels for prosperous households, but silver plate was also made for religious purposes, especially for use by the Christian Church in the later Roman period.

Silver could be hammered into shape and yet it was possible to remove all traces of hammering by careful polishing, so few signs of the manufacturing methods can be seen on Roman objects. Few craftworker's tools have been found, but the techniques were probably similar to those used today. One of the main methods of producing decoration was by the repoussé ('pushed-out') method, which was done by hammering the back of the silver so that the pattern stood out in relief on the other side. For drinking vessels, it was normal for a smooth inner lining of silver to be fitted, so hiding the identations of the repoussé work. One of the finest techniques in silverwork was its combination with glass to produce decorative vessels.

LEAD, TIN AND PEWTER

After silver was extracted from the lead ore at the mines, the lead was cast in moulds to produce large ingots (known as 'pigs'). They weighed around 86 kg (190lb), and often bore the name of the emperor and the centre of production. Lead was used extensively in the building trade for water pipes, bath linings, roofing and cisterns. It was also used for coffins, containers for cremated remains, and smaller objects such as weights and plumb-bobs.

Tin was mined for use as an alloy with other metals, and by the late 3rd century, pewter, an alloy of lead and tin, was used for the production of objects such as plates, dishes and jugs and also used as a solder. Pewter was always cast and several stone moulds have been found. These moulds consisted of two pieces, one of which fitted inside the other leaving a small gap into which the molten metal was poured.

BRONZE

Copper was rarely used on its own but was combined with other metals to form bronze. An alloy of copper and tin was suitable for working when cold to produce small, simple objects, but the most common method of manufacturing bronze objects was by casting, when lead was added to the copper instead. The *cire perdue* ('lost wax') method of casting involved making a model of the object in wax which was then coated with clay or sand with clay. This was heated so that the wax melted and ran out, leaving a hollow into which the molten bronze was poured. The outer clay covering was then broken, leaving a solid cast bronze object. For larger objects such as statues, this method was too expensive, and so the 'hollow cast' method was used. A clay model was made which was coated with a layer of wax on which all the details were sculptured. The wax was in turn coated with

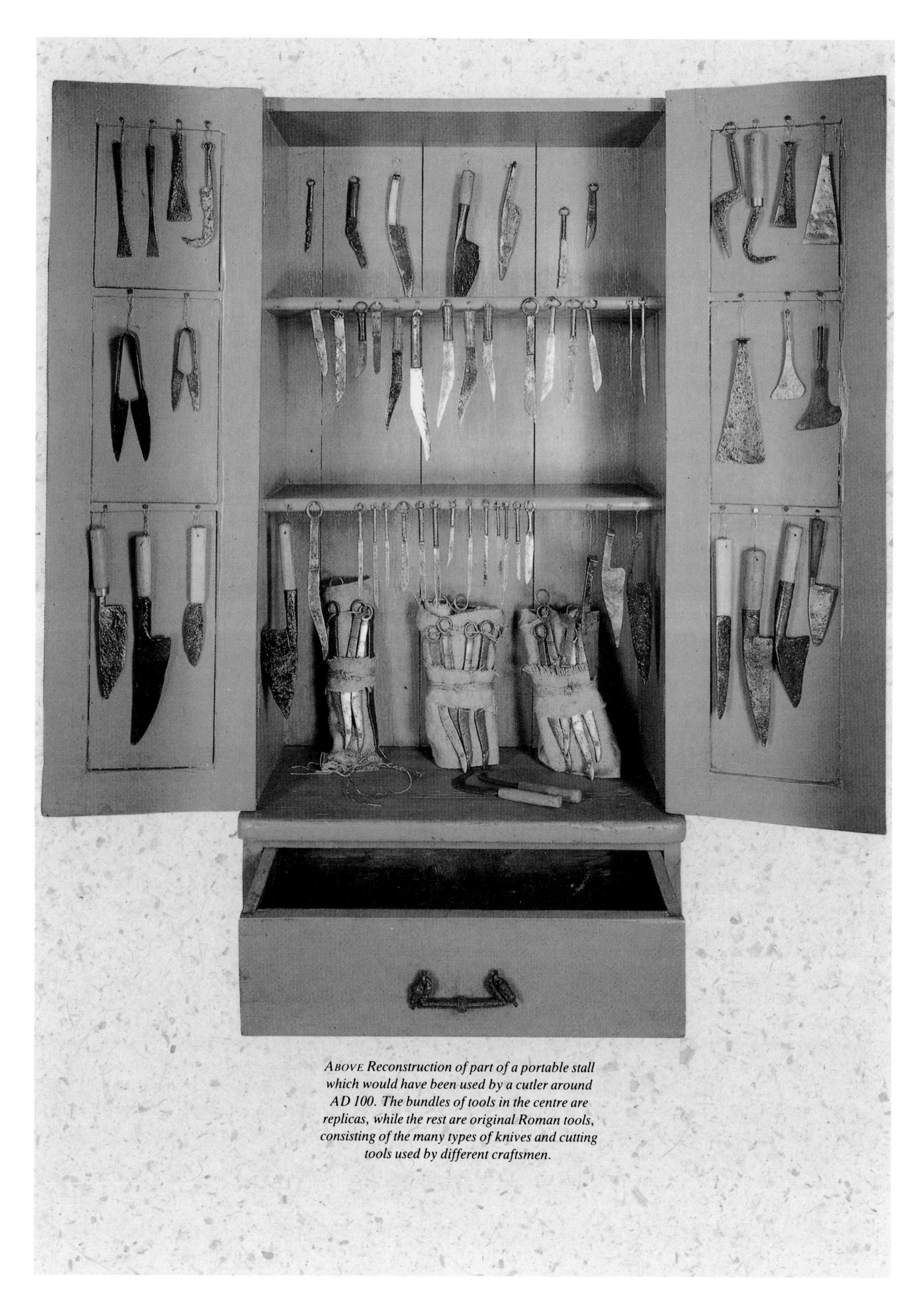

ABOVE Reconstruction of part of a portable stall which would have been used by a cutler around AD 100. The bundles of tools in the centre are replicas, while the rest are original Roman tools, consisting of the many types of knives and cutting tools used by different craftsmen.

clay, and molten bronze was poured through holes so that it replaced the wax layer, which melted away. The removal of the outer clay layer left a hollow bronze object with a solid core of clay (which was often removed). Very large objects were made in several pieces which were welded together, and some objects, including metal vessels, could be cast in reusable stone moulds.

Thousands of bronzesmiths must have been employed in workshops in the Roman period as a wide range of objects was made in bronze such as coins, pins, needles, toilet instruments, jewellery, lamp holders and tableware, as well as many items of military equipment.

Objects such as plates, brooches and armour were often tinned to make them appear to be silver by pouring molten tin over the surface. A common method of decorating small bronze objects was by enamelling, a process particularly used in the 1st–3rd centuries. Different coloured vitreous (glass) substances were placed in the separate compartments of the piece to be decorated, such as a brooch, and these melted and fused to the bronze when heated. This technique is known as champlevé, and brightly coloured objects were produced in bronze.

Iron

Iron ore was mined extensively using open-cast methods, although some mine shafts are known. The ore was 'roasted' in an open hearth and then melted in a smelting furnace constructed of clay. The molten iron was formed into ingots which could be used by blacksmiths in towns, villas and the army. The blacksmiths heated the iron in a hearth until it was red hot, and then carried it by tongs to the anvil where it was hammered into rough shape. As it cooled, the iron was reheated, and the process was repeated until the required object was formed.

The tools used by the blacksmith were very similar to those of today. Iron was widely used for everyday tools and fittings such as axes, hammers, saws, picks, horseshoes, locks and keys, hinges and nails. It was also used for military equipment including helmets, swords and daggers.

Stone

Stone was rarely used in building in many pre-Roman communities, but its use gradually increased in towns, forts and villas, and for roads. It was one of the heaviest commodities to be transported in the Roman world and so it was quarried as near as possible to where it was to be used, and then generally transported by water. The techniques of quarrying stone remained unaltered right up to the 20th century, and the quarries were mostly open cast, although some mining for rarer stones took place. Most quarries produced the blocks for

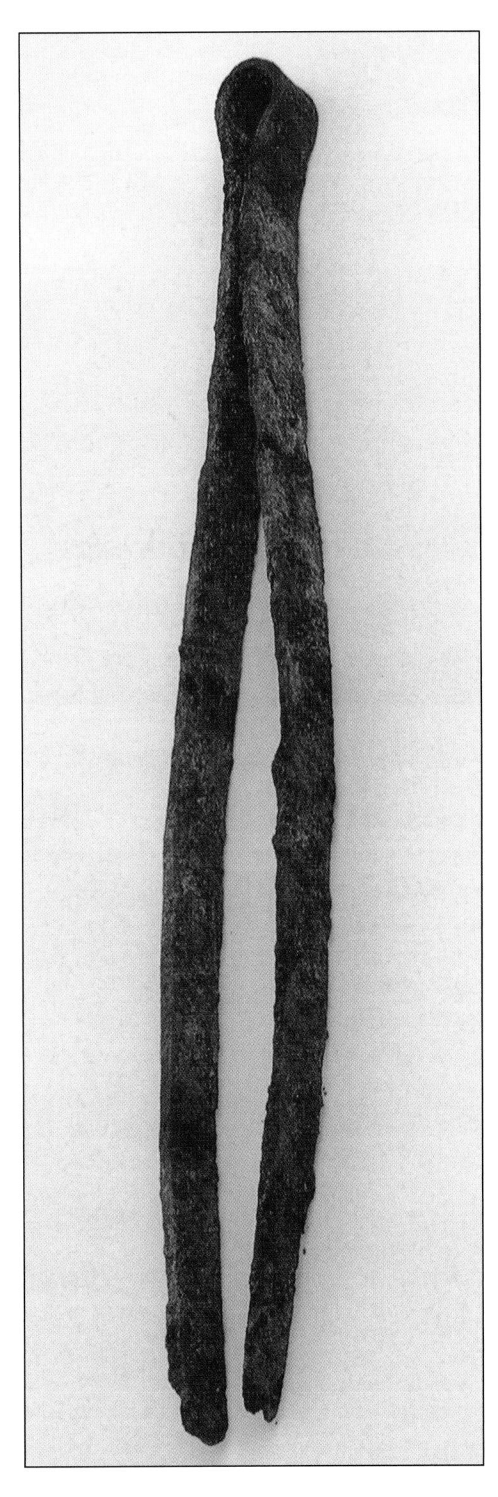

LEFT A pair of corroded iron tweezers found in London. Implements such as these tweezers are very similar to ones used today.

Right Bricks and tiles were made from clay and were then fired in kilns. Here Roman roofing tiles have remained in place from the final firing of the kiln and were never retrieved.

subsequent shaping and carving, but some stoneworking did take place there, such as the roughing out of columns and coffins. Lime production for mortar was often associated with quarrying as lime was obtained by burning limestone in large kilns.

Stone was transported to the workshops for the production of a wide range of objects such as quernstones, tombstones, altars and statues. Softer materials like jet and shale were worked into finer objects such as beads, hairpins, finger-rings, and even table legs. As well as finished objects, some stone was widely traded, particularly precious and semi-precious stones for use in jewellery, and marble and other fine stones for the decoration of buildings.

Wood

Wood was extensively used in the construction trade, in buildings and as scaffolding. Quantities of timber were also needed for ship building, wharves, and carts. Many everyday objects were also made of wood, including bowls, buckets, barrels, chests, and writing tablets. The timbers were cut initially with large saws operated by two men. Woodworking tools were very similar to those of today, including planes and chisels, and the lathe was widely used in furniture making. Very little Roman wood has survived to the present day; except where it is preserved by special conditions, such as in waterlogged deposits.

Above Bricks were often used in walls and arches. In this bath-house (viewed from the exterior) they give a pleasing and decorative effect.

Brick and Tile

A revolution in Roman construction methods was the use of baked clay bricks and tiles, which are found in vast quantities on excavations of many Roman sites, particularly in areas where suitable local building stone was unavailable. Brick and tile manufacturing was organized on a large scale, by towns and by the army, while there were also numerous smaller tileries and brickworks, some operated on a seasonal basis. The natural clay was dug out and allowed to weather over the winter, after which it was prepared for use. Bricks and tiles were made by placing the clay into moulds and left until it was dry and hard, then they were stacked in a kiln and fired. A variety of sizes of bricks was made,

LOCAL POTTERY

LEFT Most pottery consisted of simple earthenware vessels. They were made on a potter's wheel, placed on supports over a furnace in the kiln and then fired. It was normal for pottery to be supplied to fairly local markets as it was a bulky and fragile commodity to transport over long distances.

ABOVE Samian pottery was glossy fine red tableware which was made in vast quantities in the 1st and 2nd centuries and was traded all over the empire.

as well as a large range of tiles; some were marked using a finger or an official stamp, while others displayed accidental marks such as the pawprints of dogs and cats that ran across them as they were laid out to dry.

Bricks were used for walls and arches and tiles mostly for roofing. Two main types of roof tile were used – a flat tile with flanges (*tegula*) and a curved one (*imbrex*) to cover the gaps between adjoining flat tiles. Tiles were also incorporated into underfloor heating systems (hypocausts) where the floors were supported on pillars of tile (*pilae*) or stone; channels in the walls to conduct gases and hot air used specially made hollow flue tiles.

Pottery

Pottery vessels for domestic use (especially for the preparation and storage of food) had been made long before the Romans, but with increased demand large potteries grew up in areas with good quality clay. Most pottery consisted of fairly simple earthenware vessels, white, cream, orange, grey or black in colour, usually made on a potter's wheel and then fired in a kiln. This type of pottery (known as 'coarse pottery' or 'kitchen wares') was not traded over wide areas, but supplied local markets. Many shops selling pottery have been found, such as at Pompeii where shops with their contents were engulfed by the volcanic eruption of Vesuvius in 79.

Some pottery was traded over long distances, including the very large vessels known as *amphorae*. These were used as containers for wine, olive oil and fish sauce, which were traded. (Food could also be transported in barrels or sacks, but these have left virtually no trace.) Fine tablewares were popular and therefore traded widely, the most well-known type being samian ware (also known as *terra sigillata*). This was a red glossy surfaced

Below A mosaic, made from thousands of tesserae, from Hadrian's Villa at Tivoli near Rome. It depicts a finely worked bowl on which there are four drinking doves, and is a copy of a Greek original by Sosus.

ABOVE The technique of making decorative floors from pieces of marble is known as opus sectile. *This 4th-century work from the basilica of Junius Basso in Rome depicts a tiger seizing a calf.*

pottery first made in northern Italy and subsequently in Gaul and Germany. The earlier pottery was generally plain, but moulds were later used to produce vessels with decoration in relief. The samian pottery industry was organized on a massive scale, and it is found right across the empire, but from the late 2nd century the market for it declined and the North African potteries took over the production of red ware pottery.

INTER OR DECORATION

Most houses had mortar or wooden floors and plain plastered walls, but for those who could afford it interior decoration was an important aspect of life. The finest decorations were reserved for the dining and reception rooms. Skilled workers were responsible for the many mosaic floors, some fairly plain and others with elaborate scenes. The floors had to have solid foundations to prevent cracking and subsidence, and some super-imposed floors have been found where new floors were laid directly on old ones. Mosaic floors were made from small cubes known as *tesserae*, normally of stone, but with some tile, pottery, glass and other materials being used. Errors are visible on some mosaics, while others show signs of repairs. Decorative floors could also be constructed from shaped pieces of coloured marble, a technique known as *opus sectile.*

Mosaics were also used to decorate walls and, unlike floor mosaics, which had a functional purpose and had to be robust, wall mosaics were constructed of more exotic materials, in particular glass *tesserae*. However, walls were usually decorated by paintings, and the plasterer had to produce a very smooth surface on which the designs could be painted. Various pigments, generally made from natural substances, were used for the colours, and it was customary to decorate ceilings in the same way.

TEXTILES

In western Europe sheep were the major source of textile fibres and the wool was shorn with iron shears. Wool was spun with

ABOVE A reconstruction of a dining-room decorated by wall paintings and with various pieces of Roman furniture and other objects. Most wealthy Romans reclined on a couch to eat meals.

LEFT Clothing is commonly portrayed in art forms such as in this statue of a god who is wearing a toga.

hand spindles (not with spinning wheels), and then the fibres were dyed using a variety of pigments. Weaving of the woollen thread was done mainly on vertical, warp-weighted, wooden looms, none of which have survived, although they are represented in art. The woven cloth was subsequently treated by the fuller to remove grease and dirt. This was done by soaking the cloth in tanks of water mixed with 'fuller's earth' or decayed urine (which was collected in large jars provided by the fullers at street corners for the use of passers-by).

Flax was grown for linen and in the Roman period some very fine textiles were produced, including some interwoven with gold thread. Textiles were also transported over vast distances, including silk fabrics and yarn from China. A few textile fragments have survived in waterlogged conditions or as imprints on corroded metal, and clothing is often shown on mosaics and tombstones. The toga was the traditional form of dress for the upper class Roman male and consisted of a single

ROMAN SHOEMAKERS

ABOVE On the left a shoemaker sits on a stool making leather shoes, and he himself wears leather sandals. On top of his cupboard are two pairs of completed shoes. On the right another craftsman is manufacturing rope. This relief sculpture is on a stone sarcophagus.

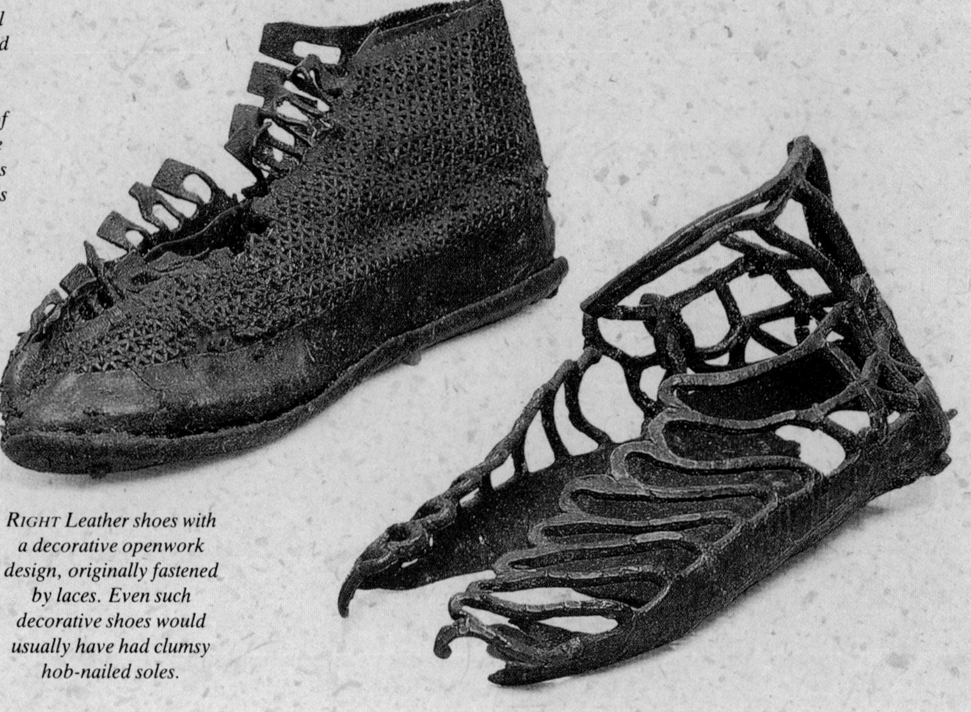

RIGHT Leather shoes with a decorative openwork design, originally fastened by laces. Even such decorative shoes would usually have had clumsy hob-nailed soles.

long piece of material carefully draped around the body. This form of dress came to be worn less frequently, and was mostly reserved for special occasions. The more common form of dress in the Roman world was the tunic, usually with sleeves, which was secured by brooches (*fibulae*) and by a girdle or belt at the waist. Tunics were worn to just below the knee, although women wore longer ones. Depending on the climate, a cloak and hooded cape was worn as an outer garment, held in place by brooches. Although the styles of clothing were fairly conservative, there was a wide range of fine to coarse materials in various colours. There is also some evidence of knitted socks or stockings worn by women, but otherwise no evidence of leg coverings except boots. Some people may have worn trousers, a north European form of dress which both Greeks and Romans held in contempt as fit only for Barbarians.

Another major product from agricultural estates was hides that were processed into leather by tanning, from which a variety of products could be made such as shoes, clothing, tents, saddles and harness. Some shoes or sandles had heavy clumsy soles with hobnails, usually for military use, but there was more elegant footwear.

Glass

The invention of glassblowing had an enormous impact on the glass industry because it enabled vessels to be produced much more rapidly and cheaply. Bluish-green glass (a colour produced by the impure raw materials) was most commonly used, but different colours and colourless glass could be achieved by the addition of various ingredients. Glass was used to manufacture vessels either by free blowing, or by blowing into a mould to produce the required shape. Window glass was made by casting in flat moulds or by blowing a cylindrical shape which was cut open and rolled out flat. Although there were other items made of glass, such as bangles and beads, the main production was of glass vessels, ranging from ones with a utilitarian domestic function to some exquisite masterpieces of art, as yet unsurpassed in technical quality and artistry.

Daily Tasks

The preparation of corn for flour was one of the most important trades, as bread was the staple item of the diet; at Pompeii actual carbonized loaves have been found. Heavy but portable rotary hand mills or querns were used, consisting of two stones with curved grinding surfaces between which the corn was ground. Corn could also be ground in larger types of rotary mills turned by slaves, or by blindfolded donkeys or horses.

Water power was used to a limited extent in the Roman world for pumping excess water out of mines and providing the power to watermills. At Barbegal in France, a large-scale 4th-century flour mill with 16 watermills arranged in a double row has been excavated. The waterwheels were over 7 ft (2 m) in diameter and the water power was provided by water from an aqueduct which descended down the waterwheels at an angle of 30°. It has been calculated that the mills could grind up to 8.8 tons (9 tonnes) of flour every 24 hours, enough to feed the inhabitants of the nearby town of Arles and surrounding district.

The concentration of watermills at Barbegal is unique in the Roman world and generally such large-scale industry and technical innovation were rare. This lack of development was probably due to the effects of slave labour and the plentiful supply of cheap labour in the cities. Roman society never fully developed an industrial economy in the modern sense, but pursued many industries on the level of crafts, which nevertheless reached technical and artistic heights.

Below Many fine vessels of glass were made in the Roman period. These three vessels (a cup with both handles broken off and bad irridescent weathering over all its surface, a long-necked flask, and a bowl with a wide flat rim and decorative handle) were all made in transparent colourless glass.

CHAPTER EIGHT

HIGHWAYS *and* BYWAYS

'All roads lead to Rome'

(ANONYMOUS, 14TH-CENTURY PROVERB)

Road Maps

The Romans were frequent travellers and undertook journeys both for military and business purposes, and for pleasure. The long-distance network of communications and transport across the vast Empire was unparalleled until modern times. To assist the traveller, numerous maps and itineraries seem to have been available, and copies of a few have survived. The *Peutinger Table* is a 13th-century copy of a late Roman map of the whole Roman Empire and beyond, from Britain to India, and survives virtually intact. It is a continuous elongated chart 22 ft (6.75 m) long and 13 in (34 cm) wide, and was a road map intended for the imperial courier service (*cursus publicus*). The map is actually a schematic diagram showing the main roads, towns, road stations, rivers, mountains and distances. In all, 555 cities are shown, each represented by small illustrations. The imperial courier service used the main roads which had official stations along them for a change of horse and an overnight halt. For the ordinary traveller there were staging posts or inns (mansiones) where the distance between two towns was too great to travel in one day.

The *Antonine Itinerary* was a 3rd-century compilation of routes all over the empire and included lists of the *mansiones* with the distances between them. Many of the roads and places have been identified. Another useful document to have survived is the *Ravenna Cosmography* which gives place-names, river names and landscape details. It was compiled by a monk in the Middle Ages from a series of much earlier documents. Roman literary accounts give some information on travel, and Diocletian's Edict on Prices, which included transport, has enabled direct comparisons of costs to be made between the Roman Empire, the Medieval period and the modern world.

Road Construction

There were roads in many places before the Romans, but these were largely local and long-distance trackways which followed the topography of the region. Roman roads were

Below Masonry road bridges of the Roman period survive throughout the Empire. This one at Vaison-la-Romaine in southern France is still used for road traffic. It was built of huge blocks of masonry held together without any mortar. Only the parapet has been replaced, having been washed away in floods in 1616. The bridge even survived a direct hit by a German bomb in 1944.

LEFT A Roman road with a paved surface running over the moor at Blackstone Edge in Greater Manchester. The central rut is thought to have been deliberately cut to hold the brake-poles of the carts.

deliberately planned and constructed, and the major routes were built initially by the army for strategic reasons. Other main roads were also constructed at State expense, although the cost of maintenance usually fell on the local community. From the main roads led a series of local roads which were financed by the local town councils, and there were also private roads across estates, built and maintained by the landowners. The number and total length of local roads must have far exceeded the major roads, although the major roads are the ones that usually survive today.

Roman roads are renowned for their straightness, but they often took detours rather than traverse difficult terrain. However, the engineers were quite capable of designing roads to cross ground such as marshland whenever necessary. The roads were laid out by surveyors and then constructed by digging down to a firm foundation which was reinforced by ramming brushwood or by driving in wooden piles. Layers of stones, sand and gravel were deposited on the foundation, and were sometimes built up as an embankment (known as an *agger*) to assist drainage, with side drainage ditches as well. The manner in which roads were constructed depended on the firmness of the subsoil and on the available materials. The final road surface often consisted of substantial paving stones held in place by a kerb on either side of the road, or otherwise crushed stones or gravel were used. Many roads display signs of subsequent repair and resurfacing.

Caravan roads in the desert have left little evidence on the ground apart from rows of small rocks and stones which were pushed to each side to make the routes easier for the pack animals. The routes can also be plotted from the existence of posting stations, wells and water tanks built by the Romans, some of which are still in use today.

Along the roads just outside the towns were the cemeteries, and funerary monuments lined the routes for all travellers to see. (It was illegal to bury the dead inside towns.) Inside old cities such as Rome, the street system was irregular, but in new towns it was carefully planned. The streets were often paved, as at Pompeii where stepping stones were provided for pedestrians. The ruts left by waggons in the streets and in the country roads indicate the great volume of traffic, although some ruts were deliberately cut to guide vehicles.

BRIDGES

Rivers could be crossed by fords, some of which were paved with stone, and ferries were also used. Many bridges were constructed of timber and were of varying complexity, some being built on piles with iron-clad tips. Timber bridges rarely survive, but they are shown in relief sculptures. Some bridges were built entirely of stone, and in the Mediterranean regions they could be constructed by erecting the piers directly on the river bed when it was dry in the summer. In temperate Europe, the piers had to be constructed with the aid of piles and timber scaffolding which was a more complex process. There were several masonry bridges in Rome, some of which survive today, while across the Empire there is evidence of many others. Some bridges were embellished by triumphal arches, and also had inscriptions and milestones.

MILESTONES

The Roman mile was a thousand Roman paces (1,611 yds or 1,472.5 m). Thus milestones were erected every thousand Roman paces, although in Gaul the league (2,430 yds/ 2221.2 m) was used as the unit of measurement. Milestones were typically cylindrical or oval-sectioned columns of stone, set on a square base, and were usually 5½–13 ft (2–4 m) in height and 20–30 in (50–80 cm) in diameter. Some had carved inscriptions giving the name of the builder or restorer of the road and distances to the nearest towns, while others had painted directions, long since worn away.

The famous 'golden milestone' was erected in Rome in 20 BC by Augustus, and consisted of a marble column to which were attached gilt-bronze plates displaying the distances from the major towns in the empire.

Over 4,000 milestones have been recorded with Latin inscriptions, and a similar number in Greek. Some milestones are still in place, but most have been re-used, sometimes as road ballast or as columns in churches. Apart from giving distances, the milestones also acted as boundary markers for farming estates and from the documentary evidence many continued to serve this purpose in the Medieval period.

ABOVE A four-wheeled carriage pulled by two horses, carved on a sarcophagus.

ROAD TRANSPORT

People travelled a great deal on foot, even for long distances, and the horse, mule and donkey were used as pack animals. Some people travelled on horseback, though, and various pieces of horse harness such as snaffle and curb-bits have been discovered in excavations. Iron horseshoes have been found, but not stirrups as these were not used.

Our knowledge of vehicles is fairly limited, mainly based on sculptures and literary evidence. Carts and chariots were well developed in the pre-Roman Celtic world, and many types of similar wheeled vehicles must have been used by the Romans. These probably ranged from large solid-wheeled carts pulled by oxen to light carriages pulled by horses. There is some evidence for the use of suspension in passenger vehicles, which may have made travelling more comfortable, but otherwise the most comfortable way to travel was probably in a litter carried by slaves.

The amount of traffic in towns was so great that in Julius Caesar's time the entry of wheeled vehicles into Rome was restricted, and these restrictions were later extended to other parts of the Empire. Wheeled vehicles were then only allowed through the city streets at night, an early example of the control of urban traffic congestion.

WATER TRANSPORT

Despite the fine roads, transport by road could still be very expensive, especially for bulky goods, and so water transport was most important. There were miles of navigable rivers, some of which had been improved by the construction of canals, and numerous flat-bottomed barges were used on them. Rafts and other boats of simple construction were also used, especially in places like Egypt, and pre-Roman techniques of boat building persisted.

In the early Republic there was hardly any tradition of seafaring, but this situation soon changed as it was quicker to travel long distances and more convenient to transport heavy goods by sea. Merchant ships became

Water Transport

ABOVE A reconstruction by Ronald Embleton of a water-front scene at the port of London at low tide. Small boats and clinker-built craft with hulls sheathed in lead are moored. Pedestrians and people on horseback are travelling across the wooden bridge over the River Thames.

RIGHT Native traditions of boat building persisted in many parts of the Roman world. This mosaic from Pompeii shows a scene from the River Nile with a native boat being used as a ferry.

LEFT This was one of two lighthouses which guarded the entrance to the harbour at Dover, England.

ABOVE Amphorae were large pottery vessels used for transporting commodities such as wine, olive oil and fish sauce.

so big that barges had to take goods from the ships up the River Tiber to Rome, leading to the growth of Ostia at the mouth of the river as a very important and busy port.

There is evidence for the appearance of ships in ancient literature and in representations in art (although quite often of a schematic nature and not accurate). This information is being supplemented by underwater excavations of Roman wrecks, and over 500 shipwrecks of this period are known in the Mediterranean. Wrecks of seafaring ships of the Roman period are virtually unknown outside the Mediterranean, although river craft have been found.

The most notable feature of Roman ships was a rigid outer shell built first, in contrast to later ships when the frame was constructed first. In the Mediterranean region, the planks of the shell were fitted edge-to-edge (carvel-built) and held in place by wooden pegs (tree-nails) or long copper nails, while north European ships were mainly constructed from overlapping planks secured by iron nails (clinker-built). The hulls of the Mediterranean ships were mostly of pine, cypress or cedar, with frames of oak; the lower part of the hull was often sheathed in lead as a defence against wood-boring sea worms. The north European ships were constructed mainly of oak.

When the shell of the ship was complete, the internal frames, strengthening timbers, decks and masts were added. There was a large mast amidships to carry a rectangular mainsail, and sometimes small masts near the stern and bow. Evidence has been found on the galley roof being covered in baked clay tiles. The ships were steered by long oars at the stern and several anchors were usually provided, particularly on the bigger ships. Anchors were of wood with lead fittings, but from the 2nd century they began to be replaced by anchors with iron fittings. Hundreds of lead stocks up to a ton in weight have been found in the Mediterranean.

CARGOES

In excavations of shipwrecks, many objects of everyday use have been found, including tableware, quernstones, and terracotta oil lamps. Most Roman merchant ships were small, carrying on average 150 tons (152.5 tonnes), but loads up to 300 tons (304.7 tonnes) could be transported. Cargoes were usually mixed, but a major commodity was wine carried in large amphorae. They were also used to carry other goods such as grain, olive oil and fish sauce (*garum*). Many amphorae have stamps on their handles, usually of the manufacturer or place of origin, especially if they contained wine, and some and some have traces of painted inscriptions giving details of the shippers, contents and date. Another clue to the date of the cargo is the style of the amphora itself which changed throughout the Roman period.

Some of the shipwrecks in the Mediterranean could carry at least 5,000 amphorae at a time. They were stacked in layers with the points of the upper layers of amphorae fitted between the necks of those below. The extensive sea trade is vividly represented by the Monte Testaccio in Rome, close to the River Tiber. It is an immense dump of amphorae fragments which is 115 ft (42 m) high and 930 yds (1,017 m) round.

HARBOURS

It was possible for small vessels to unload their cargoes on beaches but larger ships required harbours for docking and shelter from the weather. The remains of Roman harbours with monumental quays and docking areas survive all around the Mediterranean, and these involved engineering and construction work on a large scale. There were also riverside wharves in places like Rome and London, with timber-revetted waterfronts and huge warehouses. Lighthouses were an important addition to harbour entrances, and by 400 over 30 lighthouses are known to have existed in the Roman world.

CHAPTER NINE

RITUAL *and* RELIGION

"And how can man die better,
Than facing fearful odds,
For the ashes of his fathers,
And the temples of his Gods."

(LORD MACAULAY *HORATIUS*, VERSE 27)

GODS AND SOCIETY

Religion was an essential part of Roman society, and nearly every activity was governed by deities, some of which were gods and others merely vaguely defined spirits. Roman religion had many different gods, and during the Republic more gods were assimilated from the Etruscans, and later from the Greeks. Rather than simply adopt new gods, their functions were identified and combined with those of the existing Roman gods.

The main Olympian gods (so-called because they were identified with the Greek gods who lived on Mount Olympus in Greece) were Jupiter, Juno and Minerva. The Greek god Zeus was compared with the Roman god Jupiter, and became father and king of the gods, also responsible for the weather, especially storms. Juno, who became his wife and queen of the gods, was the goddess of marriage and women, and was identified with the Greek goddess Hera. Minerva (equivalent to the Greek goddess Athena) was the goddess of war and of wisdom. These three deities were often called the Capitoline triad because of shrines dedicated to them on the Capitoline Hill at Rome.

Other major Olympian deities included Mars (god of war), Mercury (god of trade and messenger of the gods) and Bacchus (god of grapes and wine production). The Greek-style gods soon became part of Rome's religious tradition, and because they were already well-developed mythological figures, it was easy to portray them in art and literature. The Romans continued to import deities, sometimes deliberately as happened in 293 BC when Aesculapius, the Greek god of medicine, was adopted because of a plague at Rome.

The Romans had a vast number of minor deities, and nearly every aspect of life had its own spirit, including personified virtues such as victory and fortune. People only worshipped those deities and spirits most closely associated with their own lives. There were spirits in the fields and woods, and each tree or stream acquired its own spirit, such as the spirit of the River Tiber. There were also spirits in the home, including Vesta who was the goddess of the hearth fire and the Penates, the spirits of the cupboard or pantry. Each household had its own Lar, a spirit or deity which guarded and protected the household and its members, and it was the responsibility of the household to maintain a shrine (*larium*) in the home, at which sacrifices were made regularly. The cautious attitude of the Romans to such spirits is exemplified by dedications of altars to the 'gods that inhabit this place', ensuring that no god could be offended by being overlooked, even if they remained unnamed.

ABOVE One of the Olympian deities was Diana, the goddess of fertility and of the hunt, who was always portrayed with arrows.

In the eastern Mediterranean, people had worshipped their kings as gods for centuries. When conquered by the Romans, they regarded their new rulers as divine figures, but this was discouraged. Instead, they were encouraged to worship 'Roma', the divine spirit of Rome, but when Julius Caesar died, he was made a god, and from then onwards it was normal practice for emperors to be deified and worshipped after their deaths (unless their memory was damned, *damnatio*

ABOVE This Classical temple at Vienne in France was originally dedicated to the imperial cult – 'Roma' and the deified Augustus – but it was later rededicated to Augustus and his wife Livia. It is one of the Empire's best-preserved temples.

ABOVE RIGHT A relief sculpture on a funerary monument depicting the construction of a Classical-style temple. A crane is being powered by slaves on a treadmill.

memoriae). The Imperial Cult and the associated worship of 'Roma' became an important element in Roman religion.

STATE OBSERVANCE

The purpose of Roman religion was to gain the goodwill of the divine forces and to keep them benevolent, since that would ensure individual and collective success and prosperity. Early Roman religion developed as part of the rituals of farming when it was essential that the rituals were performed correctly to maintain good relationships with the spirits. Roman religion was not concerned with ethical and moral behaviour, but only with the correct observance of the rituals, which in time became static and mechanical.

The State religion involved the worship of 'Roma', the Imperial Cult and the accepted classical deities, and was very much a public rather than a private religion, with the ceremonies and rituals being performed correctly to ensure the goodwill of the gods – the *pax deorum*. Temples and religious festivities received State funding, and the priests were State officials, for whom being a priest was a mark of social distinction. The emperor was the Pontifex Maximus, the head of the State religion.

The Romans communicated with the gods by sacrifice, prayer, vow and divination. There were fixed days for festivals when they could review their relationships with the various deities, and when prayers and sacrifices usually took place outside the temple of the deity. Especially at State-funded sacrifices, the main victims were cattle, sheep, goats and pigs.

On some occasions the support of the god was invoked by means of a vow rather than a prayer or sacrifice, when a gift (votive offering) was promised to the god only if the supplicant's wishes were fulfilled. In order to interpret signs sent by the gods, divination was practised, and this included inspecting the internal organs of a sacrificial animal.

TEMPLES

The style of Roman temples was much influenced by Greek architecture. Many were rectangular in shape, with an elevated podium and a portico or deep-set porch, approached by a flight of steep steps. The side and end columns could be 'engaged', that is, built into the side walls so that only part of their circumference protruded beyond the walls. During the empire, most of the columns were in the Corinthian style with ornately carved capitals.

Apart from the traditional classical design, temples were built to a variety of plans and sizes, including circular and triangular examples, culminating in the Pantheon at Rome which had a huge dome open to the sky at the very top. There were also native-style temples such as the Romano-Celtic temples in northern Europe. These were square or polygonal and surrounded by a portico consisting either of an open colonnade or a solid wall with windows. In addition, there were

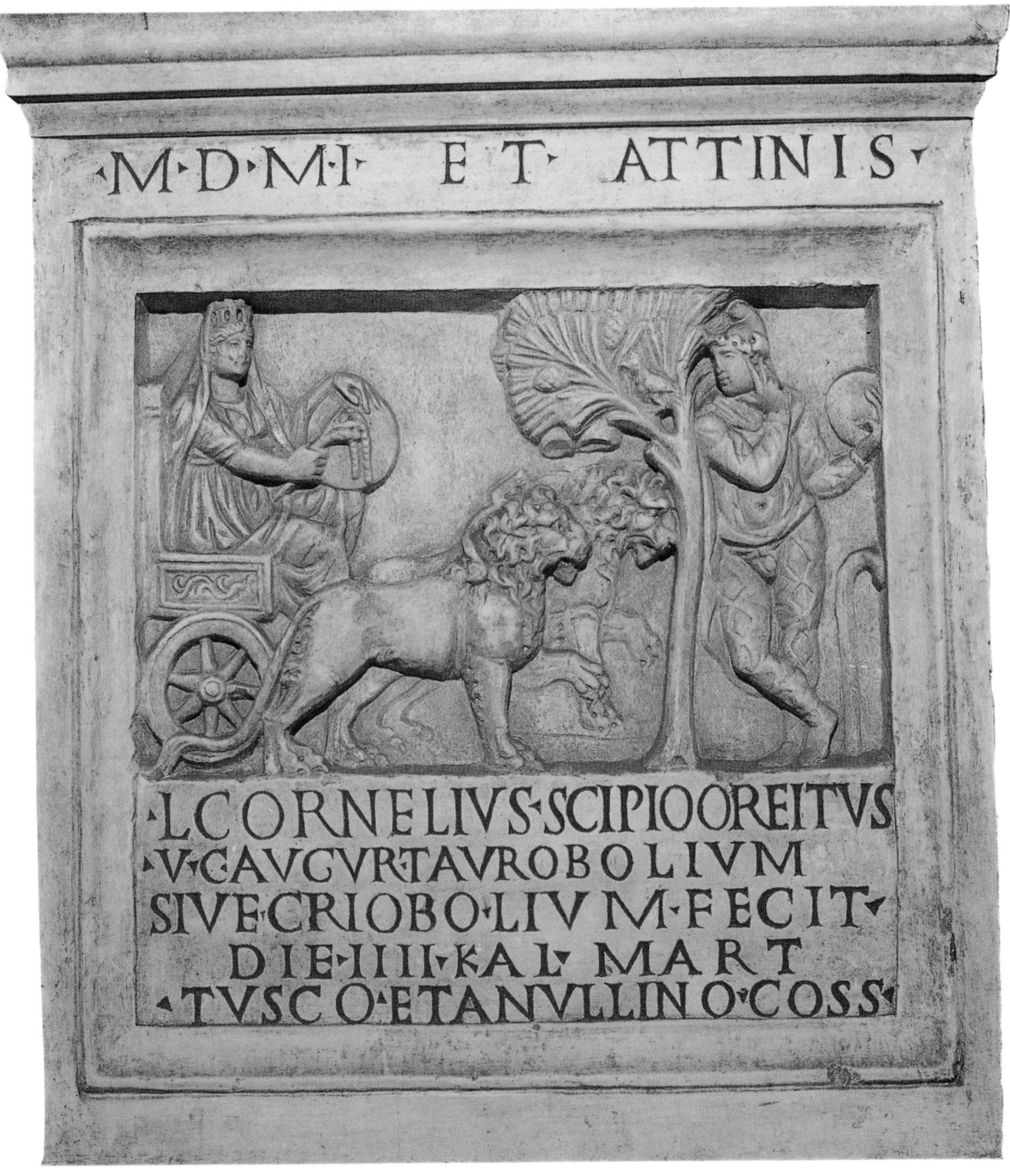

ABOVE An altar to the eastern goddess Cybele. Nearby stands her consort, the god Attis. The inscription refers to taurobolium, *a ceremony performed by several eastern cults but which originated with Cybele. The worshipper stood in a pit and was bathed in the blood of a bull sacrificed over him or her.*

many simple shrines and temples throughout the Roman world.

The main purpose of a temple was to house the cult figures and to provide an inner sanctum for the priests. The worshippers assembled outside the temple where there was usually a courtyard and the main sacrificial altar. All the public religious ceremonies took place in this area, and the courtyards were frequently surrounded by colonnades as protection against unfavourable weather.

Religious Tolerance

The Roman authorities were fairly tolerant of the religious practices of the people they conquered, although they suppressed religions that were considered to be against the State, such as the Druids in northern Gaul and Britain and also Judaism and Christianity. The Romans did their best not to offend any deity, even those of their enemies, and so instead of driving out the gods of newly conquered territory, there was often a fusion be-

ABOVE Priests performing religious rites outside a temple dedicated to the eastern goddess Isis. Most religious ceremonies took place in a courtyard outside temples. This ceremony was depicted in a wall-painting at Herculaneum.

tween local and classical gods, and the local gods continued to be worshipped as well. This can be seen at Bath in England, for example, where a Classical-style temple was dedicated to Sulis Minerva. The name Sulis is that of a local Celtic nymph who was linked with the Roman goddess Minerva.

THE MYSTERY RELIGIONS

By the late Republic, Romans became acquainted with many eastern religions from places such as Asia Minor, Egypt and beyond. These religions were very different from the Roman State religion and are often called 'mystery' religions because they involved new converts in mysterious initiation ceremonies. They offered personal salvation to individuals and appealed to all social classes and races. Most Romans did not renounce the State religion once they had been initiated into a new eastern religion, as no conflict was perceived between the two – eastern religions were private and personal while the State religion remained public and impersonal.

The main eastern cults were those of Mithras, Cybele, Isis and Bacchus. The cult of Cybele, 'The Great Mother', was the only one that was deliberately introduced into

MITHRAISM

ABOVE The god Mithras is slaying a bull from whose blood life grows. Mithraism was a popular eastern religion, particularly with the army and merchants as it was an exclusively male cult. The slaying of the bull took place in a cave, and so Mithraic temples were often built underground.

FAR RIGHT A marble head of the god Serapis, Egyptian god of the underworld. The corn measure on his head is a symbol of fertility, which Serapis represented, and is adorned by an olive tree with leaves and berries. It was buried with a group of other sculptures under the Mithraeum in London in the 4th century, possibly to prevent desecration by the Christians. It was found in 1954 and is 17 in (431 mm) high.

Rome. This happened in 205 BC in response to an oracle which required Rome to welcome the goddess if Hannibal was to be defeated.

The best-known eastern cult was that of Mithras which originated in Persia and spread across the whole Roman Empire. Mithras was a god of light, engaged in a constant struggle with Ariman, the evil prince of darkness. Mithras was often portrayed slaying a bull, symbolic of his role as a creative god, with the blood of the bull being the source of life. Mithraism was an exclusively male cult, and was especially popular in the army and with merchants.

The cult of Isis originated in ancient Egypt and reached Rome in the 1st century BC. It flourished despite being suppressed by Octavian because it was the religion of his enemy Cleopatra. Isis was a mother goddess figure and wife of the Egyptian god Serapis.

Bacchus was originally one of the Olympian gods (identified with the Greek god Dionysus), but the Bacchanalia (the often drunken celebrations in honour of the god of wine) were restricted in 186 BC by the Senate, as it was thought that the religion was becoming politically subversive. However, the religion was not totally suppressed and emerged again as one of the mystery religions, and Bacchus was even believed by many Romans to have originated from India and not to be one of the Olympian gods (where Dionysus was the twelfth of the gods of Mount Olympus).

CHRISTIANITY

The Roman world was initially tolerant of the new eastern religion of Christianity, and it became well established in Rome by the mid 1st century. However, the rites came to be misunderstood and Christians were regarded as atheists because, unlike other eastern religions, converts were expected to

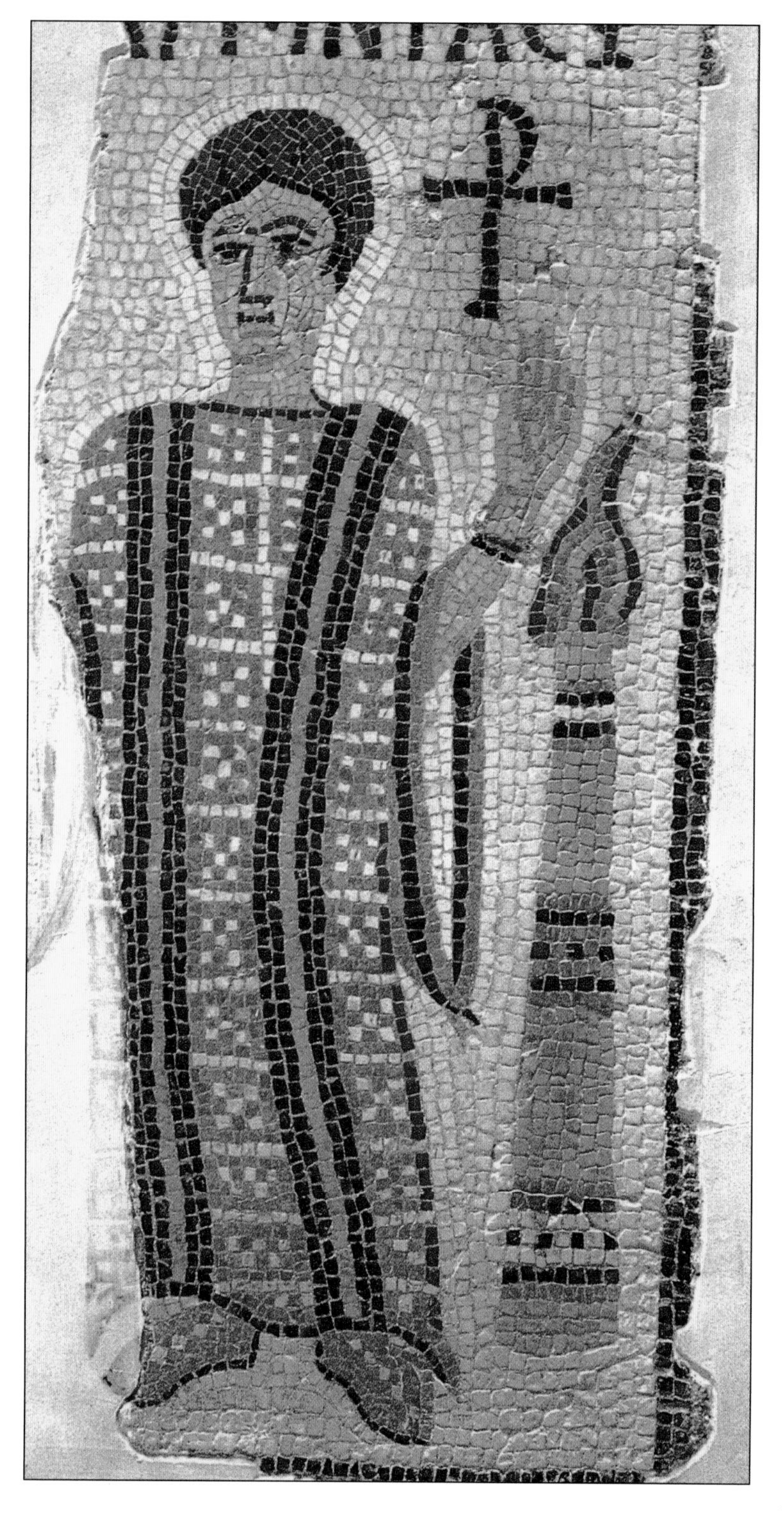

ABOVE An early Christian funerary mosaic of the 4th-5th centuries from Tunisia. The symbol is a Chi-Rho *– the first two letters of the Greek word for Christ.*

renounce all other beliefs. To the Romans this was a crime against the State, and so Christians began to be persecuted for political rather than for religious reasons. The most systematic persecutions took place from the mid to late 3rd century, but in the early 4th century the emperor Constantine was converted to Christianity. He consequently allowed Christians freedom of worship and they were no longer required to participate in the rites of the State religion.

Although Christianity began as a religion for the poorer classes, it acquired more and more wealth, and the conversion of the Roman world to this new religion was fairly rapid and extensive. At the end of the 4th century, Theodosius I abolished pagan sacrifice, closed all pagan temples (some of which were destroyed) and confiscated their estates, although the traditional games and festivals continued. Christianity became the official State religion, and followers suppressed the religious freedom of other groups and even persecuted non-Christians. The early Christian Church was from time to time rent by schisms, which caused serious political rifts, but the religion even managed to survive the Barbarian invasions.

Pagan traditions persisted as they were so deeply rooted in Roman society. It was not possible to abolish popular pagan holidays and so, instead, they were combined with Christian festivals. A popular festival in the Roman world was the Lupercalia, on 15 February, which was associated with farming and fertility. In 494 Pope Gelasius I declared that date to be the festival of the Purification of the Virgin Mary, so ensuring its success, and the eve of the festival of the Lupercalia has now become St Valentine's Day. Similarly the Saturnalia was one of the most popular festivals of the whole year, celebrated at the winter solstice. It originally took place for one day on 17 December, but by the late Republic it had extended to several days. This particular festival was not marked by public games, but was a time for family dinners, parties, gift giving, wishing friends and neighbours well, and when masters waited on their slaves. Its place was consequently taken over by Christmas in the Christian calendar, and yet the character of the celebrations has survived to the present day and these elements of ancient paganism have spread around the world.

BURIAL OF THE DEAD

The laws relating to the burial of the dead forbade interment of bodies or their cremated ashes within the boundary of a town or fort, except for children under ten days old (who had no legal existence). Cemeteries are therefore usually found lining the main roads just outside towns, and funerary monuments

LEFT The 6th-century Byzantine basilica at Porec in Yugoslavia with fine Christian wall mosaics.

BELOW A 5th-century mosaic representing an early Christian basilica with two naves and an aisle.

were erected so they could be seen from the roads. The cemetery of Alyscamps at Arles in France was just outside the Roman town on the road to Italy. It was one of the most famous sacred sites of the Roman West, and became a Christian burial ground with thousands of graves growing up around the tomb of St Geneseus.

Most Romans had fairly simple funerals but those of upper-class families could be very elaborate. It was thought that the souls went to the underworld (Hades) after death, rather than to heaven or hell. Sometimes a coin was placed in the mouth of the corpse as the fee to Charon, the ferryman of the river Styx, who carried the person to Hades. The coin was placed in the mouth as both hands would have held cakes for the three heads of the dog Cerberus, guardian of the underworld. Those souls whom the gods of the underworld would not admit were destined to wander for eternity. Consequently, it was thought that a proper burial was essential, and so many Romans belonged to funeral clubs to ensure that this was carried out.

Ashes from cremations were usually placed in containers of pottery, glass or lead which were buried. The position of the burial could be marked by an upright tombstone with a carved inscription about the dead person, and possibly a pictorial representation taken from the person's life or funerary banquet. Some cremations were placed in masonry mausolea (*columbaria*) and a few were covered by mounds of earth.

Inhumations became more popular in the later Empire and usually involved the burial of the dead in a coffin, although for the poor a sack or shroud would have been used. Coffins were of wood, lead or stone, and some bodies were partially embalmed by pouring liquid plaster of Paris around the body. Some stone coffins were extremely ornate and intended for display rather than for burial in the ground.

Grave goods were placed in cremation and inhumation burials, and often included refreshments for the journey to the underworld, shoes for travelling there, and the person's most valued possessions. Some of the coffins and mausolea were robbed in the Roman period, and as the rise of Christianity led to a decline in the use of grave goods, most Roman burials that are excavated are found to have only a few simple grave goods.

FAR LEFT An ivory diptych of the late 4th century portraying a priestess making offerings at a pagan altar. The diptych is headed "SYMMACHORUM" and there is a companion "NICOMACHORUM". Quintus Aurelius Symmachus and Nicomachus Flavianus attempted to revive pagan cults in Rome when Christianity was taking over.

LEFT Pottery vessels were sometimes decorated by schematic faces. These face pots were used as storage jars and for cooking. Some have been found buried as ritual deposits in graves, and others were used to contain cremations. It is possible that the faces were intended to resemble a particular deity.

RIGHT Les Alyscamps ('Elysian Fields') was an immense cemetery just outside Arles on the road to Italy. From the 4th century it became a Christian cemetery and expanded considerably throughout the Middle Ages. Nowadays only the plain sarcophagii have been left in place. The cemetery began to decline in the 15th century and the finest ornate sarcophagi were taken to museums, or given as gifts, and many have been lost. One consignment being loaded in a boat on the River Rhone was so heavy that the boat sank.

CHAPTER TEN

RETREAT *and* RECESSION

'While stands the Coliseum, Rome shall stand; when falls the Coliseum, Rome shall fall; and when Rome falls – the World'

(LORD BYRON, *CHILDE HAROLD'S PILGRIMAGE*, CANTO IV, CXIV)

Economic Crisis

During the first two centuries of the Roman Empire, the provinces became increasingly wealthy, but then the economy of the Empire weakened due to a variety of reasons including a rigid financial policy, the scarcity of slaves and other workers for the agricultural estates, the lack of profitable new territory to annex and exploit, increased taxation, and the immense cost of maintaining the extensive frontiers with a huge army. Matters were made worse when armies returning from the east in 166 introduced plague into the Western Empire, seriously affecting the population.

The Roman coinage was gradually debased, and instead of gold and silver coins being worth the weight of their metal content, they were replaced by a base metal token coinage. A severe shortage of precious metals in the later 3rd century forced the government to issue silver-washed bronze coins. This situation led to progressively higher prices, coins were hoarded and the economic crisis worsened. There was reduced economic activity, new public buildings became much less common, and the cities themselves were neglected. In the first half of the 4th century there was an improvement in the economy, due partly to monetary and taxation reform, but inflation was not brought to a halt.

Left The head from a giant bronze statue of Constantine I.

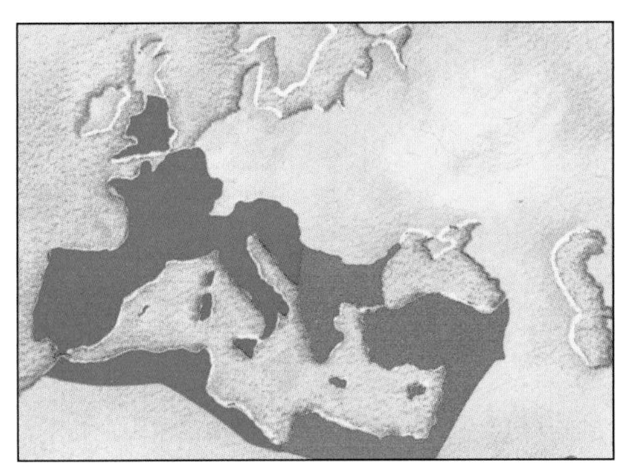

Left The division of the Roman world into eastern and western empires.

House Of Constantine

Constantine I, the Great, reunited the empire in 324 and reigned as sole Augustus until his death in 337. He was converted to Christianity, which gradually became a unifying force in the Empire. The division in the Empire between east and west still persisted in that two of his sons, Constantius II and Constantine II, served as Caesars. After his death, the Empire was again split between two Augustii; his sons Constantine II and Constans initially ruled the west and Constantius II the east, but Constantine II was eliminated after three years. In 350 Constans fell to a military usurper, Magnentius, but in an ensuing civil war, Constantius II defeated him and so was left in charge of the entire Empire.

Far Left Constans was Emperor of the Western Empire after the death of his father Constantine I in 337, but fell to the usurper Magnentius in 350.

Constantine I made Constantinople (now Istanbul) his new capital and the city continued to grow rapidly in splendour and size. In 359 Constantius II gave the city a senate, thereby awarding it constitutional parity with Rome. Meanwhile, the city of Rome was also emerging as an important centre of Christian culture and from the time of Constantine I was embellished by many religious buildings.

In 355 Constantius II appointed his nephew Julian as Caesar in Gaul, mainly to suppress the invading Germanic tribes (Alamanni and

.F L.
INTALL.
COMORD.
.PR.
othona.
Dubris.
Lemannis.
Branoduno
Garianno.
Regulbi.
Rutupis.
Anderidos.
Portu Adurni.

LEFT A page from the Notitia Dignitatum *compiled around 400 to show the various military commands and units in the western Empire. This is a schematic map of Britain showing Saxon shore forts from Brancaster in Norfolk to Portchester in Hampshire.*

Franks) who had crossed the Rhine. Two years later Julian succeeded in forcing them back across the Rhine and in 361 he rebelled against Constantius II, but the latter died of natural causes before a conflict broke out. Julian was killed two years later during a campaign against Persia, bringing the dynasty of Constantine to an end.

BARBARIAN INVASIONS

On his death, Julian's successor was Jovian, who was proclaimed by the army in Mesopotamia, but he died a few months later. Valentinian I (364–375) was then brought to power by the army as emperor of the Western Empire, while his brother Valens was chosen to rule the Eastern Empire. In 367 there was a major Barbarian invasion of Britain, but this was suppressed within two years by Valentinian's general Count Theodosius, who restored and reinforced the line of forts along Britain's northern frontier and along the coast. The reign of Valentinian I was also devoted to improving the defence of the frontiers of the Rhine and Danube.

When Valentinian I died of apoplexy in 375 he was succeeded in the west by his sons Gratian and Valentinian II, both of whom were controlled by advisers, while Valens remained emperor in the east. At this time there were large-scale movements of Germanic peoples (Barbarians to the Romans), such as the Visigoths, Ostrogoths, Alans, Alemanni, Franks, Burgundians, Vandals, and Suebi. The Huns pushed forward from even further afield, and in turn caused hundreds of thousands of dispossessed Goths (Ostrogoths and Visigoths) and Alans to flee southwards to the Danube. Valens gave permission for thousands of Visigoths to cross into the empire in 376 in order to strengthen his frontier zone and to provide new recruits for the army. However, the settlement was totally mismanaged by the Romans, and in the resulting chaos the Ostrogoths joined the Visigoths. Valens therefore marched against the Goths in 378, but on 9 August the Roman army was defeated at the Battle of Adrianople (now Edirne in European Turkey), and Valens was killed.

RIGHT Valentinian I (364–375) spent much of his reign consolidating the defences of the frontiers which had been weakened by various incursions, particularly along the Rhine and Danube.

LEFT Pevensey fort was shown in the Notitia Dignitatum *as Anderidos. The fort was positioned on the coast as a defence against Germanic invasion.*

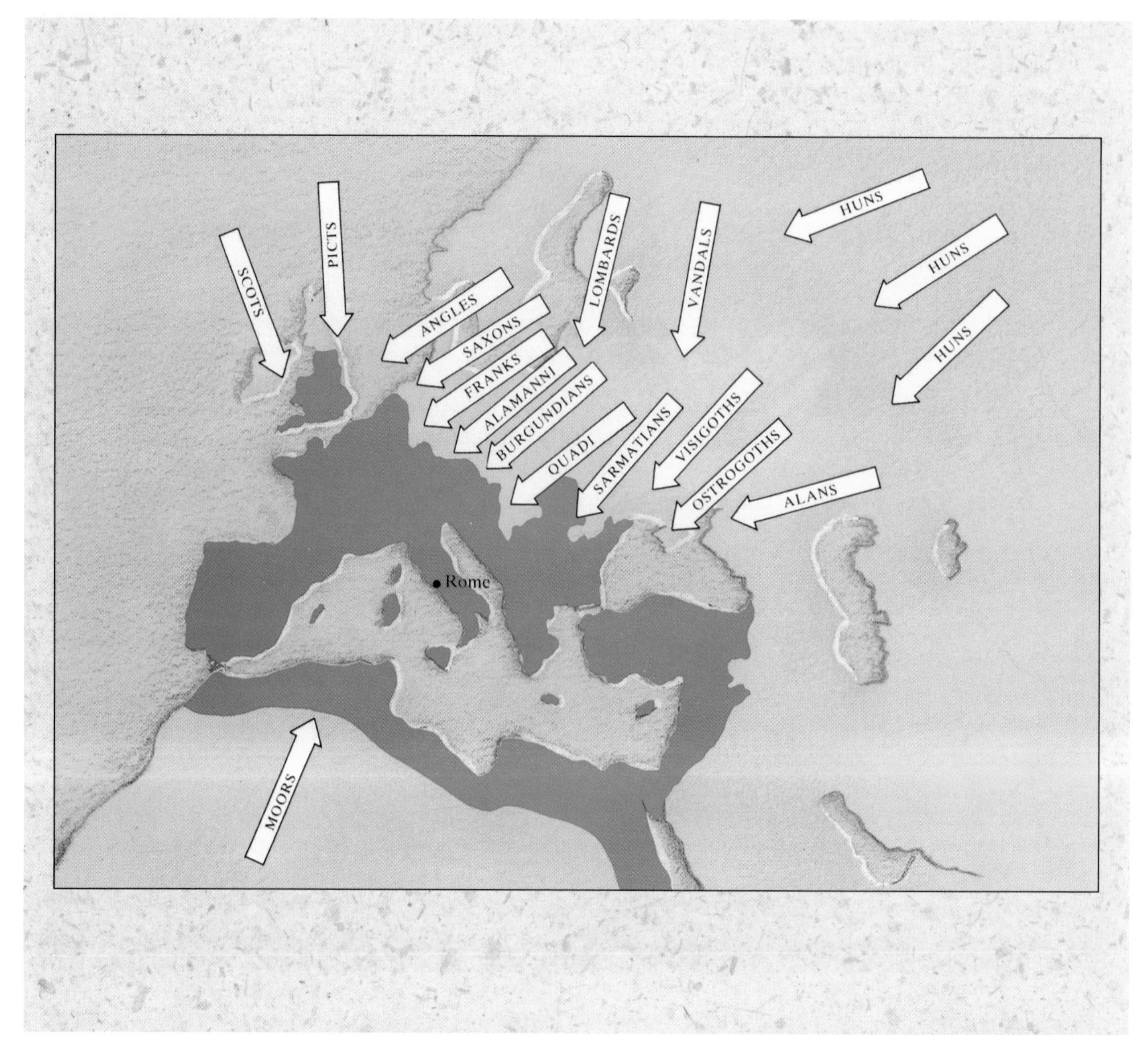

ABOVE The movement of invading tribes into the Roman Empire.

Gratian immediately appointed Theodosius (a Spanish general and the son of Valentinian's former general) to take charge in the East. Theodosius I (379–395) gradually restored order and the Ostrogoths were forced back beyond the frontier. The Visigoths were allowed to settle in the Danube provinces and to serve in the Roman army as *federates* under their own tribal leaders.

In 383 Gratian was murdered at Lyon in an army revolt led by the British usurper Magnus Maximus, who set up his court at Trier. Four years later, after he had campaigned in Gaul and Spain and restored order there, Maximus invaded Italy and deposed Valentinian II. The following year he was defeated and killed by Theodosius I, and Valentinian II was restored to power, but was found dead in 392 (possibly as a result of suicide). Theodosius I therefore took over the rule of the entire Empire. The Visigoths had helped Theodosius in his campaign against the usurper Maximus, but they then refused to return home, and wandered through Macedonia pillaging the province.

When Theodosius I died in 395, he was succeeded by his sons, 18-year-old Arcadius in the east and ten-year-old Honorius in the west. The latter was dominated by the commander Stilicho who remained in virtual control of the west for the next 13 years. Stilicho was the son of a Vandal leader who had joined the Romans and become commander-in-chief under Theodosius.

In the same year the Visigoths, under their newly elected leader Alaric, invaded Greece, and then in 401 made their way to Italy in search of new homelands, and besieged Milan. While the Western Empire began to disintegrate, the eastern empire prospered, enabling the Byzantine Empire to develop its own rich culture. In 402 Stilicho managed to beat back the Visigoths with the aid of the Alans and Vandals, who he then allowed to cross from the province of Pannonia into Noricum in return for their services.

Stilicho subsequently arranged to make use of Alaric and the Visigoths to secure control of Illyricum (modern-day Yugoslavia and Albania) over whose territory he was in dispute with Constantinople. However, he was prevented from doing this by major Barbarian invasions in Gaul and a usurpation in Britain. Alaric nevertheless demanded payment for his unused services, but this was refused, and so he invaded Italy again in 408. Stilicho was executed on the emperor's orders for alleged complicity with Alaric, and in the same year the emperor Arcadius died and was succeeded by his son Theodosius II. Alaric went on to besiege Rome, which he captured and sacked in 410.

St Jerome wrote from Bethlehem: 'When the brightest light of the whole earth was extinguished, when the Roman Empire was deprived of its head, when the whole world perished in one city, then I was dumb with silence, I held my peace even from God, and my sorrow was stirred'.

LEFT Arcadius (395–408) was Emperor of the eastern Empire, succeeding his father Theodosius I. His brother Honorius became Emperor of the western Empire.

THE COLLAPSE OF THE WESTERN EMPIRE

The fall of Rome had relatively little military significance, since the emperor and government had moved to the safety of Ravenna in northern Italy, in 402, following the siege of Milan. Ravenna became the capital city and a major centre of Christian culture for more than three centuries. The Visigoths continued moving southwards into Italy intending to proceed to Africa, but Alaric died and instead they returned northwards. In Rome there was an economic recovery, with a literary and cultural revival, and the 5th century became a time of building great monumental churches in the city.

In 412 the Visigoths seized part of south-western Gaul, but they were then forced into Spain. Eventually, in 418, they reached agreement with the Roman government to settle in Aquitaine, and from time to time they fought as *federates* on the side of Rome against other invaders.

Far worse than the sack of Rome by Alaric was the winter of 406–7, when the Rhine frontier was overrun. Hordes of Germanic peoples, mainly Vandals, Suebi, Burgundians and Alans crossed the frozen Rhine and captured cities in Gaul. There was consternation in Britain, and so the usurper Constantine III crossed from Britain to Gaul in 407 to deal with the worsening military situation. He established his court at Arles, and created a new Gallic empire, restoring order in Britain, Gaul, Germany and Spain. In the winter of 409, the Vandals, Suebi and Alans forced their way across the Pyrenees to Spain, and Constantine III's temporary Empire fell apart. Britain was never recovered, and the year 410 is usually regarded as the end of Roman Britain. Roman civilization tended to die out in northern Gaul and Germany from this time, and in the following year Constantine III was defeated by the imperial army from Ravenna and executed.

The Vandals subsequently joined forces with the Alans, whose king assumed the title '*Rex Vandalorum et Alanorum*'. In 429, led by Gaiseric, they crossed the Straits of Gibraltar into Africa. Much of North Africa then fell to the Vandals, and by 439 they had marched eastwards and taken Carthage.

In a brief period of some fifty years from 375 when the Visigoths first appeared on the Danube, the great migratory movements of the various tribes caused the disintegration of the Western Empire. The emperor Honorius, who died in 423, was succeeded by the usurper Johannes for two years, and then four-year-old Valentinian III (425–455) was installed. For a while the general Flavius Aëtius maintained Roman rule in Gaul and undertook several successful campaigns in the

ABOVE From the 6th century, after the Byzantine reconquest of Italy, Rome and other towns were neglected. Monuments and buildings disintegrated and became at least partly buried by a build-up of dirt and debris. This 18th-century etching by GB Piranesi shows the appearance of the ruins of the forum at Rome at that time.

430s and 440s. Meanwhile the Huns, under Attila, were building up strength but were defeated in 451 by a combined force of Romans, Visigoths, Franks and Burgundians near Châlon-sur-Marne. Attila retreated from Gaul and began to plunder Italy, but was persuaded to withdraw. When he died in 453, the Empire of the Huns fell apart. Aëtius was assassinated the following year at the instigation of Valentinian III, who was himself assassinated in 455. This marked the end of the dynasty of Theodosius and was followed by several short-lived emperors.

By this time, the Visigoths had penetrated into Spain, annexing most of the peninsula. The Vandals under Gaiseric advanced from Africa and in 455 spent a fortnight sacking Rome. They then left Italy, acquiring Sicily on the way. By 475 little of the Western Empire remained, although emperors of a kind continued to be nominated. Romulus Augustulus was deposed in 476, and is regarded as the last Roman emperor in the west. Rome as a state had ceased to exist 1,200 years after its legendary foundation.

From 476 Italy was controlled by Germanic kings with their court at Ravenna. The first king was Odoacer, who had been elected by his German troops. The new rulers did much to sustain the Roman way of life and its traditions, and even restored some of the public monuments. In 489 Theoderic, King of the Ostrogoths in the Balkans, was asked to recover Italy for the Eastern Empire, but instead he defeated and killed Odoacer and had himself proclaimed king, ruling from 493 to 526.

The Rise Of The East

While the west was torn apart, the Eastern Empire, usually called the Byzantine Empire, remained largely unscathed and relatively free of invasion. Under the long and stable reign of Theodosius II (who replaced the emperor Arcadius in 408), the city of Constantinople continued to grow. Many churches were constructed in this 'Rome of the East', and a colossal system of defences was built after the West had fallen. The death of Theodosius II in 450 marked the end of the dynasty of Theodosius in the east, to be replaced by a succession of military emperors. Justinian

LES ANTIQUES

LEFT The monumental arch at Glanum in southern France has survived exceptionally well as the site became virtually deserted.

then ascended the throne in 527, and in the 38 years of his reign Constantinople was transformed and the Eastern Empire rose to a powerful position. In 532 serious riots in Constantinople caused large parts of the city to be burnt, and so a phase of imposing reconstruction and building was undertaken. The most important aspect of Justinian's reign, though, was the reorganization and codification of Roman law.

The previous emperor, Justin, had tried to encourage the estranged Churches of the west to move closer to those of the east. This policy was continued by his nephew Justinian, which caused much hostility. From 533, Justinian proceeded to win back the Western Empire, including Italy, Africa and parts of Spain. Starting in Africa, his general Belisarius extended the reconquest to Italy two years later. This campaign lasted until 554 and was accompanied by much destruction and violence.

Up to that point, senatorial life had continued at Rome, and Rome and Italy had continued to flourish under the Germanic kings. However, after the Byzantine reconquest, the senatorial class disappeared, with many senators being forced to flee to Constantinople. As a result Ravenna became the seat of the new Byzantine government, while the rest of Italy, including Rome, was neglected and became impoverished. It is the demise and neglect of Rome that marks the end of the Classical world.

Justinian died in 565, but the Byzantine Empire survived for another 900 years until conquered by the Ottoman Turks in 1453. In 568 Italy was invaded by the Lombards, a west Germanic people previously settled in Pannonia (modern Hungary). Rome and Ravenna remained as Byzantine enclaves while the Lombards took over a large part of Italy, but Ravenna finally fell to the Lombards in 751 and slipped into obscurity. In the 7th and 8th centuries, much of the Eastern Empire, North Africa and parts of the Western Empire fell to invading Moors. In Constantinople, though, the walls of Theodosius II protected the city until 13 April, 1204 when armies of the Fourth Crusade broke through and devastated the magnificent city – in the name of Christianity.

ABOVE Throughout history, stone from Hadrian's Wall was re-used as building stone. Evidence of the wall and the forts can be seen incorporated into many of the buildings and castles in the area.

SURVIVAL AND LEGACY

The survival of Roman buildings and structures such as aqueducts, of movable objects such as statues, sarcophagi and jewellery, varies across the Empire. Due to a scarcity of documentary and archaeological evidence, the history of this survival through the Middle Ages to the present day is often little known. This was not helped by those excavators who removed all medieval and later layers in order to reach was what underneath.

The Romans themselves destroyed much of their own work during the process of rebuilding over the centuries. Building stone and sculptures were frequently re-used; architectural fragments are often found built into city walls, and the relief sculptures on the Arch of Constantine in Rome, for example, were taken from a previous gateway or arch. On the other hand, the Romans also restored monuments which were of special significance to them.

During the 4th and 5th centuries, town and countryside were in a state of decline and abandonment in the Western Empire. Many public buildings had already fallen into decay and disuse before the Germanic invasions, although invasion did not necessarily mean wholesale destruction. In many towns, classical buildings continued to be used and repaired, but because of a decreasing population much of the countryside was depopulated, and towns shrank in size, or were even abandoned.

In the Middle Ages many people were surrounded by reminders of their Classical past, especially by buildings and structures. Even in the Saxon period there was an awareness of the ancient civilization that had been lost, as is seen in the Anglo-Saxon poem *The Ruin* which probably describes the ruins of the Roman town of Bath. Much was still visible even up to the 18th century; it is only the present century which has destroyed Roman remains at an accelerating rate, often without record, and mainly by urban expansion and deep ploughing.

In places which were abandoned and well away from habitation, or where trading routes changed, whole Roman towns could be preserved, some in better condition than others, often depending on the climate. Les Antiques – a mausoleum and an archway – have survived virtually intact on the old Italy-to-Spain route at the town of Glanum (near St Rémy-de-Provence) in France. Other abandoned remains have decayed to such an extent that they are now mainly covered by fields, as is the case with the towns of Silchester and Wroxeter in England. Outside Europe, sculpture and architecture often survived virtually intact for centuries because population pressures tended to be much less.

Deserted sites were often used as quarries for building stone, which can then be identified in the buildings of the surrounding countryside. Some Roman towns were later reoccupied, but with a different street alignment, in ignorance of the previous grid plan. In those towns which continued to be occupied, buildings and monuments were robbed of their building materials with little regard for what was being destroyed. A number of Roman buildings do, however, survive intact, and at Arles in France the theatre and amphitheatre are still used today for performances. Some pagan games continued into the Christian era, and so amphitheatres tended to survive up to the 6th century. Theatres and amphitheatres were often incorporated into the defensive system of a town (as happened from the 8th century at Arles), and were later used as housing as well.

In the later Roman period, pagan temples were sometimes converted into churches, which assisted their preservation, as were other secular buildings such as baths. At Nîmes in France the Roman temple survives in exceptional condition; it is called the Maison Carrée, probably because of its use as the main city mosque (*cabah* or square house) in the 8th century when under Arab rule, but before then it served as a hall of justice.

OPPOSITE PAGE The Roman amphitheatre is still a symbol of entertainment at Nîmes, where the building is very well preserved allowing events to be staged – including bull fights, the modern-day equivalent of 'venationes'.

LEFT An early 19th-century watercolour by James Skene of the Maison Carrée showing the accumulation of deposits in the town. In the reign of Louis XIV it was suggested that the temple should be dismantled and re-erected at Versailles.

RIGHT The Maison Carrée temple at Nîmes survives virtually intact. It dates from the very beginning of the 1st century and was dedicated to the imperial cult. For a brief period it was converted to a mosque when the area was under Arab rule.

Some Roman towns became gradually hidden from view through decay, silting and the build-up of debris. This occurred at Rome which apparently became an unsavoury place in which to live. In many urban centres, the Roman deposits are a considerable depth below the modern-day street levels because of this build-up of debris.

In the countryside, many Roman roads continued to be used, as they are today, and Roman milestones and other monuments were retained as markers. That many Roman monuments were visible for centuries is witnessed in the many early documents relating to land where such monuments were mentioned as land markers.

Very large objects such as Trajan's Column in Rome also survived, but the fate of the enormous numbers of statues is not known except in very few cases. Many pagan statues were destroyed or defaced through religious intolerance or fear, while some were hidden and others left in place to decay. Bronze statues were melted down for their metal and marble ones were burnt in limekilns. Some statuary began to be collected during the Middle Ages, but more favoured were the sarcophagi, particularly decorated ones, which were re-used for Christian burials.

The written word has survived as inscriptions on dedications, tombstones and altars, and occasionally on parchment, papyrus and on writing tablets. Originally there must have been hundreds of thousands of manuscripts in the public and private libraries, but very few originals survive, even in fragments. Between 550 and 750 some manuscripts were copied, and the originals probably disintegrated or else the parchments were scraped clean for re-use. In the Middle Ages, however, more and more of the surviving manuscripts were copied in monasteries, ensuring the preservation of some texts today.

Throughout the Roman period, the native people gradually learned to speak and write fluent Latin, leading to the disappearance of many other languages and dialects. In the Eastern Empire Greek continued to be the main language, although the language itself underwent a continuous process of modification. In the west, the pronunciation of Latin varied regionally, but in Britain Latin died away with the Germanic invasions towards the end of the Roman period. Instead, English developed, only to be influenced by Latin and Greek during the conversion of the country to Christianity from the 6th century. Elsewhere in the Western Empire the Church helped to retain Latin and, until the end of the Medieval period, the language remained the main medium of communication of all well-educated people. By 700 everyday Latin was evolving into what are now called the Romance languages (French, Italian, Romanian, and others).

During the Renaissance classical Latin, by

RIGHT The modern-day level of many towns is considerably higher than that of the Roman remains. A mid 19th-century discovery of a mosaic at Cirencester in England was well below the level of the street.

BELOW RIGHT The amphitheatre at Arles is a popular tourist attraction. It was transformed into a fortified stronghold in the Medieval period. As well as a fort, it was also used for housing, but in 1825 the amphitheatre was cleared of all the houses and was excavated. The tower was part of the medieval fort.

then a dead language, experienced a rival. There was an awakening of interest in Classical studies, which has continued to the present day. The study of Roman architecture and art greatly influenced architectural and art styles in Europe from the Renaissance onwards. Interest in all things Roman continues to grow even though the Classics, including Latin, are rarely taught in schools. Much more than that, the Romans have affected our everyday lives, in areas such as jurisdiction, town planning, art, coinage design and even our language. It is an unfortunate irony that while there is an increasing interest in the Romans, and modern research methods add to our knowledge about them, more and more of their remains are being destroyed with little or no record.

GLOSSARY

amphitheatre: an oval arena surrounded by seats for mass entertainment.
amphorae: very large pottery vessels for transporting products such as wine, olive oil and fish sauce.
aqueduct: a system of conducting water in pipes, channels in the ground, or channels supported on arches.
Augusti: co-emperors of the Eastern and Western Empires.
auxiliaries: soldiers recruited from non-Roman citizens.
Barbarians: a Greek term adopted by the Romans to describe foreigners or non-Romans.
basilica: aisled building often associated with the forum.
Byzantine Empire: the Eastern Roman Empire from the time of Constantine I until 1453.
Caesars: co-rulers of the eastern and western empires, below the rank of Augusti.
camp: a temporary fortified enclosure with tents for housing military troops.
Carthaginians: a powerful sea-faring nation in North Africa, who were originally Phoenicians from the Lebanon.
Celtic: a term used to describe people who inhabited northern Europe in the Iron Age.
centuriation: a system of dividing the land into regular blocks.
cohort: a unit of auxiliaries or legionaries.
colonies: deliberate foundations of towns, usually settled by veteran soldiers.
contubernium: tent-party of 8 soldiers.
Etruscans: a tribe controlling much of central and northern Italy from the 8th century BC and who established many cities.
fortresses: permanent establishments for legionary troops.
forts: permanent establishments for auxiliary troops.
forum: civic centre, usually a square surrounded by offices, a temple and a basilica.
Gaul: modern-day France and Germany west of the Rhine; inhabited by Celtic peoples usually referred to as Gauls.
hypocaust: underfloor heating system.
Iron Age: a period of prehistory when iron was used as the main technological material.
latifundia: large agricultural estates.
Latin: language of the Romans. Also used to describe the people from the tribes south of Rome in the district of Latium.
legionaries: soldiers recruited from Roman citizens.
Livy: Roman historian, 59 BC–AD 17.
mausolea: stone-built structures for housing the dead, usually in coffins.
mosaic: a patterned floor or wall made from thousands of tiny cubes (usually of stone).
odeum: a small, permanently roofed theatre for musical performances and recitations.
patricians: aristocratic members of society.
Phoenicians: *see* Carthaginians.
plebeians: the urban poor.
Praetorian Guard: personal bodyguard and élite force of the emperor.
Punic Wars: fought against the Phoenicians, called *Poeni* by the Romans, which in turn gave the English term 'Punic'.
quernstones: stones for grinding grain into flour.
Romanization: the gradual adoption of the Roman way of life by non-Romans.
Sabines: a tribe to the north of Rome.
Samnites: a tribe to the south of Rome.
sarcophagi: stone coffins.
Senate: ruling council at Rome.
Tetrarchy: four-man rule of the empire.
veterans: retired soldiers.
villa: a country house, often with mosaics and wall paintings, and normally part of an agricultural estate.
votive offering: an offering or gift to a god.
wooden writing tablets: flat pieces of wood, with a layer of wax. Writing was done with a metal implement (*stylus*) on the wax, and could be erased by being heated and smoothed over. The writing sometimes scored the wood beneath, so preserving the messages.

SOME BOOKS TO READ

BOARDMAN, J., J. GRIFFIN and O. MURRAY (eds). 1988. *The Roman World* (Oxford University Press, Oxford and New York). Illustrated descriptions of the history and social life of Classical Rome, with particular emphasis on the contemporary literature.

CHEVALLIER, R. 1976. *Roman Roads* (Batsford, London). Gives much information on Roman roads, including methods of construction, bridges, life on the roads, and evidence from literature and inscriptions.

CLAYTON, P. *The Treasures of Ancient Rome* (Bison Books, London). 1986. Records Rome's artistic achievement and also an informative account of the Roman Empire as seen through its visible remains, artefacts and monuments. Heavily illustrated.

CONNOLLY, P. 1981. *Greece and Rome at War* (Macdonald, London). Vividly illustrated account of classical warfare, including numerous colour drawings and reconstructions.

CORNELL, T., and J. MATTHEWS, 1982. *Atlas of the Roman World* (Phaidon, Oxford). Charts the development of Rome and its Empire from the earliest times to the Byzantine Empire, copiously illustrated with maps, plans, photographs, and diagrams.

GREENE, K. 1986. *The Archaeology of the Roman Economy* (Batsford, London). A useful book on the economy throughout the Empire, including transport, coinage, agriculture, and industry.

GREENHALGH, M. 1989. *The Survival of Roman Antiquities in the Middle Ages* (Duckworth, London). Describes the survival into the Middle Ages of buildings and other structures, as well as smaller objects and manuscripts, from the Western Roman Empire.

HARDEN, D.B. 1987. *Glass of the Caesars* (Olivetti, Milan). Explains the wide-ranging techniques of Roman glass manufacturers, with numerous examples illustrated in colour; essentially an exhibition catalogue.

HENIG, M. 1984. *Religion in Roman Britain* (Batsford, London). Illustrated account of the many aspects of Roman religion, with evidence drawn largely from Britain.

JACKSON, R. 1988. *Doctors and Diseases in the Roman Empire* (British Museum Publications, London). Fascinating illustrated book on many aspects of Roman medicine and hygiene, from birth-control to death.

JOHNSON, A. 1983. *Roman Forts of the 1st and 2nd centuries AD in Britain and the German Provinces* (A. & C. Black, London). Well-illustrated account of various aspects of Roman forts.

JOHNSON, S. 1989. *Hadrian's Wall* (Batsford, London). History and everyday life of one of the Empire's frontiers; numerous illustrations.

PERCIVAL, J. 1976. *The Roman Villa, An Historical Introduction* (Batsford, London). Includes many details on Roman villas across the Empire.

SHELTON, J-A. 1988. *As The Romans Did. A Sourcebook in Roman Social History* (Oxford University Press, Oxford and New York). Discusses various aspects of social life, with examples in English translation from contemporary texts and inscriptions.

STRONG, D., and D. BROWN, (eds). 1976. *Roman Crafts* (Duckworth, London). An illustrated guide to the arts and crafts of the Romans.

WACHER, J. 1974. *The Towns of Roman Britain* (Batsford, London). How towns developed and what they were like in one Roman province.

Events In TheRoman World And Elsewhere

ROMAN HISTORY		EVENTS ELSEWHERE	
753 BC	Foundation of Rome	671 BC	Assyrian conquest of Egypt
		612 BC	Nimrud destroyed
		c. 600 BC	Greek colony founded at Marseille
509 BC	Foundation of the Republic	480 BC	Athens sacked by Persians
		479 BC	Death of Confucius
		432 BC	Completion of the Parthenon at Athens
390 BC	Rome sacked by Gauls	350 BC	Crossbow invented in China
		323 BC	Death of Alexander the Great
275 BC	Roman victory over King Pyrrhus of Epirus		
264–241 BC	First Punic War	221 BC	Great Wall of China built
218–201 BC	Second Punic War		
216 BC	Romans defeated at Battle of Cannae	206 BC	Chang'an becomes capital of Han dynasty in China
149–146 BC	Third Punic War		
146 BC	Corinth destroyed by Romans		
133 BC	Tiberius Gracchus' land reforms	c.112 BC	Opening of Silk Road from China to West
81 BC	Sulla becomes dictator		
60 BC	Formation of First Triumvirate		
49 BC	Julius Caesar invades Italy		
44 BC	Julius Caesar is assassinated		
31 BC	Octavian defeats Antony at Actium	31 BC	Stela of this date from the Olmec site of Tres Zapotes, Mexico
AD c.30	Crucifixion of Jesus		
43	Invasion of Britain by Claudius	c. 50	Teotihuacán in Mexico laid out as a city
64	Great Fire at Rome		
70	Destruction of Jerusalem by Titus		
79	Eruption of Vesuvius	105	First use of paper in China
166	Plague sweeps Empire		
212	Citizenship conferred throughout Empire	271	Magnetic compass in use in China
		300	Classic period of Maya civilization begins
313	Edict of Milan		
378	Romans defeated at Adrianpc		
401	Milan besieged by Visigoths		
410	Rome captured and sacked by Visigoths	c. 450	Germanic villages abandoned due to flooding
451	Attila the Hun defeated		
455	Rome sacked by Vandals		
476	Last of the western Roman emperors deposed	c. 550	Buddhism introduced into Japan
533–554	Reconquest of the western Empire		
568	Italy invaded by the Lombards	600	Mesa Verde occupied in USA

EMPERORS OF THE ROMEN WORLD	
27 BC–AD 14	Augustus
14–37	Tiberius
37–41	Gaius (Caligula)
41–54	Claudius
54–68	Nero
68–69	Galba
69	Otho
69	Vitellius
67–79	Vespasian
79–81	Titus
81–96	Domitian
96–98	Nerva
98–117	Trajan
117–138	Hadrian
138–161	Antoninus Pius
161–180	Marcus Aurelius
161–169	Lucius Verus
180–193	Commodus
193	Pertinax
193	Didius Julianus
193–211	Septimius Severus
211–212	Geta
211–217	Caracalla
217–218	Macrinus
218–222	Elagabalus
222–235	Alexander Severus
235–238	Maximinus
238	Gordian I
238	Gordian II
238	Balbinus
238	Pupienus
238–244	Gordian III
244–249	Philip the Arab
249–251	Decius
251–253	Trebonianus Gallus
2511–253	Volusianus
253	Aemilianus
253–260	Valerian
253–268	Gallienus
268–270	Claudius II, Gothicus
270	Quintillus
270–275	Aurelian
275–276	Tacitus
276	Florian
276–282	Probus
282–283	Carus
283–284	Carinus
283–284	Numerianus
284–305	Diocletian

EMPERORS OF THE ROMEN WORLD			
WEST		EAST	
286–305	Maximain (Augustus)	286–305	Dioletian (Augustus)
293–305	Constantanius Chlorus (Caesar)	293–305	Galerius (Caesar)
305–306	Constantius Chlorus (Augustus)	305–311	Galerius (Augustus)
305	Severus (Caesar)	305–309	Maximinus (Caesar)
306–307	Severus (Augustus)	309–313	Maximinus (Augustus)
306–312	Maxentius (Augustus)		
306–307	Constantine (Caesar)	308–324	Licinius (Augustus)
307–324	Constantine (Augustus)		
324–337 Constantine I			
317–337	Constantine II (Caesar)	317	Licinianus (Caesar)
337–340	Constantine II (Augustus)	317–326	Crispus (Caesar)
333–337	Constans (Caesar)	324–337	Constantius II (Caesar)
337–350	Constans (Augustus)	337–361	Constantius II (Augustus)
350–353	Magnentius (usurper, Augustus)	335–337	Dalmatius (Caesar)
353–361 Constantius II			
355–361	Julian (Caesar)	350–354	Gallus (Caesar)
361–363 Julian			
363–364 Jovian			
364–375	Valentinian I	364–378	Valens
375–383	Gratian	379–395	Theodosius I
375–392	Valentinian II		
383–388	Magnus Maximus (usurper)		
392–394	Eugenius (usurper)		
392–395 Theodosius I			
395–423	Honorius	395–408	Arcadius
423–425	Iohannes (usurper)	408–450	Theodosius II
425–455	Valentinian III	450–457	Marcian
455	Petronius Maximus		
455–456	Avitus		
457–461	Majorian	457–474	Leo
461–465	Libius Severus		
467–472	Anthemius		
472	Olybrius		
473	Glycerius		
473–475	Nepos	474–491	Zeno
475–476	Romulus Augustulus	475–476	Basiliscus
BARBARIAN KINGS OF ITALY			
476–493	Odoacer	491–518	Anastasius
493–526	Theoderic	518–527	Justin
526–534	Athalaric	527–565	Justinian
534–536	Theodahad		

INDEX

Numerals in italics refer to captions and pictures.

A

D

E

F

G

H

I

J

K

L

M

N

O

P

Q

R

S

W

X

Y

Z

Picture Credits and Acknowledgments

The material in this book previously appeared in:

AN INTRODUCTION TO GREEK MYTHOLOGY

AN INTRODUCTION TO ORIENTAL MYTHOLOGY

AN INTRODUCTION TO CELTIC MYTHOLOGY

AN INTRODUCTION TO VIKING MYTHOLOGY

AN INTRODUCTION TO EGYPTOLOGY

AN INTRODUCTION TO THE ROMANS